West Virginia
CIVIL WAR ALMANAC

Volume One

West Virginia
Civil War Almanac

Volume One

by Tim McKinney

Pictorial Histories Publishing Company, Inc.
Charleston, West Virginia

Copyright © 1998 Tim McKinney

All rights reserved. No portion of this book may be used or reproduced without written permission of the publisher

LIBRARY OF CONGRESS
CATALOG CARD NO. 97-69941

ISBN 1-57510-037-1

First Printing January 1998

Typography and book design
Arrow Graphics, Missoula, Montana

Cover design
Bill Vaughn, Missoula, Montana

PICTORIAL HISTORIES PUBLISHING COMPANY, INC.
1416 Quarrier Street, Charleston, West Virginia 25301

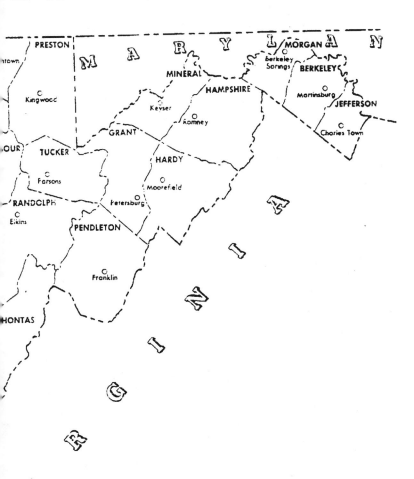

*State of West Virginia
Outline Map*

Contents

Introduction and Acknowledgments   1

Introduction 1890 Civil War Veterans Census   3

The Veteran Census Roster   7
- Barbour County   11
- Berkeley County   17
- Boone County   26
- Braxton County   29
- Brooke County   37
- Cabell County   42
- Calhoun County   57
- Clay County   63
- Doddridge County   66
- Fayette County   77
- Gilmer County   82
- Grant County   90
- Greenbrier County   93
- Hampshire County   97
- Hancock County   99
- Hardy County   104
- Harrison County   104
- Jackson County   120
- Jefferson County   136
- Kanawha County   139
- Lewis County   162
- Lincoln County   171
- Logan County   179
- Marion County   181
- Marshall County   200
- Mason County   220
- McDowell County   243
- Mercer County   245
- Mineral County   248
- Monongalia County   254
- Monroe County   267
- Morgan County   268
- Nicholas County   272
- Ohio County   275
- Pendleton County   297

Pleasants County 304
Pocahontas County 310
Preston County 314
Putnam County 341
Raleigh County 350
Randolph County 354
Ritchie County 359
Roane County 375
Summers County 384
Taylor County 386
Tucker County 395
Tyler County 399
Upshur County 410
Wayne County 422
Webster County 432
Wetzel County 434
Wirt County 450
Wood County 458
Wyoming County 484

1890 Census Confederate Index 486

Veteran Distribution by County of Residence 511

West Virginia Civil War Service Medals 512

West Virginia Soldiers and Citizens
Who Died in Federal Prisons or Military Hospitals 521

The Southern Claims Commission 531

The SCC Case Files of Joseph Caldwell and Logan Osburn 540

West Virginia Physicians in the Civil War 552

The Ft. Delaware Seventy-five 557

You Look Rather Hard 561

Introduction and Acknowledgments

HAVING RESEARCHED West Virginia's Civil War history for nearly two decades, and written and published that history since 1987, I have felt a strong need for an "Almanac" as an aid to assembling and publishing some of the vast wealth of scattered information about West Virginia in the Civil War. That desire has finally culminated in this work, which is volume one of a projected two-or three-volume series. Items selected for inclusion in this volume were chosen because of their obvious value to the historian and genealogist. It is my sincere hope that the reader and researcher will find this material to be as educational and helpful as I have found it to be.

Volume two of the *West Virginia Civil War Almanac*, will include an equally eclectic collection of previously unpublished material on the war in West Virginia, as well as a comprehensive index to the 12,683 names of Union veterans presented here.

Books and other published works concerning West Virginia's role in the Civil War have greatly increased in the past twenty years. It is one of the great pleasures of my life to have participated, to some small degree, in that achievement. The researcher of today will begin his journey far ahead of where we were a generation ago, in terms of available material. It is only proper that we study, honor, and respect the memory of our ancestors who wore the Blue and Gray.

Without the encouragement and assistance of others, an author's journey along the paths of history would indeed be short. This writer, has had the good fortune to become acquainted over the years with a number of people whose energy and talents manifest themselves through the quantity and quality of their works, and whose generosity has assisted my own efforts.

Otis K. Rice, of the WVU Institute of Technology, volunteered to edit parts of the manuscript for this work. Dr. Rice edited the manuscript for my first book, published in 1988. His friendship and advice are mutually valuable to me and gratefully acknowledged

Don and Wilma Pomeroy, of Fayetteville, West Virginia, have assisted me with several projects over the years, the present one included. Their data processing and computer skills kept this work from going completely off schedule, and I may add, kept me from going "off" as well.

Stan Cohen, Pictorial Histories Publishing Company, is always ready to offer assistance and encouragement along the way. Stan's company is largely responsible for filling the void that once existed in the publication of books about West Virginia's history, military and otherwise.

Others whose assistance with the present work is gratefully acknowledged include: (in no particular order) Fred Armstrong and the West Virginia Department of Archives and History, Charleston, WV. The West Virginia Historical Society, Charleston, WV; Bill Clements, Charleston, WV; Mike Chandler, Charleston, WV; and Geraldine Workman, Fayetteville, WV. Also helpful were the staff of Vining Library, WVU Institute of Technology, Montgomery, WV; The staff of the West Virginia and Regional History Collection, West Virginia University, Morgantown, WV; the West Virginia Division, United Daughters of the Confederacy; the West Virginia Division, Sons of Confederate Veterans; Mike Smith, Droop Mountain State Park, Hillsboro, WV; Mike Mengele, Carnifex Ferry State Park, Summersville, WV; Terry Lowry, South Charleston, WV; and Bob Krick, who is stuck in Virginia. The various staff members at the National Archives who tolerated my research. I am grateful to wife, Brenda, for patient understanding; to son, Jason, for love and inspiration; and to my parents and family for continued support of my numerous endeavors. Last but never least, I want to thank God for bringing me this far.

for my son, Jason,
who wanted to "halp Wook"
and for my wife, Brenda,
who wished he could

TIM MCKINNEY
Fayetteville, WV

June 10, 1997

Introduction
1890 Civil War Veteran Census

THE UNITED STATES Constitution provides for a federal census to be taken every ten years. Originally intended to determine the population in each state, the census gradually expanded, with more and more information being gathered. Researchers have long relied on the federal census to learn more about earlier citizens.

With the approach of the 1890 census, Congress authorized special schedules of Union Civil War veterans as a way to locate and identify veterans or their widows who might be eligible for pension or disability benefits. Although these special schedules were intended to include only Union veterans or their spouses, mistakes were made, and hundreds of Confederate veterans and widows were recorded. The author has identified nearly 1,100 Confederate veterans included on the 1890 special schedules for West Virginia. As the census taker visited each dwelling he would first ask questions from the regular population schedules, and would then ask whether or not a veteran or his widow was part of that household. If the answer was "yes," he would then complete one of the special schedules. In so doing the enumerator attempted to determine the veteran's given name, any aliases used, along with his specific branch and unit of service, period of service, and disabilities incurred as a direct result of military service, if any.

The special veterans census for West Virginia includes dozens of incomplete entries. Often, the listing will include name only, or name and a portion of the other related material. There were obviously several factors contributing to these incomplete entries. It is apparent that the veteran's physical condition sometimes prevented him from providing all of the information requested. The passage of time also contributed to loss of memory, with some veterans unable to recall specific information such as dates of service or military unit in which they had served. Occasionally, notes indicate that the veteran was away from home and his family was unable to answer the enumerator's questions, other than to say that a veteran did reside at that location.

Entries in this index total 13,780. Of that number 1,097 or 7.9% are Confederate veterans. The 1890 census statistics for West Virginia show a population of 762,794. Thus, at 13,780 the veterans identified account for 1.8% of the state's total 1890 population. The actual number would most certainly be higher, as numerous veterans were simply missed, and, of course, the vast majority of surviving Confederate veterans were intentionally omitted.

Every effort has been made to include and properly identify the veterans of these special schedules. In a few instances the faded condition of the record itself made the entry entirely unreadable. Still others were faded but sufficiently legible to allow an "educated guess." Poor hand writing was most often the problem in transcribing these records. Some enumerators wrote two or more characters or letter sequences exactly alike, and this created a sometimes insurmountable obstacle to absolute identification. Further, it is unlikely that the census taker would routinely inquire as to the correct spelling of a surname. They simply wrote what they thought they heard and, of course, this method further complicates interpretation and adds to the rate of error.

The amount of time required to read and transcribe these records far exceeded what this writer envisioned at the start of this endeavor. For example, the two counties with the largest veteran population, Kanawha and Wood, each required 17 hours total to transcribe and research individual entries. Where incomplete entries were encountered, the author has attempted by various means to determine whether or not the person listed was a Federal or Confederate veteran. When research beyond the census itself has revealed that information, it is included here in parenthesis. Parenthetical material should not he confused with data available in the actual census. More often than not, when an incomplete entry was researched the person proved to be, or very likely was, a Confederate veteran.

Divided loyalties were common in the mountain state with some men, perhaps several hundred, serving both the United States and Confederate military. Being a West Virginia/Virginia border county, Pendleton County was selected for special statistical analysis in an attempt to gauge this phenomenon. The result is quite interesting, though the sample is admittedly small, at 99 veterans listed. With the exception of the chapter on Pendleton County no attempt has been made to further identify veterans who may have served both the Blue and the Gray. A few such veterans were discovered in the course of other research and where found they have been identified in the remarks section of their respective counties.

This work does not include the names of deceased veterans or their widows found in the 1890 census. That material will be included in volume two of the Almanac along with a comprehensive name index of Union Army veterans, as well as additional statistical analysis of the data presented in this volume. This work does contain a comprehensive index of Confederate veterans. The reader may thus locate a veteran by name only and will not need to know the county of residence.

The 1890 census of Civil War veterans from West Virginia is found on microcopy M123, rolls 109 and 110. Copies of the microfilm may be purchased from the National Archives and other sources. Copies utilized by the author were purchased from the American Genealogical Lending Library, P.O. Box 329 Bountiful, Utah 84011-0329. The filmed census does contain some misplaced enumeration districts which the researcher must be wary of. This anomaly appears regardless of microfilm source, as follows:

    Berkeley Co. E.D. 8 is found after E.D. 9
    Marshall Co. E.D. 207 is found after E.D. 204
    Preston Co. E.D. 65 is found in the middle of E.D. 66.
    Randolph Co. E.D. 49 is found after Pendleton Co. E.D. 43
    Tucker Co. E.D. 68 is found before E.D. 59

An additional caveat to using these films is that there are numerous enumeration districts filmed in duplicate. This fact does not present a serious obstacle to their user but is, however, a frequent inconvenience.

IDENTIFYING CONFEDERATE VETERANS—METHODOLOGY

The author spent countless hours attempting to accurately identify Confederate veterans of the 1890 Census. When the census takers themselves discovered that a Confederate had been accidentally recorded they routinely drew a line through that veteran's name, making their identification, of course, quite simple, as long as the name was not completely obscured by the line drawn through it. This type of identification accounts for about 70% of the Confederate veterans in this work. Where the author suspected that a veteran may have been Confederate because of an incomplete entry or regimental designation beyond those mustered by West Virginia Union forces, i.e. "62 WV Infantry," the author relied first on the 1995 publication by Jack Dickinson *Tattered Uniforms and Bright Bayonets: West Virginia's Confederate Soldiers*. This ground-breaking new work attempts to list the names and counties of residence of approximately 16,000 men who enlisted into Confederate service from West Virginia. Equally valuable was *The Roster of Confederate Soldiers 1861–1865*, a transcription of the nearly 1.5 million names found on the microfilm Compiled Service Records of Confederate forces. This monumental work was undertaken by Tom Broadfoot and company of Wilmington, North Carolina, in 1995 and was completed in January 1997. Consisting of 16 hardbound volumes, this reference tool is a Godsend to countless thousands of researchers. Its availability made possible the identification of several hundred Confederate veterans included here. Also utilized were numerous volumes from the *Virginia Regimental History Series*, being published by H.E. Howard, Inc. of Lynchburg, Virginia. Several county histories and genealogical newsletters also proved valuable over the many months this work was in progress.

    Soldiers not otherwise identified were considered to be Confederate if their name appeared in one of the above reference works, and if a check of the individual's record proved that the veteran did survive the war, and could, therefore, be the person listed. Further, the name was not included unless there was found to be at least one other Confederate veteran from the same regiment, residing in that or an adjacent county. A few men with unusual names were included here as Confederate veterans although they did not belong to any military unit from western Virginia or West Virginia.

For example, the census entry for Henry Maag of Marion County is incomplete. A check of Broadfoot's roster identifies one man by that name in the entire Confederacy: "Henry Maag, Cpl. 15 Tennessee Infantry."

Where the author has attempted to identify Confederate veterans beyond the actual census, that material is included here in parenthesis. If this parenthetical material also includes a question mark, the author is less certain of accurate identification. This tentative identification is intended only as a guide to further research. It is expected and acknowledged that there will be some percentage of error in this method of veteran identification. It is further acknowledged that there are certainly some soldiers who did not meet the above criteria for inclusion, but who, with additional research will prove to be Confederate veterans. To that end the author welcomes correspondence on the subject and will gladly include subsequent identification in volume two of this work. Veterans whose military units are not identified and whose names were not found in Confederate records were tabulated as Union soldiers. At this writing Broadfoot Publishing Company is in the process of transcribing the Compiled Service Records of the Union military forces. Those records, nearly 3 million names, also published in hardbound editions, will be referred to prior to publication of volume two of this work. Of course, their availability will further diminish the number of unidentified veterans found in the 1890 census.

Two counties, Mercer and Pocahontas, list more Confederate than Union military veterans residing in those counties in 1890, while two other counties, Hardy and Webster, include no Confederate veterans. Wood County contained the largest veteran population at 777, followed by Kanawha County with 776. Hardy County contained the least, with just four veterans listed.

The original spelling of all material found in the census has been retained, with exception only for clarity. There are found in the census a very small number of veterans whose service was not Civil War related. Those names have been excluded. The author considered military service between April 1, 1861 and May 15, 1865 to be Civil War related.

The Veteran Census Roster

THE VETERANS of each county are arranged alphabetically with data in three columns. The soldiers name and rank are given first, followed by his regiment or unit of military service and the veterans date of enlistment and discharge, where found. Individual states from which a military unit was organized are identified by the first two letters of each entry, with the third or third and forth letters indicating branch of service. For example, 1 WVA indicates the First West Virginia Artillery, and 30 VASS indicates the Thirtieth Virginia Sharpshooters.

ABBREVIATIONS USED
Rank:
Pvt.—Private
Cpl.—Corporal
Sgt.—Sergeant
Lt. —Lieutenant
Cpt.—Captain
MJ—Major
Ltc.—Lieutenant Colonel
Col.—Colonel
Gen.—General
Adj.—Adjutant
QM—Quartermaster

States:
AK—Arkansas
AL—Alabama
CA—California
CT—Connecticut
DE—Delaware
GA—Georgia
IL—Illinois
IN—Indiana
IA—Iowa
KS—Kansas
KY—Kentucky
LA—Louisiana
ME—Maine

MD—Maryland
MA—Massachusetts
MI—Michigan
MN—Minnesota
MS—Mississippi
MO—Missouri
NJ—New Jersey
NY—New York
NC—North Carolina
OH—Ohio
PA—Pennsylvania
RI—Rhode Island
SC—South Carolina
TN—Tennessee
TX—Texas
VT—Vermont
VA—Virginia
WV—West Virginia

Regiment or military unit:
A—Artillery
BTN—Battalion
C—Cavalry
E—Engineers
I—Infantry
M—Militia
NG—National Guard
R—Rifleman
RG—Rangers
RS—Reserves
SS—Sharpshooters
WLA—Washington Light Artillery (one usage)
Z—Zouaves

Other:
NF—Nothing follows
CS/CSA—Confederate States of America
US/USA—United States of America
AKA—Also known as

Reading the Remarks/Disability Section

Veterans included in the census were asked if they suffered from any injury or disability directly related to their military service. If any were indicated, the enumerator wrote the complaint at the bottom of the page. Each entry has a number corresponding to the numbers on the upper half of the page. These remarks offer us a glimpse of a veterans life at that moment and will undoubtedly be a welcomed source of information for the genealogist and family historian. Civil War buffs will also benefit from veteran's remarks such as "wounded at Gettysburg," or "I deserted and ain't ashamed of it."

Some veterans took the opportunity to claim for themselves a place in history beyond their actual deeds. One man claimed he "killed Stonewall Jackson," while another said he was the "first soldier wounded at Philippi." The former is obviously false while the latter would be almost impossible to confirm.

Often the census takers themselves were so moved by a veteran's condition that they added remarks such as "he orto have a pension," or "this old soldier is nearly destitute." In one instance a woman residing in Marion County so upset the enumerator that he penned, "she is an ignorant woman and of bad repute." This entry is especially curious because widows are always so identified, whereas this woman is not shown as a widow or veteran. One veteran, when asked if he suffered any injury from his Civil War service, replied simply that he was "wounded in my character." Indeed, the entire nation was similarly wounded and its lingering effects are with us yet today.

The veteran's remarks occasionally offer information normally found at the top of the census page, such as dates of discharge or date of enlistment. It is also worth noting that the main entry for a particular man might be incomplete at the top of the page, but if you look for him in the remarks section it may say something like "deserted and joined the Confederacy," or "was in home guards 18 months." With those facts in mind the reader is advised to check the remarks section for any material relevant to the veteran he is looking for.

If the reader locates a particular veteran in the main index but finds nothing about that person in the remarks, it is because nothing was found in the census. Remarks were found for approximately 60% of the veterans listed. The author did not include such remarks as "veteran was not home at time of visit."

Abbreviations Used in Remarks

AFP—applied for pension
CDR—chronic diarrhea
CP—chicken pox
DSC—discharged on surgeon's certificate of disability

F—fever
HD—heart disease
KD—kidney disease
LD—lung disease
MP—mumps
MS—measles
POW—prisoner of war
RH—rheumatism
SS—sunstroke
TYF—typhoid fever
UFL—unfit for labor
VV—varicose veins
WIA—wounded in action
★—Confederate soldier

Some Medical Terms Used

Ague—fever with cold fits and shivering
Bright's disease—kidney disease
Catarrhus—inflamed mucous membranes usually of throat
Consumption—gradual wasting away of the body; phthisis
Dropsy—unnatural collection of water anywhere in the body
Dysentery—a flux in which the stools contain blood & mucous
Dyspepsia—indigestion; difficulty with digestion
Erysipelas—infection of mucous membranes/inflamed skin and fever
Fistula—a deep, narrow, sinuous ulcer
Lumbago—rheumatic affection of muscles about the loins and nose
Neuralgia—pain in a nerve or nerves
Piles—disease of rectum near anus; hemorrhoids
Pleurisy—inflammation of the pleura; soreness of chest/lungs
Scrofula—tumors of the lymphatic glands/a type of consumption
Scurvy—disease caused by insufficient diet
Vertigo—dizziness or swimming of the head

Barbour County

NAME/RANK	REGIMENT	WHEN SERVED
Allen, Elijah Pvt.	44 OHI	8/18/61–7/3/65
Auril, Christopher C. Pvt.	15 WVI	10/10/64–6/14/65
Ball, John D. Musician	15 WVI	9/1/62–6/14/65
Barker, Elias Pvt.	6 WVI	8/12/61–7/1/65
Barte, Henry Pvt.	— WVA	8/7/62–7/21/65
Bean, James H. Cpl.	10 WVI	2/1/62–5/1/65
Beavers, John W. Pvt.	6 WVI	9/27/61–11/25/64
Bennett, Raleigh C. Pvt.	168 PAI	9/20/62–8/20/63
Bolyaret, Elias Pvt.	4 VAC	6/12/63–3/9/64
Boyles, Andrew C. Pvt.	17 WVI	10/10/64–6/10/65
Boyles, Barnet Pvt.	14 WVI	10/10/64–6/30/65
Boyles, Daniel Pvt.	NF	
Boyles, Melker M. Pvt.	17 WVI	10/10/64–6/10/65
Brown, Henry W. Pvt.	12 WVI	8/11/62–5/26/65
Cade, Wm. Pvt.	10 WVI	6/1/62–6/26/65
Cale, Jine Pvt.	4 WVC	8/1/63–3/9/64
Carter, David G. Pvt.	———	65/65
Carter, Jasper Pvt.	1 WVA	8/62–6/65
Champ, John Bugler	6 WVC	1/1/63–5/26/66
Champ, Martin Pvt.	15 WVI	8/27/62–6/14/65
Chapman, James Pvt.	10 VAI	1/22/62–5/5/65
Chroston, Thomas Pvt.	3 WVC	3/6/65–6/30/65
Cleavinger, Minor S. Pvt.	17 WVI	9/1/64–6/28/65
Coberly, Haymond Pvt.	15 WVI	9/1/62–6/14/64
Coffman, Elijah Pvt.	15 WVI	8/23/62–6/23/65
Comer, John W. Pvt.	17 WVI	2/1/65–7/12/65
Cox, David H. Pvt.	6 WVC	10/21/62–NF
Cross, Levi Pvt.	15 WVI	3/1/63–8/1/65
Crostin, Charles M. Pvt.	17 WVI	9/8/64–7/15/65
Crouse, Squire Pvt.	10 WVI	1/22/62–5/7/65
Cummings, Lewis Pvt.	10 WVI	1/22/64–3/17/65
Currance, George W. Pvt.	4 WVC	6/7/63–3/4/64
Daugherty, Jacob A. Pvt.	6 WVI	64/65
Dawn, Marshal Pvt.	10 WVI	4/62–6/5/65
Dayton, Charles Pvt.	6 WVI	8/20/62–6/10/65
Dennison, Jeremiah Cpl.	17 WVI	2/20/65–6/30/65
Dolton, Isaac Pvt.	9 USA	8/10/64–5/29/65
Duckworth, James H. Pvt.	15 WVI	9/2/62–6/14/65
Edmond, Wm. Pvt.	10 WVI	2/22/62–5/7/65
England, Jasper Pvt.	15 WVI	5/1/63–8/9/65
Ensminger, Isaac F. Pvt.	6 WVI	1/65–6/65
Erven, Jacob E. Pvt.	6 WVC	6/28/61–NF

Evans, James Pvt.	14 INI	6/61 NF
Evans, Wm. H. Pvt.	1 WVC	6/15/64–7/8/65
Farrance, Elam Cpl.	10 WVI	9/17/62–8/9/65
Freeman, James D. Pvt.	15 WVI	8/23/62–6/23/65
Gawthrop, James W.	NF (25 VAI CSA)	
Glendenning, George M. Pvt	2 WVI	5/14/61–5/14/64
Gour, Isaac Pvt.	4 —C	8/17/63–3/6/64
Gower, John Pvt.	6 WVI	9/27/61–11/25/64
Grant, Granville A. Pvt.	7 WVI	4/7/65–7/7/65
Gregory, Mifflin G.	Santiago DeCuba	1/25/64–6/11/65
Gribble, Jonathan E. Pvt.	7 WVA	8/12/62–7/25/65
Haddox, Abram Pvt.	17 WVI	NF
Haddox, Allen P. Pvt.	15 WVI	8/23/62–6/14/65
Harrison, Benj. Pvt.	12 VAI	8/15/62–6/16/65
Harshberger, Jeremiah Pvt.	2 MDI	9/7/64–6/30/65
Hinsley, Wm. Pvt.	5 WVI	6/1/61–6/14/64
Hoffman, John J. Pvt.	——	63/65
House, Abram Pvt.	——	64/65
Hovatter, Basil Pvt.	15 WVI	62/65
Hovatter, Isaac Pvt.	15 WVI	62/65
Hovey, James M.R. Cpl.	14 WVI	8/15/62–7/3/65
Howell, John Pvt.	6 WVI	9/64–6/65
Howes, Fenilon Major	15 WVI	8/23/62–6/14/65
Hunt, John F. Pvt.	6 WVI	10/12/61–11/17/64
Hurr, Marion Pvt.	10 WVI	2/1/62–5/7/65
Jennings, James L. Pvt.	I VAC	1/62–7/65
Johnson, John Pvt.	4 WVC	11/9/63–6/23/64
Kane, Patrick Pvt.	1 WVC	8/61–7/65
Kelley, Dyer Pvt.	6 WVI	10/18/64–6/12/65
Kelley, James L.B. Pvt.	17 WVI	4/63–4/64
Kennedy, Wm. H. Pvt.	4 WVC	7/14/63–3/14/64
also	17 VAI	2/1/65–7/1/65
Kidmore, Elihu S. Pvt.	15 WVI	9/62–6/12/65
Kinolig, Same W. Bugler	21 PAC	7/16/63–7/16/65
Kisner, Elias Pvt.	15 WVI	8/23/62–3/30/65
Knight, Wm. L. Pvt.	6 WVI	9/25/61–11/17/64
Leach, Elias S. Cpl.	4 WVC	7/14/63–3/g/64
also Sgt.	17 WVI	2/13/65–6/13/65
Leonard, Bowen E. Pvt.	12 WVI	62/65
Lindsey, Zachariah Pvt.	17 WVI	NF
Lock, Isaac M. Sgt.	15 WVI	9/15/62–7/3/65
Love, Bryon Sgt.	10 WVI	1/22/62–5/7/65
Love, John J. Pvt.	10 WVI	11/7/61–8/9/65
Ludwick, Jacob M. Cpl.	12 WVI	8/16/62–6/16/65
Male, George J. Pvt.	1 WVC	3/28/63–7/8/65
Male, George W. Pvt.	17 WVI	9/26/64–6/19/65
Martin, Joab Pvt.	15 WVI	9/1/62–6/27/65

Martin, Zephaniah Pvt.	14 WVI	9/3/62–6/27/65
Mason, Harry Pvt.	17 WVI	2/13/65–6/30/65
Matlick, Joseph A. Cpl.	4 WVC	7/14/63–3/g/64
also Sgt.	17 WVI	8/27/64–6/30/65
McDaniel, Nathan Pvt.	17 WVI	8/29/64–6/30/65
McDaniel, Wm. S. Sgt.	17 WVI	8/29/64–6/30/65
McVasker, Wm. Pvt.	17 WVI	2/15/65–6/30/65
Mell, John Sgt.	6 PAC	8/8/61–6/24/65
Middleton, Mitchell Pvt.	15 WVI	8/20/62–6/14/65
Minear, Benj. F. Pvt.	6 WVC	6/22/61–8/27/65
Minerd, John Pvt.	17 WVI	1864–6/65
Mitchell, Josiah Pvt.	15 WVI	8/23/62–6/14/65
Moats, James Pvt.	6 WVC	6/21/61–8/15/64
also	7 WVI	3/29/65–7/1/65
Moats, John A. Pvt.	15 WVI	8/23/62–6/14/65
Moats, Moses Pvt.	15 WVI	1862–4/12/65
Moats, Samuel Pvt.	6 WVI	9/27/61–11/25/64
Moats, Sanford H. Pvt.	7 WVI	4/7/65–8/4/65
Moore, Isaiah Pvt.	10 WVI	6/1/62–6/26/65
Moore, Otho Pvt.	15 WVI	1/18/64–8/9/65
Moore, See M. Pvt.	4 VAC	2/1/64–10/1/64
also Cpl.	17 VAI	2/20/65–6/20/65
Moore, Silas R. Pvt.	— WVI	6/1/62–6/26/65
Moore, Wm. R. Cpl.	10 WVI	6/1/62–6/26/65
More, Joshua Pvt.	— WVA	11/61–1/8/65
Odbert, Charles "Steward"	12 VAI	8/22/62–6/65
Osborne, Zarah Pvt.	6 WVI	NF
Otterback, George W. Pvt.	3 VAI	6/15/61–7/63
Parks, John H. Pvt.	188 OHI	2/13/65–9/12/65
Payne, James A. Pvt.	6 WVI	10/6/64–6/12/65
Phelps, George A. Sgt.	15 WVI	8/23/62–6/23/65
Phillips, Granville	NF (62 VAI CSA)	
Pittman, George G. Pvt.	10 VAI	64/65
Poland, George W. Pvt.	15 OHI	3/1/64–12/5/65
Poling, A.J. Pvt.	6 VAI	8/20/62–6/10/65
Price, Isaac Pvt.	15 WVI	8/27/62–6/12/65
Price, Lewis Pvt.	10 WVI	6/15/62–6/27/65
Price, Wm. G.W. Lt.	15 WVI	8/27/62–11/24/65
Register, James K. Pvt.	18 WVI	6/15/62–6/26/65
Right, John Pvt.	10 WVI	6/13/62–6/26/65
Right, Wm. J. Pvt.	15 WVI	8/27/62–6/14/65
Robinson, Benj. F. Pvt.	4 WVC	3/20/63–3/9/64
Robinson, Cyrus V. Pvt.	13 WVI	8/26/62–6/14/65
Robinson, Jesse W. Pvt.	4 WVC	7/14/63–3/g/64
Robinson, Simon M. Pvt.	17 WVI	9/24/64–6/30/65
Robinson, Thomas B. Cpl.	4 WVC	9/63–3/20/64
also Pvt.	17 WVI	9/24/64–6/30/65

Name	Unit	Dates
Ross, Clearly	NF	
Runnisell, Samuel C.	NF	
Shaw, Hezekiah Pvt.	4 WVC	7/27/63–3/9/64
Shingleton, Abraham Pvt.	15 WVI	8/23/62–6/23/65
Shingleton, Anderson Pvt.	15 WVI	8/28/62– 6/24/65
Silcott, James H. Pvt.	6 WVI	9/11/61–6/11/65
Sipe, David T. Pvt.	6 WVI	11/5/61–6/5/65
Sipe, John L. Pvt.	15 WVI	8/27/62–6/14/65
Stalnaker, Randall T. Pvt.	27 OHI	5/31/64–9/21/65
Stansberry, Augustus Pvt.	15 WVI	8/23/62 NF
Stemple, Christopher Pvt.	15 WVI	8/23/62–6/14/65
Steward, Felix G.	NF	
Strader, Aaron Pvt.	1 WVA	8/15/62–6/28/65
Summers, Alexander Pvt.	15 WVI	1/24/64–1865
Swagger, Wm. Pvt.	12 VAI	7/62–1865
Tallman, Robert L. Cpl.	10 VAI	6/1/62–6/26/63
Taylor, Richard H. Pvt.	3 WVI	6/15/61–8/15/64
Teter, Abel Pvt.	15 WVI	8/27/62–2/26/65
Teter, Oliver Pvt.	15 WVI	8/27/62–8/64
Thorn, George Pvt.	15 WVI	9/1/62–6/14/65
Thrasher, David Pvt.	3 WVI	7/5/61–4/66
Trahern, John F. Dr.	4 VAC	7/27/63–NF
Trimbly, Adam Pvt.	4 WVC	7/27/63–3/7/64
Trimbly, Michael E. Pvt.	7 WVI	7/4/61–9/3/62
Valentine, Frank D. Pvt.	4 WVC	7/5/63–3/1/64
Votters, Wm. V.A. Sgt.	10 WVI	4/13/62–8/20/65
Walker, Samuel C.	NF	
Walter, Lewis Pvt.	17 WVI	9/20/64–6/30/65
Ware, Adam W. Pvt.	15 WVI	8/23/62–6/14/65
Weaver, Augustus J.S. Cpl.	15 WVI	8/23/62–6/24/65
Weaver, Henry Pvt.	17 WVI	2/6/65–7/22/65
Weaver, Wm. G.S. Pvt.	6 WVI	9/12/61–10/18/64
Weese, Nimrod Pvt.	10 WVC	6/15/62–8/21/65
Welch, Samuel 0. Pvt.	10 WVI	10/13/62–7/24/65
Weston, George H.	NF	
Williamson, Nathan Pvt.	15 WVI	8/27/62–5/16/65
Wilmoth, John K. Pvt.	15 WVI	8/23/62–6/23/65
Wilson, Josiah S. Pvt.	15 WVI	8/23/62–6/14/65
Windon, Wm. G. Cpl.	3 WVI	5/61–10/17/65
Winngs, Simon Pvt.	15 WVI	8/22/62–6/29/64
Wolf, Levi	NF	
Wright, John Pvt.	2 —I	5/20/61–6/14/64
Wright, Loyd Pvt.	3 VAI	6/25/61–2/28/64
also Sgt.	6 WVC	2/29/64–5/22/66
Yeager, Wm. Pvt.	15 WVI	8/23/62–6/14/65
Zircle, Jacob Pvt.	15 WVI	8/23/62–6/14/65

Barbour Co. Remarks

Allen, E.—RH & HD
Barte, H.—frozen feet
Bean, J.H.—broken leg
Boyles, D.—ague
Brown, H.W.—Shot left leg & deafness right ear
Cade, W.—injured by wagon
Carter, D.G.—WIA right hand
Carter, J.—WIA right eye
Champ, J.—WIA mouth & POW 3 months and 5 days
Coberly, H.—WIA Snicker's Ferry on left side
Coffman, E.—lost right testicle from mumps
Cox, D.H.—deserted veteran
Cross, L.—shot in head
Crostin, C.M.—CD
Crouse, S.—RH & eyes
Cummings, L.—LD/DSC
Currance, G.W.—fistula
Daugherty, J.A.—LD
Edmond, W.—CDR fall of 1864
Freeman, J.D.—right leg shot off 9/19/64
Glendenning, G.—KD & spinal trouble
Gower, J.—gunshot left elbow
Grant, G.—LD
Gregory, M.G.—RP
Hinsley, W.—WIA & KD
House, A.—RH
Hovater, B.—RP
Hovey, J.—WIA left thigh DI
Howes, F.—KD & RH
Hurr, M.—RH
Kane, P.—MP
Kisner, E.—WIA by shell
Knight, W.L.—LD & F
Lock, I.M.—RH contracted on Lynchburg raid
Love, J.J.—SS & HD
Martin, J.—WIA left leg
Mason, H.—LD
Matlick, J.A.—CD
McDaniel, W.S.—KD & piles
McVasker, Wm.—CD
Minerd, J.—MS & F
Mitchell, Md.—WIA left forearm
Moats, M.—right leg shot off 9/19/64
Moore, O.—VV & shot left leg
Moore, S.R.—shot in head

Odbert, C.H.—wounded in my character
Osborne, Z.—injury to lungs
Otterback, G.W.—KD
Phelps, G.A.—WIA left leg
Pittman, G.—Piles/DSC
Price, I.—both arms shot off
Price, L.—CDR
Register, J.—CDR & piles
Right, J.—VV & dislocation right aricle & cut wrist
Right, W.J.—thumb injured by wagon
Robinson, B.—hurt riding saddle & lame ever since
Robinson, C.V.—CD
Shingleton, A.—WIA from shell explosion
Silcott, J.H.—lost left testicle from mumps
Sipe, J.L.—RH
Skidmore, E.—TYF
Stansberry, A.—deserted 10/8/62
Strader, A.—MP
Taylor, R.H.—TYF
Teter, A.—HD
Thorn, G.—TYF
Thrasher, D.—WIA left leg
Trimbly, A.—TYF
Trimbly, M.E.—SS in army
Votters, Wm.—POW Andersonville
Weaver, A.—WIA left leg
Weese, N.—WIA Droop Mountain right side
Welch, S.A.—shot in left leg
Williamson, N.—slight wound
Wright, J.—HD & RH & piles
Yeager, W.—RH & VV

Berkeley County

NAME/RANK	REGIMENT	WHEN SERVED
Adair, George	2 NYC	63/65
Agle, George B.	CSA	NF
Ambrose, C. B. Pvt.	NF (41 VAC CSA)	
Ambrose, John W.	2 VAI CSA	4/16/61–62
Anderson, John D.	CSA	NF
Andrews, Jerimiah Pvt.	1 MDI	8/22/61–10/1/64
Armstrong, William Cpl.	15 ILI	8/7/62–1/29/63
Aued, Thomas Pvt.	CSA	NF
Bagnett, William	CSA	NF
Balons, William H.	NF	
Barger, Joseph A. Pvt.	12 PAC	2/15/63–7/7/65
Barnard, Josiah D. Pvt.	1 MDC	10/26/61–10/26/64
Barthon, Eugean Pvt.	13 MDI	2/27/64–5/29/65
Bartlett, Erastus G. Capt.	12 WVI	8/12/62–6/16/65
Beall, Edward Pvt.	138 MDI	4/64–11/64
Beard, John Pvt.	96 PAI	10/3/61–7/22/65
Beck, John Cpl.	1 MDI	12/16/61–10/25/64
Bennet, Samuel Pvt.	31 NCI CSA	6/62–8/64
Biker, William F. Capt.	87 PAI	NF
Bishop, John W. Lt.	14 WVI	8/14/62–8/14/65
Bittinger, William H. Sgt.	2 PAA	1/1/64–1/29/66
Blakeney, George W. Pvt.	NF	
Bodin, Thomas Pvt.	2 VAI CSA	61/61
Bowers, David H. Cpl.	207 PAI	8/64–5/31/65
Bown, Thomas Pvt.	7 VA CSA	61/65
Brass, John T	NF	
Braxton, Bevaley Pvt.	NF	
Bristor, Jacob H. Capt.	12 WVI	8/16/62–6/16/65
Brown, Martin Pvt.	1 MDC	9/3/61–9/3/64
Brown, Thomas G.	US	NF
Brumba, Dreen	CSA	NF
Burtram, Samuel Pvt.	33 VAI CSA	7/1/61–4/1/65
Buckerman, James Pvt.	2 PAI	8/3/61–9/28/64
Bush, Phillip Pvt.	1 NYC	8/24/61–8/29/64
Cage, James D.	NF (2 VAI CSA)	
Camey, Jacob V. Pvt.	17 VAC CSA	
Carpenter, William E. Pvt.	21 PAC	6/17/63–2/20/64
Catlett, Samuel	USA	NF
Caw, John T. Pvt.	1 MDI	10/1/62–10/16/65
Chase, William Pvt.	PAA	11/61–6/65
Claton, James Cpl.	127 PAI	64/65
Clendening, William C.	NF	
Clifford, John R. Cpl.	13 USC	3/6/65–3/18/65

Name	Unit	Dates
College, Joseph R. Pvt.	208 PAI	65/66
Combs, John L. E	NF (BUGLER 1 VAC CSA)	
Combs, Kendricks B.	NF	
Copenhaver, Jacob D.	NF (2 VAI CSA)	
Corsey, George W. Pvt.	WSC	2/27/64–8/22/65
Creast, Sumner Pvt.	NF	
Crique, Kinsey B. Cpl.	1 NYC	7/1/61–7/1/65
Cross, Daniel W. Pvt.	7 VAC CSA	8/61–4/65
Crouse, William Pvt.	6 VAC	3/13/64–6/15/65
Crump, Richard	CSA	NF
Cunningham, James N. Capt.	NF (1 VAC CSA)	
Cunningham, William L. Pvt.	1 VAC CSA	4/19/61–4/19/65
Daniels, George W. Pvt.	40 OHI	9/17/61–9/19/64
Davis, George W. Pvt.	69 OHI	11/62–4/64
Davis, John W. Cpl.	2 MDC	11/7/62–8/8/65
Deck, Ed. C.	NF (2 VAI CSA)	
Delancy, William Pvt.	202 PAI	8/18/64–8/3/65
Detter, John L. Pvt.	CSA	NF
Dixon, Samuel Vpt.	2 PAI	11/26/61–11/27/64
Donald, Enos M.	CSA	NF
Dorn, Martin L.	NF	
Douglas, Charles Pvt.	1 NYI (MULLATO)	10/9/63–12/12/64
Drenner, David F. Pvt.	1 PAI	NF
Drew, Henry	CSA	NF
Dugan, James F.	2 VAI CSA	NF
Edwards, John Pvt.	1 MDC	62/63
Erghelvrgo, Isaac Pvt.	2 PAA	62/65
Engel, James D.	NF	
Filker, Jacob Pvt.	154 PAI	11/63–6/64
Fisher, Jacob M. Pvt.	45 PAI	4/61–63
Fitz, John "Lans"	VESSEL SUAANA	5/64–8/66
Fitzgerald, Michael Pvt.	11 INI	8/11/61–8/31/64
Flick, William H. Pvt.	41 OHI	7/61–12/62
Fortex, John B.	CSA	NF
Frank, John Pvt.	14 PAC	4/20/63–8/29/65
Fravel, John H.	NF	
Freeman, Brown	NEGRO	NF
Freeze, Andrew J. Pvt.	1 VAC CSA	4/19/61–4/9/65
Friskey, Lewis Pvt.	2 MDI	9/4/61–9/4/64
Fuss, Gotleib Pvt.	2 MDC	8/61–9/64
Gallagher, Thomas Pvt.	38 MOI	62/65
Gallaher, Joshua S. Sgt.	2 MDI	8/21/61–3/13/64
Gans, John M.	NF	
Gasman, Jacob Pvt.	2 VAC CSA	
Ginn ?, James V. Pvt.	2 VAI CSA	
Girault, Edward R. Sgt.	2 MDC	9/61–9/64
Gletner, James D. Pvt.	1 MDC	9/2/61–4/13/65

Golder, Carmon	NF	
Graham, Andrew M. Sgt.	8 MDI	9/15/62–6/21/65
Green, Martin V.B. Pvt.?	PAI	8/25/61–10/1/64
Greer, Robert W. Pvt.	1 MDI	8/9/61–9/9/64
Gregory, Richard	NF	
Grimes, Robert H. Pvt.	11 PAI	4/10/61–8/12/61
Grimm, Robert H. Pvt.	1 MDI	8/26/61–5/25/65
Grozinger, John Pvt.	1 NYC	7/20/61–8/23/64
Gwinn, John Pvt.	2 VAI CSA	4/61–4/65
Hamersley, Joseph Pvt.	1 MDC	1/65–7/65
Harlow, E. B.	CSA	NF
Harlow, Marquis	NF (26 VAC CSA?)	
Harmann, William	CSA NF (2 VAI ?)	
Harmann, Jacob	NF	
Harmann, Meridith H.	NF	
Harper, Lloyd W. Pvt.	1 MDI	8/20/61–9/9/64
Harris ?, John D. Pvt.	CSA	NF
Harris, Daniel Pvt.	11? INF.	61/65
Harris, George Lt.	31 VAI? CSA	61/61
Harrison, Charles Pvt.	2 MDC	61/65
Harrison, Samuel P. Pvt.	2 VAC CSA	4/61–6/61
Hartley, James Pvt.	2 PAI	8/12/61–9/15/64
Hathaway, Orville	NF	
Hautzler, John E. Pvt.	1 MDC	62/65
Hays, James F. Pvt.	2 VAI CSA	
Hays, Joseph Pvt.	6 WVC	6/22/64–1/27/65
Heck, Joseph W.	CSA	NF
Hedges, Anthony Pvt.	1 MDC	3/13/65–6/28/65
Hedges, Bailey S.	CSA NF (1 VAA?)	
Henry, John B.	CSA NF (12 VAI?)	
Hensell, P. H. Pvt.	3 VAC	1/64–6/65
Hicks, John	CSA	NF
Hill, Ervin Pvt.	10 WVI	5/61–5/65
Hinchberger, (No First) Pvt.	NF	
Hingle, John	NF (62 VAI CSA)	
Hite, Charles A.	12 VAC? CSA	11/15/61–6/10/62
Hollida, John W. Pvt.	1 VAC CSA	6/1/61–1/1/65
Homer, Robert G. Pvt.	1 MDC	6/23/64–7/27/65
Houck, George W. Pvt.	13 MDI	2/25/65–5/29/65
Hull, Jacob Sgt.	3 MDI	9/61–5/65
Hull, John Pvt.	2 VAI CSA	4/61–4/65
Hutton, Elisha P. Pvt.	21 PAC	2/6/64–7/8/65
also Pvt.	165 PAI	10/16/62–7/28/63
Hutzler, James W. Pvt.	7 MDI	8/9/62–5/21/65
Hutzler, John C. Pvt.	1 MDI	6/8/63–7/2/65
Jack, John C. Pvt.	1 MDC	9/61–9/15/64
Jackson, Charles H.	NF	

Name	Unit	Dates
Jacobs, Thomas Pvt.	1 INI	9/61–9/64
Jennings, James W. Pvt.	13 MDI	2/1/65–5/29/65
Johnson, Seaton	NF	
Jones, Nicholas W. Sgt.	NF	
Kane, John T. Pvt.	1 MDI	11/24/61–5/29/65
Kantreer, William H. Capt.	6.WVC	6/28/61–5/65
Kearney, Miles H. Pvt.	1 NYC	9/9/61–6/27/65
Kearns, Thomas Pvt.	NF	
Keefer, Charles H.	US SCOUT	NF
Kerdy, John H. Pvt.	11 MDI	7/26/64–9/29/64
Kerfoot, James W.	CSA NF (2 VAI?)	
Kerns, George	NF	
Ketchen, Joseph G. Pvt.	1 MDC 61	NF
Keusel, John J.	CSA	11/64 NF
Keyser, Isaac Pvt.	5 WVC	1/29/64–6/30/65
Kilmer, Nary D. Pvt.	1 VAC CSA	61/65
Knapp, George Pvt.	34 MOI	12/29/63–1865
Kobius, George W. Pvt.	NF	
Kreglow, George T. Pvt.	2 VAI CSA	4/61–1/62
Lambert, George D. Pvt.	1 MDI	9/1/61–12/9/64
Lainy, Lemuel Pvt.	22 VAC CSA	4/62–5/62
Lardon, Michael	CSA	NF
Lauden, Washington Pvt.	7 INI	4/31/61–8/31/61
also 2lt.	17 INA	4/17/62–8/8/65"
Lemaster, John H. Sgt.	3 WVC	1/23/64–1/30/65
Lemen, Jacob G. Pvt.	1 MDC	9/6/61–12/3/64
Lemem, William M.D.	1 VAC CSA	4/61–4/65
Lemowith ? , W.N. ? Sgt.	2 VAI CSA	61/65
Licklider, John Pvt.	NF (12 VAC CSA)	
Lindis, Samuel Pvt.		
Long, Daniel Pvt.	PAA	5/10/64–6/20/65
Lucas, Edward Pvt.	10 VAC CSA	4/61–4/65
Lyons, John Pvt.	48 PAI	3/2/64–NF
Maconanhey, Elisha P. Lt.	9 PAC	4/61–4/64
Mann, Charles W. Pvt.	1 MDC	8/24/61–6/28/65
Manor, Charles W. Sgt.	2 VAI CSA	4/61–4/65
Marshall, George W. Pvt.	1 VAC CSA	
Marshall, Mason	NF (1 VAC CSA)	
Martin, Burrell N. Pvt.	2 MDI	6/1/63–5/29/65
Martin, George W.	NF (26 BTN VAI CSA?)	
Mason, Casper P. Pvt.	1 PAR	5/61–4/10/63
Mason, John Pvt.	USA	NF
Matthews, Benjamin F.	NF (46 VAI CSA?)	
McAneny, Frank Pvt.	6 WVI	2/3/65–6/10/65
McBee, Franklin S. Pvt.	2 MDI	6/61–10/64
McBee, William T. Pvt.	2 MDI	9/6/61–9/15/64
McBride, John H. Pvt.	1 WVC	3/24/64–7/8/65

Name	Unit	Dates
McDowell, Charles Pvt.	2 VAC CSA	
McDonald, Isaac Pvt.	1 MDC	5/8/63–6/28/65
McKee, William E. Pvt.	13 MDI	9/64–6/65
McKinney, Luke Pvt.	NF	
Merchant, John	NF (89 VAM CSA)	
Miles, John T. Pvt.	VAI CSA	4/61–9/64
Miller, Benjamine T. Pvt.	3 MDI	6/15/61–7/4/64
Miller, Daniel Pvt.	NF	
Miller, Harvey A. Pvt.	2 VAC CSA	
Miller, Henry Pvt.	CSA (89 VAM)	NF
Miller, John A. Pvt.	NF (2 VAI CSA?)	
Moser, Daniel Pvt.	7 INI	8/62–65
Munson, Calvin I. Sgt.	3 INC	9/25/63–9/65
Murphy, John W. Pvt.	8 VAI	64/65
Murphy, William Pvt.	3 VAC	1/64–6/65
Mussells, Plumer Pvt.	CSA	NF
Myers, Jacob S.	NF (25 VAI CSA)	
Myers, Samuel Pvt.	3 WVI	NF
Myers, Wm H.	NF (12 VAC CSA)	
Naggle, James Pvt.	10 —	8/62–5/65
Naggs, Joseph O.	NF······	
Neville, F. P. Lt.	15 MDI	10/11/61–2/1/65
Nikon, Timothy Pvt.	27 VAI CSA	3/62–3/65
Nipe, James P. Pvt.	2 VAI CSA	
Nokmer ? Jacob C.	12 LA CSA	4/61–4/65
Nolen, William Pvt.	WISE ARTILLERY	61/65
Noll, William T. Capt.	CSA (1 VAC)	NF
Nuger, Nicholas Pvt.	3 MDI	12/9/61–2/15/63
Oller, Samuel Pvt.	130 PAI	7/25/62–2/13/63
Orr, William Pvt.	1 MDC	9/62–6/65
Overton, George P. Pvt.	56 NYI	1/1/62–10/9/63
also Pvt.	15 NYC	1/4/64–8/9/65
Owens, James W.	NF (1 MDA CSA ?)	
Pace, James Pvt.	NF	
Palmer, Amos Pvt.	—	61/64–3/3/65
Parsons, George W. Pvt.	1 MDC	10/7/61–10/8/64
Patterson, John H. Pvt.	14 PAC	3/24/64–7/31/65
Payne, Thomas Pvt.	NF (2 VAI CSA?)	
Pearrell, Reason Sgt.	1 MDC	8/24/61–9/15/64
Peters, James Pvt.	4 WSC	9/1/63–5/6/65
Phillips, Bailey F.	NF	
Pigler, Sam B. Lt.	1 MDC	9/61–10/64
Piteo, John Pvt.	12 PAC	5/61–7/65
Pitzer, Elias M.	CSA NF (12 VAC?)	
Poisal, Adam P.S. Pvt.	2 MDI	8/26/61–9/13/64
Price, Charles Sgt.	US SIGNAL CORP	4/1/63–NF
Price, George L. Pvt.	3 WVC	1/23/64–1/30/65

Name	Unit	Dates
Randal, James Pvt.	12 VAC	61/64
Rankin, John W. Pvt.	1 MDC	9/61–9/63
Rathman, George V. Pvt.	54 PAI	9/24/61–10/12/64
Riatz ?, Hamille Pvt.	1 MDC	61/65
Riddle, Charles	CSA	NF
Riddleberger, William	CSA	NF
Ridgeway, Josiah J. Pvt.	2 VAC	62/64
Ritenhour, John Pvt.	2 VAI CSA	4/61–4/65
Roach, John W. Pvt.	2 MDI	9/18/62–6/65
Roberts, John F. Pvt.	NF (39 VAC CSA?)	
Robinson, Andrew Pvt.	3 VAI	4/63–10/65
Robinson, Armistead Pvt.	NF	
Robinson, C. R.	PAI	64/65
Robison, James Cpl.	6 ?? CSA	62/63
Rofs, Daniel R. Pvt.	7 NYC	9/11/61–3/31/62
also Pvt.	123 NYI	8/14/62–6/8/65
Roop ?, Henry Pvt.	CSA	NF
Ross, Melanthaw J. Pvt.	36 ILI	4/61–6/30/65
Rouark, William H. Pvt.	1 MDI	5/16/61–5/16/64
Russell, Thomas H. Pvt.	3 MDI	2/1664–5/25/65
Rutherford, George W. Cpl.	1 MDC	10/16/63–8/8/65
Sautman, George W. Pvt.	1 MDI	9/21/61–10/25/64
Sayles, William T.	NF (11 VAC CSA)	
Scarlett, William Pvt.	1 MDC	11/7/62–6/28/65
Schleiss, Jacob Pvt.	30 NYA	3/10/62–3/11/65
Schmidt, Adam	NF (GRAHAMS VAA CSA?)	
Schoppart, Alexandre	CSA	NF
Seonard, James M. Bugler	1 MDC	6/8/59–5/16/64
Shaw, Isaac	CSA NF (62 VAI?)	
Sherard, John M. Pvt.	16 PAC	2/12/64–8/11/65
Shipley, William Pvt.	4 MDI	12/61–5/65
Shrimp, Jonas Pvt.	54 PAI	3/62–5/65
Sibert, Eli Pvt.	1 VAC CSA	8/64–4/9/65
Simmons, Dewitt C. Pvt.	123 OHI	9/30/62–7/10/65
Small, Adam Cpl.	10 VAI CSA	4/61–4/65
Small, David H. Pvt.	1 VAC CSA	61/65
Small, George H. Pvt.	1 VAC CSA	4/62–9/62
Small, James B. Pvt.	CSA (2 VAI?)	6/64–9/64
Small, James N. Pvt.	CSA (2 VAI)	8/62–2/63
Small, John M. Pvt.	2 VAI CSA	NF
Small, Reuben W. Pvt.	2 VAC CSA	
Smith, Charles D.	NF	
Smith, John W.H.	1 MDC	9/3/61–9/15/64
Smith, Lewis Pvt.	13 MDI	5/29/63–2/65
Smith, Phillip	NF (7 VAI CSA?)	
Smith, W.D. Pvt.	4 NJI	4/1/61–7/21/61
also Sgt.	6 NJI	8/6/61–11/21/63

Name	Unit	Dates
Smith, William M. Lt.	3 MDI	NF
Smurr, Charles	NF	
Snowden, John W.	NF	
Snuirr ?, James H. Cpl.	1 MDC	10/8/61–10/8/64
Spiker, William R. Pvt.	29 ILI	2/16/64–11/22/65
Sprinkel, Adolphus N.	CSA	NF
Staff, Albert	CSA (1 VAA)	NF
Staff, Richard R. Pvt.	NF	
Stanely, Isaac W. Pvt.	2 PAI	11/26/61–11/30/64
Stanley, John Pvt.	2 NYI	2/20/64–5/24/65
Staubly, Anthony Sgt.	18 CNI	7/17/62–6/27/65
Stevens, Benjamin	USA	NF
Stevens, John Pvt.	12 PAC	63/65
Stipe, Gephart Pvt.	31 NYA	8/20/61–8/20/64
Stone, George E. Sgt.	15 PAI	8/25/62–6/65
Stouffer, John B. Pvt.	145 ILI	64/65
Strausner, Paul Pvt.	126 PAI	8/1/62–5/30/63
Studerwalt, Jacob Pvt.	6 MDI	7/62–6/65
Sullivan, David	CSA (41 VAI)	NF
Sutton, John	CSA	NF
Sutton, John D. Pvt.	10 WVI	5/1/62–5/1/65
Swisher, Charles E. Cpl.	1 PAI	7/61–11/64
Tabler, Adam Pvt.	47 VAI	61/61
Tabler, Adam A. Pvt.	VAI CSA (67 VAM?)	10/62–11/63
Tabler, Luther Pvt.	CSA (67 VAM?)	NF
Tabler, Wm M. Pvt.	1 MDI	10/13/62–8/12/65
Taylor, Otis H. Pvt.	11 MDI	64/64
Taylor, Samuel H. Pvt.	3 WVC	1/23/64–1/30/65
Taylor, James R. Pvt.	1 INC	61/65
Tebo, John A. Pvt.	NF (52 VAI CSA)	
Thompon, R. S. Pvt.	3 MDI	9/61–7/31/65
Turner, McGill Pvt.	1 VAC	6/61–9/65
Underdonk, Newton	CSA	NF
Vanmeter, Abram H. Pvt.	1 MDC	1/62–3/62
Vanmeter, Joseph	NF (2 VAC CSA)	
Vanmeter, Newton	CSA	NF
Vorhess, Abram Pvt.	VAI CSA	61/65
Vories, Ashburn Pvt.	NF	
Walburn, George E. Capt.	3 PAA	3/64–11/65
Watson, John Pvt.	1 MDC	9/1/61–10/12/65
Watson, John M. Pvt.	1 MDC	2/24/64–8/12/65
Way, George W. Pvt.	10 VAI CSA	4/62–4/65
Wayble, Cyrus N. Pvt.	1 WVI	11/7/64–5/31/65
Weaver, Abraham Pvt.	3 MDI	6/23/61–9/10/64
Welshans, John W.	CSA (67 VAM?)	NF
Welshans, Levi Pvt.	3 WVC	1/23/64–1/65
Welshans, P. H. Pvt.	3 WVC	NF

Westrater, William Pvt.	1 NYC	6/10/61–7/10/65
Wharton, Phelan	NF	
Wheeler, William Pvt.	5 ALI CSA	5/61–9/64
Wilhelm, Reason J.	1 MDI	
Williams, Alexander Pvt.	NF	
Williams, Norvel Pvt.	31 OHI	6/64–6/65
Willinghouse, James W.	2 VAI CSA	
Wilson, Charles Pvt.	NF (2 VAI CSA?)	
Wolfslagle, Phillip W.	NF	
Wormiy, John Pvt.	12 VAC CSA	62/65
Wright, William Pvt.	1 MDI	9/3/61–9/15/64
Yomery ?, Davilla Pvt.	1 VAC CSA	
Young, Martin Pvt.	1 MDC	12/28/61–2/26/64
Yountz, James Pvt.	93 PAI	10/10/61–1/15/65
Zepp, George S. Pvt.	1 NYC	NF
Zigler, Cornelius Pvt.	2 PAI	8/12/61–9/28/64
Zimmerman, Charles Pvt.	5 USC	2/5/61–2/5/64

Berkeley Co. Remarks

Ambrose, J.W.*—discharged on account of fractured arm
Andrews, J.—RH
Barnard, J.—shot in left hip
Beard, J.—gunshot arm
Brown, F.—black
Burtram, S.*—WIA finger & right thigh
Bush, P.—loss of hearing
College, J.R.—LD & piles
Crouse, W.—RH
Davis, G.A.—WIA left arm
Detter, J.L.*—surrendered at Appomattox
Douglas, C.—mulatto
Fisher, J.M.—cold settled on lungs
Flick, W.H.—gunshot left side
Free, A.J. Jr.*—WIA hip
Gallagher, T.—WIA
Hurn?, J.D.*—Surrendered at Appomattox
Jack, J.—POW escaped
Jacobs, T.—WIA left side
Leonard, J.M.—right leg shot
Lindis, S.—lost finger from gunshot

Maconanhey, E.—WIA thigh & hand
Mason, C.—ankle mashed
McBride, J.—throat infection
Merchant, J.*—RH
Miller, H.*—surrendered at Appomattox
Noll, W.T.*—Surrendered at Appomattox
Nuger, N.—HD/DSC
Pace, J.—RH
Palmer, A.—RH & CDR/DSC
Patterson, J.W.—health broken up generally
Ritenhour, J.*—WIA arm & leg
Rofs, D.R.—POW Andersonville 10 months
Ross, M.J.—total blindness
Smith, L. —shot in the house
Smith, W.D.—leg shot off
Strausner, P.—RP
Swisher, C.E.—eye out & loines injured
Tabler, W.—RH
Vearey, J.*—Confederate mulatto
Voories, A.—RH
Watson, J.—wounded at Deep Bottom on James River
Williams, H. —WIA leg
Young, M.—WIA leg
NOTE: P.H. Welshans of 3 WVC had earlier served the 67 VAM CSA.

Boone County

NAME/RANK	REGIMENT	WHEN SERVED
Adkins, Benton Pvt.	NF (50 TNI CSA?)	
Adkins, Isom Pvt.	7 WVC?	4/12/64–1865
Adkins, Sherwood Pvt.	7 WVC	1/5/63–8/10/65
Adshire, L.B. Pvt.	7 WVC	8/27/63–1865
Barker, Cumberland M. Cpl.	7 WVC	3/15/64–8/1/65
Barker, Daniel Pvt.	7 WVC	9/2/61–1/25/65
Barker, Isaac Pvt.	7 WVC	9/2/61–1/25/65
Barker, Jacob Pvt.	NF (13 VAC CSA?)	
Barker, John A.J. Pvt.	7 WVC	9/2/61–8/1/65
Basham, Nathan Pvt.	NF	
Bayes, Lewis Pvt.	11 WVI	1/1/62–7/20/65
Bias, Wm. V.B. Lt.	7 WVC	9/2/61–8/65
Bradshaw, John A. Pvt.	NF	
Bray, Joseph C.	US	NF
Chapman, John F. Blksmith	7 WVC	9/2/61–8/1/65
Cook, Henry F. Pvt.	8 WVI	12/9/61–10/29/63
Cook, James M. Pvt.	7 WVC	12/3/64–8/11/65
Cook, Wm. H. Pvt.	173 OHI	8/3/64–6/26/65
Cook, Wm. Pvt.	—WVC?	61/65
Copley, Johnson Pvt.	4 WVC	6/15/63–3/10/65
Douglas, George W. Pvt.	4 WVC	6/10/63–3/10/64
Douglas, James E. Cpl.	7 WVC	9/2/61–8/1/65
Elkins, Ryland F. Pvt.	7 WVC	12/7/61–8/1/65
Ellison, Lewis D. Cpl.	6 VAI	5/62–1865
Epling, Miles P. Pvt.	11 WVI	10/6/62–7/5/65
Epling, Philip P. Pvt.	11 WVI	7/14/62–10/4/63
Epling, Wm. T. Bugler	7 WVC	3/28/648/10/65
Evans, Mitchell Pvt.	7 WVC	10/6/61–1/26/63
Ferrell, James Pvt.	57 PAI	6/30/64–7/1/65
Gadd, James A. Pvt.	NF	
Gunnoe, Daniel H. Pvt.	4 VAC	6/15/63–3/10/64
Hager, Enoch A. Sgt.	7 WVC	10/14/61–8/10/65
Hager, Montgomery Sgt.	4 WVC	6/15/63–3/10/64
Halestine, James Pvt.	4 WVC	6/15/63–3/10/64
Hardman, Benj. G. Pvt.	11 WVI	8/62–NF
Harless, James B. Pvt.	8 WVI	9/2/61–NF
Holsten, Martin V.B. Pvt.	NF	
Holstine, Jarvis J. Pvt.	4 WVC	10/5/61–8/1/65
Holstine, John W. Pvt.	7 WVC	NF
Hunter, Francis A. Pvt.	5 MAC	10/31/62–10/31/65
Hunter, Robert Pvt.	NF (VSL 1 CAV CSA?)	
Jarrell, John Pvt.	NF (36 BTN VAC CSA)	
Javins, Francis Pvt.	45 KYI	63/65

Name	Unit	Dates
Javins, Wm. M. Pvt.	4 WVC	6/15/64–3/10/65
Keffer, Wilson Pvt.	7 WVC	9/2/61–8/1/65
Kender, Isaac Pvt.	7 WVC	3/20/64–8/1/65
Kinder, James M. Pvt.	7 WVC	12/4/62–8/1/65
Kinder, Oliver Pvt.	7 WVC	3/20/64–8/1/65
Kirse, Patrick Pvt.	66 ILI	9/11/61–9/14/64
Lewis, James H. Pvt.	7 WVC	9/2/61–9/13/62
Marrix, Patrick Pvt.	4 WVI	6/8/61–7/64
Mason, Nimrod Lt.	7 WVC?	61/65
Meadows, George Pvt.	7 WVC	9/2/61–1/25/65
Meadows, John L. Pvt.	7 WVC	1864–8/1/65
Moore, Joseph	US	NF
Mullins, Andrew J. Pvt.	55 KYI	NF
Osborn, David J. Pvt.	1 WVC	3/20/62–6/17/65
Pauley, Wm. Blksmith	7 WVC	9/3/61–7/6/63
Payne, Thornton A. Pvt.	NF	
Perry, Joseph L. Pvt.	7 WVC	2/11/65–8/1/65
Perry, Robert E. Sgt.	7 WVC	8/1/65
Pettry, James M. Sgt.	8 VAI	10/24/61–9/23/65
Pettry, Peter Pvt.	7 WVC	8/9/65
Price, Zachariah W. Pvt.	13 TNC	9/22/64–9/5/65
Price, John Lt.	7 WVC	10/24/61–4/64
Price, Wm. C. Pvt.	3 WVC	2/15/64–1865
Russell, James Pvt.	7 WVC	4/1/62–4/7/65
Scott, Isaac Jr. Bugler	1 WVC	7/27/61–8/1/65
Scott, Wm. Pvt.	7 WVC	7/27/61–6/24/65
Scraggs, Samuel	US	NF
Shaw, Elisha	US	NF
Snodgrass, Hugh Pvt.	7 WVC	9/2/61–1/25/65
Stuart, James H. Pvt.	7 WVC	10/1/64–8/1/65
Toler, Emmanuel Pvt.	NF	
Walls, John Cpl.	7 WVC	4/1/62–4/8/65
Webb, Jacob Lt.	—WVC?	61/65
Wheeler, Alexander Pvt.	NF	
White, George D. Pvt.	7 WVC	11/11/64–8/11/65
White, James A. Pvt.	7 WVC	10/61–8/65
Williams, David Pvt.	7 WVC	11/12/61–8/1/65
Williams, Loyd M. Sgt.	4 WVC	6/5/63–3/10/64
Wood, John H.	11 WVI	8/22/62–7/5/65
Workman, Amos Pvt.	7 WVC	10/5/61–8/11/61
Workman, Benj. H. Pvt.	2 WVC	62/65
Workman, Isaac Pvt.	7 WVC	12/31/62–8/65
Workman, James Sgt.	7 WVC	10/1/61–8/9/65
Workman, Jasper Pvt.	NF	
Workman, John L. Sgt.	7 WVC	10/5/51–8/1/65
Workman, Robert Pvt.	2 WVC	8/29/63–6/15/65
Workman, Tunsil P. Pvt.	7 WVC	10/3/61–5/8/65

Boone Co. Remarks

Abshire, L.B.—KD, discharge papers destroyed
Adkins, B.—thrown from vicious horse in service & breast badly injured, worst disabled ex-soldier in county
Adkins, S.—DSC
Barker, C.M.— gleydrocele
Barker, I.—broken wrist & RH
Barker, J.A.J.—catarrh & RH
Basham, N.—draws pension
Bayes, L.—CDR, gunshot wound, pensioned on disabilities
Bias, W.V.B.—hart trouble & broken toe
Bradshaw, J.A.—AFP, owns home & farm, mines coal in Kanawha
Chapman, J.F. —RH, piles & erysipelas, very badly disabled
Cook, H.F. —RH, KD, HD, pensioned on disabilities
Copley, J.—eyes, hearing, RH
Douglas, G.W.—RH
Douglas, J.E.—LD & RH
Elkins, R.F.—testikle & leg, pensioned on disabilities
Ellison, L.D. —gunshot wound
Epling, P.P. —RH, rupture, hearing, DSC, suffering disability

Braxton County

NAME/RANK	REGIMENT	WHEN SERVED
Adkinson, B.H. Pvt.	1 WVC	3/65–7/8/65
Anderson, Wm. L. Cpl.	(27 VAI CSA?)	8/11/62–6/65
Armstrong, John D. Cpl.	10 WVI	9/25/61–3/13/65
Balford, Wm. H.H. Pvt.	18 VAC CSA	3/62–4/65
Barnett, James K. Pvt.	10 WVI	6/1/62–6/27/65
Baxter, Felix G. Pvt.	3 WVC	8/10/63–7/4/65
Bender, Henry Lt.	10 WVI	1/7/62–5/3/65
Berry, James M. Capt.	25 VAI CSA	61/65
Berry, James W. Sgt.	62 VAI CSA	1861–6/23/65
Berry, Pembrook B. Pvt.	62 VAI CSA	9/1/62–1865
Berry, Thornton J. Lt.	25 VAI CSA	6/61–6/65
Bird, John W. Pvt.	31 VAI CSA	62/63
Bishop, Aaron Pvt.	23 OHI	2/1/64–3/30/65
Blagg, John W. Capt.	———	63/65
Blake, John J. Pvt.	62 VAI CSA	62/63
Boggs, Elihu J. Cpl.	91 OHI	8/15/62–6/24/65
Boggs, Paton J. Pvt.	3 WVC	1863–NF
Bolinger, Z.A. Pvt.	14 WVI	11/15/62–7/27/65
Bower, Jacob B.	US NF	
Boyles, Edgar T. Sgt.	1 WVA	6/62 6/65
Brady, Solomon B. Pvt.	10 WVI	1/11/62–5/3/65
Bragg, Edward S. Pvt.	25 VAI CSA	61/65
Brighit, Azariah H. Cpl.	10 WVI	4/15/62–5/3/65
Brohard, Taylor Pvt.	1 WVI	3/14/65–7/1/65
Brown, Allen S. Pvt.	17 VAC CSA	6/1/62–4/65
Brown, Zebeace Pvt.	6 WVI	9/2/61–6/10/65
Burns, Isaac R. Pvt.	17 WVI	64/65
Butcher, Milton Pvt.	26 VAC CSA	5/15/63–4/28/65
Campbell, David Pvt.	7 WVI	61/64
Carder, Albert F. Pvt.	15 WVI	NF
Carlin, Granville Capt.	18 VAC CSA	61/65
Carr, Francis Sgt.	10 WVI	5/3/62–6/16/65
Carr, James C. Pvt.	17 WVI	12/23/64–6/30/65
Carr, Silis Pvt.	10 WVI	5/3/62–6/22/65
Chapman, John Pvt.	7 WVC	9/26/64–6/8/65
Childers, Reuben D. Pvt.	15 WVI	8/8/62–6/5/65
Clark, T.A. Pvt.	7 WVI	3/16/65–6/27/65
Clutter, Andrew H. Pvt.	10 WVI	2/7/62–5/3/65
Clutter, John T. Sgt.	7 WVC	4/2/62–4/9/65
Cogar, Thomas Pvt.	8 WVC?	9/18/62–6/30/65
Coger, James Pvt.	62 VAI CSA	8/62–1863
Conant, Sanford Cpl.	21 OHI	8/12/62–6/18/65

Name	Unit	Dates
Cook, Samuel Pvt.	1 WVI	11/6/61–4/7/65
Crawford, Wm. "Sailor"	Steamer Janette	6/64–7/65
Criss, Benj. Pvt.	7 WVI	4/1/65–7/1/65
Criss, Peter	Teamster — VAI	5/62–8/65
Cummings, Wm. Sgt.	31 VAI CSA	9/26/61–1865
Cunningham, J.P. Pvt.	10 WVI	9/61–3/12/65
Cunningham, Jesse Pvt.	10 WVI	NF
Cunningham, Tom B. Pvt.	62 VAI CSA	8/24/62–5/24/65
Currence, L.D. Pvt.	25 VAI CSA	61/65
Daugherty, D.D. Pvt.	2 WVI	5/61–8/64
Davis, Alpheus Pvt.	17 VAC CSA	62/65
Davis, Joseph E. Pvt.	1 WVA	10/18/62–6/28/65
Dean, Richard Cpl.	—WVI	9/1/62–7/7/65
Dent, Dudley E. Pvt.	3 WVI	7/10/61–6/13/65
Detomore, Henry H. Sgt.	12 WVI	3/1/62–6/5/65
Drummond, Pendleton Pvt.	19 (VAI) CSA	NF
Duckworth, Ephraim Pvt.	6 WVC	6/25/61–8/16/64
Dunlap, Wm. B. Pvt.	17 WVI	8/30/64–6/30/65
Dyer, John J. Pvt.	62 VAI CSA	8/62–4/65
Engel, Israel G. Pvt.	10 WVI	1/8/62–5/3/65
Ewing, Robert H. Cpl.	10 WVI	11/12/62–3/12/65
Finnegan, James H. Pvt.	18 VAC CSA	61/65
Fisher, Isaac F. Pvt.	3 WVI	61/64
Flemming, Isaac Pvt.	3 WVI	10/14/61–2/28/64
also	6 WVC	2/28/64–1865
Foster, Albert Pvt.	36 OHI	8/6/61–9/3/64
Furby, Robert R. Pvt.	NF	
Garrett, H.F. Pvt.	10 WVI	3/17/62–3/63
Gerwig, Mathew Cpl.	3 WVC	9/27/62–7/31/65
Gillespie, John Z. Cpl.	9 WVI	2/29/62–7/24/65
Given, Robert P. Pvt.	10 WVI	9/1/62–7/1/65
Gochanders, Elihu H. Pvt.	10 WVI	3/16/62–3/16/65
Green, C.W. Pvt.	1 WVC	1/62–1864
Green, Johnathan Pvt.	10 WVI	8/18/62–7/19/65
Green, Thomas M. Pvt.	US	NF
Gregory, Asa B. Pvt.	62 VAI CSA	62/62
Groff, Andrew Pvt.	10 WVI	2/62–5/65
Groves, Samuel	US	NF
Hannah, John S. Pvt.	6 WVI	9/4/64–3/28/65
Harris, John Pvt.	9 WVI	12/62–6/30/65
Harrold, John C. Cpl.	10 WVI	9/20/61–3/13/65
Haymond, J.Q. Pvt.	3 WVI	6/3/61–5/31/66
Heater, Enoch Pvt.	10 WVI	5/28/63–6/16/65
Heck, Wm. S. Pvt.	CSA NF (25 VAI)	
Henderson, Samuel Pvt.	7 WVI	3/15/61–8/65
Herndon, C.W. Pvt.	1 WVA	8/14/62–6/29/65
Holland, Isaac N. Lt.	14 WVI	8/14/62–6/27/65

Name	Unit	Dates
Hudkins, James P. Pvt.	3 WVC	9/19/62–6/30/65
Hyer, John D. Pvt.	10 WVI	8/61–12/29/64
Hyer, Nimrod M. Capt.	10 WVI	2/3/62–4/30/65
Hyre, Leonard M. Pvt.	NF	
James, Johnson	NF (14 VAC CSA?)	
Johnson, Jesse Pvt.	41 PAI	10/25/64–11/1/65
Jones, C.W. Pvt.	25 VAI CSA	62/65
Jones, F.M. Pvt.	62 VAI CSA	8/62–4/65
Jones, J.W. Pvt.	44 VAI CSA	5/15/61–1865
Kelly, Alexander Pvt.	11 WVI	8/62–1865
Kitts, Andrew S. Cpl.	36 OHI	8/26/61–9/3/64
Knicely, John Pvt.	10 WVI	1/17/62–5/3/65
Knicely, Joseph H. Pvt.	10 WVI	1/6/62–5/3/65
Knicely, Samuel E. Pvt.	10 WVI	1/6/62–5/3/65
Knicely, Wm. N. Pvt.	10 WVI	1/17/62–5/3/65
Krafft, Charles F. Pvt.	10 WVI	5/20/62–6/26/65
Krafft, Wm. Pvt.	10 WVI	2/17/62–5/65
Lake, Vincent Pvt.	CSA NF (Hounshell's VAC)	
Laughary, J.C. Pvt.	67 PAI	3/9/65–6/16/65
Lenabert, Jacob Pvt.	32 OHI	5/62–1865
Lloyd, N.W. Sgt.	10 WVI	1/6/62–5/3/65
Louden, John D. Pvt.	10 WVI	9/25/61–5/14/65
Lough, A.B. Pvt.	25 VAI CSA	61/65
Lough, F.M. Pvt.	25 VAI CSA	6/61–1865
Lough, J.V. Pvt.	25 VAI CSA	62/65
Markle, John M. Pvt.	10 WVI	12/61–8/65
Marple, John M. Pvt.	10 WVI	NF
McCoy, Alpheus Pvt.	11 WVI	3/5/62–6/26/65
McLaughlin, Tom B. Cpl.	10 WVI	5/3/62–6/16/65
McMarrow, David P.	US NF	
McMarrow, Marshal Pvt.	10 WVI	4/26/62–5/27/65
McWhorter, Silvannia Pvt.	15 WVI	8/62–6/65
Mealey, John A. Pvt.	10 WVI	8/14/62–6/28/65
Metheny, John Pvt.	8 VAC	3/1/61–5/61
Miller, Lewis Pvt.	10 WVI	2/26/64–8/9/65
Mitchell, Wm. C. Pvt.	10 WVI	2/1/62–3/63
Mollohan, Harrison Pvt.	10 WVI	1/2/62–5/30/65
Montgomery, John Pvt.	3 WVC	3/22/64–5/21/65
Morris, John J.	NF	
Morris, Robert	US NF	
Morris, Thomas Pvt.	4 WVC	7/20/63–3/7/64
Morrison, George H. Pvt.	10 WVI	6/3/62–5/3/65
Morrison, Silas M. Pvt.	10 WVI	6/62–5/65
Morrison, Wm. T. Pvt.	10 WVI	4/27/62–5/3/65
Moss, Owen C. Pvt.	19 VAC CSA	4/61–1865
Mulvy, Martin Pvt.	31 VAI CSA	6/2/61–1862
also	25 VAI CSA	62/65

Name	Unit	Dates
Murphy, A.C. Pvt.	CSA NF (62 VAI?)	
Myers, S.B. Pvt.	CSA NF (62 VAI)	
Nelson, Jasper L. Pvt.	NF	
Norris, John Sgt.	25 VAI CSA	5/61–6/65
Ochletree, Wm. Pvt.	62 VAI CSA	62/64
Osborn, Laban Pvt.	7 WVC	62/65
Perkins, Weden J. Pvt.	10 WVI	4/27/62–5/3/65
Perkins, Wm. H. Pvt.	10 WVI	5/2/62–6/23/65
Persinger, John L. Pvt.	(26 BTN VAI CS)	6/5/62–9/27/62
Pettit, Mathias Pvt.	7 WVI	4/9/65–7/1/65
Phillips, George W. Pvt.	NF (31 VAI CSA?)	
Pliman, J.A. Pvt.	3 WVI	9/61–7/65
Prince, Nathan M. Pvt.	10 WVI	4/26/62–5/3/65
Propst, Levis Pvt.	14 WVI	8/17/62–6/27/65
Propst, Wm. Pvt.	10 WVI	4/62–6/65
Prunty, Francis M. Pvt.	14 WVI	3/6/65–6/27/65
Queen, A.A.M. Pvt.	CSA NF (17 VAC)	
Rexroad, Francis M. Pvt.	3 WVI	6/1/61–3/12/64
also	6 WVC	2/28/64–8/65
Rexroad, Wm. Pvt.	3 WVC	2/62–7/64
Rider, B.E. Pvt.	10 WVI	1/7/62–5/3/65
Riffe, Jacob Pvt.	10 WVI	4/13/62–10/24/64
Riffle, Isaac Pvt.	NF (62 VAI CSA)	
Riffle, Wm. C. Cpl.	10 WVI	1/2/62–5/3/65
Riffle, Wm. T. Pvt.	NF	
Robinson, J.W. Pvt.	6 WVI	61/64
Rodgers, Isaac Pvt.	98—I	8/19/62–7/6/65
Rollyson, Isaac M. Pvt.	NF	
Rollyson, John Pvt.	10 WVI	5/3/62–6/26/65
Rollyson, Wm. Major	——	65/65
Rose, Morhines Pvt.	10 WVI	4/5/62–5/3/65
Rose, Nathaniel W. Pvt.	17 WVI	12/23/64–6/30/65
Ryan, Patrick Pvt.	17 PAC	9/10/62–6/16/65
Saffle, Corbin Pvt.	17 WVI	9/2/64–6/13/65
Shaver, Harry T. Pvt.	10 WVI	1/6/62–1865
Shaver, Morgan D. Pvt.	10 WVI	8/25/62–7/7/65
Shaver, Willis P. Pvt.	10 WVI	2/16/62–5/3/65
Short, Andrew J. Pvt.	10 WVI	1/25/62–5/3/65
Skidmar, Jackson M. Pvt.	CSA NF (17 VAC)	
Skidmore, Salathiel Pvt.	10 WVI	1/27/62–5/3/65
Smallwood, Wm. H. Pvt.	16 VAI	61/65
Smith, J.W. Pvt.	CSA NF (8 VAC?)	
Smith, John M. Pvt.	11 WVI	8/17/62–6/17/65
Spaur, Abel Pvt.	26 VAC CSA	NF
Squires, Ellis W. Pvt.	10 WVI	5/5/62–5/5/65
Squires, Newlon Pvt.	10 WVI	2/6/62–5/5/65
Steers, Isaac B. Pvt.	1 PAI	6/14/61–7/14/64

Stewart, James M. Pvt.	10 WVI	9/1/62–5/15/65
Stine, G.M. Cpl. 92 OHI	NF	
Stump, Asa Pvt.	6 WVI	1/16/65–6/7/65
Suton, Taylor Pvt.	3 WVC	9/5/62–6/30/65
Tapp, Charles S.	US NF	
Taylor, Curtis F. Pvt.	CSA NF (14 VAC)	
Taylor, John C. Pvt.	14 VAC CSA	62/65
Taylor, Joseph H.	Sailor Yantic?	6/62–7/23/65
Thomas, Jacob S.	US NF	
Vawter, Julius Pvt.	10 WVI	NF
Walton, George D. Pvt.	10 WVI	8/8/62–5/8/65
Warner, E.C. Pvt.	10 WVI	3/1/63–5/3/65
Warner, Wm. Pvt.	10 WVI	8/14/63–6/65
Welling, T.M. Pvt.	39 OHI?	7/31/61–8/27/64
White, John W. Pvt.	19 VAC CSA	62/65
White, Roswell Pvt.	3 WVC	3/23/65–6/30/65
White, Thomas E. Pvt.	3 WVI	6/22/61–1/31/64
also	6 WVC	2/1/64–5/22/66
White, Wm. Teamster	3 VAI	12/62–3/1/65
Wildman, Wm. Pvt.	4 WVC	8/26/63–3/6/64
Williams, J.K. Pvt.	3 WVC	9/21/62–7/10/65
Wilson, Addison Pvt.	10 WVI	8/8/62–7/1/65
Wolf, L.C. Pvt.	(19 VAC CSA)	61/62
Woolrose?, James Pvt.	11 WVI	3/8/62–6/11/65
Woolverton, George W. Pvt.	10 WVI	5/6/62–6/13/65
Young, Benj. Pvt.	14 KYC	3/3/62–3/31/63

Braxton Co. Remarks

Adkinson, B.H. —CDR
Balford, W.H.H.*—WIA left knee
Bender, H. —disease of chest, partial deafness, sight impaired
Bird, J.W.*—catarrh in head
Bishop, A.—CDR
Boggs, P.J. —served 7 months & taken POW while on furlough
Bolinger, Z.A.—shot through body
Boyles, E.T.—sight & hearing affected
Brady, S.P.—fever left with fits, at times can hardly walk
Brighit, A.H.—hearing, now very deaf
Brohard, T.—CDR, RH, KD
Brown, Z. —CDR & HD
Butcher, M.*—gun & shell shot wounds
Campbell, D.—CDR
Carlin, G.*—WIA right arm
Carr, F.—disease right eye & partial deafness
Carr, J.C.—TYF resulting in other diseases
Carr, S.—breast hurt by shell bursting
Chapman, J.—RH
Childers, R.D.—cold on measles caused disability, now invalid
Clark, T.A.—neuralgia
Clutter, J.T.—lumbago result of smallpox & affected eyes, hearing
Criss, B.—HD & crippled
Criss, P.—disabled arm & shoulder
Cunningham, J.—KD
Cunningham, J.P.—curvature of the spine
Daugherty, D.D.—catarrh head
Davis, A.*—wounded slightly
Davis, J.E.—MS & broken leg
Dean, R.—shell wound in shoulder
Detomore, H.H. —shot in right foot, DSC
Dunlap, W.B.—LD, CDR, piles
Engel, I.G.—dropsy, catarrh head & partial loss of sight
Ewing, R.H.—gunshot in the head
Fisher, I.F.—wounded in side
Flemming, I.—injured by mumps, RH
Foster, A.—two gunshot wounds
Gerwig, M.—head & back hurt by shell burst, RH
Gillespie, J.Z.—throat trouble
Given, R.P.—gunshot wound right rist
Gochanders, E.H.—RH, gunshot wound right foot
Green, C.W.—LD
Green, J.—gunshot wound arm & leg
Gregory, A.B.*—deserter US Army & joined Confederates
Groff, A.—shot in left hand

Groves, S.—liver disease, bronchitis
Hannah, J.S. —neuralgia last four months
Harris, J.—gunshot wound right leg
Harrold, J.C.—RH, gunshot through the chest
Haymond, J.Q.—gunshot left side
Herndon, C.W.—RH
Holland, I.N.—middle finger right hand shot off & lumbago
Hudkins, J.P.—fever settled left leg, deserves pension cant get
Hyer, J.D.—LD, health is poor
Jones, J.W.★—gunshot wound
Kitts, A.S.—MS & SS
Krafft, C.F.—ague
Louden, J.D.—RH
Lough, F.M.★—WIA
Lough, J.V.★—bone scurvy
Marple, J.M.—wounded
McCoy, A.—lost left eye, contracted other diseases
McLaughlin, T.B.—gunshot right thigh & left foot
McWhorter, S.—lumbago
Mealey, J.A. —shell wound, veteran from 10/24/64 2nd Lt. to Capt.
Metheny, J.—maimed inside
Mitchell, W.C.—tumor on right leg, DSC
Montgomery, J.—the effects of lightning, discharged by telegram
Morris, T.—broken arm
Moss, O.C.★—shot in knee
Mulvy, M.★—left foot off
Osborn, L.—CDR
Perkins, W.H.—gunshot wound left thigh, TYF left me crippled
Perkins, W.J.—SS & hearing affected
Persinger, J.L.★—CDR, DSC
Pettit, M.—KD & dyspepsia
Phillips. G.W.★—WIA twice
Pliman, J.A.—gun & sabre wounds
Prince, N.M.—gunshot wound left arm & top of head, MS & LD
Rexroad, F.M.—rupture & CDR
Rexroad, W.—KD & liver disease
Rider, B.E.—RH left hip & breast, HD
Riffle, J.—gunshot wound & arm amputated, DSC
Riffle, W.C.—gunshot wound, RH & constipation
Riffle, W.T.—mumps
Robinson, J.W.—rupture
Rollyson, J.—right hand shot
Rose, M.—CDR
Rose, N.W.—measles
Ryan, P.—left arm broke
Shaver, H.T.—right leg amputated gunshot wound
Shaver, M.D.—total deaf right ear, RH

Shaver, W.P.—back & hips affected by measles, also lungs
Short, A.J.—piles
Skidmar, J.M.*—WIA
Skidmore, S.—CDR & partial loss of testicle
Smith, J.M.—RH
Squires, E.W.—CDR
Stewart, J.M.—POW Saulsbury NC 4 months 19 days, gen disability
Stine, G.M.—gunshot wound left rist
Taylor, J.H.—hearing bad on account of shell bursting
Vawter, J.—CDR
Walton, G.D.—crippled right leg
Warner, E.C.—RH & HD
Warner, W.—RH
Welling, T.M.—catarrh head & eyes, Mr. Welling is totaly blind
White, T.E. —gunshot wound left little finger
Wildman, W.—cold on mumps caused disability, now invalid
Williams, J.K. —CDR
Wilson, A.—three fingers shot off
Woolrose, J.—disabled left elbow joint
Woolverton, G.W. —gunshot left foot, ball in left side through ankle
Young, B.—wounded in foot

Brooke County

NAME/RANK	REGIMENT	WHEN SERVED
Adams, Ely Pvt.	12 WVI	5/1/62–3/14/65
Adams, John Pvt.	1 VAI	9/6/61–2/8/64
also Pvt.	2 WVI	2/8/64–7/16/65
Allen, James L. Cpl.	5 USA	1/9/62–1/9/65
Anderson, Wm. Pvt.	43 PAI	NF
Atkinson, Sam W. Sgt.	14? WVC	8/27/61–7/20/65
Atkinson, W.H. Pvt.	1 WVI	5/20/61–8/28/61
Baker, Albert Pvt.	15 NYA	8/11/63–9/2/65
Barnes, Shipley Pvt.	1 WVI	3/16/61–7/16/65
Baxter, George A. Sgt.	12 WVI	8/9/62–6/16/65
Bieter, Casper Pvt.	8 ILI	8/8/61–8/8/64
Billingsley, Wm. Pvt.	12 WVI	5/16/61–6/30/65
Bird, Francis H. Pvt.	84 OHI	5/28/62–9/20/62
also Pvt.	157 OHI	5/2/64–9/2/64
also Sgt.	57 OHI	9/2/64–5/19/65
Blankinship, George Pvt.	1 WVA	8/22/62–6/25/65
Blankinship, Peter Pvt.	6 WVI	8/25/61–11/28/64
Blankinship, Sam J. Pvt.	31 VAI CSA	9/13/61–4/9/65
Blankinship, Wm. Pvt.	6 WVI	8/25/61–11/28/64
Blankinsip, John Sgt.	1 WVI	10/30/61–11/26/64
Bradford, Melvin Pvt.	17 WVI	9/8/64–6/30/65
Britt, Elias S. Pvt.	12 WVI	8/15/62–6/16/65
Brownell, Wm. J. Cpl.	14 WVI	5/15/61–7/12/65
Brownlee, James E. Pvt.	12 WVI	8/62–6/65
Brownlee, Martin N. Pvt.	12 WVI	5/16/61–6/14/65
Bryer, Oliver 0. Pvt.	1 PAA	8/64–6/65
Bryte, Levi S. Capt.	15 WVI	6/10/61–9/16/64
Buchanan, John A. Pvt.	12 WVI	8/22/62–6/27/65
Burnett, Wm. J. Pvt.	22 PAC	10/1/62–5/10/65
Burton, Frank H. Pvt.	27 MII	12/13/63–1/3/65
Calendine, Ed M. Cpl.	6 IAC	NF
Callaway, James M. Pvt.	34 VAC BTNCSA	4/1/64–5/1/65
Campbell, John Pvt.	15 WVI	7/15/62–6/10/65
Carmichael, Moses Pvt.	4 WVC	8/25/63–7/12/65
Chamberlin, Elijah Pvt.	1 WVI	8/14/62–6/19/65
Colwell, Albert R. Cpl.	12 WVI	8/9/62–6/16/65
Colwell, Robert Pvt.	1 WVI	5/18/61–8/28/61
also Sgt.	85 PAI	9/23/61–11/22/64
Craig, Roland F. Pvt.	12 WVI	8/1/62–6/14/65
Crawford, George B. Pvt.	1 WVI	5/18/61–6/25/65
Crawford, Oscar T. Pvt.	1 WVI	10/30/61–7/16/65
Croft, Charles A. Pvt.	4 WVC	8/17/63–3/11/64
Crouch, John A. Pvt.	22 PAC	9/18/62–5/2/65

Cusick, Jacob D. Pvt.	30 OHI	8/14/62–5/31/65
Davis, John Pvt.	36 VAI CSA	5/24/61–6/2/65
Davison, George Pvt.	4 WVC	7/6/63–315/64
Deary, John H. Pvt.	66 OHI	9/27/64–6/5/65
Devore, John N. Cpl.	12 WVI	8/7/62–6/26/65
Dodd, Francis S. Pvt.	22 PAC	9/17/62–7/12/65
Dorsey, Robert G. Pvt.	1 WVC	10/15/61–7/18/65
Duval, Isaac N. Major	9 WVI	6/1/61–1/16/66
Edgell, Benj. E. Sgt.	129 OHI	6/63–3/64
English, James Cpl.	7 IAC	8/12/62–10/22/65
Erwin, Seth W. Pvt.	140 PAI	8/11/62–5/31/65
Ettier?, Joseph Cpl.	1 MDC	11/9/61–12/3/64
Fenwick, John W. Pvt.	12 WVI	9/29/63–6/14/65
Finley, Alexander Pvt.	2 WVI	2/13/65–7/65
Flemming, MattheY Sgt.	4 WVC	7/6/63–2/15/65
Forester, Sam C. Pvt.	22 PAC	8/15/62–6/1/65
Frazier, George A. Pvt.	1 WVI	5/2/61–7/16/65
George, Thomas C. Cpl.	19 PAI	9/64–6/65
Green, John W. Pvt.	12 WVI	8/23/62–6/26/65
Green, Marchell S. Pvt.	1 WVI	2/14/62–11/26/64
Hagen, John B. Pvt.	1 WVI	11/1/61–3/14/64
Hall, Augustus C. Pvt.	12 WVI	8/30/62–4/1/63
Hall, Lewis C. Pvt.	12 WVI	8/20/64–6/14/65
Hammond, Henry Pvt.	157 OHI	5/64–9/12/64
Harden, Sam Pvt.	14? WVA	1/21/64–6/25/65
Harris, Josiah	— MDI	NF
Harvey, Benj. Pvt.	12 WVI	8/22/62–1/16/65
Harvey, John H. Pvt.	12 WVI	8/1/62–6/14/65
Heingrath, Wm. Cpl.	6 WVI	9/20/61–1/9/65
Helsterne, Rinehart Pvt.	4 WVC	8/4/63–3/15/64
Hennie, James	NF	
Hervey, Henry C.	NF	
Hines, Jerry Pvt.	NF	
Hugins, Benj. Sgt.	3 WVI	6/21/61–8/15/65
Jenkins, Thomas B. Pvt.	85 PAI	9/12/61–1/31/64
also Pvt.	85 PAI	2/1/64–4/20/65
Jones, Isaac Pvt.	1 WVI	3/3/62–8/2/62
Jones, James M. Pvt.	1 WVI	9/18/61–7/28/65
Jones, Robert T.	—PA	NF
Kelley, James A. Pvt.	3 USI	2/24/64–8/22/65
Kelly, NcKendree Pvt.	12 WVI	2/63–8/65
Kelly, Wm. F. Pvt.	52 OHI	8/19/62–6/25/65
Kimberland, Cornelis Pvt.	1 WVI	9/9/61–11/26/65
Kimberland, Daniel Pvt.	1 WVI	1/31/62–6/13/65
King, George W. Pvt.	86 OHI	2/6/64–8/10/64
Kinsey, Thomas Pvt.	3 OHI	6/15/61–6/21/64
Latimer, John H. Pvt.	1 WVI	5/18/61–8/25/61

Name	Unit	Dates
Letzkus, George Pvt.	78 PAI	2/15/65–9/11/65
Letzkus, Joseph Pvt.	1 WVI	1/28/62–11/11/62
Lytel, Thomas Pvt.	1 WVI	10/30/61–6/28/62
Mack, James Pvt.	—WSA	9/9/61–6/26/65
Mahan, Richard W. Cpl.	12 WVI	8/9/62–6/27/65
Marks, Thomas H. Sgt.	12 WVI	8/1/62–6/14/65
Marsh, Cyrus C. Sgt.	2 ILC	9/28/61–1/23/65
Martin, George W. Pvt.	15 OHI	9/20/61–7/17/62
Mayo, Francis Pvt.	102 PAI	8/6/61–9/25/64
McAdoo, James Cpl.	14 PAC	9/22/62–5/28/65
McCarrmic, Frank H. Pvt.	2 WVI	11/8/62–7/16/65
McClure, Andrew J. Pvt.	14 PAC	10/5/61–1/15/63
McCreary, George W. Pvt.	4 WVC	9/23/63–3/17/64
McFadden, Sam D.	NF	
McHugh, Wm. S. Pvt.	12 WVI	8/9/62–6/27/65
McNaley, Arthur Pvt.	12 WVI	8/19/62–6/6/65
McNaley, John B. Pvt.	74 NYI	4/22/61–3/16/65
McNear, Jesse Pvt.	12 WVI	8/62–6/65
Melvin, Wm. Sgt.	1 WVI	5/2/61–7/16/65
Micholls, Alex C. Pvt.	2 CAC	9/23/61–2/9/66
Miller, George	US NF	
Miller, Joseph Pvt.	24 OHI	3/24/62–5/62
Miller, Sam Pvt.	52 OHI	5/22/62–1/3/65
Montgomery, Joseph Pvt.	12 WVI	2/4/64–8/9/65
Moran, John T. Pvt.	15 WVI	2/8/63–8/9/65
Moran, Robert Pvt.	1 WVI	10/30/61–6/25/65
Nagle, Sam C. Pvt.	1 WVI	5/9/61–8/61
also Pvt.	1 WVI	10/61–6/9/63
Nelson, Nathaniel Pvt.	12 WVI	8/8/62–6/10/65
Nicholls, Edward Musician	1 WVI	5/30/61–7/15/65
Nicholls, Robert Pvt.	1 WVI	10/30/61–6/29/62
Park, Thomas C. Capt.	1 WVI	5/16/61–7/16/65
Patterson, James Pvt.	4 WVC	7/63–3/64
Patterson, Sam Pvt.	1 WVI	5/18/61–11/28/64
Philabaum, Jacob Pvt.	10 OHC	12/24/63–8/17/65
Plummer, Wm. J. Pvt.	1 WVI	8/61–6/62
Pry, Robert A. Pvt.	140 PAI	8/8/62–5/17/65
Reese, John A. Pvt.	1 WVI	9/17/61–11/26/64
Reeves, Riley C. Pvt.	1 WVA	3/16/62–6/28/65
Reeves, Wheeler A. Pvt.	1 WVI	5/16/61–8/28/61
Richardson, Robert Pvt.	4 WVC	8/15/63–7/7/65
Riddle, Clark Pvt.	14 WVI	9/15/61–10/10/64
Ridlings, Wm. H. 1Lt.	100 PAI	4/25/61–8/28/65
Robinson, Elbert E. Cpl.	4 WVC	8/24/63–3/11/64
Rodgers, James N. Pvt.	170 OHI	5/2/64–9/24/65
Rodgers, Jonathan Pvt.	11 WVI	9/17/62–5/11/65
Russell, Granville Pvt.	1 WVI	9/8/61–7/28/65

Sanhart, George W. Pvt.	49 PAI	8/26/63–7/15/65
Schriver, Wm. Pvt.	152 PAI	NF
also Pvt.	3 PAA	1/26/64–9/22/65
Scott, Hugh Pvt.	12 WVI	8/30/62–6/14/65
Selick, Andrew Pvt.	7 WVI	9/1/61–9/1/64
Shearer, Andrew J. Pvt.	1 WVI	5/16/61–7/4/65
Shriver, Colley Cpl.	187 PAI	3/3/64–8/6/65
Shriver, Wm. L. Pvt.	1 WVI	5/16/61–7/4/65
Simms, Gilbert M. 2Lt.	6 WVI	9/9/61–6/10/65
Smith, Clarence A. Pvt.	12 WVI	8/19/62–6/25/65
Smith, John E. Pvt.	NF	
Spidel, Clement Pvt.	12 WVI	8/1/62–6/14/65
Springborn, Fred Pvt.	126 OHI	8/20/62–6/25/65
Stock, Benj. Pvt.	12 WVI	8/25/62–6/25/65
Stransbury, Hudson Pvt.	6 WVI	9/25/61–3/12/63
also Pvt.	3 WVC	1/20/64–6/30/65
Strong, George Pvt.	12 WVI	8/21/62–7/65
Suaas, Philip Pvt.	12 WVI	8/19/62–6/25/65
Taylor, Daniel Pvt.	120 INI	8/25/63–1/4/64
Thompson, Robert N. Pvt.	155 PAI	8/22/62–6/4/65
Tiffe, Joel	NF	
Timbers, George Pvt.	45 USC	7/7/64–11/4/65
Tomes, Charles S. Pvt.	150 ILI	2/2/65–1/16/66
Tucker, Wm. Sgt.	1 WVI	61–NF
Waldron, Joseph Pvt.	1 WVA	1/4/64–5/12/65
Wells, Benj. Pvt.	182 OHI	9/22/64–7/7/65
West, Henry Pvt.	32 OHI	1/30/64–7/20/65
White, Thomas J.	NF	
White, Thomas Jr. Pvt.	22 PAC	8/15/62–6/1/65
White, Thomas S. Capt.	12 WVI	9/9/61–12/19/64
Wright, David M. Pvt.	1 WVI	5/18/61–8/28/61
also Pvt.	140 PAI	8/22/62–5/31/65
Yudiker, Wm. Pvt.	15 NYA	7/6/63–7/6/65
Zink?, George W. Pvt.	4 WVC	8/10/63–8/10/64

Brooke Co. Remarks

Adams, J. — CDR & scurvy
Allen, J.L. — RH
Atkinson, S.W. — RH & cannot walk
Barnes, S. — crippled in left arm
Basford, M. — KD
Baxter, G.A. — diasbled in breast by ambulance team
Blankinsop, J. — WIA thigh & captured June 1864

Bryer, O. —RH from exposure
Burton, F.H.—gunshot left leg
Campbell, J.—WIA right arm
Chamberlin, E.—RH & injured spine
Colwell, A.R.—gunshot left side
Colwell, R.—gunshot in thigh
Duval, I. —RH & deaf WIA promoted to Brig. Gen. 9/62
Edgell, B.—left shoulder injured from ague
English, J.—CDR & piles
Flemming, M. —piles
Forester, S.C.—RH & eyes
Hall, A.C.—piles since 1864
Haney, J.H.—piles disease of rectum
Jenkins, T.B.—shot in left ankle/DSC
Jones, I. —RH/DSC 8/2/62
Kinsey, T.—piles
Letzkus, G.—fitts
Letzkus, J.—disability/DSC 11/11/62
Maban, R.W.—hip injured from a fall
Mangle, S.—gunshot left leg
Marks, T. —ruptured wounded in spine
Martin, G.W. —index finger lost to gunshot
McHugh, W.S. —asthma second year
McKendre, K. —malaria & HD
McNaley, A.—WIA left shoulder
McNaley, J.B.—wounded in head
McNear, J.—one eye lost
Melvin, W.— RH & hands crippled
Nicholls, A.C.—KD & RH
Nicholls, E. —crippled finger & defect throat
Nicholls, R.—rupture/DSC
Park, T.C.—hearing bad receiving pension
Patterson, Jm.—WIA by shell left arm/eyes hurt on picket
Pry, R.A. —gunshot left foot
Russell, T.A.—CDR & WIA right leg
Schriver, W. —F & piles
Selick, A.—RH
Shriner, W.L.— tunroy (?) rectum
Strong, G.— RH
Thompson, R.N.— left foot wounded by ax
Tomes, C. —eyes injured in army
Tucker, W.—gunshot loins
Waldron, J.—RH & captured at New Creek 11/28/64
White, T.S.—disease of blader
Wright, D.M. —gunshot in neck

Cabell County

NAME/RANK	REGIMENT	WHEN SERVED
Abshire, Wm. Pvt.	1 WVI	8/2/61–6/17/65
Adams, Edward W. Pvt.	140 OHNG	5/2/64–9/3/64
also	1 OHA	9/25/64–7/4/65
Adams, Hamilton M. Pvt.	148 OHI	2/6/63–11/5/65
Adams, James F. Pvt.	1 WVC	9/12/61–7/25/65
Adams, James K.P. Sgt.	4 WVC	7/15/63–3/9/64
Adams, Wm. E. Pvt.	13 USI?	10/28/62–10/28/65
Adams, Wm. J. Pvt.	179 OHI	7/12/64–5/12/65
Adams, Wm. S. Pvt.	1 OHA	3/3/64–7/5/65
Adkins, Albert	NF (45 BTN VAI CSA?)	
Adkins, John Pvt.	13 WVI	12/8/63–6/22/65
Aills, Christopher C.	NF	
Armstrong, Charles E. Pvt.	148 OHNG	5/2/64–9/14/64
Baker, James M. Sgt.	45 KYI	8/2/63–12/28/64
Barbour, John W. Pvt.	9 WVI	10/28/61–11/2/64
Barcus, James W. Pvt.	148 OHI	5/2/63–9/24/63
Barnes, Alexander Pvt.	USI (Negro)	5/28/64–12/26/65
AKA Alexander Jameson	NF	
Barnes, Wm. J. Pvt.	— OHC	62/65
Barnett, John C. Pvt.	3 WVC	4/25/63–6/30/65
Bartley, James Pvt.	33 OHI	12/29/61–3/65
Barton, Joseph Cpl.	11 PAC	8/5/62–6/5/65
Baumgardner, H.J. Pvt.	5 WVI	9/16/61–9/16/63
Baumgardner, John B. Lt.	13 WVI	62/63
Bayliss, Thomas H. Cpl.	7 WVC	3/14/64–8/1/65
Beach, Samuel Pvt.	9 WVI	1/1/62–6/65
Beardsley, Andrew J. Pvt.	140 OHI	4/63–12/29/65
Benedick, Sam M. Sgt.	5 VAI	8/61–7/65
Bennett, Edward A. Sgt.	6 WVI	8/10/61–2/63
also Capt.	6 WVI	2/63–4/20/65
also Major	6 WVI	4/20/65–6/10/65
Beran, Roland C. Pvt.	NF	
Berkheimer, Wm. M. Pvt.	125 PAI	8/1/62–5/10/63
also	205 PAI	8/15/64–6/2/65
Bias, James A. Pvt.	185 OHI	2/11/65–9/21/65
Bias, James L. Pvt.	1 WVC	8/15/62–6/25/64
Bias, Roland S.	NF	
Bias, Wm. A. Pvt.	9 WVI	1/1/62–6/26/65
Bias, Wm. E. Pvt.	1 WVC	9/14/61–9/14/64
Bicker, Anthony Pvt.	5 WVI	9/14/61–9/14/64
Bicker, Henry Sgt.	5 WVI	9/14/61–9/14/64
Billup, James T. Cpl.	8 WVI	1/2/62–1/2/65

Bios, Berry Pvt.	1 WVC	9/1/61–8/30/62
Bishop, Wm. A. Pvt.	194 OHI	2/24/64–10/24/65
Bishop, Wm. H. Pvt.	1 WVA	10/1/61–10/22/64
Bishop, Wm. Pvt.	91 OHI	8/10/62–7/20/64
Blackburn, John T. Pvt.	13 WVI	62/64
Blake, Andrew W. Pvt.	7 WVC	9/4/61–8/1/65
Blake, C. S. Pvt.	1 VAC	10/61–11/64
Blankenship, Andrew Pvt.	5 WVI	8/1/61–7/21/65
Blankenship, James W.	18 OHA	NF
Brown, Leon G. Pvt.	112 NYI	8/25/62–5/25/65
Brown, Philip Pvt.	10 USI	11/25/64–2/6/66
Brown, Richard Cpl.	173 OHI	8/13/64–6/29/65
Burns, John A. Pvt.	15 WVI	10/25/61–6/31/65
Butcher, James Pvt.	34 OHI	9/62–1863
Butcher, Thurman L. Sgt.	10 KYC	8/62–10/63
Caldwell, James L. Sgt.	60 OHI	2/26/64–7/28/65
Cardwell, Manoth Pvt.	194 OHI	5/4/61–7/4/65
Carvell, Wm. Pvt.	1 OHA	9/62–8/65
Cash, George W.	NF (19 BTN VAA CSA?)	
Cayslep, Carey B. Capt.	1 WVI	10/25/61–3/10/65
Chalfine, Robert A. Pvt.	14 KYI	8/63–10/65
Chapman, Johnathan Pvt.	I VAI	1/1/63–1/1/65
Childers, George W. Cpl.	13 WVI	7/62–6/65
Childers, Sam A. Lt.	3 WVC	9/17/62–6/8/65
Childers, Wm. S. Sgt.	3 WVC	9/17/62–6/30/65
Christian, James A. Pvt.	13 WVI	5/63–6/22/65
Church, John W. Pvt.	1 MOA	3/63–7/65
Clagg, Julius J. Pvt.	8 WVI	12/15/61–NF
Clark, Alexander M. Pvt.	12 OHC	10/18/63–11/14/65
Clark, Harvey Pvt.	9 WVI	10/23/61–11/19/64
Clark, Joshua M. Pvt.	1 OHA	9/20/61–1/16/65
Clark, Wm. Pvt.	13 WVI	11/8/63–6/22/65
Clay, James Pvt.	45 KYI	6/24/63–12/30/64
Clay, Michael Pvt.	188 PAI	10/24/62–10/24/65
Clutts, James H. Sgt.	14 KYI	61/65
Cobb, Joseph	NF	
Coils, John Pvt.	173 OHI	6/10/61–7/6/64
Cook, Abner J. Pvt.	3 WVC	1/3/63–6/30/65
Cook, John Pvt.	NF	
Cox, Thomas H. Sgt.	56 OHI	NF
Crandle, Shubael Pvt.	11 NYC	10/62–10/65
Crawford, Anthony Pvt.	NF	
Crawford, Wesley Pvt.	13 WVI	2/22/64–5/22/65
Cremeans, Truman Pvt.	13 WVI	9/63–8/64
Cremens, Amassa Pvt.	9 WVI	1/1/62–1/6/65
Cremens, James G. Pvt.	9 WVI	1/1/62–1/6/65
Crook, Wm. M. Sgt.	13 WVI	8/9/62–5/31/65

Cummings, Joseph Pvt.	NF (27 VAI CSA?)	
Cummins, James H. Pvt.	21 NYC	61/64
Damaron, Sylvester J. Pvt.	5 WVI	62/65
Davis, Poindexter Pvt.	7 WVC	10/12/64–8/1/65
Davis, Stephen Pvt.	12 WVI	10/27/62–11/15/63
Davis, Thomas C. Pvt.	7 WVC	1863–8/65
Dawson, Lewis J. Sgt.	7 OHC	9/7/62–7/3/65
Dawson, Martin L. Pvt.	33 OHI	8/25/61–7/25/65
Deleber, Killion Pvt.	33 OHI	8/5/61–1865
Derbyshire, Henry J.	(Ship) Huron	12/26/61–12/31/64
also Master Mate	(Ship) Gettysburg	
Dewitt, John Pvt.	173 OHI	8/19/64–6/26/65
Dicker, James A. Pvt.	5 VAI	7/18/61–7/22/65
Dicky, Hamilton L. Sgt.	193 OHI	3/1/62–9/1/65
Diehl, Louis Pvt.	Home Guards WV	NF
Dille, Amos Pvt.	36 OHI	8/15/61–6/26/65
Dillon, Charles Pvt.	15 WVI	12/26/63–5/19/65
Dillon, Wm. J. Pvt.	13 WVI	12/25/63–5/15/65
Dishman, James J. Pvt.	5 WVI	7/30/61–9/21/64
Dotson, Isaac Pvt.	56 OHI	1861–9/65
Dougherty, James	NF	
Douthet, Wm. H. Pvt.	9 VAT	10/25/61–7/25/65
Downey, Malcolm Pvt.	105 OHI	NF
Downey, Thomas	NF	
Dusenberry, Charles C.	Sutler 2 INI	11/61–7/65
also Sutler	3 VAC	NF
Earle, John S. Pvt.	9 WVI	9/61–6/5/65
Edens, Jeptha Pvt.	7 KYI	8/19/61–10/5/64
Edmonds, J.R. Pvt.	7 WVC	8/20/64–8/65
Edwards, Richard A. Pvt.	1 OHA	6/1/63–7/25/65
Eggers, Joseph Pvt.	1 WVC	9/14/61–7/65
Elkhart, George W. Pvt.	91 OHI	NF
Elkins, Alexander Pvt.	13 WVI	NF
Elkins, Alexander Pvt.	16 KYI	1/27/62–1/28/65
Elkins, Archibald Pvt.	5 WVI	8/10/61–7/27/65
Elkins, James P. Cpl.	13 WVI	62/65
Elliott, Wm. J. Pvt.	2 IAI	5/62 5/65
Emery, Wm. J. Pvt.	6 WVI	9/11/61–5/12/65
Emrick, John Cpl.	194 OHI	2/10/65–10/24/65
Eves, Thomas M. Pvt.	9 WVI	3/28/61–1865
Fawcett, Henry J. Sgt.	19 USI	6/1/63–6/1/65
Felginer, Emil Cpl.	5 WVI	9/14/61–9/14/64
Felix, Arnold Pvt.	9 WVI	61/64
Felix, Julius Pvt.	5 WVI	8/5/61–12/25/63
also	1 WVI	12/25/63–7/21/65
Fellure, Washington Pvt.	1 OHA	10/7/62–7/25/65
Fergeson, James	NF	

Name	Unit	Dates
Fergeson, Jesse	NF	
Fetty, Elmore Lt.	7 WVI	8/61–8/62
Field, Hiram K. Capt.	1 TNC	3/62–1863
Fitzgerald, Tom G. Sgt.	12 WVC	NF
Floding, George A. Pvt.	Trumbel Guards	6/13/62–6/26/65
Flowers, Fredric Pvt.	9 WVI	NF
Flowers, George W. Pvt.	9 WVI	10/28/61–11/1/64
Floyd, John H. Cpl.	13 WVI	12/3/63–5/15/65
Forbush, John Pvt.	9 WVI	6/1/62–7/4/65
Ford, Jesse Pvt.	7 WVC	2/64–1865
Foster, James M. Cpl.	5 PAC	8/12/62–6/21/65
Foster, John E. Pvt.	7 WVC	9/24/64–6/3/65
Foster, Resin Cpl.	11 WVI	8/14/62–6/17/65
France, Wm. Pvt.	10 KYC	8/4/62–9/4/63
also	148 ILI	2/2/65–9/15/65
Froidevaux, Theodore Pvt.	92 OHI	8/14/63–5/30/65
Furguson, Perceval S. Pvt.	CSA NF	
Galliway, Henry Pvt.	92 OHI	8/11/62–6/15/65
Gethard, Jeremiah Pvt.	43 OHI	11/2/64–6/25/65
Gibson, Wm. Pvt.	——	4/2/62–NF
Gilette, Arden Pvt.	114 INI	1/11/64–9/14/65
Gilkenson, Nobel Pvt.	10 KYC	8/16/62–10/16/64
Gill, Wm. Pvt.	3 WVC	10/6/62–7/15/64
Gillinghance, James Sgt.	7 OHC	8/1/62–7/4/65
Glover, Henry C. Pvt.	7 WVI	2/22/65–6/21/65
Gordon, Hamson Pvt.	3 INC	7/19/61–9/7/64
Green, Villeroy M. Pvt.	51 NYI	10/14/61–10/14/64
Greenlee, Allen Pvt.	10 WVI	1863–NF
Gregory, Peter Pvt.	53 OHI	1/62–1865
Griffin, James "Seaman"	Steamer Sebago	8/30/64–7/29/65
Gue, James Pvt.	9 WVI	61/64
Gue, Potandy Pvt.	9 WVI	63/65
Gunther, John C. Pvt.	26 OHI	8/20/61–10/31/62
Gwinn, George W. Pvt.	7 WVI	9/27/61–2/15/63
Hagley, Joseph Pvt.	13 WVI	11/1/63–6/22/68
Haley, Talbot Pvt.	5 WVI	9/1/61–3/16/65
Hamilton, John A. Pvt.	18 OHI	9/9/61–7/22/62
Hamlin, Mac Pvt.	6 OHC	10/22/61–10/22/64
Hamlin, Wm. M. Pvt.	45 KYC	12/10/63–2/64
Hanlin, Robert T. Pvt.	1 OHA	10/7/62–7/25/65
Hanner, John L. Pvt.	1 WVA	8/15/61–6/21/62
Harshbarger, John Capt.	3 WVC	9/6/62–6/65
Harshbarger, John P. Pvt.	3 WVC	8/61–8/62
Haucke, Conrad Pvt.	70 OHI	10/20/61–6/21/65
Heimrich, Gotleib Pvt.	5 WVI	9/61–1863
Henry, John W. Sgt.	1 MOI	9/16/61–6/25/65
Hensley, Fretwell G. Pvt.	11 WVI	2/11/62–5/15/65

Higgins, John T. Sgt.	176 OHI	9/5/64–6/26/65
Higgins, Josiah P. Pvt.	1 WVC	9/14/61–1/1/64
also Seaman	USS Sybil	6/4/64–7/28/65
Higgins, Wm. McD. Pvt.	173 OHI	8/26/64–6/26/65
Hilcom, Thomas	Ambulance Driver	NF
Hill, Charles M. Pvt.	13 WVC	61/65
Hinchman, Adam Sgt.	3 WVC	10/5/62–6/30/65
Holderby, Wm. R. Pvt.	6 OHC	2/29/64–6/27/65
Holland, John H. Pvt.	1 WVC	NF
Holroyd, John Cpl.	3 WVC	9/17/62–6/30/65
Hovey, Wm. M. Capt.	13 WVI	7/9/61–6/9/65
Howard, Abram W. Pvt.	7 OHC	9/30/64–6/11/65
Howes, Marcus D. Pvt.	US	NF
Huffman, Henry H. Pvt.	3 OHI	4/17/61–8/24/65
Hughes, Fleming T. Pvt.	7 WVC	8/61–8/65
Hugley, Harrison Pvt.	13 WVI	NF
Hungerford, Maurice Sgt.	186 NYI	8/23/64–8/23/65
Hunter, John Pvt.	13 WVI	8/15/62–6/22/65
Hunter, Samuel Pvt.	86 OHI	7/10/62–11/10/62
also	10 OHC	11/10/62–3/22/64
Hutchinson, George Sgt.	14 KYI	10/25/61–6/31/65
Hysell, Joseph Pvt.	1 WVI	5/1/62–5/1/65
Insco, James Pvt.	5 WVI	9/5/61–12/24/63
also	1 WVI	12/25/63–7/21/65
Jacks, Leroy Pvt.	9 OHI	3/25/62–2/1/65
Jackson, Milo B. Pvt.	140 OHI	5/1/64–9/20/64
Jackson, Roland Pvt.	14 KYC	NF
Jackson, Thomas L. Pvt.	140 OHI	5/2/64–9/20/64
Jarvis, Wm.	NF (108 VAM CSA?)	
Jeffers, Joseph Pvt.	5 WVI	8/20/61–8/20/63
Jenkins, Walter	NF	
Johnson, Christopher Pvt.	3 WVC	11/15/63–NF
Johnson, George W. Pvt.	33 OHI	64/65
Johnson, James D. Cpl.	11 WVI	62/65
Johnston, Napolean B. Sgt.	3 WVC	9/27/62–6/19/65
Jusco, Ensa Pvt.	194 OHI	2/15/65–10/24/65
Jusco, Joseph Pvt.	9 WVI	NF
Justice, V.F.? Sgt.	5 WVI	10/1/61–7/20/65
Kaul, Moses Pvt.	66 PAI	10/62–1/63
Keitz, John P. Pvt.	1 WVA	8/21/63–6/27/65
Kelley, James A. Pvt.	91 OHI	8/6/62–10/25/63
Kheunes, Solomon Pvt.	92 OHI	8/1/62–6/10/65
Koontz, Charles Pvt.	2 OHA	NF
Kratger, Henry Pvt.	7 WVC	9/62–4/65
Kuhn, James I. Capt.	1 WVI	5/18/61–NF
Landress, Allen T. Pvt.	2 WVC	9/12/62–6/30/65
Lane, Wm. H. Pvt.	2 WVC	9/12/62–6/20/65

Lapool, John Cpl.	85 ILI	NF
Lattin, David Pvt.	5 WVI	9/1/61–10/3/64
Lawhorn, George W. Pvt.	3 WVC	9/17/62–7/65
Lecky, Henry O. Pvt.	24 OHI	5/13/61–6/21/64
Lee, Franklin	NF	
Lerdy, John W. Pvt.	WV Guards	4/1/65–7/1/65
Lesage, Francis J. Pvt.	3 WVC	9/29/62–6/30/65
Lesage, Joseph A. Sgt.	1 WVC	9/26/61–11/21/64
Lewis, Clark Pvt.	9 OHC	10/1/62–7/19/65
Lewis, Wm. Pvt.	14 WVI	8/14/62–6/21/65
Luster, James T. Pvt.	3 WVC	61/65
Lute, Henry Pvt.	92 OHI	8/9/62–7/5/65
Lycon, Joseph L. Pvt.	1 WVC	10/1/61–2/17/65
Lyons, Wm. H. Pvt.	13 WVI	2/1/63–5/29/65
Mann, Thomas D. Pvt.	7 IAI	5/15/61–8/10/64
Marcum, John S. Sgt.	53 KYI	3/28/65–9/16/65
Marker, Peter Pvt.	1 NYC	7/61–7/65
Markin, John M. Pvt.	189 OHI	2/1/65–10/1/65
Marshall, Jesse Pvt.	6 VAI	61/65
Martin, George B. Pvt.	7 OHI	10/17/63–8/11/65
Martin, Zena Lt.	14 WVI	9/3/62–7/2/65
Massie, Adam Cpl.	91 OHI	8/14/62–6/24/65
Mathews, Robert A. Pvt.	25 PAI	7/18/61–4/18/62
Mays, Parker Pvt.	32 OHI	5/63–7/25/65
McArthur, Frank Pvt.	5 NYI	7/61–9/62
also Yeoman	Jean Land	9/62–5/64
McCann, Charles A. Pvt.	91 OHI	7/31/62–6/24/65
McChristian, John Pvt.	— OHI	NF
McClane, John C. Cpl.	5 WVI	6/10/61–6/26/65
McClure, Charles W. Pvt.	188 OHI	2/16/65–9/17/65
McComas, John Pvt.	3 VAC	2/28/64–6/30/65
McComas, Peyton N. Pvt.	1 WVI	3/11/62–5/21/65
McCunly, Azel Pvt.	3 WVC	10/16/62–6/12/65
McIntosh, George R. Sgt.	1 KYI	4/19/61–5/31/64
McIntosh, George R. Pvt.	NF	
McIntyre, Dews Pvt.	— MOI	5/61–7/61
McKendric, Samuel Pvt.	NF (16 VAC CSA)	
McLaughlin, James S. Pvt.	17 WVI	NF
McLean, James C. Pvt.	19 OHI	9/15/61–6/12/62
Mellen, Norman E. Pvt.	24 NYI	5/19/61–5/19/63
Melrose, Andrew H. Sgt.	8 INI	4/22/61–8/28/65
Messenger, Hira L. Cpl.	10 WVI	8/7/62–8/9/65
Miller, James T.	NF (8 VAC CSA)	
Miller, Lewis	NF (36 VAI CSA?)	
Miller, Morgan Pvt.	1 WVC	2/23/65–7/8/65
Miller, Nathan Pvt.	91 OHI	NF
Miller, Wm. B. Pvt.	7 OHC	9/3/62–7/3/65

Miller, Wm. K. Pvt.	6 OHC	3/64–7/9/65
Miser, Andrew Pvt.	6 OHI	6/18/61–6/23/64
also	70 OHI	8/9/64–8/14/65
Mitchell, Archibald M.	NF	
Mobley, James Pvt.	1 WVI	6/1/63–7/22/65
Mobley, Thomas Pvt.	16 KYI	2/16/62–2/65
Montague, John Pvt.	14 KYC	8/15/62–9/16/63
Morning, John W. Pvt.	1 WVC	8/14/62–6/3/65
Morrison, James Pvt.	5 VAI	10/1/61–6/1/63
Morrow, Charles Pvt.	173 OHI	8/64–6/26/65
Moses, John H.	NF	
Mossgrove, Thomas Pvt.	2 VAC	9/6/61–10/65
Mount, Harvey Pvt.	53 OHI	11/22/61–8/31/65
Mount, Samuel Pvt.	2 OHC	9/28/62–6/10/65
Mounts, Samuel Pvt.	2 OHC	9/22/62–6/10/65
Mourning, Andrew J. Pvt.	13 WVI	8/20/63–6/22/65
Mowry, John Pvt.	2 KYI	4/30/61–6/19/64
also Cpl.	143 OHI	2/16/65–8/4/65
Nance, Aaron Pvt.	5 WVI	8/16/61–7/15/65
Neace, George W. Sgt.	1 KYI	NF
Nelf, Louis P. Pvt.	6 WVI	8/2/61–7/21/65
Newcomb, Wm. H. Lt.	7 WVC	9/17/61–8/1/65
Newman, Albert M. Pvt.	1 OHI	8/11/61–8/14/62
Newman, John M. Cpl.	6 OHC	10/22/61–6/27/65
Newman, Milton Sgt.	3 WVC	10/17/62–7/13/65
Newmen, Leroy Cpl.	13 WVI	8/14/62–6/2/65
Nichols, McLaske Pvt.	15 WVI	8/7/62–6/14/65
Noel, Willis Pvt.	10 VAI	12/1/61–12/4/64
Nolan, David Pvt.	173 OHI	64/65
Nuller, Zachary T. Pvt.	195 OHI	2/20/65–12/18/65
Odell, Adolphus	US NF	
Orwig, Robert M. Pvt.	52 OHI	7/28/62–9/2/62
Palmer, Alonzo R.	NF	
Pancake, Abraham Sgt.	2 WVI	6/10/61–1/4/64
Panell, John I. Capt.	53 OHI	8/20/61–12/26/64
Patterson, Rush Pvt.	189 OHI	2/18/65–10/5/65
Patton, Erastus Pvt.	172 OHNG	5/2/64–9/3/64
Pemberton, Andrew Pvt.	NF	
Pemberton, David Pvt.	28 OHI	6/13/61–7/23/64
Pemberton, Jasper N. Pvt.	173 OHI	64/65
Peters, John O. Pvt.	173 OHI	8/13/64–5/11/65
Peters, Oliver H. Pvt.	21 KYI	11/7/61–11/15/64
Peyton, Charles Pvt.	9 WVI	11/61–12/64
Pitman, Moses Pvt.	38 OHI	10/4/64–7/12/65
Plybon, James C. Pvt.	13 WVI	8/14/62–6/22/65
Poling, Lloyd Pvt.	11 WVI	8/14/62–1865
Pollard, John C. Sgt.	3 WVC	9/27/62–6/19/65

Poore, Mark Capt.	1 WVI	8/15/61–7/21/65
Porter, Alexander Pvt.	3 WVC	9/17/62–6/30/65
Porter, John L. Pvt.	3 WVC	7/19/62–6/30/65
Porter, John Pvt.	14 KYC	8/16/62–11/1/65
Powell, John R. Pvt.	6 WVC	9/1/64–5/19/65
Powers, Wade H. Sgt.	39 KYI	3/8/63–9/15/65
Preston, Charles B. "Mate"	USS Gen. Meigs	7/62–9/17/65
Price, John Pvt.	131 PAI	8/27/62–6/1/63
Prince, James M. Pvt.	5 VAT	4/62–7/64
Pritchard, Charles U. Sgt.	10 KYC	8/9/62–9/17/63
Pully, John Pvt.	NF	
Randolph, James Cpl.	105 PAI	9/1/61–8/1/63
Raws, Wm. Pvt.	11 WVI	3/61–NF
Ray, Andrew S. Pvt.	7 WVC	64/65
Reynolds, Walter S. Pvt.	18 OHI	4/27/61–6/20/65
Richards, Joseph C. Pvt.	5 ILI	5/2/61–7/3/65
Ridion, Samuel Lt.	27 ILI	8/20/61–9/20/64
Riffle, John Pvt.	12 OHI	4/15/61–6/22/64
Riggs, James Pvt.	5 WVI	NF
Riggs, Robert Pvt.	15 WVI	6/63–1865
Rinnick, Wm. Pvt.	2 VAI	5/11/64–7/16/65
Roberts, Richard J. Pvt.	3 OHC	10/3/63–6/30/65
Robinson, Richard Cpl.	2 WVI	8/26/61–8/64
Rogers, Philip Pvt.	53 PAC	11/6/61–6/16/62
also Cpl.	— PAC	7/14/64–10/28/64
Rood, George W. Pvt.	5 OHI	8/1/61–5/5/65
Ross, Covington	NF	
Ross, James M. Pvt.	2 WVA	7/22/63–8/23/65
Ross, James Pvt.	2 WVA	7/22/63–8/25/65
Ross, John Pvt.	2 WVI	5/61–8/61
also	5 WVI	3/12/62–3/12/65
Rouk, Joseph Pvt.	7 WVC	12/29/62–8/12/65
Rouse, George M. Pvt.	14 KYI	2/29/64–9/15/65
Rousey, James S. Pvt.	WV Guards	2/5/64–10/5/64
Rowsey, Wm. T. Pvt.	14 KYI	8/8/62–8/2/65
Runyon, George W. Pvt.	5 WVI	10/22/62–6/25/65
Rust, George J. Pvt.	7 WVC	2/64–8/1/65
Rutherford, M. W. Pvt.	2 VAC	9/1/61–12/31/63
Rutherford, Martin W.	NF	
Rutherford, Mathew W. Pvt.	2 WVC	9/61–7/3/63
Sanford, Nathan Pvt.	5 WVI	8/13/61–10/4/64
Saunders, George W. Pvt.	36 OHC	NF
Scarberry, Elamander Pvt.	33 OHI	2/29/64–7/65
Scarberry, Noah Pvt.	89 OHI	7/28/62–2/9/65
Schultz, Jacob B. Sgt.	1 WVI	NF
Scott, George Cpl.	5 USI	7/30/63–9/20/65
Scott, James D. Sgt.	1 PAC	8/13/61–9/64

Shaw, James C. Lt.	7 WVC	8/2/62–7/4/65
Sheppard, Levi Pvt.	91 OHI	8/7/62–6/30/65
Shipe, Charles W. Sgt.	3 WVC	9/17/62–NF
Shoemaker, Joseph H. Pvt.	2 WVC	4/22/61–11/64
Short, Daniel Pvt.	173 OHI	64/65
Shorter, Wm. H. Cpl.	4 USI	10/12/64–6/6/66
Shwaebel, Jacob Pvt.	28 OHI	6/13/61–7/23/64
Sikes, Thomas Ltc.	33 OHI	4/12/61–7/12/65
Simmons, Harvey Pvt.	NF	
Simmons, Henry Pvt.	5 WVI	NF
Simmons, Martin Pvt.	122 OHI	64/65
Simpson, John B. Pvt.	15 WVI	8/11/62–6/25/65
Skidmore, Daniel Pvt.	11 WVI	8/20/62–5/12/63
Smith, Henry Cpl.	2 OHC	1862–9/65
Smith, John C. Sgt.	9 WVI	12/61–3/17/62
Smith, Michael A. Sgt.	1 WVI	4/2/62–5/2/65
Snider, Wm. T. Pvt.	7 OHI	6/10/62–9/15/62
also "Louisville Mississippi Squatter"		8/10/64–7/3/65
Snyder, Adam Pvt.	NF	
Sparks, Charles W. Capt.	73 OHI	61/65
Stanley, James Sgt.	6 NYI	4/22/61–6/11/64
Stanley, Robert Pvt.	11 KYC	9/1/62–9/1/63
Stenkey, Wm. Pvt.	5 OHI	8/1/61–5/5/65
Stephens, Jesse P.	NF	
Stephenson, Marcus Pvt.	5 WVI	7/13/61–9/24/64
Stevens, Joel Pvt.	4 MNI	1863–6/15/65
Strenk, George Pvt.	5 PAC	8/5/61–12/62
Summonds, Wm.	NF	
Swann, Roger? Lt.	5 WVI	7/17/61–2/15/62
Swann, Shelby J. Pvt.	3 WVC	12/9/62–6/30/65
Taylor, John A. Pvt.	7 PAT	4/24/61–7/65
Thompson, Amos N. Pvt.	7 OHC	11/62–7/4/65
Thompson, George W. Pvt.	29 KYI	NF
Thompson, John Pvt.	91 OHI	8/2/62–6/15/65
Thompson, Tom J. Pvt.	5 WVI	10/15/61–11/20/64
Thornton, Michael Lt.	53 PAI	9/10/61–10/30/65
Tillinghost, George Pvt.	18 OHI	4/63–10/65
Toney, Alonzo Pvt.	8 VAC CSA	62/64
Tucker, Wm. J. Pvt.	7 WVC	12/5/61–8/65
Vanata, Wm. Pvt.	8 WVI	10/5/61–11/28/62
also	7 WVC	3/28/64–8/1/65
Vanatter, Andrew J. Pvt.	8 WVI	61/62
Vanhorn, Samuel Pvt.	1 WVI	10/1/61–1/18/64
also	1 WVA	6/19/64–6/18/65
Vannater, James Pvt.	4 WVA	5/11/61–NF
Vemathis, Jackson Pvt.	7 WVC	12/15/62–8/1/65
Venoy, Anthony Cpl.	140 OHI	5/64–9/3/64

Waggoner, James Pvt.	140 OHI	5/2/64–9/3/64
Walker, James A. Pvt.	13 VAI	3/31/64–6/22/65
Wallace, Wm. F. Lt.	174 OHI	6/20/61–7/6/65
Walls, John P. Pvt.	91 OHI	8/9/62–6/30/65
Walter, Ansel Pvt.	36 OHI	10/10/61–12/64
Ward, James W. Pvt.	13 WVI	10/5/63–6/22/65
Waugh, Charles Pvt.	9 WVI	1/1/62–1/6/65
Weaks, John M. Pvt.	10 KYC	7/61–8/62
also	44 INI	9/64–8/10/65
Wellman, John D. Pvt.	5 VAI	7/18/61–7/22/65
Wells, Zackens Pvt.	173 OHI	8/64–7/65
Welsh, John H. Pvt.	4 INI	9/14/61–6/16/65
Wheeler, Edward Pvt.	107 NYI	8/4/62–5/21/65
Wheeler, Henry A. Pvt.	5 CTI	7/11/61–7/22/64
Williams, Wm. G. Pvt.	7 WVC	12/2/62–8/1/65
Willison, George W. Pvt.	3 VAC	1/1/64–7/7/65
Wills, Albert Pvt.	14 OHA	7/64–7/65
AKA William Smith	NF	
Wintz, Louis M. Pvt.	9 WVI	10/13/61–8/1/65
Wood, Jonithan E. Lt.	5 WVI	6/14/61–3/62
also Pvt.	1 OHA	9/20/63–3/11/64
also Capt.	7 WVI	3/18/64–7/65
Wood, Lyman H. Pvt.	44 OHI	8/13/61–7/30/65
Wood, Richard Pvt.	12 PAI	4/1/61–6/13/64
Woodburn, Finley Pvt.	78 OHI	8/30/62–6/30/65
Woodworth, Albert H. Cpl.	18 OHI	7/29/62–6/29/65
Wooten, Van Buren Sgt.	1 OHC	8/30/62–7/3/65
Workman, Stephen H. Cpl.	1 OHA	9/13/62–6/5/65
Wray, Isaac Pvt.	NF	
Wright, Charles Sgt.	91 OHI	8/6/62–6/24/65

Cabell Co. Remarks

Abshire, W.—RH
Adams, J.F.— lame back & limbs
Adkins, J.— LD
Baker, J.M.— RH
Barbour, J.W.—RH & LD
Barcus, J.W.—WIA arm & head
Barnes, A.— deaf in right ear
Barnes, W.J.— piles & fistula
Bartley, J.— WIA left leg, pensioner
Baumgardner, H.J.—gunshot left arm, reenlisted 9/16/63 to 8/65
Baumgardner, J.B.—fistula & stomach disease
Bayliss, T.H.—RH & HD, AFP
Beach, S.—gunshot wound right thigh
Bennett, E.A.—hemorrhoids, premature aging
Bias, J.A.— RH
Bias, J.L.— CDR
Bias, W.A.— POW 6½ months Salsbury, discharged out of 1 WVI
Bias, W.E.— testicles mashed & internal injuries
Bicker, A.— neuralgia in head
Billup, J.T.— in hospital Charleston WV 4 months with TYF, was in hospital Jan 1865 & received no discharge
Bishop, W.— shot in left leg, draws pension
Bishop, W.H.— concussion of brain
Brown, L.G.— consumption
Butcher, J.— KD, DSC
Butcher, T.L.—scrotum mashed, spinal disease
Cardwell, M.— pyles & hurt back
Cayslep, C.B.—nervous debility from measles in army
Chapman, J.— left leg broken, now lame
Childers, G.W.—POW 7 months
Childers, S.A. —hernia & RH
Christian, J.A.—shot 3 times
Church, J.W.— nervous debility & neuralgia
Clagg, J.J.— deserter
Clark, H.—WIA right leg
Clay, J. —exposure, brights disease
Clay, M.—wounded, shell top of head Drurys Bluff, pensioner
Cook, A.J.—falling back of measles
Cox, T.H.—shot in foot, draws pension
Crawford, W.—HD & arm broken, pensioner
Cremens, A.—WIA left foot
Crook, W.M.—shot in left knee
Damaron, S.J.—bronchitis
Davis, P.—piles & KD
Davis, St. —shot through right arm

Davis, T.C.—breast injured by horse
Dawson, L.J.—kicked by a horse, AFP
Dawson, M.L.—sight impaired
Deleber, K.— disentary
Derbyshire, H.J.—hearing affected
Dewitt, J.— smallpox & CDR
Dicky, H.L.— LD
Diehl, L.—organized at Wheeling was paid by state
Dille, A.—WIA left hip & right side, pensioner
Dillon, C.—bronchitis caused by measles settling on lungs
Dishman, J.J.—RH & asthma
Dotson, I.— RH & blind in one eye
Earle, J.S.— piles & shell passed through ankle
Edens, J. — indigestion
Edmonds, J.R.—RH, pensioner
Eggers, J.— POW 7 months
Elkhart, G.W.—RH, deaf from shell explosion
Elkins, J.P.— gunshot wound in side
Emery, W.J.— piles & disease of rectum
Emrick, J.— liver disease, now partially deaf
Felginer, E.— liver complaint
Felix, A.—WIA right wrist, pensioner
Felix, J. —breast & wrist injured
Fellure, W.—catarrh & lumbago
Fergeson, Je.—deserter
Field, H.K.— shot in thigh & blind
Fitzgerald, T.G.—shot in hip, AFP
Flowers, F.— CDR
Floyd, J.H.— shot in thigh at Winchester, measles, pensioner
Flowers, G.W. —shot in ankle
Ford, J. —was left sick, never discharged
Foster, J.E.—dysentary
Foster, R.—paralysis
Gethard, J.— HD
Gibson, W.— shot through hip
Gilette, A.— CDR, transferred from 72 to 114 Ind
Gilkeson, N.— leg parallized
Gill, W.—piles, spinal irritation, nervous debility
Gunther, J.C.—discharged because of deafness
Gwinn, G.W.—CDR, LD, piles, draws pension
Hagley, J. —RH & CDR
Haley, T. —consumption & pyles
Hamilton, J.A.—discharged on account of scrofula
Hamlin, W.M.—eyes were injured, AFP
Harshbarger, J.—ruptured, injured in breast
Harshbarger, J.P.—inflamation of eyes & RH, DSC
Henry, J.W.— CDR, now blind in left eye

Hensley, F.G.—RH & HD
Higgins, J.P.—CDR, AFP
Higgins, J.T.—catarrh & RH, AFP
Hill, C.M.— RH
Hinchman, A.— RH & LD
Holderby, W.R. —had fever
Holland, J.H.—wounded in arm
Hovey, W.M.— WIA through leg, formerly served 4th WVI
Huffman, H.H.—RH
Hughes, F.T.— disabled by bursting of shell near head
Hungerford, M.—HD
Hunter, J.—RH
Insco, J. —shot in right leg at Bull Run 1863, asthma
Jacks, L. —shot through left hand, KD & liver disease
Jackson, R.—thrown from his horse & head injured, AFP
Jarvis, W.*— served 3 years & deserted
Johnson, C.C.—KD
Johnson, J.D.—eye & breast injured
Johnston, N.B.—RH
Jusco, E.— KD, right eye out now
Kaul, M.—RH, was discharged or failed to pass examination
Kelley, J.A.—LD
Kheunes, S.—CDR
Koontz, C.— sprain of left ankle
Kratger, H.— brights disease of kidneys
Lane, W.H.— AFP
Lattin, D.— RH 28 years
Lawhorn, G.W.—catarrh of head
Lesage, J.A.—RH & sore eyes
Lewis, W.—TYF, spinal deformity, AFP
Lute, H. — wounded left leg, pensioner
Lyons, W.H.— HD
Mann, T.D.— CDR
Markcin, J.M.—malarial poison, dispepsia
Marshall, J.— shot in knee
Massie, A.— back disabled, AFP
McCann, C.A.— CDR
McClure, C.W.—CDR, draws pension
McComas, P.N.—WIA left leg, formerly served Co D 9 WVI
McKendric, S.*—RH & smallpox
McLean, J.C.— CDR by exposure
Messenger, H.L.—CDR & weak eyes
Miller, M.— foot strained right bone has come out, AFP
Miller, N.— feet frozen
Miser, A. — RH in hip & back
Morrow, C.— HD
Mount, S. — wounded in calf of leg

Mourning, A.J.—RH
Newman, A.M.— RH & catarrh head
Newmen, L.— broken leg, now a cripple
Nichols, M.— asthma, AFP
Nolan, D. — RH
Pancake, A.— partial deafness left ear, RH
Panell, J.I.— wound leg & breast
Patterson, R. —at present partial parallysis
Patton, E.— RH & bronchitis
Pemberton, D.—general debility, sight now very bad
Peyton, C.— POW Libby & Salsbury, RH & HD
Poling, L.— HD
Pollard, J.C.—horse fell on him, internal injury
Porter, A.— thrown from horse 3 ribs broken
Porter, J.— shoulder out of place
Porter, J.L.— lumbago & fistula
Powers, W.H.— RH & catarrh
Preston, C.B.—served on three or four vessels
Randolph, J.— HD
Raws, W. — measles settled in throat
Ray, A.S. — SS & RH
Reynolds, W.S.—HD
Riffle, J.— HD & LD
Riggs, J. — LD
Riggs, R. — shot twice, chin & hand
Rinnick, W.— now a cripple
Roberts, R.J.—LD
Robinson, R.— HD, spinal trouble, draws pension
Rogers, P.— DSC
Rood, G.W.— consumption
Ross, J. — broken leg, CDR
Ross, J.M.— now blind one eye & other defective
Rouk, J. — RH
Rouse, G.M.— gunshot wound
Rowsey, W.T.— rupture & RH, draws pension
Sanford, N.— bronchitis
Saunders, G.W.—sore eyes
Scarberry, E.—piles, pensioner
Scarberry, N.—RH & KD, POW 12 months Pemberton, Danville, Libby
Scott, G. — right eye injured
Shaw, J.C.— indigestion
Shipe, C.W.— wounded in thigh
Shoemaker, J.H.—CDR, fistula, AFP
Shwaebel, J.— CDR, HD & wound
Sikes, T. — catarrh head & gunshot wound shoulder
Skidmore, D.— injured in breast, DSC
Smith, M.A.— shot in right knee, suffering nervous debility

Snider, W.T.— rupture by bayonet wound
Stanley, J.— neuralgia
Stephenson, M.—SS
Stevens, J.— LD, pensioner
Strenk, G.— fractured leg
Summonds, W.— this man was member of Carter Co Ky homeguard
Thompson, A.N.—AFP
Thompson, G.W.—spinal disease
Thompson, T.J.—fistula & piles
Vanata, W.— DSC
Vanhorn, S.— RH
Venoy, A. —WIA
Waggoner, J.— RH, draws pension
Walker, J.A.— sunstroke received on raid from Boliver Heights to Frederick City, SS causing abcess in head
Walter, A.— ruptured & SS
Waugh, C. — lost finger right hand
Weaks, J.M.— forehead injury from mule kick causing partial deaf
Wheeler, H.A.—gunshot wound left leg, AFP
Wintz, L.M.— bronchitis & nervous disability
Wood, J.E.— hearing impaired
Wood, R.—WIA 6/30/62 at Charles City Cross Roads
Woodburn, F.— RH
Wooten, V.B.— thrown from horse, ankle out, horse kick side, AFP
Wray, I. — pensioner
Wright, C.— HD

Calhoun County

NAME/RANK	REGIMENT	WHEN SERVED
Ague, Jacob W. Pvt.	11 WVI	62/65
Allen, Joseph T. Pvt.	17 WVI	2/13/65–6/29/65
Amos, Rowley W. Pvt.	10 WVI	4/4/62–5/6/65
Badgett, Shedwick A. Pvt.	9 WVI	1/62–7/65
Ball, Jasper Pvt.	11 WVI	10/61–12/64
Barnes, William Pvt.	11 WVI	11/61–12/64
Bartrug, Peter Pvt.	7 WVI	3/13/65–6/30/65
Bauner, Josiah Pvt.	11 VAI 6	1/65
Bauner, Robert Pvt.	11 WVI	12/24/61–12/24/64
Beger, George Pvt.	85 PAI	10/1/61–2/64
Bell, James W. Pvt.	1 VAI CSA	61/63
Bell, Townsend Pvt.	—	61/64
Berkhouse, Benjamen Pvt.	NF	
Beth, John R. Pvt.	NF	
Billfie, Christopher Pvt.	NF	
Bishop, John Pvt.	53 KYI	64/65
Blake, John F. Pvt.	15 WVI	61/64
Bland, Henry H. Pvt.	1 WVI	10/14/61–11/64
Booker, Peter M. Pvt.	11 WVI	62/65
Bower, Oliver P. Pvt.	2 WVI	5/20/61–7/1/65
Brake, Jerome Pvt.	10 WVI	64/65
Brookover, Eli Pvt.	NF	
Buck, Alexander Pvt.	14 WVI	8/13/62–6/27/65
Buck, Ezekill Pvt.	7 WVI	8/8/61–8/8/64
Buck, George William Pvt.	7 WVI	62/65
Bummer, Hiram Pvt.	12 WVI	8/62–3/63
Burrous, Thomas Pvt.	—	62/65
Byner, James Pvt.	85 PAI	8/17/61–11/27/64
Cane, James M. Pvt.	WVC	8/64–8/65
Carnes, Comett Pvt.	10 WVI	8/22/62–65
Carpenter, Alfred Pvt.	3 VAC	8/62–1/65
Cheuvront, Joseph M. Pvt.	36 VAI CSA	62/65
Church, William S. Pvt.	14 WVI	61/65
Coberly, Wm J. Pvt.	6 WVI	10/4/64–5/28/65
Collins, John Pvt.	11 WVI	11/24/61–3/31/65
Cornell, John R. Pvt.	11 WVI	12/62–12/64
Cottrell, Andrew J. Pvt.	9 WVI	11/63–7/31/65
Cottrell, Thomas Pvt.	9 WVI	7/21/63–7/21/65
Cottrell, William Pvt.	1 WVI	3/1/62–7/21/65
Cox, Isaac, Sr. Cpl.	11 WVI	11/9/61–12/24/64
Cox, Windfield Pvt.	10 WVI	61/65
Cunningham, Wm L. Pvt.	11 WVI	11/10/61–12/24/64

Name	Unit	Dates
Cunningham, Wm. Pvt.	—	61/64
Davis, Jesse Pvt.	36 VAI CSA	NF
Davis, John Pvt.	31 VAI CSA	4/61–64
Davis, John Pvt.	27 OHI	6/2/65
Dillan, George Cpl.	5 WVC	6/16/61–6/16/64
Dix, Stephen S. Pvt.	9 WVI	1/22/62–7/31/65
Duein, John D. Pvt.	6 WVI	62/64
Dunn, Jacob Pvt.	11 WVI	8/21/63–8/9/65
Early, Edward Pvt.	77 OHI	4/24/64–3/5/66
Ellison, Nathaniel Pvt.	NF	
Ellison, Nathaniel Pvt.	19 VAC CSA	61/65
Ferrell, Franklin Pvt.	11 VAI	61/63
Ferrell, Henry A. Capt.	46 VAC BTN CSA	9/10/62–4/10/65
Ferrell, James Pvt.	6 WVI	10/10/61–12/24/64
Ferrell, Thomas K. Pvt.	11 WVI	2/20/62–3/20/65
Ferrell, Thornton 1 Lt.	11 WVI	12/22/61–11/24/64
Flaharty, Ulisses Pvt.	9 WVI	4/13/62–5/13/65
Freed, Jacob Pvt.	11 VAI	61/65
Gebo, Robert Pvt.	6 WVC	7/19/61–8/17/64
Gregg, Henry Pvt.	62 VAI CSA	62/64
Grim, David Pvt.	1 PAC	8/17/62–5/25/65
Gumm, Samuel Pvt.	—	64/65
Gump, Edward Pvt.	USA	8/61–7/22/65
Hall, Robert B.	NF	
Hardway, John Pvt.	9 WVI	10/14/63–7/24/65
Harshman, Oscar Pvt.	OHC	61/64
Haymaker, Francis Pvt.	PAC	8/15/64–65
Haymaker, John Pvt.	63 PAI	61/64
Heart, William A Pvt.	1 WVA	7/11/63–7/3/65
Hensley, John Pvt.	USN	4/64–8/66
Holland, William Pvt.	—	8/11/62–7/12/65
Husk, Isaac H. Pvt.	6 WVI	8/13/62–64/65
Jarvis, Kaleb Pvt.	11 WVI	61/65
Jarvis, Thomas Pvt.	1 WVI	10/20/63–6/20/65
Jones, James E. Pvt.	6 WVI	10/61–10/64
Kelley, Oscar Pvt.	11 WVI	8/18/62–6/29/65
Kelly, Lamon Pvt.	6 WVI	8/26/62–6/10/65
Kidder, Ira Pvt.	12 VAI	NF
Kincaid, James Pvt.	2 WVI	5/15/61–1/14/64
aka King, Danbarth B.	—	
King, Francis M. Pvt.	17 WVI	8/17/64–6/30/65
King, William Pvt.	7 WVI	12/62–7/65
Knight, Jeremiah Pvt.	2 WVC	9/1/61–12/1/64
Knight, John Pvt.	4 WVC	7/28/63–3/8/64
Knitz, William Pvt.	NF	
Lane, John Fifer	8 WVI	9/23/61–5/14/64
Law, Isaac T. Pvt.	11 WVI	10/9/61–8/24/65

Law, Leonard Pvt.	6 WVC	9/2/64–5/19/65
Marks, Philip C. Pvt.	1 WVI	10/63–7/65
Marshall, William Pvt.	NF	
Maze, Andrew D. Pvt.	17 VAC CSA	7/62–2/27/65
Maze, George W. 2lt.	19 VAC CSA	62/65
McClane, William Pvt.	19 OHI	9/64–10/11/65
McCoy, Henry W. Cpl.	15 OHI	9/27/61–63
McCoy, John Pvt.	6 WVI	64/65
McCoy, Samuel M. Pvt.	15 WVI	2/14/63–7/15/65
McCune, James Pvt.	9 WVI	2/11/62–2/11/65
McCune, William Pvt.	9 WVI	6/63–5/65
McDonald, James Lt.	11 WVI	12/2/61–12/64
McGee, Jesse Pvt.	11 WVI	8/26/61–12/64
Meadows, Andrew Pvt.	9 WVC	NF
Morgan, Jacob M. Pvt.	6 WVC	1/25/61–7/26/65
Morton, George W. Cpl.	18 OHI	61/64
Newell, Isaac S. Pvt.	45 OHI	NF
Norman, Alpheus Pvt.	12 WVI	62/64
Paniger, Amos Pvt.	15 WVI	8/19/62–6/23/65
Pantell, Elijah Sgt.	105 PAI	9/17/61–64
Parsons, Benjamin B. Pvt.	9 WVI	1/22/62–65
Pell, Julius Musician	6 WVI	12/24/61–1/4/65
Pettit, Nathaniel Pvt.	3 VAC	3/1/65–7/1/65
Poling, Jacob Pvt.	11 WVI	12/28/61–12/31/64
Poling, Westly Pvt.	11 WVI	8/62–6/65
Powell, Oliver Pvt.	NF	
Propst, James Pvt.	14 WVI	11/20/62–6/27/65
Raber, Jacot Pvt.	6 WVI	1/24/64–6/12/65
Richards, Adonijah Pvt.	11 WVI	11/10/61–12/24/64
Richmond, Caleb Lt.	18 OHI	8/61–11/65
Rinestone, William J. Pvt.	18 USI	11/30/61–2/10/65
Roach, George Pvt.	85 PAI	1/64–6/64
Roberts, Enoch Pvt.	7 WVI	65/65
Robinson, Francis Pvt.	11 WVI	61/65
Robinson, Harvey Pvt.	11 WVI	61/64
Rogers, Robert H. Sgt.	11 WVI	11/10/61–12/24/64
Rose, James E. 2 Lt.	CARPENTERS VAA CSA	4/22/61–1/11/65
Rostlewate, Martin Pvt.	17 WVI	3/65–7/65
Saltkill, John Pvt.	6 OHI	63/65
Shaffer, James Pvt.	12 WVI	8/9/62–7/16/65
Shaffer, John Pvt.	15 WVI	12/10/63–8/10/65
Shreconcost, Martin Pvt.	PA	NF
Sidwell, Josiah Pvt.	51 PAI	NF
Siers, John Pvt.	NF (14 VAC CSA)	
Simmers, Pladle (?) Cpl.	161 OHI	5/2/64–9/2/64
Skidd, Custill B. Pvt.	1 WVC	10/61–6/20/65

Skinner, George Sgt.	11 WVI	12/24/61–12/24/64
Smith, Barnes Pvt.	11 WVI	8/20/63–6/1/65
Smith, George Pvt.	6 WVI	8/30/64–6/10/65
Snider, John Pvt.	11 WVI	11/61–12/24/64
Snyder, Jeremiah Pvt.	20 VAC CSA	63/65
Stevens, Lindsay Cpl.	6 WVI	8/27/61–6/7/65
Stevens, Samuel W. Pvt.	1 WVI	8/18/62–6/65
Stutler, Martin Pvt.	NF	
Stutler, William B. Pvt.	19 WV?	8/61–64
Taylor, Benjamin Pvt.	—	64/65
Taylor, Wiley H. Pvt.	15 WVI	8/16/62–7/9/65
Thomas, Henry Pvt.	PAI	61/65
Thomas, Isaac H. Pvt.	2 VAI CSA	8/61–8/62
Trippett, Phillip 2 Lt.	19 VAC CSA	6/16/61–4/15/65
Tucker, John Pvt.	9 WVI	9/16/61–10/5/64
Upton, Ulyses Pvt.	9 WVI	12/15/61–6/65
Wadkins, Francis Pvt.	NF	
Welch, John R. Lt.	19 VAC CSA	62/65
Whipkey, Henry Pvt.	11 WVI	61/64
Whipkey, Jacob Pvt.	1 WVI	8/61–65
White, Francis Pvt.	18 PAC	62/65
Williams, Edward Pvt.	15 WVI	8/2/62–6/14/65
Wiseman, George Pvt.	11 WVI	62/65
Woods, William H. Pvt.	11 PAI	3/11/64–12/31/65
Yeager, Alfred Pvt.	8 WVC	63/64
Yeager, Isaac	NF	
Zumbro, Wm Pvt.	6 WVI	8/26/64–10/11/65

Calhoun County Remarks

Allen, J.T.—RH
Altkill, J.S.—piles & CDR
Badgett, S.—arm broken
Bartrug, P.—CP
Bauner, J.—scurvy loss of memory MP & POW 9 months
Bauner, R.—RH
Bell, J.W.*—gunshot wound left leg
Bell, T.—KD & LD
Blake, J.—RH by exposure
Booker, P.M.—WIA head & lost eye sight & hearing
Bower, O.—injury left knee & breast
Brookover, E.—HD
Buck, A.—KD
Buck, E.—RH & weak stomach

Buck, G.W.—WIA right index finger off & prisoner at Andersonville
Bunner, H.—HD
Byner, J.—ruptured
Carpenter, A.—right eye & finger injured
Cheuvront, J.*—broken down
Church, W.—KD
Collins, J.D.—WIA & MS
Cornell, J.R.—SS
Cottrill, A.J.—RH
Cottrill, T.— legs injured
Cottrill, W.P.— gunshot right arm
Cox, I.— RH
Cunningham, W.— RH & HD
Dillon, G.F.— partial loss of eye sight
Dix, S.S. — finger shot off
Dum, J.—MS
Ferrell, J.A.—LD
Ferrell, T.K.— RH
Ferrell, T. — RH & totally disabled
Freed, J.—eye disease RH & HD
Gebo, R.—paralysis both sides
Hardway, J. —WIA right hip
Haymaker, F.—RH incured in 1864
Haymaker, J.—WIA right arm in 1864
Hearst, W.A.—deafness origin cannonading
Husk, I.H.—weak lungs & breast hard marching
Jarvis, C.—eye disease
Jarvis, T.P.— gunshot in jaw
Jones, J.E.—affected leg
Kelley, O.—RH
King, F.M.— spinal disease
Knight, J.A.—RH
Knight, J.—wounded right eye by stone
Knitz, W. —RH
Lane, J.A.— RH
Law, I.T. —LD & RH
Law, L.F. — hurt by falling from cars
Marks, P.C.—deafness & weak eyes & is destitute
Maze, G.W.* —gunshot right arm
McCoy, H.W.—shell wound in right side of face
McCoy, Jn. —RH
McCoy, S.M.—LD & KD
McCune, J.J.— RH
McCune, W.— LD
McGee, J. —bronchitis
Meadows. A..T.—RH
Morgan, J. —TYF & RH

Morton, G.W. —deafness & eyes affected & rupture
Newell, I.S. —spinal effection by sun stroke in army
Norman, A.—RH
Pantell, E.—F & ague contracted in 1861
Parsons, B.B.— gunshot wound
Pell, J.W.— collarbone broken/was 10 yr. 3 mo & 25 days old at date of enlistment
Powell, O.—RH
Propst, J.— disease of mouth & scurvy
Raber, J.—KD
Richards, A. —fever settled in breast & stomach
Richmond, C. —WIA at Chicamauga face & jaw also piles
Rinestone, W.J.—RH
Roach, G.—lungs & liver disability by exposure 1864
Roberts, E.—RH
Rogers, R.H. —gunshot left leg & RH & testicle disease
Rose, J.E.*—shell wound in left foot
Shirner, G. —RH & nervous prostration
Shrecongrost, M. —RH incured in 1861
Smith, B.N. —gunshot & MS
Snider, Jn. —loss of sight right eye RH & HD smallpox
Stevens, L.M.— disabled right lung
Stevens, S.W.—gunshot right arm
Stutler, M.—lost eye sight & health from exposure
Stutler, W.B.—cough & weak breast incured in 1864
Taylor, B. —RH & piles
Taylor, W.H. —ulcers & VV entirely broken down
Trippett, P.*—WIA hip near Woodstock & broken down
Tucker, J.— injured by marching
Wayne, J.—RH & LD
Welsh, S.*—injured by fall from horse ruptured
Woods, W.H.—RH
Yeager, A. —RH by exposure

Clay County

NAME/RANK	REGIMENT	WHEN SERVED
Ankrum, Wm. R. Pvt.	22 VAI CSA	6/4/61–4/27/65
Arbrogast, G. W. Pvt.	7 WVC	7/31/64–8/1/65
Ashley, Jesse S. Pvt.	7 VAI	NF
Bailes, John N. Pvt.	9 WVI	7/1/62–6/28/65
Barnes, John T. Pvt.	11 WVI	NF
Blind?, Jacob Pvt.	12 VAI	8/11/62–8/19/63
Brown, Andrew	US NF	
Brown, Anthony Pvt.	7 WVC	8/1/64 8/65
Brown, Ellihu Pvt.	13 WVI	12/19/62–6/27/65
Brown, George W. Blksmith	2 WVC	9/1/62–6/30/65
Burdette, Wm. A. Pvt.	91 OHI	NF
Carpenter, Solomon Pvt.	9 WVI	3/62–1865
Davis, Stephen C. Pvt.	14 WVI	9/62–7/65
Dawson, John L. Pvt.	8 VAI	11/62–NF
Eagle, George Pvt.	7 WVC	9/26/64–8/16/65
Elerite, Henry Cpl.	1 OHA	8/23/61–7/22/65
Elliott, John M. Pvt.	1 WVA	9/26/64–7/21/65
Facemyre, John Pvt.	4 WVI	12/18/61–12/31/64
Frame, Marcellus Pvt.	173 OHI	8/64–7/26/65
Goff, George Pvt.	13 WVI	9/1/63–6/23/65
AKA George Ashby	NF	
Goldsmith, Granville Pvt.	7 WVI	12/63–NF
Griffitll, Charles P. Pvt.	4 VAI	8/18/61–2/63
Harman, Henry Pvt.	7 WVC	3/14/64–8/1/65
Hedrick, Moses Pvt.	32 IAI	7/31/62–7/13/65
Hughes, George W. Pvt.	7 WVC	4/3/62–4/8/65
Jeffrey, Shedrick Pvt.	7 WVI	10/11/64–8/1/65
Johnson, James W. Pvt.	2 WVC	9/1/62–6/30/65
Jones, Anda F. Pvt.	22 VAI CSA	7/61–4/65
Kier, Lewis Pvt.	10 WVI	2/6/64–8/9/65
King, George S. Pvt.	7 WVC	9/5/64–6/3/65
Lamby, Wm. H. Pvt.	1 WVI	10/2/61–11/15/64
Laxton, Thomas B. Pvt.	7 WVC	2/18/64–8/1/65
Lewis, Hiram Lt.	7 WVC	11/5/62–8/1/65
Lurham, Jesse P. Pvt.	2 VAI	1864–7/65
McCune, Wm. H. Pvt.	9 WVI	9/15/61–7/21/65
McKinney, John Pvt.	2 WVI	7/6/63–9/21/65
Miller, Zacahriah Pvt.	7 WVC	7/3/64–6/3/65
Minner, George W. Pvt.	2 VAC	3/30/64–6/30/65
Minner, Harper Pvt.	2 VAC	3/30/64–6/30/65
Moore, Joshuway Pvt.	7 WVC	1864–6/10/65
Moore, Metzah Pvt.	22 VAI CSA	4/25/63–12/63

Moore, Wm. H. Pvt.	7 WVC	8/15/64–6/3/65
Morton, John T. Pvt.	1 WVA	9/26/64–7/21/65
Morton, Paschal T. Sgt.	2 WVC	9/12/62–8/12/65
Mullins, James K. Pvt.	39 KYI	12/12/63–2/20/64
Mullins, Lewis S. Pvt.	4 WVC	10/62–3/65
Nichols, David Pvt.	1 WVA	12/64–8/65
Obrine, Elmore Pvt.	8 VAI	11/61–7/63
Owens, Thomas H. Pvt.	9 WVI	10/11/61–NF
also	1 WVI	1/1/63–7/24/65
Parsons, George W. Pvt.	7 WVI	62/65
Payne, James M. Pvt.	1 WVI	10/15/64–7/20/65
Procious, Adam Pvt.	78 PAI	3/28/64–9/21/65
Ramsey, Abner Pvt.	7 WVC	6/1/63–8/1/65
Reed, Levi Pvt.	9 WVI	9/16/61–10/5/64
Reed, Solomon Pvt.	7 WVC	8/15/64–6/3/65
Rodgers, John C. Pvt.	1 WVA	9/26/64–7/21/65
Rollyson, Charles M. Pvt.	10 WVI	3/31/62–5/31/65
Samples, Agrippa Pvt.	13 VAI	8/62–6/65
Samples, Andrew M. Pvt.	7 WVC	9/24/64–6/3/65
Samples, Hiram Pvt.	7 VAI	2/16/62–2/19/65
Samples, Tip? Pvt.	19 VAC CSA	9/7/62–5/26/63
Samples, Wm. Pvt.	7 WVC	9/26/64–6/19/65
Sams, Alfred Pvt.	14 PAI	7/19/63–9/5/65
Schoonover, Wm. H. Pvt.	7 WVC	11/6/62–8/1/65
Settle, James N. Pvt.	9 WVC	9/31/61–7/31/65
Sizemore, Amos Pvt.	1 VAA	9/26/64–7/21/65
Skinner, B.D. Pvt.	5 WVI	7/62–6/28/65
Smith, John Pvt.	4 WVI	7/61–7/65
Summers, David C. Pvt.	7 WVC	8/4/64–NF
Tanner, John A. Pvt.	NF	
Thompson, George W. Pvt.	20 VAC CSA	3/20/63–10/1/64
Walker, Anderson Pvt.	7 WVC	12/4/62–1865
West, Thomas Pvt.	9 WVI	NF
Westfall, Thomas Pvt.	11 VAI	2/11/62–2/10/64
also	10 WVI	2/11/64–8/9/65
Wheeler, E.B. Pvt.	10 WVI	6/1/62–6/26/65
Young, David K. Pvt.	13 WVI	12/20/62–6/22/65
Young, Samuel E. Pvt.	11 WVI	10/64–6/65

Clay County Remarks

Ankrum, W.R.*—wounded
Bailes, J.N.—injury to eyesight from measles
Blind, J.—RH
Burdette, W.A.— wounded
Carpenter, S.— hip dislocated
Davis, S.C.— HD
Elerite, H.— RH 25 years
Frame, M. — RH
Goff, G.— gunshot right jaw & right shoulder, piles, neuralgi
Goldsmith, G.— hurt by a horse
Griffith, C.P.— shot in the head
Hughes, G.W.— partial loss of eyesight caused by particle of cap penetrating the eye
Jeffrey, S.— wounded
Lamby, W.H.—gen debility
Laxton, T.B.—LD
Lewis, H. — piles & injury to feet
McCune, W.H.—wounded in shoulder
Miller, W. —RH
Moore, J. —RH
Moore, W.H.—CDR
Morton, J.T.— injury to eyesight
Morton, P.T.— wounded in shoulder
Nichols, D.—bleeding piles 25 years
Obrine, E. —HD & dropsy
Owens, T.H.—failure of eyesight
Parsons, G.W.—dislocated ankle, broken down
Payne, J.M.—CDR
Procious, A.—RH
Ramsey, A. —piles & partial loss right arm
Reed, L.—piles
Reed, S.—catarh of head
Rollyson, C.M.—LD
Samples, A.M.—drafted
Samples, H.—KD
Sams, A.—piles
Schoonover, W.H.—RH
Skinrer, B.D.—RH
Tanner, J.A.—HD
Westfall, T.—malarial Poisoning, LD, piles, brights disease

Doddridge County

NAME/RANK	REGIMENT	WHEN SERVED
Alile, Oliver Pvt.	4WVC	8/28/63–3/8/64
Allen, Francis M. Pvt.	13WVC	3/24/65–6/30/65
Allen, Israel Pvt.	6WVI	10/29/61–6/10/65
Allen, William O.	U.L.L.? (NAVY)	2/27/65–9/1/65
American, Marcus Pvt.	6WVI	NF
Amos, Benjamen S. Pvt.	10WVI	4/2/62–5/6/65
Anrett, Absolum Pvt.	14WVI	62/65
Ash, Jacob Pvt.	6WVI	8/15/62–6/12/65
Ash, Peter A. Pvt.	WV	64/64
Ash, Silas Sgt.	6WVC	6/13/61–5/19/65
Ashburn, Amaziah Pvt.	14WVI	61/64
Ashcraft, Preston Pvt.	19VAC CSA	9/15/64–4/3/65
Backus, James Pvt.	12WVI	8/15/62–6/12/65
Backus, Lewis Pvt.	6WVI	NF
Baker, Jonathan Pvt.	6WVI	10/24/61–12/1/64
Bane, Zephaniah Pvt.	WVC	61/63
Barker, William Pvt.	14WVI	8/14/62–6/24/65
Barnes, Richard L. Pvt.	7WVI	3/27/65–7/1/65
Bates, Squire Pvt.	WV	12/1/62–4/28/64
Bee, Ephram W.	4WVC	63/64
also	6WVI	NF
Beuberiage, John Pvt.	NF	
Beverlin, John W. Sgt.	WV	12/18/62–6/15/65
Beverlin, Joshual Sgt.	1WVC	8/24/61–8/24/65
Birch, Thomas Pvt.	1 PAC	7/61–NF
Black, John S. Pvt.	6WVI	8/61–8/64
Bland, Richard Pvt.	17WVI	2/11/65–6/29/65
Bland, Simon Pvt.	17WVI	2/11/65–6/29/65
Bond, Camden Pvt.	6WVI	9/4/64–6/10/65
Bonnell, Jonathan Pvt.	WV	63/64
Booker, Henry D. Pvt.	5WVC	NF
Bowen, Thomas H. Pvt.	14 PAC	3/30/64–8/2/65
Boya, Thomas Pvt.	3WVC	8/22/62–6/13/65
Boyce, William F. Pvt.	9WVI	9/15/61–7/13/65
Britton, Joseph S. Pvt.	14WVI	8/5/62–6/27/65
Brooks ?, David Pvt.	CSA	NF
Brown, Samuel V. Cpl.	6WVI	8/15/62–6/15/65
Bunnell, Charles Pvt.	6WVI	10/64–6/10/65
Caine, Silas Pvt.	14WVI	8/15/62–6/2/65
Canoll, John Capt.	6WVI	NF
Carder, John Pvt.	NF	
Cartlaw, Joseph Pvt.	6WVA	8/14/62–7/25/65
Casdor, Ruphus A. Pvt.	6WVC	3/64–6/22/66

Caton, John A. Pvt.	3 WVI	6/18/61–1/3/63
Cayler ?, George Sgt.	3 WVC	3/20/65–6/65
Celia ?, George W. Pvt.	14 WVI	7/28/62–6/27/65
Chapman, George W. Sgt.	39 OHI	7/17/61–10/64
Charter, Andrew 2lt.	14 WVI	3/15/65–6/27/65
Childers, Amos D. Pvt.	14 WVI	2/28/65–6/1/65
Childers, Jerome Pvt.	4 WVI	8/4/62–6/24/65
Childres, Cyrus S. Pvt.	14 WVI	3/6/65–7/3/65
Chipps, Samuel S. Pvt.	6 WVI	NF
Clemons, Furgeson Pvt.	6 WVI	8/64–6/65
Clovis, Sevi Pvt.	14 WVI	8/9/62–5/24/65
Cowman, John S. Pvt.	15 WVC	7/12/63–6/14/65
Cozad, Harrison J. Pvt.	6 WVI	6/61–9/64
Cuff, Samuel J.	5 VAI CSA	NF
Cumberledge, George Pvt.	6 WVI	8/28/64–6/10/65
Cunningham, John A. Pvt.	18 VAI CSA	NF
Cunningham, John W. Pvt.	77 OHI	10/7/62–8/1/63
Czigan, Isaac Pvt.	4 WVI	8/1/63–5/8/64
Czigan, Milton C. Pvt.	10 WVI	2/21/62–5/2/65
Daak, Charles Pvt.	6 WVA	8/15/62–7/25/65
Dake, Clinton Pvt.	14 WVI	7/14/62–7/2/65
Darnold, Cass M. Pvt.	6 WVI	9/8/64–6/13/65
Davis, Abner J. Pvt.	17 WVI	2/11/65–6/29/65
Davis, Christopher Pvt.	4 WVC	9/12/61–12/1/65
Davis, Ezra F. Pvt.	4 WVC	5/63–7/23/65
Davis, Granville H. Cpl.	3 WVC	7/28/62–7/3/65
Davis, Henry T. Pvt.	10 WVI	5/62 NF
Davis, Mark C.	CSA NF	
Davis, Nathan N. Pvt.	14 WVI	65/65
Davis, William E. Sgt.	6 WVI	10/2/61–1/2/64
Davis, William H. Pvt.	3 WVC	9/14/62–6/30/65
Davis, William H. Pvt	17 VAC CSA	8/20/62–1864
Davison, Franklin M. Pvt.	3 WVI	6/20/61–2/20/65
Davison, Theodore Pvt.	6 WVI	9/64–6/65
Davisson, Edgar Pvt.	10 WVI	61/65
Denison, Jonas Pvt.	14 WVI	8/14/62–6/27/65
Denison, Salatha L.	NAVY	NF
Dennison, Lewis M. Pvt.	14 WVI	8/14/62–6/27/65
Dilla ?, J. M. Pvt	16 PAC	8/62–6/20/65
Divers, Andrew J. Pvt.	3 WVC	3/24/65–6/30/65
Dorson, John N. Pvt.	10 WVI	2/25/64–8/9/65
Dotson, A. E. Pvt	6 WVI	4/18/61–6/65
Dotson, F. J. Pvt.	4 WVC	63/64
Dotson, Francis M. Pvt.	6 WVI	NF
Dotson, Israel Pvt.	4 WVC	6/63–3/64
Dotson, John C. Pvt.	6 WVI	12/61–6/65
Dotson, Spencer R. Pvt.	4 WVC	NF

aka John S. Dotson

Duckworth, Francis M. Pvt.	6 WVI	64/65
Duckworth, Wilington Pvt.	1 WVA	7/15/61–9/64
Duncan, Alva W. Pvt	6 WVI	1/64–8/12/64
Dye, John Pvt.	6 WVI	11/1/61–6/1/65
Edwards, James P. Pvt.	15 WVI	12/29/63–8/29/65
Elliott, William Pvt.	6 WVI	NF
Enlow, Henry Cpl.	141 OHI	5/2/64–9/3/64
Evans, Nimrod Pvt.	3 WVC	9/15/62–6/30/65
Fatt, Seber H. Pvt.	4 WVC	8/25/63–3/5/64
Fisher, Asa S. Pvt.	15 WVI	8/15/62–6/14/65
Fleming, Lewis S. Pvt.	6 WVI	61 NF
Flenny, Tom J. Pvt.	14 WVI	8/13/62–6/27/65
Ford, Richard Pvt.	4 WVC	9/64–4/65
Frances, William Pvt.	6 WVI	2/64–6/13/65
Frasher, Kinchelo Pvt.	11 WVI	3/15/65–7/1/65
abbert, William B. Pvt.	17 WVI	NF
Gabert, Robert S. Cpl.	3 WVC	5/20/61–6/14/64
Gain, Peter Pvt.	12 WVI	8/20/62–5/14/64
Gains, James E. Pvt.	6 WVI	10/18/64–7/18/65
Gains, George H. Pvt.	4 WVI	64/65
Gallian, James Pvt.	6 WVI	9/24/61–12/1/64
Ganison, Aaron Pvt.	4 WVC	62/65
Garner, Simon H. Pvt.	7 WVI	3/31/64–7/9/65
Gatrell ?, John W. Pvt.	25 VAI CSA	6/16/61–1865
Gatrell, Ducket W. Pvt.	6 WVI	63/65
Gatril, Absalam Pvt.	6 WVI	61/65
Glover, Vincent A. Cpl.	7 WVI	12/11/62–7/1/65
Golden, Rush W. Cpl.	10 VAC CSA	61/65
Grass, Elisha Pvt.	1 VAI CSA	NF
Grash, Andrew J. Pvt.	4 USI	11/20/63–11/27/65
Gratchouso, Albert M. Pvt.	6 WVI	9/2/62–9/10/64
Gray, David W. Pvt.	6 WVI	9/24/61–12/1/64
Gray, James W. Pvt.	6 WVI	9/21/61–12/1/64
Gray, John Jr. Pvt.	6 WVI	7/1/62–6/10/65
Gribble, John M. Sgt.	6 WVI	11/24/61–12/15/64
Gulley, Joseph N. Sgt.	20 VAC CSA	2/17/62–1865
Gum, Michael C. Cpl.	6 PAC	3/62–7/63
Gump, Benona Pvt.	17 WVI	8/30/64–6/30/65
Haddox, William Pvt.	17 WVI	9/30/64–6/30/65
Halthrop, Andrew J.	31 VAI CSA	9/61–5/65
Hardesty, Sam Pvt.	14 WVI	NF
Hart, Andy Pvt.	6 WVI	64/65
Hart, Josiah Pvt.	6 WVI	NF
Hart, Paten Pvt.	NF	
Harvey, John R. Pvt.	6 WVC	6/18/61–6/30/65
Harvey, Marcene Pvt.	6 WVI	8/15/64–7/12/65

Haught, David W. Pvt.	6 WVI	2/15/65–6/10/65
Haught, Marville S. Cpl.	6 WVI	8/29/64–6/65
Hayes, Henry Pvt.	NF	
Heflin, John S. Pvt.	6 WVI	9/3/64–6/15/65
Helmick, Jacob Pvt.	6 WVI	9/12/64–6/9/65
Henderson, John F. Pvt.	6 WVI	62/65
Henderson, Leroy Pvt.	4 WVC	7/7/63–6/65
Hess, Henry Pvt.	6 WVI	11/15/61–6/11/65
Hiley, H. Pvt.	4 WVC	7/28/63–1864
Hincle, Abraham Pvt.	3 WVC	9/15/62–6/13/65
Hinrey, David W. Pvt.	14 WVI	7/28/62–11/10/65
Holand, Patrick Pvt.	36 OHI	2/6/65–7/27/65
Holiday, Thomas E. Pvt.	14 WVI	7/28/62–7/27/65
Holmes, Alfred C. Sgt.	10 WVI	NF
Holt, William E. Sgt.	10 WVI	12/1/61–8/9/65
Hufford, Solomon Pvt.	NF	
Hugill, William M. Pvt.	NF	
Husk, Isaac Pvt.	4 WVI	8/28/63–3/8/64
Hutson, Acter F. Pvt.	4 VAC	8/25/63–3/6/64
Hyatt, William H. Pvt.	6 WVI	61/65
Hyde, Amos Pvt.	3 WVC	9/15/62–6/20/65
Hyleman, Absolem Pvt.	14 WVI	61/65
Ice, Isaac Pvt.	6 WVI	12/3/61–1/3/65
Jones, Lewis E. Sgt.	36 OHI	62/65
Jones, Montetiller Pvt.	12 WVI	62/65
King, John Pvt.	46 OHI	9/24/61–6/15/65
Kinney, John E. Pvt.	6 WVI	12/4/61–12/28/64
Kinney, Russel J. Pvt.	6 WVI	NF
Kinney, Snoden S. Pvt.	14 WVI	62/65
Kinney, William Pvt.	6 WVI	NF
Kinney, William A. Cpl.	6 WVI	9/1/64–6/10/65
Knight, Hampton S. Pvt.	14 WVI	7/28/62–6/7/65
Knight, Michael Pvt.	14 WVI	8/62–6/7/65
Knight, William B. B. Pvt.	14 WVI	3/7/65–6/7/65
Laurence, William A. Pvt.	15 WVI	8/22/62–6/22/64
Lawlis, Orlando B. Sgt.	3 WVC	9/3/62–6/6/65
Lucker, James R. Pvt.	28 ILI	61/68
Lurty, Robert D. Pvt.	CSA (20 VAC)	NF
Lyons, George W. Pvt.	6 WVI	8/15/62–6/10/65
Lyons, Richard Pvt.	3 WVC	3/24/65–8/2/65
Lyons, William A. Pvt.	6 WVI	8/31/64–6/10/65
Mailey, James Pvt.	3 WVI	5/61–7/63
Makson, Cornelius Pvt.	14 WVI	7/28/62–6/29/65
Mare, Henery Pvt.	17 WVI	2/11/65–6/13/65
Mare, Malery Pvt.	6 WVI	61/65
Maryman, Vincent C. Cpl.	21 VAI CSA	6/2/61–4/9/65
Matheny, John Pvt.	3 WVI	6/10/61–8/15/62

McClane, Preston B. Pvt.	6 WVI	NF
McCoy, John Pvt.	3 WVC	1/13/64–6/13/65
McCune, George W. Pvt.	NF	
McGill, George W. Cpl.	17 WVI	8/26/64–6/30/65
McGill, John Pvt.	OHIO	NF
McIntire, Charles T. Pvt.	14 WVI	8/22/62–6/27/65
McKeen, Samuel Pvt.	195 OHI	3/4/65–12/23/65
McMillan, John P. ? Pvt.	CSA	NF
McTe ?, Robert L. Pvt.	17 WVI	2/11/65–7/7/65
Meek, Henry T. Pvt.	—	9/24/64–12/7/64
Mitter, Willis E. Pvt.	12 WVI	9/14/62–6/27/65
Moffatt, Joseph Pvt.	6 WVI	9/1/61–12/1/64
Moon, Tabeus Pvt.	1 WVA	8/15/62–5/21/65
Morgan, Edmond Pvt.	3 WVC	10/8/61–7/21/65
Morgan, William Cpl.	WV	12/1/62–6/10/65
Morris, Daniel S. Pvt.	WVC?	3/21/65–6/12/65
Myers, Jacob Pvt.	10 WVI	2/23/62–5/29/65
Nare ?, Felix Pvt.	10 WVI	61/65
Nicholson, Ambious Pvt.	14 WVI	8/14/62–6/3/65
Nicholson, Bergman Pvt.	14 WVI	8/14/62–6/27/65
Nicholson, Colombus N. Pvt.	4 WVI	7/31/63–3/8/64
Nicholson, David H. Pvt.	14 WVI	8/15/62–7/3/65
Nicholson, James Pvt.	7 WVI	9/4/61–7/65
Nicholson, Nuten Pvt.	7 VAI	61/64
Nicholson, William Pvt.	14 WVI	8/15/62–7/3/65
Noble, Franklin Pvt.	4 WVC	7/28/63–3/8/64
Noble, Richard Cpl.	4 WVC	7/31/63–3/11/64
Norman, Thornton M. Pvt.	6 WVI	12/31/61–12/65
Nutter, Andrew J. Pvt.	6 WVI	9/2/61–6/10/64
Nutter, John Pvt.	6 WVI	61/65
Nutter, John N. Pvt.	5 WVC	3/28/64–6/8/65
Overfield, William J. Pvt.	6 WVI	9/2/61–6/10/64
Painell, Henery Pvt.	6 WVI	9/24/61–12/64
Pinell, Fielding Pvt.	4 WVC	NF
Pinnell, James Pvt.	14 WVI	NF
Planger, Phillip Pvt.	8 OHI	6/30/64–1865
Pool, Elias Pvt.	6 WVC	8/64–7/65
Powell, Benjamin C. Pvt.	6 WVI	63/65
Powell, Rubin Pvt.	7 WVI	12/25/62–5/64
Powell, Thomas Pvt.	1 WVC	9/64–7/65
Pratt, Thomas J. Pvt.	6 WVI	8/28/64–7/10/65
Pratt, William W. Pvt.	14 WVI	8/1/62–6/23/65
Prunty, George Pvt.	WV	12/1/62–6/10/65
Prunty, Nicholas Pvt.	1 WVA	8/12/61–7/25/65
Ramsey, William H. Sgt.	10 WVI	2/62–5/8/65
Randall, Melnas Pvt.	12 VAI	8/26/62–6/28/65
Reed, John W. Pvt.	10 WVI	8/16/62–7/3/65

Name	Unit	Dates
Revels ?, George Pvt.	16 OHI	NF
Richards, Jesse Pvt.	14 WVI	7/28/62–7/4/65
Richards, Lemuel Pvt.	14 WVI	7/20/62–7/3/65
Richards, Robert Pvt.	3 WVC	9/14/62–6/30/65
Richards, Samuel Pvt.	14 WVI	7/28/62–6/7/65
Riggs, William M. Pvt.	3 WVI	7/5/61–2/28/65
Robberts, David Pvt.	4 WVC	7/17/63–6/10/65
Robberts, Jeremiah	US	NF
Robinette, Thomas J. Pvt.	2 WVC	9/8/61–11/28/64
Robinson, Charles Pvt.	6 WVI	8/15/62–6/10/65
Robinson, Robert Pvt.	7 WVI	4/9/65–NF
Rollin, Wesley Pvt.	8 WVI	7/61–5/66
Rollins, Hinman Pvt.	3 WVI	NF
Rose, Ludem Pvt.	4 WVC	8/29/63–5/29/66
Rosier, William Pvt.	3 WVC	3/30/65–6/65
Ross, William Pvt.	6 WVI	64/65
Ruby ?, F. J. Pvt.	14 WVI	62/65
Ruby ?, Granville Pvt.	6 WVC	7/19/64–5/22/66
Ruigen, William H. Pvt.	6 WVI	NF
Russell, Samuel Sgt.	14 WVI	8/18/62–6/18/65
Sayre, Lemeon S. Pvt.	1 WVA	8/62–6/65
Scott, Benjamin	5 OHI	9/3/64–6/5/65
Scott, Henry Pvt.	6 WVI	9/12/64–6/10/65
Scott, Jacintha Pvt	14 WVI	8/1/62–6/20/65
Seeders, John T. Pvt.	14 WVI	NF
Sesson, Jesse Pvt.	15 WVI	11/62–6/5/65
Sheline, Michael Pvt.	4 WVI	6/13/61–4/15/62
Sherwood, Benjamine F. Sgt.	11 WVI	12/1/61–1865
Sherwood, John Pvt.	—	12/8/62–4/23/64
Shock, Perry Sgt.	3 WVC	12/25/62–6/30/65
Smith, Elias E. Pvt.	6 WVI	9/7/64–6/10/65
Smith, Frank Pvt.	6 WVI	8/29/64–6/10/65
Smith, Harey Pvt.	NF	
Smith, Harvey Pvt.	14 WVI	8/6/62–7/23/65
Smith, Jerome B. Cpl.	3 MDI	61/65
Smith, Job B. Pvt.	77 OHI	NF
Smith, John Sgt.	6 WVI	11/24/61–12/1/64
Smith, John A. Pvt.	6 WVI	NF
Smith, Moses W. Pvt.	15 WVI	9/15/62–7/3/65
Smith, Sylvester Pvt.	4 WVC	10/1/61–6/10/65
also	6 WVI	NF
Smith, Thomas J. Pvt.	14 WVI	NF
Snider, Arnold C. Pvt.	14 WVI	8/14/62–6/27/65
Snider, Isaac Pvt.	4 WVC	8/28/63–3/8/64
Snider, James E. Pvt.	14 WVI	3/6/65–6/27/65
Snider, John Pvt.	14 WVI	3/4/65–6/27/65
Snider, W? Pvt.	14 WVI	3/4/65–6/27/65

Snodgrass, Jesse F. Lt.	WV	12/1/62–6/10/65
Southworth, Benjamin C. Pvt.	3 WVI	6/4/61–1866
Southworth, George W. Pvt.	6 WVI	NF
Sowner, John Pvt.	4 WVC	8/1/63–3/8/64
Spencer, Amos T. Pvt.	4 WVC	7/17/63–3/18/64
Spencer, Moses W. Pvt.	4 WVC	7/17/63–3/18/64
Spurgeon, Jabez Pvt.	6 WVI	11/16/61–12/1/64
Squires, Isreal Blacksmith	6 WVC	6/24/63–5/22/66
Starkey, Jesse W. Pvt.	3 WVC	3/13/65–7/13/65
Starkey, Levi W. Sgt.	7 WVI	3/14/64–7/9/65
Starkey, Thomas M. Pvt.	7 WVI	3/65–7/65
Stewart, Charles	MARINE	NF
Stickle, John W. Pvt.	6 WVI	9/26/64–6/10/65
Stout, Joseph Pvt.	14 WVI	2/64–6/65
Stout, William S. Pvt.	14 WVI	3/65–6/65
Stutler, Arthur Drummer	7 WVI	12/62–4/65
Sullivan, George W. Pvt.	14 WVI	3/64–6/65
Summers, Elijah W. Pvt.	6 WVI	8/18/61–9/10/64
Sutton, Thadeus S. Cpl.	11 WVI	6/17/62–6/28/65
Swiger, Jefferson Pvt.	6 WVI	2/18/65–6/10/65
Swiger, William L.	6 WVI	10/18/64–6/10/65
Swiger, William H. Cpl.	WV	12/10/62–4/23/64
Traugh, Sirvius A. Pvt.	6 WVI	9/9/64–6/12/65
Vandevner, John H. Pvt.	1 WVI	7/61–7/65
Vanort, John Pvt.	4 WVC	6/28/63–5/9/64
Vanscay, Able Pvt.	3 WVI	6/25/61–11/26/63
Vanscay, Jesse Pvt.	5 WVI	6/25/61–8/15/64
Vanscoy, Daniel Pvt.	3 WVC	9/15/62–6/6/65
Vincent, Sanford Pvt.	7 WVI	3/20/65–7/1/65
Waldow, Francis M. Pvt.	6 WVI	2/65–6/65
Waldow, Hickman Pvt.	6 WVI	62/65
Waller, Charles L. Pvt.	14 WVI	3/10/65–6/27/65
West, Charles A. Pvt.	17 VAC CSA	8/14/62–4/6/65
White, Jadoc C. Pvt.	6 WVI	10/19/61–6/6/54
Wich, Benjamin Pvt.	14 WVI	8/62–NF
Wilctt, Nicholas J. Pvt.	6 WVI	NF
William, Hesekiah B. Pvt.	17 WVI	2/28/65–8/1/65
Williams, Israel Fifer	14 WVI	8/14/62–7/3/65
Williams, Mark Pvt.	6 WVI	9/3/64–6/10/65
Williams, Peter Pvt.	2 WVC	9/11/61–6/13/65
Williamson, George C. Pvt.	116 OHI	8/22/62–6/16/65
Wilson, James P. Pvt.	10 WVI	NF
Windon, James N. Pvt.	36 OHI	2/65–5/13/65
Wuck, Christopher C. Pvt.	10 WVI	3/62–8/65
Yerkey, Silas L. Musician	10 WVI	3/22/62–5/5/65
Yorke, Isaac Pvt.	10 WVI	1/61–8/14/65
Zinn, James J.	12 WVI	8/19/62–6/16/65

Doddridge Co. Remarks

Alile, O.—HD
America, M.—disease of head & chest
Arnett, A.—RH since 1864
Ash, J.—LD & RH
Ash, S.—disease heart & eyes
Ashburn, A.—MP
Ashcraft, P.★—gunshot wound
Backus, J.—gunshot lungs affected
Backus, L.E.—LD
Barker, W.—LD
Bee, E.—LD
Beuberidge, J.—HD
Birch, T.—HD
Bland, R.C.—chronic catarrah results of MS
Bland, S.—piles & disease of rectum results of MS
Bond, C.— CDR & RH hypertrophy left testicle
Boyce, T.J.—sprained back POW from 6/7/63 to 8/22/63
Britton, J.S.—spinal disability catarrh head
Brown, S.V.—lumbago & eye disease
Bunnell, C.—palpitalia heart & piles
Caine, S.—general disability
Carder, J.—RH
Carroll, J.—leg broke & breast mashed
Carter, G.L.—HD caused by SS
Cartlow, J.—CDR & piles
Chapman, G.W.—CDR & piles
Charter, A.—deff in right ear
Childers, A.—RH
Childres, C.—eye disease & partial deafness
Clovis, L.—sciatica
Cowman, J.—WIA leg & arm
Cozad, H.—shot in leg
Cumberledge, G.—paralysis
Czigan, I. —MP
Czigan, M.—MS & heart & kidney trouble
Dake, C.—eyes heart & lungs affected
Dakins, M.★ —HD & RH
Darnold, C.M.—disabled shoulders back head & chest
Davis, A.J. —fractured left ankle
Davis, C.—HD
Davis, G.H. —total deafness right ear injury left ear
Davis, H.T. —cold on MS
Davis, W.E. —LD

Davis, W.H.H.— eye disease LD & KD spinal effection
Davison, T. —paralacy
Denison, J.J.—insanity by fever & exposure supported by county & private individuals
Denison, S. —RH
Dennison, L.—wounded in neck defected badley
Dilla, J.—frost bite
Doak, C.—eyes & back injured
Dotson, F.M.—RH & eye disease
Dotson, J.—RH
Duncan, A.—LD
Dye, J.—disease of the eyes
Elliott, W. —spinal disease since 1865
Enlow, H.— CDR & piles
Evans, N.— HD
Fisher, A.S.—RH & MP
Fleming, L.S.— catarrah of throat & KD
Fleming, T.J.— deafness & piles since 1865
Frasher, K. —jandess & TYF
Gabbert, W. —cold on fever
Gains, J.E. —crippled hand
Gallen, J.—disease of right testicle result of mumps
Garner, S.—gunshot wound
Garrison, A.—RH
Gatril, A.—piles & LD
Gatsell, D.W.— RH
Gratehouse, A.—HD
Gray, D.W.—ruptured
Gray, J.W.—MS & weak eyes
Gray, Jn. Jr.— CDR & weak back
Gribble, J.M.— injury back & right ankle RH & dysentary
Gulley, J.* —RH
Haught, D.M.—LD
Helmick, J. —loss of hearing & eyes affected
Hess, H.—back hurt from fall
Hiley, H.— LD & HD took jandice in service
Hinde, A.— scurvy
Holiday, T.E.— loss of right testicle mumps
Holt, W.—HD & liver & stomach trouble
Hugill, W.—hurt a leg
Hutson, P.—MP left testicle
Hyatt, W.— LD & piles since 1862
Hyde, A.—complications of disease
Jones, L.— LD & hard of hearing
King, J.—rupture since 1865
Kinney, D.W.—RH
Kinney, J.—CDR

Kinsey, S.—wounded in hip 1864
Knight, H.S.—CDR & RH & catarrh head
Knight, M.—RH & HD
Knight, W.B.—CDR
Lane, Z.—CDR
Laurence, W. A.— gunshot & SS
Lawlis, O.—HD
Mailey, J.—gunshot in shoulder
Mare, H.—CDR
Mare, M.—CDR & ruptured
Marryman, V.C.*— shot in foot & ankle
Marson, C.—shot in left hip & left arm
Matheny, Jn.—shot in hand
McGill, G.W.—general disabilities from exposure
McGill, Jn. —left arm dislocated
McIntire, C.—RH & HD
McJe, R.—RH
Meek, H.F.—piles
Mitter, W.—throat & LD
Moffatt, J. —LD
Morgan, E.—catarrh head & CDR
Myers, J.— loss of right arm near Opaquen 9/19/64
Nicholson, A.B.— eyes affected
Nicholson, B.— MP
Nicholson, C.— leg fractured
Nicholson, N.— shot in left shoulder
Noble, F.— LD & eye disease
Noble, R.— eye disease
Norman, T.M.—piles
Nutter, A.J.—thrown from horse side injured
Nutter, J.—LD
Overfield, W.J.— affection of throat & lungs
Pinnell, J. —RH
Pool, E.—RH
Powell, B.C.—CDR & LD
Powell, R.—qunshot wound
Powell, T.—partly lost sight
Pratt, T.J. —lumbago & KD
Pratt, W.W.—RH
Prunty, N.—deafness
Ramsey, W.H.—MS
Randall, M. —shot in hand
Reed, J.W.—WIA both legs
Richards, R.—LD
Richards, S.—chronic gastro entritis
Riggs, W.M. —rectum RH catarrah head
Robinson, C.B.—RH

Robinson, R.—RH since 1864
Rose, L.—RH
Rosier, W.—gunshot wound
Ruly, F.J.—general break down
Russell, S. —LD
Sayre, S.— deafness caused by bursting shell over head at Gettysburg & other disabilities from chills & fever in 1864
Scott, B.— RH & LD
Scott H.—HD
Scott, I.— LD
Sesson, J.—wounded in right arm suffering RH
Shelene, M. —HD & LD
Sherwood, B.—CDR
Smith, H.— eye disease & POW Andersonville 7 months
Smith, J.B. —deafness
Smith, Jn.—eyes effected & KD
Smith, M.W. —back injured in 1862
Snider, A.C.—gunshot wound & CDR 3/4 disabled
Snider, I.—piles & KD
Snider, J.E.—RH by cold & exposure
Southworth, B.—chronic opthalma
Spencer, A. —sephna & throat trouble
Spencer, M.W.— RH
Spurgeon, J.—sore eyes
Squires, I.B.— LD & KD
Starkey, J.W.— MS affected eyes hearing lungs & kidney
Starkey, L. —gunshot wound
Stout, J.— crippled in left foot
Stout, W.S. —LD & throat trouble
Summers, E. —RH
Sutton, T.S.—LD & KD
Swiger, W.L.—dislocated ankle
Towner, J.—RH & nervousness took cold near New Creek
Traugh, S.A.—complications
Vandevner, J.— shot in hand
Vanort, J.—speach injured & KD & LD results of MS
Vanscay, A. —gunshot right leg
Vanscay, J. —gunshot & piles
Vanscoy, D. —disabled from fall
Waller, C.L.—new rolgen of head rhematis a total rock
Wendon, J.—smallpox & MP
West. W.A.*—HD
Wich, B.—MP
Wilcox, N.—ruptured
Williams, I.—HD
Williams, M.—hernia
Williams, P.—RH & HD

Williamson, G.—contracted HD on Belle Island
Wuck, C.—gunshot wound received at Kernstown Va
Yerkey, S.—ruptured
Youke, I.—shot in leg
Zinn, J. J.—shot in right shoulder

Fayette County

NAME/RANK	REGIMENT	WHEN SERVED
Ailor, Andrew J.	NF	
Allur, George W. Pvt.	31 MII	7/61–6/65
Anderson, William P.	PAI	NF
Armstrong, John Pvt.	9 MII	61/65
Arnold, James Pvt.	7 VAI	NF
Arthur, Henry W. Pvt.	7 (WVC)	10/12/64–8/1/65
Ashby, Thomas W. Pvt.	1 DEI	12/64–12/65
aka John Vanburen		
Ashley, John R. Musician	13 VAI	6/63–6/65
Baker, Absolom Pvt.	140 OHI	5/1/64–10/15/64
Bennett, Jessie Pvt.	RAMSEY'S SCOUTS	11/30/62–11/30/63
Beury, Joseph S. Cpt.	153 PAI	6/62–9/63
Bigford, Henry Pvt.	NF	
Blizzard, John H. Pvt.	7 VAI	10/4/61–6/4/65
Blume, Charles W.	1 OH?	3/1/64–7/6/65
Borton, Andy Pvt.	—	61/64–NF
Bowen, Daniel C.	NF (7 WVC)	2/29/64–5/23/65
Bowers, George M.	NF	
Bowyer, Ben R. Pvt.	11 VAI	6/15/61–8/25/65
Bowyer, Van B. Pvt.	23 OHI	8/2/65
Bradley, Silas B. Pvt.	2 WVC	4/3/63–6/30/65
Brazie, H. W. Pvt.	17 INI	6/17/61–4/10/63
also Adjutant	9 WVI	8/13/63–6/7/66
Brown, William N. Sgt.	129 PAI	8/15/62–5/25/63
Canty, John	NF	
Carlen, James Cpl.	13 WVI	9/7/62–6/21/65
Cart, James R. Pvt.	RAMSEY'S SCOUTS	3/64–12/64
Cassidy, James S.	NF (CAPT. WVI)	

Chandler, Lucious J. Pvt.	88 OHI	5/26/62–9/26/62
Cobb, Hilbever Pvt.	9 WVI	9/18/62–6/28/65
Collins, John L. Pvt.	7 WVC	3/1/62–8/11/65
Crist, Jacob K Pvt.	33 OVI	8/17/61–7/65
Crookshanks, Harvey Pvt.	—	63/64–NF
Day, Thomas A. Pvt.	22 KYI	10/21/61–1/30/65
Doolittle, George S. Pvt.	4 VAC	62/65–NF
Egbert, George T. Col.?	106 & 183 PAI	6/9/61–7/13/65
Ellis, John H. Pvt.	CSA	61/65–NF
Ellison, Felix A. Pvt.	NF	
Fitzwaters, Isiah Pvt.	155 OHI	5/2/64–8/27/64
Ford, Edward Pvt.	96 PAI	11/3/61–9/15/65
Forsythe, James Lt.	WV SCOUTS	2/1/64–5/30/65
Gilpin, George W. Pvt.	1 WVC	11/12/61–FALL 64
Gosmay, Thomas Sgt.	5 VAI	11/15/61–6/14/65
Gosnay, Joe V.	NF (174 OHI)	8/18/64–6/25/65
Gray, William Pvt.	13 WVI	8/15/62–9/2/65
Grimes, Joseph Pvt.	34 OHI	NF
Grose, Orvel B. Pvt.	RAMSEY'S SCOUTS	9/4/64–12/15/64
Hamaker, James P. Sgt.	50 VAI CSA	6/25/61–1/28/65
Hawes, Henry W.	NF (27 VAI CSA ?)	
Hawkins, William S. Pvt.	RAMSEY'S SCOUTS	1/1/64–1/1/65
Higgins, Joseph Pvt. *aka* Davis, Joseph	18 VAI	9/61–1/65
Hildreth, Horace N. Pvt.	16 MOA	1/64–7/10/65
Hinman, Edward G. Pvt.	1 OHI	9/17/61–6/13/65
Hiser, Charles W.	NF (11 OHC)	
Hodges, John W.	NF	
Hoffman, Lawrence Pvt.	187 OHI	2/65–2/65 NF
Holey, John	39 OHI	6 MO. –65
Holley, Herman D. Pvt.	NF	
House, Robert Pvt.	2 WVC	9/26/62–6/30/65
Hughes, Robert J. Pvt.	9 WVI	8/31/62–6/28/65
Hunt, Edwin R. Pvt.	2 WVC	8/15/61–6/30/65
Hunter, Willia Pvt.	8 WVI	NF
Jarrell, David Pvt.	8 WVI	9/61–65 NF
Johnson, Charles B. Cpl.	OHI	5/64–9/64 NF
Johnson, John Pvt.	NF	
Johnston, Nicholas	NF	
Jones, David Pvt.	NF	
Jones, John J. Pvt	103 PAI	3/65–7/65
Kincaid, Simon Pvt.	5 VAI	8/18/61–10/8/64
King, Lewis M. Pvt.	5 VAI	7/17/61–10/3/64
Knopp, John A. Pvt.	(10 VAC CSA ?)	63/64–NF
Koontz, Samuel B. Lt.	NF	
Legg, Benjamine T. Pvt.	RAMSEY'S SCOUTS	NF
Legg, Ephram P.	NF	

Light, Henry Pvt.	2? 8? VAC	9/62–7/65
Lissley, Lewis E.	NF	
Lively, Samuel Pvt.	7 WVI	64/65
Loomis, Samuel C. Pvt.	2 WVC	9/61–8/65
Loverly, John Pvt.	7 VAC	9/1/62–8/65
Lyons, Frank Pvt.	26 OHI	7/25/61–11/14/65
Masson, Franklin Pvt.	—	63/64–NF
McCallister, Allen Pvt.	2 WVC	9/8/61–12/4/64
McCann, Patrick Pvt.	26 VABI CSA	6/1/61–10/62
McClanahn, Thomas A. Pvt.	36 VAI CSA	62/63
Miller, Irvin E. Sgt.	10 PAI	4/61–8/4/64
Miller, James A. Pvt.	7 WVC	61/65
Miller, Wilson A. Pvt.	7 WVI	2/65–NF
Mills, Richard	CSA (8 VAC?)	64/65–NF
Mooney, Nathen Pvt.	NF	
Morten, Charles F. Pvt.	9 VAI	8/31/62–6/14/65
Muligan, Alexander Pvt.	NF	
Murphy, William F. Pvt.	NF (42 VAI CSA)	
Newton, George J.	NF	
Noble, Ed T.	NF	
Ogden, Ben	NF (49 VAI CSA?)	
Ogle, Andrew Pvt.	85 PAI	9/61–10/62
Olinger, Michael Pvt.	187 OHI	2/65–1/20/66
Owens, George H. Pvt.	4 WVI	9/11/62–6/23/65
Payne, George	(19 VAC CSA?)	61/63–NF
Perry, John R.	(26 BTN VAI CSA?)	NF
Perry, Lorenzo D. Pvt.	NF (36 VAI CSA)	
Peterson, Jackson Pvt.	4 OHI	9/17/61–6/22/65
Philips, Alfred Lt.	36 NYI	61/63
Pomeroy, John S. Sgt.	120 NYI	8/13/62–6/2/65
Pridemore, John Pvt.	54 KYI	9/3/64–9/1/65
Proctor, Nathan Pvt.	7 VAI	3/4/64–7/4/64
Propps, A. H. Pvt.	NF	2/1/64–1/1/65
Ramsey, Sam A. Pvt.	WV STATE GUARDS	3/12/64–1/1/65
Ridenour, John A. Pvt.	NF	
Rigg, Charles	8 VAC CSA	61/64–NF
Risinger, Charles A.	NF	
Rossiter, John Pvt.	NF	
Savage, Valentine Pvt.	CSA	61–NF
Sawyers, John Cpl.	CSA (27 VAI ?)	1861–NF
Scarbrough, John W. Pvt.	7 VAC	61/63
Scott, Albert Pvt.	2 WVC	9/25/61–4/9/63
Scott, Bennett Pvt.	4 OHC	61/64
Slavin, John Pvt.	18 & 173 OHI	4/61–7/65
Smith, Fred	NF	
Smith, Tom R. Pvt.	9 OHC	10/62–5/65
Stanley, Samuel K. Cpl.	26 VAI CSA	12/63–4/65

Stewart, Mathew Pvt.	10, 40, 53 KYI	9/1/63–9/15/65
Stover, Allen Pvt.	7 VAC	61/65
Stover, Massey Pvt.	7 VAC	61/65
Stover, Washington Pvt.	7 VAC	61/65
Strand, J.W. Pvt.	5 VAI	10/10/61–11/64
Sutton, John Pvt.	10 PAI	9/4/61–12/19/62
Thomas, Benjamin Pvt.	2 WVC	NF
Timberlake, Warren T. Sgt.	12 OHI	61/65
Tinsley, Thomas B. Pvt.	10 KYC	62/63
Touny, John G.	US	NF
True, George B. Pvt.	1 VAA	10/29/61–10/64
Utterback, Elias F. Pvt.	51 OHI	4/61–11/65
Vandall, Joseph D. Pvt.	60 VAI CSA	61/64
Watts, Alexander Pvt.	8 WVC	NF
Webb, Benjimine Pvt.	61 NYI	NF
Webb, John Pvt.	61 NYI	NF
Webb, John	NF (45 VAI CSA?)	
Webb, Theodore S. Lt.	24 (VAI CSA)	5/20/61–6/14/65
Wesler, William Pvt.	12 WVI	8/12/62–6/16/65
Whitaker, Edward Pvt.	2 KYC	62–NF
White, William H. Pvt.	23 OHI	11/13/63–7/10/65
Whitney, James Pvt.	NF	
Williams, Benjamine F. Pvt.	5 VAI	5/17/62–65
Williams, John Pvt.	2 VAC	63/65
Williams, Lewis Pvt.	7 WVC	12/30/62–8/5/65
Williams, Talmins Pvt.	2 USI	4/24/61–8/65
Williams, Wesley Pvt.	12 WVI	8/12/62–6/16/65
Wise, Andrew Pvt.	53 OHI	9/28/61–6/65
Wise, William I. Pvt. aka Isom Walters	7 WVC	2/3/64–9/65
Wiseman, Isaac W. Pvt.	RAMSEY'S SCOUTS	12/1/62–12/1/63
Wriston, Osten	US	NF
Wriston, William A. Pvt.	7 VAC	61/65
Wyant, William Pvt.	NF (26 BTN VAI CSA?)	

Fayette Co. Remarks

Allur, G.W. —WIA left leg, battle of Kernstown Va
Ashley, J.R.—dyspepsia
Baker, A.D. —eyesight injured
Beury, J.S. —after discharge was forge master 9th Corps
Bigford, H. —broken leg
Blizzard, J.H.—bealing in head
Blume, C.W. —piles
Bowyer, B.R.—WIA right shoulder & right leg
Bowyer, V.B.—HD & musket shot in the ankle

Brazie, H.W.—promoted to 1st Lieut. 9/20/63
Carlen, J.—shot through right knee, asthma
Chandler, L.J.—CDR
Cobb, H.—disease of eyes
Collins, J.L.—RH
Crist, J.K. —chills, fever, RH
Day, T.A.—rupture & catarrh of head
Egbert, G.T.—wounded in battle 5/64, served as Capt 57 PAI 3 mo.
Gray, W.—shot through the leg
Grimes, J.—leg crushed
Higgins, J. —RH & shot through knee
Hildreth, H.N.—hernia
Hinman, E.G.—wounded in leg
Holey, J.—wounded right knee, now totally disabled
House, R.—WIA left wrist, RH, piles, UFL
Jarrell, D. —rist sprained & collarbone broken
Johnson, C.B.—rib broke
Light, H.—KD
Lively, S.—WIA left leg & left arm
Loomis, S.C.—deafness
Lyons, F.—shot in left side of head
McCallister, A. —piles, RH, thrown from a horse
Miller, I.E.—shot in knee, now suffering lumbago
Miller, J.A.—neuralgia caused by exposure
Miller, W.A.—RH & asthma
Murphy, W.F.*—wounded in leg
Ogle, A.—HD & VV
Pomeroy, J.S.—WIA 5/3/63 served 4 months in 20 NY Militia
Propps, A.H.—piles & spleen affected
Savage, V.—gunshot left foot, piles
Sawyers, J.*—WIA & right arm amputated
Scott, A.—wounded in back by hullet
Scott, B.—thrown from horse bruising left testicle & kidney
Smith, F.—consumption
Stewart, M. —ague
Strand, J.W.—piles
Sutton, J.—shot in right leg
True, G.B.—disabled back
Watts, A.—disabled by measles
Webb, J.—wounded in leg
Webb, T.S.* —WIA left shoulder & neck
White, W.H. —CDR
Williams, J.—HD
Williams, T.—transferred from army to navy
Wise, W.I.—CDR & finger shot off

Gilmer County

NAME/RANK	REGIMENT	WHEN SERVED
Alexander, James C. Cpl.	10 WVI	3/1/62–8/9/65
Alkire, David M. Pvt.	25 VAI CSA	NF
Allen, George W. Pvt.	60 VAI CSA	6/22/61–6/65
Alltopp, Evan Sgt.	19 VAC CSA	62/65
Ayers, A. B. Pvt.	11 WVI	61/64
Bailey, Albert W. Cpl.	15 WVI	7/10/62–4/10/65
Balton, Saul ? Pvt.	NF	
Barnhouse, Sam E. Pvt.	10 WVI	3/2/62–8/25/65
Barnhouse, W. O. Pvt.	10 VAI	NF
Batton, Benjamin F. Pvt.	10 WVI	1/62–8/19/65
Beall, Alfred Pvt.	10 WVI	6/22/62–6/26/65
Beall, D. P. Pvt.	US NF	
Beall, Isaac Pvt.	US NF	
Bennett, Samuel Sgt.	15 WVI	8/15/62–7/4/65
Beslley, John Pvt.	10 VAI	4/2/62–5/15/65
Biglar, George W. Pvt.	NF	
Bircher, Nathaniel Pvt.	7 WVI	NF
Black, Winfield S. Pvt.	6 WVC	9/1/64–5/19/65
Blagg, John A. Pvt.	10 WVI	3/10/61–5/5/65
Boatwright, Daniel R. Pvt.	10 WVI	1/22/62–5/7/65
Bollinger, Thomas Pvt.	14 WVI	62/65
Bond, Nathan Pvt.	3 WVC	9/15/62–8/8/65
Bourn, John S. Pvt.	9 VAI	9/61–NF
Bowen, William C. Pvt.	168 PAI	10/15/62–7/26/63
Brake, George J. Cpl.	10 WVI	9/61–6/17/65
Brake, James J. Pvt.	1 WVI	3/30/65–7/21/65
Brammly, John A. Pvt.	6 VAI CSA	6/6/61–NF
Brannon, Hiram A. Pvt.	10 WVI	5/1/62–5/6/65
Brannon, John Sgt.	10 WVI	3/1/62–5/29/65
Brannon, Mayon T. Pvt.	10 WVI	8/15/62–6/24/65
Branson, Simon Cpl.	10 WVI	12/1/61–8/9/65
Britton, Horatio Pvt.	17 WVI	8/64–6/65
Brown, Bazil Pvt.	10 VAI	3/1/62–5/6/65
Burk, Jonathan H. Sgt.	7 VAI CSA	9/64–7/1/65
Burkhammer, William L. Pvt.	10 WVI	NF
Bush, Eli Pvt.	10 WVI	11/11/61–8/9/65
Bush, George A. Pvt.	NF (19 VAC CSA)	
Bush, George S. Sgt.	(19 VAC CSA)	9/1/62–NF
Bush, Henderson Pvt.	3 WVI	7/4/61–1/27/64
also Pvt.	6 WVC	1/23/64–5/22/66
Bush, John C.	NF	
Bush, Mandeville B. Pvt.	10 WVI	11/11/61–8/10/65

Bush, Minter Pvt.	6 WVI	9/20/64–6/10/65
Bush, Peter Pvt.	10 WVI	11/11/61–3/20/65
Bush, Samuel L. Pvt.	CSA NF (19 VAC)	
Bush, Thomas E. Pvt.	10 WVI	4/1/62–6/28/65
Cain, John W. Cpl.	10 VAI	5/1/62–5/6/65
Campbell, P. C. Pvt.	98 OHI	8/7/62–12/31/62
Carroll, James Cpl.	1 WVI	9/10/61–6/20/62
Carson, Hiram Pvt.	6 WVI	3/8/64–6/10/65
Carson, John Cpl.	6 WVI	5/31/64–6/10/65
Cather, Vespasian Sgt.	17 WVI	6/25/61–8/15/64
Cayton, Mortimon Pvt.	6 WVI	9/1/64–6/13/65
Chaplain, Edward Pvt.	3 WVC	9/14/62–6/6/65
Cheltsee, Isaac	US NF	
Clovis, Benjamin R. Pvt.	10 WVI	1/4/62–9/29/65
Coberly, Ashby M. Pvt.	19 VAC CSA	NF
Collins, Amos Pvt.	10 WVI	NF
Collins, John O. Pvt.	36 VAI CSA	6/1/61–6/22/65
Cooper, James L. Pvt.	60 VAI CSA	NF
Cooper, John M. Pvt.	60 VAI CSA	7/15/61–6/65
Cottrill, Evan Pvt.	14 VAC CSA	NF
Cottrill, William Pvt.	11 VAI	61/65
Cox, Philip Cpl.	11 WVI	9/16/62–6/17/65
Cox, Philip L. Pvt.	6 WVI	10/3/64–6/12/65
Craddock, Hugh Sgt.	11 WVI	11/7/61–8/19/65
Crites, Hamilton Pvt.	4 WVI	8/63–6/65
Culip, B. F. Pvt.	10 WVI	9/1/62–8/9/65
Cunningham, Benjamin Sgt.	10 WVI	62/63
Curry, John Pvt.	10 WVI	11/24/61–3/12/65
Danley, A. T. Pvt.	7 WVI	62/65
Dauley, Silas Pvt.	7 WVI	3/62–7/9/65
Davidson, I. S. Pvt.	19 VAC CSA	61–NF
Dennison, John	CSA NF (19 VAC?)	
Dewese, Daniel	CSA NF (19 VAC)	
Edman, J. J. Pvt.	CSA	NF
Ellyson, Robert F. Pvt.	62 VAC CSA	NF
Emerson, John	US NF	
Exline, Ebinezer Pvt.	NF	
Finn, Amos Pvt.	10 VAI	4/6/62–5/6/65
Finn, Lemeul Cpl.	10 WVI	9/20/64–2/7/65
Firestone, Michael Pvt.	6 WVI	10/61–65
Frank, Thos J. Pvt.	CSA	NF
Freeman, Lewis John Pvt.	10 WVI	3/17/62–5/29/65
Frymyer, William Pvt.	1 WVC	3/3/65–7/8/65
Furr, Lemuel Pvt.	10 VAI	1/6/62–5/6/65
Gatrell, Isaac Pvt.	11 WVI	7/12/62–6/17/65
Gragg, Jacob Pvt.	20 VAC CSA	61–NF
Greathouse, Silas Pvt.	6 WVI	2/11/65–6/10/65

Griggs, Hamilton Pvt.	1 WVC	3/4/65–7/4/65
Haddox, William Pvt.	10 WVI	12/10/61–8/9/65
Hardman, George Pvt.	10 WVI	1/4/62–8/9/65
Harris, Zack Pvt.	17 VAC CSA	62/65
Heckert, David Pvt.	6 WVI	9/24/61–6/10/65
Heckert, George E. Pvt.	10 WVI	8/15/62–6/26/65
Heckert, George V. Pvt.	6 WVI	9/5/64–6/10/65
Heckert, Henry C. Pvt.	6 WVI	9/5/64–6/10/65
Henry, Jack Sgt.	31 VAC CSA	61/63
Hess, Peter Pvt.	1 WVC	7/61–8/65
Hevitt, Roswell R.	CSA	NF
Hinzeman, Geo Pvt.	6 WVC	2/62–8/65
Holbert, B. F. Pvt.	10 WVI	5/12/62–6/26/65
Holbert, Wm. M. Pvt.	—	5/6/64–5/6/65
Holt, John Sgt.	11 WVI	12/2/61–65
Hoover, George Pvt.	62 VAI CSA	61/65
Jeffries, John Pvt.	15 WVI	8/15/62–6/14/65
Jones, Benjamen Pvt.	15 WVI	62/65
Keith, Andrew Pvt.	7 WVI	9/23/64–7/1/65
Keller, Frederick Pvt.	10 WVI	1/64–7/65
Kelly, James Pvt.	1 WVC	4/1/65–7/9/65
Keyseeker, Henry Pvt.	3 MDI	1/28/63–5/27/65
Kick, Simon H. Pvt.	7 WVI	7/4/61–11/25/65
King, Elijah Pvt.	10 WVI	11/11/61–3/21/65
King, John Pvt.	1 WVC	12/30/61–7/8/65
Knisely, Adam Pvt.	6 WVI	1/3/62–1/3/65
Knisely, Henry Pvt.	10 WVI	11/11/61–3/65
Kulh, Christian Sgt.	31 VAI CSA	5/31/61–65
Kuhl, William Pvt.	WVI	4/4/62–5/6/65
Lamb, John A. Pvt.	6 WVI	10/64–6/15/65
Lockard, Levi Pvt.	10 WVI	4/2/62–6/65
Lowther, Joseph Pvt.	NF	
Marks, Ezekial Pvt.	19 VAC CSA	NF
Matheny, James Blacksmith	4 WVC	7/17/63–3/6/64
Matheny, John E. Pvt.	1 WVC	3/3/65–7/8/65
Matthews, Silas Pvt.	11 WVI	61/65
McClung, James Pvt.	12 WVI	8/13/62–6/26/65
McCullugh, John Cpl.	3 WVC	10/61–6/30/65
McDonald, Elexander ?	3 VAI CSA	9/1/62–3/1/63
McNorman, Charles Lt.	2 VAC CSA	8/62–5/5/65
Mick, Solomon Pvt.	1 WVA	8/12/62–7/1/65
Miller, George Pvt.	10 VAI	5/12/62–5/6/65
Miller, Henry H. Pvt.	NF	
Mitchell, Layfette Pvt.	17 WVI	3/1/65–6/30/65
Moneypenny, Henry Pvt.	15 WVI	8/14/62–6/9/65
Moneypenny, James Pvt.	15 WVI	8/21/62–6/14/65
Moneypenny, Perry Pvt.	6 WVI	9/5/64–6/10/65

Montgomery, James E. Cpl.	3 WVI	7/61–10/62
Moody, John Pvt.	1 WVA	8/12/62–6/30/65
Moore, Adam Pvt.	CSA NF (62 VAI)	
Moore, George M. Pvt.	NF	
Moore, Owen A. Pvt.	8 WVI	2/62–6/65
Moss, George Pvt.	10 WVI	5/1/61–5/31/65
Neal, John Pvt.	2 WVI	4/61–6/64
Nelson, Abraham Pvt.	10 WVI	4/4/62–5/25/65
Nicholson, Shaderie Pvt.	7 WVI NF	
Norman, Richard Pvt.	1 VAI	10/1/61–5/6/62
Nutter, Josiah Pvt.	6 WVI	9/24/61–6/11/65
Patterson, Thomas Cpl.	10 WVI	10/20/61–8/9/65
Paugh, James Pvt.	10 WVI	2/28/62–5/7/65
Paw, Benjamin F. Pvt.	1 WVA	8/20/62–6/30/65
Pearcy, Albert F. Pvt.	20 VAC CSA	9/62–11/64
Perkins, Perry Pvt.	26 VAC CSA	62/65
Peter, Francis Pvt.	1 WVA	8/14/62–6/28/65
Pinkard, Branon Pvt.	6 WVI	9/6/64–6/10/65
Pitsinger, Judson Pvt.	10 WVI	5/2/62–6/28/65
Powell, William Pvt.	3 WVC	6/13/63–7/65
Powell, John R. Pvt.	6 WVI	9/5/64–6/10/65
Pritchard, Philip Pvt.	6 WVC	6/61–10/16/65
Pritt, Robert Pvt.	10 WVI	61/65
Queen, Benton Cpl.	10 WVI	12/2/61–8/9/65
Rader, George Pvt.	7 WVI	64/65
Rainey, Eli Pvt.	NF	
Ratcliff, John Pvt.	7 WVI	3/25/65–8/8/65
Reaser, James Pvt.	CSA NF (26 BTN VAI)	
Reaser, Sam S. Pvt.	26 BTN VAI CSA	62/65
Reynolds, S.W. Pvt.	1 WVA	8/13/62–6/28/65
Riddle, John Pvt.	10 WVI	8/10/62–2/63
Roach, Jacob Pvt.	1 WVC	NF
Roach, Jonithan Pvt.	NF	
Roberts, Uriah Pvt.	10 WVI	3/5/64–8/65
Robinson, Ed S.	US NF	
Rogers, Lias Pvt.	NF	
Rogers, George Pvt.	14 PAC	3/25/64–8/24/65
Sandy, John W. Pvt.	3 WVC	64/65
Seal, James W. Pvt.	CSA NF (HOUNSHELL'S BTN VAC)	
Short, Hiram Pvt.	10 WVI	3/3/62–3/14/64
also	17 WVI	2/29/65–8/9/65
Siers, William Pvt.	36 BTN VAC CSA	NF
Sisk, Christopher Cpl.	15 WVI	1/25/65–4/9/65
Sisk, Meridith Pvt.	6 WVI	9/26/64–6/10/65
Skinner, Lewis Pvt.	10 VAI	4/1/62–3/1/63
Smarr, John W. Pvt.	9 WVI	12/6/61–7/21/65
Smarr, Meckee Pvt.	10 VAI	4/6/62–6/4/63

Smith, Charles A. Pvt.	6 NHI	63/65
Smith, Christian Pvt.	6 WVI	62–6/15/65
Snider, John Pvt.	7 WVI	9/23/64–7/1/65
Speirs, James Pvt.	10 WVI	9/1/62–6/30/65
Spounagle, George Pvt.	18 VAC CSA	5/18/61–65
Stalnaker, A. H. Pvt.	11 WVI	8/62–6/65
Stalnaker, John Sgt.	6 WVI	9/5/64–6/10/65
Stalnaker, Mascelum Pvt.	30 OHI	11/8/61–8/19/65
Stalnaker, N. C. Sgt.	20 VAC CSA	4/61–65
Stern, Israel Sgt.	10 WVI	2/22/62–8/65
Stout, Abner Pvt.	14 WVI	3/5/65–7/3/65
Stout, Michael	CSA	NF
Stump, Allen Pvt.	19 VAC CSA	1/62–5/65
Stump, Levi Pvt.	31 VAI CSA	6/61–4/65
Stutler, John Cpl.	3 WVC	9/14/62–6/6/65
Sullivan, Ottawey E.	NF	
Taylor, George W. Sgt.	10 WVI	5/1/62–9/9/65
Taylor, Morris J. Pvt.	15 WVI	8/15/62–2/23/63
Tomblin, George B. Cpl.	6 WVC	11/63–8/1/65
Townsend, Eliot O. Pvt.	9 WVI	12/22/62–2/28/64
Turner, John E. Sgt.	10 VAI	12/22/61–8/65
Varner, Phillip Pvt.	11 OHC	6/3/63–6/26/66
Varner, Samuel L. Sgt.	10 WVI	11/11/61–8/16/65
Waldick, Francis Pvt.	15 WVI	8/13/62–6/14/65
Wallirs, Christopher Pvt.	6 VAI	8/27/62–6/13/65
West, James Pvt.	6 WVI	9/20/64–6/10/65
West, Stephen Pvt.	10 WVI	3/10/62–6/30/65
Westfall, Adam Pvt.	10 VAI	61/63
Westfall, John Pvt.	10 WVI	2/2/64–8/9/65
Wiant, Andrew Pvt.	10 VAI	6/11/62–5/11/65
Wilfong, William Sgt.	3 WVC	7/10/63–6/31/65
Williams, Aaron Pvt.	5 USA	12/64–12/67
Williams, George Pvt.	1 WVC	6/6/62–7/17/65
Williams, Isaac Pvt.	10 WVI	5/1/62–5/65
Williams, Isaac Pvt.	10 WVI	2/22/62–5/2/65
Willson, H. T. Pvt.	10 VAI	3/64–65
Willson, William Pvt.	62 VAI CSA	8/61–4/65
Wilson, D. D. Pvt.	10 WVI	64/65
Wyers, Ben F. Pvt.	CSA NF (19 VAC)	
Yerkey, Thomas Pvt.	19 VAI CSA	63–NF
Zinn, Marion Pvt.	6 WVI	8/7/62–6/10/65

Gilmer Co. Remarks

Allen, G.W.*—POW at Ft. Delaware
Altop, E.*—flesh wound
Bailey, A.—gunshot wound left leg DSC
Barnhouse, S.—gunshot left leg
Batton, B.F.—Numony fever
Beall, A.—gunshot wound right side 7/7/64
Bennett, S.—disabled third finger left hand
Biglar, G.—wounded in breast
Bircher, N.—gunshot wound back & leg
Black, W.—gunshot left arm LD
Blagg, J.A.—gunshot wound in eye sight
Boatwright, D.—qunshot in riqht hand
Bond, N.—RH & KD shell wound
Bowen, M.C.—RH & neurelgia of head & neck
Brake, G.J.—two gunshots right leg & right arm
Brake, J.J.—hearing in left ear affected
Bramly, J.A.*—wound in the arm
Brannon, J.S.—loss rite leg below knee
Brannon, M.T.—disability TYF 4 months
Britton, H.—CDR & nervous prostration
Burk, J.H.*—CDR & RH & KD
Bush, Eli—shell wound right arm
Bush, M.B.—right lung affected from fever
Bush, P.—three gunshot wounds
Bush, T.E.—gunshot wound in side
Cain, J.W.—flesh and bone wound
Campbell, P.—shot in right elbow
Carroll, J.—thrown from horse hurt in back
Cather, V.—CDR and results now chronic
Cayton, M.—granulated eyes deaf in left ear
Chaplain, E.J.—ruptured
Collins, J.O.*—POW Ft. Delaware 3 months & 20 days
Cooper, J.L.*—right arm amputated at elbow
Cottril, I.*—RH
Cox, P.L.—RH
Cox, P.—loss of hearing
Craddock, H.—defective in hip & shoulder & voice
Crites, H.—cold settled on breast
Culip, B.—disabled left breast by ball at Hatcher's Run, Va 3/31/65
Cunningham, B.—HD
Curry, J.—eyes affected from MS 3 ruptures
Firestone, M.—ruptured
Freeman, L.—gunshot in left eye
Furr, A.—wound on left side

Furr, L.—sore feet
Gatrell, I.N.—neuratrophy
Gragg, J.*—POW Camp Chase 24 mo. & Rock Island 13 mo
Haddox, W.—WIA by spent ball
Hardman, G.—LD
Heckert, G.E.—gunshot wound head
Heckert, G.—RH
Heckert, H.C.—deaf right ear
Hess, P.—ruptured
Hinzeman, G.—disabled left leg, right side of head
Holt, J.—POW Bell Island 6 months
Jeffries, J.S.—RH result in scrofula
Keck, S.—shot left arm & thigh
Keller, F.—gunshot right leg blind right eye from MS
Kelley, J.B.—ruptured wounded in right arm
Keyseeker, H.—gunshot & shell wounds hip & foot
King, J.—gunshot right arm right shoulder saber
Knisely, A.—partial deafness
Knisely, H.—gunshot and shell wound
Lamb, J.—loss of left testicle from smallpox
Lockard, L.—hip dislocated lameness
Matthews, S.—shot in left arm
McClung, J.A.—bad eyes
McDonald, E.*—POW Camp Chase one month
McNorman, C.*—blow on head
Mick, S.—partially lost hearing
Miller, G.W.—wound in back
Moneypenny, H.—RH & scurvy POW 6 months Saulsbury, NC
Moneypenny, J.—RH & scurvy POW 6 months Saulsbury, NC
Montgomery, J.—gunshot wound in head
Moody, J.W.—RH
Moore, O.—RH
Moss, G.P.—wounded in hip by shell
Nicholson, S.—gunshot wound in arm
Norman, R.K.—LD & RH
Patterson, T.C.—LD
Paugh, J.—MS & F broken down
Peters, F.M.—HD & RH
Pitsinger, J.—VV "Judson is in a helpless condition...he orto have a pension"
Pritchard, P.—weak eyes from measles
Ratcliff, J.—TYF & RH
Reaser, J.*—POW
Roach, Jacob—WIA by bayonet left hip at Antietam, MD
Roberts, U.—LD
Sandy, J.W.—mashed instensines
Short, H.H.—shot in left great toe
Siers, W.*—sore feet

Simon, B.R.—gunshot wound shoulder
Sisk, C.—LD receiving pension
Sisk, M.—neuralgia & etc.
Skinner, L.—RH
Smarr, J.W.—catarrh in head & side pleurisy
Smarr, M.—HD
Smith, C.A.—gunshot 3rd finger
Smith, Chris.—camp fever (TYF) 6 weeks
Snider, J.A.—RH
Speirs, J.B.—RH & chronic pleurisy
Stalnaker, N.*—2 months POW at Pt. Lookout, MD
Stout, M.*—vertigo & RH
Stump, L.*—indigestion of the stomach
Stutler, J.C.—horse shot & left foot mashed by fall
Taylor, G.W.—WIA right knee by ball Hatcher's Run, Va
Taylor, M.J.—asthma
Turner, J.—blYdrocela
Waldeck, F.—RH & piles
West, S.—TYF
Wiant, A.C.—gunshot wound & RH
Williams, A.—blood vessels of both legs ruptured
Williams, I.—RH
Williams, I.—VV right leg
Willson, H.—left leg shot by ball
Wilson, A.—SS & chills fever & snake bite
Zinn, M.—RH

Grant County

NAME/RANK	REGIMENT	WHEN SERVED
Amtower, George	NF	
Armuntrout, Solomon Pvt.	18 VAC CSA	6/2/61–1863
Ault, Martin	NF	
Baker, Samuel C. Pvt.	14 PAC	10/4/64–8/24/65
Bean, George Lt.	18 VAC CSA	6/2/61–5/20/65
Becker, Henry Pvt.	NF	
Bergdall, Henry Pvt.	CSA	62–NF
Berges, John Pvt.	7 WVI	8/17/61–1/9/63
Berze, Henry Pvt.	7 WVI	2/4/62–12/2/62
Boring, John Pvt.	10 KYC	9/62–NF
Buckbee, Jesse M. Pvt.	7 WVI	11/22/61–7/1/65
Burgess, Christopher C. Pvt.	7 WVI	12/30/61–7/10/65
Carroll, James P. Pvt.	1 WVC	9/16–7/8/65
Caton, Jacob J. Pvt.	6 WVC	3/20/64–5/22/66
Cirtes, David Pvt.	11 VAC CSA	62/64
Conell, William P. Pvt.	7 WVI	8/17/61–1/9/63
Conell, William P. Cpl.	3 MDI	1/63–5/18/65
Conrad, Isaac Pvt.	NF	
Davis, A. W. Pvt.	18 VAC CSA	6/2/63–9/10/64
Delay, Wm T. Pvt.	18 VAC CSA	6/2/61–5/20/65
Dolty, Abijah Pvt.	7 WVI	7/61–1864
Gouldizen, Gabrid Pvt.	US SCOUT	8/64–5/65
Gouldizen, Wm. Pvt.	18 VAC CSA	62/65
Hamstead, Charles Pvt.	7 WVI	8/28/61–2/28/62
Harness, George S. Pvt.	McNEILL'S RANGERS CSA	6/61–5/65
Harness, Henry C. Sgt.	5 MOC CSA	61/65
Haslacker, Anthony Pvt.	2 MDI	9/18/61–6/10/65
Heavner, Amos Pvt.	62 VAC CSA	5/61–6/65
Hilkey, William I.	NF (17 VAC CSA?)	
Hill, Wm B. Pvt.	18 VAC CSA	6/2/61–5/20/65
Hiser, Jonathan	NF (62 VAI CSA)	
Hogbin, James C. Sgt.	18 VAC CSA	61/65
Hutton, Isaac W. Pvt.	18 VAC CSA	6/2/61–5/65
Jordan, Wm P. Sgt.	10 VAC	63/64
Judy, Isaac	NF (McNEILL'S RANGERS CSA)	
Keplinger, John J. Pvt.	7 WVI	8/28/61–1/9/63
also	3 MDI	1/15/63–5/29/65
Kimble, John	NF (62 VAI CSA)	
Kitzmiller, Jacob Pvt.	3 WVC	10/11/62–6/30/65

Kitzmiller, Lloyd A. Pvt.	2 WVI	3/22/64–7/16/65
Knotts, Absolom Pvt.	6 WVI	8/22/64–6/10/65
Lakman, John A. Pvt.	2 OH	8/10/63–8/23/65
Lemon, George L. Sgt.	7 WVI	11/22/61–6/31/65
Leikins, James Pvt.	164 OHI	2/11/64–9/13/65
Lipscomb, David H. Pvt.	6 WVI	9/30/61–6/10/65
May, Philip Cpl.	7 WVI	11/27/61–7/1/65
Mace, John Pvt.	McNeill's Rangers CSA	62/65
McDonnel, John Pvt.	7 WVI	8/27/61–2/14/63
Meyers, Arlando J. Pvt.	7 IAI	7/28/61–12/16/61
aka Alanzo Huffman Pvt.	11 USI	4/26/62–5/4/65
Moyers, Abijah Pvt.	NF	
Moyers, Phelix	7 VAI	8/10/61–9/1/62
Myers, James Pvt.	2 MDI	8/29/61–5/6/65
Neil, Washington C. Pvt.	62 PAI	7/61–7/65
Nelson, Sam H. Pvt.	10 VAI CSA	63/64
Nordeck, John F. Cpl.	6 WVI	10/5/61–6/10/65
Orris, William C. Pvt.	115 PAI	9/3/63–7/11/65
Parsons, Adam H. Pvt.	11 VAC CSA	62/65
Ratliff, Wm. B. Pvt.	7 WVI	3/17/63–9/7/65
Ridings, Peter D. Pvt.	14 WVI	4/17/63–7/3/65
Roberts, Archable Pvt.	NF	
Roberts, Jeramiah Pvt.	184 OHI	2/9/65–9/20/65
Rogers, Albert Pvt.	10 VAI CSA	61/65
Rohrbaugh, Wm. H. Pvt.	18 VAC CSA	63/65
Sandes, Martin Pvt.	7 VAI	11/22/61–5/23/62
Sears, John T. Pvt.	2 MDI	9/18/61–1864
Shell, Daniel Sgt.	7 WVI	11/27/61–9/7/63
Shell, Job W. Pvt.	7 WVI	11/22/61–7/1/65
Shobe, Isaac N. Pvt.	18 VAC CSA	4/14/63–5/20/65
Shobe, Martin H.C. Pvt.	18 VAC CSA	4/15/63–5/20/65
Siles, Jacob Pvt.	7 VAI	11/22/61–11/22/64
Simmons, Lysus	NF	
Sims, George G. Pvt.	2 MDI	2/13/65–6/7/65
Smith, Lafayette Pvt.	18 VAC CSA	62/63
Smith, Morgan P. Pvt.	1 OHC	2/11/64–9/13/65
Souia, Henry Pvt.	22 MDC	62/65
Stager, Jacob Pvt.	NF	
Stonebreaker, Voiden Pvt.	14 WVI	6/10/63–6/27/65
Stonestreet, Martin Cpl.	7 WVI	12/4/61–3/15/65
Strother, William Pvt.	18 VAC CSA	62/65
Sypolt, Christopher C. Pvt.	NF	
Taylor, Alphonso Pvt.	1 ILA	1/11/64–6/23/65
Taylor, Harrison Sgt.	McNeill's Rangers CSA	61/65
Thalaker, Henry Pvt.	18 VAC CSA	6/2/61–5/20/65

Tittinboon, August Pvt.	7 WVI	11/23/61–7/4/65
Turner, John S. Pvt.	7 WVI	11/22/61–8/1/65
Wainer, John M. Pvt.	149 INI	2/1/65–9/27/65
Welton, Able S. Pvt.	18 VAC CSA	6/6/62–5/20/65
Welton, Isaac S. Pvt.	18 VAC CSA	6/2/61–5/20/65

Grant Co. Remarks

Berze, H.—gunshot right arm
Boring, J.—thrown from horse & hurt in breast
Buckbee, J.M—ankle broken
Burgess, C.C.—WIA left shoulder & left leg
Caton, J.J.—POW 4 months & WIA gunshot
Conell, W.P.—contracted neuralgia POW 16 months 7 days
Hamstead, C.—total blindness
Hilkey, W.—RH & dyspepsia since 1863
Keplinger, J.—POW 16 months 9 days & RH
Leikins, J.—gunshot left ankle & thigh disabled by manual labor
Lipscomb, D.H.—RH & LD
May, P.—WIA left leg
McDonnel, i.w.—POW 16 months 8 days & MS
Meyers, A.J.—POW Andersonville RH & DSC/LD
Neil, W.—wounded right hand & left leg
Nordeck, J.—RH
Orris, W.C.—contracted poisonous malaria
Ratliff, W.B.—POW 1 month 13 days
Ridings, P.D—LD contracted cold April 1865
Roberts, J.—POW 16 months 7 days, general disability
Sears, J.T.—shot through left hand
Shell, D.—RH
Shell, J.W.—CDR wounded right arm
Smith, M.P.—disabled liver spine & lungs
Stonebreaker, N.—LD
Stonestreet, M.—LD & TYF in 1863
Taylor, A.—right arm & shoulder hurt in fall from horse
Tittinboon, A.—wounded in breast
Turner, J.S.—shot through left leg

Greenbrier County

NAME/RANK	REGIMENT	WHEN SERVED
Adwell, Robert A. Sgt.	7 WVI	5/63–7/65
Allen, George W. Pvt.	CSA (BRYAN'S BATTERY VAA)	
Baldwin, Owen Pvt.	1 KYI	4/9/64–4/9/65
Beat, Elery C. Pvt.	PAI	1864–NF
Betts, David Lt.	5 PAI	6/7/61–1865
Blake, Benjamin F. Pvt.	4 WVC	10/1/63–NF
Blake, William B.	NF (CSA ?)	
Blake, William B. Musician	154 OHI	64/65
Blankenship, Hiram B. Pvt.	1 KYI	7/9/64–4/9/65
Blankenship, Joseph Pvt.	22 VAI CSA	6/9/61–4/9/65
Boon, John A. Pvt.	CSA (26 BTN VAI)	62/63
Brant, Mason M. Pvt.	26 VAI CSA	1862–4/9/65
Broofman, David Pvt.	27 VAI CSA	5/11/61–1864
Brown, Austin M. Pvt.	10 WVI	1/27/62–5/3/65
Burns, James L. Pvt.	7 WVC	NF
Callison, Isaac A. Pvt.	I (60 VAI CSA?)	6/64–9/64
Callison, Madison Pvt.	? (60 VAI CSA?)	64/65
Carter, Martin D. Pvt.	NF	
Caseboalt, George M. Pvt.	60 VAI CSA	62/64
Chambers, Hugh Pvt.	39 KYI	4/9/62–4/9/65
Chatterton, Alphons Pvt.	27	9/5/61–1/16/62
Coleman, Elexiond Sgt.	39 KYI	12/10/62–9/25/65
Cooke, James H. Pvt.	14 INI	5/1/63–2/3/64
Correll, William M. Pvt.	14 VAC CSA	5/62–4/9/65
Cousins, Franklin A.	TEAMSTER	NF
Crane, Charles L. Pvt.	91? (14 VAC CSA?)	64/65
Crookshanks, Tyree H. Pvt.	WV GUARDS	3/10/65–7/1/65
Curry, Samuel H. Pvt.	132 OHI	NF
Cutlip, James D. Pvt.	2 WVC	6/20/63–7/4/65
Dancy, James M. Pvt.	4 TNI US ?	3/11/63–8/2/65
Deitz, James Pvt.	79 VAI CSA	5/61–6/62
Depriest, Joseph Pvt.	NF (79 VA MILITIA CSA)	
Ellis, Abram S.	NF	
Ferrar, Peter Pvt.	23 OHI	63/65
Fewell, Patrick H. Pvt.	7 WVC	9/1/64–6/3/65
Fink, A. L. Capt.	36 OHI	5/62–11/65
Fisher, Christopher Pvt.	22 VAI CSA	1862–4/65
Fitzgerald, George W. Pvt.	50 VAI CSA	4/9/62–4/9/65
Fleshman, Van Buren R. Pvt.	14 VAC CSA	62/63
Ford, John Pvt.	2 WVC	6/7/63–6/20/65
Ford, Michael Pvt.	14 VAC CSA	61/62
Fravel, Israel Pvt.	122 PAI	9/64–7/65

Fuller, Amazi S. Capt.	2 PAA	6/62–1865
Gabert, John L. Pvt.	14 VAC CSA	61/65
Gardner, Rufus Pvt.	13 VA ?	5/62–1865
Hagar, Amzi Pvt.	105 PAI	7/63–5/65
Hall, Robert E. Pvt.	1 USI	64/65
Hall, Thomas A. Pvt.	27 VAI CSA	5/61–1862
Hamer, David Pvt.	WV GUARDS	12/1/64–7/1/65
Hamrick, Charles W. Cpl.	7 WVC	3/28/62–4/9/65
Hanfin, Patrick	TEAMSTER	NF
Hanna, Andrew M. Pvt.	14 VAC CSA	62/63
Hanna, Michael E. Pvt.	WV GUARDS	1/1/64–12/31/64
Hanna, Samuel Pvt.	2 WVC	7/63–7/65
Harris, David Pvt.	2 WVC	63/65
Hayes, Benjamin Pvt.	60 VAI CSA	6/19/61–6/19/65
Hinkle, Amos S. Pvt.	60 VAI CSA	61/64
Hoke, Christopher C. Pvt.	NF (19 VAC CSA)	
Hoke, Henry A. Pvt.	7 WVC	8/24/64–8/11/65
Hoover, Samuel Pvt.	2 MDI	4/65–6/65
Hunley, Silas Pvt.	2 WVI	11/62–7/18/65
Johnson, Samuel Pvt.	119 KYI	1/64–5/65
Kincaid, Alexander Pvt.	10 VAC CSA	7/61–8/13/62
Kincaid, Lemia G. Pvt.	NF	
Kramer, Ephrain L. Cpl.	132 PAI	8/14/62–5/63
Layton, David M. Pvt.	25 VAI CSA	5/61–4/9/65
Lee, Christopher Pvt.	23 TNC US ?	11/1/63–8/3/65
Legg, John W. Pvt.	14 VAC CSA	5/23/61–7/8/64
Legg, Samuel D. Pvt.	— I	6/61–5/63
Lewis, George H. Pvt.	CSA (14 VAC)	61/62
Livesay, George W. Pvt.	60 VAI CSA	6/61–4/9/65
Livesay, John Pvt.	91 OHI	4/9/64–6/24/65
Long, Napolean B. Pvt.	132 OHI	NF
McCling, Cyrus Pvt.	14 VAC CSA	61/62
McClung, Alphius P. Capt.	14 VAC CSA	61/65
McClung, Cyrus R. Sgt.	27 VAI CSA	5/11/61–1862
McCleary, Joseph K. Pvt.	2 WVI	NF
McLaughlin, Harvey J. Pvt.	7 WVC	9/15/64–6/3/65
McMillion, James W. Pvt.	60 VAI CSA	6/61–10/7/64
Metsinger, Jacob Pvt.	44 PAI	NF
Milem, James B. Pvt.	NF	
Moxloye, Thomas Pvt.	55 MAI	NF
Myles, Ruben C. Pvt.	14 VAC CSA	62/65
Nicholas, Michael Pvt.	60 VAI CSA	61/65
Parker, William H.	NYC	4/61–4/64
Peck, Joseph L. Pvt.	5 MAC	4/18/64–10/4/64
Pickering, John Pvt.	10 VAC CSA	5/3/61–4/9/65
Price, Charles E. Pvt.	126 OHI	3/1/64–6/30/65
Price, James W. Pvt.	60 VAI CSA	6/24/61–6/24/64

Name	Unit	Dates
Price, Joseph D. Pvt.	126 OHI	2/20/64–1/1/65
Puse, Robert R. Pvt.	VAC CSA	6/20/61–6/5/65
Rader, Charles H. Pvt	7 VAC CSA	1861–4/9/65
Rapp, Joseph A. Pvt.	2 WVC	6/7/63–6/30/65
Raymond, Edward Capt.	CSA	63/65
Reese, Charles Pvt.	33 PAI	4/15/61–7/1/65
Rider, James R.T. Pvt.	WVI	4/21/65–6/10/65
Rogers, George M. Pvt.	WVI	4/4/64–4/6/65
Rucker, William Major	13 WVI	5/6/62–11/64
Scudder, Fulton Pvt.	27 VAI CSA	61/65
Shafer, Joseph	NF	
Shawver, Andrew C. Capt.	27 VAI CSA	4/14/61–6/65
Shawver, John T. Pvt.	27 VAI CSA	5/11/61–NF
Shields, William H. Lt.	60 VAI CSA	61/65
Sizemore, Jacob Pvt.	37 VAC CSA	6/62–3/65
Smales, John Teamster	USI	63/65
Smith, Franklin Pvt.	9 WVI	3/1/62–3/8/65
Smith, James Pvt.	27 VAI CSA	5/11/61–NF
Smith, Shorten	NF	
Snedegar, James A Pvt.	7 WVC	8/15/64–6/13/65
Spinke, Allen Pvt.	NF	
Sunders, Edward Pvt.	NF	
Surber, Thomas C.	NF (SGT. 14 VAC CSA)	
Taylor, Samuel W. Pvt.	WV GUARDS	12/1/64–7/1/65
Thomas, John (B) Pvt.	NF (19 VAC & 31 VAI CSA)	
Tincher, Christopher Cpl.	187 OHI	3/14/65–1/26/66
Via, Wesley F. Pvt.	25 VAI CSA	5/61–6/64
Via, James T. Pvt.	14 VAC CSA	62/65
Wade, Morgan Pvt.	5 OHI	8/18/64–6/24/65
Weaver, David W. Pvt.	200 PAI	8/26/64–5/30/65
Wendall, James W. Pvt.	1 USA	NF
White, Charles	NF	
Williams, Benjamin F. Pvt.	WV GUARDS	12/1/64–7/1/65
Wilphong, John Pvt.	31 VAI CSA	61/65
Woodley, Alexander W. Pvt.	15 OHI	10/1/64–10/31/65
Woodward, John R. Pvt.	14 VAC CSA	1/64–6/10/64
Yoakum, George W. Pvt.	US SCOUTS	8/15/64–4/15/65

Greenbrier County Remarks

Blake, B.—swelling in right leg, enlisted navy discharged 65
Callison, I.A.*—W R Ramseys Scouts Nicholas Co. (also 60 VAI CSA)
Chatterton, A.—CDR & fistula
Coleman, E.—HD & LD
Cooke, J.H.—asthma & bronchitis

Crane, C.L. —shot in left thigh, discharge stolen
Deitz, J.*—discharged from militia
Depriest, J.*—crippled leg
Ferrar, P.—suffering from effects of camp fever
Fink, A.L.—RH, deafness, pneumonia, LD, discharge burnt with House in 1888
Fuller, A.S.—mustered out as Lt. Col. of the 4th PAA
Hagar, A.—wounded in arm
Hall, R.E.—crippled hand & feet
Hanfin, P.—RH
Hanna, S.—blindness
Hoke, H.A.—internal injury from horse falling
Hoover, S.—abscess in right side
Hunley, S.—fracture of right clavicle
Legg, J.W.*—gunshot in right arm
Legg, S.D.*—eyesight injured, in Ramseys company ind scouts Nicholas Co. (also served first the 79 VAM CSA)
Livesay, J.—shot through left shoulder, left knee, right thigh
McCleary, J.K.—catarrh
Metsinger, J.—flesh wound right leg
Parker, W.H.—4 wounds, 1 shot in leg, 3 saber, served as B Smith under Gen. Grant, discharged burned in house fire
Price, C.E.—RH result of measles
Puse, R.R.*—gunshot in side
Rapp, J.A.—loss of speech
Reese, C.—has other discharge says Col John Appleton Union WV
Rider, J.—Isaac W Allens State Troops
Rogers, G.M.—Isaac W Allens State Troops
Scudder, F.*—left the army
Shafer, J.—claims to have been a US soldier
Shawver, A.C.* —shot through left leg, POW Ft Delaware
Smith, J.*—run off
Smith, S.—claims to have been a US soldier
Tincher, C. —asthma & foot disease
Wade, M. —toes frozen off
Weaver, D.W.—effects of malarial fever
Wendall, J.W.—LD
White, C.—claims to have been a US soldier
Williams, B.F. —right eye affected by bursting percussion gun cap?
Wilphong, J.*—gunshot in both thighs
Woodley, A.W.—flesh wound in arm, Woodley is a clergyman
Woodward, J.R.*—gunshot in right thigh
Yoakum, G.W.—crippled hip from MS, served Capt John Yoakums co. Ind. Scouts Hardy Co WV

Hampshire County

NAME/RANK	REGIMENT	WHEN SERVED
Abell, Lemuel T. Pvt.	2 MDI	6/2/62–5/65
Abvel, Wm. E. Pvt	2 MDA	4/7/63–5/29/65
Agnew, Dan C. Pvt.	22 PAC	NF
Arnold, Joshua R. Pvt.	110—I	7/9/61–6/21/64
Barker, L. C. Pvt.	10 WVI	8/5/62–6/28/65
Bauer, Peter Pvt.	1 WVC	NF
Beal, Wm	Surgeon 39 ?	9/15/61–NF
Beatly, Henry Pvt.	3 MDI	61–NF
Beckman, Lewis Pvt.	NF (1 BTN VAI CSA?)	
Berkeley, Benjamin	Surgeon 68 OHI	61/65
Berkheimer, Henry Pvt.	202 PAI	9/1/64–8/8/65
Bobo, Joseph Pvt.	10 WVI	NF
Bowman, Peter Pvt.	NF (37 VAI CSA ?)	
Brannon, William E. Pvt.	1 D.C. VOL?	8/23/61–9/12/65
Brown, Alfred	Seaman SHIP/ESTRELLA	2/9/64–7/14/66
Bullsford, James W. Pvt.	10 WVI	2/29/64–8/9/65
Chraston, John W. Cpl.	1 MDI	61/65
Chraston, James S. Pvt.	2 MDI	6/62–1/65
Cobun, Isaac B. Sgt.	3 WVI	6/61–1865
Cook, Thomas J. Pvt.	5 OHC	10/1/63–6/27/64
Crabtree, John D.	NF (63 VAI CSA?)	
Davis, William F. Sgt.	16 PAC	1/4/64–7/24/65
Dawson, Huson B. Pvt.	3 MDI	62/65
Dicken, David M. Pvt.	2 PAC	5/11/64–7/20/65
Dicken, Tolbert Pvt.	NF (24 VAC CSA?)	
Durst, Henry Pvt.	NF	
Eckheardt, Frederick Pvt.	6 WVI	3/24/64–4/10/65
Everett, Louis Pvt.	4 VAI	6/17/61–1/20/64
Fearnow, Chas W.	NF	
Hansell, Joseph T. Pvt.	2 MDI	8/14/62–4/25/65
Harding, George Pvt.	NF (41 VAI CSA?)	
Heath, Wm. D. Pvt.	NF	
Johnsen, James Pvt.	2 MDI	61/65
Kesner, Soloman Pvt.	NF	
Kidwell, Evan H. Pvt.	10 WVI	2/29/64–8/9/65
Laven, Henry Pvt.	3 MDI	3/26/64–5/25/65
Ludwick, Thomas Pvt.	5 VAI	5/2/63–9/10/64
Mahew, Joshua Pvt.	10 VAI	NF
McAtee, John D. Cpl.	2 MDI	2/63–6/65
McCone, Wm	9 PAI?	NF
McDowel, Hugh Pvt.	2 WSC	11/28/62–8/12/65

McGee, Charles Pvt.	3 PAC	NF
McKinley, N. Capt.	MDI	1864–NF
Muller, John H. Pvt.	16 PAC	7/14/63–4/10/65
Montgomery, James W. Pvt.	4 PAC	10/10/61–2/63
Parker, P.	MDI	8/30/61–NF
Pepper, John W. Lt.	ILI	8/16/61–4/14/65
Pierce, J. W. Sgt.	103 PAI	10/16/61–NF
also	2 PAC	65/65
Poling, John G. Pvt.	13 OHI	1/62–4/65
Rinehart, Jeremiah Pvt.	NF	
Shoemaker, Jasper Pvt.	168 OHI	5/2/63–9/10/66
Shumate, Joseph	NF (61 VAI CSA?)	
Simpson, William S. Pvt.	3 WVI	9/8/62–7/13/65
Sirbaugh, George W. Pvt.	NF	
Staub, Christian Pvt.	1 MDC	11/6/61–8/12/65
Suter, Wm. S.	NF	
Thomas, Abram Pvt.	NF	
White, S. P. Pvt.	54 PAI	1/9/62–4/11/65
Wingfield, John Pvt.	NF	
Wolf, Joseph Pvt.	NF	
Young, David Pvt.	16 MII	8/13/61–8/8/65

Hampshire County Remarks

Arnold, J.R.—RH
Baker, L.C.—scalp disease
Beatly, H.—SS
Berkhimer, H.—rupture
Brannon, W.—wounded slightly in side
Bullsford, J.—thumb disabled health deranged
Coburn, I.B.—POW 13 months
Cook, T.J.—shot in right leg & left foot
Dawson, H.B.—TYF & pneumonia
Dicken, D.M.—RH
Kidwell, E.—toe split open
Ludwick, T.—shell wound in leg & pensioner
Mahew, J.—drawinq pension
McAtee, J.D.—kicked in head by horse & RH
McDowel, H.—fell from horse very weak back
Muller, J.H.—shot through both thighs
Pierce, J.W.—fracture of ribs
Poling, J.G.—shot through chin
Shoemaker, J.—general disability
Staub, C.—contracted erysiplous & tula
White, S.P.—gunshot in arm
Young, D.—shot through left leg

Hancock County

NAME/RANK	REGIMENT	WHEN SERVED
Allison, A. B. Pvt.	12 WVI	8/12/62–6/65
Allison, James Pvt.	12 WVI	1/1/64–8/20/65
Allison, W. H. Pvt.	12 WVI	1/64–1865
Armstrong, Henry Pvt.	40 OHC	7/1/63–2/22/64
Bailey, Joseph Pvt.	12 WVI	8/62–6/16/65
Barton, George W. Pvt.	65 OHI	61/65
Baxter, William H. Pvt.	12 WVI	8/12/62–9/8/63
also	179 OHI	9/12/64–6/17/65
also	Cpl. 34 USI	9/3/66–4/1/69
Beebout, Samuel Pvt.	1 VAI	5/61–8/61
also	12 WVI	8/16/62–6/16/65
Bernard, Van B. Cpl.	12 WVI	8/12/62–6/16/65
Bervinkle, George Cpl.	2 PAI	8/16/61–8/65
Bowen, James H. Cpl.	4 WVC	7/3/64–5/65
Bradley, James Pvt.	1 WVI	10/10/62–7/16/65
Brandon, George W. Pvt.	1 VAA	7/6/62–6/27/65
Brandon, Richard E. Pvt.	NF	
Brown, James W. Pvt.	2 WVI	3/5/64–5/25/65
Brown, R. H. Lt. Col	12 WVI	5/21/61–6/16/65
Brown, William F.	NF	
Chapman, Bazzelleel W. Capt.	1 VAI	5/221/61–8/27/61
Chapman, William M. Pvt	1 VAI	9/8/61–1864
Clark, George W.	NF	
Clutter, Martin V. Pvt.	77 OHI	12/20/61–3/8/66
Cochran, Friend Pvt.	189 OHI	2/22/65–9/28/65
Cooper, W. G. Pvt.	17 PAI	8/25/62–6/16/65
Cornell, Joseph Sgt.	10 INI	1861–NF
also Lt.	10 INI	1861–9/18/64
Connell, William B. Pvt.	114 OHI	8/13/62–7/17/65
Crawford, Lewis Pvt.	1 VAI	NF
Croasman, William Pvt.	74 PAI	3/65–9/65
Cullen, Isaac N. Pvt.	1 VAI	5/61–8/61
also	12 WVI	8/12/62–6/16/65
Cullen, Isreal H. Pvt.	17 WVI	8/24/64–6/30/65
Cullen, John M. Pvt.	1 VAI	5/4/61–8/61
Cullen, Mathew M. Cpl.	12 WVI	8/12/62–6/16/65
Cullen, Samuel H. Pvt.	12 WVI	8/12/62–6/16/65
Devers, William Pvt.	3 OHI	5/15/62–10/29/62
Daughty, James Pvt.	155 PAI	8/15/62–5/31/65
Dufford, Samuel J. Pvt.	67 PAI	4/1/65–7/24/65
Elliott, Ross B. Pvt.	1 VAI	9/8/61–7/62
Erskine, John US	NF	
Farnsworth, John Pvt.	39 OHI	7/22/61–7/22/65

Fisher, William E. Cpl.	1 OHI	10/21/61–10/6/64
Flowers, John W. Pvt.	12 WVI	12/26/63–8/9/65
Freeman, James K.	NF	
Freshwater, John C. Pvt.	12 VAI	8/8/62–6/6/65
Frymen, Alexander Pvt.	43 OHI	2/28/65–7/13/65
Fullerton, George W. Pvt.	2 WVC	7/10/61–7/3/65
Gamble, Thomas Pvt.	78 OHI	12/27/61–1865
Garel, Robert Pvt.	1 WVC	10/10/64–7/8/65
Gatrell, Campbell US	NF	
Geer, E. W. Pvt.	1 WVI	5/21/61–8/27/61
Gibbins, Edward J. Pvt.	30 OHI	8/17/61–1865
Girth, George Pvt.	2 INC	61/63
Glass, Lanford Pvt.	8 MII	6/14/61–5/16/62
Gray, Philip Pvt.	77 OHI	3/65–4/65
Grimes, James Pvt.	1 VAI	5/21/61–8/27/61
Hare, Jackson Pvt.	1 VAC	61/65
Harris, E. S. Pvt.	6 NCI CSA	5/12/61–4/7/65
Hawthorn, Frank Pvt.	13 OHI	6/22/61–9/64
Hewitt, R. B. Lt.	4 WVI	8/62–3/4/65
Hewitt, William Lt.	12 WVI	5/21/61–6/16/65
Holmes, John Pvt.	12 VAI	2/16/65–7/8/65
Howard, A. P. Pvt.	15 PAC	62/64
Howard, Harvey Pvt.	12 WVI	8/16/62–6/16/65
Hubley, Samuel "Landsman"	(SHIP) REINDEER	NF
Hunter, George W. Pvt.	1 WVI	9/8/61–8/65
Joseph, John A. Pvt.	20 OHI	4/22/61–8/23/61
also	14 PAC	11/3/62–8/8/65
Keggy, David H. Pvt.	23 PAI	8/6/62–8/1/65
Kennedy, Edward W. Drummer	45 PAI	7/12/62–9/63
also Pvt.	77 PAI	2/3/63–2/3/64
Kenney, Joseph Sgt.	3 WVC	3/20/63–6/30/65
Kincaid, McArthur	NF	
Kline, John R. Pvt.	85 PAI	9/13/61–11/22/64
Lainer, Lewis Pvt.	1 USA	NF
Lambert, George Lt.	102 PAI	6/14/61–6/14/64
Lambright, William F. Pvt.	32 OHI	7/62–6/8/65
Lee, Oliver G.	MARINE/MOA	2/1/63–2/64
Lockhart, Joseph Cpl.	1 ILI	2/24/62–7/14/62
Lockhart, Thomas J. Pvt.	1 VAI	4/61–7/64
Loliday, Abraham Pvt.	PAI	5/61–8/61
Lwaney, Tom R. Sgt.	1 WVI	NF
Mahan, William C. Pvt.	12 WVI	8/21/62–6/16/65
Markes, W. H. Ferrier	5 PAC	7/5/61–10/15/64
Martin, Allison Capt.	WHITE CLOUD?	2/62–8/64
Martin, John Pvt.	1 OHI	8/5/61–9/13/63
McBee, Jesse Pvt.	1 OHI	9/61–3/65
McCoy, James Pvt.	62 PAI	7/4/61–7/13/64

McGrew, Alfred Pvt.	5 OHC	2/6/64–10/30/65
McGrew, Nathan Cpl.	39 OHI	12/15/64–NF
McIntoish, John Pvt.	52 OHI	8/22/62–6/3/65
McLain, Richmond W. Pvt.	2 OHI	9/25/61–5/5/63
McLane, Porter C.	US SURGEON	5/15/62–10/2/65
McNicol, George	NF	
McSwergin, W. R. Cpl.	4 WVC	9/23/63–3/4/64
McSwigin, J. D. Sgt.	5 OHC	6/15/61–6/20/64
also	31 OHI	2/14/65–10/30/65
Melvin, John H. Capt.	12 WVI	8/12/62–6/16/65
Miller, Morgan H. Pvt.	12 WVI	8/12/62–6/16/65
Miller, Thomas Cpl.	1 VAI	5/21/61–8/27/61
Mills, J. B. Capt.	78 OHI	12/23/61–7/16/65
Minesinger, George Pvt.	140 PAI	8/9/62–5/31/65
Moore, Ezekiel J. Pvt.	4 VAC	1863–NF
also	186 OHI	NF
Moore, George H. Pvt.	15 IAI	10/21/61–10/17/62
also Wagoneer	9 IAC	10/3/63–2/3/66
Morris, Mathias K. 2lt.	30 PAI	6/11/62–7/28/63
Morrow, Samuel Pvt.	VAI	1862–NF
Munford, Jacob N. Pvt.	5 OHI	8/64–7/65
Orvic, Thomas Pvt.	1 OHI	10/17/61–9/22/64
Patterson, David M. Pvt.	12 WVI	8/12/62–6/16/65
Penney, Joseph Pvt.	NF	
Peterson, Joshua Pvt.	1 WVI	9/23/61–6/1/62
Plattenburg, Jesse Capt.	2 WVI	4/15/61–8/65
Porter, James Sgt.	12 WVI	8/62–6/65
Pugh, A. H. Wagoneer	119 ILI	8/22/62–8/26/65
Pugh, Robert W. Pvt.	12 WVI	8/12/62–6/16/65
Ramsey, Wm. J.	NF	
Randolph, Milton Pvt.	16 OHI	9/63–1/65
Reed, George B. Pvt.	1 WVA	7/20/62–6/27/65
Richey, Joseph T. Pvt.	18 PAC	63/65
Rinard, Richard Pvt.	236 OHI	2/22/65–7/27/65
Robb, William B.	NF	
Robinson, Alfred Pvt.	52 OHI	8/9/62–1863
Rosr, S. F. Cpl.	1 VAI	10/1/61–12/31/63
Ruggles, Jesse M.	NF	
Sardner, Thomas	US NF	
Scott, John R. Pvt.	1 WVI	5/31/61–8/27/61
Scott, William R. Sgt.	12 WVI	8/16/62–6/16/65
Settle, J. N. Pvt.	178 OHI	8/17/64–7/9/65
Shimer, James H. Pvt.	40 OHI	8/22/62–6/20/65
Smith, James A. Pvt.	22 IAI	NF
Smith, Jesse M.	NF	
Snider, George Pvt.	98 NYI	8/5/64–8/31/65
Snowden, Robert	US NF	

Stevenson, Thomas Pvt.	PAA	9/64–6/65
Stewart, W. W. Pvt.	12 WVI?	1/1/64–5/12/65
Swearingen, S. M. Pvt.	1 WVA	8/11/62–8/7/65
Thayer, Milton H. Cpl.	179 OHI	9/12/64–6/17/65
Thomas, William Pvt.	1 WVI	2/15/64–7/21/65
Trout, Samuel Pvt.	1 VAI	5/61–8/61
also	12 WVI	8/11/62–4/25/65
Tyler, Henry E.	NF	
Watson, William A.	NF	
Weaver, Jeol L. Pvt.	144 OHI	5/1/64–8/11/64
Weekly, Francis Pvt.	7 VAI	2/16/64–7/5/65
Weekly, George W. Pvt.	7 VAI	8/7/61–7/1/65
West, Henry B. Sgt.	40 OHI	11/9/61–12/6/64
Wright, Robert Pvt.	5 PAA	8/17/64–6/30/65
Wylie, Daniel M. Pvt.	1 VAI	5/21/61–8/27/61
Yankings, Andrew J. Pvt.	2 VAI	6/14/61–1/4/64
Yant, Daniel H. Lt.	15 WVI	8/28/62–NF
Young, Intrepid Pvt.	12 WVI	8/12/62–6/16/65

Hancock County Remarks

Allison, A.B.—deafness from ereysipilas
Allison, W.H.—gunshot left elbow, pensioner
Armstrong, H.—thrown from horse ribs broken
Bailey, J.—TYF & ague
Barton, G.W.—LD from exposure
Baxter, W.H.—contracted sore eyes
Beebout, S.—wounded in head made him deaf in right ear
Berwinkle, G.—POW Belle Island & others contracted asthma
Bowen, J.H.—RH
Chapman, W.—WIA three times
Clutter, M.V.—left side shoulder & breast crushed
Cochran, F.—chronic pleurisy & RH
Connell, W.B.—contracted phthisic
Cooper, W.C.—CDR
Croasman, W.—RH & piles
Cullen, I.H.—RH
Cullen, M.M.—CDR & SS still afflicted at short intervals
Daughty, J.—WIA ring finger left hand
Elliott, R.B.—left breast injured DSC
Farnsworth, J.—disabled by MS & stvitis, ears hurt artillery fire
Flowers, J.—RH
Frymen, A.—kicked by a horse
Fullerton, G.—frozen feet
Gamble, T.—RH
Gibbins, E.J.—head spine & breast fractured by falling tree
Girth, G.—gunshot wound left limb

Glass, L.—DSC
Hare, J.—breast mashed by horse UFL
Harris, E.S.*—WIA left hand, gunshot twice surrenddred Appomattox
Hawthorn, F.—DSC
Hewitt, R.B.—RH
Hewitt, Wm.—WIA left thigh gunshot
Holmes, J.—injured shoulder
Howard, H.—POW Lynchburg & Danville
Hunter, G.W.—POW Andersonville & disease of hips, knees, stomach
Joseph, J.A.—POW Andersonville 11 months, lost hearing right ear
Kennedy, E.W.—wounded by saber on wrist & DSC
Kenney, J.—piles & CDR UFL
Lainer, L.—RH
Lambright, W.F.—consumption from exposure
Lee, O.G.—catarrh & piles transferred to 1st Missouri Arty
Lockhart, T.J.—RH unable to work
Markes, W.H.—gunshot wound & CDR
McBee, J.—draws pension
McGrew, A.—sight of left eye destroyed & RH
McLain, R.—RH & HD trouble hearing
McSwigin, J.D.—WIA twice left thigh & left elbow
Miller, T.—contracted piles still afflicted
Mills, J.B.—back injury
Moore, E.J.—broncitis & catarrh
Moore, G.H.—injury of left arm UFL
Morrow, S.—was punished for strict obedience
Munford, J.N.—HD
Penney, J.—draws pension of $12 per month
Peterson, J.—LD from exposure
Plattenburg, J.W. - qunshot wound left arm
Randolph, M.—piles
Reed, G.B.—sore throat & piles
Richey, J.T.—gunshot wound in breast
Robinson, A.H.—chest trampled, left lung injured RH long time UFL
Rose, S.F.—general disability
Scott, J.R.—SS
Smith, J.A.—POW Andersonville contracted RH unfit for occupation
Stevenson, T.—RH & HD disabilities causing nervousness
Thomas, W.—RH
Troup, S.—asthma
Watson, W.A.—asthma caused by exposure
Weaver, J.L.—contracted erysipelas
Weekley, F.—both arms injured
West, H.B.—WIA three times seriously once unfit for labor
Wright, R.—F settled in back & limbs supported by family UFL
Wylie, D.M.—injured in burying comrad a few days after discharge
Yankings, A.—knee dislocated & mashed up in a collision

Hardy County

NAME/RANK	REGIMENT	WHEN SERVED
Evans, Benj Sgt.	7 WVI	12/30/61–7/1/65
Fishel, John Henry Pvt	51 INI	2/62–NF
Fisher, Adam Capt.	?	3/17/63–3/12/66
Mongale, Michel	US	NF

Harrison County

NAME/RANK	REGIMENT	WHEN SERVED
Adams, Abraham Pvt.	7 WVI	3/65–7/4/65
Allen, John B. Pvt.	3 WVI	5/61–8/65
Allen, Lafayette J. Pvt.	3 WVC	3/15/65–6/30/65
Anderson, Benjamin F. Pvt.	7 WVI	3/14/65–7/14/65
Anderson, James R. Sgt.	12 WVI	8/11/62–6/16/65
Armour, John W. Pvt.	NF	
Armstaid, John J.	NF	
Ash, Isaac	US NF	
Asmor, James R. Pvt.	NF	
Ayers, Lasander J. Pvt.	3 WVC	4/4/64–6/30/65
Backus, Sanford Pvt.	6 WVI	9/15/64–6/10/65
Bailey, Adam Pvt.	7 WVI	3/65–NF
Bailey, John Sgt.	3 WVI	6/25/61–8/15/64
Bailey, John F. Pvt.	12 WVI	NF
Bailey, John W. Sgt.	4 WVC	8/2/63–3/9/64
Bailey, Marshal Pvt.	2 WVI	5/20/61–6/14/64
Bailey, William N. Pvt.	10 WVI	10/17/61–8/9/65
Baltzley, John Pvt.	US	NF
Barnes, Albert L. Pvt.	3 WVC	3/14/65–7/14/65
Barnes, William Pvt.	4 WVC ?	7/21/63–3/9/64
Barrett ?, Michael Pvt.	1 WVC ?	2/15/62–11/2/62
Bartlett, Hiram L. Pvt.	7 WVI	65/65
Bartlett, Julius C. Pvt.	3 WVC	3/21/65–7/9/65
Bates, Notley S. Pvt.	6 WVI	9/9/64–6/9/65
Bayles, Edmund D. Pvt.	1 WVI	8/11/62–6/28/65
Bee, William Pvt.	7 WVI	9/61–7/65
Benedum, John H. Pvt.	6 WVI	9/10/64–6/10/65
Bennett, Ar ? P. Pvt.	6 WVC	3/18/64–8/12/65
Bennett, Theodore C.	NF	
Bennett, Theron D. Pvt.	12 WVI	8/15/62–5/23/65
Bennett, William O. Pvt.	12 WVI	8/12/62–4/8/63

also	12 WVI	9/64–6/65
Bice, Jacob W. Pvt.	3 WVC	3/14/65–7/14/65
Blackwell, Enoch F. Pvt.	12 WVI	2/27/64–5/13/65
Blenshaw, James Pvt.	1 WVA	9/9/61–6/19/65
Boughner, Oliver P. Lt.	10 WVI	1/18/62–3/7/65
Bowen, Lot Major	3 WVC	10/17/62–12/12/64
Boyer, James T. Pvt.	3 WVC	3/10/65–6/16/65
Boyles, Samuel J. Pvt.	2 WVI	5/25/61–6/14/64
Bradford, Corbin B. Pvt.	7 WVI	3/14/65–7/1/65
Brake, David C. Pvt.	12 WVI	2/24/64–8/9/65
Brent, Clabren? Pvt.	41 PAI	6/16/61–8/16/64
Brent, Jefferson Pvt.	8 MAC	3/21/64–10/21/65
Brohard, George W. Pvt.	3 WVI	6/25/61–8/15/64
Brook, Matthew S. Pvt.	6 WVI	8/12/61–8/20/64
Broun?, Henry S. Pvt.	9 LAI CSA	7/19/61–9/1/61
Brown, John	US NF	
Brown, William K. Sgt.	1 WVC	12/23/63–7/8/65
Bryant, Templeton C. Pvt.	17 WVI	9/1/64–7/10/65
Bumgardner, John Q. Pvt.	6 WVI	8/20/61–6/10/65
Bumgarner, James Surgeon	WVC NF	
Bussey, Edward Pvt.	NF (20 VAC CSA)	
Butler, Julius Pvt.	45 USI	5/62–3/65
Callahan, James Pvt.	5 WVC	5/20/61–2/5/65
Carder, John W. Sgt.	12 WVI	8/9/62–6/16/65
Carder, Thomas Pvt.	6 WVI	8/20/61–6/10/65
Casseday, Thomas Pvt.	6 WVC	6/21/61–8/21/64
Castard?, George W. Cpl.	33 VAI (CSA?)	6/25/61–8/12/63
Cattrill, Tom J. Pvt.	12 WVI	NF
Chaplin, Thomas J. Pvt.	4 WVC	7/18/63–3/8/64
Childers, Asher S.	NF	
Childers, Enoch Pvt.	3 WVC	9/15/62–6/13/65
Christner, Jacob Pvt.	3 MDI	2/20/61–5/29/65
Clazier, Joseph Pvt.	12 WVI	8/11/62–6/16/65
Cochran, Isaac R. Pvt.	108 OHI	2/8/64–7/22/65
Coffman, Elmore P. Pvt.	7 WVI	3/18/65–7/16/65
Coffman, George W. Cpl.	6 WVC	6/25/63–5/25/66
Coffman, John M. Pvt.	12 WVI	8/26/62–6/16/65
Coffman, Theodore Pvt.	12 WVI	12/28/63–8/8/65
Coffman, Thomas C. Pvt.	3 WVC	3/14/65–6/13/65
Combs, Francis I. Pvt.	3 WVC	9/6/62–6/6/65
Conaway, John C. Pvt.	7 WVI	4/1/65–7/1/65
Conrad, Alexander Sgt.	85 PAI	10/15/61–10/17/64
Conred, John	CSA NF (62 NCI)	
Coon, Robert W. Sgt.	12 WVI	8/13/62–6/16/65
Coonrine, Thomas Pvt.	10 WVI	12/61–8/65
Cork, Andrew J. Pvt.	11 WVI	3/1/65–6/30/65
Cork, Harrison Pvt.	12 WVI	8/16/62–6/16/65

Cork, John W. Pvt.	3 WVC	9/14/62–6/13/65
Cornewelle, Ashum Cpl.	6 WVI	1/30/63–6/10/65
Cornewelle, George Pvt.	6 WVI	6/14/63–6/31/65
Cottrail, George W. Pvt.	6 WVC	8/8/64–9/18/65
Cottrill, David Pvt.	6 WVC	6/10/61–8/16/64
Cox, Bernard D.	14 ZOUAVE	NF
Cramp, William N. Pvt.	12 WVI	8/7/62–6/16/65
Crim, Jacob	3 WVC	3/14/65–6/30/65
Crim, James E. Pvt.	12 VAI	8/9/62–1865
Criss, Aaron Pvt.	1 WVC	2/15/65–7/15
Cross, Samuel S. Pvt.	1 WVC	3/3/65–7/8/65
Cullison, William N. Sgt.	7 WVI	7/5/61–7/4/65
Cuningham, Elkania T.	NF	
Cunningham, Daniel Pvt.	14 WVI	8/20/62–6/27/65
Cunningham, Walter J. Pvt.	3 WVC	3/25/65–7/20/65
Cutwright, Salathial Pvt.	4 WVC	7/14/63–3/6/64
Daugherty, Norval Pvt.	3 VAI	6/1/61–2/5/64
David, James N. Pvt.	22 PAC	9/6/62–5/25/65
Davidson, Lathan A. Pvt.	5 IAI	7/61–NF
Davis, Daniel T. Pvt.	3 WVC	9/15/62–6/30/65
Davis, George H. Pvt.	2 MDI	9/61–9/64
Davis, George W. Pvt.	10 WVI	2/23/64–8/19/65
Davis, Henry H. Pvt.	NF	
Davis, John W. Pvt.	6 WVC	8/11/64–9/15/65
Davis, Joshua F Pvt.	NF	
Davis, Nire S. Pvt.	2 MDI	8/8/61–9/29/64
Davis, Owen Pvt.	6 WVI	9/23/61–6/9/65
Davis, Van B. Pvt.	3 WVC	3/14/65–7/14/65
Davison, Josiah Pvt.	6 WVI	9/10/64–6/10/65
Davisson, John H. Pvt.	3 WVC	10/14/62–10/30/64
Dawson, William H. Pvt.	3 WVI	8/18/61–8/18/64
Dawson. William	NF	
Day, Benjamine F. Pvt.	12 WVI	8/18/62–5/12/65
Day, John D. Pvt.	12 WVI	2/23/64–5/29/65
Day, Morgan Pvt.	14 WVI	3/24/65–6/27/65
Day, Solomon Pvt.	WVI	NF
Dayton, George W. Pvt.	1 WVA	12/5/62–11/30/65
Dillon, Silas Pvt.	4 WVC	NF
Doughtery, John A. Pvt.	61 PAI	5/64–4/23/65
Drain, Presley Pvt.	12 WVI	8/16/62–6/16/65
Drummond, Burton Pvt.	1 WVC	61/61
Drummond, Wilford Pvt.	2 WVI	4/4/65–7/18/65
Dudley, Fleming Sgt.	1 WVC	7/18/61–7/8/65
Duff, Alexander Pvt.	7 WVI	3/14/65–7/1/65
Duncan, Moses S. Sgt.	6 WVI	8/20/61–8/20/64
Edgell, William N. Pvt.	WVI	12/3/62–3/14/64
also Cpl.	2 WVI	3/15/64–7/16/65

Exline, Joseph Pvt.	12 WVI	8/16/62–5/16/65
Finlen, James	NF	
Firush ?, George Pvt.	3 WVI	6/10/61–1/31/64
Fittro, Andrew Pvt.	1 WVC	3/2/65–7/8/65
Fittro, James J. Pvt.	3 WVC	8/14/62–6/18/65
Fittro, Oliver J. Pvt.	3 WVC	2/23/65–6/30/65
Fittro, Watson Pvt.	NF	
Flanigan, James Pvt.	15 WVI	7/62–/65
Flannagan, William J. Pvt.	3 WVC	3/14/65–6/30/65
Fleming, Eli B. Sgt.	6 WVI	8/18/64–6/10/65
Fleming, William H. Musician	3 WVI	9/15/61–3/15/62
Fletcher, David F. Pvt.	12 VAI	8/11/62–11/6/63
Fletcher, John T. Pvt.	3 WVC	9/14/62–6/30/65
Flowers, Lawson J. Pvt.	3 WVI	5/12/61–10/16/65
Fogg, Benjamin F. Pvt.	14 PAC	3/24/64–9/24/65
Fond ?, Michael Pvt. *aka* Wallace Thomas	57 PAI	4/13/65–6/29/65
Ford, Thomas L. Pvt.	7 WVI	3/15/65–7/1/65
Fordyre, John	NF	
Fortney, Hiram J. Pvt.	3 WVC	3/9/65–7/31/65
Fortney, Joshua D. Pvt.	12 WVI	8/63–3/64
Fortney, Joshua Pvt.	12 WVI	8/13/62–7/1/65
Fowler, Nathan M. Cpl.	3 WVC	7/3/63–6/30/65
Fox, George F. Pvt.	12 WVI	7/1/62– NF
Franklin, Joe Pvt.	NF	
Frazier, Granville W.	NF	
Frazier, James Pvt.	— I	3/15/65–5/29/65
Freeman, John T. Sgt.	15 WVI	8/15/62–6/21/65
Frush ?, John U. Pvt.	6 WVI	9/1/64–6/10/65
Fry, James H. Pvt.	8 WVI	3/13/63–7/3/65
Fulkeneer ?, William H. Pvt.	3 WVC	9/15/62–6/30/65
Fulkineer, John M. Pvt.	3 WVC	11/22/62–7/18/65
Furnes ?, John H. Pvt.	12 WVI	8/15/62–7/15/65
Gabert, George C. Pvt.	6 WVC	8/18/61–8/11/65
Gadd, John B. Pvt.	152 OHI	5/28/64–9/2/64
Gain, Elias Pvt.	6 WVI	8/31/64–6/10/65
Gain, John J. Pvt.	12 WVI	61/65
Gawthrop, John A. Capt.	119 VAM	7/8/58–1866
George, Maulsby Pvt.	3 VAI	61/65
Gifford, Waldo W. Pvt.	12 WVI	8/13/62–6/16/65
Gilmore, Francis Pvt.	1 WVC	12/17/62–7/8/65
Goff, Nathan Gen.	NF (BREVET BRIG. GEN FROM WV)	
Goldsborough, Townsend	NF	
Goodwin, Eppa D. Pvt.	14 WVI	3/14/65–6/27/65
Gordon, Robert T. Sgt.	3 WVI	7/4/61–5/9/63
Gordon, Samuel Cpl.	60 OHI	2/64–7/65
Grant, John Q ?. Pvt.	29 KYI	2/6/65–7/18/65

also Sgt.	GUNBOAT KINEA?	12/26/62–11/26/64
Gray, Andrew C. Pvt.	14 WVI	8/8/62–6/27/65
Green, John Sgt.	6 WVI	12/1/62–6/10/65
Gribble, C. G. Pvt.	6 WVI	8/26/61–12/26/63
Grieve?, James A. Pvt.	81 PAI	8/24/61–7/27/62
Griffin, Isaac H. Pvt.	3 WVC	9/15/62–6/30/65
Grimes, David H. Pvt.	10 WVI	5/18/62–6/28/65
Gum, Andrew J. Pvt.	10 VAI	61/65
Gum, B. W. F. Pvt	10 WVI	61/65
Hagerty, Delilia A. Pvt.	6 WVC	3/13/64–7/22/65
Hagerty, Fred M. Pvt.	HOME GUARD	63/65
Hagerty, Jesse M. Cpl.	3 WVC	3/15/65–6/30/65
Haley, Henry H. Pvt.	3 WVC	2/23/65–6/30/65
Hall, Flavius E. Pvt.	12 WVI	8/6/62–6/16/65
Hall, Jordan C. Cpl.	3 WVC	8/29/64–6/10/65
Hall, Oscar F. Pvt.	7 WVI	NF
Hall, Silas J. Pvt.	6 WVI	9/12/64–6/10/65
Hamrick, Robert Pvt.	3 WVC	9/15/62–6/11/65
Haney, John L. Pvt.	3 WVC	12/15/63–6/30/65
Harbest, John A. Pvt.	6 WVC	6/18/61–3/30/65
Harden, James C. Pvt.	12 WVI	8/15/62–6/16/65
Harden, John W.	NF	
Hardman, Joseph D. Pvt.	12 WVI	8/14/62–4/3/63
Hardman, Nicholas Pvt.	12 WVI	8/15/62–6/16/65
Hardman, Peter Pvt.	3 WVI	61/64
Haroker, William Pvt.	3 WVC	3/9/65–6/13/65
Harris, Moses Pvt.	77 OHI	2/16/64–8/12/65
aka Moses Cox		
Harrison, Benjamin F.	US	NF
Harrison, James A. Pvt.	22 PAC	2/10/64–5/13/65
Harrison, James T.	14 WVI	3/14/65–6/27/65
Harrison, Joseph B. Pvt.	12 WVI	8/15/62–7/1/65
Harrison, Samuel Pvt.	NF	
Haymond, Henry Capt.	18 USI	10/26/61–1870
Haymond, Lee Capt.	3 WVC	4/11/63–6/10/65
Haymond, Rufus Sgt.	12 WVI	8/15/62–6/16/65
Healdreth, Benjamin H. Pvt.	12 WVI	8/18/62–6/16/65
Heckman ?, Miranda Pvt.	14 WVI	65/65
Heflur, William Pvt.	6 WVI	9/12/64–6/10/65
Heldreth, David Pvt.	17 WVI	9/5/64–6/30/65
Heldreth, David G. Pvt.	14 WVI	8/5/62–6/27/65
Henderson, Alexander Pvt.	6 WVI	9/62–6/65
Henderson, Eli Pvt.	6 WVI	5/10/61–8/10/65
Hendrickson, Thomas Pvt.	3 WVC	3/17/63–6/30/65
Hess, Jeremiah W. Sgt.	6 WVC	6/27/61–5/22/66
also	3 WVI	NF
Hess, William P. Pvt.	1 MDI	6/9/64–6/14/65

Hickman, Sam B. Pvt.	1 WVA	NF
Higginbotham, Henry W. Pvt.	25 PAI	1/30/64–12/6/65
Hill, Emanuel Pvt.	32 PAI (NEGRO)	NF
Holmes, John M. Pvt.	14 PAC	9/62–9/65
Hooper, John Pvt.	6 WVI	9/10/64–6/10/65
Horbert, Luther C. Pvt.	12 WVI	8/15/62–6/16/65
Huff, Ai ? Pvt.	6 VAI	62/65
Huff, Austin A. Pvt.	6 WVI	9/10/64–6/10/65
Hugill, Asa Capt.	7 WVI	7/16/62–9/17/64
Hursey, William L.	NF	
Jackson, Adam L. Pvt.	1 WVA	8/21/61–9/14/64
Jackson, Irvin Pvt.	12 WVI	8/16/62–5/29/65
Jackson, Roby Pvt.	12 WVI	8/13/62–6/16/65
Janes, Henry E. Pvt.	3 WVI	6/10/61–8/16/64
Jarbo ?, James H. Pvt.	6 WVI	8/4/62–6/10/65
Jaws ?, Edward	NF	
Jeffers, John M. Lt.	14 WVI	8/12/62–7/3/65
Jenkins, James Pvt.	1 WVA	NF
Jett, James E. Pvt.	6 WVI	64/65
Johnson, George A. Pvt.	6 VAC CSA	62/65
Jones, Nathan M. Sgt.	17 WVI	10/64–6/65
Keesy, Noah Pvt.	6 WVI	9/10/64–6/10/65
Kellar, Jacob R.	NF	
Kellison, A. J. Pvt.	3 INC	5/8/63–6/6/66
Kelly, Stephen Pvt.	6 WVI	7/22/62–6/10/65
Kennedy, James T. Pvt.	7 WVI	3/15/65–7/1/65
Kennedy, Richard Pvt.	11 WVI	9/20/62–6/30/65
Kidd, Jonathan Pvt.	6 WVC	9/9/64–5/19/65
Kildow, Daniel Pvt.	NF	
Knox, William Lt.	3 WVC	3/14/65–7/14/65
Kuhn, Eli Pvt.	1 WVC	8/8/61–9/16/64
Lang, Fred A. Sgt.	18 PAC	10/14/62–6/29/65
Lang, Sebastian Cpl.	1 WVA	6/62–6/65
Lanham, William Pvt.	7 WVI	3/15/65–7/1/65
Laugh, Jacob J.	US NF	
Law, James S. Pvt.	3 WVI	6/10/61–3/23/65
Law, Jesse D. Pvt.	6 WVI	9/10/64–6/10/65
Leo, Michael Pvt.	7 WVI	4/15/65–7/19/65
Lepley, Josiah Pvt.	12 WVI	8/10/62–9/22/64
Limer, Daniel Pvt.	12 WVI	8/8/62–7/65
Lindsey, James M. Pvt.	6 WVI	8/18/64–6/10/65
Linville, Constantine H. Pvt.	9 WVI	2/25/62–2/28/64
Linville, John A. Pvt.	1 WVI ?	2/15/65–7/8/65
Litchnell ?, Dan Pvt.	12 WVI	NF
Long, Syloamus Pvt.	3 WVC	3/14/65–6/30/65
Longenette, James W. Pvt.	10 VAI	12/3/61–8/9/65
Loomon, James Pvt.	7 WVI	4/11/65–5/31/65

Name	Unit	Dates
Lorentz, George O. Pvt.	1 WVA	8/62–7/65
Lorentz, Marcellus Pvt.	3 WVC	9/15/62–6/30/65
Louchery, Daniel C. Pvt.	6 WVI	8/26/64–6/10/65
Lovett, William E. Pvt./Lt.	3 WVC	9/62–1/9/65
Lowe, David Pvt.	14 WVI	3/6/65–6/27/65
Lunum, James P. Pvt.	3 — C	3/5/65–6/5/65
Lyons, Christoper N. Pvt.	6 WVI	9/19/64–6/10/65
Madden, Jesse H. Sgt.	12 WVI	9/15/62–5/14/65
Madison, William Pvt.	NF	
Manear, Samuel W. Pvt.	12 WVI	8/17/62–6/16/65
Mann, Patric ? Pvt.	3 WVI	NF
Martin, Abia Pvt.	6 WVI	9/12/64–6/165
Martin, Elisha N. Pvt.	3 WVI	6/27/61–5/8/63
Martin, Felix W. Pvt.	17 WVI	8/24/64–6/30/65
Martin, Homer D. Pvt.	40 IAI	9/15/64–9/15/65
Martin, Lorenza D. Pvt.	6 WVI	9/10/64–6/15/65
Martin, Silas E. Cpl.	WVI	12/2/62–4/23/64
also Pvt.	3 WVC	3/21/65–6/13/65
Martin, William H. Pvt.	3 VAI	6/27/61–5/27/66
Martin, William H. Pvt.	6 WVC	6/8/61–8/12/64
Mason, Asa C. Sgt.	87 INI	8/13/62–7/5/65
Matheny, John W. Sgt.	4 VAI	7/16/63–3/6/64
Matthey, Ame ? Pvt.	4 WVC	7/25/63–3/10/64
aka Mathey, Henry		
Maxon, Herman Pvt.	10 WVI	5/64–5/65
Maxson, Sanford S. Pvt.	85 NYI	9/16/64–7/16/65
Maxwell, David Pvt.	7 WVI	4/2/65–7/65
Mayer, Henry F. Sgt.	3 WVI	NF
McAtee, James W. Pvt.	NF	
McAteer, A. J. Cpl.	6 WVI	7/23/62–6/10/65
McCarty, Enoch D. Pvt.	1 WVC	65/65
McCarty, Stephen F. Pvt.	1 WVC	3/3/65–7/8/65
McClung, Marcelous Pvt.	3 WVC	3/14/65–6/30/65
McClung ?, William H. Pvt.	12 WVI	8/3/62–7/65
McCord, Henry R. Adj.	12 WVI	8/15/62–6/15/65
McCord, John T. Pvt.	10 WVI	8/15/62–5/16/65
McElfresh, Sanford Pvt.	6 WVI	3/3/65–6/10/65
McGee, William B. Pvt.	17 WVI	3/12/65–7/9/65
McIntire, Isaac N.	NF	
McMillan, Samuel J. Cpl.	20 WVC	4/63–4/65
McNemar, Beckwith A. Pvt.	6 WVI	8/4/62–6/10/65
Miley, Joseph Pvt.	7 WVI	3/65–6/65
Miller, Abel E. Pvt.	6 WVI	9/15/64–6/10/65
Mills, James A.	NF (16 VAC CSA?)	
Minter, Guinn Pvt.	10 WVI	61/65
Monroe, John W. Pvt.	VAI CSA	5/1/61–2/26/62
Monroe, Riley Pvt.	12 WVI	8/9/62–6/15/65

Moore, Alexander C. Major	3 VAI	6/28/61–9/23/62
Moore, Daniel H. Pvt.	14 WVI	1/16/64–7/2/65
Moore, Elias Pvt.	6 WVI	9/3/64–6/10/65
Moore, Ricard V. Pvt.	1 WVA	6/12/61–9/14/64
Moore, Thomas Pvt.	6 WVI	7/12/62–6/65
Moran, Hesekiah H. Pvt.	10 WVI	6/62–2/25/63
Morgan, David P.	NF	
Morris, James H. Pvt.	7 WVI	3/15/65–7/1/65
Morris, James M. Pvt.	10 WVI	5/62–1865
Morris, Walter M. Pvt.	3 WVC	10/15/62–7/10/65
Morrison, Alva Pvt.	3 WVC	5/1/63–6/30/65
Morrow, David M. Pvt.	19 VAC CSA	5/62–1865
Munday, Hiram Sgt.	6 WVC	6/11/61–3/12/64
Murphy, Samuel Pvt.	1 WVC	12/1/61–9/6/62
Myers, John J. Pvt. *aka* James Myers	3 WVI	6/61–6/23/65
Nay, Fielding Pvt.	12 WVI	8/16/62–6/16/65
Nay, Fred M. Blacksmith	3 WVI	9/15/62–6/30/65
Nay, Lewis F. Pvt.	14 WVI	8/21/62–1/27/65
Nay, Silas J. Pvt.	14 WVI	8/16/62–6/27/65
Neeper, Hugh Pvt.	23 OHI	2/3/63–7/25/65
Nesbit, Richard Pvt.	5 NJI	8/24/61–8/24/64
Norman, Seymour Pvt.	7 WVI	3/28/65–8/3/65
Northcott, Robert Ltc.	12 WVI	8/6/62–1/5/65
Nutter, Henry Pvt.	7 WVI	3/14/65–7/15/65
Nuzum, Thomas N. Sgt.	3 WVC	9/15/62–6/13/65
Ogden, Madison S. Pvt.	3 WVC	3/14/65–6/30/65
Ogden, William R. Cpl.	12 WVI	8/13/62–7/1/65
Osborn, Alexander H. Sgt.	17 WVI	2/15/65–6/30/65
Parson, Benjamin F. Pvt.	17 WVI	10/64–7/8/65
Patton, Richard Pvt.	MOC	62/65
Peck, John C. Cpl.	12 WVI	8/28/62–6/28/65
Pepper, James B. Pvt. *also*	4 WVC 17 WVI	7/14/63–3/9/64 6/30/65–11/9/65
Perine, Isaac W. Pvt.	NF	
Perry, Isaac C. Pvt.	VAI (14 VAC CSA)	NF
Pettit, Mannon Pvt.	1 WVC	8/8/61–7/8/65
Pinchean ?, Layfiett Pvt.	12 WVI	8/24/62–6/20/65
Price, William Pvt.	1 WVA	8/14/62–6/28/65
Prim, Charles E. Pvt.	12 WVI	8/8/62–6/10/65
Prine, John D.	NF (19 VAC CSA?)	
Pritchard, George W. Pvt.	7 WVI	NF
Radabaugh, Jacob M. Pvt.	1 WVA	8/13/62–6/28/65
Rager, William J. Sgt.	7 VAI	7/3/61–6/62
Randall, George F. Sgt.	14 WVI	8/5/62–6/27/65
Randolph, David F. Pvt.	14 WVI	8/20/62–6/27/65
Reed, Alexander Pvt.	7 WVI	NF

Reed, Neyin Pvt.	1 WVC	61/62
Reeder, Benjamine A. Pvt.	3 WVI	6/27/61–10/31/62
Reeder, Charles A. Cpl.	12 WVI	8/16/62–6/16/65
Reynolds, William B. Cpl.	1 MDC	3/64–7/65
Rheul, John L. Pvt.	196 OHI	3/65–10/65
Rhoades, John Pvt.	7 WVI	3/15/65–7/1/65
Riblett, Daniel A. Cpl.	3 WVI	6/19/61–8/12/64
Riblett, George J. Pvt.	19 VAC CSA	6/19/63–1/19/65
Richards, Lewis B. Pvt.	7 WVI	3/64–NF
Rider, John G. Pvt.	12 WVI	2/25/64–8/9/65
Riley, Moses S.	NF	
Robey ?, James M. Pvt.	1 WVC	2/16/65–7/16/65
Robey, Andrew J. Pvt.	12 VAI	3/64–9/65
Robey, James A. Pvt.	10 WVI	2/1/64–8/9/65
Robey, Tom J. Pvt.	3 WVI	6/17/61–3/9/64
also	6 WVC	3/9/64–10/16/65
Robinson, Burgess Pvt.	6 WVC	6/19/61–1/22/64
also	3 WVI	1/22/64–10/16/65
Robinson, Edmund Pvt.	1 WVA	8/13/62–6/28/65
Robinson, Frederick Pvt.	1 WVC	8/11/64–7/65
Robinson, Jack Pvt.	106 I	3/64–10/65
Robinson, James Sgt.	3 WVC	3/9/65–7/9/65
Robinson, John N. Pvt.	1 WVC	2/27/65–7/10/65
Robinson, William P. Cpl.	4 WVC	7/12/62–3/10/63
Rogers, Stephen Pvt.	6 WVI	9/1/64–6/10/65
Rollins, Leroy Pvt.	1 VAI	8/18/61–9/14/64
Ross, Henry C. Pvt.	6 WVI	9/3/64–6/10/65
Ross, John H. Pvt.	36 OHI	3/15/65–7/28/65
Ross, William F. Pvt.	3 WVC	3/21/65–6/30/65
Rousle, Moton Pvt.	45 PAI ?	5/13/64–11/4/65
Ruckman, John Pvt.	7 WVI	3/15/65–7/1/65
Ruckman, William B. Pvt.	3 WVI	64/65
Rule, Charles J. Pvt.	7 WVI	3/15/65–7/1/65
Rumble, Thornton A. Pvt.	6 WVI	9/1/64–6/10/65
Sandy, Moses A. Pvt.	3 VAI	6/27/61–8/17/64
Sandy, William Pvt.	6 VAI	62/65
Sapp, Alison Pvt.	3 WVC	3/14/65–7/14/65
Sapp, John M. Pvt.	3 WVC	3/14/65–7/14/65
Schutte, Gotlieb Pvt.	12 WVI	8/11/62–6/16/65
Sheets, John Pvt.	7 WVI	9/61–8/65
Sheets, Samuel Pvt.	1 WVC	2/24/64–7/8/65
Shiin ?, Dexter L. Pvt.	12 WVI	8/14/62–6/16/65
Shinn, Albert T. Pvt.	3 VAI	6/27/61–8/17/64
Shinn, Alphus Pvt.	3 WVI	9/1/61–3/1/62
Shinn, Frank G. Sgt.	34 OVI	9/6/61–9/13/64
Shinn, Leander Pvt.	12 WVI	8/20/62–6/16/65
Shinn, Oliver W. Pvt.	3 WVI	6/10/61–8/10/64

Shrader, David Pvt.	3 ILC	3/15/65–10/19/65
Shrader, William L. Pvt.	12 WVI	8/18/62–3/25/63
Shuttleworth, N. A. Capt.	3 WVI	6/10/61–6/5/62
Silcott, Emanuel B. Pvt.	6 WVI	2/16/65–6/12/65
Silcott, Lewis T. Pvt.	6 WVI	2/23/64–6/10/65
Sletzer, Jacob M. Pvt.	5 VAI CSA	3/1/62–6/20/65
Smallwood, Elisha Pvt.	7 WVI	NF
Smallwood, John W. Pvt.	6 WVI	9/11/64–6/10/65
Smith, Cyrus W. Pvt.	10 WVI	12/28/62–3/28/65
Smith, James H. Pvt.	1 WVI	2/8/65–7/8/65
Smith, Josiah D. Pvt.	6 WVI	9/7/64–6/65
Smith, Lemuel Pvt.	10 WVI	62/65
Smith, William D. Pvt.	12 WVI	8/13/62–6/16/65
Smith, William J. Pvt.	7 WVI	3/28/65–7/1/65
Smoot, Thomas A. Pvt.	19 VAC CSA	6/62–3/64
Snodgrass, Jesse Lt.	WV	62/65
Sommerville, James W. Pvt.	3 WVC	3/18/64–6/30/65
Sprout, Jesse A. Pvt.	NF	
Stansburry, Justus Cpl.	6 WVI	8/6/61–8/15/64
Stark, Elias Pvt.	6 WVC	9/64–NF
Starks, Silus Pvt.	12 WVI	8/18/62–6/16/65
Stealy, Granville Pvt.	3 WVC	9/14/62–6/30/65
Stealey, George J. Capt.	—	61/65
Steel, Samuel N. Capt.	USA	8/61–7/14/65
Stephens, David E. Pvt.	4 WVC	8/4/63–3/9/64
Stewart, Oscar T.	12 VAI	62/65
Stewart, Richard Pvt.	7 PAC	7/15/63–5/10/65
Stitlze ?, John Pvt.	1 WVA ?	9/13/62–7/28/65
Stonestreet, Sameul C. Pvt.	7 WVI	3/15/65–6/22/65
Struetaler ?, James Pvt.	5 VAA CSA	9/1/62–6/25/65
Stuck, Hezekiah Pvt.	7 WVI	3/14/65–7/1/65
Stutler, Charles W. Pvt.	3 WVC	9/14/62–6/6/65
Stutler, Stephen Pvt.	15 WVI	62/65
Sulivan, Enoch Pvt.	3 WVC	3/14/65–6/23/65
Sullivan, Thomas Pvt.	7 WVI	3/20/65–7/1/65
Sutton, Andrew N. Pvt.	3 WVC	3/10/64–6/30/65
Sutton, John Pvt.	12 WVI	1/3/64–7/19/65
Swartz, Jacob M. Pvt.	6 WVI	8/8/62–6/15/65
Swiger, Calvert Pvt.	19 VAC CSA	7/63–5/12/65
Swiger, Elias Jr. Pvt.	3 WVC	3/23/65–7/8/65
Swiger, Fredric L. Pvt.	6 WVI ?	9/3/64–6/10/65
Swiger, John B. Pvt.	1 WVC	3/4/65–7/8/65
Swiger, Matthew Pvt.	3 WVI ?	12/29/63–3/7/64
Swiger, Solomon R. Pvt.	3 WVC	3/21/65–6/15/65
Tate, Oscar H. Pvt.	1 WVC?	3/4/63–7/8/65
Thompson, Joe A. Pvt.	10 WVI	11/61–5/64
Thompson, Joseph Pvt.	1 WVA	8/61–8/64

Name	Unit	Dates
Tucker, Benjamin F. Pvt.	19 VAC CSA	8/62–4/16/65
Tyson, Daniel M. Pvt.	14 WVI	3/16/65–6/27/65
Vanhorn, John A ?. Pvt.	20 VAI CSA	3/63–1865
Vanpelt, Robert Pvt.	1 VAA	7/18/61–2/1/65
Vernon, Abner Pvt.	6 WVI	9/10/64–6/10/65
Wagner, George W. Pvt.	20 WVI	3/14/65–5/1/65
Wagner, Wilbur Cpl.	6 WVI	8/20/61–6/10/65
Wallace, Richard Chaplain	12 WVI	9/10/62–6/30/65
Wallen, George W. Pvt.	3 PAC	2/25/64–10/31/65
Warner, John S. Pvt.	1 WVA	8/14/62–5/29/65
Washburn, Anson L. Pvt.	7 WVI	3/65–8/65
Washington, George M.	NF	
Webb, John Sgt.	6 WVC	6/15/61–8/15/64
Webb, Joseph Pvt.	6 WVI	64/65
Welsh, Elim Pvt.	6 WVI	9/61–6/16/65
Welsh, Laman Pvt.	4 WVC	8/1/63–3/8/64
Whitehair, John J. Pvt.	6 WVI	8/29/64–6/10/65
Whitehair, Levi Pvt.	NF	
Whitehair, Salathael J. Pvt.	17 WVI	2/15/65–6/30/65
Wilcox, Isaac N. Pvt.	6 WVI	9/5/64–6/12/65
Williams, Noah Pvt.	10 WVI	2/20/62–5/7/65
Williams, Samuel Cpl.	3 WVC	3/9/65–6/30/65
Willis, George E. Pvt.	14 WVI	3/13/65–6/27/65
Willis, Henry H. Cpl.	12 WVI	8/1/62–6/16/65
Wilmoth, George W. Pvt.	10 VAI	NF
Wilson, Thomas R. Pvt.	1 WVC	2/28/65–7/8/65
Windon, Charles Pvt.	1 VAI	NF
Winmiller, Adam Pvt.	12 WVI	8/16/62–6/16/65
Wires, William H. Pvt.	186 OHI	2/13/65–9/18/65
Wise, Pleasant W. Pvt.	12 WVI	62/65
Wiseman ?, Job Pvt.	15 WVI	8/13/62–6/6/65
Wolf, Elias Pvt.	1 WVC	2/28/65–7/8/65
Woodfield, Joseph Pvt.	12 WVC	3/31/65–6/30/65
Wright, Benjamin Pvt.	12 WVI	8/27/62–4/1/63
Wright, Nathan Pvt.	14 WVI	2/65–6/27/65
Young, John T. Cpl.	1 WVC	9/9/61–7/8/65

Harrison County Remarks

Allen, J.B.—WIA by shell at Bull Run in hospital Ft. Levenworth?
Anderson, J.A.—rupture right side
Bailey, A.—no discharge was home on leave with sick soldier
Bailey, J.F.—LD
Bailey, J.W.—SS
Bailey, Jn.—RH
Bailey, M.—RH
Barrett, M.—gunshot wound right leg
Bates, N.S.—RH
Bee, Wm.—POW 5 months
Benedum, J.H.—epilepsy
Bennett, A.P.—RH & gunshot
Bennett, T.D.—LD & HD
Bennett, W.O.—MS & DSC
Bice, J.W.—catarrh
Blackwell, E.F.—gunshot wound left leg
Boughner, O.P.—wounded in left arm
Bowen, L.—DSC
Brake, D.C.—right foot mashed
Brook, M.S.—cold on MS etc.
Bryant, T.C.—hurt by log while building fortifications
Bumgardner, J.Q.—RH & stomach trouble
Bumgarner, J.—injured by fall from horse
Bussey, E.—POW 6 months Camp Chase & Ft. Delaware
Butler, J.—RH
Carder, J.W.—CDR
Chaplin, T.J.—CDR & catarrh
Childers, E.—eye injured by bursting of cap
Christner, J.—shot through lungs
Coffman, J.M.—KD
Coffman, Theo.—bronchitis sequal of measles gets $4 pension
Combs, F.I.—WIA twice, right foot & left hip
Conaway, J.C.—RH
Conrad, A.—CDR & RH
Coon, R.W.—KD & HD
Coonrine, T.—LD & throat trouble, POW Libby prison
Cork, A.—paralysis
Cottrail, G.W.—eyesight injured by saber wound
Cottrill, D.—eyesight
Criss, A.—injury of back & hip caused by fall gets $4 pension
Cullison, W.H.—piles
Cunningham, D.—mumps settled in right side
Cunningham, W.J.—RH
Cutwright, S.C.—LD
Daugherty, N.—RH

David, J.N.—CDR
Davidson, L.A.—detailed hospital duty by Capt. Grubb no discharge
Davis, D.T.—RH & crippled
Davis, G.W.—shell wound right foot gets $4 pension
Davis, J.F.—HD & RH
Davisson, J.H.—RH & frozen feet
Dawson, W.H.—vercale & injury left side
Day, M.—cold on measles
Drain, P.—CDR & TYF at Winchester, VA
Drummond, B.—ruptured, TYF gets $2 pension
Drummond, W.—rupture & piles
Duff, A.—VV & catarrh
Duncan, M.S.—brain fever causing deafness gets pension
Edgell, W.N.—fracture right ankle
Exline, J.—gunshot wound
Flanigan, J.—hernia, in 17 battles
Fletcher, D.F.—fever settled on lungs
Flowers, L.J.—spinal affection from enlargement of spleen & heart
Fogg, B.F.—piles & bronchitis also pleurisy in left side
Ford, T.L.—piles, CDR & RH
Fortney, J.D.—HD
Fox, G.F.—deserted
Freeman, J.T.—piles
Fulkineer, J.M.—left leg shot off, POW at Richmond 73 days
Furnes, J.H.—HD
Gabert, G.C.—RH
Gain, J.J.—gunshot wound right hand
George, M.—one eye injured
Gifford, W.W.—CDR
Gilmore, F.—pneumonia & gunshot wound in right foot
Goff, N.—POW
Grant, J.g.—Mr. Grant served 2 years in navy
Gray, A.C.—loss of hearing
Green, J.—HD, RH & cold on mumps
Grimes, D.H.—broken heart
Gum, A.J.—ruptured
Hamrick, R.—fractured right leg, POW Andersonville 11 months
Hagerty, D.A.—hurt in train collision in ILLs
Hagerty, J.M.—defective eyes
Hall, F.E.—eye disease through piles gets $12 pension
Hall, S.J.—VV
Haney, J.S.—hemerrhoids & rupture
Harbest, J.A.—RH thrown from horse gets $4 pension
Harden, J.C.—RH & HD
Hardman, J.D.—urenary affection
Hardman, P.—SS gets $6 pension
Harris, M.—gunshot wound

Harrison, J.—hearing affected
Haymond, H.—WIA Stone's River knee, right leg & hernia
Haymond, R.—KD & indigestion, POW 7 months
Healdreth, B.H.—parralisis
Heflur, W.—catarrh of head & chest gets $4 pension
Heldreth, D.G.—KD & HD
Heldreth, D.—stomach & effected eyes
Henderson, A.—gunshot wound in foot
Henderson, E.—head & back afflicted
Hendrickson, T.—CDR & piles POW 10 months
Hess, J.W.—RH & CDR
Hess, W.P.—gunshot left shoulder, this man gets only $6
Higginbotham, H.—wounded foot
Holmes, J.M.—hernia
Horbert, L.C.—MS & TYF
Hugill, A.—RH
Jackson, R.—RH & helpless now
Janes, H.E.—piles & asthma
Jeffers, J.M.—CDR & piles
Johnson, G.A.'—shot through hand
Keesy, N.—knee dislocated
Kellison, A.J.—deafness & RH
Kelly, S.—RH, rupture, partial blindness
Kuhn, E. —RH
Lang, F.A.—POW 14 months
Lang, S. —impared eyesight, RH & rupture gets $6 pension
Lanham, W.—total deafness in left ear
Law, J.S.—promoted to captain
Lindsey, J.M.—disabled 3/4 gets small pension
Lorentz, G.—gunshot wound above eye & deafness
Lowe, D. —RH
Lunum, J.P.—LD
Lyons, C.N.—gunshot wound left leg
Moore, A.C.—bleeding piles, Capt. WV light artillery
Madden, J.H.—rupture of legs
Manear, S.W.—piles & RH
Martin, E.N.—WIA
Martin, F.W.—catarrahl conjunctivitis nose, stomach disease & MS
Martin, H.D.—RH
Martin, L.D.—MS, LD, KD
Martin, W.H.—rectum & eye sight injured
Mason, A.C.—slight wound on legs POW 7 months at Saulsberry
Matheny, A.—RH while POW
Matheny, J.W.—RH & HD
Maxon, H.—ankle injury
Maxson, S.S.—CDR & piles
Maxwell, D.—afflicted side, cold on measles

McCarty, S.F.—RH
McElfresh, S.—RH
McNemar, B.A.—erysipelas rupture incurred
Miley, J.—RH & MS
Miller, A.E.—RH
Minter, G.—promoted to captain
Moore, D.H.—VV & RH gets $4 pension
Moore, E.—RH
Moore, R.V.—CDR & injured hands
Moore, T.—skin disease & KD gets $6 pension
Moran, H.H.—gunshot wound in hand
Morris, J.H.—sight affected
Morris, J.M.—gunshot wound left hand
Morris, W.M.—severe freezing, was in 38 engagements
Morrow, D.M.*—gunshot wound
Murphy, S.—DSC
Nay, F.—gunshot wound
Nay, F.M.—RH, piles & LD
Nay, L.F.—side pleurasy & KD gets pension
Nay, S.J.—shot through right arm
Nesbitt, R.—gunshot wound right leg
Nesbitt, R.—gunshot wound right leg gets $4 pension
Norman, S.—disease of respiratory organs
Northcott, R.—heat & inflamation stomach
Nuzum, T.A.—RH & hearing
Ogden, W.R.—thum shot off
Osborne, A.H.—served in WV militia
Parsons, B.F.—palpitation & piles gunshot right ankle partly deaf
Perry, I.C.*—desertion
Pettit, M.—disabled right eye, HD & piles gets $16 pension
Prim, C.E.—sight affected & gunshot wound left knee cap
Pritchard, G.W.—piles, RH & catarrh in head
Radabaugh, J.M.—eyesight injured by measles
Rager, W.J.—CDR & palpitation gets $8 per month pension
Randall, G.F.—shot 3 times
Reeder, B.A.—HD & stomach
Reynolds, W.B.—TYF & pneumonia
Rhoades, J.—CDR
Riblett, D.A.—RH & hearinq
Richards, L.B.—home sick when army disbanded, no discharge
Rider, J.G.—chills & fever
Robey, A.J.—CDR & catarrh draws $2 per month pension
Robey, J.A.—catarrh of head & chest gets $6 pension
Robey, T.J.—SS & scurvy, loss of teeth & catarrh
Robinson, B.—cold on measles
Robinson, F.—cold on measles
Robinson, Jm.—naso catarrh & deafness

Robinson, W.P.—wound in right arm
Rogers, S.—disabled around lef nee
Rollins, L.—CDR, 6 VA Inf. Com. E. also
Ross, J.H.—TYF & MS
Ross, W.F.—RH
Ruckman, J.—VV left leg
Rule, C.J.—loss of fore finger on left hand
Rumble, T.A.—RH
Sandy, M.A.—SS & piles WIA
Sandy, W.—fever & ague
Sheets, J.—left ear destroyed
Shinn, F.G.—CDR, RH & catarrh, disease left testicle
Shinn, O.W.—both eyes injured
Shrader, D.—loosing speech 2 weeks caused by cold
Shrader, W.L.—VV & LD
Sletzer, J.M.'—joint of finger injured, POW Ft. Delaware 13 months
Smith, J.D.—RH
Smith, L.—broken right leg
Smith, W.D.—MS
Snodgrass, J.—bronchitis
Sommerville, J.W.—WIA by shell
Sprout, J.A.—cold on measles
Starks, S.—cold on measles
Stealey, G.J.—catarh & bronchitis
Stutler, C.W.—WIA by shell
Sutton, J.—intermittent fever leaving weak lungs & eyes
Swiger, E. Jr.—gunshot right leg
Swiger, M.—LD
Swiger, S.R.—MS & HD
Thompson, J.A.—loss of sight
Thompson, J.—frozen foot & finger mashed right foot & right hand
Wagner, G.W.—piles
Washburn, A.—CDR, HD & RH
Webb, J.—RH & HD
Webb, J.—WIA left thigh POW at Richmond 7 months
Wilcox, I.N.—bronchial catarrh
Williams, N.—wounded in right leg
Willis, G.E.—catarr
Wilson, T.R.—RH
Winmiller, A.—diseased head resulting from SS
Wiseman, J.—HD & disability of legs from wound
Woodfield, J.—wounded right ankle
Wright, B.—LD
Wright, N.—N. catarrh & deafness of both ears

Jackson County

NAME/RANK	REGIMENT	WHEN SERVED
Abbott, James D. Pvt.	187 OHI	2/28/64–3/1/65
Adams, Isaac M. Sgt.	10 WVI	9/7/62–5/2/65
Adams, Wm. A.S. Pvt.	6 WVI	9/12/64–6/10/65
Alvis, John W. Cpl.	7 WVI	9/1/61–7/3/65
Amos, Franklin M. Pvt.	7 WVC	7/1/62–8/1/65
Anderson, Bicknel Pvt.	4 WVC	8/25/63–3/14/64
Anderson, C.M. Pvt.	7 WVC	2/65–8/65
Anderson, Wm. C.	US NF	
Andrews, John G. Pvt.	1 WVI	6/5/64–7/25/65
Angus, Wm. Pvt.	10 WVI	2/25/64–8/9/65
Antill, John Pvt.	11 WVI	8/14/62–6/17/65
Archer, Eliskey Pvt.	66 OHI	9/64–6/20/65
Archer, J.C. Pvt.	20 OHI	2/29/64–7/15/65
Archer, John M. Pvt.	176 OHI	8/23/64–6/14/65
Archer, Peter Pvt.	176 OHI	8/22/64–5/20/65
Armstrong, Richard J. Pvt.	180 OHI	9/23/64–7/12/65
Arnold, Louis A. Pvt.	13 WVI	3/29/64–6/22/65
Ascher, Vincent Pvt.	66 OHI	9/28/64–6/3/65
Ashby, T. Pvt.	7 WVC	2/2/62–8/1/65
Aten, Peter Pvt.	9 WVI	10/1/62–8/65
Bachus, George W. Sgt.	VA Rangers	10/6/64–5/31/65
Baker, Elijah Sgt.	4 WVC	6/63–3/64
Baleh, Samuel Sgt.	7 OHA	6/22/63–8/22/65
Barber, Samuel L. Capt.	11 WVI	7/10/62–6/17/65
Barnes, Charles W. Pvt.	92 OHI	7/8/64–7/65
Barnett, Kendall Pvt.	11 WVI	8/14/62–6/17/65
Barnett, Preston Pvt.	13 WVI	8/10/63–6/10/65
Barnheart, Jacob Pvt.	11 WVI	3/26/65–8/9/65
Barnheart, John L. Cpl.	11 WVI	8/63–6/17/65
Barr, Lewis Pvt.	NF	
Bartlett, Daniel W. Pvt.	11 WVI	10/15/62–8/15/65
Bates, George W. Pvt.	11 WVI	8/11/62–6/17/65
Bates, Jacob Pvt.	11 WVI	8/9/62–6/17/65
Batton, Aaron Pvt.	92 OHI	8/4/62–6/10/65
Beaver, Peter Pvt.	116 OHI	12/1/63–12/8/65
Begal, David Pvt.	9 VAI	5/10/63–3/10/64
Bereslin, Granville Pvt.	11 WVI	10/26/61–11/9/64
Beymer, Wm. Pvt.	25 OHI	2/16/62–6/18/66
Bias, Franklin Pvt.	4 WVC	8/20/63–3/8/64
Black, James H. Pvt.	7 OHC	10/22/62–6/20/65

Name	Unit	Dates
Black, John S. Pvt.	73 OHI	1/1/61–3/10/63
Blagg, Abraham S. Pvt.	3 WVI	10/12/61–7/8/65
Blankenship, Levi Pvt.	4 WVI	6/16/61–3/64
Board, Andrew J. Pvt.	11 WVI	10/24/61–8/14/65
Bonnett, Martin Pvt.	9 WVI	11/61–7/65
Boon, Nathan Pvt.	4 WVC	3/11/64–NF
Boone, Andrew H. Pvt.	4 WVC	6/30/63–8/1/65
Boso, James W. Pvt.	36 OHI	9/17/61–8/27/65
Boso, Silvester G. Pvt.	4 WVI	7/61–8/64
Boute, Henry Pvt.	2 WVC	10/63–7/64
Bowen, Ezra Pvt.	4 WVI	7/20/61–8/29/64
Boyce, Marcellus S. Pvt.	6 WVI	10/15/61–6/10/65
Boyd, E. Pvt.	17 PAC	62/65
Boyer, Solomon S. Pvt.	58 OHI	12/4/61–9/16/65
Braden, Samuel Pvt.	11 WVI	7/17/62–6/17/65
Brannon, Lorenzo D. Pvt.	—	8/21/64–5/20/65
Brooks, Samuel G. Pvt.	25 OHI	6/26/61–6/18/66
Brooks, Wm. Pvt.	170 OHI	5/64–9/11/64
Brownell, George W. Sgt.	4 WVC	7/63–3/64
Buchannan, Wm. Pvt.	11 WVI	8/30/64–6/30/65
Buckelew, James Pvt.	11 VAI	10/6/62–7/7/65
Buffington, Wm. Sgt.	11 WVI	1861–NF
Bull, Reson H. Lt.	92 OHI	8/8/62–6/30/65
Bumgardner, John Pvt.	7 WVC	7/27/61–8/16/65
Burns, Joseph T. Pvt.	62 PAI	7/4/61–11/21/62
Calvert, Marchel Pvt.	11 WVI	11/1/61–8/9/65
Calwill, Howard Pvt.	2 OHC	7/61–2/63
Campbell, J.H. Pvt.	4 PAC	8/16/62–7/12/65
Canter, Jonas Pvt.	9 WVI	2/9/62–2/5/65
Carl, Daniel	NF	
Carl, John M. Pvt.	63 OHI	61/62
Carll, Wm. T. Pvt.	9 VAI	1/1/62–1/1/64
also	1 VAI	1/1/64–7/31/65
Carpenter, A. Pvt.	60 VAI CSA	9/1/62–6/10/65
Casto, David Pvt.	9 WVI	1/30/62–1/30/65
Casto, G.W. Pvt.	8 WVI	1/64–8/1/65
Casto, G.W. Sr. Pvt.	13 WVI	9/13/63–6/22/65
Casto, J.H. Pvt.	8 WVC	2/1/61–10/1/65
Casto, Jacob B. Pvt.	9 WVC	6/10/64–11/15/65
Casto, James Pvt.	8 WVI	2/1/64–8/1/65
Casto, Jonathan H. Pvt.	13 WVI	5/17/63–5/65
Casto, Mark Pvt.	9 WVI	2/22/62–2/22/65
Casto, Mason Pvt.	13 WVI	8/6/62–6/14/65
Casto, N.L. Cpl.	7 WVC	10/1/61–8/1/65
Cattrell, Henry M. Pvt.	7 WVC	3/20/64–8/1/65
Chambers, Z.T. Pvt	61 PAI	8/20/61–1865
Chancey, John Cpl.	9 WVI	11/21/61–1/1/63

Chaney, Ranswell Pvt.	9 VAI	2/1/64–7/1/65
Chevront, James M. Pvt.	4 WVC	NF
Chisslin, Samuel P. Pvt.	62 OHI	10/61–1862
also	7 OHC	1/2/64–6/29/65
Ciders, G.H. Cpl.	7 WVC	9/15/61–8/9/65
Ciders, J.P. Pvt.	7 WVC	2/2/65–8/1/65
Clark, James W. Pvt.	12 WVI	8/13/62–7/2/65
Cleek, Francis M.	NF	
Cleek, P.E. Sgt.	9 WVC	11/1/61–1/30/64
Cline, Theodore P. Pvt.	187 OHI	2/14/65–6/20/65
Cobb, Hiram Pvt.	9 WVI	2/2/62–8/1/65
Cobb, J.M. Cpl.	9 WVI	2/28/62–2/28/65
Cochran, James E. Pvt.	4 WVC	6/12/62–3/11/63
Coe, Lisander M. Cpl.	11 WVI	8/14/62–6/26/65
Comer, Noah M. Pvt.	8 WVI	11/1/61–8/28/63
Compston, Alex Pvt.	9 WVI	9/1/61–7/21/65
Compston, John Pvt.	9 WVI	9/1/61–3/1/63
Conger, E.D. Pvt.	9 VAI	2/19/62–2/19/65
Conner, John S.	NF	
Conner, John W. Pvt.	155 ILI	2/25/65–9/18/65
Cooper, Artemus Cpl.	53 KYI	3/18/65–9/15/65
Cooper, Wm. Pvt.	22 KYI	9/61–6/10/65
Cooper, Wm. W. Pvt.	11 WVI	8/31/62–9/15/64
Cougnor, Jasper M. Pvt.	6 WVI	2/29/64–1865
Craig, Samuel Pvt.	12 WVI	8/13/62–6/16/65
Crihfield, W.B. Pvt.	14 OHC	61/64
Crites, Wm. H. Pvt.	7 VAC	8/29/64–6/3/65
Cunningham, Allison Sgt.	15 WVI	8/22/62–6/29/65
Cunningham, Benj. R. Lt.	16 INA	11/28/62–7/25/65
Cunningham, Elias Pvt.	NF	
Cunningham, Isiah Pvt.	9 WVI	10/7/61–7/21/65
Dailey, Aaron Pvt.	115 OHI	10/16/64–6/8/65
Davis, Aaron W. Lt.	3 WVC	11/21/62–6/30/65
Davis, James W. Pvt.	18 OHI	4/28/61–9/64
Davis, Marcean Pvt.	NF (17 VAC CSA)	
Davis, S.F. Pvt.	4 WVI	7/3/61–7/8/65
Dearman, A. Pvt.	11 WVI	9/1/63–6/10/65
Delaney, John H. Pvt.	43 OHI	6/64–7/65
Delaney, Wm. Pvt.	194 OHI	2/25/65–10/24/65
Deniberger, George P. Cpl.	11 WVI	8/14/62–6/22/65
Depal, Daniel D. Pvt.	11 WVI	9/63–8/65
Dewees, Wm. J. Pvt.	11 WVI	8/14/62–6/27/65
Dixon, James Pvt.	- USI	10/6/64–11/6/65
Donelson, Alexander W.	4 PAC	5/23/65–NF
Donohue, Daniel D. Pvt.	4 WVC	8/30/63–3/11/64
Donohue, James Pvt.	75 OHI	12/9/61–8/9/62
Dopp, David Pvt.	26 NYC	2/16/65–7/3/65

Name	Unit	Dates
Dotson, James Pvt.	39 OHI	12/27/64–6/14/65
Draggoo, E.W.	NF (20 VAC CSA)	
Drick, George W. Pvt.	11 WVI	8/8/62–6/17/65
Dudgeon, James M. Pvt.	11 WVI	8/16/62–6/17/65
Dulin, Kingsbury Pvt.	11 WVI	7/3/62–6/17/65
Easlep, Benj. F. Sgt.	7 WVC	10/15/61–8/1/65
Edwards, John C. Pvt.	66 OHI	12/25/61–12/7/65
Ellis, Eathen Pvt.	2 OHA	6/27/63–8/23/65
Ent?, Wm. A. Pvt.	Wilder Battery	5/27/61–6/11/64
Escue, Wm. Pvt.	7 WVI	65/65
Evans, James Pvt.	CSA (129 VAM)	9/9/62–5/12/65
Ewing, Joel Pvt.	NF	
Faber, Wm. F. Pvt.	3 WVC	8/29/63–7/10/65
Farley, James S. Pvt.	176 OHI	8/27/64–6/14/65
Finch, Wm. Pvt.	-WVI	4/13/61–6/18/65
Fish, B.F. Pvt.	1 WVI	10/17/61–NF
Fisher, Martin Pvt.	8 WVI	7/2/61–1/31/64
Fisher, Samuel Pvt.	3 WVC	8/9/63–6/30/65
Flesher, Henry C. Major	5 VAC	6/28/61–7/1/63
Flowers, John W. Pvt.	4 WVI	10/7/61–7/12/65
Franklin, John Pvt.	18 OHI	61/64
Fulton, Samuel Pvt.	77 OHI	10/2/61–3/8/66
Gardner, John H. Lt.	15 INI	5/61–8/24/64
Garnes, Jackson Pvt.	3 WVC	8/9/63–7/20/65
Garnes, Vincent E. Pvt.	7 VAC	2/25/64–8/1/65
Garrett, James H. Cpl.	7 WVC	11/12/61–8/1/65
Gasten, Olin C. Pvt.	39 OHI	3/10/65–7/10/65
Gatchel, Charles S. Cpl.	11 WVI	8/31/62–NF
Gibbs, Prescott B. Pvt.	39 OHI	1/19/61–2/3/62
Gillispie, Joseph Pvt.	11 WVI	8/14/62–6/17/65
Gilpin, Alfred B. Sgt.	11 WVI	8/11/62–4/13/65
Givens, Oliver Sgt.	92 OHI	2/1/64–7/20/65
Godby, J. Pvt.	7 VAC? CSA	11/1/61–1/30/65
Good, John W. Pvt.	13 WVI	8/12/62–6/26/65
Gorrell, Abraham Pvt.	3 WVC	5/25/63–7/28/65
Gorrell, Stephen Pvt.	3 WVC	2/25/63–6/25/65
Gorrell, Thomas Pvt.	3 WVC	2/3/63–6/30/65
Gould, Wm. H. Cpl.	6 WVC	9/3/64–5/19/65
Granden, Wm. Pvt.	186 OHI	1/19/65–9/18/65
Grayson, Wm. Pvt.	9 WVI	4/21/63–7/21/65
Greenlee, Morris C.	Gunboat Alice	9/27/64–3/1/65
Griffiths, James W. Cpl.	7 WVI	3/7/65–7/1/65
Grimes, G.S. Pvt.	NF	
Gruber, David Pvt.	40 OHI	8/20/62–6/27/65
Hall, Bazel Pvt.	3 WVC	9/62–8/63
Hall, Henry Pvt.	3 WVC	9/62–1865
Hamilton, John Pvt.	11 WVI	3/30/62–6/17/65

Name	Unit	Dates
Hamrick, Mark B. Pvt.	9 WVI	9/16/61–10/5/64
Harfoold, Lemeul Major	13 VAI	8/9/62–6/23/65
Hargrove, John Pvt.	8 MNI	8/20/62–8/1/65
Harpold, J.A. Pvt.	9 VAC	12/1/61–7/1/65
Harris, D.E. Pvt.	45 PAI	3/65–12/65
Harrison, G.W.H. Pvt.	7 WVC	11/1/61–8/1/65
Harrison, Henderson Pvt.	7 WVC	10/61–8/65
Harvey, James E. Pvt.	NF	
Hassler, Ferdinand R. Col.	6 NYA	1861–8/65
Hawk, Adam Pvt.	6 KSI	NF
Hawk, Solomon F. Pvt.	2 WVC	8/61–7/65
Hebussy, Adolphus Pvt.	4 WVI	7/25/61–8/22/64
Hendershot, Brown	NF	
Henderson, James A. Pvt.	— WVI	10/62–8/9/65
Herenberger, E. Pvt.	4 WVC	NF
Hickell, Wm. G. Pvt.	11 VAI	8/14/61–6/17/65
Hickman, M. Pvt.	27 OHC	6/1/61–6/1/65
Hill, Felix M. Pvt.	5 WVC	6/16/61–6/16/64
Holey, John W. Cpl.	7 OHA	12/15/61–1862
Holland, Wm. A. Pvt.	77 OHI	2/15/64–3/26/66
Hopkins, Wm. B. Pvt.	11 VAI	8/15/62–5/27/65
Horne, James E. Pvt.	9 VAI	12/6/61–7/21/65
Horne, John H.P. Pvt.	9 VAI	12/7/61–7/21/65
Houston, George A. Pvt.	28 OHI	1864–7/65
Houston, John A. Pvt.	25 OHI	6/28/61–1864
Huffin, Marian Pvt.	20 OHI	2/65–7/65
Hunter, Andrew J. Pvt.	13 WVI	6/22/62–9/13/65
Hunter, J. Pvt.	6 WVI	9/61–1865
Hupp, Casey Pvt.	92 OHI	8/6/62–6/10/65
Hurd, Jacob S. Pvt.	116 OHI	8/19/62–6/30/65
Iman, J.E. Sgt.	7 WVC	7/21/61–8/1/65
Jarrott, Cyrous Pvt.	179 OHI	9/16/64–6/17/65
Jenkins, John Pvt.	7 WVI	2/65–7/3/65
Johns, (Wm.) L. Pvt.	19 VAC CSA	10/1/62–6/1/65
Johnson, Peter W. Pvt.	1 WVI	2/9/64–11/17/65
Jones, Enos Pvt.	18 OHI	1861–2/8/64
Jordan, Wm. Pvt.	63 OHI	10/1/61–7/28/65
Kedden, Uriah Pvt.	116 OHI	1/4/64–6/15/65
Keefer, Benj. F. Pvt.	7 WVC	1/4/62–8/1/65
Keel, Solomon Pvt.	3 WVC	9/12/62–6/12/65
Kelbaugh, Joseph Pvt.	20 OHI	4/62–7/65
Kennedy, John Pvt.	27 OHI	7/19/64–9/21/65
Kerns, G. Pvt.	1 WVI	11/1/64–8/1/65
Kessel, Abraham Pvt.	13 WVI	12/1/63–6/22/65
Keyes, Henry Pvt.	38 OHI	63/65
Kimes, Samuel R. Pvt.	13 WVI	8/15/62–6/25/65
King, Dixon R. Capt.	11 WVI	11/1/61–1/29/65

King, John W. Lt.	11 WVI	3/20/62–6/17/65
King, John W. Pvt.	4 WVC	7/10/62–3/10/64
King, Winfield S. Pvt.	11 WVI	1861–8/9/65
Knopp, Henry Pvt.	VAC CSA (17)	6/15/62–7/4/65
Knox, Samuel Pvt.	6 WVC	1862–1/4/64
Koonts, Edwin G. Pvt.	7 WVC	8/27/64–6/3/65
Lane, John S. Cpl.	11 WVI	8/14/62–6/17/65
Lane, Washington Pvt.	4 WVI	9/61–10/64
Lanham, Aberham Pvt.	7 WVC	4/14/61–8/28/65
Lanham, John N. Pvt.	13 WVI	10/1/63–6/22/65
Lathem, Elias A. Pvt.	11 WVI	6/16/62–6/16/65
Lathem, W.F. Pvt.	7 WVC	2/20/65–8/2/65
Lee, Charles H. Cpl.	30 OHI	7/25/61–8/13/65
Lemley, Thomas H.A. Lt.	1 WVC	7/18/61–7/8/65
Lewis, Ring Pvt.	26 OHI	8/62–NF
Lewis, Wm. Pvt.	7 WVC	3/9/65–7/1/65
Linscott, A.W. Pvt.	11 ILI	7/3/61–6/9/63
Litton, John J. Pvt.	13 WVC	11/20/63–8/20/65
Lloyd, N.S. Pvt.	4 WVC	6/8/63–3/11/64
Lloyd, Wm. Pvt.	9 WVI	2/9/62–NF
Lmoey?, Wm. Pvt.	75 OHI	11/25/61–7/26/65
Logston, John E. Pvt.	11 WVI	1/5/64–8/9/65
Love, John M. Sgt.	11 WVI	8/14/62–6/1/65
Lucicom, Levi Pvt.	62 OHI	3/9/64–6/9/65
Ludwig, Daniel Pvt.	116 OHI	1/1/63–5/14/65
Lynch, James	NF (31 VAI CSA?)	
Lytle, Uriah Lt.	11 WVI	6/28/62–12/26/64
Mahan, Richard G. Cpl.	11 WVI	8/14/62–6/28/65
Mahon, John 11. Pvt.	7 WVC	9/4/64–6/3/65
Manges, Chester B. Pvt.	4 WVI	9/15/62–8/9/65
Mason, Perry Pvt.	4 WVI	7/4/61–7/16/65
Masters, Thomas Pvt.	161 OHI	5/63–3/65
Mayse, J.H. Pvt.	27 VAI CSA	10/1/61–6/1/65
McBride, Samuel Cpl.	20 OHI	12/16/61–12/19/64
also Sgt.	186 OHI	1/19/65–9/18/65
McBrien, Henry Cpl.	11 WVI	9/14/62–6/24/65
McCollins, Daniel Pvt.	77 OHI	12/61–12/64
McCord, Arthur Pvt.	7 WVI	12/15/61–12/24/64
McDonough, Enoch C. Pvt.	7 IAI	3/31/64–7/22/65
McGraw, J.W. Pvt.	9 WVI	2/29/64–7/21/65
McGrew, J.P. Pvt.	7 WVC	11/11/64–8/1/65
McKinley, James Sgt.	11 WVI	8/14/62–6/17/65
McKitrich, David H. Pvt.	129 OHI	8/2/63–3/5/64
McKoy, James R. Pvt.	13 WVI	11/10/63–6/21/65
McLaughlin, J.L. Pvt.	11 WVI	3/3/62–6/14/65
McMurray, John L. Pvt.	3 WVC	9/61–10/8/62
also	9 WVI	2/12/63 6/30/65

Name	Unit	Dates
McMurray, Wm. Pvt.	9 WVI	11/26/61–12/31/63
also Cpl.	1 WVI	1/1/64–7/21/65
McPherson, Jesse Pvt.	4 WVC	7/20/63–3/11/—
McPherson, Joseph Pvt.	186 OHI	2/13/65–9/18/65
McRay, Edgar M. Pvt.	4 WVC	7/63–7/7/65
Menear, Daniel F. Pvt.	4 VAI	7/15/61–6/9/65
Mercer, H.H. Pvt.	9 WVI	9/17/61–6/18/64
Michell, Ezekiel Pvt.	6 WVC	1/15/62–7/15/65
Miller, Bartlett F. Pvt.	7 WVC	NF
Miller, Bob Pvt.	13 OHI	62/64
Miller, Hampten Pvt.	9 WVI	3/6/62–5/5/65
Miller, J.J. Pvt.	12 OHC	8/1/61–8/1/64
Miller, John Pvt.	13 VAI	8/16/62–6/22/65
Miller, Monroe Sgt.	4 WVC	6/6/63–3/11/64
Miller, Perry Pvt.	11 WVI	8/6/62–6/6/65
Moore, Charles Pvt.	CSA (18 VAC?)	2/1/65–7/27/65
Moore, James W. Pvt.	9 VAI	NF
Moore, Nathan Pvt.	116 OHI	8/11/64–6/14/65
Moors, Mordecai Pvt.	128 INI	3/11/64–8/4/65
Moran, Robert Pvt.	176 OHI	8/10/64–6/23/65
Morgan, David S. Pvt.	7 OHC	9/20/62–7/3/65
Morgan, James B. Cpl.	11 WVI	2/26/63–8/9/65
Morgan, Ralph S. Pvt.	15 WVI	3/18/62–5/29/65
Morris, Joab Pvt.	13 VAI	12/26/63–6/8/65
Morris, Thomas Pvt.	3 WVC	9/10/62–1/22/65
Morson, Joseph Pvt.	176 OHI	8/23/64–6/14/65
Mounday, John R. Pvt.	8 WVI	2/1/64–8/1/65
Mourhouse, Chasin C. Pvt.	36 OHI	2/20/65–7/27/65
Mourhouse, Josiah P. Pvt.	4 WVI	7/15/61–7/65
Mullinex, Jason Pvt.	11 WVI	8/22/62–6/26/65
Myre, Arjalon P. Pvt.	146 OHNG	5/2/64–9/7/64
Neff, John A. Pvt.	- INA	1/64–8/10/65
Nichols, John W. Pvt.	2 MEC	11/2/62–12/6/65
Odell, John Pvt.	6 WVI	7/4/61–8/16/64
Ohse, Wm. Pvt.	4 WVI	7/10/63–3/11/64
Orem, Henson Pvt.	10 WVI	7/1/63–8/9/65
Osburn, George Pvt.	1 WVC	3/63–7/8/65
Painter, Barney Pvt.	7 WVC	2/22/61–8/1/65
Parson, A.R. Pvt.	3 WVC	8/9/63–6/30/65
Parsons, F. Pvt.	11 WVI	NF
Parsons, G.W. Pvt.	8 WVI	8/1/61–7/16/65
Parsons, Hirram Pvt.	11 VAI	8/14/62–6/6/65
Parsons, John Pvt.	3 WVC	8/9/62–7/1/65
Patterson, O. Pvt.	7 WVC	4/1/64–7/12/65
Patterson, James Pvt.	11 WVI	7/22/62–6/17/65
Payne, John Pvt.	6 WVI	1/15/62–7/15/65
Peden, John Cpl.	36 OHI	8/12/61–7/25/65

Name	Unit	Dates
Peppers, Alfred Pvt.	186 OHI	2/4/65–9/18/65
Pernell, Meredith A. Pvt.	11 VAI	7/30/62–7/4/65
Peters, Michael M. Pvt.	185 OHI	2/6/65–9/26/65
Petty, J.A. Musician	6 WVI	8/61–10/64
Phillips, Andy J. Pvt.	11 WVI	11/2/61–8/9/65
Pickering, Charles R. Pvt.	11 WVI	10/26/61–11/11/64
Powers, Wm. Pvt.	11 WVI	8/18/62–6/25/65
Pratt, James G. Pvt.	134 OHI	3/23/65–7/19/65
Pratt, John Pvt.	7 VAI	8/61–2/13/63
Priddy, John W. Pvt.	4 WVI	7/25/61–7/22/65
Priddy, W.B. Pvt.	4 WVI	7/25/61–8/26/64
Pringle, Barzilid M. Pvt.	11 WVI	8/31/62–6/31/65
Pruden, W.M. Cpl.	4 WVC	3/11/64–NF
Rains, George W. Pvt.	10 WVI	11/11/61–3/17/65
Rake, John A. Pvt.	NF	
Rand, Kinsey Pvt.	4 WVI	7/25/61 8/26/64
Randolph, C. Pvt.	7 WVI	9/10/64 8/2/65
Rankins, Thomas B. Pvt.	-WVI	8/14/62–6/28/65
Rankins, Thomas J. Cpl.	11 VAI	8/14/61–6/17/65
Rarden, Thomas Pvt.	11 WVI	8/20/62–6/29/65
Rawlings, George W. Pvt.	7 WVC	8/8/64–6/25/65
Ray, J.M. Pvt.	8 WVI	10/1/61–6/1/65
Redding, Charles Pvt.	1 WVC	8/30/61–12/30/65
Redding, W.H. Cpl.	11 WVI	8/18/62–6/65
Redman, James W. Pvt.	7 WVI	NF
Reed, Henry N. Sgt.	2 WVC	7/5/61–7/4/65
Rhodes, Abijah Pvt.	13 WVI	8/13/62–6/22/65
Rhodes, Ira Pvt.	39 OHI	3/23/65–7/9/65
Rhodes, Solomon D. Pvt.	13 WVC	8/20/63–11/20/65
Ridenour, Benj. J. Pvt.	9 WVI	2/9/62–8/24/65
Riell, Daniel B. Pvt.	193 OHI	3/6/65–NF
Riffle, David Pvt.	9 WVI	2/20/62–7/30/65
Riley, Millard F. Pvt.	7 WVC	2/8/65–8/1/65
Robinson, Benj. Pvt.	36 OHI	4/61–6/1/65
Robison, Allen Pvt.	4 VAI	9/15/61–7/15/65
Robison, John A. Pvt.	176 OHI	8/22/64–6/14/65
Rodgers, Ashbel T. Pvt.	3 WVI	6/21/61–8/15/64
Rodgers, George W. Pvt.	9 WVI	9/15/61–7/18/65
Roseberry, J.L. Sgt.	9 WVI	12/25/61–1/1/65
Rowan, Archibald Pvt.	11 WVI	9/1/62–6/29/65
Rowley, G.C. Pvt.	11 WVI	8/62–6/9/65
Rowley, H.C. Pvt.	4 WVI	7/25/61–8/26/64
Ruben, Cooper Pvt.	11 WVI	8/14/62–6/17/65
Safereed, B.F. Pvt.	4 WVI	2/20/62–2/12/64
Safreed, Wm. L. Pvt.	4 WVI	7/12/61–7/18/65
Sands, Alexander Pvt.	186 OHI	2/4/65–9/18/65
Sarver, David H. Pvt.	75 OHI	9/1/62–1/31/65

Sayre, Andrew J. Pvt.	11 WVI	8/2/62–3/30/64
Sayre, Isaac Pvt.	2 WVI	5/1/64–7/18/65
Sayre, Lafayette Pvt.	7 VAC	2/10/64–8/10/65
Sayre, Robert F. Pvt.	92 OHI	8/8/62–1/13/65
Shafer, Jacob C. Pvt.	1 VAI	10/17/64–6/10/65
Shamblin, Thadeus Pvt.	7 WVC	3/25/64–8/65
Shank, Calvin C. Pvt.	13 WVI	12/11/63–6/22/65
Sharp, Granville E. Pvt.	141 OHI	5/2/64–9/3/64
Shatto, Philip Pvt.	4 WVC	7/15/63–3/20/64
Shaver, Henry Pvt.	11 WVI	7/62–6/18/65
Shepherd, Francis M. Cpl.	1 WVI	9/19/61–7/25/65
Shepherd, McDonald Pvt.	2 WVI	2/16/65–7/20/65
Shepherd, Wm. Pvt.	1 VAI	4/19/61–11/24/64
Shine, Nehemiah S. Pvt.	13 WVI	8/8/62–6/22/65
Shinn, Charles P. Cpl.	9 WVI	3/62–6/65
Silket, M. Pvt.	7 WVC	2/2/65–8/10/65
Simons, Thomas J. Pvt.	11 WVI	NF
Skidmore, A.S. Pvt.	13 VAI	1/1/64–6/22/65
Skinner, Joel Pvt.	11 WVI	8/7/62–6/17/65
Slaughter, David P. Pvt.	13 VAI	8/4/63–NF
Slaughter, Elijah Pvt.	11 WVI	8/22/62–6/27/65
Slaughter, F.M. Pvt.	9 WVI	12/1/61–12/17/64
Slaughter, John J.C. Pvt.	—	1/6/64–5/6/64
Slaughter, Wm. B. Pvt.	9 VAI	2/2/62–7/23/65
Smith, Charles Pvt.	25 OHI	6/4/61–8/13/62
Smith, Cummings Pvt.	11 WVI	11/1/61–12/26/64
Smith, David Pvt.	3 VAC	8/15/62–7/14/65
Smith, David Pvt.	9 WVI	2/22/62–2/28/65
Smith, George W. Cpl.	16 OHI	7/62–4/65
Smith, Henderson M. Sgt.	1 WVC	9/9/61–7/19/65
Smith, Williams Pvt.	17 WVI	9/64–8/65
Smith, Wyatte Pvt.	13 WVI	8/12/62–6/20/65
Snider, Michael Pvt.	13 VAI	9/10/63–6/22/65
Snider, Thomas H. Pvt.	73 OHI	8/31/62–4/17/65
Snodgrass, Silas W. Cpl.	6 WVI	8/12/61–8/12/64
Southal, Alexander F. Pvt.	13 OHC	3/28/64–8/17/65
Staats, Rudolf Pvt.	11 WVI	8/14/62–NF
Starcher, L. Pvt.	7 WVC	7/21/61–8/1/65
Stephens, Francis M. Pvt.	92 OHI	8/9/62–6/10/65
Stevens, Wm. Pvt.	4 VAI	7/2/61–9/15/63
Stewart, Elisha Pvt.	13 VAI	1/4/64–6/25/65
Stewart, Enoch Pvt.	9 VAI	3/4/62–3/4/65
Stewart, Lemeul C. Pvt.	9 WVI	10/14/61–NF
Stoats, Benj. Pvt.	4 VAC	8/1/63–3/1/64
Stoats, George W. Pvt.	4 WVC	7/10/63–3/11/64
Stone, James F. Pvt.	4 WVI	7/25/61–7/18/65
Summerfield, Thomas Lt.	70 INI	7/61–6/65

Name	Unit	Dates
Sutton, H.H. Pvt.	25 OHI	7/27/61–12/18/66
Swain, James Sgt.	13 WVI	9/23/63–6/25/65
Swain, Numan Pvt.	13 WVI	9/20/62–7/27/65
Swartwood, Levi Pvt.	1 OHA	11/15/61–1/15/65
Thomas, A.C. Pvt.	9 WVI	2/1/61–7/1/65
Thomas, Calvin H. Pvt.	4 WVI	6/18/61–7/4/64
Thomas, Enoch W. Pvt.	100 PAI	8/29/61–8/29/64
Thomas, George W. Pvt.	7 WVC	7/27/61–8/1/65
Thomas, John Pvt.	176 OHI	8/27/64–6/14/65
Thomas, Peter P. Pvt.	13 WVI	10/1/63–6/25/65
Thomas, Wm. A. Pvt.	13 WVI	8/22/62–6/22/65
Tidd, Samuel Pvt.	116 OHI	8/15/62–7/15/65
Tribett, George W. Pvt.	63 OHI	9/61–1/62
Tuttle, John Pvt.	15 WVC	6/10/61–9/9/65
Walker, Francis Pvt.	39 OHI	5/10/61–7/22/65
Wallace, Isaac M. Pvt.	80 OHI	2/24/64–8/13/65
Wallis, Andrew W. Pvt.	25 OHI	7/8/61–7/26/64
Walls, George W. Pvt.	23 OHI	9/4/63–7/26/65
Warfield, Nelson D. Pvt.	20 OHI	12/16/64–2/27/65
Warner, George R. Pvt.	10 WVI	10/2/61–10/20/64
Waterman, Marvin Pvt.	23 OHI	11/3/64–4/16/65
Watkins, Francis M. Pvt.	NF	
Watts, Wm. G. Pvt.	11 WVI	8/28/62–6/27/65
Waundling, Adam Pvt.	63 OHI	10/3/61–2/6/63
Weakley, Levi Pvt.	66 OHI	1862–7/7/65
Webb, John G. Pvt.	10 WVI	1/29/64–8/9/65
West, Robert W. Pvt.	NF	
West, Stephen A. Pvt.	77 OHI	11/61–12/16/63
also	18 OHI	3/28/64–10/29/65
Whetstone, Sam H. Pvt.	4 WVI	6/61–7/65
White, J.M. Pvt.	20 OHI	2/29/64–7/15/65
White, John C. Pvt.	11 WVI	8/14/62–6/17/65
White, John J. Cpl.	13 WVI	12/15/62–6/22/65
Whitney, George W. Pvt.	137 NYI	9/10/64–5/10/65
Wickley, Benj. Pvt.	32 OHI?	64/65
Williams, Daniel S. Pvt.	77 OHI	10/2/61–3/8/66
Williams, James A. Pvt.	130 INI	1/1/63–9/1/65
Williams, W.W. Pvt.	17 VAC CSA	4/1/62–3/1/63
Williamson, James W. Capt.	11 WVI	8/20/62–3/20/65
Williamson, John M. Pvt.	9 WVI	2/14/62–2/15/65
Williamson, Wm. Pvt.	4 WVI	7/16/61–8/25 64
Wilson, George J. Cpl.	17 WVI	8/30/64–6/30/65
Wimer, John Pvt.	16 PAC	2/20/65–8/11/65
Winten, Clark Sgt.	194 OHI	3/1/61–11/4/65
Wise, Thomas, W. Pvt.	13 WVI	12/20/63–5/29/65
Wolf, John W. Sgt.	7 WVC	11/12/61–8/65
Wolf, Wm. H. Pvt.	13 WVI	8/16/62–6/25/65

Woodruff, Wm. Pvt.	73 OHI	NF
Woods, James F. Pvt.	11 WVI	NF
Worley, Jacob Pvt.	194 OHI?	3/65–11/65
Wright, Charles C. Cpl.	126 NYI	7/22/62–11/62
Wright, Harrison Pvt.	6 WVI	9/3/64–6/10/65
Yates, E. W. Pvt.	1 WVC	61/62
Yates, Warren M. Pvt.	43 OHI	3/62–7/65
Young, David Pvt.	7 OHC	10/1/62–NF
Zeper, Samuel Pvt.	110 OHI	4/64–9/64

Jackson County Remarks

Abbott, J.D.—deafness from measles
Adams, I.M.—chronic costiveness
Adams, W.A.S.—bronchitis & HD
Alvis, J.W.—gunshot wound left shoulder
Amos, F.M.—pleurisy & rupture
Anderson, B.—CDR
Anderson, C.M.—hand iniured bY horse
Antill, J.—RH
Archer, J.C.—crippled in knee
Arnold, L.A.—gunshot wound right shoulder
Ashby, T.—gunshot wound
Aten, P.—CDR
Bachus, G.W.—RH & piles
Baleh, S.—eye disease
Barber, S.L.—RH & catarrh
Barnett, K.—LD
Barnett, P.—hurt in right testicle
Barnheart, J.L.—gunshot wound right knee
Bartlett, D.W.—RH & piles
Bates, G.W.—deaf left ear, piles
Batton, A.—gunshot left side
Beaver, P.—gunshot wound
Begal, D.—ruptured
Bereslin, G.—right leg shot off
Black, J.H.—RH
Blagg, A.S.—ID
Blankenship, L.—spinal & kidney disease
Board, A.J.—CDR & HD
Boone, A.H.—dyspepsia
Boute, H.—ruptured
Boyer, S.S.—WIA right arm
Braden, S.—deaf left ear
Brooks, S.G.—RH & wolmds

Brooks, W.—dispepsia
Buckelew, J.—liver disease
Bull, R.H.—KD
Burns, J.T.—gunshot wound right arm
Campbell, J.H.—bleeding piles, now nearly disabled
Canter, J.—gunshot through both cheeks
Carl, J.M.—stomach disease
Carll, W.T.—bronchitis
Carpenter, A.*—gunshot wound of leg
Casto, D.—thumb shot off
Casto, G.W. Sr.—hernia
Casto, J.H.—HD & LD
Casto, M.—gunshot wound
Casto, M.—pleurisy
Cattrell, H.M.—RH & MS
Chambers, Z.T.—WIA left foot
Chancey, J.—RH
Chisslin, S.P.—gunshot wound left hand
Ciders, G.H.—shell wound right shoulder
Clark, J.W.—gunshot wound right side
Coe, L.M.—RH & HD
Conger, E.D.—gunshot left leg, now suffering RH, eyes, dropsy
Cooper, A.—HD, eyelid granulated
Cooper, W.—liver disease
Cooper, W.W.—St Anthonys disease (?)
Crites, W.H.—cold in head & eyes
Cunningham, B.—RH
Cunningham, E.—hurt in left leg
Cunningham, I.—piles
Davis, A.W.—gunshot wound right wrist
Davis, J.W.—MS
Dearman, A.—gunshot wound
Depal, D.D.—spinal trouble & CDR
Dixon, J.—RH
Donelson, A.W.—CDR, hard of hearing
Donohue, D.D.—feet frozen
Donohue, J.—two fingers shot off right hand
Dopp, D.—old & feeble
Drick, G.W.—injured by shell
Dudgeon, J.M.—gunshot wound left arm
Dulin, K.—right thumb shot off
Easlep, B.F.—CDR & TYF
Edwards, J.C.—hemorrhoids & wounds
Ent, W.A.—piles
Escue, W.—nervous trouble
Ewing, J.—catarrh & piles
Finch, W.—piles & CDR

Fish, B.F.—POW Libby 6 months & 4 days
Fisher, M.—RH
Fisher, S.—RH
Flesher, H.C.—RH
Flowers, J.W.—CDR
Garnes, J.—apoplexy & RH
Garnes, V.E.—RH
Garrett, J.H.—general disability
Gatchel, C.S.—gunshot wound left leg
Gillispie, J.—catarrh & RH
Gilpin, A.B.—injury to right hip joint
Godby, J.*—gunshot wound in hand
Gorrell, A.—lump in stomach
Gorrell, S.—loss of left eye
Gorrell, T.—loss of left eye
Gould, W.H.—POW Richmond 3 months
Grayson, W.—CDR
Greenlee, M.C.—catarrh in head
Griffiths, J.W.—LD, catarrh, RH
Grimes, G.S.—hernia
Gruber, D.—left shoulder & breast injury, RH & HD
Hall, B.—rupture
Hall, H.—rupture
Hamilton, J.—RH
Hamrick, M.B.—deafness
Harpold, J.A.—gunshot wound
Harqrove, J.—CDR & piles
Harris, D.E.—black
Harrison, G.W.H.—CDR & LD
Hawk, S.F.—crushed by fall of horse, lost testicle
Henderson, J.A.—RH
Hickell, W.G.—CDR & sore eyes, disease of rectum
Hickman, M.—flesh wound
Holland, W.A.—RH, piles, constipation, POW Tyler Texas 311 days
Hopkins, W.B.—asthma & 2 flesh wounds
Horne, J.E.—liver & stomach trouble
Horne, J.H.P.—RH, piles, indigestion
Houston, G.A.—RH
Houston, J.A.—crippled left hip
Hunter, A.J.—gunshot wound
Hurd, J.S.—wounded
Iman, J.E.—mashed foot
Jenkins, J.—black
Kelbaugh, J.—MS
Kessel, A.—piles
Keyes, H.—RH & HD
King, D.R.—CDR

King, J.W.—CDR, LD, HD
Knopp, H.*—RH
Koonts, E.G.—feet frozen
Lane, J.S.—crippled right arm & shoulder
Lane, W.—sight badly impaired
Lathem, W.F.—loss of left eye
Lee, C.H.—WIA twice
Lewis, W.—eye disease
Linscott, A.W.—loss of left eye
Ludwig, D.—HD
Lytle, U.—RH & HD
Mahan, R.G.—RH both legs & left shoulder
Mahon, J.H.—RH & catarrh, left arm injured by horse kick
McBride, S.—gunshot wound left foot
McBrien, H.—gunshot wound left thigh
McCollins, D.—hurt in back
McCord, A.—partial deafness
McGrew, J.P.—hernia
McKoy, J.R.—gunshot right arm
McLaughlin, J.L.—WIA right hip
McMurray, J.L.—WIA breast, right shoulder, left arm, right leg
McRay, E.M.—liver & kidney disease
Menear, D.F.—wounded through both hips
Mercer, H.H.—blind & helpless
Miller, B.—stomach disease
Miller, J.—RH & wound left hand
Miller, M.—deafness
Miller, P.—disabled left shoulder
Moore, C.*—bronchitis & deafness
Moore, J.W.—weak eyes
Moore, N.—stomach disease
Morgan, D.S.—RH
Morgan, R.S.—WIA right arm, totally disabled
Morris, J.—piles & disease of rectum
Morris, T.—RH
Mullinex, J.—nervous prostrations & rupture
Neff, J.A.—HD & KD, ruptured also
Nichols, J.W.—RH
Ohse, W.—LD
Osburn, G.—RH
Painter, B.—pluracy left side
Parsons, F.—shot in forehead
Parsons, H.—CDR, weak back, KD
Parsons, J.—gunshot wound in thigh
Peden, J.—gunshot wound in left side of head
Pernell, M.A.—eye disease
Phillips, A.J.—gunshot wound abdomen, forearm & hand

Powers, W.—gunshot wound right side
Pratt, J.G.—catarrh in head
Pratt, J.—rupture in stomach, DSC
Priddy, J.W.—catarrh of head
Priddy, W.B.—gunshot wound in breast
Pringle, B.M.—wounded in left breast
Rains, G.W.—gunshot wound in left shoulder
Rake, J.A.—WIA caused fits
Rand, K.—erysipelas & catarrh head
Randolph, C.—RH
Rankins, T.J.—RH, wound in shoulder
Rawlings, G.W.—ruptured & falling mumps
Ray, J.M.—gunshot wound in hand
Redding, C.—wounded in thigh
Redding, W.H.—CDR & piles
Reed, H.N.—left eye injured by sun pain
Rhodes, A.—piles, feet frozen
Rhodes, I.—catarrh in head
Ridenour, B.J.—hernia & LD
Riffle, D.—gunshot wound in ankle
Robinson, B.—HD
Robison, A.—WIA left shoulder & lost third finger left hand
Robison, J.A.—RH of heart
Rodgers, A.T.—piles & CDR
Rodgers, G.W.—broken constitution
Rowan, A.—CDR
Rowley, G.C.—wounded left leg, now suffering HD
Rowley, H.C.—CDR 3/4 disabled
Safereed, B.F.—wound in knee
Safreed, W.L.—gunshot wound left hand
Sarver, D.H.—HD & bronchitis
Sayre, A.J.—piles
Sayre, ~.—left leg fractured
Sayre, R.F.—disabled in back
Shafer, J.C.—shoulder injured
Shamblin, T.—RH
Shank, C.C.—dyspepsia
Sharp, G.E.—KD
Shatto, P.—gunshot in right leg
Shepherd, F.M.—POW
ShePherd, M.—head affected
Shepherd, W.—RH & constitutional trouble
Shine, N.S.—wounded in head & leg
Shinn, C.P.—wounded in neck
Simons, T.J.—blind right eye
Skidmore, A.S.—CDR
Slaug~ter, W.B.—WIA left breast & right shoulder

Slaughter, D.P.—diserter from army never was discharged
Slaughter, E.—CDR
Slaughter, F.M.—spinal trouble of back
Slaughter, J.J.C.—gunshot left cheek, enlisted as teamster
Smith, Ch.—WIA right hand
Smith, D.—catarrh, disease of chest
Smith, G.W.—spinal trouble, LD, HD, now paralyzed & helpless
Smith, H.M.—gunshot wound right hand
Snider, M.—injury in back & head
Snider, T.H.—WIA right breast
Snodgrass, S.W.—deaf left ear
Southal, A.F.—gunshot right shoulder
Stevens, W.—LD
Stewart, E.—piles & asthma
Stewart, E.—RH & weak eyes
Stewart, L.C.—WIA left arm
Stoats, B.—catarrh in head
Stoats, G.W.—enlargement of tonsils
Stone, J.F.—catarrh & deafness
Summerfield, T.—wounded in hand
Swain, J.—gunshot wound right foot
Swartwood, L.—disabled in back & hip
Thomas, A.C.—RH & CDR
Thomas, C.H.—CDR
Thomas, E.W.—granulated sore eyes
Tidd, S.—shot in right hip
Tribett, G.W.—gunshot wound left shoulder
Walker, F.—wounded in face & leg
Warfield, N.D.—RH & HD
Warner, G.R.—blind in right eye
Watkins, F.M.—bayonet wound
Watts, W.G.—LD, WIA left arm
Waundling, A.—right hip & back injury
Weakley, L.—gunshot wound in right arm
Webb, J.G.—shell wound left knee
Whetstone, S.H.—bronchitis
White, J.C.—LD
Whitney, G.W.—bronchitis & HD
Wickley, B.—RH
Williams, J.A.—fistula 27 years
Williamson, J.M.—piles
Williamson, W.—CDR
Winten, C.—piles & bronchitis
Wise, T.W.—RH & catarrh in head
Wolf, J.W.—liver complaint
Woodruff, W.—gunshot wound in face
Zeper, S.—CDR

Jefferson County

NAME/RANK	REGIMENT	WHEN SERVED
Arnett, Daniel W.	5 OHI?	63/65
Benatt, Henry W. Pvt.	100 PAI	8/28/61–2/3/62
Black, George W.	NF (27 VAI CSA?)	
Blincol, James Pvt.	1 MDC	11/61–6/1/65
Bond, John H. Pvt.	Loudans VAC	1/3/65–5/31/65
Boyd, Sam J. Pvt.	1 PAI	7/6/63–1/6/64
Briggs, Charles H. Capt.	1 CTC	10/26/61–1/20/65
Brown, Joseph F.	NF (2 VAI CSA)	
Brown, Machall	NF	
Brumaman, Adam Pvt.	19 PAI	2/27/65–7/1/65
Butts, James H. Pvt.	1 WVC	10/1/63–6/65
Buzzard, Albert Pvt.	1 MDC	63–7/65
Chambers, Charles H. Pvt.	NF	
Colty, Robert Pvt.	NF	
Corey, George H. Lt.	17 VTI	12/24/63–7/14/65
Covert, Tunis Pvt.	1 NYI	61/64
Crane, Ezekial C. Pvt.	63 PAI	8/27/61–12/27/62
Cummings, Edward S. Pvt.	5 NYA	62/65
Daniels, Henry V. Sgt.	4 NJI	4/25/61–7/31/61
Dearing, Elias Pvt.	——	61/62–NF
Debenshere, Thomas Pvt.	30 USI?	1864–NF
Dorsey, John A.	NF (16 VAI CSA?)	
Dudrow, Charles E. Saddler	14 PAC	8/26/62–5/31/65
Duey, Hiram Pvt.	NF	
Dusing, Jacob Pvt.	3 MDI	8/19/62–5/24/65
Fayman, James D. Lt.	1 VAI	4/25/61–1862
also	3 MDI	1862–NF
Foreman, James Pvt.	Loudan VAC	2/3/65–5/31/65
Frame, John H. Pvt.	43 USI	3/8/65–10/20/65
Gibson, Samuel Pvt.	—C	7/1/61–7/10/62
Gore, Wm. Pvt.	NF	
Graham, George W. Lt.	144 NYI	8/12/62–9/12/64
Grubb, James W. Pvt.	Coles MDC	NF
also Capt.	Loudans VAC	9/4/61–5/31/65
Harris, John	NF (2 VAI CSA)	
Harrison, John L. Bugler	1 MDC	1862 NF
Hawk, James W.	NF	
Higinbotham, Samuel Pvt.	16 PAC	11/15/62–1/15/63
Hines, Martin H. Pvt.	3 MDI	3/64–5/65
Johns, Gibson C. Pvt.	87 PAI	10/12/61–9/7/64
Johnson, Edward W. Pvt.	(64 VAI CSA?)	8/10/61–9/63

Jones, Samuel	NF (1 VAC CSA?)	
Kilham, John T. Pvt.	1 MDI	NF
Kirby, Edward T. Pvt.	2 OHC	9/9/61–2/26/63
Lancaster, John J. Pvt.	NF (13 BTN VAA CSA?)	
Lattersall, Edward Pvt.	5 USC	9/18/60–/1/67
Lee, Edgar Pvt.	1 PAI	6/10/61–7/26/62
also Lt./Capt.	101 PAI	11/5/62–6/25/65
Liggett, Tom W. Pvt.	3 MDI	62/65
Lightner, Scott W. Pvt.	133 PAI	62/63
also	149 PAI	63/65
Mansfield, James Pvt.	18 USI	1/27/63–1/1/64
McArthur, John	NF	
McCaully, Wm. Pvt.	NF	
Melton, Binjiah F. Pvt.	17 KSI	5/64–5/65
Moler, William J. Pvt.	– MOI	61/62
Moller, Rollin V.	NF (12 VAC CSA)	
Moore, Samuel	NF (2 VAI CSA)	
Nicewarner, Henry C. Pvt.	1 MDC	11/7/62–6/28/65
Nyers, Robert L. Pvt.	8 ILC	7/10/63–7/15/65
Page, John B. Pvt.	3 — ?	3/1857–5/1866
Porter, Charles	NF (7 VAI CSA?)	
Robinson, James Pvt.	1 OHA	7/13/63–7/25/65
Ruse, John Pvt.	43 INI	11/15/64–6/14/65
Sager, Solomon J. Pvt.	— MDI	62/64
Shaw, William A. Sgt.	8 MSI CSA	8/31/62–5/17/65
Shewbridge, Benj. Pvt.	2 MDI	NF
Shipley, Fenrose	NF	
Sisler, Abraham	NF	
Snyder, John Pvt.	1 MDC	2/26/64–NF
Soudes, Micheal Pvt.	2 MDC	11/1/61–5/1/65
Sponseller, Stockton Pvt.	Loudans VAC	3/31/65–5/31/65
Staphera, Abram Pvt.	2 VA- ? CSA	5/61–NF
Stover, Sheyer Pvt.	2 MDI	8/13/61–10/25/64
Stump, Abner Pvt.	13 PAC	9/1/62–7/20/65
Surner, Henry Pvt.	1 —?I	61/65
Synder, Peter Pvt.	1 MDC	NF
Taylor, James R. Sgt.	1 MDC	9/17/61–11/19/65
Upwright, Lewis F. Bugler aka Ludwig Rupbrecht	1 USA	1860 NF
Wachter, Elijah R. Pvt.	1 MDI	9/1/61–12/9/64
Washington, Lawrence	NF (9 VAC CSA?)	
Watterman, William Pvt.	13 MDI	2/28/65–5/29/65
White, Benjamin F. Pvt.	NF (Sgt. 2VAC CSA)	
Williams, George W. Pvt. aka George Beanes	3 MAI	62/65
Wilson, John A. Pvt.	210 PAI	9/13/64–5/30/65
Woodard, George L. Pvt.	11 MDI CSA	5/63–9/63

Jefferson County Remarks

Arnett, D.W.—lost his hearing
Benatt, H.W.—wounded right thigh
Blincol, J.—epilepsy
Bond, J.H.—KD
Boyd, S.J.—failing health account exposure during war
Briggs, C.H.—wounded, also in company E 2d Conn. Inf.
Corey, G.H.—RH
Covert, T.—ruptured, shot in side
Crane, E.C.—shot through left lung
Cummings, E.S.—service about 2 1/2 years
Daniels, H.V.—hemorrhoids, also in civil capacity till close
Frame, J.H.—ruptured
Gibson, S.—thumb broken & rupture
Graham, G.W.—CDR resigned on disability
Hines, M.H.—chronic neuralgia
Johns, G.C.—fistula, RH, HD & DSC
Kirby, E.T.—HD
Lattersall, E.—HD & RH
Liqqett, T.W.—LD, KD, throat trouble
Mansfield, J.—CDR, DSC
McCauley, W.—blind left eye
Moler, W.J.—hearing affected
Nicewarner, H.C.—RH
Page, J.B.—ruptured
Ruse, J.—RH
Sager, S.J.—thrown from horse ruptured right side
Shaw, W.A.*—gunshot wound left hand
Shrewbridge, B.—hemorrhoids DSC
Snyder, J.—defective in mind
Snyder, P.—rupture & RH
Soudes, M.—kneecap knocked off
Stover, S.—right leg shot
Stump, A.—throat infection
Taylor, J.R.—deaf one ear
Upwright, L.F.—ruptured by shell
Wachter, E.R.—shot in head
White, B.F.*—his house burned & his discharge burned with it

Kanawha County

NAME/RANK	REGIMENT	WHEN SERVED
Abbott, Daniel H. Cpl.	7 WVC	7/1/61–8/13/65
Abbott, Henry Pvt.	7 WVC	7/27/61–8/1/65
Abbott, Smith Pvt.	7 WVC	9/61–8/65
Abbott, Wilson Sgt.	7 WVC	61/65
Abshire, Simeon Pvt.	7 WVC	9/1/61–8/1/65
Adkins, Alex J. Pvt.	7 WVC	4/24/64–8/9/65
Adkins, Isaac Pvt.	7 VAI	62/65
Adkins, Lorenzo Pvt.	7 WVC	3/28/64–8/1/65
Adkins, Marion F. Pvt.	7 WVC	2/21/65–8/1/65
Akers, Adam	NF	
Akers, Wm. T. Pvt.	(24 VAI CSA?)	61/65
Akyers, M.D. Pvt.	NF	
Allen, Frank N. Pvt.	22 PAC	62/65
Allen, James H. Pvt.	13 VAI CSA	62/65
Amos, Benj. T. Pvt.	7 WVC	9/17/61–8/1/65
Anderson, Charles Pvt.	7 WVC	9/1/61–1/31/64
Anderson, Silas M. Lt.	37 VAC CSA	5/25/62–1865
Andred?, Edgar A. Pvt.	156 ILI	NF
Angel, Charles W. Lt.	7 WVC	9/5/61–8/1/65
Armstrong, James M. Pvt.	Jones VAA (CSA)	4/15/61–12/3/63
Arter, Theadore Adj/Gen.	143 OHI	NF
Astep?, Martin Pvt.	22 VAI CSA	61/65
Baldwin, David Sgt.	8 WVI	10/61–8/1/65
Baldwin, Edward A. Pvt.	9 NYI	1864–6/29/65
Balklap?, Wm. Pvt.	1 VAI	10/22/62–7/25/65
Barker, James H. Pvt.	7 WVI	9/2/61–7/5/65
Barlew, Nayes Pvt.	126 PAI	61/63–
Barnett, Eliott Pvt.	13 WVI	12/12/63–7/22/65
Barringer, Wm. Pvt.	4 VAI	5/61–7/65
Bayo, Joseph Pvt.	7 WVC	11/1/64–8/1/65
Bays, James M. Pvt.	7 WVC	9/5/61–9/10/63
Bays, John H. Pvt.	8 WVI	10/15/61–8/15/65
Beasley, Robb Pvt.	7 WVC	8/25/64–6/3/65
Bess, Charles H. Pvt.	2 VAC	2/64–7/4/65
Bias, Everminst R. Pvt.	7 WVI	2/65–7/65
Bias, John B.C. Cpl.	7 WVC	11/7/61–/1/65
Bibby, Robert Lt.	59 VAI CSA	61/62
Bird, Charles W. Pvt.	62 VA? (162 VAM CSA)	62/65
Blackburn, John E. Pvt.	7 WVC	61/65
Blackburn, M.W. Cpl.	4 VAI	6/17/61–4/17/63

Blackburn, W.H. Sgt.	—WVC	9/1/61–8/15/64
Blackshire, James A. Pvt.	7 WVC	11/1/61–1/65
Blackwell, Lewis Y. Pvt.	4 VAI	8/18/61–8/26/64
Blackwood, Wm. R. Lt.	45 VAI BTN CSA	10/62–7/11/65
Blake, Henry Pvt.	1 WVC	4/1/63–1865
Boggess, James Pvt.	7 WVC	3/27/64–8/1/65
Boggess, John G.	NF	
Boggs, Levi J. Pvt.	4 WVI	8/18/61–8/19/64
Bohnet, Joseph Pvt.	3 OHI	7/4/61–7/12/65
Bonham, Jasper A. Pvt.	4 WVI	9/10/61–7/27/65
Bonham, Powhattan L. Sgt.	7 WVC	7/25/61–8/25/65
Bonham, Wm. H. Blksmith	8 WVI	7/27/61–8/11/65
Booker, James A. Pvt.	13 VAI	12/17/62–6/27/65
Booker, Wm. L. Pvt.	4 VAI	8/18/61–1/19/64
also	2 WVI	1/20/64–7/16/65
Bostic, Alexander Pvt.	13 WVI	NF
Bostic, John H. Pvt.	7 WVC	11/4/61–6/26/65
Bowles, Woodford W. Pvt.	7 VAI	62/65
Bowls, Allen Pvt.	7 WVI	NF
Bradley, John L. Sgt.	8 WVI	11/2/61–8/9/65
Brewer, Smith	US NF	
Brogan, James Pvt.	7 WVC	10/64–8/1/65
Brown, George E. Pvt.	13 VAI	8/5/63–6/5/65
Brown, James O. Pvt.	67 OHI	10/15/64–8/15/65
Brown, Jonathan Pvt.	2 WVI	8/25/62–7/11/65
Brown, Robert Pvt.	11 WVI	62/65
Brown, Samuel H. Pvt.	Navy	62/63
Brumley, Joseph Lt.	13 VAI	9/2/62–6/23/65
Bryant, Josiah P. Pvt.	7 VAC	8/64–1/65
Buckner, James M. Pvt.	19 VAC CSA	NF
Buckner, John R. Pvt.	4 WVI	8/18/61–6/3/65
Burdett, Amanda J. Pvt.	7 WVC	11/23/61–8/1/65
Burdett, James M. Pvt.	7 WVC	7/27/61–1/24/65
Burdett, James S. Pvt.	7 WVC	NF
Burdett, John S. Capt.	——	2/62–6/65
Burdett, Wm. H. Pvt.	4 VAI	7/25/61–8/24/64
Burditt, Eli Pvt.	4 VAI	8/62–8/65
Burgess, Amos Pvt.	4 WVI	8/18/61–8/26/64
Burgiss, George L. Pvt.	4 VAI	1863–NF
Burke, Michael Pvt.	83 OHI	8/6/62–7/24/65
Burnes, John A. Pvt.	2 VAC	3/64–7/4/65
Bury, Wiley A. Pvt.	7 WVC	11/1/61–8/1/65
Butler, Wm. Pvt.	NF	
Buttan, Louis D. Capt.	27 NYI	4/61–5/65
Butterfield, George Pvt.	12 OHI	6/22/61–6/24/64
Buttrick, Edwin L. Col.	39 WSI	8/22/62–9/22/64
Cager, Mitchel Pvt.	7 WVC	64/65

aka Myres Cager	NF	
Canterbery, Anthony Pvt.	4 WVC	NF
Canterbery, Samuel H. Pvt.	NF (22 VAI CSA?)	
Canterbery, Wm. A. Sgt.	7 WVC	12/62–1865
Canterbury, Thompson	NF	
Carel, Frederick Pvt.	4 VTI	NF
Carl, Richard D. Pvt.	4 WVI	1861–7/65
Carl, Wm. C. Pvt.	4 VAI	8/18/61–8/26/64
Caron, Jacob C.	Teamster	63/63
Carpenter, Thomas Pvt.	Kanawha Guard	62/65
Carr, David	NF	
Carr, Francis M. Pvt.	8 WVI	9/6/61–NF
Carr, James G. Pvt.	7 WVC	9/2/61–2/8/64
Cart, John W. Pvt.	22 VAI CSA	5/61–4/11/65
Cart, Mathew C. Cpl.	7 WVC	1/6/65–8/1/65
Carter, Albert G. Pvt.	7 WVI	2/65–7/65
Carter, Henry L. Pvt.	7 WVC	10/18/61–8/1/65
Carter, Wm. Pvt.	13 WVI	1/30/65–6/28/65
Carter?, Virgil? Pvt.	1 ILA	5/16/64–6/25/65
Casdorph, Caleb H. Lt.	7 WVI	7/27/61–3/12/65
Cassa, John W. Pvt.	13 VAI	11/61–7/26/65
Chandler, Abraham E. Cpl.	3 WVI	8/10/63–6/22/65
Chandler, Wm.	US NF	
Chandler, Wm. A. Sgt.	7 WVC	9/5/61–8/1/65
Cheek, John Pvt.	8 WVC	11/1/61–1865
Childress, Adison Pvt.	7 WVC	3/29/64–8/1/65
Childress, Daniel Pvt.	13 WVI	8/22/62–6/5/65
Childress, Wm. L. Cpl.	7 WVC	3/31/64–8/1/65
Christopher, Michael Lt.	4 WVI	8/18/61–1864
Clark, Jacob C. Sgt.	6 WVC	7/6/61–8/17/64
Cline, John Pvt.	34 VAC CSA	6/61–3/64
Clingher, Isaac N. Pvt.	26 OHI	6/30/61–4/10/64
Cobb, Charles A. Pvt.	7 WVC	9/23/64–6/3/65
Cobb, John M. Pvt.	13 WVI	12/13/62–5/25/65
Cobb, Joseph M. Pvt.	13 WVI	6/11/63–2/20/65
Cobb, Wm. Pvt.	13 VAI	8/1/63–6/23/65
Coffman, Henry C. Pvt.	7 WVC	7/27/61–8/1/65
Collin, Daniel Pvt.	NF	
Collins, Jesse Pvt.	4 VAI	8/18/61–8/18/64
Comer, George W. Pvt.	7 WVC	61/65
Comer, Isaac Pvt.	13 WVI	12/20/63–6/22/65
Conaway, W. H. Pvt.	2 WVC	6/20/61–1865
Conely, George N. Pvt.	7 WVC	10/64–8/65
Coney, George Cpl.	22 VAI CSA	5/61–12/63
Conway, Harry Pvt.	4 VAI	1/5/61–7/6/64
Cook, James Pvt.	7 VAI	3/3/62–6/65
Cook, Thomas A. Lt.	4 OHC	9/61–2/64

Cooper, Bayless Pvt.	2 WVC	63/65
Cooper, George W. Pvt.	7 WVC	NF
Cooper, Jacob Pvt.	7 VAI	7/27/61–8/12/65
Copen, Augusta Sgt.	NF	
Copla, Thomas Cpl.	4 WVC	6/15/63–3/10/64
Cordill, Abner Pvt.	CSA (63–VAI)	61/64
Cornwell, George C. Pvt.	2 VAI	9/61–11/64
Cox, Samuel D. Pvt.	NF	
Crabtree, Henry Sgt.	45 KYC	63/64
Cummings, John	NF	
Cunningham, Henry C. Pvt.	7 WVI	9/5/61–8/1/65
Cuthrie, John Jr. Pvt.	7 WVC	7/27/61–1/25/65
Dailey, Isaac Pvt.	7 WVC	10/1/64–8/1/65
Dailey, John Cpl.	7 WVC	10/4/64–8/1/65
Dame, Marcus P. Pvt.	NF	
Dana, Eugene I. Cpl.	3 NYA	61/65
Danbenspeck, Jacob Cpl.	1 PAC	2/29/64–7/13/65
Daniel, David O. Pvt.	7 WVC	9/5/61–1/31/64
Daniels, Frank J. Pvt.	51 MAI	9/62–8/63
Danner, George Pvt.	13 WVI	8/15/62–6/20/65
Danniels, Thomas Pvt.	NF	
Darnell, Arthur W. Lt.	13 VAI	8/15/62–2/27/65
Darnell, Samuel Pvt.	—WVC	11/6/62–6/30/65
Darr, Manly G. Pvt.	3 USI	10/31/64–11/29/65
Davis, John H. Lt.	13 WVI	12/3/62–6/22/65
Davis, Wm. H. Pvt.	7 OHI	12/18/63–6/26/65
Davis, Wm. T. Pvt.	17 VAC CSA	10/62–5/65
Dawson, Noah W. Pvt.	7 WVC	11/4/61–5/1/65
Dawson, Robert C. Lt.	7 WVC	11/5/618/1/65
Dayton, Giles A. Sgt.	137 NYI	5/62–12/65
Debolt, Jacob Pvt.	62 TNI	9/14/61–3/26/63
Deel, James E. Pvt.	9 VAI	10/12/63–7/25/65
Deel, Levi Pvt.	9 VAI	3/31/64–7/25/65
Deitz, John K. Pvt.	NF	
Dew, James Pvt.	7 WVI	1/19/65–8/1/65
Dew, Windsor Pvt.	7 WVC	9/2/61–8/1/65
Dickinson, Wm. T. Sgt.	7 VAC	4/17/61–10/65
Dodd, Felix Pvt.	7 WVI	9/12/64–6/10/65
Dodson, Andrew J. Pvt.	13 WVI	5/64–8/65
Dodson, James R. Pvt.	7 WVC	10/23/64–8/1/65
Dodson, Thomas W. Pvt.	7 WVC	10/12/64–8/1/65
Dolton, Robert Pvt.	7 WVC	4/8/62–4/8/65
Dougherty, Henry C. Pvt.	NF	
Douglas, John Sgt.	4 VAI	8/18/61–5/13/65
Drake, Admiral D. Cpl.	9 WVI	9/18/61–7/25/65
Drake, Lorenzo D. Pvt.	4 VAI	12/22/61–7/16/65
Dunbar, John M. Pvt.	22 VAI CSA	61/63

Dye, Cummings Pvt.	19 VAC CSA	62/65
Earley, Edward Pvt.	13 – (Negro)	12/17/64–1/18/65
Eary, Anthony R.	US NF	
Eckenrodd, Silas Pvt.	2 IAI	7/61–12/63
Edens, Benj. Pvt.	7 WVC	3/64–1865
Edens, Clarkson Pvt.	7 WVC	7/27/61–8/1/65
Edens, Jesse Pvt.	7 WVC	7/26/61–8/1/65
Edens, John W. Pvt.	13 WVI	8/17/62–5/30/65
Edens, Jonathan Pvt.	8 WVI	7/27/61 1/17/63
Edens, Philip Pvt.	7 WVC	7/27/61–8/11/65
Elliott, Nathan Pvt.	1 VAC	8/6/61–6/7/65
Elswick, Harvey G. Pvt.	39 KYI	8/13/63–8/65
Elswick, Michael Pvt.	7 WVC	9/26/64–6/3/65
Elswick, Wm. M. Pvt.	7 WVI	2/23/65–7/1/65
England, Julias G. Pvt.	13 VAI	11/26/62–6/22/65
Eplin, Miles H. Pvt.	7 WVC	9/2/61–6/25/65
Eskew, Andrew J. Pvt.	7 WVC	10/7/64–8/1/65
Estep, J. W. Pvt.	7 WVC	10/15/61–1/31/64
Ewars, Lewis H. Pvt.	1 WVI	62/65
Fauber, Jesse Pvt.	7 WVC	61/65
Fawber, George N. Pvt.	13 VAI	8/15/62–7/65
Fellows, James D. Lt.	7 WVC	3/2/62–8/65
Ferguson, Charles D. Pvt.	57 VAI CSA	4/62–1865
Ferrell, Francis M. Pvt.	7 WVC	10/1/64–8/1/65
Fisher, Emberson Cpl.	2 WVI	8/12/62–7/11/65
Fisher, James A.L. Pvt.	7 WVC	7/27/61–8/3/65
Flora, Leonidas Pvt.	5 OHI	9/23/63–12/9/65
Ford, Timothy Pvt.	NF	
Foster, Joseph H. Cpl.	7 WVC	9/2/61–8/1/65
Fridley, John C. Pvt.	7 WVC	11/61–1/65
Fronts, Wm. W. Pvt.	1 WVI	3/23/64–7/16/65
Gales, Lovell C. Pvt.	144 OHI	9/62–8/63
Garnette, John E. Pvt.	5 VAI CSA	1864–4/11/65
Garretson, Perrey	US Transportation Service NF	
Garton, Stephen Cpl.	13 WVI	1/3/64–6/22/65
Gates, James M. Pvt.	4 WVI	NF
Gates, Virgil A. Pvt.	4 WVI	61/63
Gatewood, Perry Pvt.	13 VAI	8/14/62–6/12/65
George, Richard Pvt.	13 WVI	8/62–6/65
George, Wm. H. Pvt.	13 WVI	8/62–6/29/65
Gibson, Charles A. Pvt.	12 OHI	61/64
Gibson, John A. Pvt.	13 WVI	62/65
Gibson, Samuel Pvt.	NF	
Glover, Charles Pvt.	7 WVC	9/5/61–8/1/65
Godint, James H. Pvt.	23 OHI	5/61–7/64
Gollion, Gilbert J. Cpl.	23 KYI	10/4/61–10/4/64
Grass, Richard Pvt.	11 WVI	2/20/62–8/15/65

Grayhm, John Lt.	7 WVC	10/61–1865
Green, Eli Cpl.	7 WVC	61/65
Green, Frank Sgt.	5 USI (Negro)	10/11/63–9/20/65
Green, John Pvt.	7 WVC	11/27/61–8/1/65
Greenway, John Pvt.	54 VAI CSA	8/61–1865
Griffith, Thomas H. Cpl.	57 INI	11/16/61–2/14/65
Gunno, John Pvt.	7 WVC	4/64–8/65
Gunter, James G. Pvt.	13 WVI	8/62–6/65
Gunter, John W. Pvt.	13 WVI	64/65
Haas, James Pvt.	NF	
Hage?, Charles H. Pvt.	4 WVI	8/18/61–8/26/64
Hager, Michael Pvt.	7 WVC	9/2/61–8/12/65
Haid, Benedict Pvt.	NF	
Haldway, Wm. P. Pvt.	9 WVI	1/22/62–11/65
Haley, Joseph A. Pvt.	7 VAC	3/64–8/65
Hall, Anthony Pvt.	7 WVC	11/9/61–1/26/65
Hall, Commodore P. Pvt.	4 WVI	6/61–6/65
Hall, Jobe Pvt.	13 WVI	8/15/62–6/22/65
Hall, John W. Cpl.	7 WVC	9/5/61–8/1/65
Hall, Wm. H. Pvt.	7 WVC	9/5/61–8/1/65
Hall, Wm. J. Pvt.	24 — (VAI CSA)	NF
Hall, Wm. Pvt.	4 WVI	12/18/61–6/4/64
Hall, Woodson B. Pvt.	13 WVI	1862–6/20/65
Haller, Coscius C. Pvt.	13 OHC	64/65
Halley, John H. Pvt.	7 WVC	3/31/64–8/4/65
Hamilton, James M.	NF (20 VAC CSA)	
Hamilton, Lewis H. Pvt.	56 OHI	11/61–1/63
Hammack, Andrew J. Pvt.	4 WVI	9/13/62–7/11/65
Hammack, Lewis A. Pvt.	4 WVI	8/18/61–8/26/64
Hanna, David Pvt.	7 WVI	NF
Hanna, Harvey	NF	
Hannagan, Alexander Pvt.	140 PAI	7/11/62–6/4/65
Hannah, Wm. M.	NF	
Hanshaw, James W. Cpl.	7 VAC	6/6/64–1/6/65
Hanshaw, Perry Pvt.	7 WVC	63/65
Hanshaw, Silas S. Pvt.	22 VAI (CSA)	NF
Harding, John Sgt.	13 WVI	9/1/63–6/30/65
Harless, Leroy Sgt.	7 WVC	9/6/61–8/10/65
Harless, Wm. A. Pvt.	7 WVC	9/6/61–8/10/65
Harliss, J.H. Pvt.	7 WVC	3/64–8/7/65
Harlon, Thomas C. Pvt.	1 WVC	10/12/61–6/25/65
Harold, Irdell Pvt.	13 WVI	4/62–6/28/65
Hawkins, W.N. Lt.	13 WVI	8/12/62–6/22/65
Haynes, Crocket J. Pvt.	7 WVI	7/27/61–8/1/65
Haynes, John R. Pvt.	13 WVI	8/16/62–6/25/65
Haynes, Samuel Pvt.	7 WVC	4/18/64–8/1/65
Haynes, Wm. M. Pvt.	13 WVI	8/18/62–6/22/65

Hays, David A. Pvt.	4 VAI	8/15/61–8/15/64
Hays, John Pvt.	13 WVI	9/12/62–4/14/63
Hays, Vincent A. Sgt.	13 WVI	8/22/62–6/22/65
Hemmings, Levi Pvt.	13 WVI	NF
Henderson, Massey	US NF	
Henley, Nemiah S. Pvt.	49 OHI	2/2/62–2/1/65
Henneman, George Sgt.	39 OHI	8/13/61–9/64
Herald, Wm. Pvt.	13 VAI	NF
Hess, David Pvt.	NF	
Hess, Henry	NF	
Higgthum, S.A. Pvt.	8 WVC	3/4/64–8/19/65
High, James M. Pvt.	13 WVI	NF
High, John H.	US NF	
Hight?, Andrew J. Pvt.	CSA NF	
Hill, Aaron B. Pvt.	7 WVC	9/5/61–8/1/65
Hill, George W. Pvt.	62–OHI	9/15/62–9/15/64
Hill, Jenifer Cpl.	7 WVC	10/4/64–8/1/65
Hill, Wm. H. Pvt.	7 WVC	9/5/61–6/30/65
Hill, Wm. S. Pvt.	7 WVC	9/2/64–6/3/65
Hodges, Wm. 0. Pvt.	7 VAI	NF
Holcomb, James Pvt.	13 WVI	11/21/62–6/22/65
Holcomb, James T. Pvt.	7 WVC	11/6/61–8/1/65
Holley, Charles Pvt.	7 WVC	11/16/61–8/1/65
Holley, John Pvt.	13 WVI	11/1/63–6/22/65
Holstain, Henry H. Pvt.	NF	
Holstine, Daniel Pvt.	—WVC	1/15/63–8/1/65
Holstine, James H. Pvt.	7 WVI	3/2/65 7/1/65
Holstine, Peter L. Pvt.	4 WVC	6/15/63–3/20/64
also	7 WVC	11/10/64–8/1/65
Holstine, Wm. Pvt.	7 WVC	62/65
Holt, John Pvt.	7 WVC	NF
Honaker, Thomas D. Sgt.	8 WVI	11/61–1863
Hoppenstoll, Frank Sgt.	13 VAI	8/13/62–6/22/65
Hornsby, Thomas J. Pvt.	NF	
Houston, Samuel W. Lt.	25 OHI	6/61–8/65
Hudnall, John T. Pvt.	36 OHI	9/27/61–7/6/64
Hudson, John T. Cpl.	7 WVC	8/13/61–8/1/65
Huff, Edward Pvt.	5 VAC CSA	6/1/62–6/20/65
Huffman, Adam Pvt.	2 VAI	1/20/64–7/16/65
Huger, John G. Pvt.	NF	
Hughart, Henry H.	NF	
Hughes, Charles A. Pvt.	7 WVC	8/15/64–6/3/65
Hughes, Lafayette Pvt.	5 OHI	7/12/61–8/10/63
Hughes, Thomas J. Pvt.	13 WVI	8/12/62–6/65
Hughey, George K. Pvt.	7 WVC	3/1/64–8/1/65
Hull, Wm. C. Pvt.	7 WVC	10/17/64–8/5/65
Hulsey?, James H. Pvt.	NF	

Humbles, Wm. Pvt.	27 —	64/65
aka William Carter	NF	
Hundley, James H. Pvt.	4 VAI	7/22/61–4/18/65
Hunley, Christopher Pvt.	4 VAI	12/10/62–7/6/65
Hurt, Edward F. Capt.	(3 VARS CSA?)	61/65
Hutson, Anderson Sgt.	7 WVC	10/8/64–8/1/65
Ide, Nathan E. Pvt.	NF	
Imhoff, Henry Pvt.	155 PAI	7/25/62–7/3/65
Innman, Bezaleel Pvt.	4 WVI	11/17/61–2/64
Jackson, James A.	NF	
Jackson, Wm. Pvt.	17 MEI	7/22/61–2/27/63
Jacobs, George R. Pvt.	— WVA	NF
James, Davis H. Pvt.	11 WVI	2/18/62–7/28/65
James, Davis Sgt.	7 WVI	2/23/65–7/1/65
James, Samuel Pvt.	13 WVI	9/4/62–6/22/65
James, Thomas Pvt.	7 WVI	8/8/64–6/3/65
Jarrett, Anderson Pvt.	7 WVC	9/15/61–8/1/65
Jarrett, John Y. Sgt.	4 WVI	8/18/61–8/26/64
Jarvis, John W. Pvt.	9 WVI	63/65
Jeffers, Wm. H. Pvt.	7 WVC	11/1/62–8/1/65
Jenkins, George W. Pvt.	7 WVI	8/27/64–8/1/65
Jenkins, Robert T. Pvt.	8 VAI	7/61–1/63
Johnson, Alfred Pvt.	NF	
Johnson, Clark Cpl.	7 WVI	2/1/64–8/1/65
Johnson, Jackson Pvt.	1 WVI	10/7/61–7/21/65
Johnson, John Sgt.	5 VAC	6/16/61–6/16/64
Jones, Lemon Pvt.	140 OHI	5/64–9/10/64
Jones, Nowel Pvt.	NF	
Jones, Samuel Pvt.	7 WVC	12/3/62–8/1/65
Jones, Alfred Pvt.	NF	
Jones, Calvin Pvt.	7 WVI	8/18/64–6/3/65
Jones, Elisha T. Pvt.	13 WVI	8/22/62–7/11/65
Jones, Francis M. Pvt.	7 WVC	2/17/65–8/1/65
Jones, Robert W. Sgt.	7 WVC	61/65
Jones, Samuel L. Pvt.	7 VAI	3/6/65–7/1/65
Jones, Wilson Pvt.	13 WVI	12/27/63–6/26/65
Jones, Wm. Pvt.	13 VAI	8/12/62–7/26/65
Jones, Wm. Pvt.	8 VAI	12/31/61–8/1/65
Joplin, Francis M. Pvt.	7 WVC	6/61–8/1/65
Jopling, Jesse Pvt.	13 WVI	8/15/62–6/13/65
Jordan, Wm. G. Pvt.	13 WVI	6/22/62–6/22/65
Kalahan, James Pvt.	NF	
Kanty, James? J. Pvt.	7 WVI	11/1/61–1/31/64
Karnes, Granville G. Pvt.	7 WVC	9/17/61–8/11/65
Katcere?, Aaron N. Pvt.	13 OHC	2/26/64–8/10/65
Keeley, Wm.	NF	
Keely, George "Stewart"	13 MEI	11/29/61–8/9/65

Keeney, Woodford W. Pvt.	7 WVC	4/25/64–8/2/65
Keller, Alexander Pvt.	91 OHI	8/62–1865
Kelley, Aldrich J. Lt.	60 VAI CSA	2/62–4/9/65
Kelley, James H. Pvt.	5 WVI	8/61–12/63
Kelley, James M.	US NF	
Kennedy, David M. Pvt.	4 WVI	9/1/62–1865
Kenny, Wm. R.	NF	
Kesterson, Francis	US NF	
Keyser, Dewit Pvt.	11 VAC CSA	4/1/61–4/1/65
Keyser, Hezekiah Pvt.	11 VAC CSA	4/1/61–1865
King, James P. Pvt.	11 WVI	61/65
King, Wm. Pvt.	7 WVC	NF
Kinsey, Samuel Pvt.	2 VAC	4/7/63–6/30/65
Kirk, James Pvt.	8 WVI	7/27/61–10/18/62
Kirk, James Pvt.	8 WVI	9/2/61–9/18/62
Kurtz, Isiah	US NF	
Lacy, George W. Pvt.	13 WVI	8/22/62–6/22/65
Laline?, Wm. Pvt.	7 VAI	61/65
Lambert, James K.	US NF	
Landers, Meredith Pvt.	13 VAI	8/22/62–6/13/65
Lands, Charles "Marine"	(Ship) Dictator	NF
Lanham, Columbus C. Pvt.	36 VAC CSA	10/62–4/65
Lanham, John W. Pvt.	13 WVI	12/24/63–6/22/65
Larrence, James R. Cpl.	8 VAI	10/61–10/62
Layne, Robert T. Cpl.	—WVC	7/61–1/24/65
Layton, Joseph Pvt.	7 WVC	NF
Leavett, Alonzo Pvt.	5 OHI	6/1/64–5/65
Lee, R.H. Capt.	8 VAI	7/21/61–10/10/64
Legg, Francis M. Pvt.	4 WVI	7/16/62–7/11/65
Legg, John C. Pvt.	7 WVC	2/2/65–8/1/65
Leonard, John Pvt.	139 PAI	4/61–5/63
Leuper, John W. Pvt.	91 OHI	8/61–5/9/65
Levins, Charles W. Pvt.	12 OHI	8/20/61–NF
Lewis, Wm. Pvt.	13 WVI	NF
Linville, Andrew J. Pvt.	67 OHI	4/64–4/65
Lowenstein, Sam M. Pvt.	23 OHI	5/20/61–6/30/64
Loyd, Andrew I. Cpl.	36 OHI	7/10/61–12/28/62
Lynch, Joseph Sgt.	22 VAI CSA	6/61–9/62
Lynn, Wm. H. Pvt.	26 VAI BTN CSA	7/1/61–7/5/65
Lyons, Hiram Pvt.	9 VAI	3/9/62–7/21/65
Lyons, Joseph Pvt.	9 VAI	2/1/62–2/1/65
Mace, Jacob Pvt.	7 WVC	9/15/61–1/24/65
Magruder, Fredrick	Navy	NF
Malone, Wm. R. Lt.	4 WVI	61/65
Mandiville, Massey J. Pvt.	2 WVC	4/63–7/65
Martain, Samuel	NF (58 VAI CSA?)	
Martin, Charles Pvt.	7 WVC	10/4/64–8/1/65

Martin, Erasmus Sgt.	7 WVC	2/29/64–8/65
Martin, Lewis A. Lt.	7 WVC	2/29/64–8/1/65
Mason, Joseph S. Pvt.	CSA NF (Hoole's Co. MSA?)	
Mason, Thomas J. Pvt.	10 VAC CSA	3/13/64–4/19/65
Masters, Richard	— OHI	NF
Matheny, James A. Pvt.	NF (10 VAC CSA?)	
Matheny, John C. Pvt.	—	8/16/61–2/6/64
Matheny, Michael Pvt.	13 VAI	8/22/62–5/25/65
Matheny, Samuel D. Pvt.	4 WVI	9/61–9/64
Matheny, Wm. T. Pvt.	7 WVC	2/7/65–8/1/65
Mayer, Daniel Ast/Surgeon	5 VAI	8/10/61–9/14/64
McCallister, Corydon Pvt.	8 INI	8/20/61–8/20/65
McCan, Amos Pvt.	7 WVC	4/63–8/65
McClaskie, James Pvt.	7 WVC	9/5/61–8/1/65
McComack, Burnette Pvt.	7 WVC	9/2/64–6/3/65
McConnick, Warren M. Pvt.	126 OHI	5/12/64–3/26/65
McCracken, P.H. Sgt.	55 PAI	7/20/61–7/30/65
McCracken, Wm. Pvt.	140 OHI	4/64–8/64
McCrea, Robert P. Pvt.	NF	
McDonald, John S. Lt.	13 WVI	61/65
also LTC	17 WVI	NF
McIntosh, Curtis B. Pvt.	23 OHI	4/17/61–8/3/65
McNeff, James Pvt.	1 WVI	6/6/61–9/12/64
McVay, John L. Pvt.	8 WVC	7/27/61–8/1/65
McVey, Henry T. Sgt.	7 WVC	7/27/61–8/1/65
McWhorter, Henry C. Lt.	9 VAI	3/62–12/62
Meanes, George W. Pvt.	7 WVC	NF
Means, John Pvt.	7 WVC	9/3/64–6/3/65
Means, John R. Pvt.	7 WVC	9/6/61–8/1/65
Medley, John A. Pvt.	7 WVI	2/24/64–7/1/65
Meibler, Harrison Pvt.	13 WVI	8/16/62–10/14/63
Mices, John Pvt.	7 WVC	5/28/64–8/1/65
Michaelson, Charles J. Pvt	14 WVI	9/3/64–6/27/65
Michaelson, Otto H. Pvt.	14 WVI	8/62–1865
Middleton, George O. Pvt.	4 CTI	1861–NF
also	1 CTA	12/62–5/64
Midkiff, Allen Pvt.	7 WVC	10/10/64–8/1/65
Midkiff, Davis M. Pvt.	7 WVC	9/64–6/65
Midkiff, Levi Pvt.	13 WVI	8/8/62–6/22/65
Midkiff, Lorenzo D. Pvt.	7 WVC	12/4/62–8/1/65
Midkiff, Montgomery Cpl.	7 WVI	9/28/64–6/3/65
Midkiff, Morris Pvt.	7 WVC	9/11/61–8/1/65
Milam, Wm. T. Pvt.	36 VAC CSA	6/6/61–5/64
Miller, Absalom Pvt.	7 WVC	8/31/64–1/3/65
Miller, Augustine	NF	
Miller, Henry C. Pvt.	13 WVI	11/11/63–6/22/65
Miller, Thomas Pvt.	2 WVC	8/23/61–7/4/65

Mitchell, Eli Pvt.	23 VAI CSA	61/65
Monday, Mitche O. Pvt.	7 WVC	7/21/61–8/1/65
Monk, James N. Sgt.	7 WVC	12/61–2/1/65
Monroe, Edmond Pvt.	13 CTI	11/7/61–1/6/65
Mooney, Alfred Pvt.	23 OHI	12/31/63–6/7/65
Moore, Mel Pvt.	9 WVI	7/13/62–4/13/65
Morgan, John Lt.	NF (24 VAI CSA?)	
Morris, Joshua Pvt.	Marine Corp	9/16/64–9/16/68
Morris, Lewis Pvt.	— WVI	2/15/64–2/22/65
Morris, Richard Pvt.	7 WVI	2/23/65–7/1/65
Morris, Wm. H. Pvt.	NF (7 VAC CSA?)	
Morton, G.W.T. Pvt.	2 WVC	9/12/62–7/1/65
Moses, James R. Cpl.	11 VAI	8/15/62–7/5/65
Mowlton, John Pvt.	2 MEI	7/5/61–7/11/65
Mullens, Marshall Pvt.	39 KYI	4/62–1865
Mullins, Isam Pvt.	39 KYI	62/65
Mullins, Sherwood Pvt.	39 VAI (CSA?)	63/65
Murdock, Joseph A. Pvt.	NF (34 VAC CSA?)	
Murphey, Henry Pvt.	34 VAC CSA	5/62–1864
Myers, Abraham Pvt.	7 WVC	65/65
Myers, Charles Pvt.	NF	
Myers, Jackson Pvt.	7 WVC	8/15/64–6/3/65
Myres, Levi QM/Sgt.	7 VAC	10/5/64–8/1/65
Naylor, John M. Pvt.	13 WVI	8/62–5/11/65
Naylor, John Y. Sgt.	9 VAI	9/19/61–9/19/64
Neal, Enoch Pvt.	2 WVC	4/63–7/65
Newhouse, Benj. S. Pvt.	4 WVI	61/64
Newhouse, Edmond Pvt.	7 WVI	2/23/61–8/8/65
Newhouse, John S. Pvt.	13 WVI	12/6/62–6/22/65
Newhouse, Lewis M. Pvt.	8 WVI	12/63–1/65
Nichels, Andrew J. Pvt.	CSA NF (28 VAI?)	
Nicholas, Lewis Pvt.	7 —	NF
Nichols, Isaac Pvt.	5 WVI	8/61–3/65
Nichols, John W. Pvt.	11 WVI	10/6/61–8/6/65
Nichols, Wm. Pvt.	2 VAC	9/61–7/4/65
Noble, David R. Lt.	8 VAI	61/63
Nolder, James Pvt.	168 OHI	5/2/64–9/9/64
Norton, Andrew J. Lt.	1 KYI	1/4/65–3/11/66
Nunley, Adolphus Pvt.	NF	
Nunley, John P. Sgt.	7 WVC	10/1/61–8/31/65
Odell, John S. Cpl.	7 WVC	3/28/64–8/25/65
Oiler, James Pvt.	NF	
Oliver, Samuel Pvt.	4 WVI	8/9/61–9/10/64
Orcutt, Augustus C.	US Navy	NF
Orth, John Pvt.	13 WVI	8/15/62–6/22/65
Padgett, John J. Pvt.	11 VAI (CSA)	6/6/61–4/1/65
Page, Charles H. Pvt.	4 WVI	8/18/61–8/26/64

Page, Cornelius Pvt.	13 VAI	8/62–5/65
Page, John E. Pvt.	7 WVI	3/25/65–9/2/65
Pance, Chapman Pvt.	7 WVC	8/23/64–8/1/65
Panley, Charles A. Pvt.	7 WVC	9/6/64–6/13/65
Parker, George Pvt.	3 VAC	1864–7/65
Parson, Merideth Pvt.	7 WVC	9/64–8/1/65
Parsons, John A. Cpl.	7 WVC	10/10/64–8/1/65
Parsons, Richard A. Pvt.	7 WVC	9/5/61–8/1/65
Patton, George W. Pvt.	236 PAI	6/63–10/63
Pauley, Anderson Pvt.	7 WVC	9/5/61–8/1/65
Pauley, Cornelius Cpl.	13 WVI	8/2/62–6/22/65
Pauley, Dryden L. Pvt.	7 WVC	9/5/61–2/65
Pauley, James Pvt.	4 WVI	5/29/62–5/29/65
Pauley, John A. Pvt.	7 WVC	9/5/61–8/1/65
Pauley, John F.	NF	
Pauley, Oscar F. Pvt.	4 VAI	8/18/61–8/26/64
Pawley, Madison Pvt.	7 WVI	64/65
Pawliene, Augustine W.	Comodere Bay	61/65
Payne, George	NF	
Paynter, Wm. Pvt.	NF (36 BTN VAC CSA?)	
Peck, Elijah Pvt.	196 OHI	2/65 4/65
Pence, Henry Pvt.	4 WVI	8/18/61–8/26/64
Perry, Ephram Pvt.	2 WVC	8/22/62–12/25/62
Perry, James J. Pvt.	8 WVI	7/61–10/62
Perry, Wm. E. Pvt.	7 WVC	9/61–8/65
Peters, John Pvt.	7 VAC	7/27/61–6/24/65
Phillips, Peter Pvt.	194 OHI	2/65–11/65
Phillips, Robert H. Pvt.	7 WVC	9/5/61–8/1/65
Pickering, Martin W Pvt.	54 VAI CSA	5/4/61–4/65
Pilchard, Henry L. Pvt.	7 WVC	NF
Pilchard, John W. Cpl.	3 WVI	10/6/62–6/30/65
Pitzer, Cary A. Pvt.	60 VAI CSA	6/20/61–5/1/65
Porter, Andrew Sgt.	7 WVC	61/65
Porter, Crockett Pvt.	1 KYI	7/29/61–7/2/64
Porter, George W. Pvt.	87 OHI	5/62–10/64
Porter, Noah Pvt.	7 WVC	2/1/64–8/1/65
Porter, Robert C. Pvt.	42 INI	9/26/64–6/18/65
Porter, Thomas Pvt.	7 WVC	2/21/65–8/1/65
Presce, Wm. R.	NF	
Price, John B. Pvt.	19 VAC CSA	10/61–5/65
Price, Squire Pvt.	19 VAC CSA	5/24/61–1865
Pridemore, Joseph Sgt.	7 VAC	12/1/61–8/1/65
Prince, Washington H. Pvt.	11 VAI	5/1/61–1865
Pritt, Wm. Pvt.	7 WVI	NF
Quick, Thomas F. Pvt.	7 WVC	9/3/64–6/3/65
Quigly, Charles P. Pvt.	13 WVI	8/18/62–5/16/65
Rackey, Thomas J. Sgt.	1 PAC	8/8/61–9/12/64

Name	Unit	Dates
Rader, James Cpl.	13 VAI	9/15/62–6/22/65
Radford, Wm. Pvt.	CSA NF (166 VAM)	
Rake, David M. Pvt.	45 KYI	11/3/63–2/14/65
Ramsey, Asher Sgt.	13 VAI	8/15/62–6/22/65
Ramsey, Wm. Pvt.	4 VAI	8/18/61–1864
Randalls, Samuel Pvt.	1 WVI	61/65
Rangon, John F. Pvt.	7 WVI	7/27/61–1/24/65
Ranse, James D. Pvt.	7 WVC	8/1/61–1862
Rathburn, John Q. Sgt.	11 PAC	8/26/61–8/13/65
Reed, Alexander Pvt.	4 WVI	9/13/62–7/12/65
Reed, Edward N. Pvt.	7 WVC	8/61–8/8/65
Reid?, George W. Pvt.	27 VAI (CSA?)	4/12/62–10/3/64
Reynolds, Hiram Sgt.	7 WVC	10/15/61–1/31/64
Reynolds, John P. Pvt.	7 WVC	8/20/64–8/1/65
Reynolds, Preston Pvt.	4 WVI	8/18/61–4/13/65
Richards, Isaah-	NF	
Richards, Moses Pvt.	5 MAC (Negro)	6/64–10/65
Riley, Wm. W. Pvt.	13 WVI	8/15/62–6/1/65
Rippitte?, Edmund Sgt.	1 OHI	8/7/62–1/26/65
Ritchardson, John W. Pvt.	CSA NF	
Ritz, George L. Pvt.	4 WVI	6/5/61–7/4/64
Roberts, James Pvt.	NF (34 BTN VAC CSA?)	
Roberts, Townsend Pvt.	7 WVC	64/65
Robins, Samuel P. Pvt.	13 WVI	9/21/62–6/22/65
Robinson, Charles Pvt.	4 WVI	1861–2/18/63
Robinson, George W. Pvt.	15 WVI	9/8/62–6/15/65
Robinson, Moses H. Cpl.	7 WVC	9/61–8/1/65
Robson, Joseph Pvt.	2 WVC	7/63–7/11/65
Rollins, James Pvt.	NF	
Rose, David Pvt.	7 WVC	9/9/62–8/1/65
Ross, John W. Pvt.	Clay Co. Guard	2/12/65 5/30/65
Ross, Michael R. Pvt.	— WVI	NF
Rucker, George Pvt.	13 VAI	9/19/62–6/26/65
Rucker, John	NF	
Rucker, Milton W. Pvt.	4 VAI	8/18/61–10/8/61
Rucker, Wesley Pvt.	2 WVI	5/28/62–7/11/65
Rumbaugh, James Pvt.	137 PAI	8/63–1865
Saers, Mathias Pvt.	7 WVC	8/1/61–6/3/65
Sampler, Thomas P. Pvt.	7 WVC	11/23/61–8/1/65
Samples, Lafayette S. Pvt.	7 VAC	2/61–8/65
Sampson, John Pvt.	4 VAI	6/17/61–7/22/65
Sampson, Samuel Pvt.	4 VAI	8/18/61–8/18/65
Samuels, Caleb G. Pvt.	13 WVI	8/22/62–6/25/65
Sands, Matthew	NF	
Savage, Jesse S. QM/Dept.	—	8/63–1/64
Savage, Wm. A. QM/Dept.	—	8/63–1/64
Schath, Martian Pvt.	1 WVA	7/22/63–7/22/65

Name	Unit	Dates
Schoolcraft, George A.	36 VAC CSA	62/65
Schoolcraft, Jacob Pvt.	14 VAC CSA	8/62–4/5/65
Schoolcraft, Polser F.	9 VAI	3/62–3/65
Scott, Hesihap Lt.	13 WVI	8/12/62–10/65
Shafer, Henderson Pvt.	7 WVC	NF
Shafer, Oliver Pvt.	1 WVI	1864–6/21/65
Shafer, Salathiel Pvt.	1 WVI	2/24/62–7/21/65
Shaffer, George W. Pvt.	9 WVI	4/61–7/65
Shamblin, Jesse Sgt.	22 VAI CSA	6/1/61–3/2/65
Shank, Charles "Bugler"	7 VAC	2/1/63–8/1/65
Shaver, Abram C. Pvt.	141 OHI	5/2/64–6/2/65
Shaver, Joe K. Lt.	149 PAI	8/62–7/65
Shaver, Lafayette Cpl.	7 WVC	12/61–8/1/65
Sherkey, James L. Pvt.	7 WVC	64/65
Shreeves, Abraham Pvt.	14 VAI	8/20/62–6/22/65
Shultz, George Pvt.	7 WVC	4/64–8/1/65
Shultz, Joshua Pvt.	7 WVC	9/5/61–8/1/65
Shumake, Hezekiah Pvt.	NF	
Sigmon, Wm. Pvt.	13 WVI	8/62–6/25/65
Sigmone, Shields Pvt.	13 WVI	8/16/62–6/22/65
Sigmund, John G.	NF	
Simmons, Cannan Pvt.	7 VAC	62/65
Simmons, Jesse Pvt.	7 WVC	61/65
Simpkins, Marinda J.	NF	
Sines, Henry J. Sgt.	13 WVI	8/19/62–6/22/65
Skees, Robert R. Sgt.	18 OHI	61/61
Slack, Hedgeman Major	7 WVC	9/5/61–8/1/65
Slack, John N. Pvt.	3 MOC	11/61–5/66
Slack, Wm. H. Pvt.	8 WVI	10/23/62–9/14/65
Slater, Thomas J. Pvt.	7 WVC	2/24/—NF
Smith, David K. Cpl.	4 WVC	8/1/63–3/10/64
Smith, George H. Pvt.	7 WVC	2/65–8/1/65
Smith, George K. Pvt.	23 OHI	6/7/61–7/9/65
Smith, George W. Pvt.	13 WVI	63/65
Smith, Henry Pvt.	7 VAC	NF
Smith, John M. Pvt.	11 VAI	9/11/62–6/65
Smith, Lewis C. Pvt.	—	8/61–8/64
Smith, Lorenzo D.	NF	
Smith, Owen Pvt.	7 WVC	1861–8/65
Smith, Squire Pvt.	4 VAI	8/25/61–7/16/65
Smith, Wm. H.	US NF	
Smith, Wm. H. Pvt.	7 WVC	9/61–8/1/65
Sneed, John W. Pvt.	13 WVI	11/13/63–6/22/65
Snider, Milton E. Pvt.	13 WVI	9/15/62–6/22/65
Snodgrass, Leonard Pvt.	7 WVC	8/6/64–6/3/65
Snodgrass, Martin Pvt.	13 WVI	NF
Snodgrass, Nathan Pvt.	13 WVI	8/15/62–7/22/65

Songher, John H. Pvt.	7 WVI	11/1/61–1/5/65
Spencer, Ahus Pvt.	7 WVC	2/23/64–6/6/65
Spradling, James Pvt.	13 VAI	7/61–7/64
Stafford, James Pvt.	7 WVC	10/14/61–8/1/65
Stanley, Jackson Pvt.	7 WVC	61/65
Stephens, Columbus C. Pvt.	7 WVC	2/17/65 8/1/65
Stephens, John D. Pvt.	13 WVI	62/65
Stephenson, Thomas Pvt.	7 WVC	11/10/61–5/17/64
Stevens, Jett S. Sgt.	178 PAI	10/62–7/63
Stone, John A. Pvt.	7 WVC	4/3/65 8/1/65
Stover, Eli Pvt.	7 WVC	9/4/61–8/1/65
Strickland, Wm. W.	NF (36 BTN VAC CSA)	
Strickland, David Pvt.	13 VAI	NF
Strickland, Ephram H. Pvt.	4 VAI	8/18/61–5/18/62
Strickland, John Pvt.	4 VAI	NF
Strickland, Lewis M. Pvt.	13 VAI	NF
Suder, Jacob Pvt.	18 PAC	3/64–10/22/65
AKA Karl Gallus	NF	
Summers, Edgar A. Ast/Srgn	—	3/62–6/65
Summers, James C. Cpl.	4 WVI	8/18/61–8/26/64
Surface, Augustus L. Pvt.	7 WVC	10/19/64–8/7/65
Surgeon, Jacob Pvt.	22 NJC	NF
Surratt, Benomis Pvt.	22 OHI	1/1/61–9/1/61
Swaar, John E. Lt.	7 VAC	8/12/62–8/1/65
Swinburn, Thomas Pvt.	7 WVC	9/5/61–1/24/65
Swinney, Wm. R. Pvt.	23 VAI (CSA)	4/62–3/19/64
Tate, George W. Pvt.	7 WVI	65/65
Taylor, Homer Cpl.	7 WVI	3/5/64–8/1/65
Taylor, Horace Pvt.	7 WVC	2/15/65–8/65
Taylor, Janus O. Pvt.	13 WVI	8/1/63–6/22/65
Taylor, John J. Pvt.	7 WVC	61/65
Taylor, Joseph Pvt.	NF (62–VAI CSA?)	
Taylor, Stephen Pvt.	9 WVI	12/18/61–2/28/64
Taylor, Wm. H. Pvt.	1 VAI	61/65
Teel, James H. Pvt.	7 WVC	9/5/61–8/1/65
Teel, John F. Pvt.	13 VAI	8/12/62–1/25/65
Teel, Samuel Pvt.	13 VAI	8/15/62–6/22/65
Terill, Squire Pvt.	7 WVC	64/65
Thaxton, James D. Pvt.	7 WVI	7/27/61–1/24/65
Thaxton, John R. Pvt.	8 VAC	6/1/61–5/1/65
Thaxton, Monroe S. Pvt.	7 WVC	7/27/61–1/24/65
Thomas, Andrew J. Pvt.	11 WVI	8/14/62–6/17/65
Thomas, David C. Pvt.	NF	
Thomas, Jesse A. Cpl.	7 WVC	7/27/61–1/31/64
Thomas, Joel P. Cpl.	13 VAI	8/62–7/10/65
Thomas, John A. Pvt.	13 WVI	8/27/62–6/22/65
Thomas, Robb Pvt.	7 WVI	3/64–8/65

Name	Unit	Dates
Thomas, Winsom Pvt.	NF	
Thumm, Jacob F. Pvt.	107 OHI	8/22/62–7/10/65
Tincher, John	NF	
Todd, Isaac N. Pvt.	13 WVI	3/1/64–11/27/65
Toler, Wm. H. Pvt.	8 VAI NF	
also	7 WVC	1862–8/1/65
Toney, David J. Pvt.	4 VAI	12/18/61–7/16/65
Toney, Levi Pvt.	7 WVC	3/11/64–8/1/65
Toney, Robert Pvt.	7 WVC	9/1/61–8/1/65
Toothman, James W. Pvt.	13 WVI	8/62–7/65
Traub, Albert	NF	
Trust, Peter Pvt.	27 USI (Negro)	63/65
Tucker, Calvin Pvt.	7 WVI	11/28/64–8/1/65
Tucker, Fultan Pvt.	1 WVA	8/9/61–6/28/65
Turley, Andrew J. Cpl.	13 WVI	8/8/62–6/22/65
Turley, Andrew J. Pvt.	7 WVC	9/5/61–6/31/64
Turley, Christopher Pvt.	7 WVC	2/14/65 8/1/65
Turley, Jackson D. Sgt.	1 WVC	9/5/61–8/1/65
Turley, Larison Pvt.	7 WVC	8/64–8/1/65
Tyree, Wm. P. Lt.	7 WVC	12/25/61–7/31/65
Vance, John Pvt.	4 VAI	61/65
Vaught, D.H. Pvt.	NF (Lowry's VAA CSA)	
Walker, Ansel Pvt.	36 OHI	2/29/64–8/65
Walker, Augustine Sgt.	16 MEI	5/61–10/65
Walker, Charles F. Pvt.	55 OHI	1/3/62–7/27/65
Walker, George W. Pvt.	13 WVI	8/1/62–6/29/65
Walker, James P. Sgt.	1 PAC	8/9/61–3/65
Wall, Absalom Pvt.	7 WVI	2/17/62–8/1/65
Wall, Asbury Pvt.	11 VAI	8/15/63–8/5/65
Wall, Augustus Pvt.	11 WVI	8/15/62–7/5/65
Walls, Wm. H. Pvt.	7 WVC	9/12/61–8/1/65
Walton, J.W. Pvt.	7 WVC	2/22/63–8/9/65
Walton, Wesley A. Pvt.	NF	
Wanner, Alexander	US NF	
Watrous, Albert W.	— NYI	NF
Watson, Wm.	NF (22 VAI CSA?)	
Weaver, George W. Pvt.	7 WVI	64/65
Weaver, Samuel Pvt.	13 WVI	9/15/62–5/25/65
Welch, Edmond G. Pvt.	Roane Co. Guard	6/62–9/64
Welch, Edward G. Pvt.	Roane Co. Guard	6/62–9/64
Welcher, John Pvt.	8 VAI	10/61–12/19/65
Wertz, Cassius C. Pvt.	201 PAI	8/29/64–NF
Westbay, George Pvt.	7 WVC	10/64–8/65
White, C.F. Pvt.	7 WVC	2/27/65–6/22/65
White, John Pvt.	8 WVI	11/6/61–11/6/62
White, Wm. P. Cpl.	13 VAI	9/2/62–6/22/65
Whitington, James C. Pvt.	13 WVI	8/18/62–6/22/65

Whitlock, John P. Pvt.	28 WVI?	5/61–7/61
Whittington, Wm. H. Pvt.	13 WVI	3/61–8/1/65
Wildman, Joseph Pvt.	49 PAI	9/3/61–11/64
William, Belcher Pvt.	7 WVC	9/26/64–6/3/65
Williams, Alford Pvt.	2 WVC	2/64–1/65
Williams, Augustus B. Pvt.	14 WVI	5/2/64–8/64
Williams, Sanford Pvt.	13 WVI	12/11/62–6/65
Williams, Walter Pvt.	7 WVC	7/27/61–1/24/65
Williams, Willy P. Pvt.	22 VAI CSA	6/15/61–7/10/61
Williams, Wm. F. Pvt.	142 PAI	8/8/62–5/29/65
Williams, Wm. N. Pvt.	4 VAI	8/12/62–8/12/65
Willson, David Pvt.	7 WVC	10/64–6/65
Willson, Fulding B. Pvt.	7 WVI	9/5/61–8/65
Wilson, Samuel H. Pvt.	12 WVI	6/12/62–5/18/65
Wilson, Wm. R. Pvt.	9 WVI	2/2/62–7/22/65
Wines, Wm. Cpl.	7 WVC	12/3/62–8/1/65
Wiseman, Almedous Cpl.	8 WVI	9/15/61–11/14/62
Wiseman, Augustus A. Pvt.	4 WVI	8/18/61–8/26/64
Wiseman, John Pvt.	85 PAI	2/24/62–6/18/65
Withrow, John N. Pvt.	7 WVC	9/1/64–6/3/65
Withrow, Wm. A. Pvt.	34 OHI	1/1/63–4/1/63
Woodrum, Archibald Pvt.	13 WVI	7/27/63–6/22/65
Woods, Lewis Pvt.	7 WVI	2/23/65–7/1/65
Woodson, Blake	US NF	
Woody, Fleming G. Sgt.	7 WVC	7/27/61–1/24/65
Wootton, John F. Sgt.	73 OHI	7/63–6/65
Workman, Abram Pvt.	8 WVI	7/27/61–10/18/62
Yonell?, James Pvt.	5 WVI	61/64

Kanawha County Remarks

Abbott, H.—received 6 gunshot wounds
Abshire, S.—RH
Adkins, I.—LD
Akers, W. T.—hearing affected 1863
Akyers, M. D.—shot left leg, shot through lungs
Allen, F. N.—broken down
Amos, B. T.—RH, vertigo, hearing, nervousness
Anderson, C.—lung trouble & other diseases
Angel, C. W.—gunshot wound & rupture
Baldwin, D.—gunshot wound right leg
Barnett, E.—gunshot wound left leg
Bayo, J.—deaf in both ears from military service
Bays, J. M.—gunshot left leg at Cedar Creek 10/19/64

Bias, E.R.—piles
Bibby, R.*—blind of left eye
Blake, H.—gunshot wound in left leg
Bonham, W.H.—neuralgia
Bostic, A.—collarbone broken
Bowles, W.W.—general disability from prison life (POW)
Bowls, A.—RH
Bradley, J.L.—wounded in leg
Brogan, J.—blind partially
Brown, G.E.—HD
Brown, S.H.—measles settled in ??
Burdett, W.H.—shot in right shoulder & foot
Burditt, E.—gunshot through hips
Burgess, A.—wounded right hand
Burke, M.—catarrh, hemora~, piles
Burnes, J.A.—slight wound right leg
Canterbery, S.H.*—bloody piles
Canterbery, W.A.—disabled right arm
Carl, R.D.—SS
Carpenter, T.—served under Capt Wood Blake
Carr, F.M.—blind
Carter, W.—old & blind in right eye
Casdorph, C.H.—catarrh in head 25 years
Cassa, J.W.—MS
Chandler, A.E.—hip & kidneys, gunshot wound arm & side
Chandler, W.A.—RH & partially blind
Cheek, J.—shot in left leg while on duty
Childress, A.—HD
Childress, D.—enlargement of liver
Christopher, M.—gunshot in left leg
Clark, J.C.—broken down
Clinqher, I.N.—right leg off
Cobb, J.M.—shot through right arm
Coffman, H.C.—failure of eye sight
Conely, G.N.—frozen feet & legs, sight
Conway, H.—shot through lung
Cunninqham, H.C.—fracture right nee, chronic pleurisy 24 years
Cuthrie, J.—HD 25 years
Dailey, I.—breast & kidneys, now has HD
Dailey, J.—CDR, stomach disease
Danner, G.—CDR, piles, deaf
Darnell, A.W.—gunshot wound left thigh
Darr, M.G.—catarrh
Dawson, N.W.—POW Richmond & Andersonville, 1 year 2 mos 13 days
Dawson, R.C.—gunshot left side & arm
Deel, J.E.—HD & LD
Deel, L.—shot through right shoulder

Dew, J.—RH, leg broken in coal mine
Dew, W.—disabled back, hip while dress parade at Charleston
Dodson, A.J.—eyes, back, heart, hearing
Dodson, J.R.— crippled in hack & left shoulder
Dodson, T.W.—LD, CDR, piles, spine
Drake, L.D.—lost smell caused by smallpox
Dye, C.*—CDR
Eckenrodd, S.—gunshot in left ankle
Edens, J.—HD & deafness 1 year
Edens, J.—RH
Edens, P.—RH in back & right hip
Elliott, N.—RH
Elswick, M.—RH
Eskew, A.J.—weak eyes result of smallpox
Estep, J.W.—TYF
Ewars, L.H.—catarrh
Fawber, G.N.—mind
Ferrell, F.M.—UFL
Fisher, E.—dropsy, KD, result of measles
Fisher, J.A.L.—loss eye sight
Flora, L.—rupture
Fridley, J.C.—KD & sight
Fronts, W.W.—shot in left leg
Garton, S.—wounded in hip
Gatewood, P.—old & UFL
George, R.—gunshot right hand, wounded testicles, RH & sight
George, W.H.—wounded
Gibson, C.A.—old & not able to work much
Gibson, S.—this man draws a pension of $24 per month & was never a soldier
Glover, C.—piles, KD, bladder
Griffith, T.H.—burned left foot & ankle
Gunno, J.—wounded left foot
Gunter, J.G.—loss of eye sight & hearing to some extent
Haas, J.—shot in arm
Hager, M.—piles & RH
Haldway, W.P.—POW Andersonville, catarrh, scurvy, CDR
Hall, A.—gunshot in left breast & shoulder
Hall, J.W.—RH
Hall, W.B.—thumb & finger shot off right hand
Hall, W.H.—piles, SS & LD
Hammack, L.A.—wounded right hand
Harless, L.—RH & HD
Harlon, T.C.—shot in left hand
Hawkins, W.N.—shot through right breast
Haynes, J.R.—catarrh
Haynes, W.M.—SS
Hays, V.A.—shot through left side

Hemmings, L.—CDR
Higgthum, S.A.—rupture
Hill, A.B.—deaf & blind partially
Hill, J.—disease of back & hip
Hill, W.H.—piles, RH, HD, sight
Hill, W.S.—right eye out
Holstine, D.—frosted feet
Holstine, P.L.—shot in ankle & finger off
Holstine, W.—shot in foot
Honaker, T.D.—RH, maimed, DSC
Hudnall, J.T.—shot through right arm
Hudson, J.T.—disease of breast & side, deaf
Huff, E.*—nerves affected
Huger, J.G.—contracted cough
Hughes, L.—DSC, by losing an eye
Hughey, G.K.—SS while on duty
Hulsey, J.H.—in commissary department
Hundley, J.H.—POW Andersonville 14 months discharged for insanity
Hunley, C.—CDR
Hutson, A.—LD & RH
Jackson, W.—spinal affection
James, D.H.—LD, KD, HD, RH right shoulder
Jarrett, A.—KD
Jarrett, J.Y.—gunshot wound in right thigh
Johnson, C.—RH
Johnson, J.—RH
Jones, E.T.—RH
Jones, W. (13 VAI)—shot in left thigh
Jones, W.—crippled shoulder & breast
Joplin, F.M.—foot mashed
Jopling, J.—gunshot in left thigh, entirely disabled in leg
Jordan, W.G.—injured by log, wood from waggon
Kanty, J.J.—disabled
Karnes, G.G.—CDR, asthma, piles, gunshot wound
Katcere, A.N.—SS & phtisic
Keeney, W.W.—RH, LD, liver disease
Keyser, H.*—injury
King, W.—lame in right knee
Kirk, J.—piles & CDR
Kirk, J.—shot in left shoulder
Lacy, G.W.—RH
Landers, M.—gunshot in thigh
Lanham, J.W.—TYF
Layton, J.—wounded foot
Leuper, J.W.—shot riqht hip
Levins, C.W.—POW, lost an eye & when released never got to regt
Loyd, A.I.—gunshot wound left hand

Lynn, W.H.*—shot in the hand
Lyons, H.—gunshot in neck May 1862
Lyons, J.—piles
Mace, J.—gunshot wound left arm
Martin, C.—liver & lung disease
Matheny, S.D.—RH & HD
McCan, A.—weak eyes
McClaskie, J.—loss of testicle by mumps
McComack, B.—weak eyes & lungs
McNeff, J.—jaw broken & wounded in breast
McVay, J.L.—hurt back & lower bowels & neck by horse falling
McVey, H.T.—RH
McWhorter, H.C.—gunshot
Means, J.—nasal catarrh & RH
Means, J.R.—RH, lame shoulder & breast
Meibler, H.—cold on measles caused nervous disability
Michaelson, O.H.—shell wound in hand
Midkiff, A.—LD 24 years
Midkiff, L.D.—liver disease & epleptic fits
Midkiff, L.—rupture & stiff finqer
Midkiff, M.—neuralgia & weak eyes
Midkiff, M.—wounded in left shoulder
Miller, Au.—DSC
Monday, M.O.—defective sight from measles
Monroe, E.—RH
Mooney, A.—vericiceal partial (?) feet & eyes
Moore, M.—shot through left hand
Morris, J.—RH
Morris, L.—shot in the foot
Morris, R.—blind of left eye
Mullens, M.—piles & RH
Myers, A.—lame in right foot
Naylor, J.M.—SS
Naylor, J.Y.—nervous disability
Nichols, I.—scrofula, broken down, entirely disabled
Noble, D.R.—spinal disease
Nolder, J.—shot middle finger right hand in Ky 6/19/1864
Norton, A.J.—was in 4 VAI 3 years
Nunley, A.—left leg broke falling on a bridge
Odell, J.S.—disease of throat & lungs
Orth, J.—SS on Lynchburg raid
Padgett, J.J.*—shot
Page, C.—old & UFL
Parson, M.—blind in left eye from measles
Parsons, J.A.—HD & catarrh
Parsons, R.A.—LD & piles
Pauley, C.—RH

Pauley, J.A.—crippled foot & knee
Pauley, O.F.—injured right foot
Pawley, M.—CDR, deaf right ear
Pence, H.—fractured thy
Perry, E.—lungs affected & RH
Perry, J.J.—RH
Perry, W.E.—smallpox
Phillips, R.H.—shot through right hip
Pilchard, H.L.—SS & injured by explosion of gunpowder
Porter, A.—RH
Porter, C.—eyes effected & RH & ruptured
Porter, N.—broken down from exposure
Porter, T.—broken
Pridemore, J.—hurt by a stirrup
Quigly, C.P.—ruptured 1863
Rader, J.—RH
Ramsey, A.—RH
Rangon, J.F.—blindness
Ranse, J.D.—RH
Rathburn, J.Q.—POW at Libby, injured head & foot cron malarial
Reed, E.N.—fever sore caused to be crippled
Riley, W.W.—RH & HD
Roberts, J.—leg broke by horse falling
Robins, S.P.—RH resulting in spinal affection
Robinson, C.—woonded with shell
Robinson, G.W.—gunshot right thigh, dislocated left elbow joint dislocation caused by fall while making charge
Robinson, M.H.—hearing affected
Robson, J.—disabled from measles
Rose, D.—scull fractured
Saers, M.—wounded by horse falling
Samples, L.S.—LD
Sampson, J.—gunshot wound in hand & shoulder
Samuels, C.G.—gunshot cross small of back, CDR
Schoolcraft, P.F.—LD
Shafer, H.—old & feeble
Shaffer, G.W.—gunshot in left foot
Shamblin, J.*—shot through the breast
Shaver, A.C.—injured back
Shultz, G.—right leg amputated from effects of gun explosion
Shultz, J.—KD
Sigmund, J.G.—piles & sunstroke
Simmons, C.—mumps
Simpkins, M.J.—AFP
Sines, H.J.—CDR 1864
Smith, G.H.—lumbago
Smith, J.M.—disabled by fever falling in left side

Smith, O.—RH
Smith, Sq.—pleurisy of side
Smith, W.H.—LD
Sneed, J.W.—2 gunshot wounds leg & head
Snodgrass, M.—RH, general dibility
Snodgrass, N.—overheat, DSC
Stanley, J.—LD
Stephenson, T.—SS
Stover, E.—loss of 4th finger left hand
Surratt, B.—RH & HD
Swaar, J.E.—piles
Swinney, W.R.—overheat
Taylor, H.—RH
Taylor, S.—jarred by cannon ball
Teel, S.—wound in right leg
Thaxton, J.R.—shot in finger
Thomas, J.A.—RH
Thomas, W.—RH
Thumm, J.F.—shot through right shoulder
Tincher, J.—defective in sight
Todd, I.N.—DSC
Toler, W.H.—paralysis & RH
Toney, L.—asthma
Toney, R.—back & kidney disease
Toothman, J.W.—old & UFL
Tucker, C.—piles
Turley, A.J.—disease of breast, stiff ankle & hip
Turley, A.J.—HD
Turley, J.D.—gunshot in right side
Walker, A.—WIA left hip, enlisted recent time (?) Sgt Critfeal
Wall, Au.—old & blind
Welcher, J.—gunshot wound both legs
Wertz, C.C.—hearing affected
Westbay, G.—lungs, feet, legs & eyes
Whitington, J.C.—SS
Whittington, W.H.—LD
William, B.—sore eyes & measles
Williams, A.—broken down
Williams, S.—broken wrist
Williams, W.P.—POW Camp Chase 10 months
Willson, D.—KD, sight, kicked by horse
Wilson, S.H.—sick, not able to work at present
Wines, W.—left leg broken, CDR
Wiseman, A.—RH
Withrow, J.N.—RH
Woodrum, A.—RH & weak back
Workman, A.—CDR & weak eyes

Lewis County

NAME/RANK	REGIMENT	WHEN SERVED
Abel, William M. Pvt.	4 VAC	8/17/63–2/6/64
Alfred, James Sgt.	10 WVI	3/2/62–3/19/65
Alfred, Pleasant Pvt.	10 WVI	12/15/61–3/15/65
Anderson, Charles E. Major	3 WVC	4/63–6/30/65
Anderson, James J. Sgt.	10 WVI	9/25/61–3/13/65
Anderson, Sorengo D. Pvt.	3 WVC	9/15/62–7/8/65
Anderson, William D. Pvt.	10 WVI	9/25/61–3/12/65
Arbogast, Daniel Pvt.	15 WVI	8/16/62–6/14/64
Archer, John	NF	
Aspurall, William H.(?) Lt.	8 OHC	8/19/61–7/19/65
Atkins, John G. Sgt.	11 WVI	12/61–8/10/65
Atkinson, Travers T. Pvt.	3 WVC	3/61–6/64
Bailey, Elam	NF	
Bailey, John H. Capt.	10 WVI	10/17/61–3/25/65
Ballard, Edward H. Pvt.	10 WVI	12/16/61–3/20/65
Ballard, James A. Pvt.	3 VAC	/24/62–/13/65
Ballentine, John T. Pvt.	6 WVI	10/1/61–10/15/64
Baram, F. M. Pvt.	15 WVI	3/63–65
Barnes, Josephes Sgt.	12 VAI	8/15/62–6/16/65
Barnett, Elias Pvt.	6 WVI	9/20/64–6/10/65
Barnett, Samuel Pvt.	10 WVI	10/61–6/12/65
Barnette, William C. Pvt.	10 WVI	9/25/61–3/12/65
Barrickman, John S. Pvt.	4 WVC	8/3/63–3/6/64
Batten, William C. Lt.	15 WVI	8/61–4/63
Bauserman, Joseph F. Pvt.	1 WVC	8/5/63–7/18/65
Bean, John Pvt.	10 WVI	5/25/63–8/10/65
Bee, Benjamin W. Pvt.	14 WVI	3/5/65–6/17/65
Bee, Richard Pvt.	6 WVI	9/24/61–6/10/65
Bennett, Elijah Pvt.	1 WVA	8/62–6/28/65
Bennett, Nathan D. Sgt.	10 WVI	1/2/62–8/65
Bennett, Salem Pvt.	10 WVI	1/11/62–3/17/65
Bird, Samuel R. Pvt.	10 WVI	8/9/64–6/20/65
Blake, Clark C. Pvt.	9 WVI	6/27/62–7/21/65
Boggs, Washington Pvt.	10 WVI	9/25/61–3/13/64
Bonnel, Floud M. Pvt.	6 VAI	2/28/61–10/6/64
Bonnett, Henry Pvt.	10 WVI	10/2/61–8/19/65
Bounds, James	US NF	
Brag, William Pvt.	3 WVI	1861–NF
Brake, Granville Pvt.	15 WVI	8/14/62–65
Brison, James E. Pvt.	12 WVI	62–65
Brison, William E. Lt.	3 WVI	6/12/61–6/24/65
Broash, Thomas	NF	
Brown, Alexander Cpl.	15 WVI	8/16/62–6/14/65

Name	Unit	Dates
Brown, Frank	US NF	
Brown, Jesse Pvt.	15 WVI	8/7/62–6/14/65
Bunten, Watson M. Sgt.	40 ILI	7/25/61–3/13/64
Burkhammer, John Pvt.	10 WVI	6/1/62–6/28/65
Burkhammer, Joseph Pvt.	15 VAI	8/11/62–6/18/65
Burley, Albert Pvt.	15 VAI	8/11/62–6/16/65
Burnsides, William H. Pvt.	15 WVI	8/16/62–6/14/65
Burrough, David H. Pvt.	15 WVI	8/16/62–6/14/65
Bush, John J. Pvt.	15 WVI	NF
Butcher, George W. Cpl.	4 WVC	7/63–3/64
Butcher, Jasper N. Pvt.	NF	
Butcher, Michael E. Pvt.	15 WVI	8/2/62–3/65
Cane, F. M. Pvt.	3 WVC	4/3/65–6/30/65
Carder, Jacob H. Pvt.	3 WVI	4/10/61–8/16/64
Cayner, Archibald Pvt.	15 WVI	1/22/64–8/9/65
Chalfont, Robert	US NF	
Clark, Bart Lt.	3 WVI	61–65
Clemans, John Pvt.	17 OHI	9/61–10/62
Clifton, Joseph H. Pvt.	12 PAI	61–62
Clifton, Wm	US NF	
Clinger, John	US NF	
Cloud, G. D.	US NF	
Coburn, John W. Sgt.	10 WVI	61–65
Colter, Edward Pvt.	10 WVI	12/15/61–3/65
Conley, Jacob C. Pvt.	15 VAI	8/10/62–6/12/65
Conrad, George W. Pvt.	15 WVI	8/11/62–6/14/65
Courtright, William Pvt.	17 WVI	8/29/64–6/30/65
Crawford, John Pvt.	3 WVI	6/61–7/23/65
Crawford, Noah Pvt. *aka* Crawford, William N.	10 WVI	8/12/62–7/5/65
Crofford, Charles A. Pvt.	10 VAI	64–65
Cunningham, Enoch G. Sgt.	10 WVI	9/25/61–3/12/65
Curry, Farleton	NF	
Dadson, Charles E. Pvt.	15 WVI	2/26/64–5/9/65
Daugherty, Charles C. Pvt.	6 WVC	9/1/64–4/8/65
Davis, George W. Pvt.	3 MDI	4/10/64–7/64
Davis, James T. Sgt.	15 WVI	8/62–5/25/65
Davis, Nathaniel Pvt.	3 MDI	1862–NF
Davis, Thomas S. Pvt.	10 WVI	7/4/62–4/20/65
Debar, Benjamin Pvt.	15 WVI	8/14/62–6/14/65
Detamone, John W. Lt.	15 VAI	8/11/62–/8/64
Devall, A. G.	NF	
Dinsmore, Robert G.	US NF	
Doddry, John Pvt.	15 WVI	8/14/62–6/14/65
Doughlas, Lansh	NF	
Douglas, Gared A. Cpl.	3 VAI	6/22/61–8/11/63
Draper, Mitchel C. Pvt.	10 WVI	3/18/62–8/9/65

Duncan, James W. Pvt.	10 WVI	6/1/62–6/5/65
Elsey, Abram	US NF	
Ervin, Marshall M. Musician	15 WVI	4/62–12/63
Fisher, Zebadu Pvt.	15 NYI	8/20/62–6/23/65
Flecher, Robert P. Pvt.	1 WVC	9/7/61–7/8/65
Fleming, Wm	US NF	
Frame, Erastus	NF	
Fretwell, Frank Pvt.	1 WVA	8/14/62–6/28/65
Fulkineer, James Pvt.	3 WVC	9/15/62–6/30/65
Gall, Lafayette E. Major	169 USI	6/57–4/65
Garton, James Pvt.	15 WVI	8/7/62–6/14/65
Garton, William T. Pvt.	1 WVC	1/1/62–6/12/65
Gaston, Thomas M. Pvt.	1 WVA	9/14/62–6/28/65
George, John	NF	
Gibson, J. J. Pvt.	11 MNI	8/25/64–6/26/65
Giggins, Isaac Pvt.	4 WVC	63/65
Gochenour, William M. Pvt.	10 VAI	3/64–8/18/65
Goff, E.	NF	
Goodwin, Ambrose Pvt.	10 WVI	11/12/61–12/29/64
Graves, Albert L. Pvt.	3 WVI	2/18/62–6/30/65
Grogg, Jacob Pvt.	6 WVI	1865
Gunn, John Sgt.	NF	
Hall, James F. Pvt.	15 WVI	8/15/62–6/14/65
Hall, Joseph Pvt.	15 VAI	8/10/62–6/12/65
Harman, P. G. Cpl.	10 WVI	1/20/62–8/7/65
Harper, William B. Pvt.	10 WVI	1/17/62–3/12/65
Heinzman, Alfred Pvt.	15 WVI	8/14/62–6/14/65
Helmick, William Pvt.	6 WVI	10/64–6/65
Henline, Andrew J. Pvt.	15 WVI	8/16/62–4/14/65
Henry, David Pvt.	3 WVI	6/4/61–5/30/66
Henry, Hugh B. Pvt.	3 WVI	9/24/63–5/22/65
Hersman, Mark Pvt.	NF	
Highland, Calvin Pvt.	3 WVC	3/65–7/65
Hornbeck, William Pvt.	1 WVA	9/13/62–6/29/65
Houth, Louis	US NF	
Hughes, Henry Pvt.	39 OHI	7/16/61–7/22/65
Hughes, Houston Cpl.	15 WVI	8/16/62–6/9/65
Hurst, Darius L. Pvt.	10 WVI	11/22/61–3/21/65
Hyre, David H. Pvt.	4 WVC	8/2/63–3/6/64
Jarvice, Hugh Pvt.	10 WVI	61/65
Jarvice, Acy S. Pvt.	10 WVI	12/62–3/65
Jeffries, Levi B. Pvt.	15 WVI	63/65
Jett, Wm	NF	
Jones, Samuel C. Pvt.	1 WVA	8/19/62–6/30/65
Jordan, John P. Pvt.	10 WVI	11/61–3/16/65
Kerins, John Pvt.	5 VAC	61/65
Kirtpatric, C. B.	US NF	

Name	Unit	Dates
Lahan, Michael L. Pvt.	10 WVI	12/61–8/9/64
Lamb, John W. Pvt.	3 WVC	3/4/64–6/30/65
Lamb, Skidmore Pvt.	15 WVI	8/21/62–6/14/65
Langford, Pleasant Pvt.	10 WVI	3/4/62–3/17/65
Lansford, J. A.	US NF	
Lawman, J. S. Pvt.	1 WVA	9/13/62–6/29/65
Lawson, Benj F. Cpl.	3 WVC	4/13/62–3/11/65
Lawson, Daniel B. Pvt.	15 WVI	8/14/62–6/14/65
Layfield, William Asst/Surgeon	82 PAI	10/17/64–6/17/65
Lewis, Gilbert Pvt.	NF	
Lightburn, J.A.J. General	WVI	8/28/61–6/22/65
Losh, Joseph Pvt.	15 WVI	8/15/62–6/15/65
Lovett, James B. Pvt.	3 WVC	9/15/62–6/13/65
Malia, Patrick. Pvt.	15 VAI	8/11/62–7/11/65
Markly, Joseph Pvt.	3 WVI	1/24/62–5/22/66
Marsh, Spencer C.	US NF	
Martin, James A. Pvt.	6 WVI	2/16/65 6/10/65
Maxson, James K. P. Pvt.	15 WVI	8/15/62–6/23/65
May, Lorentz Sgt.	15 WVI	8/15/62–6/14/65
McCartney, Elijah W. Pvt.	10 WVI	11/25/61–5/24/65
McDermott, Thomas Pvt.	NF	
McHenry, Wilson	NF	
McNemara, David C. Pvt.	6 WVI	6/14/62–6/10/65
McNemer, Wm B.	NF (18 VAC CSA)	
McQuain, William C. Pvt.	3 WVC	2/27/64–6/30/65
McWhorter, John S. Cpl.	3 WVC	61/65
Mead, Jackson	US NF	
Means, William Pvt.	47 OHI	10/1/61–10/15/65
Melt, John Pvt.	?	62/65
Mick, William E. Pvt.	3 WVC	3/10/64–6/12/65
Mills, Aleck Pvt.	US NAVY	1/64–9/65
Minear, John Pvt.	3 WVI	1/1/61–8/65
also	6 WVC	
Minnich, Elbridge G. Sgt.	44 OHI	61/65
Mitchel, Benjamine Pvt.	10 WVI	3/3/62–3/1/63
Mitchel, John A. Pvt.	3 WVC	3/20/64–6/30/65
Moneypeny, Asa Pvt.	10 WVI	11/20/61–8/9/65
Moneypeny, Thomas W.J Cpl.	15 WVI	8/11/62–6/14/65
Moneypeny, William R. Pvt.	10 WVI	61/65
Monneypeny, William J. Pvt.	15 WVI	8/15/62–6/15/65
Montgomery, Henry Cpl.	15 VAI	8/11/62–/12/65
Moore, James S. Pvt.	10 WVI	6/28/62–6/28/65
Moore, Levin W. Pvt.	VAA	8/7/61–/26/65
Moore, William N. Pvt.	3 VAC	2/11/64–6/13/65
Morris, Curtis Pvt.	15 VAI	8/17/62–6/16/65
Morris, William N. Pvt.	1 WVA	2/26/64–/28/65
Mullinax, Samuel B. Pvt.	15 WVI	8/15/62–6/14/65

Name	Unit	Dates
Murphy, Michael Pvt.	1 ILI	9/64–7/65
Neely, Gill Pvt. (Negro)	6 USC	9/26/64–12/9/65
Nicoll, William J. Capt.	15 WVI	8/14/62–6/14/65
Nuzum, Jessie	US NF	
Olds, William C. Lt.	105 OHI	8/3/62–8/3/65
Osburn, John W. Pvt.	6 WVI	10/14/64–6/10/65
Palmer, Gabriel Y. Cpl.	36 OHI	8/26/61–8/64
Peerey, James S. Pvt.	3 VAC	61/63
Peterson, David F. Lt.	10 WVI	9/8/61–8/9/65
Peterson, Jasper Capt.	15 WVI	8/14/62–9/17/63
Pickens, Jonathan Pvt.	1 WVC	1/27/65–7/8/65
Pritcard, Charles C. Pvt.	3 WVI	7/10/61–2/65
Raitt, Thomas	NF (36 VAI CSA?)	
Raysen, Albert F. Sgt.	15 WVI	8/15/62–6/14/65
Reece, A. R. Pvt.	15 WVI	8/6/62–6/29/65
Reger, William Cpl.	1 WVA	8/12/62–6/14/65
Rexroad, Uriah Pvt.	15 WVI	8/11/62–6/18/65
Rexrode, Nathan Lt.	3 WVC	62–65
Riffee, Benjamin Cpl.	15 WVI	8/16/62–6/14/65
Riffee, John R. Cpl.	15 WVI	8/15/62–6/14/65
Riffle, Jonathan M. Pvt.	10 WVI	9/8/61–12/30/64
Ring, Daniel W. Pvt.	10 WVI	/29/63–8/9/65
Rohrbough, Antoney E. Cpl.	15 VAI	8/11/63–6/16/65
Rohrbough, Jacob M. Pvt.	1 VAC (?)	8/17/62–6/7/65
Rohrbough, John G. Pvt.	15 WVI	8/15/62–6/14/65
Rose, William	NF (22 VAI CSA?)	
Sandy, Michael Pvt.	6 VAC	3/8/65–8/8/65
Sandy, Ulyssis Pvt.	6 WVI	NF
Shakelford, James W. Pvt.	8 WVI	10/4/62–5/20/64
Shea, John Sgt.	10 VAI	3/19/62–6/28/65
Shearer, William Pvt.	1 WVC	1/1/62–1/6/65
Shelton, W. J. Pvt.	4 WVI	62/63
Shinn, Harrison O. Pvt.	(?) 15 WVI	8/11/62–6/14/65
Simon, Christian Pvt.	10 WVI	9/12/61–3/12/65
Simpson, Alpheus F. Pvt.	15 WVI	8/22/62–9/10/65
Simpson, Marshal Cpl.	10 WVI	10/17/61–8/9/65
Simms, Alfred Pvt.	3 WVC	2/27/64–6/12/65
Siron, Henry F. Pvt.	3 WVI	2/2/64–6/65
Smith, Benjimin Pvt.	16 WVI	NF
Smith, Ellis S. Pvt.	10 WVI	61/65
Smith, Joseph Pvt.	10 WVI	1/1/62–7/28/66
Smith, Thomas G. Pvt.	10 VAI	/8/61–8/14/65
Smith, William M. Pvt.	7 VAC	/25/63–8/1/65
Snell, Guthen	US NF	
Spiers, William B. Pvt.	10 VAI	2/17/62–5/16/65
Stalnaker, Newton J. Pvt.	7 WVI	3/16/65–6/16/65
Stark, Henry Pvt.	10 WVI	1/19/62–3/19/65

Starkey, John C. Pvt.	6 WVI	9/30/64–5/24/65
Starcher, George W. Pvt.	15 WVI	8/15/62–6/3/65
Stalnaker, M. W. Sgt.	10 WVI	3/18/62–8/9/65
Stealy, Jacob Cpl.	10 WVI	7/17/62–7/18/65
Steele, Edward	US NF	
Steambeck, George W. Pvt.	15 WVI	62/65
Strader, John Pvt.	3 WVI	6/22/61–5/22/66
Summerville, Thomas	US NF	
Swecker, Manley Pvt.	15 WVI	8/11/62–6/14/65
Swisher, James P. Pvt.	15 WVI	2/14/63–11/18/65
Taft, Sam B. Pvt.	153 KYI	2/10/65–/18/66
Taylor, Albert Pvt.	15 WVI	8/16/62–6/14/65
Taylor, Bradley Pvt.	15 WVI	8/14/62–6/14/65
Taylor, George A. Cpl.	15 WVI	8/16/62–6/14/65
Taylor, Noah Pvt.	15 WVI	8/14/62–6/14/65
Taylor, Samuel Pvt.	10 WVI	3/61–7/64
Timms, Michal Pvt.	10 VAI	1/1/62–5/16/65
Turner, James Sgt.	10 WVI	3/17/61–3/17/64
Turner, Johnson V. Pvt.	15 VAI	8/15/62–6/15/65
Turner, Sanford B. Pvt.	10 VAI	6/10/61–3/17/65
Underwood, Charles S. Pvt.	10 WVI	9/26/61–3/12/65
Underwood, James S. Pvt.	10 WVI	12/11/61–8/9/65
Waggoner, Martin J. Pvt.	15 WVI	8/14/62–6/14/65
Waggoner, Oliver Sgt.	15 WVI	8/14/62–6/14/65
Ward, Harvey Pvt.	15 VAI	8/11/62–1/16/65
Ward, John D. Sgt.	15 VAI	8/11/62–6/16/65
Warner, G. M. Pvt.	WV NF	
Warner, Granville	US NF	
Warner, Tom M. Pvt.	10 WVI	9/26/61–3/12/65
Warner, William D. Pvt.	15 VAI	8/17/62–6/16/65
Weaver, John W. Pvt.	1 WVA	8/12/62–6/28/65
Wells, John Pvt.	1 WVC	7/18/61–7/18/65
West, C. T.	US NF	
West, Luther H. Pvt.	6 WVI	2/7/65 6/10/65
West, Richard	US NF	
Westfall, Peter Pvt.	10 VAI	10/16/61–5/17/65
Whetzel, George Pvt.	10 WVI	62/65
White, James Pvt.	12 WVI	63/65
Williams, George W. Pvt.	3 WVC	11/62–65
Wilson, J.H.S. Pvt.	16 PAC	8/18/62–65
Wilson, James C. Pvt.	10 WVI	9/25/61–3/12/65
Wilson, Jasper Pvt.	15 WVI	8/15/62–6/14/65
Wimer, Ellihu Pvt.	10 WVI	9/25/61–3/13/65
Wimer, Leonard R. Pvt.	3 WVI	6/10/61–9/29/65
Wimer, Morgan Pvt.	10 WVI	8/18/62–6/28/65
Windmiller, Walter Pvt.	3 WVC	9/22/62–1/27/65
Winemiller, Henry Pvt.	3 WVC	9/21/62–6/30/65

Wiseman, Samuel H. Pvt.	12 WVI	5/62–4/65
Wood, Andrew J. Sgt.	15 WVI	8/11/62–6/65
Wood, William V. Pvt.	3 WVI	6/10/61–5/22/66
Woofter, Marian Pvt.	(?) 10 WVI	2/15/62–3/15/65
Wright, J. B.	US NF	
Yates, James W. Pvt.	1 VAC	2/15/63–2/11/65
Yates, John B. Cpl.	17 VAI	4/2/64–1/30/65
Yoake, William J. Pvt.	15 WVI	3/4/64–8/9/65
Young, John C. Pvt.	12 WVI	8/11/62–5/25/65
Zinn, John W. Pvt.	6 WVI	8/18/61–9/10/64

Lewis Co. Remarks

Alfred, J.—gunshot wound 11/6/63 & wounded 9/22/64
Anderson, L.D.—fever settled in limbs
Arbogast, D. —cause of disability dropsy & smallpox
Atkinson, T.T.—piles
Bailey, J.H.—disease of throat
Ballard, E.H.—RH
Barnes, J.—RH
Barnett, E.—health destroyed
Barnett, S.—POW Danville 9 months 20 days
Barnette, W.C.—heat disease & RH & womded in hand
Barrickman, J.S.—eresiphelas
Bean, J.—broken rib
Bee, B.W.—piles & injured in hip
Bee, R. —LD
Bennett, E.—shot right thigh
Bennett, N.D.—VV & gunshot wound shoulder
Bennett, S.— RH & piles wounded in foot
Blake, C.C.— hernie
Boggs, W. —RH
Brake, G.—loss of leg by amputation
Brison, J.E.—hernia
Brison, W.E.—eriupolis face & head
Brown, A.—malarial poising resulting disease of spine epilepsy
Brown, J.—hernie Sept 19 1864 Winchester Va
Bunten, W.M. —wounds & VV
Burkhammer, J.—affection of head & back
Burnsides, W.H. —lumbargo
Bush, J.J.—RH
Butcher, G.W.—LD & crippled in hand
Butcher, M.E. —shot twice left hand
Cane, F.M.—CDR
Carder, J.H.—RH
Cayner, A.—RH & piles
Clemans, J—reinlisted Sept 1864 discharged June 1865, LD

Coburn, J.W. — RH & catarrh
Conrad, G.W. —LD
Crawford, J.—wounded in back
Crawford, N. —gunshot wound in the leg
Cunningham, E.G. —KD & LD
Dadson, C.E. —bronchitis, transferred to Co. B 10 WVI June 1865
Daugherty, C.C. —disability caused by TYF
Davis, G.W. —general disability
Davis, J.T.—RH
Davis, N. —piles
Davis, T.S. —throat & stomach disease
Detamone, J.W.—HD
Doddry, J. — RH
Douglas, G.A.—RH
Draper, M.C. —hurt by shell
Duncan, J.W. —shell wound head & breast causing loss of left eye
Ervin, M.M.—RH
Fretwell, F.—RH
Fulkineer, J. —neuralgia & HD
Garton, W.T. —deafness & piles
Gochenour, W.M. —CDR
Goodwin, A.—general disability
Graves, A.L. —RH
Hall, J.F.—bronchitis
Harman, P.G. —leg broke by wagon
Harper, H.B.— astbm
Helmick, W.—pneumonia
Henry, D. —shot through leg, mounted & changed to 6 WVC
Henry, H.B.—RH, changed to 6 WVC
Hughes, H. —RH
Hyre, D.H.—LD & HD
Jarvice, A.S.—shell wound of left arm
Jones, S.C.—CDR & stomach trouble
Jordan, J.B. —shot left hand crippled left leg
Lightburn, J.A.J.—gunshot wound of head
Losh, J.—SS
Lovett, J.B.—pneumonia followed by weak lungs
Martin, J.A. —TYF never had good health since
Maxson, J.K.P.—wound left ankle, injury to head & severe deafness
McCartney, E.W. —wounded in back & shoulder
McNemara, D.C.—RH
McQuain, W.C.—KD
McWhorter, J.S.—gunshot left temple
Means, W.—derangement of stomach & KD
Minear, J.—wounds & piles
Mitchel, B.—RH
Mitchel, J.A. —scurvy

Monneypenny, T.—disease of back 1862
Monneypenny, A.—syphlus from Sept 1863
Monneypenny, W.—right finger shot off
Mullinax, S.B.—RH & LD
Nicoll, W.J.—gunshot left side of head
Osburn, J.W.—dispepsy & RH
Peterson, D.F.—gunshot left hip
Pleasant, A.—shot left hand & left side
Pritchard, C.C.—left leg amputated
Raysen, A.F.—RH & KD
Reece, A.R.—wounded thigh
Rexroad, U.—KD
Riffee, J.R.—RH & piles
Riffle, J.M.—RH
Rohrbough, J.G.—constipation & LD
Shackelford, J.W.—RH
Shea, J.—shot in left lung
Shearer, W.—gunshot right shoulder Sept 1864
Simon, C.—RH & LD
Simpson, M.—partial loss sight
Sims, A.—RH & KD
Siron, H.F.—deafness & RH
Smith, E.S.—wounded right thigh
Smith, J.—shot through ankle at Winchester
Spiers, W.B.—dyspepsia
Starkey, J.C.—smallpox & bronchitis
Stealy, J.—gunshot wound left hip
Strader, J.—ruptured, feet frozen, and eyes injured
Swecker, M.—CDR
Taylor, A.—deafness
Taylor, G.A.—RH, run over by dispatch carrier
Taylor, S.—hemorhages
Underwood, C.S.—RH & KD
Underwood, J.S.—wounds foot & arm
Waggoner, M.J.—CDR & piles
Wells, J.—foot broken by horse falling
West, L.H.—catarrh of head
Wilson, J.—epilepsy
Wilson, J.C.—catarrh & CDR
Wimer, E.—KD
Wimer, L.R.—CDR, piles, malarial poison
Wimer, M.—RH & LD
Windmiller, W.— defness & wounded
Wood, W.V.—hurt Feb 1864, reinlisted in 6 WVC
Yates, J.B.—KD, LD, RH & lack of eyesight
Yoake, W.J.—deafness
Young, J.C.—RH

Lincoln County

NAME/RANK	REGIMENT	WHEN SERVED
Abbott, Braden A. Pvt.	7 WVI	1861–NF
Adkins, Aaron Pvt.	34 VAC CSA	11/62–4/15/65
Adkins, Anderson Pvt.	7 WVC	2/1/63–8/1/65
Adkins, Andrew Pvt.	7 WVC	8/23/64–1/3/65
Adkins, Burrell Pvt.	— VAI CSA	7/62–1863
Adkins, Caleb Pvt.	7 WVC	62/65
Adkins, Eliott Pvt.	7 WVC	1862–8/65
Adkins, Enos Pvt.	CS (45 BTN VAI)	63/64
Adkins, Gorden Pvt.	US NF	
Adkins, Greenville	7 VAC	NF
Adkins, Hiram Pvt.	7 WVC	2/5/62–8/65
Adkins, Jacob Pvt.	1 WVA	10/1/61–7/11/62
also	173 OHI	8/13/64–6/26/65
Adkins, John H. Pvt.	CSA (129 VAM)	63/65
Adkins, John N. Pvt.	7 WVI	NF
Adkins, Joshua Pvt.	7 WVC	10/24/61–8/1/65
Adkins, Kenos M. Pvt.	7 WVC	1/11/65–8/1/65
Adkins, Lewis	US NF	
Adkins, Luke G. Pvt.	7 WVC	12/61–8/65
Adkins, Martin Pvt.	7 WVC	1/10/65–8/1/55
Adkins, Mathew Pvt.	7 WVI	64/65
Adkins, Mathias Pvt.	7 WVC	1/28/65–8/1/65
Adkins, Milton Pvt.	7 WVI	11/20/64–8/1/65
Adkins, Perry G. Pvt.	3 USI	10/7/64–12/12/65
Adkins, Samuel Pvt.	NF	
Albright, James A. Pvt.	4 WVI	6/15/63–NF
Arthur, Wm. J. Pvt.	7 WVC	3/22/64–8/1/65
Baisden, James Pvt.	CS (25 BTN VAI)	62/63
Baker, John L. Pvt.	5 VAI	12/1/62–7/21/65
Bias, Enos Sgt.	3 WVC	10/17/62–6/30/65
Bias, John M. Pvt.	3 WVC	4/27/63–6/30/65
Bias, Linville Cpl.	3 WVC	10/17/62–6/30/65
Bills, John L. Pvt.	11 WVI	7/11/62–6/17/65
Black, John W. Pvt.	3 WVI	3/23/64–6/30/65
Boothe, Wm. A. Pvt.	1 VAI	1/1/62–1/6/65
Bosten, George Pvt.	36 OHI	10/62–7/63
also Lt.	2 OHA	8/63–9/65
Bowman, Beverly B. Sgt.	7 WVC	9/5/62–1865
Bowman, James Pvt.	8 WVI	10/1/61–2/4/63

The Veteran Census Roster 171

Bragg, James C. Pvt.	7 VAC	NF
Brewer, Edward Pvt.	4 WVC	63/64
Brock, Jordan Pvt.	54 KYI	9/64–9/65
Browning, Charles Sgt.	36 VAC CSA	6/61–4/65
Browning, Francis Pvt.	CSA (129 VAM)	NF
Browning, Jackson Pvt.	36 VAC CSA	NF
Browning, James Pvt.	VAC CSA (34?)	10/1/62–8/1/63
Browning, Miles B. Pvt.	39 KYC CSA	10/62–1865
Brumfield, John S. Pvt.	VAC CSA	64/65
Brumfield, Parish Pvt.	— VA CSA	62/65
Bryant, James Pvt.	CSA (129 VAM)	NF
Calahan, Andrew E.	NF	
Camron, David C. Sgt.	45 KYI	8/3/63–12/24/64
Carroll, Wm. A. Pvt.	173 OHI	8/25/64–6/26/65
Chandler, Richard A. Pvt.	7 WVC	11/6/61–8/1/65
Clark, Alexander Pvt.	13 WVI	1862–6/65
Clark, John Pvt.	75 OHI	11/61–3/65
Clark, Samuel Pvt.	14 KYI	6/63–9/65
Collins, Levi Cpl.	34 VAC CSA	12/61–1863
Collins, Michael Pvt.	8 WVI	9/2/61–11/26/64
Cooper, Silas Pvt.	8 WVI	10/62–10/63
Cremeans, Preston L. Pvt.	7 WVC	8/31/62–6/15/65
Crum, Silas	US NF	
Cummings, James D. Pvt.	8 WVI	11/31/62–8/1/65
Curry, George I. Pvt.	1 WVC	2/65 7/3/65
Curry, Granville Lt.	3 WVC	10/17/62–6/30/65
Dailey, John B. Pvt.	173 OHI	8/13/64–6/26/65
Davis, Jiles Pvt.	36 VAC CSA	9/61–1864
Dillon, Marshall Pvt.	1 OHA	7/21/63–7/25/65
Dingess, Henderson Pvt.	36 VAC CSA	9/63–1864
Dottson, Andrew J. Pvt.	7 VAC	NF
Dunlap, Addison Pvt.	7 WVC	9/22/64–6/13/65
Dunlap, Piner Pvt.	7 WVC	1/21/65–8/1/65
Dunlop, Maurice Pvt.	NF	
Duty, Wm. Pvt.	36 VAI CSA	6/22/61–1865
Egnor, Josiah Pvt.	11 OHC	6/9/63–5/20/66
Eliott, Joseph Pvt.	NF (Byrnes KYA CSA?)	
Elkins, Andrew	CSA NF (34 BTN VAC)	
Elkins, Boyd W. Pvt.	7 WVC	11/62–8/65
Elkins, Jacob Pvt.	7 VA-	NF
Erving, Lucas Pvt.	36 VAI CSA	6/61–1864
Evans, Wm. R. Pvt.	22 KYI	10/22/61–1/25/65
Fowler, John P. Pvt.	VAC CSA (1)	62/62
Fowler, Wm. T. Pvt.	CSA (129 VAM)	62/62
Fry, Lewis Pvt.	VAC CSA (1)	11/63–1864
Gary, Wm. H. Pvt.	7 WVC	3/4/65 8/5/65
Gorden, Isaac G. Lt.	1 VAC CSA	62/63

Name	Unit	Dates
Grass, Lacy Pvt.	3 USI	10/31/64–11/29/65
Griffith, Joseph A. Pvt.	11 WVI	3/27/62–5/16/65
Hagar, Rilan Pvt.	1 KYI	NF
Hagar, Silas Pvt.	7 WVI	NF
Hager, Fernando Pvt.	14 KYI	1861–9/25/65
Hager, Henderson Pvt.	8 VAC	61/64
Hager, Russell Pvt.	8 VAI	61/62
Hall, Moses B. Sgt.	13 WVI	8/22/62–6/22/65
Hall, Wm. P. Pvt.	7 WVC	1/1/62–8/65
Harless, James Pvt.	7 WVI	NF
Heck, John Pvt.	91 OHI	8/15/62–6/28/65
Hill, Wehster L. Pvt.	91 OHI	8/9/62–6/24/65
Hill, Isarah Pvt.	7 WVC	9/20/64–6/3/65
Hills, Nimrod Pvt.	7 WVC	9/16/64–6/3/65
Hokins, Hamilton Pvt.	7 WVC	8/15/62–8/1/65
Holley, Edgar D. Cpl.	14 KYI	10/20/61–1/31/65
Holton, Wm. A. Pvt.	7 WVI	8/17/64–8/1/65
Honaker, Martin W. Pvt.	14 KYI	10/61–6/65
Hood, George W. Pvt.	7 WVC	7/4/64–8/15/65
Howard, Samuel B. Pvt.	11 WVI	8/1/62–6/17/65
Hudson, Ithamer T. Sgt.	7 WVC	9/4/61–1/23/65
Jackson, Isaac Pvt.	3 WVC	11/22/62–NF
Jackson, John Cpl.	14 KYC	12/18/62–3/24/64
Johnson, Thomas Pvt.	1 WVI	2/15/64–7/21/65
Jones, Thomas E. Pvt.	88 OHI	1/64–7/65
Justice, George M. Pvt.	7 WVC	9/2/61–7/1/65
Keck, Daniel B. Pvt.	9 WVI	12/25/61–8/15/65
Keck, Wm. T. Pvt.	3 WVC	11/63–6/65
Keeney, Neri Pvt.	7 WVC	9/12/62–6/3/65
Kid?, Work Pvt.	7 WVC	1/65 8/65
Kinder, Henry J. Pvt.	7 WVC	3/21/62–4/8/65
Kingcaid, John W. Pvt.	13 WVI	6/62–6/65
Kusser, David Pvt.	1 VAC CSA	62/65
Lacy, James P. Pvt.	7 WVC	7/20/64–6/3/65
Lambert, Hiram Pvt.	36 VAI CSA	63/65
Landeman, Boye B. Pvt.	11 VAI	8/1/62–6/17/65
Lane, Thomas R. Pvt.	12 PAC	1/3/63–NF
Lewis, Robert A.	—	63/65
Lias?, Henry C. Pvt.	7 WVC	1/25/65 8/31/65
Lias, James W? Pvt.	2 WVC	7/61–NF
Lively, Mark Cpl.	7 WVC	9/5/61–8/9/65
Lovejoy, David Pvt.	7 VAC	61/65
Lovejoy, Richard Cpl.	7 WVC	10/61–8/65
Lovejoy, Wm. P. Pvt.	7 WVI	NF
Lucas, David D. Pvt.	5 VAI	1862–NF
Martin, Thomas	US NF	
May, Jacob C. Pvt.	11 WVI	3/27/62–5/16/65

Name	Unit	Dates
McClure, George W. Pvt.	7 WVC	10/4/64–8/9/65
McClure, Harrison Pvt.	7 WVC	7/20/62–8/15/65
McClure, Joseph R. Pvt.	7 WVC	8/22/64–6/3/65
McClure, Nelson Pvt.	7 WVC	10/5/64–8/7/65
McComas, Blackburn Pvt.	3 WVC	1/63–7/65
McComas, Elisha A. Pvt.	3 WVC	1/63–7/65
McComas, George R. Pvt.	9 VAI	12/16/61–12/31/63
McComas, Wilson Pvt.	3 VAC	2/28/64–7/13/65
McCormic, John Pvt.	7 WVC	9/2/64–6/3/65
McCormic, Jurden Pvt.	7 WVC	9/3/61–6/15/65
McGraw, Charles Pvt.	5 VAI	7/61–11/63
McMullion, James W. Pvt.	9 VAI	12/25/61–4/7/64
Meek, Wm. Pvt.	8 VAC CSA	5/61–1865
Menely, Rilan F. Pvt.	7 WVI	NF
Midkiff, Wm. G. Pvt.	7 WVC	12/3/61–1/24/65
Mitchell, John J. Pvt.	8 WVI	2/6/62–12/31/62
Mulens, Henry Pvt.	34 VAC CSA	NF
Mulens, Van B. Cpl.	CS (Swanns VAC)	1863–NF
Mullens, J.M.P. Pvt.	1 KYI	63/65
Mullins, Spencer Pvt.	39 KY-	NF
Nelson, Wm. L. Pvt.	7 WVC	3/29/65 7/6/65
Oillon, John Cpl.	62–OHI	9/30/62–6/17/65
Orr, Mills? Cpl.	7 WVC	10/14/61–8/1/65
Paine, Simeon Pvt.	9 WVI	10/61–7/65
Parsons, Edward M. Pvt.	3 USI	10/27/64–11/24/65
Pauley, Allen H. Pvt.	7 WVC	10/8/61–8/9/65
Pauley, Daniel Pvt.	7 WVC	12/15/62–8/5/65
Pauley, Henry A. Pvt.	7 WVC	2/2/65 8/1/65
Pauley, Joseph Pvt.	7 WVC	9/5/61–6/24/65
Pauley, Lafayette W. Pvt.	7 WVC	9/5/61–8/15/65
Pauley, Nelson Pvt.	7 WVC	9/2/64–6/3/65
Pauley, Sanford Pvt.	1 WVI	9/2/64–6/13/65
Pauley, Wm. W. Pvt.	7 WVC	10/64–8/9/65
Payton, Wm. M. Pvt.	7 WVC	3/24/64–8/15/65
Peck, Wm. B.P. Pvt.	1 WVC	10/63–6/65
Pennington, Isaac G. Pvt.	5 WVI	9/14/61–7/10/62
Perry, I.G. Pvt.	36 VAI CSA	6/3/61–7/61
Plumley, Calaway Pvt.	7 WVC	1/25/65 8/1/65
Plumley, Melvin Pvt.	7 VAC	NF
Porter, Greenville Pvt.	49 KYI	1863–NF
Powell, Henry A. Pvt.	5 WVI	8/10/61–10/4/64
Pridemore, Daniel Pvt.	4 KYI	7/29/62–12/30/64
Prutley, Marshal B. Pvt.	7 WVI	2/25/65 7/1/65
Rakes, Richard Pvt.	39 KYI	NF
Rank?, Henry Pvt.	7 WVC	8/20/62–6/3/65
Ratliff, John	CSA NF (24 VAI?)	
Ray, Isaac W. Capt.	14 KYI	8/63–6/65

Reynolds, Wm. A. Pvt.	173 OHI	8/14/64–6/26/65
Rice, Wm. Pvt.	6 OHC	62/65
Robinson, A.D. Pvt.	45 KYI	8/8/63–12/24/64
Roby, John Pvt.	7 WVC	9/5/61–6/15/65
Ross, Samuel H. Pvt.	167 VAM (CSA?)	8/7/63–2/7/64
Roy, Charles B. Pvt.	9 VAI	12/16/61–12/16/64
Rrowning, Mitchel Pvt.	36 VAI CSA	10/62–1865
Scites, Canada Pvt.	7 WVC	1862–NF
Scites, Christopher A. Pvt	3 WVC	3/1/63–6/30/65
Scites, Hiram Pvt.	3 WVC	3/1/64–6/30/65
Shultz, Johrl Pvt.	7 WVC	9/13/64–6/3/65
Sias, A.L. Pvt.	34 BTN VAC CSA	5/28/61–5/2/65
Sizemore, Edward W. Pvt.	4 VAI	62/63
Skenes, James Pvt.	14 KYI	8/62–8/63
Smith, Albert P. Pvt.	11 WVI	1862–NF
Smith, Daniel M. Pvt.	7 WVC	2/14/65 8/1/65
Smith, George W. Pvt.	7 WVC	8/22/64–6/3/65
Smith, Luke S. Pvt.	13 WVI	10/63–7/65
Smith, Wm. S. Pvt.	3 WVC	12/64–7/65
Sowards, David W. Pvt.	20 OHI	12/16/64–7/18/65
Spears, Henry Pvt.	91 OHI	7/63–7/65
Spears, Preston Pvt.	9 VAI	5/61–5/64
Spears, Wesley Pvt.	9 OHI	NF
Spurlock, Eli Pvt.	8 WVI	61/62
Spurlock, Eliphas Pvt.	8 VAI	9/1/61–NF
Spurlock, John Pvt.	8 WVI	9/1/61–8/1/65
Spurlock, Seth Cpl.	8 WVC	9/1/61–8/2/65
Spurlock, Wm. Pvt.	8 WVI	9/61–1865
Steed, Wm. H. Pvt.	25 OHI	63/66
Stewart, Frank Pvt.	NF	
Stone, Christopher M. Pvt.	7 WVC	6/20/61–5/24/65
Stroud, Harmon Pvt.	NF	
Swanson, Joseph Pvt.	16 KYI	62/65
T,ovejoy, Joseph Pvt.	7 WVC	12/22/62–8/1/65
Tacket, Samuel A. Pvt.	NF	
Tackett, Eliga Pvt.	7 WVC	9/5/61–6/24/65
Thompson, Hasting	NF	
Thornton, James G. Pvt.	91 OHI	8/6/62–6/13/65
Tomland, Alfred Pvt.	16 VAI CSA	62/65
Tomlin, Alfred Sr.	—VA CSA	NF
Tona?, Squire	—VAC CSA	63/64
Turley, Hezekiah Pvt.	7 WVC	3/64–8/1/65
Turley, John H. Pvt.	7 WVC	8/6/64–6/3/65
Turley, Noah Pvt.	7 WVC	7/4/64–6/3/65
Ullom, Andrew J. Pvt.	14 KYI	10/25/61–6/31/65
Vance, A.J. Pvt.	VAC CSA (34?)	8/62–4/65
Vance, Francis Pvt.	34 VAC CSA	8/62–10/64

Vance, Marvel Pvt.	36 VAI CSA	6/61–12/64
Vance, Wm. Pvt.	27 VAI CSA	63/65
Vannatter, Samuel Pvt.	1 VAI CSA	64/65
Vest, Crawford E. Pvt.	3 WVC	1/1/64–6/30/65
Wall, Joshua Cpl.	36 VAI CSA	7/1/61–2/16/64
Watson, Daniel Pvt.	45 KYI	7/63–11/64
Williams, Spencer Pvt.	9 WVI	61/65
Williamson, Joseph Pvt.	45 KYC	NF
Williamson, Wiley Pvt.	8 VAI	5/61–1865
Wilson, David Pvt.	129 OHI	8/27/63–6/21/65
Woodson, Richard S. Pvt.	7 WVC	9/11/64–8/1/65
Workman, Wm. Pvt.	34 VAC CSA	3/62–1864
Yeager, John F. Pvt.	14 MOC	2/61–2/65

Lincoln County Remarks

Adkins, A.*—eyes affected, WIA 3 times, arm, leg & side
Adkins, H.—loss of speech
Adkins, J.—HD, pensioner
Adkins, M.—mumps
Adkins, Mat.—affected in hip
Bias, L.—LD
Black, J.W.—CDR, diseased testicles from mash on saddle, UFL
Bosten, G.—piles & LD
Bowman, J.—general derangement
Bragg, J.C.—sore leg below knee
Browning, M.*—shot in right arm
Calahan, A.E.—he claims his eyes were injured permanently
Camron, D.C.—gunshot wound left thigh
Carroll, W.A.—diseased testicles & RH
Clark, A.—fistula & CDR
Clark, J.—gunshot wound, pensioner
Collins, L.*—shot through knee
Collins, M.—diseased
Cremeans, P.L.—piles & partial paralasis
Curry, G.—deafness
Curry, G.I.—lame back
Dailey, J.B.—crippled lmee
Dillon, J.—respiratory organs diseased, pensioner
Dillon, M.—catarrh of head
Dottson, A.J.—effects of pneumonia in side
Dunlap, P.—rupture
Duty, W.*—finger broke
Gary, W.H.—neuralgia & catarrh

Grass, L.—CDR, diseased rectum, pensioner
Hager, H.—loss of one eye & mumps fell
Hall, M.B.—RH
Hills, N.—loss of right eye
Honaker, M.W.—relapse of measles settled in back
Howard, S.B.—scrofula
Hudson, I.T.—lame back
Jackson, I.—diseased, pensioner
Jackson, J.—right leg, ankle & head hurt by fall from horse
Johnson, T.—shot through thigh
Justice, G.M.—I.D
Keck, D.B.—CDR, liver disease, fistula
Keck, W.T.—loss of left testicle & eyes permanently injured
Kinder, H.J.—rupture from kick of horse
Landeman, B.B.—gunshot wound in left ear
Lewis, R.A.—shot through calf of leg
Lively, M.—hearing
Lovejoy, D.—KD
Lucas, D.D.—freezing
May, J.C.—right ankle mashed
McClure, G.W.—lungs, head & eyes affected
McClure, J.R.—piles
McClure, N.—LD & RH
McComas, E.A.—stricture of the bladder
McComas, G.R.—gunshot wound right knee
McMullion, J.W.—dishonorably discharged
Midkiff, W.H.—disease of respiratory organs
Mitchell, J.J.—left shoulder & hand shot
Mullins, S.—fever fell in legs & back
Orr, M.—CDR
Paine, S.—RH & HD
Pauley, A.H.—dropsy
Pauley, D.—catarrh of head
Pauley, N.—piles & KD
Pauley, S.—nervous dibility
Porter, G.*—(served first the 34 VAC CSA deserted 1/1863)
Powell, H.A.—disease of testicles & back, pensioner
Pridemore, D.—CDR & LD
Rakes, R.—crippled in hip
Rank, H.—crippled from horse throw
Ratliff, J.*—crippled in hip
Reynolds, W.A.—diseased
Rice, W.—LD
Robinson, A.D.—piles
Scites, C.A.—RH
Shultz, J.—hurt from horse throw
Skenes, J.—strained hip joint

Smith, L.S.—rupture & sore in small of back following measles
Sowards, D.W.—RH
Spears, H.—RH
Spurlock, E.—fistula
Spurlock, J.—one eye almost put out in the war
Spurlock, S.—crippled shoulder, mustered out of duty health bad
Spurlock, W.—shot through neck, injured by shell in side
Steed, W.H.—smallpox & gunshot wound, pensioner
Stewart, F.—drafted but deserted in a short time
Stroud, H.—sick on disability when regt discharged
Swanson, J.—diseased
Thompson, H.—now in the WV lunatic asylum
Turley, H.—rupture
Ullom, A.J.—LD
Vance, F.*—shot 3 times
Vannatter, S.*—piles
Vest, C.E.—smallpox & lame back
Wall, J.*—piles
Williams, S.—gunshot wound left shoulder
Williamson, W.—LD

Logan County

NAME/RANK	REGIMENT	WHEN SERVED
Anderson, Robert Sgt.	1 KYI	8/7/64–1865
Baldwin, Shadrack Pvt.	7 WVI	11/10/61–12/27/62
Ballard, Curtis Pvt.	8 VAI	2/6/62–9/10/63
Baughman, Isaac Pvt.	11 PAC	1862–8/65
also	133 PAI	NF
Blankenship, Jacob Cpl.	39 KYI	7/7/63–9/12/65
Bragg, David Sgt.	7 WVI	10/63–6/5/65
Brewer, Aaron Pvt.	45 KYI	5/63–12/65
Browning, Allen K.M. Pvt.	9 WVI	1/15/62–NF
Buchanan, James A.	NF (45 VAI CSA?)	
Buchanan, Thomas Lt.	4 WVI	6/1/64–12/18/64
Burgess, Cornelius Sgt.	7 WVC	12/9/62–8/1/65
Burgess, John W. Cpl.	8 WVI	12/9/62–8/1/65
Chaffin, Christopher Pvt.	13 —?	6/61–4/65
Damron, George W. Cpl.	45 KYI	12/11/63–2/14/65
Daniels, Thomas	US NF	
Dempsey, Joseph	NF	
Elkins, Charles K. Pvt.	7 WVC	NF
Ellis, Abner A. Pvt.	8 WVI	8/1/64–8/15/65
Elswick, George W. Pvt.	2 WVC	3/15/63–6/25/65
Eskins, Dewitt C. Pvt.	7 WVI	12/8/62–8/1/65
Estep, Jonathan Sgt.	(13 KYC CSA)	8/19/63–12/24/64
Hannah, Isaac	NF	
Hatfield, Johnson Pvt.	39 KYI	10/62–10/65
Jeffery, Bird L. Pvt.	7 WVI	2/16/65 8/1/65
Kelley, Wm. Pvt.	41 KYI	11/4/62–8/15/65
Lackey, Solomon	CSA NF	
Lanaghan, John Sgt.	32 OHI	8/4/62–6/18/65
Meade, Wm. Pvt.	5 OHI	4/15/64–1/14/65
Mounts, Charles W. Pvt.	(45 BTN VAI CS)	1/1/63–9/13/65
Mounts, Jackson A. Pvt.	39 KYI	1/62–9/65
Mounts, Wm. H. Pvt.	(45 BTN VAI CS)	5/62–11/63
Nelson, Inin Pvt.	7 WVI	11/10/61–8/18/65
Pack, James A. Pvt.	(Swanns VAC CS)	11/63–1864
Parsley, Jolin W. Pvt.	5 VAI	NF
Parsley, Moses Pvt.	14 KYI	3/20/64–9/65
Perry, Jasper Cpl.	7 WVC	1/62–8/1/65
Perry, Rhodes B. Pvt.	8 VAI	2/6/62–10/13/62
also Cpl.	4 WVC	6/15/63–5/30/64
also Pvt.	7 WVC	11/17/64–8/1/65

Pomith, James Pvt.	8 WVI	10/15/64–NF
Prince, Van B. Pvt.	5 VAI	8/10/61–6/26/63
Riffe, Gordon Pvt.	7 WVC	NF
Riffe, Patterson Pvt.	7 WVC	9/62–8/65
Spaulding, A. Pvt.	45 KYI	8/1/61–11/64
Starr, Wm. Cpl.	14 KYI	61/65
Thompson, Henry	NF (Swann's BTN VAC CSA)	
Vance, John P. Pvt.	4 VAC	6/15/63–3/10/64
White, Benj. W.	NF (129 VAM CSA)	
White, Francis M. Pvt.	8 WVI	6/9/62–8/1/65
White, John Pvt.	7 WVI	6/27/64–8/1/65
Woody, Sidney T. Pvt.	—	64/65
Workman, James A. Pvt.	38 VAI CSA	63/65 NF

Logan County Remarks

Baldwin, S.—spinal affection
Ballard, C.—gunshot wound in left side
Blankenship, J.—RH & HD
Brewer, A.—wounded
Browning, A.K.M.—ruptured
Burqess, C.—now suffering from disease
Damron, G.W.—hearing & left leg injured
Estep, J.★—POW at Camp Morton Indiana (served 13 KYC CSA)
Lackey, S.★—surrendered (CSA, name not found in CSR)
Meade, W.—exposure
Mounts, C.W.★—partial loss of sight & HD (45 BTN VAI CSA 5/1/63 to 1/28/64 deserted)
Mounts, J.A.—RH
Mounts, W.H.★—RH (enlisted 45 BTN VAI CSA 5/1/63 to 7/10/63 AWOL and into 60 VAI CSA 1864)
Pack, J.A.★—deaf in left ear, paroled (served Swanns VAC CSA)
Parsley, J.W.—Capt Murray's home guards subject to orders 5 VAI
Parsley, M.—exposure to cold
Perry, R.B.—RH & weak lungs, now infirm
Riffe, P.—disabled by horse falling on his leg
Spaulding, A.—thrown from horse, discharged
Starr, W.—exposure caused RH
Workman, J.A.★—surrendered

Marion County

NAME/RANK	REGIMENT	WHEN SERVED
Adams, George Pvt.	6 WVC	6/7/61–2/1/64
also Blacksmith	6 WVC	2/1/64–7/15/65
Ammons, Albert Pvt.	6 WVI	1/30/65–6/10/65
Amos, Enoch K. Pvt.	NF	
Amos, Thornton Cpl.	14 WVI	8/14/62–6/27/65
Anderson, Enos Pvt.	14 VAI	2/14/64–6/27/66
Anderson, Henry Pvt.	12 VAI	NF
Anderson, John Pvt.	6 WVA	8/7/61–2/23/64
also	1 WVA	2/22/64–7/21/65
Anderson, Newton B. Pvt.	12 WVI	8/4/62–6/16/65
Anderson, Robert Pvt.	12 VAI	8/17/62–6/65
Arnet, Elbert M. Pvt.	17 WVI	2/28/65–6/30/65
Arnett, Eber Pvt.	6 WVI	9/1/64–6/10/65
Arnett, Franklin Cpl.	6 WVI	9/3/64–6/10/65
Arnett, John Pvt.	12 WVI	8/13/62–6/13/65
Arnett, Riley Pvt.	6 WVI	9/1/64–6/13/65
Ashcraft, Armistead Pvt.	12 WVI	12/28/63–6/14/65
Atha, Elihu Cpl.	14 WVI	8/16/62–6/27/65
Atha, Ulyssus S. Pvt.	6 WVI	9/1/64–6/10/65
Atha, Wm. M. Pvt.	7 WVI	3/24/65–7/8/65
Austin, Joseph Pvt.	14 WVI	8/20/62–6/28/65
Baker, Elias Pvt.	6 WVI	8/12/62–7/2/65
Baker, James H. Pvt.	4 WVI	1/17/61–1/20/64
Baker, James Pvt.	6 WVI	2/14/65–6/10/65
Barnes, Harvey R. Pvt.	NF	
Barnes, Peter T. Pvt.	17 WVI	2/17/65–6/30/65
Barr, Benjamin Pvt.	50 PAI	8/64–8/23/65
Barthelow, George Cpl.	7 WVI	6/8/61–10/13/62
Bartholow, James O. Pvt.	4 VAI	7/12/63–3/17/64
also Cpl.	6 VAI	9/9/64–6/20/65
Batson, John W. Pvt.	17 VAI	8/64–7/6/65
Batson, Washington B. Pvt.	6 WVC	6/25/61–5/25/66
Beall, John T. Pvt.	20 VAC CSA	6/10/62–5/10/65
Bean, Joseph Pvt.	1 WVI	4/14/62–4/30/65
Bennett, Frank Pvt.	3 WVC	2/24/64–6/30/65
Berry, Tom L. Pvt.	6 WVC	1/1/61–8/13/64
Billinglea, Ellis Sgt.	16 OHI	6/8/62–12/20/64
also Pvt.	6 WVI	1/17/65–6/10/65
Billingsley, John E. Cpl.	12 WVI	8/18/62–6/16/65
Binns, John H. Pvt.	4 WVC	7/13/63–3/7/64
Blaker, Lindsey Pvt.	22 PAC	9/15/62–7/19/65

Boggers, Caleb Pvt.	14 WVI	8/16/62–6/27/65
Boggess, John W. Bugler	1 WVA	8/7/62–7/21/65
Boggess, Tom C. Pvt.	3 WVC	2/62–6/65
Boice, Isaac Pvt.	3 WVC	9/3/62–6/5/65
Boler, John Pvt.	1 WVI	4/2/61–7/1/61
also	6 WVI	9/25/61–6/7/65
Bolton, James W. Chaplain	5 WVC	8/20/61–6/14/64
Bowman, Lewis Pvt.	1 VAA	11/4/61–1/18/65
Bowman, Wm. H. Pvt.	10 WVI	2/24/64–8/9/65
Boyce, Ezekial Pvt.	3 WVC	3/21/65–6/30/65
Brand, Tom Pvt.	4 WVC	7/1/63–3/64
Brannon, Willis T. Pvt.	6 VAI	3/8/63–6/10/65
Brown, Abner Pvt.	15 WVI	12/18/62–5/27/65
Brown, Francis M. Pvt.	12 WVI	8/18/62–6/16/65
Brown, George W. Pvt.	3 WVI	6/10/61–2/1/64
also	6 WVC	2/1/64–8/7/65
Brown, James Pvt.	14 WVI	3/4/65–6/27/65
Brown, Levi Pvt.	14 WVI	2/24/65–6/27/65
Brown, Stephen T. Pvt.	10 WVI	2/24/64–8/3/65
Brown, Wm. M. Pvt.	6 WVI	11/61–11/64
Brownfield, James Surgeon	14 WVI	4/7/64–6/27/65
Brumage, David W. Pvt.	6 WVC	3/10/64–7/24/65
Brummage, Elisha Pvt.	14 WVI	8/5/62–6/27/65
Brummage, Isaac Pvt.	20 VAC CSA	10/62–6/10/65
Brummage, James R. Pvt.	14 WVI	8/18/62–6/27/65
Brummage, Perry L. Cpl.	15 WVI	11/27/63–8/9/65
Brunner, John Pvt.	46 PAI	7/12/65–6/16/65
Burgoyne, Lewis E. Sgt.	12 WVI	1/2/64–8/20/65
Burns, Zebulon M. Pvt.	3 WVI	6/1/61–8/16/64
Burt, Franklin Capt.	89 NYI	7/21/61–1/29/64
Campbell, James F. Cpl.	14 WVI	8/14/62–6/27/65
Campbell, Robert A. Cpl.	7 WVI	65/65
Carothers, Andrew J. Pvt.	3 WVC	3/9/65–6/30/65
Carpenter, David Pvt.	7 WVI	4/9/65–7/1/65
Carpenter, John Pvt.	15 WVI	9/17/62–6/11/65
Carpenter, Tom W. Pvt.	2 WVI	1/1/62–1/7/65
Carter, Eldridge Lt.	17 WVI	9/8/64–6/30/65
Carter, Madison Lt.	1 WVA	8/6/61–10/3/64
Cartright, Thornton Pvt.	7 WVI	3/15/65–NF
Chisler, Mortimer Pvt.	NF	
Churty, James F. Pvt.	6 WVI	2/13/65–6/10/65
Clayton, Alpheus Pvt.	7 WVI	65/65
Clayton, Edgar L. Lt.	3 WVC	9/62–7/65
Clayton, Edward B. Pvt.	20 VAC CSA	4/18/62–2/28/64
Clayton, Usisses A. Sgt.	14 WVI	10/15/62–6/27/65
Cobb, John A. Lt.	7 WVC	12/2/61–1/18/65
Cochran, Nathaniel C. Sgt.	1 WVA	7/18/61–9/14/64

Cole, Nimrod Pvt.	3 WVC	9/3/62–6/6/65
Colebern, Wm. Pvt.	203 PAI	9/5/64–6/21/65
Compston, Philoros B. Sgt.	6 WVI	8/6/61–8/15/64
Comwell, Wm. E. Pvt.	17 WVI	8/20/64–6/30/65
Conaway, George F. Pvt.	3 VAC	2/22/65–6/30/65
Conaway, James E. Major	31 VAI CSA	5/61–6/10/65
Conaway, Joseph Pvt.	14 WVI	1/18/64–7/27/65
Conely, James Bugler	1 WVC	9/6/61–6/22/62
Constable, George Pvt.	6 VAI	9/64–6/65
Coogle, Benj. Lt.	6 WVI	8/6/61–8/15/64
Courtney, Tom P. Cpl.	6 WVI	8/7/61–9/6/64
Crain, John B. QM Sgt.	17 WVI	9/6/64–7/6/65
Cremeans, Luther Pvt.	22 VAI CSA	1861–4/9/65
Crim, Henry T. Pvt.	6 WVI	10/12/64–6/4/65
Crim, Joseph T. Pvt.	3 WVC	3/9/65–6/4/65
Crim, Wm. H. Pvt.	7 WVI	4/11/65–6/6/65
Crouser, Lafayette Pvt.	7 WVI	4/1/65–6/8/65
Crowell, Griffin Pvt.	12 WVI	8/15/62–6/15/65
Cunningham, Benj. Pvt.	22 VAI CSA	12/7/63–6/14/65
Cunningham, Daniel Pvt.	— WVA	8/12/61–9/14/64
Cunningham, David L. Pvt.	6 WVI	9/5/64–6/10/65
Cunningham, Eber Pvt.	7 WVI	4/11/65–6/65
Cunningham, John Pvt.	17 WVI	2/21/65–6/30/65
Cunningham, Martin V. Pvt.	14 WVI	8/14/62–8/1/65
Cunningham, Nelson Pvt.	17 WVI	NF
Curry, David J. Sgt.	1 WVC	8/6/61–8/6/64
Dailey, Andrew Pvt.	8 PAI	6/61–1865
Darn, Samuel S. Pvt.	3 MSA? CSA	6/22/61–1/65
Daugherty, Wm. C. Sgt.	1 WVA	8/7/61–7/21/65
Davis, Daniel H. Pvt.	10 WVI	1/14/64–8/9/65
Davis, George Pvt.	7 WVI	4/11/65–7/1/65
Davis, Henry T. F. Sgt.	6 WVI	4/1/62–4/17/65
Davis, Jacob B. Cpl.	17 WVI	2/28/65–6/30/65
Davis, John B. Pvt.	12 WVI	1/1/64–8/21/65
Davis, Jonathan B. Pvt. *aka* Persie Davis	12 VAI	NF
Davis, Josiah Cpl.	3 WVI	5/28/61–6/2/65
Davis, Samuel S.	6 WVC	8/20/64–6/26/65
Davis, William L. Pvt.	6 WVI	1/16/65–6/10/65
Davis, Wm. Pvt.	3 WVC	9/14/62–6/30/65
Dean, James Pvt.	1 WVC	7/18/61–7/3/65
Debery, James Pvt.	16 PAC	9/15/62–6/30/66
Denham, Robert J. Pvt.	8 NYA	2/9/63–2/9/68
Devore, James Pvt.	17 WVI	10/1/64–6/30/65
Dick, James Pvt.	6 WVI	NF
Dodd, John E. Pvt.	1 WVI	8/7/61–1864
also	1 WVA	64/64

Name	Unit	Dates
Dotts, Toliver Pvt.	22 PAC	8/30/62–7/19/65
Downey, Eli Pvt.	6 VAI	8/6/61–9/2/64
Downey, John T. Pvt.	15 VAI	9/1/64–6/13/65
Downey, Wm. H. Cpl.	6 WVI	9/12/64–6/10/65
Downs, John S. Pvt.	6 VAC CSA	4/5/63–5/22/64
Drain, Isaac Pvt.	12 WVI	8/15/62–6/16/65
Dunnington, Robert Lt.	6 WVI	8/30/64–6/10/65
Ellis, Samuel Pvt.	6 WVI	9/5/64–6/5/65
Ensingmer, Jacob S. Pvt.	6 WVI	1/16/65–6/10/65
Farrance, Granville Pvt.	12 WVI	8/18/62–6/16/65
Fast, Jonathan W. Pvt.	1 WVA	8/21/61–9/27/64
Ferrell, Elias S. Cpl.	1 WVA	8/61–9/20/64
Ferrell, Heil E. Pvt.	6 WVI	8/13/61–6/10/65
Fetty, Joseph L. Pvt.	15 WVI	62/65
Fisher, John Capt.	6 WVI	8/6/61–6/10/65
Fisher, Wesley Pvt.	6 WVI	8/6/61–8/15/64
Fleming, Charles L. Cpl.	6 WVI	8/6/61–8/6/64
Fleming, Darian Pvt.	7 VAI	4/2/65–7/28/65
Fleming, Emory J. Pvt.	6 WVI	10/15/64–6/10/65
Fleming, Festus R. Pvt.	7 WVI	3/11/65–6/6/65
Fleming, Frank M. Pvt.	6 WVI	2/16/65–6/10/65
Fleming, George J. Cpl.	2 WVI	3/1/65–7/18/65
Fleming, Robert J. Sgt.	6 WVC	6/3/61–2/12/68
Fleming, Rufus E. Col.	6 WVC	6/27/61–5/28/66
Fleming, Sanford Pvt.	6 WVI	8/26/64–6/10/65
Fleming, Tom A. Capt.	12 WVI	8/18/62–6/16/65
Fleming, Tom T. Sgt.	12 WVI	1/5/64–8/9/65
Fleming, Wm. A. Pvt.	12 WVI	8/11/62–6/16/65
Fletcher, Benj. E. Pvt.	19 VAC (CSA)	4/63–4/64
Fletcher, Jesia B. Pvt.	6 WVI	1/16/65–6/10/65
Floyd, James H. Pvt.	7 WVI	4/9/65–NF
Floyd, Robert P. Pvt.	14 WVI	8/9/62–6/13/65
Fluharty, James S. Pvt.	14 WVI	8/17/62–8/16/65
Freeland, Emanuel M. Pvt.	6 VAI	4/13/63–6/10/65
Fry, Chrisitan Cpl.	7 WVI	8/7/61–3/62
Gain, Harrison Pvt.	7 WVI	3/22/65–7/8/65
Gains, William L. Pvt.	14 WVI	6/26/63–6/27/65
Gallahue, Charles A. Pvt.	17 WVI	NF
Garlow, Levi Pvt.	7 WVI	4/9/65–7/1/65
Gaskins, A. J. Pvt.	17 WVI	9/64–7/65
Gaskins, George H. Pvt.	191 PAI	7/7/63–6/28/65
Geldbaugh, John Pvt.	15 WVI	8/22/62–6/14/66
Gilpin, Amos Pvt.	1 WVA	8/14/62–7/25/65
Glover, Richard M. Pvt.	7 WVI	7/1/65–NF
Goodwine, Wm. Pvt.	5 MAC	4/18/64–10/31/65
Grandstaff, Wm. H. Pvt.	7 WVI	1/4/64–7/1/65
Gray, Hannams Pvt.	6 WVI	8/15/61–8/18/64

Gray, John B. Pvt.	3 WVC	8/62–1/16/64
Gray, Wm. Sgt.	1 WVI	5/21/61–10/2/62
Grubb, Benj. Pvt.	12 WVI	8/16/62–5/16/65
Guernsey, Wm. S. Musician	18 NHI	7/20/64–12/12/65
Gump, Philip H. Pvt.	6 WVI	2/18/65–6/10/65
Gump, Silas J. Pvt.	6 WVI	2/18/65–6/10/65
Hall, Jabez L. Pvt.	6 VAI	8/6/61–8/15/64
Hall, Jeptha Pvt.	6 WVI	6/11/62–6/10/65
Hall, John Pvt.	6 VAI	8/12/61–7/28/65
Hall, Wilson Pvt.	6 WVI	9/7/64–6/10/65
Hall, Wm. Capt.	WVI "Exempts"	62/65
Hall, Wm. H. Pvt.	6 WVI	8/27/64–1/10/65
Hamilton, Ashbel F. Pvt.	14 WVI	8/20/62–6/27/65
Hamilton, Elijah C. Pvt.	— WVI	10/1/63–11/16/65
Hanes, David Pvt.	6 WVI	1/16/65–6/10/65
Harbert, Stephen S. Pvt.	1 WVC	3/8/65–7/9/65
Harden, Tom D. Pvt.	14 WVI	4/14/62–6/27/65
Hare, James Pvt.	8 PAI	6/21/61–11/3/62
Harlow, John A. Pvt.	12 VAA CSA	4/62–6/65
Harr, Rufus E. Pvt.	12 WVI	8/26/62–1865
Harrison, George W. Pvt.	3 WVI	6/27/61–9/12/65
Hartley, James R. Pvt.	7 WVI	4/9/65–6/1/65
Hartley, Joe M. Cpl.	17 WVI	9/3/64–7/3/65
Hartley, T.A. Pvt.	17 WVI	8/16/64–5/25/65
Harvey, Basil L. Pvt.	12 WVI	8/12/62–6/12/65
Harvey, Pruit Pvt.	3 WVI	6/18/61–6/8/64
Haught, Gideon N. Pvt.	7 WVI	4/4/65–7/1/65
Haught, John Pvt.	9 WVI	4/4/62–5/1/65
Haught, Levi Pvt.	6 WVI	1/30/65–6/10/65
Haun, Levi Pvt.	1 WVA	9/7/61–9/14/65
Hawkenberry, John Pvt.	15 WVI	10/28/63–8/9/65
Hawkenberry, Zedkiah Pvt.	15 WVI	12/8/62–8/9/65
Hawkenbery, Tom F. Pvt.	15 WVI	2/19/64–6/14/65
Hawkins, John Cpl.	10 WVI	2/20/64–8/9/65
Hawkins, John L. Pvt.	12 WVI	4/1/65–7/1/65
Hawkins, Marion Pvt.	3 WVC	3/26/64–6/30/65
Hayhurst, David P. Pvt.	6 WVI	2/17/65–6/10/65
Hayhurst, John Pvt.	6 WVI	2/17/65–6/10/65
Hays, Bennett S. Pvt.	14 WVI	8/62–8/65
Hays, Horatio Pvt.	7 WVI	3/1/65–7/1/65
Hays, Nimrod Pvt.	7 WVI	4/1/65–NF
Heill, Robert M. Sgt.	7 VAI	4/9/65–7/3/65
Helem, John H. Pvt.	6 WVC	4/20/64–5/22/66
Helmick, David S. Cpl.	17 WVI	8/17/64–6/13/65
Helmick, Nathaniel Capt.	17 WVI	8/24/64–6/30/65
Helsley, Nimrod Pvt.	1 WVA	8/8/61–9/4/64
Henderson, Haymond Pvt.	12 WVI	NF

Hendrixson, George Pvt.	6 WVI	8/12/61–8/20/64
Heston, David Pvt.	17 WVI	8/3/64–6/30/65
Hews, Rober Pvt.	6 VAI	7/15/61–6/62
Hibbs, Eugene Pvt.	—WVI	65/65
Hibbs, Thomas W. Pvt.	12 WVI	8/13/62–6/16/65
Hibbs, Wm. H. Pvt.	12 WVI	8/15/62–6/16/65
Hill, Jacob Pvt.	6 WVI	7/28/63–6/10/65
Hill, Joseph A. Pvt.	1 WVA	8/14/62–7/21/65
Hirons, John Pvt.	7 WVI	4/9/65–7/1/65
Hockinbery, Francis Pvt.	15 WVI	12/8/62–8/9/65
Hoffman, Amso Cpl.	7 WVI	4/1/65–7/7/65
Holmes, Calvin A. Pvt.	14 WVI	8/62–7/65
Horner, Jacob D. Pvt.	20 VAC CSA	9/15/63–5/25/65
Hough, John Pvt.	6 WVI	8/15/61–8/15/64
Huey, Alexander C. Pvt.	WVI "Exempts"	62/65
Huey, David H. Pvt.	17 WVI	10/1/64–6/30/65
Huey, James H. Pvt.	WVI "Exempts"	62/65
Huffman, Asa Pvt.	7 WVI	3/64–6/12/65
Hughes, John H. Pvt.	18 PAC	3/20/65–NF
Hunter, Daniel Pvt.	9 VAI	1/1/62–7/25/65
Hunter, George W. Pvt.	6 VAI	9/15/61–10/8/64
Hunter, William H. Pvt.	9 WVI	1/15/62–2/28/64
Hunter, Wm. Pvt.	6 WVI	8/12/62–8/20/64
Huskill, Robert L. Pvt.	12 WVI	8/14/62–6/16/65
Ice, Fielding R. Pvt.	7 WVI	4/11/65–6/10/65
Ice, Henry M. Capt.	14 WVI	8/9/62–2/28/65
Ice, Isaac H. Pvt.	6 WVI	2/65–6/65
Ice, Jesse M. Pvt.	14 WVI	8/20/62–6/27/65
Jackson, George D. Sgt.	15 WVI	10/1/62–6/22/65
Jackson, Thomas Pvt.	1 OHI	12/64–9/65
Jenkins, Benj. Pvt.	45 USI (Negro)	7/20/64–12/12/65
Jenkins, Ezekiel Pvt.	6 WVI	11/21/61–1/18/65
Jenkins, Levi Pvt.	1 WVC	6/22/61–11/20/63
Jennison, John F. Sgt.	12 WVI	8/18/62–6/16/65
Johnson, Harrison W.	NF (45 VAI CSA?)	
Johnson, Robert Pvt.	7 WVI	3/65–7/9/65
Jones, Andrew Pvt.	6 WVI	8/2/61–8/15/64
Jones, C.J. Pvt.	14 WVI	2/16/64–6/27/65
Jones, Hiram E. Cpl.	12 WVI	8/10/62–6/15/65
Jones, John C. Cpl.	6 WVI	8/15/61–8/18/64
Jones, John N. Cpl.	7 WVI	8/61–7/1/65
Jones, Sam E. Sgt.	140 OHI	NF
Jumbro, George B. Cpl.	6 WVI	8/29/64–6/10/65
Keener, John D. Cpl.	6 WVI	9/12/64–6/10/65
Kellar, James C. Pvt.	12 WVI	8/14/62–5/28/65
Keller, Fielden Pvt.	6 WVI	1/1/65–NF
Kendall, Cornelius Pvt.	14 WVI	8/5/62–1/27/65

Kerns, Wm. J. Sgt.	6 WVC	6/10/61–8/16/64
King, Andrew Pvt.	6 WVI	8/23/64–6/13/65
Kinkaid, David M. Cpl.	4 WVC	9/22/63–6/23/64
Kintyhtt, Leroy Pvt.	18 PAC	9/26/62–7/10/65
Koon, Isaac Pvt.	6 WVI	9/3/64–6/10/65
Koon, O. A. Pvt.	6 WVI	8/12/61–8/12/64
Latham, John T. Lt.	NF	
Laulis, John Pvt.	1 VAC	7/18/61–7/8/65
Layman, Jacob Pvt.	12 WVI	8/16/62–4/1/63
Layman, Joshua Sgt.	17 WVI	8/19/64–6/30/65
Lee, Jacob J. Pvt.	6 WVI	8/7/61–NF
also	1 WVA	1861–9/14/64
Lemasters, Sam K. Pvt.	11 WVI	10/8/61–11/14/64
Lemley, Abraham Pvt.	14 WVI	9/6/62–7/3/65
Leonard, Bernard F. Pvt.	3 WVC	10/16/62–NF
Leonard, Harvey F. Pvt.	1 WVA	7/11/62–7/21/65
Leonard, John A. Pvt.	6 WVI	8/10/61–NF
also	1 WVA	7/3/62–12/23/62
Levell, Jeremiah B. Pvt.	6 WVI	8/7/61–7/14/62
Levell, John Q. Pvt.	1 WVA	11/10/61–1/18/65
Levell, Morgan T. Pvt.	73 ILI	8/5/62–6/12/65
Linn, Samuel Pvt.	17 WVI	2/15/65–6/13/65
Linn, Wm. Cpl.	14 IDI?	12/13/61–6/11/65
Lloyd, Wm. S. Pvt.	WVI "Exempts"	9/63–1865
Longsten, John P. Pvt.	NF	
Looman, Frank Pvt.	——	62/65
Loonan, Henry Pvt.	6 WVI	8/10/61–9/64
Loonan, Joshua Sgt.	11 WVI	10/26/61–8/9/65
Loonan, Robert Pvt.	6 WVI	8/12/61–8/20/64
Lough, Calvin J. Cpl.	12 WVI	8/16/62–6/16/65
Lough, Hezekiah T. Pvt.	12 WVI	8/13/62–6/16/65
Luper, Wm. M. Pvt.	12 WVI	8/13/62–6/16/65
Mahanna, Neeley Sgt.	3 WVC	9/3/62–6/6/65
Maphis, Harrison A. Pvt. AKA Adam Frankhouser	3 PAC	11/21/63–11/9/65
Markley, Joshua Pvt.	10 WVI	2/3/64–8/9/65
Marr, James B. Major	3 DEI	1861–3/4/63
Martin, Benj. F. Pvt.	5 WVI	10/22/63–5/30/66
Martin, Elias Pvt.	6 WVI	9/3/64–6/10/65
Martin, Elihu Pvt.	12 WVI	8/15/62–6/16/65
Martin, Gideon Chaplain	15 WVI	1/23/63–6/14/65
Martin, Isaac N. Lt.	14 WVI	8/16/63–6/27/65
Martin, Jesse T. Pvt.	12 VAI CSA	5/20/62–8/19/62
Martin, John O. Pvt.	12 WVI	3/64–8/9/65
Mason, John R. Pvt.	14 WVI	2/24/65–6/27/65
Mason, Peter Pvt.	7 WVI	4/1/65–6/22/65
Mason, Richard J. Pvt.	19 VAC CSA	63/65

Maulsby, Tom A. Capt.	1 WVA	8/7/61–10/14/63
May, Jacob W. Pvt.	1 WVA	8/7/61–9/14/64
McCray, Raymond R. Cpl.	12 WVI	2/1/64–8/9/65
McDonald, John I. Pvt.	12 WVI	8/18/62–6/16/65
McGee, George W. Musician	6 WVC	NF
McGill, Joseph M. Pvt.	7 WVI	4/9/65–8/14/65
McIntire, Elias Pvt.	12 WVI	8/14/62–6/15/65
McIntire, George L. Pvt.	7 WVI	3/64–7/10/65
McKinney, Haymond	NF	
McVicker, Hillery A. Pvt.	9 WVI	3/11/62–4/30/65
Means, James C. Lt.	6 WVA	8/7/61–8/19/64
Meniner, Stephenson Pvt.	4 WVC	6/63–3/64
Mercer, John W. Cpl.	12 WVI	8/18/62–6/16/65
Mercer, Waitman W. Pvt.	17 WVI	8/31/64–6/30/65
Merrifield, Edward Pvt.	1 WVA	8/14/62–7/21/65
Merrifield, James E. Pvt.	15 WVI	11/22/62–6/11/65
Merrifield, Newton Pvt.	1 WVA	8/14/61–9/16/64
Merrifield, Sidney Pvt.	6 WVI	2/65–6/65
Merrill, John N. Pvt.	7 WVI	4/9/65–NF
Millan, John M. Cpl.	1 WVA	8/12/61–6/22/65
Miller, Enos Pvt.	17 WVI	2/23/65–6/30/65
Miller, Samuel Pvt.	28 ILI	9/16/61–1/4/64
Miller, Tom C. Cpl.	7 WVI	4/1/65–7/10/65
Minnear, Henry H. Pvt.	14 WVI	8/15/62–6/27/65
Minnear, Wm. H. B. Pvt.	6 WVI	4/1/62–4/3/65
Monroe, Josiah Pvt.	12 WVI	8/9/62–6/16/65
Moore, Caleb Cpl.	14 WVI	8/16/62–6/27/65
Moore, Jeptha M. Pvt.	3 WVI	6/15/61–6/15/65
Moore, Jesse Pvt.	14 WVI	2/24/65–6/27/65
Moore, Theophilus Cpl.	7 WVI	9/1/61–7/1/65
Moore, Thornton H. Pvt.	14 WVI	2/26/64–6/27/65
Moran, Zachariah Pvt.	15 WVI	8/11/62–5/21/65
Morgan, Aaron C. Pvt.	6 WVI	9/3/64–6/10/65
Morgan, Archie Pvt.	12 WVI	12/24/63–8/9/65
Morgan, Eber D. Pvt.	12 WVI	8/18/62–6/16/65
Morgan, John R. Pvt.	6 WVI	3/6/65–6/10/65
Morgan, John S. Pvt.	20 VAC CSA	8/10/64–6/26/65
Morgan, John W. Pvt.	6 WVI	9/25/64–6/10/65
Morgan, Marcus Drummer	6 WVI	9/12/64–6/10/65
Morgan, Oliver P. Pvt.	6 WVI	8/13/61–4/17/63
Morgan, Silas Pvt.	6 WVI	2/13/65–6/10/65
Morgan, Wm. C. Pvt.	6 WVI	9/3/64–6/10/65
Morhead, Miner Pvt.	127 VAI	8/22/64–9/8/65
Morley, Joseph Pvt.	6 WVI	9/12/64–6/10/65
Morley, Wm. A. Pvt.	1 WVA	8/14/62–7/21/65
Morris, Andrew J. Pvt.	1 WVC	9/5/64–7/8/65
Morris, Charles E. QM	3 WVC	9/3/62–6/6/65

Name	Unit	Dates
Morris, Eli C. Pvt.	6 WVI	2/17/65–6/10/65
Morris, George S. Pvt.	62 VAI CSA	5/20/61–5/1/65
Morris, Josephus Pvt.	12 WVI	8/14/62–6/12/65
Morris, Levi Pvt.	7 WVI	4/9/65–7/9/65
Morris, Richard S. Pvt.	6 WVI	4/6/63–6/10/65
Morris, Sam H. Pvt.	14 WVI	8/22/62–6/27/65
Morris, Wm. G. Pvt.	7 WVI	8/18/61–2/18/64
Mort, John Pvt.	6 WVI	8/6/61–10/10/63
Motter, Jerome B. Sgt.	6 WVI	8/12/61–8/12/64
Murdock, Wm. Pvt.	45 USI (Negro)	7/20/64–12/5/65
Musgrave, Eli Sgt.	179 OHI	8/4/64–6/17/65
Musgrave, James Pvt.	6 WVI	10/28/61–2/16/64
Musgrave, John C. Pvt.	12 WVI	8/31/62–6/16/65
Musgrave, John S. Lt.	WVI "Exempts"	1/9/63–6/10/64
Myer, Tom P. Cpl.	7 WVI	1/1/62–7/5/65
Nutter, Calvin Pvt.	147 PAI	9/6/64–7/1/65
Nuzum, Edwin T. Cpl.	5 WVC	5/20/61–6/14/64
Nuzum, James H. Pvt.	2 WVI	2/14/65–9/12/65
Nuzum, John S. Pvt.	3 WVC	9/3/62–6/6/65
O'Dell, Joshua D. Pvt.	6 WVI	9/5/64–6/10/65
Oakley, Randol Pvt.	6 WVI	6/16/63–6/10/65
Ott, John Pvt.	17 WVI	8/30/64–6/30/65
Palmer, George W. Cpl.	16 PAC	9/19/62–2/16/65
Parker, Eli L. Capt.	6 WVC	8/15/62–6/1/66
Parker, Lewis W. Pvt.	116 NYI	8/62–12/10/62
Parker, William C. Cpl.	6 WVI	9/3/64–6/10/65
Phillips, Wm. O. Pvt.	17 WVI	2/16/65–6/30/65
Pierce, Morgan Pvt.	6 WVI	12/22/62–6/10/65
Piett, James Pvt.	184 OHI	2/65–8/65
Pitcher, Martin V. Pvt.	12 WVI	8/15/62–6/16/65
Poling, Richard Pvt.	12 WVI	4/16/62–4/2/63
also	7 WVI	4/11/65–7/1/65
Pollitt, Wm. H. Pvt.	111 NYI	8/8/62–1/8/65
Powel, James G. Pvt.	1 WVA	8/9/61–9/14/64
Powell, Francis M. Pvt.	17 WVI	9/4/64–7/1/65
Powell, Francis M. Pvt.	17 WVI	8/20/64–6/30/65
Price, Merriam Pvt.	6 WVI	8/15/61–8/20/64
Prichard, Amos N. Capt.	12 WVI	8/26/62–3/24/65
Prickett, Richard W. Pvt.	14 WVI	8/14/62–6/29/65
Prickett, Wm. H. Pvt.	14 VAI	8/14/62–7/3/65
Pride, John Pvt.	6 WVI	9/3/64–6/10/65
Raber, Christopher Pvt.	9 WVI	NF
Randall, Norvil G. Pvt.	14 WVI	8/16/62–6/15/65
Raney, Wm. Pvt.	3 WVI	6/10/61–11/28/62
Reed, Frank B. Pvt.	47 ILI	8/13/62–3/17/63
Reed, Thomas Capt.	1 WVI	10/29/61–11/26/64
Rex, Eli H. Pvt.	31 VAI CSA	8/28/61–4/10/65

Rex, Francis M. Pvt.	12 WVI	8/9/62–6/16/65
Reynolds, Joel B. Cpl.	6 WVI	NF
Rice, Isaac N. Pvt.	12 WVI	8/18/62–6/16/65
Richards, Wm. R. Sgt.	3 WVC	8/25/62–6/6/65
Richardson, George H. Pvt.	6 WVI	9/23/61–NF
also	1 WVA	— 7/23/65
Richardson, Mark W. Pvt.	7 WVI	65/65
Richman, Tailor Pvt.	4 WVC	7/8/63–3/10/64
Riddel, Daniel C. Pvt.	1 VAC	7/18/61–6/17/64
Ritzer, John F. Sgt.	12 WVI	8/18/62–6/16/65
Rober, Wm. M. Pvt.	7 WVI	1/63–9/65
Roberts, David T. Sgt.	14 WVI	8/11/62–6/25/65
Robinson, Dennis M. Pvt.	12 WVI	8/27/62–6/65
Robinson, Franklin Cpl.	14 WVI	8/20/62–6/27/65
Robinson, Ithanner Pvt.	3 WVI	7/3/61–8/12/64
Rogers, James Pvt.	3 WVC	10/13/62–1/18/65
Ross, Henry Cpl.	17 WVI	9/3/64–6/30/65
Ruble, Henry M. Pvt.	7 WVI	7/3/61–2/4/64
also	7? WVA	2/17/64–7/1/65
Rush, John W. Pvt.	85 PAI	9/28/61–11/22/64
Rutherford, Fred T. Pvt.	7 WVI	4/9/65–7/1/65
Sample, Woodman Musician	61 PAI	5/15/61–7/3/65
Samsel, Wm. H. Pvt.	1 WVI	3/23/64–7/16/68
Sandy, Newton B. Pvt.	3 WVI	6/6/61–10/5/62
Sandy, William J. Pvt.	6 WVI	9/13/64–6/10/65
Satterfield, Columbus Pvt.	6 WVI	8/6/61–8/13/64
Satterfield, Eusebius Pvt.	6 WVI	4/63–6/65
Satterfield, John N. Pvt.	6 WVA	8/61–9/14/64
Satterfield, Newton Pvt.	17 WVI	— 6/31/65
Satterfield, Sam L. Pvt.	15 WVI	11/27/62–8/9/65
Satterfield, Sidney W. Sgt.	6 WVI	8/13/61–1/13/65
Scott, Phelix Pvt.	14 WVI	8/20/62–6/20/65
Shanks, John Pvt.	6 WVI	1/24/65–6/10/65
Sharp, George W. Pvt.	14 WVI	8/20/62–6/27/65
Sharp, James L. T. Pvt.	7 WVI	4/1/65–7/1/65
Shaw, Joshua Cpl.	12 WVI	8/14/62–6/16/65
Shaw, Lemeul R. Pvt.	12 WVI	8/15/62–6/16/65
Shaw, Tom W. Sgt.	4 WVC	7/13/63–3/7/64
Shear, Frank M. Pvt.	6 VAI	8/6/61–8/15/64
Shingleton, John Pvt.	12 VAI	8/61–6/64
Shoemaker, Joseph Pvt.	10 VAI	6/7/62–8/65
Shores, Simon F. Pvt.	12 WVI	8/18/62–6/16/65
Shrayer, James W. Capt.	14 WVI	8/22/62–6/27/65
Shroyer, Alexander Pvt.	6 WVI	8/15/61–8/15/64
Shroyer, Andrew M. Pvt.	12 WVI	8/9/62–3/5/65
Sigler, Philip Pvt.	1 WVA	8/14/62–7/21/65
Smith, George W. Pvt.	6 WVC	6/27/61–5/28/66

Smith, John L. Pvt.	—WVC	6/15/64–5/22/66
Snider, James R. Sadler	6 WVC	9/3/64–5/19/65
Snodgrass, Enos E. Pvt.	6 VAI	2/18/65–6/10/65
Spears, Aaron A. Pvt.	29 MEI	1/1/64–6/21/66
Spencer, Benj. T. Pvt.	6 WVI	8/62–6/65
Spencer, John W. Pvt.	3 WV "Exempts"	8/17/63–4/23/64
Spencer, Zinn H. Pvt.	3 WVI	5/1/61–7/7/65
Springer, James D. Pvt.	3 WVC	11/16/63–6/30/65
Springer, Zacheus Pvt.	17 WVI	8/27/64–6/13/65
Stanton, David Pvt.	3 WVC	10/26/62–6/6/65
Starkey, George W. Pvt.	WVI "Exempts"	4/23/64–NF
Stealy, Perry G. Pvt.	3 WVI	6/27/61–6/19/65
Stevens, Allen Pvt.	6 WVC	2/26/64–9/7/65
Stirett, James W. Pvt.	7 WVI	3/17/65–7/9/65
Straight, Wm. G. Cpl.	20 VAC CSA	4/1/63–6/65
Strait, Jacob M. Pvt.	14 WVI	8/9/62–6/27/65
Sturgeon, Jacob Sgt.	3 WVC	8/22/62–6/3/65
Sturgeon, Jacob Sgt.	3 WVC	8/22/62–6/5/65
Sturm, Jesse F. Pvt.	7 WVI	4/7/65–7/11/65
Sturn, Lemeul Sgt.	107 ILI	7/62–7/28/65
Summers, George P. Pvt.	1 WVA	9/5/61–10/31/64
Surgher, Alpheus Pvt.	1 WVA	8/14/62–6/14/65
Swindler, John J. Cpl.	7 WVI	7/3/61–8/18/64
Swisher, John W. Pvt.	6 WVI	8/29/64–6/10/65
Tennant, Ziniry Pvt.	17 WVI	8/28/64–6/30/65
Thomas, James H. Pvt.	6 WVC	2/18/64–5/22/66
Thompson, Wm. Pvt.	3 VAC	9/62–6/15/65
Toothman, Elias L. Pvt.	6 WVI	12/30/64–6/11/65
Toothman, James W. Pvt.	— MOI	62/64
Toothman, Josephus	NF	
Toothman, Samuel Pvt.	7 WVI	4/11/65–7/1/65
Toothman, Wm. A. Pvt.	14 WVI	9/1/62–NF
Tory, James L. Pvt.	35 MAI	8/6/62–6/28/65
Travis, Harman Pvt.	6 WVC	8/28/64–5/19/65
Tucker, Nathan Pvt.	US Navy West Indian Squadron	1863
Turner, George T. Pvt.	14 WVI	8/8/62–6/27/65
Upton, James R. Pvt.	6 WVI	8/15/61–8/15/64
Vandergrift, Calvin Pvt.	3 WVC	8/62–6/65
Vandergrift, Marshall Pvt.	12 WVI	8/15/62–6/16/65
Vanderwort, Norval Pvt.	6 VAI	5/20/64–6/10/65
Vangilder, James Pvt.	6 WVI	3/1/65–6/10/65
Vangilder, Joseph Pvt.	6 WVI	3/1/65–6/10/65
Vangilder, Philip Pvt.	6 WVI	9/12/64–6/10/65
Veach, John Pvt.	17 WVI	2/23/65–7/30/65
Veach, Samuel Pvt.	17 WVI	2/23/65–6/30/65
Vilt?, Washington F. Pvt.	10 VAI	2/3/62–8/9/65

Vincent, Obediah Pvt.	31 VAI CSA	5/24/61–4/9/65
Vincent, Riley Pvt.	6 WVI	4/62–4/65
Walker, Wm. H. Pvt.	3 MDI (Negro)	7/15/64–5/11/65
Walls, Archibald H. Pvt.	7 WVI	4/4/65–7/1/65
Watkins, Ed Pvt.	6 WVI	2/65–6/10/65
Watson, Charles B. Pvt.	3 WVC	3/6/65–7/10/65
Watson, Mark S. Pvt.	3 WVC	3/6/65–6/12/65
Watson, Robert Pvt.	12 WVI	8/27/62–6/8/65
Watts, Charles E. Bugler	6 WVC	6/20/61–8/13/64
Weaver, Frank C. Pvt.	———	63/65
Weekley, Wm. J. Pvt.	3 WVC	3/9/65–6/30/65
Weekly, James K. Pvt.	7 WVI	4/9/65–7/1/65
Wells, Charles E. Pvt.	17 WVI	2/22/65–7/7/65
Wells, Francis M. Sgt.	7 WVI	65/65
Wells, Richard D. Cpl.	12 WVI	8/13/62–6/16/65
Wells, Richard Musician	12 WVI	8/18/62–6/16/65
West, John J. Musician	15 WVI	11/18/62–8/9/65
West, Johnithan J. Pvt.	12 WVI	1/4/64–7/19/65
West, Perry G. Capt.	WVI "Exempts"	4/23/64–NF
Westfall, Solomon Pvt.	NF	
Whiteman, Abel C. Pvt.	6 WVI	9/5/64–NF
Wilkinson, Tom M. Pvt.	14 PAC	3/28/64–8/16/65
Williams, Eli Pvt.	12 WVI	8/14/62–6/16/65
Wilson, Benjamin Pvt.	6 WVI	1/16/65–6/10/65
Wilson, Eli Cpl.	17 WVI	9/3/64–7/1/65
Wilson, Francis A. Pvt.	17 WVI	8/24/64–6/30/65
Wilson, Jacob N. Pvt.	———	63/65
Wilson, Jeremiah Pvt.	9 WVI	3/29/62–4/30/65
Wilson, Nusum M. Pvt.	6 VAI	8/13/61–8/13/64
Wilson, Stephen S. Pvt.	7 WVI	8/12/61–7/1/65
Wiseman, Joshua Pvt.	19 VAC CSA	9/62–6/22/65
Wolf, John Pvt.	6 WVI	9/12/64–6/10/65
Wood, Elijah T. Pvt.	6 WVI	2/65–6/65
Wood, John N.	1 WVA	2/17/61–7/21/75
Woodruff, Charles H. Pvt.	6 WVI	9/25/61–11/17/64
Wright, Eli Pvt.	14 WVI	8/14/62–6/27/65
Wright, Thomas Pvt.	22 VAI CSA	4/24/61–7/13/63
Wright, Wm. Pvt.	1 WVA	8/12/61–9/14/64
Wyckoff, Solomon Pvt.	3 WVI	6/1/61–8/1/64
Yager, Frederick Pvt.	14 WVI	8/20/62–6/27/65
Yates, Elza Pvt.	1 WVC	7/61–11/62
also	11 USC	11/18/62–11/18/65
Yates, Wm. M. Pvt.	5 USA	8/5/61–12/64
Youst, Emory D. Pvt.	6 WVI	8/24/64–6/15/65
Youst, Martin Pvt.	6 WVI	1/16/65–6/10/65

Marion County Remarks

Amos, T.—ruptured
Arnett, J.—CDR
Arnett, R.—CDR
Ashcraft, A.—CDR
Atha, E.—HD & RH
Atha, U.S.—CDR & catarrh nasal
Atha, W.M.—CDR & piles
Austin, J.—wound of back & hand
Baker, E.—bronchitis & nasal catarrh
Baker, J.H.—hempligia right side
Barnes, P.T.—injury by fall from horse
Barr, B.—dyspepsia, irregular act of heart
Barthelow, G.—CDR, KD & LD
Batson, J.W. Jr.—deafness
Bean, J.—HD
Blaker, L.—lumbago
Boggess, C.—gunshot wound left shoulder
Boggess, J.W.—injury by fall from horse
Bolton, J.W.W.—gunshot right ankle, in hospital until 3/24/65
Bowman, L.—VV & RH
Bowman, W.H.—CDR & loss of finger
Boyce, E.—KD
Brannon, W.T.—catarrh, RH
Brown, A.—loss of 4th finger right hand
Brown, G.W.—RH
Brown, J.—lumbago
Brown, L.—bronchitis
Brown, S.T.—CDR
Brown, W.M.—chrushed and catarrh
Brummage, E.—general disability
Brummage, J.R.—CDR
Brummage, P.L.—lumbago
Burgoyne, L.E.—injury of left leg
Carothers, A.J.—RH
Carpenter, T.W.—RH & dyspepsia
Cartright, T.T.—CDR, left army on order of Sec. Stanton
Churty, J.F.—nasal catarrh
Clayton, A.—CDR
Clayton, E.L.—RH & lumbago
Cole, N.—hernia & hepatic disease
Compston, P.B.—fistula, KD & LD
Comwell, W.E.—neuralgia
Conely, J.—HD, now in his 70th year
Courtney, T.P.—deafness

Crim, H.T.—HD & LD
Crim, W.H.—bronchial catarrh
Crouser, L.—fistula
Crowell, G.—CDR & HD
Cunningham, D.L.—HD
Cunningham, Dan—brights disease
Cunningham, E.—drafted, no discharge
Cunningham, M.V.—gunshot wound
Curry, D.J.—RH
Dailey, A.—gunshot in hip, POW 5 months 21 days
Davis, D.H.—ague
Davis, H.T.F.—RH & piles
Davis, J.B.—diseased stomach & rupture
Davis, J.B.—partial blindness
Davis, W.L.—RH all over
Dean, J.—gunshot wounds
Denham, R.J.—RH
Devore, J.—RH & hemorrhoids
Dick, J.—pthisis pulmonalis
Dodd, J.E.—saber cut in head, transferred to Batt F 1862
Dodd, J.T.—drafted, left and came home
Dotts, T.—RH
Downey, E.—RH
Downey, J.T.—RH
Drain, I.—shot through hand
Edwards, Eveline—she is an ignorant woman and of bad repute [NOTE—E. Edwards not listed as widow or soldier?]
Fast, J.W.—gunshot wound in left shoulder & arm, draws pension
Ferrell, E.S.—lumbago & renal disease
Ferrell, H.C.—HD
Fetty, J.L.—RH & HD applied for pension
Fleming, F.R.—RH
Fleming, R.E.—shot through right thigh at 2nd Bull Run
Fleming, R.J.—left eye out
Fleming, S.—catarrh in head & deafness
Fleming, T.A.—RH
Fleming, T.M.—CDR & piles, drawing pension
Fleming, W.A.—injury to back, disease of stomach & bowels
Fletcher, B.E.—abcess & ribs broken
Floyd, J.H.—cold on measles, deserted at Alexandria, VA
Floyd, R.P.—VV
Fluharty, J.S.—RH
Freeland, E.M.—dyspepsia
Fry, C.—RH
Gain, H.—CDR
Gains, W.L.—RH
Garlow, L.—dyspepsia neuralgia

Gaskins, G.H.—shot under the arm
Gideon, M.—partily paralized
Glover, R.M.—RH
Gray, H.—injury of left side & hip
Gray, J.B.—lumbago
Gray, W.—gunshot left knee, amputated
Grubb, B.—asthma
Gump, S.J.—piles
Hall, J.C.—RH
Hall, J.L.—deafness
Hall, Jep.—TYF
Hall, Jn.—HD
Hall, W.H.—bronchial catarrh
Hamilton, A.F.—RH & nasal catarrh
Hanes, D.—RH, HD & LD
Harbert, S.S.—RH
Harden, T.D.—gunshot in both arms
Hartley, J.M.—CDR
Harvey, B.L.—rupture
Harvey, P.—RH
Haught, G.N.—substitute
Haught, J.—wound of left arm & chest
Haught, L.—LD
Hawkenberry, J.—disease of eyes
Hawkenberry, Z.—gunshot wound of shoulder
Hawkenbery, T.F.—RH
Hawkins, J.—shot through left arm at Lynchburg, 6/18/64
Hawkins, J.L.—at home on furlough when co discharged
Hawkins, M.—bronchial catarrh
Hays, B.S.—hernia & hemorrhoids
Hays, N.—running sore on leg
Heffron, M.—now disabled, brights disease
Heill, R.M.—RH
Helem, J.H.—CDR, piles & RH
Helsley, N.—injured by horse, hernia
Hendrixson, G.—RH
Heston, D.—RH & HD
Hews, R.—RH
Hibbs, T.W.—CDR & stomach trouble
Hibbs, W.W.—wound of right face & head
Hockinbery, F.M.—RH & HD
Holmes, C.A.—hernia
Huffman, A.—weak eyes, almost blind
Hunter, D.—RH
Hunter, G.W.—frozen feet & RH
Hunter, W.—CDR
Hunter, W.H.—stomach trouble & disease of eyes

Huskill, R.L.—index finger off right hand, CDR & enlarged joints
Ice, J.M.—piles
Jackson, T.—disease of stomach, in hospital at Covington
Jenkins E.—RH
Jenkins, L.—gunshot, chest chrushed with horse
Jennison, J.F.—hernia left side
Johnson, H.W.—RH
Jones, A.—ankle sprained
Jones, C.J.—LD
Jones, J.N.—catarrh
Jones, S.E.—HD
Jumbro, G.B.—RH
Keller, F.—piles, now nearly deaf
Kendall, C.—bronchitis & sore legs
Kinkaid, D.M.—neuralgia
Kinq, A.—CDR & KD
Kintyhtt, L.—LD
Layman, J.—CDR
Layman, J.—epilepsy & hemorrhoids
Lee, J.J.—RH & piles
Lemasters, S.K.—crippled in knee
Leonard, H.F.—dispepsia, Batt A and F consolidated 1864
Leonard, J.A.—crushed hip joint
Levell, J.B.—dyspepsia & piles, discharged from hospital
Levell, J.Q.—injury to back lifting cannon
Levell, M.T.—gunshot in right leg & 2 shell wounds
Lloyd, W.S.—RH
Looman, J.—LD & struck by shell
Looman, R.—piles
Loonan, H.—RH
Lough, C.J.—shot in left arm
Lowden, G.W.—hernia
Mahanna, N.—cramp & stiffness in right leg, now in his 74th year
Markley, J.—RH
Marr, J.B.—diseased rectum, memoranda captured at Warrenton Curry,
Martin, B.F.—saber wound
Martin, I.N.—LD
Martin, J.O.—scurvy, shot through right leg
Martin, Jn.—dislocation of great toe & back injury
Mason, P.—dyspepsia
Maulsby, T.A.—gunshot wound of right leg & CDR
McGill, J.M.—catarrh & bronchitis
McIntire, G.L.—CDR & RH
McKinney, H.—LD
McKinney, J.C.—fistula & CDR
McVicker, H.A.—HD
Mercer, J.W.—gunshot left leg

Mercer, W.W.—weak lungs
Merrifield, J.E.—stomach trouble
Merrifield, N.—RH & piles
Merrifield, S.—strain of left hip
Merrill, J.N.—hepatic disease
Millan, J.M.—partial deafness
Miller, Sam J.—SS & wound in left eye
Mininer, S.—RH & bronchitis
Minnear, H.H.—sciatic RH
Monroe, J.—SS & RH
Moore, C.—VV
Moore, J.—piles
Moore, T.—injury of ankle
Moore, T.H.—asthma
Morgan, A.—LD
Morgan, E.D.—CDR
Morgan, W.C.—catarrh deafness
Morley, W.A.—prisoner 6/14/63
Morris, A.J.—RH
Morris, C.E.—POW at Danville
Morris, E.C.—asthma
Morris, J.—RH
Morris, L.—CDR
Morris, R.S.—RH
Morris, S.H.—hemorrhoids & disease of rectum
Mort J.—hernia, DSC
Motter, J.B.—hernia
Musgrave, J.C.—disease of rectum
Musgrave, J.S.—pluerisy
Myer, T.P.—RH
Nutter, C.—general disability
Nuzum, E.T.—catarrh
Nuzum, J.S.—RH
O'Dell, J.D.—RH & dispepsia
Orr, M.D.—gunshot left leg
Ott, J.—RH
Palmer, G.W.—deafness
Parker, E.L.—disabled right hand & arm, hernia of r&l side
Parker, W.C.—rupture, piles & HD
Phillips, W.O.—nasal catarrh
Piett, J.—affliction of eyes, LD & RH
Pitcher, M.V.—piles & loss of speech
Poling, R.—RH & HD, breast disabled
Powel, J.G.—RH
Powell, F.M.—deafness & stomach trouble
Price, M.—RH
Prickett, W.H.—broken jaw by ball

Raber, C.—epilepsy & lumbago
Raney, W.—deafness & general disability
Reynolds, J.B.—scurvy, piles, MS, POW Andersonville
Rice, I.N.—CDR
Richman, T.—neuralgia
Ritzer, J.F.—shot in right ankle
Rober, W.M.—hernia, heart & spinal disease
Roberts, D.T.—lumbago
Robinson, D.M.—LD
Robinson, F.—lumbago, wounded by shell right thigh
Robinson, I.—wounded in back
Rogers, J.—asthma & CDR
Ross, H.—RH & stomach disorder
Ruble, H.M.—HD & piles, in hospital six weeks
Rush, J.W.—lumbago & wound left side
Sample, W.S.—blindness, deafness, VV, in first battle of the war
Sandy, N.B.—gunshot wound
Sandy, W.J.—asthma
Satterfield, C.F.—strain of ankle, crippled finger
Satterfield, E.—knee injured & rupture
Satterfield, J.N.—RH & loss of left eye
Satterfield, J.W.—bronchitis & CDR
Satterfield, S.L.—asthma
Satterfield, S.W.—RH, catarrh & bronchitis
Scott, P.—WIA Cedar Creek, 10/19/64 left thigh
Shanks, J.—CDR
Sharp, J.L.T.—disease of stomach and bowels
Shaw, J.—gunshot in left side
Shaw, L.R.—HD
Shaw, T.W.—partial deafness
Shear, F.M.—piles & deafness
Shingleton, J.—neuralgia
Shroyer, A.I.—blindness & HD
Shroyer, A.M.—neuralgia & HD
Smith, J.L.—malaria & CDR
Snodgrass, E.E.—lumbago
Spears, A.A.—CDR, lumbago, piles & dyspepsia
Spencer, J.W.—RH
Spencer, Z.H.—piles
Starkey, G.W.—disease of eyes
Stevens, A.—RH & hernia
Strait, J.M.—rupture
Sturgeon, J.—piles
Sturgeon, J.—piles
Swindler, J.J.—flesh wound in thigh
Swisher, J.W.—RH & HD
Tennant, Z.—renal disease

Thomas, J.H.—disease of stomach, POW 2 1/2 months
Toothman, S.—CDR & stomach trouble
Toothman, W.A.—gunshot through neck
Tory, J.L.—hard hearing, injured unloading boat at Vicksburgh
Tucker, N.—hearing affected
Upton, J.R.—piles, sore eyes & general disability
Vandergrift, C.—gunshot in right shoulder
Vandergrift, M.—scurvy, piles, MS, POW Andersonville
Vincent, R.—bladder & kidney trouble
Walls, A.H.—SS
Watts, C.E.—saber wound in head & hip
Weekley, W.J.—RH
Weekly, J.K.—RH
Wells, C.E.—hernia & disease of rectum
Wells, F.M.—gunshot wound of right chest
West, J.J.—disease of throat, loss of voice
West, Perry G.—LD & spinal disease
Wilkinson, T.M.—throat & lung trouble
Williams, E.—dyspepsia
Wilson, B.—catarrh of head & chronic dysentary
Wilson, J.—catarrh
Wilson, J.R.—bunion on left great toe
Wilson, N.M.—piles & CDR
Wilson, S.S.—disease of eyes & disability
Wood, E.T.—RH
Wood, J.N.—general disability
Wright, E.—rupture
Wright, W.—ague
Wyckoff, S.—deafness & catarrh
Yager, F.—RH & HD

Marshall County

NAME/RANK	REGIMENT	WHEN SERVED
Adams, Elijah Pvt.	18 PAC	2/28/64–10/28/65
Allemong, C. L. Pvt.	26 INI	8/6/61–4/26/62
Allen, John P. Cpl.	1 WVI	10/15/61–11/64
also	17 WVI	2/65–6/13/65
Alley, William L. Pvt.	6 WVI	12/31/61–6/10/65
Allison, James M. Pvt.	47 ILI	8/16/61–10/9/64
Allman, Joshua Pvt.	12 WVI	62/65
Ally, Uriah P. Pvt.	6 WVI	1/10/64–6/10/65
Anderson, Benjamine Sgt.	6 WVI	9/1/61–10/22/64
Anderson, Edmond Pvt.	5 PAA	9/3/64–6/30/65
Armstrong, John Pvt.	15 WVI	8/11/62–66
Arndt, David Pvt.	6 WVC	6/5/61–6/5/64
Arnold, John B. Pvt.	4 WVC	6/2/63–3/28/64
Ashby, Thomas J. Pvt.	6 WVI	9/25/61–6/10/65
Ashton, Ruben K. Pvt.	170 OHI	5/14/64–9/10/64
Aston, Thomas Pvt.	12 WVI	7/30/62–6/16/65
Baird, Joseph H. Pvt.	12 WVI	8/13/62–9/8/63
Baker, Arthur O. Capt.	17 WVI	8/30/64–6/30/65
Baker, James E. Pvt.	7 WVI	1/16/62–7/8/62
Baker, Timothy B. Pvt.	12 WVI	8/15/62–6/16/65
Baldwin, Francis W. Ltc.	7 WVI	8/7/61–7/1/65
Bane, Henry Sgt.	12 WVI	8/14/62–6/16/65
Bane, Jesse Pvt.	12 WVI	8/14/62–6/17/65
Barcs, Louis Pvt.	116 OHI	8/19/62–6/14/65
Barker, James K. P. Pvt.	15 OHI	10/25/63–11/25/64
Barnet, William Pvt.	NF	
Barnett, Jesse L. Capt.	7 WVI	8/7/61–7/1/65
Basset, Jacob W. Pvt.	12 WVI	2/64–6/65
Baton, Jerome Pvt.	14 WVI	61/63
Baton, John Pvt.	14 WVI	64/65
Baumberger, Vincent Pvt.	15 OHI	9/61–7/65
Beck, Henry Pvt.	11 ILC	9/23/61–10/15/65
Bennett, William Pvt.	52 OHI	NF
Beyer, John Pvt.	1 WVI	9/61–8/65
Billick, William Pvt.	7 WVI	8/6/61–5/9/63
Black, Charles L. Pvt.	22 PAC	8/6/62–6/2/65
Blair, James M. Pvt.	12 WVI	8/13/62–6/19/65
Blake, John Pvt.	1 WVI	10/17/61–7/21/65
Blake, John Pvt.	11 WVI	11/61–12/64
Blake, Robert Pvt.	15 WVI	8/15/62–6/30/65

Blake, Thomas Sgt.	12 WVI	8/11/62–6/16/65
Blake, Thomas Pvt.	11 WVI	6/13/63–6/17/65
Blakemore, William Sgt.	6 WLA CSA (6 WASHINGTON VAA)	6/15/61–4/15/65
Bloom, Chas J. Pvt.	17 OHI	NF
Bogard, Saml Pvt.	61 PAI	7/17/63–9/12/65
Boggess, Benjamin S. Pvt.	13 WVI	5/1/64–6/22/65
Bonar, John W. Sgt.	17 WVI	2/18/65–7/30/65
Bonar, Thomas S. Sgt.	1 WVI	10/8/61–11/28/64
Bond, George W. Pvt.	—	8/12/61–8/27/64
Bond, Jacob Pvt.	7 WVI	8/7/61–7/18/64
Boner, William N. Pvt.	12 WVI	7/22/62–6/28/65
Boston, James W. Pvt.	25 OHI	3/27/65–7/5/65
Bowen, Jobe Pvt.	17 WVI	/16/65–7/2/65
Bowers, N. J. Capt.	7 WVI	7/61–7/63
Bowers, John Pvt.	17 WVI	2/17/65–6/5/65
Bozard, Jeremiah Pvt.	1 WVC	7/64–7/3/65
Bozard, Levi Pvt.	39 OHI	7/4/61–7/9/65
Brandon, Charles Pvt.	15 OHI	9/6/61–1/19/65
Brandon, Evan Pvt.	15 OHI	9/6/61–11/21/65
Brandon, Hiram Pvt.	38 OHI	9/27/64–9/10/66
Brantner, David A. Sgt.	17 WVI	2/17/65–6/13/65
Brock, Levi G. Pvt.	15 OHI	9/6/61–8/29/62
Brooks, John	NF	
Brown, Frederick M. Pvt.	1 WVA	2/15/64–6/25/65
Bruce, Nathan T. Pvt.	15 WVI	8/13/62–6/30/65
Bryant, James Pvt.	—	61/64
Bryner, George W. Pvt.	118 PAC	10/8/62–6/8/65
Bryson, Abram Sgt.	12 WVI	8/28/62–6/15/65
Bumgardner, William Pvt.	97 OHI	8/6/62–6/25/65
Burch, Talbott Pvt.	12 WVI	8/13/62–4/7/63
Burge, Elijah	NF (46 BTN VAC CSA)	
Burge, James K. Pvt.	6 WVI	12/6/64–6/10/65
Burgess, Isaac Pvt.	32—I	2/16/64–8/22/65
Burgess, William Pvt.	6 WVI	2/15/65–5/10/65
Burghardt, Frederick Pvt.	NF	
Burket, William W. Pvt.	4 WVC	7/2/63–3/10/64
Burley, John A. Pvt.	2 WVI	2/16/64–7/16/65
Burley, Linsey Pvt.	17 WVI	64–7/7/65
Burly, William J. Major	12 WVI	8/16/62–6/16/65
Burris, William Pvt.	10 WVI	9/10/62–6/30/65
Burt, Robert Pvt.	7 WVI	62/65
Bush, John W. Pvt.	17 WVI	7/1/64–6/30/65
Buskirk, Mortimer Pvt	77 OHI	10/31/61–12/20/63
Butcher, Jonas Pvt.	23 OHI	5/62–9/63
Buzzard, John Pvt.	1 WVI	3/17/64–7/65
Buzzard, Theodore Pvt.	17 WVI	9/2/64–6/30/65

Byard, William Pvt.	6 WVI	3/7/63–7/30/63
Byrnes, William F. Pvt.	12 WVI	8/16/62–6/15/63
Cane, Alexander M. Pvt.	NF	
Carmichael, Silas Pvt.	4 WVC	7/63–3/64
Carnahan, William Pvt.	195 OHI	5/2/64–12/18/65
Carothers, William H. Sgt.	5 NY Zouave	5/61–NF
Carr, Joseph Pvt.	6 WVI	61/62
Carr, William Pvt.	15 WVI	10/11/62–NF
Carroll, James Sgt.	NF	
Catlett, Alfred Pvt.	25 OHI	10/63–8/2/65
Catlett, Peter B. Pvt.	3 WVI	7/4/61–4/63
Chaddock, Richard Cpl.	17 WVI	2/65–6/65
Chambers, Amos Pvt.	17 WVI	8/30/64–5/19/65
Chambers, Caleb Pvt.	7 WVI	8/7/61–63
Chambers, Henry Pvt.	6 WVI	10/1/61–6/10/65
Chambers, James A. Pvt.	7 WVI	8/7/61–7/1/65
Chambers, James A. Pvt.	7 WVI	2/19/64–7/1/65
Chambers, James E. Pvt.	17 WVI	8/30/64–6/30/65
Chambers, Wilson Pvt.	12 WVI	8/62–NF
Chambers, Wm	NF	
Chapman, John Pvt.	9 OHC	11/62–7/65
Chase, Wilson C. Pvt.	1 WVC	2/7/64–7/8/65
Chattock, Joseph Pvt.	12 WVI	8/23/62–NF
Clark, Thomas Pvt.	7 WVI	8/7/61–12/18/63
Clark, Thomas R. Pvt.	12 WVI	2/64–8/19/65
Clark, Wm H. Pvt.	7 WVI	8/61–6/65
Clayton, John W. Pvt.	12 WVI	6/14/64–NF
Clayton, William Pvt.	3 WVI	6/61–NF
also	6 WVC	7/64–NF
Clegg, John Pvt.	12 WVI	1/64–8/65
Clouston, James Cpl.	7 WVI	8/5/61–7/8/65
Coats, Benjamin Pvt.	30 OHI	9/3/62–6/65
Coleman, William Pvt.	1 WVI	5/15/61–6/20/65
Comer, William S. Pvt.	17 WVC	NF
also	4 WVI	NF
Connelly, James C. Lt.	1 WVI	4/24/61–2/63
aka Connelly, Celest Pvt.	17 WVI	2/65–7/65
Conner, Ephram D. Pvt.	3 WVC	3/7/65–5/31/65
Conner, George W. Pvt.	1 WVA	8/5/63–NF
also Sgt.	17 WVI	2/5/65–6/25/65
Copper, John Pvt.	15 WVI	9/62–6/65
Coutz, John V. Pvt.	15 WVI	9/9/62–6/30/65
Cox, Harry H. Sgt.	27 PAC	8/15/62–5/20/65
Craft, Samuel Pvt.	NF	
Craig, Ira Pvt.	1 MDI	10/11/61–9/31/62
Crawford, Jacob M. Pvt.	1 MDC	10/12/62–8/8/65
Criswell, Lloyd Pvt.	1 WVI	10/62–7/16/65

Criswell, Harrison Pvt.	77 OHI	9/20/61–6/30/63
Criswell, John W. Pvt.	17 WVI	8/25/64–7/1/65
Criswell, William Pvt.	6 WVI	10/1/61–11/12/64
Crow, Absalom Pvt.	12 WVI	8/13/62–7/19/65
Crow, Harman Pvt.	12 WVI	8/15/62–6/16/65
Crow, Henry Pvt.	12 WVI	8/13/62–6/22/65
Crow, Isaac Pvt.	4 WVC	10/18/63–3/15/64
Crow, John S. Pvt.	12 WVI	8/13/62–6/1/65
Crow, John W. Pvt.	4 WVC	7/63–3/15/64
Crow, John W. Pvt.	12 WVI	8/15/62–6/16/65
Cunningham, George Pvt.	15 WVI	10/11/62–NF
Cunningham, John W. Pvt.	17 WVI	2/22/65–6/30/65
Cunningham, Phillip Pvt.	17 WVI	2/18/65–6/30/65
Dague, Frederick A. Cpl.	17 WVI	2/18/65–6/3/65
Dague, Frederick Sgt.	15 WVI	8/13/62–7/7/65
Dague, William Pvt.	17 WVI	2/18/65–6/30/66
Dailey, Thomas A.	Telegraph Operator	NF
Dakin, Joshua D.	NF	
Dardinger, John S. Pvt.	11 WVA	6/29/61–11/26/63
Darrah, William Pvt.	6 WVI	10/1/62–11/12/64
Darrah, William Pvt.	17 WVI	9/23/64–6/30/65
Daugherty, William H. Pvt.	3 WVI	7/2/61–8/7/65
David, John L. Pvt.	6 WVI	7/7/61–8/15/65
Davis, John E.	US NF	
Davis, John H. Pvt.	15 WVI	8/12/62–2/24/63
Davis, John R. Pvt	10 VAC CSA	4/6/63–4/6/65
Davis, Lindsey Pvt	48 PAI	9/20/64–7/17/65
Davis, Robert R. Pvt.	3 WVI	7/22/61–8/17/64
Davis, Thomas J. Pvt.	17 WVI	2/18/65–6/30/65
Davis, William D.	NF	
Davis, William G. Pvt.	38 OHI	NF
Deitz, Andrew Pvt.	12 WVI	8/5/62–6/16/65
Dennis, Abraham Pvt.	4 WVC	7/4/63–3/64
Derrow, Jacob Pvt.	6 WVI	11/11/61–11/12/64
Dickey, David Pvt.	6 WVI	10/1/61–11/12/64
Dickey, Robert Pvt.	6 WVI	10/14/61–3/12/64
Dorsey, Cornelius Pvt.	4 WVC	7/2/63–5/10/64
Doolen, Edward Pvt.	17 WVI	2/65–7/65
Dorsy, William H. Pvt.	12 WVI	8/16/62–NF
Doughirtz, James W. Cpl.	10 WVI	8/13/62–6/30/65
Dowler, Gustavue Pvt.	1 WVA	2/15/64–6/27/65
Dowler, John W. Pvt.	1 WVI	3/17/64–7/22/65
Drake, Samuel Pvt.	11 VAI	6/29/61–6/29/64
Duncan, William H.	NF (8 VAC CSA)	
Earnest, Henry Pvt.	17 WVI	2/14/65–7/7/65
Eckels, John P. Pvt.	43 OHI	10/1/61–7/14/62
also	43 OHI	1/1/63–7/14/65

Edwards, John W. Pvt.	12 WVI	8/16/62–6/16/65
Edwards, William L. Pvt.	1 WVA	6/10/61–6/20/65
Elder, Daniel W. Pvt.	18 PAC	4/7/64–11/17/65
Engle, Jeremiah Lt.	34 OHI	8/5/61–9/29/64
Erlewine, Stewart Pvt.	17 WVI	8/9/64–6/65
Evans, Gains W. Pvt.	1 WVI	9/17/61–5/11/62
Evans, George W. Cpl.	4 WVC	8/63–3/64
Evans, George W. Pvt.	3 WVI	6/28/61–8/17/64
also	6 WVC	NF
Evans, John Pvt.	1 WVI	9/17/61–1/17/62
Evans, Stephen? Pvt.	6 WVI	6/25/63–6/12/65
Evans, William Pvt.	12 WVI	8/10/62–6/28/65
Ewing, George M. Cpl.	15 WVI	8/13/64–6/30/65
Ewing, William W. Pvt.	17 WVI	2/28/65–6/13/65
Fair, Martin W. Pvt.	12 ILC	1/15/62–5/29/66
Fierheller, August Cpl.	25 OHI	1/1/64–6/18/66
Finn, Thomas Lt.	7 WVI	9/61–12/15/64
Fitzgerald, George W. Sgt.	63 PAC	8/1/61–8/1/64
Flanigan, John M. Pvt.	12 WVI	8/9/62–6/65
Fletcher, Abraham Pvt.	17 WVI	2/17/65–6/30/65
Ford, H. L. Lt.	129 OHI	6/19/63–11/5/64
Founds, John W. Pvt.	12 WVI	8/14/62–6/16/65
Fountain, James H. Pvt.	3 WVI	7/1/61–3/20/64
Fox, Jeremiah Pvt.	1 WVC	8/61–4/63
Fox, Washington Pvt.	6 WVI	1/16/65–6/10/65
Frances, Emaneul Pvt.	12 WVI	8/11/62–5/19/65
Francis, Joseph T. Pvt.	12 WVI	8/12/62–4/28/65
Fry, William H. Pvt.	92 OHI	9/8/62–6/10/65
Fry, James W. Pvt.	7 WVI	9/22/61–9/22/64
Fuchs, Albert C. Pvt.	20 NYI	5/6/61–1/1/65
Gaines, David A. Pvt.	6 WVC	7/6/61–8/17/64
Gamble, James L. Pvt.	17 WVI	2/14/65–6/27/65
Gamble, William C. Pvt.	12 WVI	8/11/62–6/15/65
Games, Alfred Sgt.	12 WVI	8/30/62–6/15/65
Games, John D.	NF	
Gaines, William F. Pvt.	1 WVC	10/9/61–2/28/65
Gardner, William W. Pvt.	15 WVI	8/13/62–2/25/64
Gatts, William S. Pvt.	17 WVI	2/18/65–6/30/65
Gill, Benjamin Pvt.	85 PAI	9/22/61–4/4/62
Givens, Joseph N. Pvt	2 WVI	NF
also	179 OHI	NF
Goff, Charles Pvt.	17 WVI	64/65
Goke, Louis Pvt.	1 WVA	6/28/61–8/8/64
Goodrich, Nelson Pvt.	12 WVI	8/13/62–6/16/65
Goodwin, John A. Pvt.	17 WVI	2/14/65–6/30/66
Gorby, David Pvt.	11 WVI	10/4/61–8/9/65
Gordon, George C. Lt.	170 OHI	5/13/64–9/67

Gossett, George Pvt.	12 WVI	8/12/62–6/16/65
Goudy, William Cpl.	1 WVI	9/23/61–11/26/64
Granstaff, Jacob Pvt.	11 VAI	7/5/61–NF
Granstaff, John R. Pvt.	7 WVI	3/28/64–4/15/65
Graves, William P. Pvt.	1 WVC	NF
Gray, Bushrod Pvt.	139 ILI	5/16/64–10/28/64
Gray, Francis M. Pvt.	12 WVI	8/9/62–5/15/65
Gray, William Pvt.	1 WVA	8/13/63–4/15/64
Grayham, Wm T.	NF	
Greathouse, Harmon Pvt.	6 WVC	8/4/64–5/19/65
Gregg, Gaus Pvt.	12 VAI	8/16/62–3/1/63
Greggs, Isaac Pvt.	12 WVI	8/13/62–6/16/65
Grim, Abraham Pvt.	7 WVI	12/20/61–10/9/62
also	15 WVI	1/28/64–6/14/65
Grim, George W. Pvt.	15 WVI	1/28/64–6/14/65
Grimes, James Pvt.	12 WVI	8/62–6/65
Grimes, John W. Pvt.	4 WVC	8/20/63–3/15/64
aka R? Beteran?	17 WVI	9/2/64–6/20/65
Grimes, W. O. Pvt.	3 WVI	7/61–64
also	17 WVI	3/65–7/65
Grindle, Levi Pvt.	7 WVI	NF
Grist, Isaac Pvt.	61 OHI	2/9/62–7/24/65
Groves, William Pvt.	1 WVI	NF
Gump, Braley Pvt.	6 WVI	10/2/61–6/13/65
Guss, William Drummer	23 USI	10/1/63–5/1/65
Hadsall, John E. Sgt.	12 WVI	8/15/62–6/16/65
Hager, Jacob Sgt.	1 WVI	4/61–8/61
Hager, James S. Pvt.	2 WVC	9/1/64–6/1/65
Hager, N. Cpl.	1 WVI	5/16/61–8/16/61
also Capt.	85 PAI	12/1/61–3/9/63
Hall, George Pvt.	37 IYI	7/23/63–12/29/64
Hall, George W. Pvt.	10 WVI	12/13/63–8/9/65
Hall, Regin W. Qm Sgt.	6 WVI	4/1/62–4/4/65
Halpin, Robert J. Pvt.	12 VAC CSA	NF
Hamilton, John Pvt.	8 PAC	4/62–5/65
Hammond, Johnson Pvt.	52 OHI	8/22/62–6/22/65
Hammond, Thomas G. Pvt.	1 WVA	3/22/64–6/27/65
Hammond, William Pvt.	3 WVI	7/61–6/64
Hanen, Samuel R. Lt.	3 WVI	7/10/61–1/30/64
also	6 WVC	1/31/64–7/13/65
Harbinson, Thomas B. Pvt.	17 WVI	8/20/64–6/30/65
Harbinson, Iven F. Pvt.	NF	
Harbison, Iven F. Pvt.	7 WVI	9/61–7/65
Harris, Amos Pvt.	1 WVI	10/1/61–11/26/64
Harris, Eli Pvt.	4 WVI	7/8/63–3/10/64
Harris, Elias R. Pvt.	1 WVI	4/21/61–8/7/61
also	17 WVI	2/65–7/7/65

Harris, George C. Pvt.	17 WVI	2/65–7/65
Harris, George W. Pvt.	12 WVI	8/17/62–6/65
Harris, Henry Pvt.	1 WVI	9/17/61–11/26/64
Harris, James P. Pvt.	17 WVI	9/2/64–6/30/65
Harris, John C. Pvt.	17 WVI	2/18/65–6/30/65
Harris, John F. Pvt.	4 WVC	7/8/63–3/10/64
Harris, John M. Pvt.	6 WVI	5/23/64–7/10/65
Harris, John W. Pvt.	17 WVI	9/5/64–6/30/65
Harris, Samuel Pvt.	12 WVI	8/16/62–6/16/65
Hart, Amos J. Pvt.	44 PAI	7/14/63–7/16/65
Hart, Jacob Pvt.	14 PAI	8/62–5/65
Hartley, Newton Lt.	NF	
Hartzell, John Pvt.	17 WVI	9/6/64–NF
Haught, Joshua Pvt.	36 OHI	10/64–6/65
Heartly, Samuel Pvt.	11 WVI	8/62–NF
Heath, John Pvt.	77 OHI	9/15/62–7/18/65
Heatherington, Edward D. Capt.	4 IAC	10/9/61
also	8 MOC	8/16/62–3/4/63
Helmes, George M. Pvt.	1 WVI	10/17/61–63
Helms, Martin B. Lt.	1 WVI	10/8/61–3/11/65
Henry, Alexander Pvt	12 WVI	8/13/62–4/7/63
Heston, William Pvt.	6 WVI	9/27/61–11/25/64
Hicks, Jacob B. Sgt.	4 WVC	NF
Hicks, James W. Pvt.	1 WVI	2/26/64–7/17/65
Hicks, John A.	US NF	
Hicks, W. B. Pvt.	4 WVC	8/19/63–NF
also	17 WVI	9/2/64–NF
Hicks, William R. Cpl.	12 WVI	8/13/62–7/19/65
Hildebrand, Henry Pvt.	6 WVI	61–2/1/64
Hill, Isaac Pvt.	77 OHI	2/22/64–5/9/65
Hilton, Joseph (?) Pvt.	6 USI	7/13/63–9/21/65
Hoffman, Brice Pvt.	18 PAC	11/1/62–8/24/65
Hoffmann, Jacob T. Pvt.	62? WVC	5/62–65
Hooth, George Pvt.	1 WVI	9/61–63
Hopkins, Mark Lt.	7 WVI	7/7/61–7/1/65
Howard, George M. Pvt.	1 WVI	9/61–2/24/65
Howard, James A. Sgt.	1 WVI	10/17/61–3/11/65
Howard, Thomas Pvt.	17 WVI	2/65–7/7/65
Hubbs, George W. Pvt.	17 WVI	8/64–7/7/65
Hubb, Isaac H. Pvt.	12 WVI	8/14/62–6/16/65
Hubbs, William H. Cpl.	1 WVI	10/18/61–10/18/64
Hugins, Eli Pvt.	17 WVI	2/17/65–6/30/65
Humphries, William B. Pvt.	WVA	8/11/62–6/18/65
Hunt, David Pvt.	7 WVI	8/7/61–6/15/65
Hunter, Hanson W. Major	6 WVC	7/6/61–8/17/64
Israel, Jacob E.	NF	
Jackson, Harrison Pvt.	3 WVC	10/62–7/65

Johnson, Abram Pvt.	11 WVI	7/11/62–8/9/65
Johnson, Alexander Pvt.	2 WVI	3/21/64–7/16/65
Johnson, Anthony Pvt.	17 WVI	2/18/65–6/13/65
Johnson, George W. Pvt.	77 OHI	12/29/61–3/8/66
Johnson, Morris Pvt.	WVI "Exempts"	10/1/62–7/5/65
Johnston, David B. Pvt.	4 WVC	7/8/63–3/4/64
also Cpl.	17 WVI	8/14/64–7/13/65
Jolinken, Daniel Pvt. (?)	1 WVC	8/6/61–12/28/62
also	6 WVC	6/64–5/25/66
Jones, Abraham Cpl.	12 WVI	8/13/62–6/1/65
Jones, Daniel Pvt.	17 WVI	2/18/65–6/30/65
Jones, George A. Sgt.	12 WVI	8/16/62–6/20/65
Jones, John E. Pvt.	14 WVI	7/14/62–7/3/65
Jones, John G. Sgt.	12 WVI	8/13/62–7/19/65
Jones, Louis B. Pvt.	130 OHI	5/2/64–9/22/64
Jones, Moses Pvt.	7 WVI	4/61–7/65
Jones, William P. Cpl.	17 WVI	NF
Jorlus, Zachariah Pvt.	7 WVI	8/7/61–8/12/62
Juergens, Arnold Cpl.	6 WVI	9/62–7/16/65
Kearns, Andrew Pvt.	NF	
Keene, John Cpl.	77 OHI	10/26/61–3/8/66
Kellar, Charles Sgt.	17 WVI	8/30/64–6/30/65
Keller, David V. Pvt.	1 WVI	11/27/61–7/16/65
Keller, Henry Pvt.	1 WVI	61–NF
Keller, John Pvt.	77 OHI	10/18/61–3/8/66
Keller, John W. Pvt.	17 WVI	NF
Keller, John W. Pvt.	4 VAC	8/63–1/64
Kemple, Otis Pvt.	1 WVI	10/7/61–7/16/65
Kepple, August Pvt.	NF	
Kerns, David W. Pvt.	1 WVA	3/24/62–6/28/65
Keyser, John S. Pvt.	6 WVI	8/21/62–6/10/65
Kimmins, Samuel W. Pvt.	1 WVI	11/1/62–7/22/65
King, W. H. Pvt.	8 PAI	9/20/63–2/65
Kirkman, George W. Pvt.	18 OHI	8/15/61–10/14/62
Kliensorge, William Pvt.	6 WVI	9/15/61–11/15/64
Knapp, Robert Pvt.	1 WVI	5/21/61–8/27/61
also Cpl.	12 WVI	7/30/62–6/16/65
Knox, William A. Pvt.	17 WVI	2/15/65–6/30/65
Law, Nathaniel B. Pvt.	7 WVI	8/7/61–7/1/65
Leach, Benjamin Pvt.	1 WVI	10/1/61–7/16/65
Lewis, France Pvt.	77 OHI	9/4/62–6/65
Lilly, T. W. A. Musician	5 WVI	6/16/61–6/16/64
Litten, Anthony	NF	
Littleton, James Pvt.	15 WVI	63/65
Livsly, William Pvt.	NF	
Lockwood, John H. Col.	7 WVI	NF
Loges, Frederick Sgt.	6 WVI	9/28/61–12/1/64

Logsdan, John T. Pvt.	12 WVI	8/13/62–6/16/65
Logsdon, Joseph Pvt.	4 WVC	7/2/63–3/5/64
also	17 WVI	10/4/64–6/30/65
Lowe, David L. Pvt.	1 OHSS	12/3/62–6/12/63
Lowe, Thomas Pvt.	43 OHI	11/20/63–7/13/65
Lucas, Alexander Pvt.	149 OHI	64/65
Lucas, Charles H. Pvt.	179 OHI	64/65
Lucas, Samuel S. Pvt.	19 OHI	10/9/64–6/2/65
Majors, John W. Pvt.	1 WVI	10/1/61–7/16/65
Majors, William Cpl.	12 WVI	8/13/62–6/1/65
Manfried, John S. Pvt.	1 WVA	1/1/64–7/21/65
Manning, Franklin Pvt.	4 WVC	7/2/63–3/10/64
Manning, Tom W. Lt.	12 WVI	8/19/62–11/8/64
Mariner, Charles Pvt.	12 PAI	4/16/61–7/12/61
also	62 PAI	7/15/61–9/27/64
Maris, William T. Pvt.	17 WVI	7/64–6/13/65
Marple, Joel D. Pvt.	17 WVI	NF
Marple, Joseph Pvt.	17 WVI	NF
Marple, William H. Pvt.	17 WVI	2/14/65–6/14/65
Marquis, Amos Pvt.	45 ILI	9/21/61–1/3/65
Marsh, John W. Pvt.	15 WVC	10/11/62–NF
Marshall, James W. Pvt.	17 WVI	2/17/64–65
Martin, Andrew J. Pvt.	1 WVI	10/18/61–11/18/62
also	1 WVC	11/19/62–11/19/65
Martin, Levi Pvt.	18 VAC	5/62–9/64
Mathews, A. D. Pvt.	17 WVI	2/18/65–6/30/65
Mathews, Andrew J. Cpl.	12 WVI	8/62–6/65
Mathews, Christopher Sgt.	12 WVI	8/9/62–6/29/65
Mathews, Samuel W. Pvt.	1 WVC	2/64–7/65
May, Levi Pvt.	4 WVC	8/30/63–3/15/64
McCardle, Christopher Pvt.	WVI	10/30/63–NF
McCombs, Alexander	NF	
McCombs, Joseph T. Pvt.	1 WVA	2/22/64–6/25/65
McCulley, James Pvt.	1 WVI	4/61–8/65
McCullough, James	NF	
McCully, Hugh Pvt.	1 WVI	4/14/62–4/65
McDaid, Michael S. Sgt.	1 WVC	NF
McFarland, Tom B Pvt..	4 WVC	7/4/63–3/64
McGary, John Pvt.	7 WVI	8/61–7/65
McGary, Thomas Pvt.	12 WVI	8/8/62–12/19/64
McGill, James H. Sgt.	WV SCOUTS	4/22/61–11/62
also Lt.	11 WVI	11/62–5/64
McGill, William Pvt.	3 WVC	7/12/61–5/66
McGown, Patrick Pvt.	6 WVC	7/19/61–3/20/64
McHenry, James N. Pvt.	12 WVI	8/11/62–1/1/65
McLlvain, James W. Pvt.	6 WVI	10/12/61–11/12/64
McNeil, John Pvt.	17 USI	6/64–6/25/68

Name	Unit	Dates
McNeill, Hugh B. Cpl.	85 PAI	10/15/61–7/4/63
McPeek, Joseph B. Pvt.	3 WVI	7/6/61–8/17/64
Mealey, John Pvt	6 WVC	10/20/62–11/65
Merinar, George Pvt.	15 WVI	2/14/64–6/25/65
Messenger, John Pvt.	1 WVC	8/6/61–7/8/65
Messiker, Thomas Pvt.	4 WVC	7/2/63–3/10/64
Mickey, Samuel Pvt.	171 PAI ?	10/24/62–8/6/63
Mille, Abraham Pvt.	140 PAI	8/18/62–12/1/63
Miller, Micheal Pvt.	12 WVI	8/18/62–6/16/65
Mills, James D. Pvt.	3 WVI	7/10/61–NF
Moore, John Pvt.	116 OHI	8/20/62–6/20/65
Moore, Thomas Pvt.	7 WVI	8/7/61–3/30/63
Morgan, John V. Pvt.	6 WVC	NF
Morris, Daniel Pvt.	12 WVI	8/62–6/65
Morris, Hiram	NF	
Morris, Samuel Pvt.	6 WVI	6/30/62–6/12/65
Morris, William Pvt.	NF	
Muldrew, Abram Pvt.	6 WVI	9/12 61–11/12/64
Muldrew, Andrew Pvt.	12 WVI	NF
Muldrew, Josephus Pvt.	3 WVC	12/13/62–7/17/65
Murphy, David L. Pvt.	1 WVI	5/21/61–8/27/61
Murray, George H. Pvt.	22 PAC	8/7/61–10/17/64
Murray, Thomas Pvt.	NF	
Murry, Frederick	NF	
Myers, Emory P. Pvt.	7 WVI	2/24/64–7/1/65
Myers, George M. Pvt.	1 WVI	9/17/61–9/64
Niedmyer, Fredrick Pvt.	1 WVI	4/15/61–7/15/61
Newton, Edward Pvt.	6 WVI	61/64
Nicolls, Olier G. Pvt.	7 WVC	62/65
Noice, Thomas Pvt.	12 WVI	8/17/62–6/16/65
Nowel, Wm Cpl.	161 OHI	5/2/64–9/2/64
also Sgt.	185 OHI	2/13/65–9/26/65
Oden, Jonathan Pvt.	1 MDC	12/3/61–12/3/63
O'hare, Patrick Pvt.	14 PAC	61/64
Orr, Hiram Pvt.	15 WVI	8/62–6/65
Orum, Lloyd Pvt.	11? WVI	5/19/61–8/27/61
also	1 WVA	8/26/64–7/11/65
Osborne, Markes L. Pvt.	171 OHI	5/1/64–9/1/64
Owens, Milton Cpl.	11 WVI	6/25/61–10/62
Parriott, Robert A. Pvt.	17 WVI	2/65–6/30/65
Parriott, S. A. Pvt.	4 WVC	8/30/63–3/10/64
also	17 WVI	9/2/64–6/30/65
Parsons, Thomas Pvt.	12 WVI	8/62–5/65
Patterson, Harrison Pvt.	1 VAA	8/63–4/64
Patterson, Hugh H. Pvt.	4 OHI	4/22/61–7/8/61
Paull, Richard T. Pvt.	11 WVI	8/2/62–6/65
Peabody, Benjamin F. Pvt.	2 NJI	5/30/61–5/30/64

Peabody, Horatio N. Cpl.	2 NJI	5/30/61–5/30/64
Pearl, Edward Pvt.	2—C	1/1/62–3/1/65
Pelley, Philip M. Pvt.	12 WVI	8/8/62–6/16/65
Pelly, James S. Sgt.	2 WVI	2/15/64–7/17/65
Peters, Robert S. Cpl.	—	8/7/62–6/24/65
Peters, Samuel Pvt.	12 VAI	2/16/64–8/19/65
Pettit, Levi Pvt.	3 PAC	3/15/64–10/31/65
Pierce, Arthur D. Sgt.	—	7/6/61–8/17/64
Pinnock, Jacob S.	NF	
Poiles, Clyde Pvt.	10 VAI	1/5/64–8/9/65
Porter, Abner S. Pvt.	6 WVC	7/6/61–8/17/64
Powell, Melvin Pvt.	12 WVI	8/15/62–6/16/65
Powell, Tom W. Pvt.	17 WVI	65–NF
Price, Moses B. Sgt.	3 WVC	7/10/61–8/20/64
Price, Thomas J. Pvt.	17 WVI	2/17/65–6/13/65
Prosser, Washington Pvt.	6 CTA	9/15/64–6/19/65
Purdy, Louis B. Capt.	3 WVI	7/6/61–8/17/64
Pyles, James W. Pvt.	15 PAC	8/25/62–6/26/65
Pyles, Lu Pvt.	4 WVC	7/63–3/64
Queyley, John Pvt.	1 WVI	3/64–7/65
Raper, John M. Pvt.	92 OHI	8/15/62–6/17/65
Ray, Ebinezer Pvt.	6 WVI	6/25/63–6/13/65
Redd, John S. Pvt.	12 WVI	8/23/62–5/65
Reid, John Pvt.	17 WVI	2/17/65–6/30/65
Renforth, Franklin Pvt.	15 WVI	61/65
Reynold, Lewis Pvt.	17 WVI	8/30/64–6/30/65
Reynolds, William Pvt.	17 WVI	9/4/64–6/13/65
Rice, Isaac S. Lt.	6 USC	6/16/61–10/5/65
Rice, James A. Pvt.	7 WVI	8/26/61–9/63
Richardson, Elizah Pvt.	77 OHI	2/13/64–3/8/65
Ricey, George Pvt.	17 WVI	2/65–6/65
Rigby, Thomas Pvt.	7 WVI	9/61–6/65
Riggle, Jacob	US NF	
Riggs, Elias E. Pvt.	1 WVI	5/30/64–7/11/65
Riggs, Lemuel Pvt.	1 WVI	3/1/64–5/1/65
Riggs, William Pvt.	85 PAI	4/24/61–3/25/64
Rine, David Pvt.	12 WVI	8/14/62–6/15/65
Risinger, Sivith ? Cpl.	9 PAC	61/64
Roberts, Irvin F. Sgt.	4 WVC	7/2/63–3/10/64
Roberts, John C. Capt.	12 WVI	8/62–1/65
Roberts, W. W. Pvt.	1 WVC	2/2/64–7/8/65
Robinson, Philip Pvt.	12 WVI	8/12/62–7/65
Rodacker, William Pvt.	17 WVI	2/17/65–6/7/65
Rolen, John L. Pvt.	11 PAI	9/20/64–6/8/65
Ross, Joseph Pvt.	17 WVI	8/30/64–6/30/65
Ruble, Jacob Pvt.	50 PAI	9/3/64–7/7/65
Ruckman, Isaac D. Pvt.	12 WVI	8/7/62–6/16/65

Rulong, Manson Pvt.	12 WVI	62/65
Russel, John W.	NF	
Rutan, John H. Pvt.	17 WVI	2/18/65–6/30/65
Rutencutter, Winfield Pvt.	10 WVI	11/24/63–8/9/65
Sajocts, Josiah V. Pvt.	1 WVI	11/6/62–8/9/65
Samuel, A. Pvt. *aka* Alexander Comer	12 WVI	8/13/62–6/16/65
Schaub, Jacob Pvt.	39 OHI	6/61–8/65
Seng, John Pvt(?)	1 WVI	11/8/61–11/26/64
Scisson, Andrew Pvt.	12 WVI	8/23/62–NF
Shepherd, Henry C. Pvt.	1 WVI	3/22/64–7/65
Siburt, Barney Pvt.	17 WVI	8/30/64–6/30/65
Sinclair, Josiah Lt.	129 OHI	6/19/63–11/5/63
Sims, Newton G. Pvt.	6 WVI	11/5/61–7/26/65
Sindsey, W. H. Pvt.	3 WVI	5/1/61–8/64
Sivert, David A. L. Sgt.	3 WVC	10/8/61–6/5/65
Sloan, Henry Pvt	17 WVI	2/25/61–6/30/65
Sloan, Samuel Pvt.	6 WVI	12/6/61–6/10/65
Smalley, Jacob M.	NF	
Smith, Jacob Pvt.	12 WVI	8/15/62–6/65
Smith, John A. Sgt.	6 WVC	4/20/64–5/22/66
Smith, Joseph Pvt.	1 WVA	8/12/63–7/25/65
Smith, William W. Pvt.	142 PAI	8/8/62–5/15/65
Snedaker, Henry N. Pvt.	161 PAI	63/64
Sogsdon, James N. Pvt.	12 WVI	8/62–6/65
Sogsdon, Thomas Pvt.	17 WVI	2/65–6/65
Sowery, Benjamin C. Pvt.	12 WVI	8/7/62–"deserted"
Spear, Joseph J. Sgt.	116 OHI	8/21/62–6/14/65
Sphar, John Pvt.	12 WVI	8/7/62–3/16/65
Spoon, Jacob Cpl.	4 WVC	7/21/63–4/10/64
Sproul, Henry Sgt.	3 WVC	9/12/62–6/30/65
Staley, James Cpl.	17 WVI	2/65–7/65
Standiford, Jacob Pvt.	12 WVI	3/12/64–NF
Standiford, Skelton Pvt.	6 WVI	10/14/61–11/11/64
Steel, George K. Pvt.	2 IAI	5/10/61–8/1/65
Stewart, George Pvt.	1 WVA	6/13/63–6/27/65
Stewart, Irvin Pvt.	4 WVC	8/2/63–3/4/64
Stewart, Irvin Pvt.	7 WVI	8/7/61–8/8/64
Stewart, James Pvt.	5 PAA	7/64–6/30/65
Stewart, James P. Pvt.	4 WVC	7/2/63–3/10/64
Stewart, P P. Pvt. *also*	7 WVI 6 WVC	7/7/61–7/7/64 8/27/64–5/15/66
Stewart, Robert W. Sgt.	6 WVI	10/14/61–11/12/64
Stewart, Samuel M. Cpl.	6 WVI	8/12/61–9/20/64
Stewart, W. A. Pvt.	6 WVI	10/1/61–11/12/64
Stillivell, Timothy Pvt.	17 WVI	2/17/65–6/13/65
Stilwell, Elias Cpl.	17 WVI	2/17/65–7/25/65

Stiliwell, Joseph R. Pvt.	12 VAI	2/16/64–8/9/65
Stillwell, Tim S. Pvt.	12 WVI	2/4/64–8/18/65
Stine, William Pvt.	12 WVI	7/31/62–6/16/65
Stonaker, David Pvt.	2 WVI	2/17/64–7/16/65
Strait, Henry Pvt.	18 PAC	10/27/62–6/13/65
Suter, Jacob Cpl.	12 WVI	8/20/62–6/15/65
Sutten, Benjamin Pvt.	7 WVI	10/61–64
Sutten, Isaac N. Pvt.	7 WVI	10/61–62
Talbert, Anthony W. Pvt.	1 WVI	5/21/61–8/27/61
also	17 WVI	9/64–7/65
Talbert, James Sgt.	24 INI	7/8/61–11/15/65
Taylor, Frances Pvt.	12 WVI	8/12/62–6/16/65
Taylor, Harrison Pvt.	1 WVI	4/15/61–7/15/61
Taylor, John Cpl.	10 WVI	8/13/62–6/30/65
Taylor, Joseph Sgt.	1 MIC	3/14/62–4/66
Taylor, William H. Pvt.	1 WVI	5/61–9/61
Terrell, Thomas Pvt.	4 WVC	7/2/63–3/10/64
Thatcher, Salathiel Pvt.	10 OHC	2/12/64–7/24/65
Thomas, Ebenezer Surgeon	3 WVI	8/15/61–8/17/64
Thomas, Phillip Pvt.	5 PAA	8/15/64–7/7/65
Thompson, Henry W. Sgt.	1 WVA	8/1/63–7/11/65
Tibbs, Napoleon Pvt.	—I	NF
Todd, Martin C. Pvt.	6 WVI	2/13/65–7/10/65
Tomilson, Alfred Pvt.	6 WVC	12/12/61–NF
Tomilson, Joseph Sgt.	12 WVI	8/62–6/65
Tomilson, William P. Pvt.	3 VAI	12/4/61–1/16/63
Tomlinson, John G. Pvt	3 WVI	7/1/61–12/1/66
Tracy, David W. Pvt.	NF	
Treadway, William M. Capt.	6 WVI	10/14/61–11/12/64
Trinter, John A. Pvt.	12 WVI	8/9/62–7/1/65
Truman, Henry D. Pvt.	11 WVI	7/22/62–6/17/65
Turner, A. Adjutant	5 NYA	3/17/64–7/17/65
Turner, Samuel Pvt.	15 WVI	3/13/62–65
Tuttle, Jesse Pvt.	1 WVC	2/6/64–7/8/65
Vanata, Thomas D. Sgt.	18 PAC	9/8/62–7/11/65
Velton, Phillip	NF	
Virgin, Nelson Pvt.	76 PAI	7/15/63–6/27/65
Waits, Albert B. Cpl.	25 OHI	2/4/64–6/18/66
Washington, George Pvt.	18 PAC	NF
Wasmuth, John Pvt.	6 WVI	9/28/61–6/16/65
Watson, Robert Pvt.	18 PAC	2/27/64–10/31/65
Weekly, James A. Pvt.	15 OHI	1/20/65–11/26/65
Weekly, Thomas B. Sgt.	15 OHI	9/6/61–11/21/65
Weidebusch, Adolph L. Pvt.	25 OHI	11/24/62–11/23/64
Welch, Samuel Pvt.	15 WVI	61/64
Welch, William Sgt.	36 VAICSA	NF
Wells, David Pvt.	17 WVI	3/13/65–7/13/65

Wellwy, Henry H. Pvt.	17 WVI	2/26/65–6/30/65
Welsh, Thomas D.	17 WVI	8/29/64–6/30/65
West, Simon S. Pvt.	140 PAI	9/4/62–6/8/65
Wetzel, Martin Cpl.	12 WVI	8/13/62–6/10/65
Whellatch, George W. Pvt.	17 WVI	2/65–7/65
Whipkey, Jacob Sgt.	18 PAC	8/18/62–16/65
Whipkey, Jonas Cpl.	18 PAC	8/18/62–7/65
White, George W. Pvt.	6 PAI	8/12/61–9/13/64
White, Henry S. Sgt.	6 WVI	9/61–6/20/65
White, John W. Pvt.	1 WVI	5/21/61–8/27/61
White, Joseph C. Pvt.	193 OHI	3/4/65–8/4/65
Whiteman, William A. Sgt.	15 WVI	8/19/62–6/14/65
Whitlatch, Jacob Pvt.	7 WVI	3/10/64–6/13/65
Williams, Edward Pvt.	17 WVI	2/16/65–6/30/65
Williams, Normal Pvt.	17 WVI	8/64–7/7/65
Wilson, James F. Pvt.	1 WVA	63/65
Wilson, John F. Pvt.	6 WVI	11/61–64
Wilson, Samuel Pvt.	12 VAI	8/12/62–6/16/65
Wilson, Samuel W. Pvt.	17 WVI	2/18/64–6/6/65
Winesburgh, Barney Pvt.	17 WVI	2/17/65–6/30/65
Winget, John M. Pvt.	85 PAI	2/16/62–9/63
Winter, Isaac D. Lt.	15 WVI	8/11/62–6/11/65
Winter, William H. Pvt.	NF	
Winters, Alonzo Sgt.	15 WVI	8/13/62–6/65
also	10 WVI	NF
Winters, Joshua Pvt.	1 WVI	9/23/61–3/26/64
Wolfe, John Pvt.	17 WVI	2/18/65–6/30/65
Wooton, James E. Lt./Qm	14 WVI	8/22/61–7/3/63
Workman, Lewis B. Pvt.	6 WVI	1/1/62–1/8/64
Woyt, Joseph B. Gm Sgt.	6 WVC	7/1/61–7/15/65
Wright, Oscar Pvt.	5 OHI	8/30/64–7/1/65
Wyley, Archibald J. Pvt.	2 WVI	2/24/64–7/16/65
Yancey, John Pvt.	6 WVI	8/22/62–3/20/63
Yink, Joseph Pvt.	17 WVI	2/17/65–6/30/65

Marshall County Remarks

Allen, J.P.—two ribs broken
Alley, W.L.—POW & RH
Allison, J.M.—broken down in health
Anderson, B.—LD
Ashby, T.J.—blood vessel ruptured in leg
Aston, T.—POW Libby prison 18 days
Baird, J.H.—DSC by reason of phthisic & pneumonia
Baker, A.O.—fracture of knee caps
Baker, J.E.—wounded in back, pension $8
Baker, T.B.—weak eyes
Bane, J.—shell wound in head
Barcas, L.—shot through right leg
Barker, J.K.P.—disease of breast & eye sight affected
Barnett, J.L.—WIA shell in hand, 12/13/62 Fredericksburg, WIA right arm 10/27/64 at Hatchers Run Va, now paralyzed
Basset, J.W.—wounded left arm
Baton, J.—two gunshot wounds
Baumberger, V.—rupture
Bennett, W.—SS
Beyer, J.—shot in the arm contracted RH
Billick, W.—gunshot wound, UFL
Blair, J.M.—back injured on duty
Blake, J.—WIA gunshot left hand New Creek, WV
Blake, R.—broken down in health
Bonar, T.S.—WIA
Bond, G.W.—RH
Boner, W.N.—gunshot wound neck & shoulder
Boston, J.W.—blood poison, never mustered into service
Bowen, J.—deafness in right ear & CDR
Bowers, N.J.—wounded in throat
Bozard, J.—hurt by fall of horse in Shenandoah Valley
Brandon, C.—RH & exzena
Brandon, E.—shot through right shoulder joint
Brandon, H.—leg poisoned
Brock, L.G.—gunshot wound
Bruce, N.T.—leg broken
Bryson, A.—CDR & RH
Bumgardner, W.—hemoroids, in hospital 6 months
Burch, T.—DSC, RH & dropsy
Burghardt, F.—RH
Burket, W.W.—eyes affected
Burly, W.J.—chronic dispepsia
Burris, W.—plearisy & HD
Burt, R.—cold on flux, consumption of bowels
Bush, J.W.—asma

Butcher, J.—reinlisted spring of 1864 same company
Byrnes, W.F.—wounded in hand, DSC
Carnahan, W.—hurt on head, battle of Piedmont, captured
Carr, J.—DSC
Catlett, A.—both collar bones broken
Catlett, P.B.—RH & tumer
Chambers, C.—gunshot wound in left knee
Chapman, J.—injured by fall of horse 9/21/64
Clark, T.R.—blind from fever, pension $24
Clayton, W.—struck on head by stone on guard duty mind affected
Clegg, J.—blindness
Clouston, J.—gunshot left leg
Coleman, W.—RH, health reduced
Conner, G.W.—kidney trouble & general disability
Copper, J.—ruptured by kick of mule
Coutz, J.V.—TYF & asthma
Cox, H.H.—TYF & ague
Craig, I.—DSC
Criswell, H.—KD & nasal catarrh, reinlisted 2/16/65
Criswell, J.W.—LD
Criswell, L.—WIA at Snickers Ferry 7/18/64, pension $4
Crow, H.—injured in breast by wagon falling on him
Crow, J.S.—wounded in right thigh
Cunningham, P.—POW Andersonville 8 months & rupture
Dague, F.—SS
Dardinger, J.S.—both hands shot off
Darrah, W.—piles & general disability
Daugherty, J.W.—broken down in health
Daugherty, W.H.—gunshot wound left thigh, contracted RH in 1863
Davis, J.H.—HD & liver disease
Davis, L.—had lung fever now in poor health
Davis, R.R.—general disability
Deitz, A.—gunshot wound right arm
Derrow, J.—shot through hand & collar bone broken falling
Dowler, J.W.—pension $6
Drake, S.—MS reinlisted Co E 10 WVI 12/28/63 discharged 8/9/65
Edwards, J.W.—CDR & weak back
Edwards, W.L.—chronic desenterry & piles
Elder, D.W.—VV right leg, pension $24 per month
Evans, G.W.—bone disease right arm & leg, DSC
Evans, G.W.—injured by fall of horse reulting piles
Evans, Jn.—disease of bowells
Ewing, G.M.—breast injured & piles
Finn, T.—loss of left leg
Founds, J.W.—shot throuqh hand & ruptured
Fountain, J.H.—RH thrown from horse, scurvy, reinlisted 3/20/64
Fox, J.—crushed by a horse in a stable

Fox, W.—LD & KD, proper name George W. Fox
Francis, E.—eye disease, total blindness
Francis, J.T.—general disability
Gaines, W.F.—wounded in left hip
Gains, D.A.—RH & CDR
Games, J.D.—HD & piles
Gardner, W.W.—LD & HD
Gatts, W.S.—RH & MS
Goodrich, N.—lost right eye & deaf right ear
Goodwin, J.A.—RH
Gordon, G.C.—catarrh
Goudy, W.—CDR
Granstaff, J.R.—WIA leg amputated below the knee
Granstaff, J.—RH, DSC
Gray, B.—broken down in health
Gray, F.M.—gunshot left thigh at Piedmont Va 6/5/64
Greathouse, H.—thrown from horse right arm disabled
Gregg, G.—MS, DSC
Greggs, I.—POW Bell Island four weeks
Grimes, J.—RH & MS, defective hearing
Hager, J.B.—piles, 3 month service
Hager, J.S.—HD & eyes affected by MS & wounded in the foot
Hall, G.—dyspepsia & HD
Hall, R.W.—chronic catarrh & RH
Hamilton, J.—shot in left hip
Hammond, J.—disease of eyes & urinary organs
Hammond, W.—RH
Harbinson, T.B.—ruptured in service
Harbison, I.F.—gunshot both shoulders, pension $8
Harris, A.—POW Bell Island 6 months
Harris, E.R.—breast & back affected by measles
Harris, G.W.—injured in left hand by gunshot
Harris, H.—gunshot wound in head
Harris, J.P.—RH
Hart, A.J.—wounded in the chin at Resaca in Ga.
Hart, J.—RH & HD
Heartly, S.—breast injured
Heath, J.—POW 10 months Tyler Texas
Heatherington, E.—RH & CDR
Heston, W.—fever left him feeble
Hicks, W.R.—gunshot in hand
Hildebrand, H.—weak lungs
Hill, I.—CDR & RH, pension $14
Hilton, J.—injured in right knee pension $6
Hoffman, B.—wound in hand, pension $4
Hopkins, M.—shot through right eye, lost sight
Hunt, D.—right arm amputated at shoulder gunshot, pension $45

Jackson, H.—HD
Johnson, An.—RH & asma
Johnson, G.W.—WIA left hand & right leg
Jones, A.—injured from effects of mumps
Jones, J.G.—wounded by gunshot in left hand
Jones, L.B.—lost right eye from measles
Jones, M.—WIA near Petersburg Va 6/64 pension $6
Jones, W.P.—POW Andersonville 9 months now has CDR
Jonhson, A.—spinal disease
Jorlus, Z.—scarfula left leg, DSC
Jounken, D.—WIA by fall from horse Aug 1862 Racoon Ford, DSC
Juergens, A.—RH
Keene, J.—chronic disease & RH of back
Keller, D.V.—left knee injured
Keller, J.—gunshot wound
Keller, J.W.—HD, several injuries, not on muster rolls
Kepple, A.—RH
Kimmins, S.W.—POW Belle Isle 6 months, injured in right leg
Kirkman, G.W.—MS settled on lungs, reinlisted 9/1/64
Kliensorge, W.—RH
Knapp, R.—POW Richmond 18 days
Leach, B.—HD & RH
Lockwood, J.H.—RH
Loges, F.—RH
Logsdon, J.N.—gunshot right arm, disease left breast
Logsdon, T.—abscess of liver, discharge lost in flood
Lowe, D.L.—hurt by fall
Lowe, T.—double hernia
Lowery, B.C.—deaf left ear, reinlisted in 130 INI
Lucas, S.S.—right leg crushed, bronchitis & RH
Majors, J.W.—rupture & piles
Majors, W.—HD & LD
Manning, T.W.—RH & CDR
Maris, W.T.—now crippled, RH
Marple, J.D.—left leg hurt from long march
Marple, W.H.—RH
Marquis, A.—broken down in health
Marsh, J.W.—stummick disease & general disability
Martin, A.J.—WIA shell right shoulder New Market 6/64 pension $4
Mathews, S.W.—piles
McCully, H.—deafness caused by firing cannon
McGary, T.—loss of right arm, DSC
McGill, J.H.—disease of stomach
McGill, W.—RH
McGown, P.—reinlisted 3/27/64
McNeill, H.B.—spine partial paralysis of the lower limbs
Mealey, J.—injury to right eye

Merinar, G.—head hurt by shell
Messenger, J.—injured by horse crushing knee & frozen foot
Morris, H.—dispepsia, RH & HD
Myers, G.M.—CDR, HD, POW 6 months captured at Moorefield, 9/1863
Nicolls, O.G.—TYF, proper name John OG Nicholls
Oden, J.—thrown from horse captured POW Libby prison
Orr, H.—shot in the thigh
Orum, L.—POW Pemberton prison three months
OsBorne, M.L.—chronic desenterry
Parsons, T.—CDR, cold on measles
Patterson, H.H.—now nearly blind
Paull, R.T.—CDR & RH
Pelley, P.M.—right eye shot out, gun ball still in head
Peral, E.—eye injured & RH
Peters, R.S.—wounded in foot & RH
Peters, S.—RH, CDR & asma
Pierce, A.D.—rupture
Poiles, C.—CDR, wounded right hip & frozen feet
Porter, A.S.—spinal disease
Powell, M.—POW Libby prison 21 days, MS
Powell, T.M.—LD from MS
Price, M.B.—HD & RH, asthma
Price, T.J.—RH & dyspepsia
Prosser, W.—bronchitis, catarrh & sight impaired
Raper, J.M.—RH & VV
Ray, E.—stummick disease
Redd, J.S.—gunshot wound left leg
Reid, J.—RH & HD
Renforth, F.—hearing affected & RH
Renolds, W.—RH
Rice, I.S.—piles & fistula
Rice, J.A.—WIA by shell in hips at ? WIA gunshot Fredericksburg
Riggs, E.E.—3 months in Richmond prison, catarrh of stomach
Riggs, L.—RH
Roberts, I.F.—RH
Roberts, J.C.—gunshot wound in right knee
Rodacker, W.—deafness & blindness from measles
Rolen, J.L.—weak eyes from fever, ruptured by fall, DSC
Ruckman, I.D.—general disability
Rutencutter, W.—LD & stummick disease
Sajocts, J.V.—knee disabled by fall, discharged from 10th WVI
Schaub, J.—shot through right leg
Shepherd, H.C.—SS
Sims, N.G.—WIA Cloyd's Mountain Va 5/9/64
Sivert, D.A.L.—gunshot wound right lung
Smith, J.A.—partial loss of eye sight
Smith, Jo.—back injured

Smith, W.W.—general disability & piles
Sphar, J.—CDR
Spoon, J.—shot through seat of left ear
Stewart, J.P.—LD, reinlisted Co. A 17 WVI
Stewart, S.M.—eyesight impaired
Stiliwell, J.R.—disease of head, kidney affected
Stillivell, T.—evil effects from mumps in service
Stillwell, E.—caught cold in my eyes from exposure
Stine, W.—shot in the leg & stomach disease
Stonaker, D.—hemorage of the bowels, pensioner
Strait, H.—general disability from fever, pension $4
Talbert, J.—TYF left feeble and lung trouble
Taylor, J.—shot in left leg
Thomas, P.—Veslega & deafness, pension $22
Thompson, H.W.—rupture
Tibbs, N.—HD
Tomilson, J.—HD & RH
Tomilson, W.P.—CDR & spinal affection, DSC
Trinter, J.A.—RH & HD
Truman, H.D.—lost first finger of right hand
Turner, A.—POW Libby & salisbury prison, captured at Cedar Creek Oct 19, 1864 paroled 2/22/65 & HD
Turner, S.—POW Louivill for 8 months & RH
Vanatta, T.D.—wound in face, detached on staff duty
Virgin, N.—frozen feet, POW at Libby Prison, Andersonville & Florence, SC in all 9 months, pension $12
Waits, A.B.—dispepsia & premature decay of all physical faculty
Weekly, T.B.—CDR, wound in hip 6/8/62 slight
Welch, W.*—wounded twice
Wellwy, H.H.—WIA right foot 4/2/65 near Fort Gregg, Va
Whipkey, J.—pension $8
Whipkey, Jonas—pension $4
White, H.S.—gunshot right elbow
Wiedebusch, A.—shell wound left shoulder, piles & KD
Wilson, J.F.—bad eyesight
Wilson, S.—RH & piles
Winget, J.M.—injured in back by log building road pension $4
Winter, I.D.—RH
Winters, J.—gunshot wound in hand
Wyley, A.J.—finger shot off, RH
Yancey, J.—double hernia
Yink, J.—RH

Mason County

NAME/RANK	REGIMENT	WHEN SERVED
Ailor, John Pvt.	13 USI	8/64–9/65
Allemany, Eri Pvt.	33 OHI	8/26/61–7/12/65
Allen, Alexander Lt.	34 ILI	9/7/61–8/22/65
Allen, Wm. J. Pvt.	4 VAI	6/21/61–5/9/65
Allen, Wm. M. Pvt.	198 OHI	4/5/65–5/18/65
Alshire, Wm. Pvt.	7 MOM	5/20/62–4/6/65
Armstrong, Benj. E. Pvt.	7 WVC	10/1/61–8/1/65
Arthurs, Lafayette Pvt.	7 WVC	11/29/62–8/1/65
Asbury, Thomas Pvt.	13 WVI	8/21/62–6/22/65
Bable, John Pvt.	2 OHC	9/23/62–5/12/65
Bader, Rudolph Pvt.	75—	4/27/61–7/16/64
Bailes, John Pvt.	4 WVI	6/20/61–7/16/65
Bailes, Joseph Pvt.	4 WVI	7/61–6/64
Baker, Elisha E. Pvt.	1 KYI	NF
Ball, John W.	NF (30 BTN VASS CSA?)	
Ball, Thomas E. Cpl.	7 WVC	9/4/61–8/1/65
Ball, Wm. Pvt.	3 WVC	10/2/63–6/30/65
Barnell, Wm. Pvt.	13 WVI	8/62–6/65
Barnett, James Pvt.	13 WVI	62/65
Barnett, John Pvt.	CSA NF (8 VAC?)	
Barnett, Samuel Pvt.	13 WVI	8/8/62–7/17/65
Bartram, Leonard	NF	
Baxter, John W. Cpl.	13 WVI	8/14/62–6/28/65
Beach, John B. Sgt.	77 OHI	10/15/61–3/8/66
Beaver, George W. Pvt.	77 OHI	10/16/62–10/15/65
Bennett, Richard Cpl.	1 WVC	9/20/61–1/23/65
Birchfield, John H.	NF	
Birchfield, Nathaniel Pvt.	13 WVI	8/11/62–6/22/65
Birchfield, Wm. Pvt.	13 WVI	8/15/62–6/2/65
Blazer, Philip Lt.	7 OHC	10/8/62–7/3/65
Blessing, C.L. Cpl.	13 WVI	NF
Boardman, James W. Pvt.	2 MNA	1862–7/65
Boggens, John A. Pvt.	13 WVI	NF
Boggers, Robert O.	US NF	
Boird, George W. Cpl.	11 WVI	1861–7/65
Boso, Frncis M. Pvt.	10 WVI	62/65
Bowins, James M. Pvt.	44 —	NF
Bowles, Francis M. Pvt.	7 WVC	2/64–8/65
Brannon, John S. Pvt.	9 WVI	3/31/64–6/27/65
Bright, Andrew J. Pvt.	NF	
Bright, E.S. Pvt.	104 OHI	8/11/62–7/12/65
Brown, Charles W. Pvt.	4 WVI	7/23/61–7/18/65

Brown, James	CSA NF (14 VAC?)	
Brown, Joseph A. Pvt.	9 WVI	2/28/64–7/21/65
Broyles, James M. Pvt.	7 OHC	8/30/62–7/3/65
Bumgarner, Calvin S. Pvt.	4 WVI	6/9/61–7/16/65
Burdett, James P. Pvt.	11 WVI	8/14/62–6/17/65
Burk, John S. Pvt.	122 OHI	5/12/62–5/30/66
Burns, Harvey Pvt.	11 WVI	1/15/62–5/15/65
Burns, James	NF	
Burnside, Hugh A. Pvt.	1 WVA	8/15/62–6/65
Burnside, Joseph Pvt.	15 OHC	6/19/63–3/1/65
Burwell, Spurlock Pvt.	7 WVC	3/10/64–8/1/65
Bush, Jesse F. Pvt.	63 OHI	10/4/61–7/22/65
Butcher, John Pvt.	45 KYI	NF
Butcher, Wm. H. Pvt.	53 OHI	10/26/61–8/11/65
Byers, Wm. A. Pvt.	7 WVC	10/14/61–8/5/65
Cable, Abner H. Sgt.	4 WVI	7/17/61–8/25/64
Cable, Wm. B. Pvt.	4 VAI	9/62–9/65
Caloway, Eli	NF	
Cariends, John C. Pvt.	18 OHI	9/20/61–11/9/64
Carlile, Calvin Pvt.	13 WVI	62/65
Carroll, Thomas Cpl.	4 WVI	6/5/61–7/4/64
Carry, Alonzo Pvt.	92 OHI	62/65
Carson, Benj. R. Pvt.	4 WVC	8/1/63–3/10/64
Carson, W. A. Pvt.	NF	
Carter, John	NF (22 VAI CSA?)	
Cartwright, Albert H. Pvt.	197 OHI	3/17/65 7/31/65
Cartwright, Wm. H. Pvt.	92 OHI	8/5/62–2/25/65
Casey, Madison Pvt.	15 WVI	4/14/64–6/23/65
Casto, Jacob A. Pvt.	13 WVI	12/25/63–6/22/65
Chambers, Richard F. Pvt.	5 WVI	1/1/63–7/21/65
Chambers, Wm. Cpl.	5 WVI	10/8/61–1/1/65
Chapman, John W. Pvt.	8 WVI	NF
Chapman, W. H. Pvt.	4 WVI	61/65
Chattan, John H. Pvt.	7 WVC	1861–NF
Cherrington, Charles Sgt.	23 OHI	63/65
Childers, Charles Pvt.	13 WVI	9/9/62–6/22/65
Childers, John P. Pvt.	7 WVC	3/24/64–8/1/65
Childers, Robert L. Pvt.	13 WVI	11/10/63–6/22/65
Circle, Charles E. Pvt.	4 WVI	6/5/61–7/4/64
Circle, John Pvt.	4 WVI	6/5/61–7/4/64
Clagg, Lorenzo S. Pvt.	8 WVI	12/31/61–6/31/64
also Cpl.	7 WVC	6/31/64–8/1/65
Clark, Allen Pvt.	7 OHC	9/62–7/5/65
Clendenin, Joseph S. Pvt.	4 WVI	6/17/61–7/17/65
Clouch, Alexander Pvt.	13 WVI	8/8/62–6/22/65
Cochran, Caleb Pvt.	7 WVC	12/2/61–6/18/63
Cole, Joseph Sgt.	62 PAI	4/14/61–6/25/65

Cole, Wm. W. Cpl.	5 PAA	8/29/64–6/13/65
Coleman, Wm. L. Pvt.	9 WVI	2/28/62–7/2/65
Collins, Richard Pvt.	4 WVI	6/17/61–8/19/63
Congo, Zachariah Pvt.	4 WVC	8/29/63–NF
also	187 OHI	2/18/65–6/20/66
Conley, John B. Pvt.	9 WVI	2/2/62–NF
Conrad, Andrew Pvt.	2 WVI	5/18/61–10/30/62
Conway, Charles W. Pvt.	7 WVC	4/64–8/1/65
Cooper, George Pvt.	NF	
Cooper, Jeremiah I. Pvt.	11 PAC	8/30/62–6/9/65
Cornelius, Wm.	CSA NF (55 VAI?)	
Cosset, Daniel Pvt.	11 VAI	61/61
Cossin, George Pvt.	11 WVI	11/20/62–8/9/65
Cottrell, Eliza W. Pvt.	11 WVI	3/30/62–6/17/65
Cox, Augustus C. Pvt.	122 OHI	63/65
Crawford, John Pvt.	NF (45 BTN VAI CSA?)	
Crawford, Samuel Pvt.	4 WVI	6/17/61–7/6/64
Cremeans, Wm. H. Pvt.	13 WVI	11/9/63–6/22/65
Crosier, Richey	NF	
Crump, James Pvt.	13 WVI	8/20/62–6/20/65
Crump, Thailes Pvt.	3 WVC	9/62–6/65
Cumberledge, Isaac Cpl.	4 WVC	7/25/63–3/8/64
Cundiff, Charles B. Pvt.	198 OHI	4/5/65–5/18/65
Cundiff, George W. Pvt.	197 OHI	3/31/65 7/31/65
Cunningham, Henry Pvt.	9 WVI	12/25/61–12/25/64
Curry, Timothy	NF	
Curtis, Jarvis A. Pvt.	140 OHI	5/2/64–9/3/64
Dains, Andrew D. Pvt.	7 OHC	9/3/62–7/3/65
Daniel, Henry Pvt.	2 OHA	6/23/63–8/31/65
Daniel, Keefer Pvt.	15 WVI	1/4/64–6/23/65
Darst, Samuel Pvt.	91 OHI	2/6/64–6/9/65
Davis, Benj. C. Pvt.	8 WVI	NF
Davis, Elias Pvt.	4 VAI	7/14/61–12/30/63
Davis, Thomas Pvt.	98 OHI	NF
Dawson, George Pvt.	— VAA	1863–4/65
Dean, Samuel B. Pvt.	112 OHI	2/11/65–9/1/65
Dewault, Ashby G. Pvt.	4 WVI	NF
Dewees, Wm. F. Pvt.	13 WVI	8/8/62–6/22/65
Dolmer, Henry Pvt.	3 OHI	5/23/61–8/14/64
Doolittle, David W. Pvt.	13 WVI	9/63–6/22/65
Dormick, John Pvt.	1 WVC	9/4/61–11/29/64
Doss, James M. Cpl.	1 WVI	9/4/61–NF
also Sgt.	7 WVC	1862–8/7/65
Downs, Robert O.	NF	
Duncan, Benj. Pvt.	NF	
Duncan, Daniel J. Pvt.	26 VAI CSA	4/10/61–5/25/65
Duncan, George W.	NF (25 BTN VAI CSA?)	

Name	Unit	Dates
Dunlap, Creal Pvt.	13 WVI	3/21/64–6/22/65
Dunlop, John	NF	
Dunn, James	NF (26 BTN VAI CSA?)	
Dunn, John Pvt.	27 VAC (CSA?)	NF
Dwight, Stephen Pvt.	18 BAT?	8/12/62–6/29/65
Dye, James P. Pvt.	4 CAI	9/27/61–11/1/62
Dyke, Amos Pvt.	7 OHC	9/3/62–6/20/65
Eader, James	NF	
Eads, Charles C. Pvt.	NF	
Eckard, Calvin J. Pvt.	13 WVI	8/3/62–6/23/65
Edward, Albert Pvt.	1 WVI	8/13/61–7/2/65
Edwards, A.E. Pvt.	141 OHI	5/64–9/64
Edwards, Harrison Pvt.	13 WVI	3/31/64–6/22/65
Edwards, James Pvt.	13 WVI	9/9/62–6/22/65
Edwards, John R. Pvt.	1 VAA	7/20/62–6/28/65
Edwards, Lewis W. Sgt.	13 WVI	12/10/63–6/21/65
Edwards, Thomas Pvt.	13 WVI	6/5/61–6/17/64
Edwards, Wm. L. Pvt.	13 WVI	8/4/62–6/22/65
Egan, James G. Pvt.	174 OHI	8/13/64–6/28/65
Elliott, Philip Pvt.	4 VAI	7/16/6–4/13/65
Ellis, Richard L. Pvt.	13 WVI	8/62–5/65
Ellison, Horace W. Cpl.	10 PAA	5/21/61–6/13/65
Ely, Washington Pvt.	7 OHA	10/28/63–6/27/65
Farwer, Monroe Pvt.	13 WVI	8/8/62–6/22/65
Ferguson, John H. Cpl.	13 WVI	8/8/62–5/22/65
Ferguson, Wm. A. Pvt.	13 WVI	12/25/63–6/22/65
Fisher, John M. Pvt.	13 WVI	8/62–7/5/65
Fisher, John W. Pvt.	7 WVC	3/63–1865
Fisher, Thomas H. Sgt.	13 VAI	9/2/62–6/22/65
Fisher, Gideon Pvt.	8 WVC	61/65
Fletcher, Joseph Pvt.	7 WVI	NF
Flint, Samuel Pvt.	4 VAI	3/65–9/65
Foreman, Wm. Pvt.	5 WVI	9/16/61–5/5/63
Forest, Jasper Pvt.	52 KYI	10/4/63–2/18/65
Fowler, Jesse B. Pvt.	4 WVI	6/61–NF
French, Robert Cpl.	4 WVI	6/5/61–7/4/64
Fry, Gideon Pvt.	NF	
Fry, Marion Sgt.	13 WVI	8/15/62–6/22/65
Fuller, James F. Pvt.	53 KYI	4/4/65–9/15/65
Garden, Alexander Pvt.	4 VAI	9/1/61–4/14/62
Gardner, George P. Cpl.	1 WVA	9/62–6/28/65
Gardner, Leonidas Pvt.	4 WVC	7/63–4/64
Gardner, Peter A.	NF	
Garrison, James H. Sgt.	15 WVI	8/11/62–6/14/65
Gaskins, James H. Pvt.	13 WVI	8/9/62–6/22/65
Gibb, Sheldon Pvt.	13 WVI	8/62–5/24/65
Gibbons, John A. Sgt.	31 OHI	8/4/61–5/30/62

Gibbs, Andrew J. Pvt.	13 WVI	8/19/62–6/22/65
Gibbs, Archibald Sgt.	9 WVI	12/9/61–12/26/64
Gibbs, G.W. Pvt.	10 WVI	8/18/62–6/26/65
Gibbs, James R. Cpl.	13 WVI	8/19/62–6/22/65
Gibbs, Joseph F. Pvt.	13 WVI	10/28/63–10/22/65
Gibbs, Michael Pvt.	4 WVI	6/5/61–7/64
Gibbs?, Andrew J. Pvt.	188 PAI	2/1/64–12/14/65
Gibson, Norman	NF	
Gilbe, John R. Sgt.	7 WVC	NF
Gilliam, E.L. Ast/Surgeon	2 WVC	8/61–6/30/65
Gillingham, Milton Pvt.	1 OHC	NF
also	18 OHI	NF
Gillis, Roger Pvt.	174 OHI	8/18/64–6/28/65
Gillis, Thomas Pvt.	4 WVI	6/11/61–3/14/64
Glenn, Alvaro Pvt.	11 WVI	62/65
Gobert, Wm. H.H. Pvt.	196 OHI	2/9/65–10/9/65
Goble, Andrew J. Sgt.	63 OHI	11/11/61–6/18/65
Goodall, Wm. T.	NF	
Goodrich, Lewis Pvt.	4 WVI	6/15/61–7/15/65
Gouin?, Joel	NF	
Gould, Andrew	NF	
Graham, George Pvt.	18 OHI	NF
Graham, John M. Sgt.	13 WVI	8/24/62–10/26/63
Graham, Ransler Pvt.	73 OHI	8/9/62–8/13/65
Granstoff, Adam Pvt.	122 OHI	1/5/64–6/19/65
Gray, Paris Pvt.	13 WVI	12/5/63–6/10/65
Green, Hugh G. Sgt.	13 WVI	NF
Green, John T. Sgt.	4 WVI	8/1/61–8/24/64
Green, Oscar Pvt.	13 WVI	NF
Green, Wm. E. Pvt.	7 WVC	8/31/64–6/3/65
Greenlee, George A. Pvt.	13 VAI	2/11/65–6/65
Greenlee, George B. Pvt.	13 WVI	12/1/63–5/15/65
Greenlee, Hesekiah Pvt.	13 WVI	2/14/65 6/22/65
Greenlee, John M. Pvt.	13 WVI	5/11/63–6/22/65
Greenlee, Martin Pvt.	13 WVI	2/65–5/65
Greenlee, Wm. P. Capt.	13 WVI	8/8/62–6/22/65
Gregory, David	NF	
Groynn, Amos Pvt.	4 WVI	6/61–7/64
Guard, John W. Pvt.	18 — BTN	7/62–6/29/65
Guthrie, Francis A. Capt.	111 PAI	9/10/61–8/2/63
Haley, Daniel G. Pvt.	18 OHI	9/20/64–7/11/65
Halfhill, John W. Pvt.	4 WVI	1/2/62–6/20/65
Hall, Daniel J. Pvt.	7 WVC	1861–8/65
Hall, John Pvt.	101 PAI	61/63
Hall, Joseph J.	NF	
Hampton, James Pvt.	36 OHI	NF
Haning, Eliva Pvt.	7 OHI	NF

Hankins, Wm. Pvt.	14 WVI	9/5/62–8/65
Hanna, James W. Lt.	13 WVI	8/15/62–6/24/65
Hanna, Samuel D. Pvt.	13 WVI	8/15/62–6/22/65
Hannis, Thomas C. Pvt.	39 OHI	6/21/61–7/4/65
Harbour, Thomas Pvt.	7 WVI	10/22/64–8/1/65
Harris, Bartholomew Pvt.	7 WVC	12/10/61–8/1/65
Harris, Daniel Pvt.	7 OHI	8/15/62–6/29/65
Harris, Wm. Pvt.	13 WVI	NF
Harrison, George W. Pvt.	7 WVC	3/29/64–8/10/65
Hart, Calvin Pvt.	11 WVI	1/28/64–8/9/65
Hawkins, Peter F. Pvt.	13 WVI	63/65
Hawthorne, George W.	NF	
Hayes, Levi Pvt.	166 OHNG	5/64–9/64
Haynes, Sheldon H. Pvt.	2 WVC	8/5/61–10/15/62
Hays, Joseph L. Pvt.	5 OHC	7/63–1/65
Heatherington, Hamden Capt.	43 OHI	2/17/62–7/23/65
Hein, Joseph Lt.	1—A	9/8/61–9/27/65
Henderson, Donnally F. Lt.	4 WVI	4/1/61–12/8/62
Henry, Darius Pvt.	7 WVC	61/63
Henry, Hugh Pvt.	173 OHI	8/5/64–6/26/65
Henry, John W.	NF	
Hess, John H. Sgt.	13 WVI	8/18/62–6/22/65
Hesson, John Pvt.	13 WVI	8/62–6/22/65
Higginbotham, John Cpl.	7 WVC	10/23/61–8/1/65
Higginbottom, John Pvt.	11 WVI	12/4/61–5/23/65
Hill, Andrew C. Pvt.	13 WVI	12/24/63–6/22/65
Hill, Andrew J.	NF (Chapman's VAA CSA)	
Hill, Daniel Pvt.	14 WVI	12/31/63–6/22/65
Hill, George W. Pvt.	13 WVI	12/24/63–6/22/65
Hill, Jonathan Pvt.	13 WVI	12/18/63–1/18/65
Hinkle, James R. Pvt.	9 WVI	12/28/61–7/21/66
Hobbs, Squire T. Pvt.	1 WVI?	7/18/63–7/23/65
Hoffman, Robert H. Pvt.	7 WVC	8/63–8/65
Hoffman, Samuel Pvt.	4 WVI	8/61–8/64
Hogg, John F. Pvt.	13 WVI	12/7/63–7/11/65
Holley, Andrew Pvt.	NF	
Holley, George W. Pvt.	10 WVI	8/24/62–7/5/65
Holley, Joseph S. Pvt.	13 WVI	8/27/63–6/22/65
Holstein, Perry Pvt.	7 WVC	9/64–8/65
Holt, Rutter Pvt.	12 WVI	10/8/64–NF
Hoplite, Charles	NF	
Hoschar, Andrew K. Pvt.	13 WVI	10/1/63–6/22/65
Houghton, H.H. Pvt.	2 USSS	11/61–6/65
Howard, Hiram R. Pvt.	11 OHI	4/21/61–6/25/64
Howard, McDonald Cpl.	18 OHI	4/63–11/65
Howel, Elias Pvt.	13 WVI	8/24/63–2/24/65
Howerty, Daniel S. Lt.	11 WVI	10/26/61–6/7/65

Name	Unit	Dates
Hudson, David Pvt.	13 WVI	8/22/62–7/18/65
Hudson, Preston Sgt.	4 VAI	7/3/61–7/18/65
Hugh, Graham Pvt.	12 WVI	62/65
Hughes, James Pvt.	4 WVC	7/4/63–3/64
Hummel, Wm. C.B. Pvt.	2 NYC	4/62–6/65
Huston, Archable Chaplain	122 OHI	8/62–6/65
Hyatt, Albert Pvt.	13 WVI	10/9/63–6/17/64
Hyatt, Emanuel Pvt.	13 WVI	8/8/62–6/22/65
Hyatt, Richard R. Pvt.	12 KSI	5/61–6/65
Hylton, Ira Pvt.	13 VAI	8/62–6/22/65
James, George W. Pvt.	6 WVI	8/31/64–6/12/65
James, Levi W. Pvt.	33 OHI	8/25/61–7/25/65
Jeffries, Felix Pvt.	13 WVI	8/8/62–6/30/65
Jinkins, Daniel P. Pvt.	4 VAI	8/14/61–1/19/64
Jinnings, Peter	NF	
Jividen, Jonathan Pvt.	13 WVI	10/9/63–6/22/65
Johnson, David B. Sgt.	13 WVI	8/15/62–6/22/65
Johnson, George E.	NF	
Johnson, Jeremiah H. Sgt.	13 VAI	9/9/62–6/22/65
AKA Johnson, J. Hamilton	NF	
Johnson, Joseph W. Pvt.	73 OHI	8/1]/61–7/11/65
Johnson, Noah Pvt.	18 OHI	9/20/61–11/9/64
Johnson, Suman Pvt.	18 OHI	10/16/61–11/9/64
Johnson, Valentine E. Pvt.	73 OHI	11/7/62–5/18/65
Jolley, Norvel N. Pvt.	91 OHI	NF
Jones, A.P. Pvt.	2 WVI	7/61–7/8/65
Jones, Thomas E. Pvt.	12 ILI	8/28/61–2/15/62
Jonnson, Asa S. Pvt.	13 WVI	12/11/62–6/22/65
Jordan, John W. Pvt.	7 WVC	3/1/65–8/1/65
Jordan, Samuel J.	NF (Pegram's VAA CSA?)	
Jordon, Wm. H.	NF	
Jordon, Wm. M. Pvt.	15 KSC	8/18/63–6/20/65
Jourdan, James H. Pvt.	2 WVC	7/63–7/4/65
Kanode?, Marshal Pvt.	CSA NF	
Kauff, Jacob Pvt.	66 PAI	3/63–NF
Kearns, Jesse Pvt.	9 VAI	12/25/61–12/18/62
also	3 VAC	6/20/63–7/15/65
Kearns, Thomas Cpl.	9 WVI	12/61–7/65
Kelley, James S. Sgt.	13 WVI	8/15/62–6/22/65
Kent, Hugh Sgt.	9 USA	8/64–8/65
Kernes, Wm. Cpl.	13 WVI	8/15/62–6/22/65
Kidwell, Franklin C. Pvt.	14 WVI	8/14/62–6/14/65
Kilen?, Lewis D. Pvt.	2 WVC	9/20/61–11/29/64
Kimberling, Wm. Pvt.	4 WVI	7/19/61–9/4/64
King, Ephraim Pvt.	4 WVI	10/4/61–1/24/64
also	2 WVI	1/24/64–7/16/65
King, Nicholas Pvt.	36 OHI	8/1/61–9/64

Name	Unit	Service Dates
King, Wm. W. Pvt.	175 OHI	6/63–6/65
Kinser, Michael Pvt.	1 KYI	6/18/61–7/64
Kirk, Thomas B. Pvt.	5 WVI	8/5/61–8/5/64
Kirkpatrick, James A. Pvt.	7 WVC	NF
Klaus, Jacob Pvt.	1 TXA CSA	9/61–6/20/65
Kleen, Patrick Pvt.	13 WVI	8/22/62–6/22/65
Klingensmith, David Pvt.	4 WVI	6/16/61–7/6/64
Klingensmith, Wm. Pvt.	4 WVC	1863–3/10/64
also	187 OHI	2/10/65–6/26/65
Klinzing, Henry Pvt.	87 PAI	2/23/65–6/29/65
Knap, Sam P. Pvt.	9 VAI	5/62–1864
KnapenbercTer, Jacob Pvt.	11 WVI	3/29/62–6/20/65
Knapp, Francis	NF	
Knapp, Moses Pvt.	4 WVI	8/25/61–8/8/64
Knapp, Wm. Pvt.	13 WVI	8/4/62–6/22/65
Koreins?, Adonis W. Capt.	9 WVI	11/61–3/64
Krepps, Joshua Pvt.	6 USC	9/21/61–7/22/62
Kroft, Charles Pvt.	140 OHNG	5/2/64–9/3/64
Lambe, Wm. A. Pvt.	6 WVI	9/7/64–6/10/65
Lampirt, Andrew Pvt.	55 KYI	3/65–8/65
Latham, Charles T. Lt.	13 WVI	8/4/62–1/18/65
Lathey, Alexander Pvt.	188 OHI	2/24/65–9/21/65
Lawson, Wm. Cpl.	13 WVI	8/10/62–6/22/65
Lee, Benj. Pvt.	5 OHI	5/20/64–8/65
Leopard, Thomas E.	NF	
Lerner, Herman Pvt.	107 PAI	9/19/64–6/6/65
Lewis, Allen Cpl.	13 WVI	3/31/64–6/22/65
Lewis, Benj. F. Pvt.	13 WVI	12/63–6/65
Lewis, Isaac A. Pvt.	13 WVI	2/1/64–6/22/65
Lewis, Isaac N. Pvt.	4 WVI	6/17/61–7/13/65
Lewis, James W. Pvt.	1 MOC	11/63–6/65
Lewis, Sines Pvt.	9 WVI	2/10/62–2/10/65
Long, Benj. Pvt.	9 WVI	2/62–7/65
Long, Edmond Pvt.	55 KYI	3/8/65–9/19/65
Long, Wm. A. Pvt.	1 KYI	2/1/64–12/14/65
Loosier, Bert	NF	
Love, C. C. Pvt.	4 WVI	7/5/61–1865
Love, James L. Cpl.	4 WVI	6/16/61–7/6/64
Love, Wm. P. Sgt.	140 OHNG	5/2/64–9/3/64
Lowry, Alonzo A. Pvt.	7 OHC	9/2/62–7/3/65
Luce, Algunon Pvt.	46 PAI	9/62–4/65
Lutton, Mathew Pvt.	13 WVI	62/65
Lyda, Andrew J. Chaplain	3 WVI	8/10/62–4/29/64
also	6 VAC	NF
Lyon, Rulof Pvt.	50 NYE	2/13/64–6/16/66
Lyons, John W. Pvt.	9 WVI	9/3/61–7/25/65
Lyons, Joseph Pvt.	7 WVI	63/65

Malone, Charles B. Pvt.	4 WVI	8/14/62–6/16/65
Marks, Henry A. Pvt.	13 WVI	8/4/62–6/22/65
Martin, Franklin Sgt.	9 VAI	12/16/61–7/21/65
Martin, John H. Pvt.	18 OHA	8/13/62–6/29/65
Martin, Preston Pvt.	91 OHI	8/15/62–10/14/63
Mathews, Philip Pvt.	4 WVI	6/14/61–1/6/64
Mattox, Josiah Pvt.	13 WVI	8/9/62–6/65
Mauck, Robert Cpl.	141 OHI	5/2/64–9/3/64
Mayes, Charles W. Pvt.	7 WVC	1864–8/9/65
McCallester?, Peary?	CSA NF	
McCloud, John Pvt.	13 VAI	10/10/62–NF
McCloud, Redford Pvt.	7 WVC	NF
McCollock, J.S. Pvt.	13 VAI	8/22/62–6/25/65
McComb, John	NF	
McComb, Thomas	NF	
McDade, George Pvt.	7 WVC	12/61–1/31/64
McDade, Jackson Pvt.	7 WVI	12/10/61–6/22/65
McDaniel, Alexander Pvt.	13 WVI	8/9/62–6/22/65
McDaniel, George W. Pvt.	13 WVI	9/29/63–6/22/65
McDaniel, John Pvt.	13 WVI	8/5/62–6/22/65
McDaniel, Ruben Pvt.	13 WVI	8/5/62–6/22/65
McKindley, Philip H. Pvt.	7 WVC	3/1/64–6/17/65
Meek, Samuel	NF	
Meeks, Richard W. Cpl.	13 WVI	8/15/62–6/22/65
Meriston?, Husekiah	NF	
Messick, Jacob W. Pvt.	13 WVI	8/22/62–6/22/65
Metheny, Daniel B. Pvt.	13 WVI	1/63–1/22/65
Metheny, George W. Pvt.	NF (Chapmans VAA CSA?)	
Micheltree, James H.	NF	
Middlecoff, James L. Pvt.	— OHA	1/23/63–7/12/65
Miller, Wm. A. Pvt.	6 WVI	8/20/61–8/27/64
Miller, Wm. A. Pvt.	9 WVI	1/15/62–7/21/65
Mitchell, Dandy J.	NF	
Mitchell, Isaac Pvt.	15 USI (Negro)	8/15/64–8/25/65
Mitchell, Philip Sgt.	4 WVI	6/20/61–5/2/65
Modderspaugh, George Pvt.	2 OHI	10/18/64–8/23/65
Molden, Frank Pvt.	184 OHI	2/1/65 9/14/65
Moore, Isaac H. Capt.	4 OHC	10/30/61–7/15/65
Moore, Joseph Pvt.	63 OHI	12/16/61–7/8/65
Morgareige, Daniel J. Pvt.	2 WVI	8/30/61–6/23/65
Moriarty, John Pvt.	13 WVI	8/22/62–6/22/65
Morris, Robert F.	NF	
Morris, Van B. Lt.	11 WVI	8/22/62–6/24/65
Morrow, Gideon	NF	
Morrow, Henry C. Pvt.	173 OHI	8/5/64–6/26/65
Morrow, John F. Pvt.	18 OHI	4/22/61–7/28/65
Morrow, Robert L?	NF	

Moulden, James W. Pvt.	1 WVC	3/10/64–NF
Mourning, George W. Pvt.	13 WVI	8/8/62–6/22/65
Mulfreed, Wm. H.H. Pvt.	13 WVI	10/7/62–6/22/65
Natross, Martin Pvt.	4 WVI	6/17/61–7/5/64
naviS, Winfield 5. Pvt.	7 WVC	9/10/— 8/1/65
Neal, Daniel C. Pvt.	6 INC	6/23/63–9/15/65
Neale, John W. Lt.	2 WVC	11/21/61–5/5/62
also Pvt.	140 OHI	5/2/64–9/3/64
Nease, Harvey	NF	
Needham, James M. Pvt.	1 WVA?	10/10/62–7/3/65
Neek, Jasper N. Pvt.	129 OHI	6/23/63–7/4/65
Nelson, Mark Pvt.	7 KYI	NF
Newbraugh, James A.	Wagonmaster	NF
Newell, Elijah F. Pvt.	13 WVI	8/62–12/64
Newland, John Pvt.	116 OHI	8/15/62–6/14/65
Nickelson, Joseph Pvt.	4 VAI	8/2/61–8/13/63
Noble, Anson Pvt.	13 WVI	11/1/63–6/22/65
Noble, Erastus	NF	
Nye, Tobias S. Pvt.	9 PAI?	7/15/61–11/11/62
Nyers, Wm. Pvt.	6 WVI	64/65
Oliver, Eli Pvt.	7 OHI	1861–3/28/63
Oliver, John C. Pvt.	13 WVI	2/65–6/22/65
Oliver, John Pvt.	4 VAI	6/9/61–7/16/65
Oliver, Thomas Pvt.	13 VAI	10/13/62–6/22/65
Onail, Wm. Pvt.	7 WVI	62/65
Owens, Wm. Pvt.	2 WVC	9/6/61–11/28/64
Palmer, Andrew J. Pvt.	36 OHI	2/23/65–7/27/65
Parsons, Elias Pvt.	193 OHI	3/3/65–8/4/65
Parsons, Travers Pvt.	—	1864–6/65
Patterson, James W. Pvt.	13 WVI	8/9/62–6/22/65
Patterson, John A.	NF (23 VAC CSA?)	
Pearl, John Pvt.	41 USI	8/62–6/65
Pearson, Wm. H. Pvt.	9 WVI	61/65
Peck, Andrew J. Cpl.	2 WVC	1/1/64–7/4/65
Pegram, Pinkerton	NF (8 VAC CSA?)	
Perry, David Pvt.	4 WVI	6/5/61–7/4/64
Phelps, Oliver Capt.	1 WVI	6/22/61–7/17/65
Philips, Squire J. Sgt.	13 WVI	9/9/62–6/22/65
Phillips, John F. Pvt.	CSA NF (22 VAI)	
Pickens, H.G. Pvt.	9 WVI	62/65
Pickens, Spencer Pvt.	13 WVI	8/12/62–6/22/65
Pierce, Indian Pvt.	13 WVI	12/28/63–6/22/65
Pierce, Lanson C.	NF	
Pillow, Wm. J.	NF	
Pinnick, John T. Pvt.	4 WVI	6/16/61–7/16/65
Plants, Chrisitan Pvt.	4 WVI	NF
Plantz, George W. Pvt.	13 WVI	8/1/62–6/25/65

Name	Unit	Dates
Plantz, George W. Pvt.	140 OHI	5/2/64–9/3/64
Pluntz, John Sgt.	13 WVI	8/62–6/20/65
Polk, Gideon Pvt.	4 WVI	7/20/61–8/29/64
Porter, John C.	NF	
Porter, Lewis Pvt.	9 WVI	11/3/61–6/5/65
Pounds, Joseph Lt.	13 VAI	9/9/62–6/22/65
Prebbs, Charles Cpl.	13 WVI	9/9/62–6/22/65
Preston, Newell Pvt.	13 WVI	8/8/62–6/22/65
Pritchard, James	NF	
Pullin, Jonathan Pvt.	1 WVA	8/18/62–6/28/65
Pullin, Tonathe Lt.	7 WVI	11/15/61–2/28/65
Pullin, Wm. Pvt.	NF	
Racy, John D. Pvt.	1 VAC	11/21/61–6/14/65
Rainlen?, Wm. Pvt.	1 OHA	7/26/63–7/25/65
Ramsey, Thomas Pvt.	47 KYI	9/63–12/26/65
Ravidon, Henry C. Pvt.	1 OHA	8/30/62–7/10/65
Rayburn, Gilbert Pvt.	4 VAI	6/5/61–7/5/64
Rayburn, Griff Pvt.	13 WVI	1863–6/22/65
Rayburn, James A. Cpl.	13 VAI	8/5/62–6/22/65
Rayburn, James R. Pvt.	13 WVI	8/62–6/22/65
Rayburn, John R. Pvt.	13 WVI	9/63–6/22/65
Rea, Robert Pvt.	197 OHI	3/27/65 7/31/65
Redman, Shank	NF	
Reed, Park Pvt.	73 OHI	8/5/62–5/30/65
Regents?, John R.	CSA NF	
Rice, Harrison Cpl.	13 WVI	8/9/62–6/22/65
Rice, Vincent D. Pvt.	13 WVI	8/7/62–1863
Rickard, George Pvt.	13 VAI	12/10/63–6/21/65
Rickerd, Michael Pvt.	4 WVI	6/5/61–7/24/65
Riffle, Charles Pvt.	13 WVI	9/9/62–6/22/65
Riffle, Henry Cpl.	7 WVC	10/1/61–1/1/65
Riffle, Louis E. Pvt.	13 WVI	9/9/62–6/12/65
Riggs, Augustus Pvt.	36 OHI	8/12/61–9/3/64
Riggs, Wm. A. Pvt.	45 OHI	63/65
Riley, Marion Pvt.	1 WVI	NF
Rimmey?, George W.	NF	
Robberts, Andrew J. Pvt.	4 WVI	6/21/61–6/10/65
Robinson, Andrew Pvt.	140 PAI	NF
Robinson, Spurloc~ Sgt.	7 WVC	9/1/61–8/1/65
Robson, Anthony Cpl.	5 OHI	8/64–12/64
Rock, M.W. Pvt.	1 WVC	9/20/61–7/18/65
Rogers, Josiah C. Pvt.	—Army	8/22/62–6/23/65
Rosebery, Michael Capt.	4 WVI	8/18/62–6/21/65
Roush, Jonas Pvt.	13 VAI	10/10/62–1863
Roush, Joseph M. Pvt.	4 WVI	7/61–1865
Roush, Moses Pvt.	13 VAI	8/18/62–6/22/65
Rowley, Emanuel Pvt.	15 WVI	9/9/62–6/22/65

Name	Unit	Dates
Rowsey, Henry J. Cpl.	7 WVC	2/28/64–8/1/65
Rowsey, Wm. H. Sgt.	7 WVC	2/28/64–8/1/65
Roy, Wm. H. Pvt.	7 WVI	3/14/64–8/2/65
Rulen, Joshua	NF	
Russell, Hiram Pvt.	13 WVI	9/9/62–5/22/65
Ryan, Thomas Sgt.	4 WVI	6/9/61–7/6/64
Sands, George W. Pvt.	13 WVI	8/9/62–6/20/65
Sayer, Daniel Pvt.	187 OHI	64/65
Sayre, Andrew Sgt.	3 WVC	9/2/62–6/26/65
Sayre, Hiram Pvt.	13 WVI	9/9/62–5/25/65
Sayre, J.O. Cpl.	140 OHI	64/64
Sayre, John W. Pvt.	4 WVI	7/25/61–8/24/64
Sayre, Mark G. Pvt.	13 WVI	8/29/62–6/22/65
Sayre, Pleasant Pvt.	4 VAI	7/18/61–7/29/64
Scantlin, John Pvt.	2 WVI	11/1/64–7/19/65
Schools, Paul O. Pvt.	13 WVI	8/6/62–6/22/65
Schultz, August Pvt.	204 PAA	8/64–7/4/65
See, Wm. Pvt.	13 WVI	12/25/63–6/22/65
See, Wm. W. Pvt.	15 WVI	11/26/63–6/22/65
Selby, C.H. Pvt.	NF	
Sewell, Andrew H. Pvt.	NF	
Sharp, —— Pvt.	146 OHNG	5/2/64–9/7/64
Sheline, Andrew J.	NF	
Sheppard, Andrew J.	NF (51 VAI CSA?)	
Sheppard, John T. Pvt.	8 VAC CSA	1862–NF
Shindle, Sam J. Pvt.	2 VAC	9/1/61–11/22/64
Shively, Benj. T. Pvt.	4 WVI	6/61–7/27/65
Shoemaker, Joseph Pvt.	4 WVI	6/5/61–3/10/63
Shrewsbury, Columbus Lt.	4 WVI	6/5/61–5/26/63
Shuler, George W.	NF	
Sieving, Fred	Artillery	4/17/61–6/28/65
Sims, Wm. Pvt.	4 WVI	6/20/61–7/16/65
Sines, Peter Pvt.	4 WVI	6/61–7/16/65
Skidmore, Chapin J. Pvt.	39 OHI	6/22/61–9/4/62
Slayton, Daniel W. Pvt.	141 OHI	5/1/64–9/1/64
also	11 MII	2/25/65–7/29/65
Slayton, James W. Pvt.	141 OHI	5/1/64–9/1/64
Smith, Daniel Pvt.	13 WVI	11/26/64–6/22/65
Smith, David Pvt.	9 WVI	12/7/61–7/22/65
Smith, Elisha Pvt.	2 WVC	1864–6/65
Smith, George E. Cpl.	9 PAI	5/24/61–3/25/63
Smith, George Pvt.	4 VAI	6/15/61–7/22/65
Smith, James W.	CSA NF (8 VAC)	
Smith, John H. Pvt.	13 WVI	8/22/62–1865
Smith, Samuel Pvt.	13 WVI	8/8/62–6/22/65
Smith, Wm. H. Pvt.	3 WVC	3/1/63–6/30/65
Smith, Wm. P. Pvt.	13 WVI	8/8/62–6/22/65

Name	Unit	Dates
Smith, Wm. Pvt.	4 WVC	63/64
Smith, Wm. Pvt.	7 WVC	2/1/64–8/1/65
Snider, Jobe Pvt.	11 WVI	8/14/62–6/6/65
Snyder, Elias Pvt.	11 WVI	8/14/62–6/65
Snyder, John E. Pvt.	4 WVI	6/1/61–3/62
also	13 WVI	10/62–1865
Sonesby, Edward Pvt.	2 WVC	3/6/64–6/30/65
Spann, Lemeul	13 WVI	7/11/61–8/65
Spencer, John Pvt.	13 WVI	8/18/62–6/26/65
St. Clair, Alfred Pvt.	13 VAI	NF
Stagg, Alfred G.	26 NJI	NF
Stanley, Edward Pvt.	60 OHI	8/4/62–11/10/62
Stephens, Thomas Pvt.	9 OHC	10/62–1865
Stewart, Adam Pvt.	13 WVI	8/4/62–6/22/65
Stewart, George Cpl.	13 WVI	8/8/62–6/22/65
Stewart, John Pvt.	7 WVC	10/1/61–8/1/65
Stiles, John C. Pvt.	36 OHI	NF
Stone, John Pvt.	11 WVI	8/14/62–6/25/65
Stone, John T. Lt.	NAVY	1/22/63–6/65
Stone, Richard "Engineer"	US Key West	11/13/63–10/1/65
Stover, James L. Pvt.	4 WVI	6/5/61–7/5/64
Stover, Wm. P. Pvt.	4 WVI	7/26/61–7/26/64
Strater, Wm. Pvt.	87 PAI	9/5/61–10/13/64
Stricklen, Jasmer D. Cpl.	7 WVC	10/15/61–8/1/65
Sullivan, Alfred T. Lt.	13 WVI	12/26/63–6/22/65
Sullivan, Joseph E. Pvt.	7 WVC	11/61–2/65
Taylor, John M. Pvt.	13 WVI	3/13/63–6/22/65
Taylor, John Pvt.	26 OHI	6/8/61–8/1/65
Taylor, Wesley B. Pvt.	3 WVC	1862–1/25/65
Teeters, Marcellus Pvt.	1 WVC	64/65
Terry, Edward	NF	
Thomas, Allen Pvt.	195 OHI	NF
Thomas, F. Blksmith	7 WVC	3/28/64–8/1/65
Thomas, James G. Pvt.	9 WVI	61/63
Thomas, Rubin Pvt.	13 WVI	10/4/62–7/1/64
Thomas, Samuel Cpl.	9 WVI	2/62–2/64
Thorn, Joshua L. Cpl.	80 INI	63/65
Thornton, Allen Pvt.	7 WVI	3/22/64–NF
Thornton, Charles W. Pvt.	7 VAC	12/24/61–1/4/65
Thornton, Francis Pvt.	13 WVI	8/3/62–6/26/65
Thornton, Wm. Pvt.	13 WVI	10/1/63–6/16/65
Tillis, Smith Pvt.	13 WVI	8/12/63–6/22/65
Tolliver, John R. Pvt.	1 OHC	8/15/61–9/8/62
Troeger, Ernest	NF	
Tulley, Andrew Pvt.	13 WVI	7/26/63–6/22/65
Turley, Claiborne C. Cpl.	170 OHI	8/16/64–6/26/65
Turnbull, Thomas Pvt.	4 WVC	1/1/63–3/10/64

Turner, Henry C. Pvt.	4 WVI	6/5/61–7/4/64
Turner, Jacob C. Pvt.	8 WVI	2/15/62–8/65
Tweksburry, Aaron Pvt.	36 OHI	7/15/63–11/63
Vangilder, Amasa C. Pvt.	4 VAI	10/30/61–10/25/62
VanMatre, Jacob Pvt.	4 —	7/1/61–7/14/64
VanMatre, Leonard Pvt.	13 WVI	10/12/62–6/27/65
VanMatre, Rockway Pvt.	7 OHA	12/2/61–1/6/65
VanMatre, Wm. J. Pvt.	13 WVI	9/9/62–6/22/65
Vanmeter, Perry Pvt.	1 WVA	8/4/62–6/28/65
Vanmeter, Reasin	7 OHA	12/2/61–1/6/65
Varian, Daniel Pvt.	2 WVC	1/15/63–7/10/65
Vickers, Sam C. Pvt.	13 WVI	3/25/64–6/22/65
Villars, James A. Sgt.	11 WVI	6/16/61–B/9/65
Vincent, Lewis F. Pvt.	13 WVI	8/15/62–6/22/65
Wade, Isaac Pvt.	4 INC	8/14/62–11/5/62
Walker, Frank Pvt.	18 OHA	7/62–6/22/65
Wallace, Wm. T. Pvt.	7 WVC	2/17/65 8/65
Wamsley, Wm.	NF	
Warden, Sebert Cpl.	7 WVC	3/15/64–8/10/65
Warth, Charles S. Pvt.	19 VAC CSA	5/64–4/65
Watterson, Andrew Pvt.	140 PAI	8/15/62–5/19/65
Waugh, Silvester	NF	
Weigand, Adam Cpl.	13 WVI	8/62–6/65
Werner, Wm. Pvt.	155 PAI	8/62–1863
Whealdon, Isaac H. Pvt.	63 OHI	5/61–1863
White, Overton Pvt.	18 MOI	10/1/61–5/63
Whitt, Archibald Pvt.	36 OHI	1862–7/65
Wilcoxen, John S. Sgt.	9 WVI	3/61–7/65
Wildman, Hiram Pvt.	36 OHI	8/10/61–9/13/64
Wiles, G. W. Pvt.	12 WVI	61/65
Williams, Boyd Pvt.	7 VAC	10/1/61–1/25/65
Williams, Gideon H. Pvt.	4 WVI	6/13/61–7/5/64
Williams, Ira Pvt.	13 WVI	NF
Williams, Simon Capt.	13 WVI	8/15/62–12/16/65
Williamson, Henry C. Pvt.	4 WVC	7/61–8/64
Wilson, Edward R. Sgt.	19 VAC CSA	64/65
Wilson, G. W. Pvt.	13 WVI	1862–NF
Wilson, Wm. H. Pvt.	32 OHI	8/1/61–7/20/65
Winebrewer, Alex H. Pvt.	13 WVI	8/8/62–6/22/65
Wires, Thomas Pvt.	7 WVC	3/64–8/65
Wise, John Pvt.	7 OHC	7/20/62–7/3/65
Wiseman, Henry B. Pvt.	5 VAI? CSA	5/10/61–4/1/65
Wolf, David Pvt.	13 WVI	8/12/62–6/26/65
Wolf, Harvey Pvt.	60 OHI	3/62–1865
Wolford, Calvin Sgt.	7 OHC	8/1/62–7/4/65
Wood, Elijah J.	NF	
Woodrum, Richard Sgt.	13 WVI	9/9/62–6/24/65

Woods, Wm. F. Pvt.	13 WVI	8/12/62–5/19/65
Work, Franklin A. Cpl.	53 OHI	9/5/62–8/25/65
Worley, W.H.H. Cpl.	9 WVI	12/25/61–12/31/63
also	1 WVI	1/1/64–7/21/65
Young, Franklin D. Pvt.	6 WVI	8/6/61–8/6/64
Young, Robert Blacksmith	13 WVI	8/8/62–6/22/65
Zeiher, Peter Pvt.	1 WVC	9/8/61–10/28/62
Zerkle, Wm. Pvt.	13 WVI	1863–6/22/65

Mason County Remarks

Ailor, J.—legs swollen to knees
Allemany, E.—broken left leg
Allen, A.—RH & gunshot wounds
Allen, W.J.—kicked in back by horse
Alshire, W.—WIA left leg shot
Amsbury, H.—bronchitis
Armstrong, B.E.—asthma
Asbury, T.—LD
Bable, J.—CDR
Bailes, J.—eye disease
Bailes, Jn.—back & HD
Baker, E.E.—catarrh
Ball, W.—kicked on ankle by horse
Barnell, W.—disease of back, kidneys & leg wound
Barnett, S.—gunshot wound
Bartram, L.—hronchitis
Baxter, J.W.—deafness
Beaver, G.W.—liver complaint & rupture
Birchfield, N.—gunshot wound
Blazer, P.—frozen feet, catarrh & HD
Blessing, C.L.—gunshot wound in ankle
Boggens, J.A.—HD & SS
Boird, G.W.—wounded & HD
Bowins, J.M.—RH
Bowles, F.M.—piles
Bracy, J.D.—nervous debility
Bright, A.J.—diseased testicle
Bright, E.S.—plurasy & catarrh of head
Brown, C.W.—LD & piles
Brown, J.A.—hip & knees
Bumgarner, C.S.—RH & HD

Burk, J.S.—partial blindness
Burns, H.—WIA
Burns, J.—RH
Burnside, J.—LD
Burwell, S.—RH
Bush, J.F.—gunshot wounds right shoulder & left ankle
Butcher, J.—LD & sore eyes
Butcher, W.H.—deafness
Cable, W.B.—deafness
Caloway, E.—demented
Cariends, J.C.—wounded in arm
Carlile, C.—wounded in head & foot
Carroll, T.—shot in right arm above wrist
Carry, A.—combination of diseases
Carson, B.R.—LD & RH
Carter, J.*—LD
Cartwright, W.H.—served 4 months previous to term
Casey, M.—RH
Chambers, R.F.—KD, liver disease, result of jaundice
Chambers, W.—disease head & eyes, RH, result measles & fever
Chapman, W.H.—bayonet wound side
Chattan, J.H.—RH
Cherrington, C.—WIA left cheek by shot
Childers, J.P.—CDR result of flucks
Childers, R.L.—frozen feet
Circle, C.E.—RH
Clendenin, J.S.—CDR
Clouch, A.—HD & LD
Cole. W.W.—deafness
Coleman, W.L.—WIA left knee & right thigh resulting VV
Collins, R.—POW Libby prison
Congo, Z.—LD
Conrad, A.—WIA left leg
Conway, C.W.—bronchitis
Cooper, G.—tramp not home at present
Cooper, J.I.—RH & catarrh
Cottrell, E.W.—wounded right foot
Crawford, J.*—CDR
Crosier, R.—HD 25 years
Crump, C.—LD
Cunningham, H.—RH
Curtis, J.A.—RH
Darst, S.—CDR, gunshot wound
Davis, E.—disease of back & side, cold on measles
Davis, T.—breast trouble
Davis, W.S.—injury to back
Dewault, A.G.—general disability

Dolmer, H.—gunshot wound
Doolittle, D.W.—wounded in left arm
Duncan, B.—CDR
Duncan, G.W.*—catarrh head & sight
Dwight, S.—spinal disease
Dye, J.P.—ruptured 28 years
Eader, J.—LD, hearing
Eckard, C.J.—RH, right ear off
Edward, A.—RH
Edwards, A.E.—RH
Edwards, J.R.—LD
Edwards, L.W.—RH & HD
Edwards, T.—CDR
Egan, J.G.—gunshot wound left thigh
Ellison, H.W.—HD
Farwer, M.—breast trouble
Ferguson, J.H.—wounded in leg
Ferguson, W.A.—liver complaint
Fisher, G.—catarrh
Fisher, J.M.—piles & HD
Fisher, J.W.—RH
Fisher, T.H.—fever, CDR
Fletcher, J.—gunshot wound in chin
Flint, S.—catarrh, sight
Forest, J.—RH
Fowler, J.B.—deafness
French, R.—wounded in testacle
Fry, G.—nervous debility
Fry, M.—gunshot through left shoulder
Garden, A.—RH
Gardner, G.P.—total deafness one ear
Gardner L.—asthma
Gardner, P.A.—bleedinq Piles
Garrison, J.H.—wounded in head
Gaskins, J.H.—disease of urinary organs, now has consumption
Gibbons, J.A.—LD & CDR
Gibbs, A.J.—CDR & piles
Gibbs, A.J.—hearing
Gibbs, A.—sycovitis of left knee & RH
Gibbs, G.W.—CDR
Gibbs, J.F.—CDR
Gibbs, J.R.—RH & frozen feet
Gibson, N.—HD
Gilliam, E.L.—CDR, knee & breast injury
Gillis, R.—SS
Glenn, A.—nervousness from shell
Goodall, W.T.—CDR

Goodrich, L.—grovel (?)
Gouin, J.—liver disease
Gould, A.—injured back
Graham, G.—piles
Graham, R.—RH
Granstoff, A.—gunshot wound
Green, H.G.—CDR
Green J.T.—WIA hand & foot
Greenlee, G.A.—deafness both ears
Greenlee, H.—lungs & stomach result of measles
Greenlee, J.M.—LD
Greenlee, M.—CDR
Greenlee, W.P.—catarrh in head
Groynn, A.—KD
Guard, J.W.—blood poison left leg 25 years
Haley, D.G.—KD & spinal disease 25 years
Halfhill, J.W.—bronchitis
Hall, D.J.—plurasy
Hall, J.—fistula
Hall, J.J.—shell wound
Haning, E.—injured by exposure
Hanna, J.W.—gunshot in right arm
Hanna, S.D.—spinal disease
Harbour, T.—CDR
Harris, B.—piles & RH
Hawkins, P.F.—severe combination
Hays, J.L.—head & spine disease
Heatherington, H.—CDR & RH
Hein, J.—CDR & RH resulting in HD
Henry, H.—CDR
Henry, J.W.—HD
Hess, J.H.—deafness left ear & LD
Higginbottom, J.—WIA at Cedar Creek 10/19/64
Hobbs, S.T.—paralysis of bowels
Hoffman, R.H.—hernia
Hoffman, S.—RH
Hogg, J.F.—LD & eyes
Holt, R.—piles, bronchitis, asthma
Hoschar, A.K.—CDR
Houghton, H.H.—WIA lower jaw & left breast
Howard, H.R.—wounded in leg
Howard, M.—CDR & piles
Howel, E.—St. Vitus Dance (?) result of exposure
Howerty, D.S.—catarrh & LD
Hudson, D.—foot injured by a jump in army
Hudson, P.—dysentary & lumbago of back
Hugh, G.—piles

Hummel, W.C.B.—deafness
Huston, A.—RH
Hyatt, R.R.—deafness
Hylton, I.—affected eyesight
James, G.W.—general disability
James, L.W.—CDR & RH
Jeffries, F.—gunshot wound
Jinkins, D.P.—gunshot wound
Jinnings, P.—qunshot wound
Jividen, J.—RH & neuralgia, result of exposure
Johnson, A.S.—CDR
Johnson, D.B.—wounded in neck
Johnson, J.H.—affects of starvation, POW Saulsbury & Richmond
Johnson, J.W.—gunshot wounds
Johnson, N.—CDR
Johnson, S.—gunshot wound & RH
Johnson, V.E.—liver complaint
Jones, A.P.—SS
Jones, T.E.—shot in leg
Jordan, S.J.*—RH
Jourdan, J.H.—LD
Kanode, M.*—gastrophy
Kauff, J.—in camp as regt mustered out discharge not given
Kearns. J.—deafness
Kearns, T.—neuralgia & loss of one eye
Kernes, W.—RH & MS
Kilen, L.D.—spinal disease
Kinser, M.—WIA left hip
Kirk, T.B.—LD
Klingensmith, D.—neuralgia
Klingensmith, W.—frozen feet, breast hurt
Knapenberger, J.—scrofula
Knapp, S.P.—teamster
Koreins, A.W.—catarrh
Krepps, J.—dislocation of left ankle
Lampirt, A.—thrown from horse right shoulder dislocated
LatheY, A.—CDR
Lee, B.—CDR
Lewis, B.F.—CDR
Lewis, I.A.—RH & HD
Lewis, I.N.—CDR & RH
Lewis, S.—RH
Long, B.—shot through breast & other wounds POW Andersonvile
Long, E.—lower limbs & side affected from measles
Long, W.A.—CDR
Love, C.C.—neuralgia & RH

Lowry, A.J.—plurasy of right side
Luce, A.—CDR
Lutton, M.—neuralgia
Lyon, R.—lung & throat disease
Lyons, J.—left leg off
Lyons, J.W.—RH & HD
Marks, H.A.—kidneys, result of TYF
Martin, J.H.—spine disease & RH
Martin, P.—WIA left hip
Mathews, P.—LD
Mattox, J.—measles cough
Mauck, R.—pneumonia
McCallester, P.*—HD
McCloud, J.—loss of left eye, sore eyes, deserted
McCloud, R.—HD
McCollock, J.S.—RH
McComb, J.—atrophe
McComb, T.—spinal disease
McDade, J.—RH
McDaniel, A.—CDR, piles, RH
McDaniel, G.W.—LD from measles
McDaniel, R.—bronchitis
McKindley, P.H.—KD
Meek, J.N.—catarrh
Meek, S.—spinal disease & sight
Meriston, H.—RH
Messick, J.W.—CDR & sight
Middlecoff, J.L.—RH & piles
Mitchell, P.—wounded in knee & piles
Modderspaugh, G.—RH
Moore, I.H.—WIA left arm
Morgareige, D.J.—horse fell on right leg resulting in necrocous
Morris, R.F.—bronchitis, sight
Morris, V.B.—wounded by shell left shoulder & right leg
Morrow, G.—CDR
Morrow, H.C.—RH
Morrow, J.F.—chronic pneumonia
Morrow, R.L.—gunshot wound
Moulden, J.W.—thrown from horse & back injured
Mourning, G.W.—CDR, deafness
Mulfreed, W.H.H.—RH, piles
Neale, J.W.—dislocation of right elbow
Needham, J.M.—HD
Nelson, M.—LD from measles
Newbraugh, J.A.—CDR
Newell, E.F.—RH 27 years
Nickelson, J.—loss of left leg by gunshot

Noble, A.—gunshot wound in head, CDR
Nye, T.S.—breast trouble
Oliver, E.—right arm off
Oliver, J.C.—disease of hip & spine from fall
Onail W.—strain in ankle
Parsons, T.—WIA right leg & shoulder
Patterson, J.A.*—HD
Patterson, J.W.—fistula
Pearl, J.—RH
Peck, A.J.—fracture of leg
Pegram, P.*—CDR
Perry, D.—injury to right arm
Philips, S.J.—RH & HD
Phillips, J.F.*—RH
Pierce, L.C.—HD
Pinnick, J.T.—gunshot left leg & CDR
Plants, C.—general disability
Plantz, G.W.—liver & heart disease, weak eyes
Pluntz, J.—gunshot wound in arm, DSC
Porter, J.C.—shell wound
Pounds, J.—neuralgia
Pritchard, J.—disease of chest & sight
Pullin, J.—disease of back & feet
Pullin, T.—wound in left side
Pullin, W.—CDR
Ramsay, T.—defect in hearing
Ravidon, H.C.—frozen hands
Rayburn, J.A.—RH & HD
Rayburn, J.R.—breast & spinal complaint
Rayburn, J.R.—HD & RH of back
Redman, S.—LD
Rice, H.—RH & CDR
Rice, V.D.—LD & HD
Rickard, G.—RH & HD
Rickerd, M.—gunshot through right lung, deaf right ear
Riffle, H.—frozen feet
Riggs, A.—loss of right thumb from gunshot wound
Riggs, W.A.—blindness & deafness, partial
Riley, M.—breast & heart disease
Rimmey, G.W.—diseased eyes & 2 fingers off
Robberts, A.J.—gunshot wound
Robinson, A.—deafness incurred hy bursting of shell
Robinson, S.—head & eyes
Rock, M.W.—gunshot wound left shoulder
Rosebery, M.—disease of right testicle
Roush, J.—CDR & tumor in the breast
Roush, J.M.—broken ankle & RH

Rowley, E.—wounded back & leg
Roy, W.H.—hearing
Russell, H.—blind right eye
Sands, G.W.—dropsy
Sayer, D.—CDR
Schools, P.O.—CDR & piles
See, W.—RH
See, W.W.—disease of breast, disabled ankle
Sewell, A.H.—CDR
Sheline, A.J.—liver trouble
Sheppard, A.J.—LD
Sheppard, J.T.—diseased liver
Shindle, S.J.—rupture & hernia
Shively, B.T.—KD
Sines, P.—CDR & RH
Skidmore, C.J.—CDR, hemorrhoids, DSC
Slayton, D.W.—RH
Smith, D.—gunshot left shoulder
Smith, El.—RH
Smith, G.E.—WIA left thigh & back
Smith, G.—partial paralasis
Smith, J.H.—W
Smith, W.—HD & liver complaint
Smith, W.P.—wounded in side
Snider, J.—RH
Snyder, J.E.—RH, KD, liver complaint, deafness & eye disease
Sonesby, E.—W & lumbago
Spann, L.—CDR
Spencer, J.—CDR
St. Clair, A.—CDR, rupture, wounded
Stanley, E.—spinal disease
Stewart, J.—HD & LD
Stone, J.T.—deafness & RH, served on Retre (?) Chocktaw
Stone, J.T.—eye, back & kidney disease, result of measles
Stone, R.J.—in service before 4/63 WIA left arm by cannon ball
Stover, J.L.—catarrh & RH
Strater, W.—wounded in ankle
Stricklen, J.D.—bronchitis
Sullivan, A.T.—spinal iritation
Sullivan, D.M.—loss of eye
Taylor, J.—HD
Taylor, W.B.—gunshot wound in head & thigh
Teeters, M.—LD, eyes & ears
Terry, E.—LD & RH
Thomas, A.—CDR
Thomas, F.—liver complaint
Thomas, J.G.—double rupture

Thomas, R.—HD, gunshot wound
Thorn, J.L.—CDR
Thornton, A.—wounds throat & neck
Thornton, C.W.—ruptured
Thornton, F.—RH
Thornton, W.—gunshot wound right arm
Tolliver, J.R.—gunshot wound left knee
Turley, C.C.—asthma & piles
Turnbull, T.—catarrh resparatory organs
VanMatre, J.—shot in leg, bullet in yet
Varian, D.—wounded right arm by fall from wagon
Vickers, S.C.—wound in right foot
Villars, J.A.—loss of thumb
Vincent, L.F.—head, throat & breast
Walker, F.—piles
Wallace, W.T.—hips & spinal injury
Wamsley, W.—LD
Waugh, S.—bronchitis
Weigand, A.—ruptured
Whealdon, I.H.—HD
White, O.—WIA
Whitt, A.—shot in hand
Wilcoxen, J.S.—HD & RH
Wiles, G.W.—gunshot wound
Williams, B.—plurasy of side
Williams, G.H.—piles
Williams, S.—gunshot in lower jaw
Williamson, H.C.—piles
Wilson, E.R.*—HD
Wilson, G.W.—eyes & hearing
Wilson, W.H.—nervous affection of left side
Winebrewer, A.H.—piles & CDR
Wires, T.—wound in head & thigh
Wise, J.—two fingers shot off, injured below knee right leg
Woods, W.F.—gunshot wound
Work, F.A.—piles, CDR
Young, F.D.—CDR, broken leg
Young, R.—CDR

McDowell County

NAME/RANK	REGIMENT	WHEN SERVED
Asbury, James H. Pvt.	24? VA BTN CSA	4/10/62–1865
Barlow, Alfred	NF	
Belcher, Andrew	NF	
Belcher, Daniel S.	NF	
Belcher, John F.	NF (26 BTN VAI CSA?)	
Blakely, Hiram	NF	
Coleman, Curtis Cpl.	39 KYI	10/10/63–9/15/65
Coleman, Wm. Pvt.	39 KYI	1863–NF
Dillon, James C. Pvt.	1 KYI	1/1/64–7/20/65
Fields, Gabriel C. Pvt.	1 USI	6/20/63–10/12/65
Goff, Samuel W. Pvt.	3 WVC	6/29/64–6/30/65
Green, Leonard Pvt.	8 VAI?	3/24/62–7/62
Hagerman, John Pvt.	39 KYI	9/14/62–9/15/65
Hagerman, Wm. Jr. Cpl.	39 KYI	10/8/62–9/15/65
Hagerman, Wm. Sr. Lt.	39 KYI	11/30/62–4/1/65
Hatllaway, John C. Capt.	4 MIC	61/65
Hicks, Harrison Pvt.	39 KYI	6/63–9/15/65
Hood, George W. Pvt.	——	64/65
Justice, Daniel Pvt.	39 KYI	63/65
Kelly, Wm. C.	NF (64 VAI CSA?)	
Lambert, Joseph Pvt.	7 WVC	2/18/65–8/1/65
Lambert, Hiram Cpl.	39 KYI	6/20/63–9/15/65
Lester, Abner	NF (54 VAI CSA?)	
Leviden, Louis Pvt.	182 OHI	8/64–1865
Malone, Wm.	US Navy	NF
Moore, Wm. F. Pvt.	4 PAI	2/16/64–7/13/65
Mullins, Allen Pvt.	39 KYI	11/24/62–9/15/65
Muncy, Archibald Pvt.	79 KYI	11/17/62–9/15/65
Murphy, John	NF (25 VAI CSA?)	
Payne, John D. Pvt.	39 KYI	2/10/63–9/15/65
Payne, Wm. Pvt.	39 KYI	6/1/64–9/15/65
Pucket, Malki Pvt.	39 KYI	9/14/62–9/15/65
Roberts, Adam	NF (46 BTN VAC CSA?)	
Rose, Eli B.	NF (34 BTN VAC CSA)	
Rowe, Joel N. Pvt.	39 KYI	7/28/63–9/15/65
Rowe, John Pvt.	——	61/65
Sherry, Henry	NF	
Shumate, Mark H.	NF	
Simmons, James H. Pvt.	5 MIC	63/65
Simpson, Wm. L.	NF	
Spince, Edward Pvt.	49 KYI	2/63–NF
Teale, Comings Pvt.	39 KYI	2/65–9/15/65

Totten, John	NF	
Vanover, Elijah	NF (French's BTN VAI CSA)	
Woolcock, John	NF	
Woosley, Benj. F. Pvt.	2 TNI?	11/9/61–11/9/64
also	55 KYI	64/65
Yates, John D.	NF	

McDowell County Remarks

Blakely, H.—KD & liver disease
Fields, G.C.—gunshot in war
Goff, S.W.—left leg off
Green, L.—WV troops
Hagerman, J.—RH
Hood, G.W.—RH, I think I am entitled to pension
Murphy, J.*—went home on sick furlough
Payne, J.D.—shot in back
Pucket, M.—LD, shot in back, run a rammer through hand
Rose, E.B.*—very old & needy
Spince, E.—RH, LD, deafness
Woosley, B.F.—wounded in right hip

Mercer County

NAME/RANK	REGIMENT	WHEN SERVED
Adkins, Preston Pvt.	34 BTN VAC CSA	1861–4/9/65
Akers, Henry H. Pvt.	VAA CS (Fry's)	3/62–5/65
Akers, Nathaniel B. Pvt.	60 VAI CSA	63/65
Allen, John G. Pvt.	(Thurmond VARG)	64/65
Bailey, George E. Pvt.	9 PAC	2/17/64–7/65
Basham, John Pvt.	60 VAI CSA	9/61–4/65
Bennett, Lyman M. Pvt.	NF	
Bicknele, Adolphus Major	2 NCI CSA	8/63–4/5/65
Bowling, Charles A. Pvt.	60 VAI CSA	9/62–4/5/65
Brians, James A.	NF	
Broyles, Andrew W. Pvt.	—WVI	4/1/65–6/20/65
Buchanan, George Pvt.	NF (23 BTN VAI CSA)	
Burgess, James Pvt.	21 KYI	9/64–10/65
Burton, Elias Pvt.	60 VAI CSA	1862–3/2/65
Clark, Elijah Sgt.	34 BTN VAC CSA	12/5/63–4/5/65
Clark, Henry Pvt.	23 VAI CSA	6/61–4/65
Claugh, Dewitt C.	NF	
Cook, George W. Pvt.	17 VAC CSA	8/62–4/24/64
Cook, Theodore S. Pvt.	197 OHI	3/14/65–4/15/65
Crain, Louis G. Sgt.	39 OHI	7/14/61–8/9/65
Croy, Isaac Pvt.	36 VAI CSA	8/61–11/61
Davis, Paryas S. Lt.	2 WVI?	63/65
Day, Joshua Pvt.	7 WVC	2/17/65–8/1/65
Demagan, Lewis D.	CSA NF	
Dodd, Anderson A. Pvt.	8 VAC CSA	61/65
Duhring, Casper H. Capt.	32 PAI	6/62–11/63
Epling, Lewis A. Pvt.	36 VAI CSA	62/64
Evans, Joseph Pvt.	NF	
Faulkner, Gorden Blksmith	—(17 VAC CSA?)	2/1/64–1865
Ferguson, Elkanah R. Pvt.	34 BTN VAC CSA	1/65–4/13/65
Fitzwater, Isaac N. Pvt.	7 WVI	3/7/65–7/1/65
French, Russell G. Capt.	25 OHI	4/1/62–1864
Gadd, Andrew P. Pvt.	23 VAI CSA	9/62–4/65
Garlic, James F. Pvt.	4 TNC (CSA)	5/3/64–7/2/65
aka James Floid	NF	
Gilmore, Milton Pvt.	32 OHI	1/5/65–7/20/65
Godfrey, Augustus C. Pvt.	34 OHI	8/6/63–NF
Gunther, John J. Pvt.	27 IAI	8/14/62–11/25/62
Hatcher, Edmond H. Cpl.	23 VAI CSA	8/61–10/64
Heath, John T. Pvt.	68 OHI	11/2/61–3/19/64
Hewitt, John D. Pvt.	13 PAC	9/1/64–7/25/65
Hodge, David Cpl.	7 PAI	61/61

Holdren, James H. Pvt.	8 WVC?	12/12/64–8/1/65
Houchins, George H. Sgt.	30 VAI CSA	6/61–7/63
Hubbard, Paten A. Sgt.	23 VAI CSA	61/64
Jewel, John G. Pvt.	45 VAI CSA	62/64
Johnson, Richard Pvt.	NF	
King, James M. Pvt.	54 VAI CSA	11/61–6/10/64
Lilly, James Pvt.	CS (23 BTN VAI?)	1/15/65–4/65
Lilly, James W. Pvt.	23 VAI CSA	1862–5/8/64
Lilly, John E. Pvt.	23 VAI CSA	12/62–6/63
Lilly, Rufus B. Pvt.	VAI CS (23 BTN)	9/62–9/62
Lilly, Wm. H. Pvt.	36 VAI CSA	6/61–1865
Lilly, Wm. P. Pvt.	17 VAC CSA	7/30/62–6/29/65
Lyon, John D. Pvt.	23 VAI CSA	9/62–9/64
McBride, John Pvt.	VAI CSA (57?)	64/65
McBride, Taswell W. Pvt.	34 BTN VAC CSA	1863–4/65
McBride, Thomas Pvt.	60 VAI CSA	6/2/61–4/9/65
McToor?, Charles Pvt.	NF	
Meadar, Creed T. Pvt.	2 VAC CSA	63/65
Meadar, Green W. Pvt.	23 VAI CSA	8/61–4/65
Meadar, Lycurges Pvt.	23 VAI CSA	2/63–8/63
Meadows, Harvey S. Pvt.	1 USI	1/25/64–12/5/65
Meadows, Samuel D. Pvt.	34 BTN VAC CSA	64/65
Melon, Napolean B.	NF	
Meyer, Israel Pvt.	1 PAC	61/64
Mills, Anderson Pvt.	2 VAC	1862–7/4/65
Mills, Huah G. Pvt.	23 VAI CSA	10/62–3/65
Moten, James W. Pvt.	11 VAI CSA	3/4/62–8/62
Mullen, Thomas J. Pvt.	NF	
Oaks, Jesse Pvt.	9 VAI CSA	10/24/64–4/9/65
Oaks, Wm. Pvt.	9 VAI CSA	64/65
Paddock, Frederick S. Pvt.	7 DEI	64/64
Pendegraff, Patrick	NF	
Pennington, Gordon W. Sgt.	7 VAC (CSA?)	3/64–5/13/65
Phillips, Wm. P. Lt.	2 KSI	5/11/61–6/22/65
Pierce, Samuel H. Pvt.	1 PAI	5/31/61–8/19/61
Price, Henry D. Pvt.	(4 VAI CSA?)	63/65
Reed, James B. Pvt.	58 VAI CSA	9/15/61–6/10/65
Rose, Bryant Pvt.	51 VAI CSA	4/64–11/9/64
Rumburg, Wm. J. Pvt.	23 VAI CSA	8/61–4/65
Shrewsbery, James W. Pvt.	(151 VAM CSA)	64/65
Swader, David Pvt.	CSA (11 BTN VARS?)	
Tabor, George O. Sgt.	59 VAI CSA	6/61–12/63
Taylor, Joseph Pvt.	22 PAI	1/63–11/6/65
Thomas, Wayne	NF (23 BTN VAI CSA?)	
Thompson, Dallas	Ironclad Roanoke	NF
Tiller, John M. Pvt.	6 WVC	5/15/62–1864
Vaught, Ransom Pvt.	22 OHA	6/13/63–7/15/65

Walters, John P. Pvt.	NF (29 VAI CSA?)	
White, George W.P.	NF (30 BTN VASS CSA)	
Wiley, James Pvt.	19 INI	4/29/65–5/13/65
Winters, Frank Pvt. *aka* Ceribus Winters	23 OHI NF	7/6/64–NF
Wood, Crofford Pvt.	60 VAI CSA	63/64
Wood, German Pvt.	34 BTN VAC CSA	64/65
Workman, Levi C. Pvt.	6 PAI	9/20/62–3/20/63

Mercer County Remarks

Akers, N.B.*—shot in thigh
Brians, J.A.—RH, at times nearly disabled
Broyles, A.W.—white swelling, company not part of any regiment
Cook, T.S.—RH
Crain, L.G.—right leg shot off
Croy, I.*—right fingers shot off
Davis, P.S.—CDR, he surely deserves a pension
Day, J.—gunshot wound second toe left foot
Dodd, A.A.*—health much impaired
Faulkner, G.—in service at Kettetsburg 3 months at Chas WV 8 mo. drove a team the winter of 1863 for U.S.
French, R.G.—gunshot wound in thigh
Gadd, A.P.*—5 months in prison
Garlic, J.F.*—crippled leg
Heath, J.T.—VV, he ought to have a pension
Hodge, D.—deformed by RH contracted in service
Holdren, J.H.—RH
King, J.M.*—I deserted & aint ashamed of it
Lilly, W.P.*—health lost in prison, POW 7 months Pt. Lookout
Meadar, C.T.*—WIA head & back
Meadows, H.S.—RH
Mills, A.—bloody piles
Mills, H.G.*—shot on left shoulder
Moten, J.W.*—paralized in one side
Phillips, W.P.—fistula, he deserves a pension
Pierce, S.H.—LD & asthma, I think he deserves a pension
Rose, B.*—POW 7 months Pt. Lookout
Rumburg, W.J.*—shot in right arm
Swader, D.*—shot in left side
Taylor, J.—wounded in leg at Winchester
Thompson, D.—RH
Workman, L.C.—shot in face

Mineral County

NAME/RANK	REGIMENT	WHEN SERVED
Abernathy, Ephriam Pvt.	3 MDI	9/20/61–5/30/65
Adison, Martin Pvt.	2 MDI	8/2/62–6/15/65
Barnhouse, William L. Pvt.	6 WVI	3/1/62–65–NF
Barrick, James S. Pvt.	10 WVI	6/20/62–6/25/64
Berry, Hyde N.	NF (14 VARS CSA?)	
Bice, William Pvt.	2 MDI	8/20/61–5/29/65
Binnear, James Pvt.	2 MDI	11/6/62–5/25/65
Blackburn, Benjamine T. Pvt.	3 MDI	7/1/61–6/20/65
Bly, William E. Pvt.	7 VAA CSA	8/17/62–5/25/65
Boyd, Peter Pvt.	32 PAI	5/62–8/11/65
Broden, Thomas J. Pvt.	10 WVI	2/1/62–5/2/65
Brady, Michael T. Pvt.	3 MDI	9/20/61–5/30/65
Brannon, Patrick M. Pvt	2 MDI	7/29/61–9/29/64
Brobst, Cormany Pvt.	168 PAI	10/16/62–5/18/65
Brown, Daneil S.	CSA NF (34 VAI?)	
Brown, James Pvt.	3 MDI	9/20/61–5/30/65
Bruce, William N. Drummer	2 MDI	8/14/62–5/24/65
Buneuf, William G. Pvt.	5 MDI	10/8/61–12/1/65
Burke, Richard G. Sgt.	1 MDC	2/24/64–6/28/65
Butler, John S. Pvt.	178 PAI	10/10/61–8/25/63
Byer, John Sgt.	1 VAC	6/18/61–7/17/65
Calery, Patrick Pvt.	2 MDI	8/3/61–9/29/64
Campbell, Robert Pvt.	2 MDI	8/12/61–9/29/64
Canan, John J. 2lt.	1 MDI	9/61–4/62
Case, Watson Rev.	NF	
Castle, Glen H. Pvt.	3 WVI	6/22/61–6/22/65
Cherry, J. Charles Pvt.	10 PAI	6/12/61–6/11/64
Clark, Andrew J. Pvt.	5 MDI	9/19/64–6/14/65
Clayton, Martin H. Pvt.	31 VAI CSA	5/15/61–5/17/62
Cleque, Robert Pvt.	NYI	2/11/64–6/13/65
Conners, George W. Pvt.	6 WVI	3/12/63–6/10/65
Connoly, Charles C. Cpt.	69 NYI	1864–1866
Connoly, Matthew Pvt.	NF	
Cook, Timothy Pvt.	7 VAC	9/9/61–NF
Crawford, David K. Cpl.	10 WVI	4/22/62–5/13/65
Creal, Edward B. Pvt.	5 WVC	5/20/61–12/31/64
Cunningham, James W. Pvt.	CSA NF (7 VAC?)	
Daugherty, John Pvt.	122 OHI	8/22/62–8/31/65
Dean, Richard D. Pvt.	2 MDI	9/9/62–12/9/62
Dennison, Samuel S. Pvt.	2 MDI	7/27/61–9/20/64

Durham, Nelson Pvt.	2 MDI	8/12/61–9/29/64
Duval, Henry Pvt.	2 PAC	2/12/63–9/12/66
Easter, Jacob H. Cpl.	3 MDI	3/28/64–5/29/65
Elifritz, Edward S. Pvt.	1 WVA	6/15/64–6/11/65
Ellis, John W. Pvt.	15 WVI	11/4/63–9/24/65
Evans, Benjamin Pvt.	2 MDI	9/8/61–4/29/65
Falk, Thomas J. Pvt.	2 MDI	9/23/61–2/64
Fazenbaker, George W. Pvt.	2 MDI	7/24/61–9/29/64
Fisher, Conrad Pvt.	2 MDI	10/2/61–10/1/64
Fisher, John H.	NF	
Fisk, Marcus "Bugler"	3 MDC	9/25/61–12/31/64
Flick, Jackson	1 WVC	1/1/64–7/8/65
Fraizer, James M. Pvt.	6 WVC	6/21/61–8/15/64
Friend, Benjamine F. Pvt.	3 MDI	11/19/61–5/29/65
Fussner, George W. Cpl.	2 MDI	8/1/61–10/13/64
Gardner, John W. Pvt.	3 WVI	2/23/62–6/1/65
Hall, Peter W. Pvt.	27 ? INF	8/13/62–5/29/65
Harden, Orland E. Cpl.	12 MII	10/17/63–NF
Harrison, Forsythe Qm.	—	1861–1865 NF
Harrison, George W. Cpt.	Aqm.	61/65
Harrison, Reynolds Pvt.	10 VAI	9/10/61–1865
Harrison, William H. Pvt.	6 WVI	1/11/63–1865
Heck, John Sgt.	1 MDC	8/3/61–9/3/64
Heckert, John H. Pvt.	17 WVI	2/13/64–7/7/64
Helms, Charles M. Pvt.	6 WVC	6/21/61–8/15/64
Hershberger, John S. Sgt.	6 WVC	5/1/61–5/22/66
Hickle, John W. Pvt.	13 VAI CSA	5/18/60–2/18/62
Himuel, Lemuel F. Pvt.	3 WVC	64/65
Hodges, Milton Sgt.	2 MDI	8/21/61–9/28/65
Houblt, Jacob Pvt.	188 OHI	2/18/64–11/19/64
Jackson, William H. Sgt.	2 MDI	7/12/61–5/28/65
Johnstone, James 1st. Class Boy	Flagship Blackhawk	64/65
Kelly, Daniel Sgt.	4 NYA	11/20/63–9/26/65
Kennedy, George F. Cpl.	16 MDI	2/3/65–2/28/65
Kerns, Elisha Sgt.	2 MDI	8/12/61–9/29/64
Kight, Lewis F. Pvt.	2 MDI	7/18/61–5/29/65
Kight, Oliver	NF	
Kight, William G. Pvt.	10 WVI	4/4/62–6/24/65
Kilroy, Thomas M. Pvt.	3 MDI	12/24/61–3/16/65
Kitsmiller, John H. Pvt.	10 WVI	4/1/62–5/10/62
Kuhnle, John C. Pvt.	6 WVI	4/8/62–4/8/65
Lee, Jesse A. Pvt.	54 PAI	8/11/62–5/31/65
Level, Edmond Sgt.	1 WVA	8/7/61–10/14/64
Lieberman, Carl A. Sgt.	1 LA ZOUAVES CSA	4/3/61–4/10/65
Limebauugh, Daniel Pvt.	7 MDI	8/18/61–7/13/65
Lowry, Walter Sgt.	32 OHI	8/1/61–7/20/65
Martin, Daniel Pvt.	3 IN?	9/25/61–3/16/65

Martin, John Pvt.	41 PAI	9/22/63–8/22/65
Mattick, John W. Pvt.	3 WVI	6/29/61–3/19/63
Mayhue, Garrett Pvt.	62 VAC CSA	5/8/62–4/3/65
McDermott, Peter Pvt.	PAA	NF
McGinnis, David E. Lt.	3 VAI	6/28/61–11/9/64
McGuinness, John J. Sgt.	165 NYI	9/12/62–9/1/65
McIntire, Elias Pvt.	14 WVI	8/16/62–6/27/65
McKinzie, George H. Pvt.	2 MDI	9/11/62–5/29/65
Metcalf, Samuel	NF	
Middleton, William Pvt.	2 MDI	8/20/61–5/29/65
Miller, Gilead Pvt.	2 MDI	8/6/61–5/29/65
Miller, William B. Pvt.	1 MDC	8/27/64–6/28/65
Mills, William Pvt.	1 MDI	10/23/61–9/13/64
Minnear, Zacaria Pvt.	6 WVI	8/29/64–6/10/65
Molter, Samuel A. Pvt.	1 WVI	9/2/61–9/28/64
Moorain, John Pvt.	13 INI	6/19/61–2/26/63
Mullen, Patrick Cpl.	2 MDI	7/29/61–9/29/64
Mulvey, Charles Pvt.	2 MDI	8/1/61–9/29/64
Murphy, James Pvt.	28 PAI	8/23/61–11/25/62
Myers, David H. Pvt.	2 NJC	8/29/64–8/29/65
Myers, Harry Pvt.	2 WVI	5/10/61–1865
Nim, Eli F. Sgt.	6 WVI	8/29/61–6/10/65
O'Connor, Patrick J. Cpl.	39 ILI	10/28/62–10/28/65
Parris, William R. Pvt.	3 MDI	10/23/61–3/16/65
Paugh, William H. Pvt.	3 MDI	3/26/64–5/29/65
Perry, John W. Capt	3 WVI	6/1/62–7/5/65
Phillips, Jacob L. Pvt.	1 VAA	12/17/62–4/1/63
Pippin, Robert H. Pvt.	1 MDI	10/1/62–6/15/65
Plush, William Pvt.	1 ILA	12/1/61–7/10/65
Pringle, John Sgt.	2 MDI	7/19/61–9/29/64
Purdy, Richard Pvt.	9 MDI	1862/63
Ravenscraft, James Pvt.	3 MDI	10/16/61–3/1/65
Reynolds, William F.	NF (27 VAI CSA?)	
Riddington, Thomas Sgt.	18 ILI	61/65
Rise, Charles Pvt.	2 WSV	6/11/61–6/20/62
Rowe, Charles C. Pvt.	11 MDI	11/15/64–6/29/65
Sayles ?, William Capt.	CSA	8/7/61–?/23/65
Seaman, William F. Pvt.	25 VAI CSA	5/15/61–4/19/65
Sears, Josiah Pvt.	NF	
Sever, Geroge F. Pvt.	11 NYI	8/18/62–6/11/65
Shaffer, William L. Pvt.	10 WVI	12/5/63–8/9/65
Shaw, Henry C. Sgt.	3 MDI	2/1/62–5/1/65
Shea, John	NF	
Sheets, Fredrick W.	CSA NF (50 VAI)	
Shillingburg, Isaac N. Pvt.	10 WVI	4/1/62–5/10/65
Shoemaker, John Pvt.	168 OHI	5/1/64–9/8/64
Shrout, George Pvt.	193 OHI	2/22/65–8/4/65

Name	Unit	Dates
Simons, Alfred E. Cpl.	10 WVI	3/22/62–5/23/65
Simpson, Elisha Pvt.	2 MDI	8/16/61–9/28/64
Simpson, James Pvt.	2 MDI	8/16/61–9/28/64
Smith, Phillip K. Cpl.	WVI	1/22/62–2/22/65
Snider, William Cpl.	2 MDI	8/21/61–9/28/64
Snyder, John W. Pvt.	7 WVI	12/3/61–12/30/64
Sour, John W. Cpl.	125 PAI	8/7/62–5/18/63
Sparks, Uriah Sgt.	107 PAI	3/11/62–6/13/65
Spencer, Jerome Pvt.	12 INC	1/1/64–9/4/65
Stiers, Lafayette C. Pvt.	12 WVI	8/20/62–6/16/65
Strain, John H. Pvt.	2 MDI	61/63
Stump, William J. Pvt.	154 OHI	5/2/64–9/20/64
Tasker, Benjamin Pvt.	10 WVI	5/19/63–10/13/65
Taylor, William A. Capt.	4 VAC	8/7/61–6/23/65
Thompson, James Capt.	17 MDI	8/18/62–3/16/64
Trass, Andrew Pvt.	127 PAI	NF
Trout, James H. Pvt.	2 WVI	NF
Turner, John Pvt.	2 MDI	8/22/61–5/24/65
Wagley, Edward H. Sgt.	3 WVC	6/23/64–7/10/65
Walker, Samuel J. Sgt.	14 PAC	12/29/61–9/64
Wallace, Thomas Pvt.	2 USI	2/21/60–2/21/65
Walsh, Robert R. Cpl.	4 WVI	7/19/61–7/18/65
Welch, James P.	NF (McNeill's Rangers CSA)	
Welch, Louis	CSA NF (7 VAC?)	
Welch, Patrick P. Pvt.	3 VAC	3/17/62–7/3/65
Welch, Robert B.	CSA NF (7 VAC)	
Wells, Benjamine F. "Drummer"	7 MDI	8/16/62–7/1/65
Wenner, Henry W. Pvt.	2 MDI	8/27/61–9/27/65
Wigley, George Lt.	2 MDI	7/26/61–9/64
Wildman, Thomas Pvt.	3 WVI	6/14/61–7/15/65
Wilson, Henry I. Pvt.	NF (22 VAI CSA?)	
Wilson, James I. Col.	30 MDI	2/25/62–12/27/64
Wiseman, James H. Sgt.	7 VAI	10/16/61–3/16/65
Woodrow, George "Clerk" QM	DEPT.	NF
Yanta, Daniel Pvt.	1 MDC	5/23/61–6/28/64
Yull, George W. Pvt.	3 WVI	6/28/61–8/1/64
Yull, Libbus W. Pvt.	6 WVC	10/22/64–3/19/65

Mineral County Remarks

Barnhouse, W.L.—RH
Bice, W.—wounded in heel
Blackburn, B.T.—SS, dyspepsia & RH
Brannon, P.M.—RH
Buneuf, W.G.—brights disease
Campbell, R.—entirely broken down, malarial poison
Case, W.—Penn militia crossed into Md & enlisted as McClinnan
Castle, G.H.—POW 6/26/64 released 3/1/65
Cherry, J.C.—wounded in right leg
Cook, T.—wounded in knee, pensioner
Crawford, D.K.—gunshot wound head & leg
Creal, E.B.—POW Andersonville, CDR
Dean, R.D.—DSC
Elifritz, E.S.—RH
Ellis, J.W.—wounded in left leg badly crippled
Evans, B.—badly crippled from prison life
Falk, T.J.—throat
Fisher, C.—catarrh head
Frazier, J.M.—pluersay
Harrison, R.—eye injured & RH
Harrison, W.H.—wounded & lost right eye battle of Moorefield, Va
Helms, C.M.—cataract of eye
Hodges, M.—grandular inflamation
Johnstone, J.—ague
Kelly, D.—now paralyzed in spine
Kerns, E.—sight of left eye gone
Kilroy, T.M.—wounded in left leg
Lee, J.A.—blind in right eye
Limbaugh, D.—POW Salisbury NC 6 months
Lowry, W.—gunshot wound right leg near total deafness from TYF
Mayhue, G.*—wounded in left hip
McDermott, P.—gave discharge papers to pension agent
McGinnis, D.E.—wounded in left hand
Molter, S.A.—deaf riqht ear from exposure
Moorain, J.—WIA right leg & left shoulder
Mulvey, C.—RH & hearing
Murphy, J.—wounded in left side
Myers, H.—head wounded
Nim, E.F.—wounded in left hand by explosion of gun
O'Connor, P.J.—RH
Perry, J.W.—wounded side of head
Pippin, R.H.—disease of respiratory organs
Plush, W.—disabled firing canon & laying under canon on cars
Pringle, J.—bronchitis
Reddington, T.—LD

Rise, C.—DSC
Seaman, W.F.*—wounded on head
Sever, G.F.—WIA five times
Shaw, H.C.—taken prisoner at Harpers Ferry 1862
Shillingburg, I.—RH badly crippled
Simons, A.E.—shot through both thighs
Smith, P.K.—hearing affected
Snyder, J.W.—WIA right hip, Gettysburg 7/3/63
Sparks, U.—WIA left hip, Gettysburg
Tasker, B.—WIA battle of Cedar Creek, Va 1864
Taylor, W.A.—wounded in right hand
Walker, S.J.—wounded in right shoulder
Wallace, T.—wounded in left testicle
Wildman, T.—wounded in left hip
Wiseman, J.H.—abdominal rupture & RH now bed riddin & crippled
Yull, G.W.—WIA left knee battle of McDowell, Va 1863

Monongalia County

NAME/RANK	REGIMENT	WHEN SERVED
Ammons, Corbly Pvt.	14 WVI	4/7/62–5/24/65
Arnett, Isaac E. Pvt.	6 WVI	8/20/61–7/25/62
also Capt.	14 WVI	7/25/62–3/6/65
Arnett, William C. Cpl.	6 WVI	9/1/64–6/10/65
Arnett, William H. Pvt.	14 WVI	8/14/62–8/1/65
Auston, Nimrod Pvt.	10 WVC	6/11/61–NF
Baily, John T. Sgt.	3 WVC	5/31/61–8/8/65
Ball, Andy Pvt.	20 PAI	12/63–11/65
Bane, Joseph Cpl.	140 PAI	8/18/62–5/15/65
Barb, George Pvt.	14 WVI	3/18/65–6/27/65
Barker, Shelby P. Sgt.	1 WVC	61–7/8/65
Barnes, James A. Pvt.	14 WVI	8/7/62–7/3/65
Barrackman, Greenbury Pvt.	14 WVI	8/18/62–4/13/65
Barrickman, Jacob Pvt.	3 WVC	8/62–6/65
Barthlow, William L. Pvt.	3 WVC	9/16/61–6/13/65
Bavemore, Milton Pvt.	14 PAC	9/22/62–5/20/65
Bayles, Jonah Pvt.	7 WVI	7/31/61–8/7/64
Beall, John	NF	
Beatty, John Pvt.	14 WVI	8/62–7/65
Beatty, James G. Pvt.	7 WVI	1861–NF
Beatty, William Pvt.	14 WVI	NF
Bell, John Pvt.	3 WVC	6/8/61–8/31/65
Berkley, Robert Pvt.	11 VAI CSA	6/61–3/65
Berry, Richard B. Pvt.	3 WVC	9/1/64–7/65
Blaney, Henry C. Pvt.	14 PAC	3/9/64–9/5/65
Blaney, Sam J.	1 WVC	6/1/61–7/65
Boggess, James N. Pvt.	1 WVA	8/7/61–9/14/64
Bolyard, Jacob Pvt.	NF	
Bowman, Moses Pvt.	15 WVI	8/62–9/4/65
Boyd, James Pvt.	3 WVC	3/3/65–7/65
Breakison, Daniel W. Pvt.	14 WVI	8/22/62–5/25/65
Breakison, Frederick Pvt.	14 WVI	8/22/62–7/27/65
Bricker, William H. Pvt.	7 WVI	7/2/61–8/7 64
Brook, James Pvt.	1 WVC	6/61–7/8/65
Brook, St. George S. Pvt.	2 VAC	5/63–4/65
Brooks, Robert Pvt.	14 WVI	8/18/62–7/3/65
Brown, Granville Lt.	14 WVI	8/14/62–6/30/65
Brown, Johnathan Pvt.	3 WVC	9/3/62–6/6/65
Buey, William A. Pvt.	4 WVC	7/13/63–2/29/64
Burnes, Francis M. Pvt.	3 WVC	3/22/65–6/22/65
Cage, James G. Pvt.	85 PAI	2/7/63–2/7/65

Cain, William W. Pvt.	6 WVI	3/62–6/7/65
Carothers, John E. Cpl.	3 WVI	6/4/61–NF
also Cpl.	6 WVC	61–5/22/66
Carpenter, Ashman Pvt.	15 WVI	9/17/62–7/3/65
Carrico, John W. Pvt.	17 WVI	9/2/64–6/30/65
Carroll, William Pvt.	14 WVI	8/14/62–6/27/65
Chaplin, Albert J. Pvt.	8 PAI	8/25/62–9/25/63
Chisler, Stephen Pvt.	6 WVI	9/27/61–6/28/65
Clisler, Lewis Musician	7 WVI	9/61–4/3/65
Cole, John Pvt.	7? WVI	62/64
Cole, John S. Pvt.	14 WVI	8/62–6/65
Cole, William P. Pvt.	14 WVI	4/1/65–6/27/65
Colebank, Thomas J. Pvt.	7 WVI	7/3/61–2/12/63
Conn, Garrett Cpl.	14 WVI	8/14/62–6/27/65
Conn ?, Jacob L. Pvt.	14 PAC	9/4/64–5/13/65
Cordray, David E. Cpl.	3 WVC	9/3/62–6/6/65
Core, Benjamine Pvt.	3 WVC	3/26/64–6/30/65
Core, Christopher Pvt.	3 WVC	8/22/62–6/3/65
Cox, Eli Pvt.	14 WVI	2/14/65–6/27/65
Crop, Francis Pvt.	14 WVI	8/28/62–6/27/65
Cumberledge, Simon Pvt.	14 WVI	6/62–7/3/65
Cuningham, John W. Pvt.	7 WVI	7/4/61–1863
Dalton, Solomon Pvt.	17 WVI	8/64–7/65
Davis, Bella Pvt.	1 WVC	3/6/63–7/8/65
Davis, James N. Pvt.	17 WVI	9/64–7/65
Davis, John C. Lt.	3 WVC	6/7/61–4/62
Dawson, George W. Cpl.	14 WVI	8/21/62–6/27/65
Debolt, George W. Sgt.	6 WVC	6/8/61–8/13/64
Deets, William Cpl.	3 WVC	10/61–1/65
Dolton, William H. Pvt.	NF	
Dougherty, Joseph Cpl.	3 WVI	10/15/62–6/6/65
Douney, James G. Pvt.	10 WVI	NF
Dunaway, William H.	97 PAI	9/15/64–7/65
Duncan, Charles H. Pvt.	2 CAC	8/61–10/64
Dunn, Jackuel Pvt.	14 WVI	8/61–6/64
Eaglew, Jacob T. Pvt.	1 WVC	7/18/61–7/8/65
Eddy, Isaac S. Pvt.	6 WVI	2/2/65–6/12/65
Eddy, Pinkney Pvt.	6 WVI	2/3/65–6/10/65
Eichlebewrger, Jacob T. Pvt.	140 OHI	5/2/64–5/22/65
Emerson, John P. Pvt.	7 WVI	6/61–3/63
Emory, Abraham Pvt.	14 PAC	3/22/64–5/17/65
Ferrel, Michael Pvt.	3 WVC	9/61–6/65
Fetty, Francis M. Pvt.	14 WVI	9/3/62–5/28/65
Fields, Thomas D. Pvt.	17 WVI	61/62
Fisher, Leonard Pvt.	17 WVI	8/64–6/6/65
Fleming, Silas W. Pvt.	6 WVC	2/27/64–5/22/66
Fletcher, Benjamin F. Pvt.	14 WVI	3/10/64–6/27/65

Name	Unit	Dates
Flumm, Thomas Pvt.	17 WVI	7/64–7/3/65
Ford, Adam H. Pvt.	3 IAC	2/1/63–8/9/65
Ford, Dabing K. Pvt.	6 WVI	12/15/63–6/10/65
Forst, Elis J. Pvt.	9 WVI	3/8/62–5/20/65
Fowler, William Pvt.	7 WVI	61/62
Frankenberry, Josiah B. Pvt.	62 PAI	7/61/63–1/9/64
Frederic, Jacob Pvt.	14 WVI	8/14/62–6/29/65
Furman, David D. Pvt.	14 WVI	8/62–6/65
Furman, Simeon Pvt.	1 WVC	9/63–7/64
Gapen, Joseph	50 —	9/2/64–6/8/65
Garrittson, James T. Pvt.	57 PAI	10/4/61–9/1/62
Garrison, Alpheus Capt.	17 WVI	9/10/64
Glasscock, Arnett Sgt.	6 WVI	9/5/64–6/10/65
Glasscock, William J. Pvt.	3 WVC	9/3/62–6/6/65
Gould, Samuel Pvt.	14 WVI	6/18/62–6/29/65
Grimm, John Pvt.	14 WVI	8/14/62–6/27/65
Grubb, George Pvt.	NF	
Gunp, Henry Pvt.	17 WVI	9/3/64–6/30/65
Gunp ?, Peter Pvt.	14 WVI	8/20/62–6/9/65
Guthry, William H. Pvt.	1 WVC	7/18/61–8/8/64
Hale, Morgan B. Pvt.	14 WVI	8/14/62–6/27/65
Halfin, Joseph F. Cpl.	3 WVC	9/3/62–6/6/65
Haney, John W. Pvt.	14 WVI	8/2/62–7/4/63
Hare, Silas W. Lt.	14 WVI	8/16/62–6/27/65
Harker, Eugene Pvt.	WVI	2/14/65–6/27/65
Harris, William	3 WVC	61/63
Hart, Arthur Pvt.	1 WVC	7/15/61–7/16/65
Hart, Elza Pvt.	1 VAC	9/61–7/17/65
Hart, Jacob H. Pvt.	3 WVC	9/30/61–6/21/65
Harter, William N. Pvt.	1 WVA	3/23/64–7/11/65
Hastings, Isaac Pvt.	7? WVI	7/61–5/62
Haught, William G. Pvt.	17 WVI	2/13/65–6/28/65
Hayhurst, Eli Pvt.	12 WVI	8/14/62–6/16/65
Hays, George C. Cpl.	17 WVI	8/64–7/65
Headley, Thomas T. Pvt.	18 PAC	9/62–9/64
Henderson, Asa Pvt.	3 WVC	7/6/62–6/1/65
Hennen, William O. Sgt.	6 WVI	9/25/61–6/10/65
Henry, James M. Pvt.	3 WVC	8/62–4/63
Hess, Francis M. Cpl.	6 WVI	11/18/61–NF
also Sgt.	1 WVA	61–1/18/65
Hess, J. Steen Sgt.	1 WVC	6/21/61–7/8/65
Hess, Stephen G. Pvt.	3 WVC	9/62–7/65
Hoffman, John Pvt.	1 WVA	8/17/61–9/14/64
Hoffman, Nimrod H. Lt.	1 WVC	11/24/61–1/2/65
Holland, Capell Pvt.	1 WVA	8/62–7/14/65
Holland, Thomas G. Pvt.	36 OHI	8/13/61–11/10/64
Holland, William E. Sgt.	4 WVC	7/12/63–3/64

Name	Unit	Dates
Holt, William B. Pvt.	10 WVI	9/61–3/15/65
Hoskinson, Eliem Sgt.	14 WVI	8/20/62–5/20/65
Hostetler, James	7 WVI	NF
Hought, Edward Pvt.	6 WVI	1/12/65–6/12/65
Howard, John Pvt.	NF	
Howell, John H. Pvt.	14 WVI	8/14/62–6/27/65
Irwin, William Blacksmith	3 WVC	10/16/62–6/6/65
Jacobs, Jacob Pvt.	14 WVI	8/14/62–6/27/65
James, Jessie Sgt.	81 PAI	9/61–11/64
Jarett, Jacob Pvt.	7 WVI	8/61–8/64
Jenkins, Bartholomew	1 — C	61/64
Jenkins, John Pvt.	7 WVI	7/61–7/65
Jennewine, Bartholomew Pvt.	6 WVC	2/64–5/66
Johnson, Charles J. Pvt.	3 WVC	62/65
Jolliffe, James S. Pvt.	14 WVI	8/2/62–6/65
Jolliffe, John M. Pvt.	14 WVI	8/14/62–6/27/65
Jolliffe, John M. Cpl.	14 WVI	8/14/62–6/29/65
Jolliffe, Oliver P. Capt.	14 WVI	8/14/62–6/27/65
Jolliffe, William R. Pvt.	14 WVI	8/14/62–6/27/65
Jonn, Isaiah Pvt.	14 WVI	8/28/62–6/27/65
Jones, Nathaniel Pvt.	7 WVI	9/1/61–6/12/62
Jones, Wilson Pvt.	1 WVC	6/61–9/8/63
Kelley, Joseph Pvt.	4 WVC	7/13/63–3/7/64
Keldin, William W. Qm/Sgt.	3 USA	6/62–6/65
Kelly, Asa S. Pvt.	17 WVI	9/64–7/65
Kerns, Nathan Pvt.	14 WVI	8/14/62–6/27/65
Kidwell, James H. Pvt.	1 WVC	NF
King, Alexander Pvt.	7 WVI	1/16/62–1/16/65
King, George D. Pvt.	7 WVI	3/64–6/64
King, George N. Pvt.	14 WVI	8/14/62–6/27/65
King, Jessie Pvt.	186 OHI	2/17/65–9/18/65
Koontz, Andrew J. Pvt.	1 WVC	6/22/61–9/64
Kramer, Samuel E. Sgt.	19 WVI	8/27/64–6/30/65
Lanham, Thomas Pvt.	17 WVI	9/3/64–6/30/65
Laury ?, Isaiah Pvt.	81 PAI	NF
Lawlis, Job Pvt.	3 WVC	8/64–6/6/65
Lazier, Henry B. Capt.	7 WVI	7/1/61–1/1/63
Lemley, Titus Pvt.	3 WVI	6/7/61–8/13/64
Lewellen, William A. Pvt.	3 WVC	10/3/62–6/3/65
Lewelly, Anothy G. Pvt.	62 PAI	7/63–7/65
Linch, William E. Pvt.	1 WVC	8/25/64–7/8/65
Long, John L. Pvt.	NF (25 VAI CSA ?)	
Lorigh, Elery J. Pvt.	3 WVC	9/3/62–6/6/65
Lough, George W. Pvt.	8 PAI	1/2/61–7/18/65
Lough, Samuel Pvt.	6 WVI	8/28/64–6/10/65
Lyons, Alphes Pvt.	14 WVI	8/62–5/65
Mackey, Horatio N. Lt.	1 WVC	6/22/61–3/12/62

Manear, Thomas Pvt.	1 WVC	6/1/61–7/65
Martin, Charles Pvt.	3 WVI	7/25/61–2/15/63
Martin, John W. Cpl.	14 WVI	8/22/62–5/25/65
Martin, Washington Pvt.	3 WVC	9/3/62–6/6/65
Mayfield, Eugenius Pvt.	7 WVI	7/1/61–6/30/65
Mayfield, George W. Pvt.	3 WVC	3/20/65–6/30/65
Mayfield, James A. Pvt.	6 WVC	3/4/64–6/66
Mayfield, Sylvester Pvt.	3 WVC	3/20/65–7/3/65
McBee, Thomas H. Pvt.	3 WVI	6/7/61–8/14/64
McCord, James Pvt.	17 WVI	2/15/65–6/30/65
McDahel, William Pvt.	1 WVC	3/28/65–7/8/65
McElroy, Daniel Drummer	14 WVI	8/16/62–6/27/65
McElroy, Samuel Pvt.	14 WVI	8/14/62–6/26/65
McGallagher, Isaac Pvt.	2 USA	9/10/61–10/63
also	17 WVI	9/5/64–6/30/65
McGraw, Silas Pvt.	3 WVC	9/62–6/65
McGruder, Perry	NF	
McRae, Oliver P. Pvt.	17 WVI	8/30/64–7/7/65
McVicker, George W. Capt.	3 WVC	9/3/62–7/3/65
McVicker, James M. Pvt.	3 WVI	62/63
Middlton, Roby Cpl.	3 WVC	10/30/61–10/10/63
Meeks, Thomas J. Yeoman	Gunboat N6 USN	7/1/64–6/65
Michael, Reason S. Pvt.	1 WVC	9/5/64–7/8/65
Mitchell, Ellis B. Pvt.	10 WVI	2/10/64–4/27/65
Moore, Adam Pvt.	17 WVI	8/29/64–6/30/65
Moore, Daniel V. Pvt.	9 WVI	4/5/62–4/30/65
Moore, Gilbert T. Pvt.	17 WVI	8/29/64–6/30/65
Moore, Jonathan S.	6 WVC	3/4/64–6/3/65
Moran, Joseph Pvt.	62 VAI CSA	8/10/62–5/10/65
Morris, David Pvt.	1 WVA	61/65
Murry, Arthur Pvt.	14 WVI	8/18/62–7/27/65
Murry, Robert Pvt.	17 WVI	2/15/65–7/4/65
Neeley, Irvin Pvt.	6 WVI	1/24/65–6/10/65
Neely, Nimrod Pvt.	1 WVC	9/5/64–7/8/65
Nelson, David Pvt.	3 WVC	9/23/62–6/30/65
Newzum, Joel D. Pvt.	17 WVI	8/64–6/65
Nicholson, Albert Pvt.	6 PAA	8/24/64–6/20/65
Nuce, Abram Pvt.	14 WVI	8/62–7/65
Nuce, George W. Pvt.	14 WVI	8/62–7/28/65
Odbert, Robert Pvt.	NF	
Orvin, Smith R. Pvt.	7 WVI	7/28/61–12/12/63
Parkhurst, Grant Pvt.	111 PAI	8/13/62–1/18/63
Pethetel, James Pvt.	6 WVI	9/25/61–11/64
Philips, James K. Pvt.	17 WVI	1/19/65–6/65
Phillips, Benjamin Pvt.	6 WVI	7/24/62–6/10/65
Phillips, William H. Pvt.	4 WVC	NF
also	17 WVI	6/63–6/30/65

Phillips, William P. Pvt.	3 WVC	2/64–7/1/65
Piles, Jacob Pvt.	1 WVA	6/1/64–7/21/65
Plumm, Elza Pvt.	17 WVI	9/64–6/30/65
Pogger, John T,. Pvt.	14 WVI	9/61–10/12/64
Pool, William L. Pvt.	14 WVI	8/19/62–5/14/65
Porter, James F.	14 WVI	61/65
Powell, Robert Pvt.	14 WVI	7/18/62–6/25/
Price, John E. Pvt.	6 WVC	8/21/62–5/20/65
Price, Michael Pvt.	14 WVI	8/14/62–7/3/65
Pride, John Pvt.	14 WVI	3/29/65–6/27/65
Protzman, Marion Pvt.	17 WVI	8/28/64–6/65
Pride, William Pvt.	6 WVI	2/14/65–6/10/65
Protzman, Nimrod Musician	17 WVI	9/64–7/65
Protzman, William G. Cpl.	3 WVC	9/61–11/62
Rager, Alexander Pvt.	3 WVC	62–7/65
Reppert, Sylvanius Pvt.	4 WVC	7/13/63–3/7/64
Rexroad, Balsor Pvt.	10 WVI	11/25/61–3/14/65
Reynolds, John Cpl.	15 WVI	63/65
Rice, Michael Pvt.	14 WVI	8/18/62–7/3/65
Ridgway, George D. Pvt.	WVC	61/64
Robe, Isaiah Pvt.	17 WVI	9/1/64–6/14/65
Robe, Robert Cpl.	6 WVI	8/7/61–9/14/64
Roberson, Mentererast Pvt.	7 WVI	7/61–6/64
Roberts, Daniel Pvt.	37 BTN VAC CSA?	9/61–11/64
Robinson, George W. Pvt.	3 WVC	8/61–7/65
Robinson, John R. Sgt.	17 WVI	8/30/64–6/30/65
Robinson, Solomon Pvt.	4 WVC	9/23/63–5/31/66
Robison, Philip M. Pvt.	7 WVI	7/31/61–1/1/63
Rogers, Allen A. Pvt.	6 WVC	2/64–7/65
Rogers, James V. Pvt.	1 WVA	11/6/61–6/18/65
Rose, Edward Pvt.	8 PAI	8/25/62–3/10/63
Ruble, Edward Pvt.	7 NF	
Rude, George W. Pvt.	3 WVC	9/61–2/63
Rumble, Alexander Pvt.	17 WVI	9/2/64–7/1/65
Runner, David Pvt.	21 IAI	8/15/63–7/15/65
Sauders, John Cpl.	14 WVI	8/2/62–6/27/65
Sanders, Samuel Pvt.	3 WVI	6/18/61–7/65
Scott, Marshall Pvt.	3 WVI	5/61–6/66
Scott, William T. Lt.	18 PAC	9/22/62–11/10/65
Seargeant, William J. Pvt.	NF (23 VAI CSA?)	
Selby, Edward Pvt.	1 WVC	6/61–7/8/65
Selby, Leonard Cpl.	17 WVI	8/24/64–6/30/65
Shafer, Nelson Pvt.	7 WVI	7/2/61–8/12/64
Shafferman, William Pvt.	7 WVI	2/15/65–6/30/65
Shanks, Andrew Pvt.	17 WVI	9/11/64–6/30/65
Shanks, Leonard Pvt.	6 WVI	6/7/61–NF
Shanks, William Pvt.	7 WVI	9/1/61–5/15/62

Name	Unit	Dates
Shaw, David Pvt.	1 WVC	2/65–7/65
Shaw, John L. Capt.	8 ILI	5/20/61–11/63
Sheets, Albert G. Pvt.	14 PAC	9/62–7/1/65
Sherman, William R. Pvt.	14 WVI	4/7/62–5/24/65
Shisler, Charles B. Pvt.	3 WVI	6/2561–5/65
Shisler, Jacob S. Pvt.	1 USC	11/12/62–11/12/65
Shomaker, Leviah Pvt.	1 WVC	6/12/61–7/8/65
Shriver, John I. Pvt.	17 WVI	1864–6/5/65
Shriver, William H. Pvt.	3 WVI	8/11/62–5/19/65
Shuman, Eli Pvt.	9 WVI	NF
Simmons, Jacob Pvt.	7 WVI	7/61–1864
Shriver, Lester Pvt.	17 WVI	2/13/65–6/28/65
Shriver, William H. Pvt.	3 WVI	8/11/62–5/19/65
Simpson, James Pvt.	14 WVI	8/28/62–6/27/65
Sine, Jacob C. Pvt.	168 PAI	10/16/62–7/25/65
Sisler, George Pvt.	PAI	10/16/62–3/18/64
Six, Jocephus Pvt.	6 WVI	2/26/63–6/10/65
Smith, George W. Cpl.	6 WVC	7/1/61–7/1/65
Smith, George W. Pvt.	61 PAI	7/16/63–11/11/65
Snider, George W. Pvt.	3 WVC	9/22/62–6/11/65
Snider, Joseph Col.	7 WVI	9/2/62–4/15/64
Snider, Ralley Pvt.	6 WVI	8/7/62–6/10/64
Snowden, William H. Pvt.	14 WVI	8/14/62–6/27/65
Staggers, Harry Lt.	17 WVI	7/64–7/65
Stanberry, Hose Pvt.	1 WVC	6/22/61–6/8/64
St. Clair, James P. Sgt.	3 WVC	9/61–1862
St. Clair, Silas M. Pvt.	3 WVC	3/65–6/30/65
Stephen, Simon Pvt.	6 WVI	1/6/65–6/10/65
Stewart, Andrew A. Pvt.	8 PAI	8/25/62–12/6/64
Stewart, Elisha T. Ptv.	6 WVI	3/11/65–6/13/65
Stewart, William J. Pvt.	14 PAC	9/22/62–5/30/65
Steyvesant, Peter Pvt.	5 HA	8/64–6/65
Stiles, George Pvt.	6 WVI	9/25/61–11/17/65
Stokes, Jackson Cpl.	14 —	8/22/62–6/27/65
Stoneking, Lewis S. Pvt.	3 WVC	10/61–6/64
Strobridge, John Pvt.	3 WVC	3/18/65–7/6/65
Strosmeler, Arthur Pvt.	10 PAC	4/18/61–6/11/64
Summers, Jonaly T. Pvt.	14 WVI	8/9/62–6/29/65
Sutton, Joseph Pvt.	6 WVI	8/30/64–6/18/65
Sypult, William Pvt.	3 WVC	9/15/62–7/1/65
Taylor, George Pvt.	61 PAI	NF
Tennant, Amon J. Pvt.	17 WVI	9/3/64–6/19/65
Tennant, Simon J. Pvt.	17 WVI	8/29/64–6/30/65
Thomas, Jocephus Pvt.	6 WVI	3/62–6/7/65
Thompson, Frank W. Col.	3 WVC	6/8/61–8/13/64
Thompson, James J. Capt.	3 WVI	6/7/61–8/13/64
Thompson, John A. Pvt.	17 WVI	9/2/63–6/10/65

Name	Unit	Dates
Tichener, William W. Pvt.	6 WVI	8/12/61–8/20/64
Titus, Benjamin Pvt.	85 PAI	10/15/61–11/15/64
Toothman, Christopher Pvt.	3 WVC	9/3/63–6/6/65
Trainer, Thomas H. Chaplain	12 WVI	62–12/25/62
Tweeksperry, John Pvt.	18 PAC	8/23/62–7/10/65
Vandevort, William I. Cpl.	17 WVI	8/24/64–9/24/65
Varner, Enos Pvt.	9 WVI	4/30/62–4/3/65
Walker, James S. Pvt.	9 WVI	3/14/62–5/6/65
Walker, William W. Pvt.	6 WVI	2/8/65–6/17/65
Wallace, William Pvt.	79 PAI	10/61–10/63
Warman, Thomas Pvt.	2 WVC	12/61–11/64
Watkins, Caleb	14 WVI	8/62–6/65
Watkins, George W. Pvt.	14 WVI	8/14/62–7/1/65
Watson, James S. Pvt.	14 WVI	8/14/62–6/27/65
Watton, Thomas P. Pvt.	3 WVC	2/1/64–6/65
Watts, Joseph E. Musician	17 WVI	9/2/64–6/30/65
Wear, Robert Pvt.	7 WVI	9/61–1/4/64
Weekly, George W. Pvt.	3 WVC	10/16/62–6/6/65
Wells, Michael P. Cpl.	1 WVI	7/18/61–7/8/65
West, Alpheus Pvt.	17 WVI	8/20/64–6/30/65
West, John D. Pvt.	168 PAI	10/16/62–7/26/63
White, William Pvt.	NF	
White, William Pvt.	101 PAI	12/63–1/66
Widdows, George W. Pvt.	7 WVI	7/61–6/65
Wiedman, David Qm/Sgt.	3 WVC	9/15/62–11/14/65
Willard, Archibald Pvt.	17 WVI	9/11/64–6/30/65
Williams, James Pvt.	17 WVI	8/30/64–7/7/65
Williams, Thomas B. Pvt.	116 PAI	6/31/63–7/18/65
Wilson, Alphius Pvt.	6 WVI	9/61–NF
Wilson, Archa Pvt.	17 WVI	9/2/64–7/6/65
Wilson, Benjamine T. Pvt.	9 WVI	4/30/62–7/22/65
Wilson, Fletcher B. Pvt.	6 WVI	1/16/65–6/10/65
Wilson, John N. Pvt.	1 WVA	8/8/61–9/14/64
Wilson, Josephus Pvt.	17 WVI	8/27/64–6/30/65
Wilson, Sylvester Pvt.	9 WVI	4/5/62–4/30/65
Wilson, Virginius Pvt.	17 WVI	7/64–7/65
Wining, Peter J. Pvt.	3 WVC	9/3/62–6/6/65
Woodruff, Erastus Pvt.	6 WVI	8/7/62–6/10/65
Woody, Thomas J. Pvt.	3 WVC	5/25/63–7/15/65
Wright, Jeremiah Pvt.	17 WVI	8/27/64–6/30/65
Wright, John B. Pvt.	17 WVI	9/3/64–6/13/65
Yost, Jacob Pvt.	17 WVI	2/14/65–6/28/65
Yost, James E. Pvt.	17 WVI	8/27/64–6/30/65
Yost, Louis S. Pvt.	3 WVI	3/14/62–NF
Yost, William Pvt.	7 WVI	62/65

Monongalia Co. Remarks

Austin, W.H.—gunshot left thigh, in southern hospital
Baily, J.T.—bronchitis
Baremore, M.—shot through arm
Barnes, J.A.—atrophy testacle, TYF
Barrackman, G.—bronchitis
Barrickman, J.—hernia
Barthlow, W.L.—shoulder hurt
Bayles, J.—gunshot wound
Beatty, J.—catarrh
Beaty, J.G.—wounded in hip
Beaty, W.—RH
Blaney, H.C.—POW Andersonville 5 months
Boggess, J.N.—loss of eye & hernia
Bolyard, J.—sent home TYF
Bowman, M.—shot right thigh
Breakison, D.W.—CDR
Bricker, W.H.—catarrh in head
Brook, St. G.*—wounded in foot
Brown, G.—CDR & piles
Brown, J.—hernia
Burnes, F.M.—pensioned
Cage, J.G.—rupture
Cain, W.W.—measles & 2nd left toe shot off
Carothers, J.E.—CDR & liver disease
Carrico, J.W.—deafness
Chaplin, A.J.—tumer under arm
Cole, J.S.—spinal disease
Colebank, T.J.—RH & HD
Conn, G.—WIA left thigh & deafness
Cordray, D.E.—lumbago
Core, C.—spinal affection, POW 1863
Cumberledge, S.—left shoulder dislocated
Cuningham, J.W.—RH
Davis, B.—RH
Davis, J.B.—pensioned
Debolt, G.W.—CDR
Deets, W.—hernia
Dolton, W.H.—RH
Douney, J.G.—piles & injury to eyes, discharge at pension office
Dunaway, W.H.—RH
Eaglew, J.T.—ruptured by fall of horse
Eddy, P.—HD
Emerson, J.P.—DSC
Emory, A.—LD

Ferrel, M.—fall of a horse
Fetty, F.M.—CDR
Fields, T.D.—RH
Fisher, L.—HD
Fleming, S.W.—RH, CDR & piles
Fletcher, B.F.—gunshot left thigh
Ford, D.K.—CDR
Fowler, W.—KD
Frankenberry, J.—HD & LD
Furman, D.D.—KD
Furman, S.—absces in left ear
Garritson, J.T.—catarrh
Glasscock, A.—RH, dispepsia & HD
Glasscock, W.S.—RH
Gould, S.—pensioned
Gunp, P.—wounded in left hand
Halfin, J.F.—SS
Haney, J.W.—eyes afflicted by burstinq of a shell
Hare, S.W.—CDR
Harris, W.—RH & HD
Hart, J.H.—pensioned
Harter, W.N.—SS
Headley, T.T.—RH
Henderson, A.—RH
Hennen, W.O.—measles
Henry, J.M.—RH & HD, DSC
Hess, F.M.—HD & deafness
Hess, S.G.—catarrh in head
Hoffman, J.—RH
Hoffman, N.H.—paralysis wounded in hip & ankle
Holland, T.G.—shot through thigh
Holt, W.B.—shoulder mashed
Hoskinson, E.—wounded in arm
Hostetler, J.—lost an arm
Howell, J.H.—toe shot off
Irwin, W.—chronic disease
Jenkins, B.—RH
Jenkins, J.—piles
Johnson, C.J.—piles, pensioned
Jolliffe, J.M.—shot through thighs
Jolliffe, J.S.—POW Andersonville 7 months
Jolliffe, W.R.—shell wound shoulder
Jones, J.—wounded in hand, crippled in knee & hips
Jones, W.—pensioned, krippled in foot
Keldin, W.W.—spinal trouble
King, G.D.—one finger shot off
Lazier, H.B.—CDR

Lemley, T.—RH & SS
Lewellen, W.A.—Pneumonia
Long, J.L.—discharge at pension office
Lough, S.—RH
Lyons, A.—wounded
Manear, T.—krippled in leg
Martin, C.—flesh wound on the neck
Martin, J.W.—RH
Martin, W.—HD & RH
Mayfield, E.—pensioned
Mayfield, G.W.—applied for disability pension
McCord, J.—disabled in back
McDahel, W.—pensioned
McElroy, D.—RH
McGallagher, I.—catarrh in head
McGraw, S.—CDR & loss of left eye
McVicker, J.M.—rupture
Mddlton, R.—RH
Meeks, T.J.—application for disability pension
Mitchell, E.—fractured skull
Moore, D.V.—wounded in hand
Moore, G.T.—diabetes
Moore, J.S.—RH & MS
Moran, J.*—POW Camp Chase Ohio
Murry, A.—pensioned, left lower jaw bone shot off
Neeley, I.—collarbone broken
Neely, N.—neuralgia & deafness
Nelson, D.—RH
Newzum, J.D.—RH
Nicholson, A.—CDR
Nuce, A.—knocked down by shell
Pethetel, J.—RH
Philips, J.K.—RH
Phillips, W.H.—CDR, MS, TYF & hospital
Piles, J.—defection in speech
Plumm, E.—TYF
Porter, J.F.—wounded twice
Powell, R.—pensioned
Price, J.E.—CDR
Protzman, M.—pensioned on disability
Protzman, N.—RH
Protzman, W.I.—atrophy in hips
Rager, A.—POW Libby prison 1 month, finger shot off
Rexroad, B.—lumbago
Reynolds, J.—RH & rupture
Rice, M.—pensioned on disability
Ridgway, G.D.—piles

Robe, I.—DSC
Robe, R.—RH & DSC
Roberson, M.—pensioned on disability
Robinson, G.W.—RH
Robinson, J.R.—eresyphelas fever
Rogers, A.A.—piles
Rose, E.J.—shot in right leg
Rude, G.W.—fall of a horse injured back
Runner, D.—pensioned
Sauders, J.—shot in left thigh
Scott, M.—POW Richmond 3 months
Scott, W.T.—catarrh
Selby, E.—pensioned for disability
Selby, L.—hurt in back
Shafer, N.—nothing but RH
Shanks, A.—throat trouble from mumps
Shanks, L.—reinlisted in 1864
Shanks, W.—RH
Shaw, D.—hearing affected & sore eyes
Shaw, J.L.—pensioned
Sheets, A.G.—chronic disease
Sherman, W.R.—stomach & lung trouble
Shisler, C.B.—POW Andersonville 5 months 15 days
Shriver, W.H.—scurvy, POW from April 8 to Sept 26, 1864
Shuman, E.—discharge at pension office
Simmers, J.—ruptured
Simpkins, J.N.—fever & ague
Smith, G.W.—gunshot right hip
Smith, G.W.—wounded in both legs
Snider, Jo.—RH & WIA
Snowden, W.H.—gunshot ankle
Staggers, H.—rupture
Stanberry, H.—LD, pensioned
StClair, J.P.—horse falling mashed back
Stewart, A.A.—bronchitis
Steyvesant, P.—RH & piles
Stokes, J.—mashed foot
Stoneking, L.S.—back injury by fall from horse
Strosmeler, A.—CDR
Summers, J.T.—pensioned
Sutton, J.—left lung affected
Tennant, A.J.—KD
Tennant, S.—liver complaint
Thomas, J.—wounded in left arm
Thompson, F.W.—shot in shoulder
Thompson, J.J.—RH & hemorrhoids
Tichener, W.W.—fits

Titus, B.—wounded in arm
Tweeksperry, J.—RH
Varner, E.—injury to back
Walker, J.S.—wounded in side
Wallace, W.—general disability
Warman, T.—pensioned
Watton, T.P.—pensioned on disability
Watts, J.E.—CDR
Wear, R.—left arm shot off
Weekly, G.W.—CDR
West, J.D.—rupture
White, W.G.—wounded left leg
Widdows, G.W.—RH
Wiedman, D.—HD
Willard, A.—CDR & SS
Williams, T.B.—wounded in foot
Wilson, Al.—discharge at pension office
Wilson, B.T.—CDR
Wilson, J.N.—injury to left side
Wilson, Jos.—neuralgia in head
Wilson, S.—injury to head & eyes
Wining, P.J.—RH
Woody, T.J.—shot through leg & thigh
Wright, J.—catarrh
Wright, J.B.—RH
Yost, J.E.—injury to eyes
Yost, L.S.—wounded

Monroe County

NAME/RANK	REGIMENT	WHEN SERVED
Appleton, John W.M. Major	34 MAI	5/26/62–8/13/65
also	1 MAA	NF
Ballard, Wm. A. Pvt.	137 OHI	5/1/64–8/10/64
Beck, Jacob Pvt.	5 VAI (BTN CSA)	2/61–7/65
Bostick, Joseph Pvt.	7 WVC	8/23/64–8/1/65
Clarkson, Louis O.	NF	
Dowdy, Henry Pvt.	22 OHI	6/63–6/65
Duncan, John E. Pvt.	22 NYC	12/4/63–4/27/65
Eads, Joseph H. Pvt.	(26 BTN VAI CS)	11/1/63–4/5/65
Falls, Wm. T. Pvt.	4 USI	10/64–6/10/66
Jones, James W. Pvt.	7 WVC	8/23/64–8/1/65
Kelly, Abraham Pvt.	195 OHI	3/9/65–7/20/65
Maguire, Charles E.	NF (21 VAI CSA)	
Nicholson, Alexander Pvt.	9 WVI	2/29/64–6/26/65
Pate, Anthony Pvt.	"Rattler" (58 VAI CSA?)	6/10/63–4/20/65
Porter, Calender Pvt.	25 TNI (CSA)	3/1/62–1865
Webb, Telverton Pvt.	—WVI	63/65
Woolwine, Henry H. Pvt.	13 WVI	8/15/62–6/22/65

Monroe Co. Remarks

Appleton, J.W.M.—spinal injury
Beck, J.*—shot in hand & otherwise disabled
Bostick, J.—Confederate & U.S. (also served 60 VAI CSA)
Dowdy, H.—RH & rupture
Duncan, J.E.—shot, ball entering left side nearing heart
Falls, W.T.—injured right knee & foot, pensioner
Jones, J.W.—Confederate & U.S. (also served 22 VAI CSA)
Kelly, A.—disability incurred on 4/8/1865
Nicholson, A.—crippled in shoulder & arm, pensioner
Porter, C.*—WIA hip & scalp, both flesh wounds
Woolwine, H.H.—saber wound left knee at Winchester Va 9/19/64, wounded in back at Harpers Ferry 1865

Morgan County

NAME/RANK	REGIMENT	WHEN SERVED
Ashkettel, John N. Pvt.	1 MDC	2/11/65–6/28/65
Barker, George R. Pvt.	2 MDI	8/26/61–9/64
Bayer, Robert Pvt.	12 MDC	11/10/62–11/65
Beall, William Md	—	9/1/61–9/30/63
Bechtol, John W. Pvt.	1 MDC	10/10/61–64
Becktol, H. C. Pvt.	2 MDI	8/26/61–9/26/64
Bernhard, Samuel Pvt.	3 MDC	9/4/63–9/7/65
Biddle, David W. Capt.	9 USI	4/26/61–5/24/64
Bird, John N.	NF (31 VAI CSA?)	
Bishop, George W. Pvt.	56 PAI	9/19/64–5/31/65
Blackwood, William J.	12 PAC	NF
Blake, George Pvt.	1 VTC?	9/19/61–11/19/64
Bowles, John T. Sgt.	1 MDI	8/1/61–9/64
Boxell, James Pvt.	2 MDI	8/12/61–9/28/64
Burke, Abert L. Pvt.	2 MDI	NF
Butts, William H. Pvt.	1 MDC	8/30/61–8/15/64
Buzzard, George D. Sgt.	2 MDI	8/26/61–6/65
Campton, George Pvt.	1 MDC	8/26/61–12/15/64
Chase, Samuel Pvt.	1 MDI	8/21/61–5/29/65
Childers, Benjamine F. Pvt.	14 WVI	8/6/62–6/27/65
Clingerman, Harrison Pvt.	149 PAI	8/26/63–6/24/65
Conley, James P. Lt.	10 WVI	9/12/61–9/12/64
Coughlan, Peter J. Pvt.	1 MDC	8/10/61–8/18/64
Crabtree, Eli Pvt.	2 MDI	8/12/61–9/28/64
Cross, James F. Sgt.	2 MDI	8/26/61–5/29/65
Cross, Noah Pvt.	7 PAC	4/63–10/65
Culp, Lewis Pvt	10 WVI	1/1/64–8/8/65
Dawson, Samuel Pvt.	3 MDI	4/62–5/29/65
Dawson, Thomas H. B. Pvt.	2 MDI	10/13/61–10/13/64
Disher, Henry W. Pvt.	182 OHI	NF
aka Anderson, James	105 OHI	8/19/64–7/7/65
Divilbyss, Frederick Pvt.	3 MDI	10/61–5/29/65
Divilbyss, John H. Pvt.	3 MDI	10/61–5/29/65
Eckard, Samuel Pvt.	15 WVI	1/1/63–8/9/65
Eppinger, William Sgt.	54 PAI	9/4/61–3/11/64
Everett, John H. Pvt.	1 MDI	8/21/61–5/9/65
Faris, John Pvt.	2 MDI	61–NF
Filler, John H. Sgt.	2 MDI	9/25/61–5/29/65
Frederick, John Cpl.	1 MDI	9/15/62–5/29/65
Fritzman, John Pvt.	3 MDI	4/14/62–5/29/65
Frushmar, Wm. H. Pvt.	(?) 3 WVC	1/3/64–6/13/65

Name	Unit	Dates
Gaither, John R. Pvt.	15 WVI	6/3/63–8/9/65
Gale, John Sgt.	136 USI (NEGRO)	64–1/1/66
Gyeke, Loni Capt. (?)	2 MDC	9/13/61–10/14/62
Hanes, Elisha Cpl.	2 MDC	8/26/61–9/20/64
Hare, Hinman W. Cpl.	2 MDI	8/12/61–9/28/64
Harley, Peter N. Pvt.	5 MDI	9/20/64–6/20/65
Hasenbuhler, Louis Sgt.	21 PAI	4/27/61–8/7/61
Hauscholder, George Pvt.	1 MDI	8/21/61–5/20/65
Heavring, Peter Pvt. (?)	3 MDI	10/19/61–2/8/65
Hedding, Ephraigm G. Lt.	3 MDI	9/28/61–6/65
Hedding, Noah Pvt.	3 MDI	9/28/61–6/65
Heenry, Nicholas Pvt.	1 MDC	11/28/61–11/28/62
Henry, George	US	NF
Henry, Levi Pvt.	2 MDI	8/26/61–9/26/64
Hensrote, John Pvt.	2 MDI	9/4/61–9/28/64
Hiett, Asa L. Pvt.	10 WVI	3/8/64–8/9/65
Hinds, Charles E. Pvt.	3 MDI	4/14/62–5/29/65
Hinds, Michael J. Pvt.	3 MDI	8/4/61–5/29/65
Homiby, Reuben A. J. Pvt.	ROANOKE	1/64–6/27/65
House, William H. C. Pvt.	2 MDI	8/12/61–9/28/64
Housholder, Henry C. Pvt.	15 WVI	5/18/63–8/19/65
Hovermale, Nathaniel Pvt.	1 MDC	10/5/61–8/22/63
Johnson, John W. Pvt.	1 MDI	8/63–5/64
Keeseeker, Thomas H. Pvt.	NF	
Keller, John Pvt.	2 MDI	8/12/61–9/28/64
Kemp, Hiram W.	WAGON MASTER	NF
Kerns, John W. Pvt.	3 WVI	3/31/64–5/29/65
Kesecker, William Pvt.	100 PAI	2/18/65–7/24/65
Keslor, John Pvt.	2 MDI	8/12/61–9/28/64
Kidwell, John N. Pvt.	15 WVI	NF
King, George W. Pvt.	15 WVI	62–8/65
King, John Pvt.	15 WVI	62–8/65
Lanehart, Denis Pvt.	15 WVI	63–7/3/65
Lintz, Peter Pvt.	3 MDI	4/15/62–5/29/65
Lutman, David H. Pvt.	2 MDI	9/6/61–9/13/64
Lutman, George W. Pvt.	2 MDI	9/6/61–9/13/64
Macandles, John Pvt.	1 MDC	NF
May, Francis S. Pvt.	54 PAI	11/13/61–12/5/64
McAdams, John Pvt.	12 PAC	NF
McBee, Henry C. Pvt.	2 MDI	9/6/61–5/29/65
McBee, Joseph H. Cpl.	2 MDC	9/6/61–9/13/64
McCollough, William H. Sgt.	19 PAI	7/19/64–9/3/64
McKshives, Thomas Pvt.	—	8/24/65–NF
Michall, Henry H. Pvt.	2 MDI	9/6/61–5/29/65
Moss, Sylvester Pvt.	3 MDI	2/22/64–5/29/65
Newell, George W. Pvt.	MDI ?	2/24/65–5/24/65
North, Samuel Pvt.	126 PAI	8/2/62–5/20/65

Parker, Thomas J. Pvt.	NF (37 VAC CSA ?)	
Pemberton, Edmond	NF	
Plotner, Samuel Pvt.	1 MDI	8/1/61–9/64
Post, Abraham Pvt.	NF (20 VAC CSA)	
Potter, William H. Pvt.	1 MDI	8/21/61–9/4/64
Price, Samuel S. Pvt.	63 OHI	1/1/62–1/10/65
Pritchard, Parker Pvt.	MDI ?	8/30/61–9/30/64
Read, John Qm (?)	ARTILLERY CSA	9/61–64
Reece, Pritchard	US	NF
Roach, Joseph B. Pvt.	2 MDI	8/61–9/26/64
Schooley, John V. Pvt.	79 PAI	62–7/12/65
Shriver, George Pvt.	115 OHI	8/9/62–8/14/65
Smith, Emanuel Pvt.	49 PAI	1/62–2/63
Smith, Harison Pvt.	1 MDC	8/61–9/64
Snidemiller, Henry Pvt.	1 MDC	10/4/61–12/9/64
Spring, Apollos Pvt.	2 MDI	8/12/61–5/29/65
Swanger, John W. Pvt.	12 PAC	1/1/62–7/20/65
Thomas, John W. Pvt.	82 INI	8/62–5/64
Titepoe, William Pvt. (?)	2 MDI	8/26/61–9/26/64
Titerhoe, George P. Pvt. (?)	1 MDC	10/10/61–64
Turner, John Pvt.	14 WVI	8/12/62–7/27/65
Turner, John Pvt.	2 MDI	8/12/61–9/28/64
Walters, Edward Pvt.	2 MDI	8/26/63–6/8/65
Walters, James P. Pvt.	1 MDI	9/4/63–6/19/65
Waugh, George L. Pvt.	2 MDI	NF
Waugh, John Pvt.	2 MDI	9/6/61–5/29/65
Waugh, Thomas J. Pvt.	2 MDI	9/11/61–5/11/64
Weaver, Gotleib Drummer	3 MDI	4/14/62–6/6/65
Webster, William H.	NF (1 MDC CSA?)	
Whitford, John K. Capt.	3 MDI	11/11/61–2/8/65
Whorrel, William Pvt.	1 MDC	9/2/64–6/28/65
Yost, John W. Pvt.	2 MDC	8/26/61–10/64
Ziler, George W. Pvt.	2 MDI	9/13/61–9/30/64

Morgan Co. Remarks

Beall, W.—ruptured & paralyzed
Bernhard, S.—CDR & moon (?) blindness
Bishop, G.W.—RH from measles
Bowles, J.T.—asma & HD
Butts, W.H.—gunshot right side
Conley, J.P.—TYF, RH & CDR
Cross, J.F.—wounded in face, gunshot
Culp, L.—KD, dispepsia
Dawson, T.H.B.—wounded in foot shot Smithfield, Jefferson Co. Va.
Divilbyss, J.H.—claims to have contracted LD in 1862
Everett, J.H.—bronchitis & LD
Faris, J.—receives a pension
Filler, J.H.—CDR
Frederick, J.—POW Andersonville 9 months
Fritzman, J.—catarrh, RH & fractured side from horse kick
Frushmer, W.H.—HD
Gale, J.—shot right leg
Homiby, R.A.J.—right hip injured, blowed up by torpedo
Householder, H.C.—RH, piles & defect eyesight
Kerns, J.W.—abscess on back & RH
Kesecker, W.—epilepsy
Lintz, P.—RH for six years
Lutman, D.H.—ribs broken, LD, badly disabled from army service
Lutman, G.W.—LD, piles & RH
May, F.S.—chronic lumbago & RH
McBee, H.C.—disabled eyes, RH & piles
Michall, H.H.—MS, RH & bronchitis
Newell, G.W.—ruptured
Plotner, S.—crippled in back by teams running away dragging him
Potter, W.H.—LD, hernia, MS & gunshot wound at Gettysburg
Pritchard, P.—arm dislocated
Shriver, G.—vertigo & HD
Smith, E.—leg broken by wagon
Waugh, J.—LD
Weaver, G.—piles & CDR

Nicholas County

NAME/RANK	REGIMENT	WHEN SERVED
Adkins, James S. Cpl.	6 WVI	8/63–4/65
Amick, Jacob Pvt.	14 VAC CSA	6/61–4/65
Amick, Jos. M. Pvt.	60 VAI CSA	6/61–4/65
Boley, Wm. M. Pvt.	36 VAI CSA	6/61–1865
Brown, Joseph Pvt.	NF (8 VAC CSA?)	
Bryant, John J. Pvt.	36 OHI	10/15/61–5/15/62
Buckle, Charles H. Pvt.	———	4/63–1864
Burns, Wm. H. Pvt.	13 PAI	4/24/61–8/61
Cassaday, Rawley Pvt.	3 VAI	5/61–8/64
Casto, David Pvt.	13 WVI	62/65
Champion, Clifton H. Pvt.	CSA	6/63–4/65
Chapman, James W.	NF (22 VAI CSA)	
Clark, John Pvt.	10 WVI	8/8/62–5/65
Clawson, George Pvt.	43 OHI	12/1/61–1862
Cook, Edward C. Pvt.	7 WVC	1/1/62–8/16/65
Craig, James S. Pvt.	141 OHNG	11/64–NF
Craig, Peter H. Pvt.	2 WVC	9/9/62–6/30/65
Davis, Francis M. Pvt.	6 VAC?	8/20/64–5/20/65
Davis, Robert C. Pvt.	22 VAI CSA	4/63–1865
Dawson, Wm. A. Pvt.	7 WVC	3/17/64–8/9/65
Dempsey, James H. Pvt.	CSA (8 VAC)	NF
Donnohue, John O. Pvt.	34 OHI	NF
Dorsey, John F. Pvt.	126 (VAM)	11/62–11/64
Eagle, Philip R.	NF	
Egle, John A. Sgt.	126 (VAM)	11/63–6/65
Eye, Christopher Pvt.	36 VAI CSA	NF
Fran?, Seward Pvt.	13 WVI	9/25/63–6/8/65
Grose, Jacob C. Pvt.	60 OHI	2/12/62–11/10/63
Groves, John Sgt.	36 OHI	NF
Halfpenny, Lewis Pvt.	2 WVC	6/13/62–6/13/65
Halstead, Wm. A. Pvt.	(22 VAI CSA)	6/5/61–4/65
Hinkle, Philip Pvt.	7 WVI	11/1/64–8/1/65
Howell, John S. Pvt.	2 VAI	3/16/63–7/14/63
Hughes, John W. Pvt.	26 WV?	NF
Hurley, James H. Pvt.	3 WVI	6/1/61–8/8/64
Jarvis, Wm. A. Pvt.	7 WVC	11/1/61–8/9/65
Johnson, James E. Pvt.	34 INI	9/14/61–2/14/65
King, Wm. Capt.	4 WVC	8/1/63–7/27/64
Malcom, Joseph A. Pvt.	36 VAI (CSA)	3/1/64–6/30/65
Martin, John Pvt.	36 VAI CSA	6/61–6/62
McClung, Adoniram J. Pvt.	36 VAI CSA	6/6/61–4/65

McClung, Wm. J. Pvt.	—	3/1/65–6/30/65
McClung, Wm. W. Pvt.	22 VAI CSA	61/62
McCutchen, Rufus Pvt.	35 IAI	7/19/62–5/24/65
Moor, Perry Pvt.	17 VAI	63/65
Mullins, James Pvt.	—	61/61
Mullins, John H. Pvt.	2 WVC	8/29/63–6/30/65
Mullins, Sanders Pvt.	34 OHC	4/3/63–10/65–
Nichols, George W. Pvt.	8 WVI	62/65
Nichols, Isaac R. Pvt.	9 WVI	9/20/63–7/21/65
Osburn, James H. Pvt.	2 WVC	2/2/63–6/25/65
Patton, Charles R. Pvt.	—	65/65
Penny, Huston Pvt.	6 VAI?	10/1/64–6/1/65
Persinger, Louis J. Pvt.	11 WVI	9/62–6/20/65
Pierson, David N. Pvt.	1 WVI	7/1/62–7/1/65
Pierson, John A. Pvt.	9 WVI	7/1/62–7/1/65
Pierson, Jonathan B. Pvt.	7 OHC	8/62–7/65
Rader, A.C.	NF (22 VAI CSA?)	
Rader, Michael Pvt.	(22 VAI CSA)	3/1/64–7/1/65
Rader, Robinson Pvt.	126 (VAM)	9/1/63–7/1/65
Rader, Wm. C. Pvt.	— VAI	2/1/64–6/30/65
Ramsey, Charles Pvt.	126 (VAM)	62/63
Ramsey, Edward C? Pvt.	— WVI	61/63
Ramsey, John R. Pvt.	126 (VAM)	12/62–12/63
Ramsey, Thomas A. Pvt.	126 (VAM)	12/1/61–1865
Reedey, James	NF	
Rhodes, Thomas Pvt.	7 WVC	9/62–6/65
Riger, John Pvt.	— WVC	10/5/62–8/1/65
Rosenburger, John B. Pvt.	62 PAI	7/3/63–6/65
Samples, Robert Sgt.	13 WVI	12/27/62–6/22/65
Samples, Samuel H. Pvt.	7 VAC	8/15/64–6/9/65
Seay, Mathew W. Sgt.	57 VAI CSA	5/19/61–4/9/65
Shackleford, Fountain Pvt.	36 VAI CSA	6/61–4/12/65
Shelton, Wm. Pvt.	119 KYI	NF
Spencer, Samuel H. Pvt.	9 VAI	5/1/62–3/1/65
Stephanson, John D. Pvt.	11 WVI	9/23/64–6/17/65
Stewart, Thomas Pvt.	— WVI	11/64–4/65
Tanner, James "Seaman"	Oshita?	7/26/64–8/3/65
Trent, Thomas W. Pvt.	CSA (26 BTN VAI)	NF
Tygret, John A. Pvt.	VAM CSA (79)	61/63
White, Silvester Pvt.	37 KYI	9/62–10/65
Williams, Samuel F. Pvt.	2 WVC	9/10/62–6/30/65
Williams, Sheldon P. Pvt.	2 USI?	9/62–6/30/65
Wiseman, John N. Pvt.	36 VAI CSA	6/10/61–4/65
Wolf, Malory Pvt.	4 WVI	7/1/61–7/13/64
World, Granville Musician	173 OHI	NF
Young, Silas Pvt.	8 WVI	9/61–1/65

Nicholas County Remarks

Bryant, J.J.—RH, spine out of joint
Buckle, C.H.—Discharged by parole (CSA?)
Casto, D.—WIA right hip
Clark, J.—KD, AFP 1881
Clawson, G.—feet frozen
Cook, E.C.—ruptured
Fran, S.—dropsy, DSC
Grose, J.C.—CDR & injuries from mumps
Groves, J.—catarrh head & CDR
Hinkle, P.—RH
Howell, J.S.—wounded in throat, captured by Confederates (POW)
Hurley, J.H.—RH
Jarvis, W.A.—ulcer of legs
Johnson, J.E.—measles
King, W.—shell wound & bleeding piles
McClung, A.J.*—shot in the arm
McCutchen, R.—dislocation of left shoulder
Moor, P.—discharged by paroll (CSA?)
Mullins, J.—fever, discharged at close of war
Mullins, S.—ruptured, DSC
Nichols, G.W.—RH, AFP 1889
Nichols, I.R.—CDR, RH, sore leg
Osburn, J.H.—disabled in back thrown from horse, AFP 1889
Penny, H.—small pocks
Pierson, J.A.—piles, RH, dyspepsia
Pierson, J.B.—RH June 1863 & bleeding piles
Ramsey, C.—shot in the leg
Samples, R.—RH
Samples, S.H.—convulsion of brain
Shackelford, F.*—WIA jaw & side
Shelton, W.—eyes affected
Spencer, S.H.—breast fractured
Stephanson, J.D.—injury of small of back & urinary disease, dropsy
Tanner, J.—asthma
Trent, T.W.*—wounded in the foot
White, S.—measles
Williams, S.F.—malarial poison
Wiseman, J.N.*—RH
Wolf, M.—TYF, SS, pneumonia
World, G.—epilepsy
Young, S.—neuralgia

Note: James S. Adkins apparently was first in the 22 VAI CSA, deserted and was discharged from the 6 WVI April 1865

Ohio County

NAME/RANK	REGIMENT	WHEN SERVED
Adams, Townsend Cpl.	1 WVC	2/11/64–7/8/65
Agnew, R.S. Pvt.	4 WVC	7/6/63–3/15/64
Albinger, Henry Pvt.	6 WVI	61/64
Allen, Charles E. Pvt.	2 WVI	6/14/61–6/19/63
also Cpl.	4 WVC	7/6/63–3/15/64
also Sgt.	3 WVC	2/15/65–6/30/65
Arkle, Joseph A. Pvt.	3 WVC	3/2/63–3/2/68
Armbruster, Frank F. Pvt.	17 WVI	2/25/65–6/20/65
Armbruster, John Pvt.	6 VAI	10/1/64–11/17/64
Armbuster, Jacob Pvt.	1 WVA	8/20/62–7/21/65
Armstrong, Andrew Pvt.	1 WVI	5/10/61–8/27/61
Armstrong, James Pvt.	3 VAC	2/3/65–7/8/65
Ashley, Andrew J. Pvt.	1 WVA	8/16/62–5/22/65
Atkinson, David T. Pvt.	- WVI	2/20/64–7/22/65
Aul, Conrad Pvt.	67 PAI	11/16/64–7/14/65
Ayers, Ephraim Drummer	24 NJI	9/1/62–6/29/63
Babcock, Henry M. Pvt.	11 —I	9/6/62–7/9/63
Backer, Levi Pvt.	77 OHI	10/28/61–3/8/66
Baggs, George W.	NF	
Bailey, John B.W. Pvt.	— OHI	62/65
Baker, George Pvt.	1 WVA	9/1/61–9/1/64
Baker, Henry J. Pvt.	186 OHI	2/15/65–9/8/65
Baker, John Pvt.	39 OHI	4/1/65–11/65
Baker, Louis Pvt.	6 WVI	10/17/61–11/12/64
Barber, Andrew M. Pvt.	5 OHI	8/31/64–6/22/65
Barber, Henry M. Pvt.	80 OHI	6/23/62–2/10/66
Barr, James C. Pvt.	100 PAI	8/27/61–12/31/63
Barr, John A. Pvt.	50 OHI	8/14/62–5/24/65
Barrett, Gregory Ltc.	4 MDI	8/15/62–5/30/65
Barriss, Engelbert Pvt.	1 VAA	9/1/61–11/15/62
Bartholomaus, Wm. Pvt.	8 OHA	61/65
Batchelor, John Pvt.	12 NYI	4/21/61–8/16/61
also	133 NYI	10/1/64–6/15/65
Bath, Michael	NF	
Bauer, Wilhelm Pvt.	6 VAI	10/7/61–1864
Baukard?, Adulph M. Pvt.	62 PAI	1/29/62–2/20/65
Bell, David Lt.	11 WVI	1/2/62–1/3/65
Bennett, Mathew	NF (4 VAI CSA?)	
Bennett, Thomas D. Pvt.	2 WVI	2/16/65–7/16/65
Biddle, Lloyd A.	US NF	
Biggs, Benj. Pvt.	135 OHI	5/2/64–6/22/65

Biggs, James H. Sgt.	1 WVA	8/17/62–6/27/65
Bilby, James S. Pvt.	16 PAC	4/20/64–8/11/65
Billick, John G. Pvt.	140 PAI	8/16/62–3/10/64
Birch, John	NF	
Birch, John J. Pvt.	1 WVA	8/62–6/65
Bistel, Samuel Pvt.	168 PAI	10/16/62–1/20/63
Blan, Wm. H. Pvt.	77 OHI	2/3/64–4/8/66
Blayney, David M. Capt.	12 WVI	8/11/62–6/16/65
Bliss, Isaac N. Pvt.	1 WVI	NF
Blowers, John Q. Pvt.	1 WVI	5/17/61–8/27/61
also	46 PAI	7/14/63–4/20/65
Boddy, Byron Sgt.	18 PAC	1861–5/15/65
Bode, Henry Pvt.	13 OHC	NF
Bodley, Wm. J. Sgt.	1 WVA	8/4/63–4/15/64
Boettcher, Henry Pvt.	1 NJA	11/18/63–3/22/65
Boice, George Pvt.	7 WVI	7/19/61–7/65
Bolte, George Pvt.	—WVA	NF
Bonar, John Pvt.	1 —I (Negro)	6/27/62–6/64
Bonenberger, Peter	Marine NF	
Bowers, Gersfaous? Sgt.	93 PAI	1861–6/20/65
Bowman, George Pvt.	88 PAI	10/4/61–4/26/64
Boyd, Abraham Pvt.	WVI "Exempts"	9/24/63–5/12/65
Boyd, James N. Pvt.	3 OHC	1/63–7/64
Boyd, Manuel Pvt.	13 WVI	11/22/63–6/17/65
Boyd, Sylvester W. Pvt.	122 OHI	8/22/62–6/26/65
Boylan, Thomas Pvt.	6 WVI	11/1/61–2/11/63
Brady, John Cpl.	6 VAI	10/1/61–11/17/64
Brahler, Henry Pvt.	1 WVI	10/1/61–12/31/64
Breion, Thomas O. Pvt.	——	5/61–NF
Bremer, Wm. Pvt.	6 WVI	9/28/61–12/1/64
Bremson, Wm. Pvt.	1 ILC	6/61–1864
Brice, Sylvester L. Capt.	52 OHI	8/15/62–6/5/65
Brimer, George Pvt.	1 WVC	9/8/61–11/28/64
Britt, Andrew H. Capt.	1 VAI	5/10/61–8/10/61
Britt, John T. Sgt.	1 WVI	5/10/61–8/27/61
Britt, Tom G. Pvt.	1 WVI	5/10/61–8/27/61
Broest, Daniel Pvt.	5 WVC	5/15/61–6/14/64
also	6 WVC	8/13/64–5/19/65
Brosius, James	Recruiting Officer	62/62–NF
Brown, James Pvt.	140 PAI	62/64
Brown, John J. Pvt.	6 WVI	8/18/62–1O/20/64
Brown, Joseph W. Pvt.	8 WVI	61/65
Brown, Soloman	US NF	
Brubaker, Samuel B. Pvt.	163–OHI	NF
Bruno, Napolean Pvt.	3 WVC	3/9/65–6/30/65
Bryson, Joseph Pvt.	82 OHI	12/13/61–12/11/62
Buckholz, Joseph A. Pvt.	108 OHI	12/18/63–7/22/65

Budka, Wm. A. Pvt.	1 WVA	6/28/61–8/8/64
Buey, Zachariah	1 WVI	NF
Burdatts, Oscar S. Pvt.	1 WVC	9/8/61–12/31/63
Burdett, Wm. H. Pvt.	2 OHI	6/61–9/61
also	1 WVC	9/61–7/8/65
Burke, James S.	NF	
Burley, Joseph A. Pvt.	6 WVC	7/6/61–8/17/64
Burt, Joseph H. Pvt.	102 PAI	8/19/61–6/28/65
Busbey, Lenn L. QM/Sgt.	1 WVI	8/16/62–6/27/65
Buswinkle, George W. Cpl.	2 MDI	8/16/61–9/28/64
Butler, James J. Pvt.	3 WVC	2/20/65–6/30/65
Bye, Frederick Pvt.	1 WVC	8/28/61–9/20/64
Caldobaugh, Phillip Pvt.	128 OHI	2/15/64–2/27/65
Caldwell, George B. Ltc.	12 PAI	4/24/61–1/21/65
Campbell, Robert	US NF	
Canson, Robert Pvt.	12 WVI	8/20/62–6/16/65
Carroll, Orville Pvt.	12 WVI	6/62–6/65
Case, Wm. Pvt.	14 OHI	8/11/62–6/16/64
Casteel, Wm. H.	NF	
Ceeders, Wm. H. Pvt.	4 WVC	7/22/62–3/9/63
Chalfant, Dock	NF	
Chambers, Alexander Pvt.	17 WVI	9/26/64–6/22/65
Chambers, Tom J. Sgt.	6 VAI	9/23/61–11/17/64
Chapman, Wm. H. Sgt.	1 WVI	10/1/61–11/25/64
also Lt.	2 WVI	11/30/64–7/21/65
Chippy, Samuel W.	NF	
Chort, Fred Pvt.	NF (7 VAC CSA?)	
Chromiger, Sam B. Pvt.	1 PAA	5/23/64–9/6/64
Church, Marcus W. Pvt.	168 PAI	10/16/62–7/24/63
also	97 PAI	9/30/64–6/28/65
Clark, Daniel	NF	
Clark, George W. Pvt.	1 VAI	8/27/62–6/28/65
Clatterbuck, Wm. H. Pvt.	1 WVI	3/15/64–7/19/65
Clifton, George W. Pvt.	1 WVC	8/62–6/65
Cline, Joseph C.	Ambulance Driver	NF
Cline, Sam H. Pvt.	6 WVI	NF
Coen, James N. Pvt.	15 WVI	8/14/62–6/14/65
Conant, George W. Pvt.	NF	
Condon, Wm. Pvt.	24 OHI	5/15/61–5/15/64
also	178 OHI	9/29/64–6/29/65–
Conkle, Henry	NF	
Connelly, Benj.	NF	
Connelly, Joseph H. Sgt.	1 WVA	8/20/62–6/27/65
Conwell, John Pvt.	1 WVI	8/17/61–9/1/64
Cook, Charles W. Pvt.	9 PAI	7/1/61–1/19/63
Cook, Lewis Pvt.	6 WVI	61/65
Cooper, Sam H. Pvt.	7 WVI	NF

Cowan, Robert Capt.	2 MDI	8/16/61–5/29/65
Cowden, Wm. J. W. Pvt.	——	10/63–7/65
Cox, Richard	NF	
Cox, Thomas Pvt.	52 OHI	NF
Cox, Wm. M. Pvt.	12 INI	4/19/61–5/19/62
also	49 INI	4/1/65–9/17/65
Craft, James Pvt.	1 WVI	9/10/61–11/26/64
Crags, Phelix H. Lt.	22 PAC	9/6/62–5/24/65
Craig, Daniel W. Pvt.	6 OHC	5/2/61–6/17/65
Craiz, Wm. Pvt.	6 WVI	10/2/61–6/10/65
Crew, Sam B. Cpl.	129 OHI	7/63–3/64
Crum?, George Pvt.	1 WVI	11/14/61–1/27/63
Crumbaeher, George Pvt.	1 WVI	5/10/61–8/27/61
Culver, George W. Pvt.	1 VAI	9/62–7/65
Culver, John Pvt.	2 WVI	1/1/62–7/16/65
Culver, Simeon Pvt.	1 WVC	61/63
Cunningham, Charles Pvt.	6 WVC	2/12/64–7/8/65
Cunningham, Duncan Capt.	10 WVI	8/18/62–6/9/65
Cunningham, Sam W. Pvt.	1 WVI	2/23/64–7/23/65
Curtis, Wm. B. Gen.	Brevet Gen. US	8/25/62–6/20/65
Dailey, Hamilton Pvt.	25 OHI	2/29/64–6/18/66
Damenberg, Henry	NF	
Daugherty, John H. Pvt.	15 WVI	8/15/62–7/30/65
Davis, Charles L. Cpl.	3 NJI	4/24/61–1864
Davis, James Pvt.	188 OHI	1/65–5/65
Davis, James W. Pvt.	7 WVI	7/29/62–9/15/63
Davis, John A. Blksmith	1 WVC	8/14/61–7/8/65
Davis, Sam P. Pvt.	5 OHI	8/15/62–6/26/65
Dayel, Benj. E. Pvt.	77 OHI	NF
Dean, Abraham Pvt.	1 WVI	10/17/61–11/26/64
Dean, Joseph M. Pvt.	1 VAI	10/1/61–7/29/62
Deekes, Jacob Pvt.	1 WVC	2/10/65–7/8/65
Defibaugh, George W. Pvt.	15 WVI	8/18/62–10/13/63
Deiters, Charles H. Sgt.	1 WVA	8/20/62–6/27/65
Delibaugh, Solomon Pvt.	15 WVI	8/11/62–6/14/65
Dennis, Edgar L. Pvt.	1 WVC	2/25/64–7/8/65
Dillon, Peter Capt.	116 OHI	9/18/62–NF
Dittmore, John Pvt.	1 VAI	9/16/61–11/26/64
Dobbins, Peyton B. Sgt.	1 VAI	3/2/64–7/21/65
Doman, George W. Pvt.	140 PAI	8/18/62–5/17/65
Donnelly, John H. Pvt.	NF (2 VAI CSA?)	
Dorsey, Bassiel Pvt.	12 WVI	8/14/62–6/18/65
Dougherty, Robert M. Pvt.	15 WVI	8/13/62–6/30/65
Douglas, Edward S. Pvt.	46 IAI	5/14/61–10/20/61
Dovener, Blackburn B. Capt	15 WVI	8/30/62–1/1/65
Downing, Joseph B. Pvt.	1 WVA	8/15/63–1/3/64
also Cpl.	1 WVA	1/3/65–7/11/65

Doyle, George Pvt.	2 WVI	1/31/65–7/65
Doyle, John Pvt.	1 WVC	8/13/61–12/31/63
Dugan, Edward Sgt.	1 NYC	6/1/62–6/64
Dunlap, Benj. F. Pvt.	77 OHI	10/28/61–3/8/66
Dunlap, Wm. M. Pvt.	12 WVI	2/15/64–8/9/65
Dye, Enoch	US NF	
Dyson, James Pvt.	1 VAA	8/16/62–8/27/65
Echols, Wm. W. Pvt.	77 OHI	NF
Eikey, Charles Pvt.	2 WVC	10/1/61–11/28/64
Elliott, Charles H. Pvt.	85 PAI	NF
Engelhart, Frederick Pvt.	1 MOC	63/65
Esmins, Lewis Pvt.	1 OHA	10/17/61–10/16/64
Estrusth, Charles Cpl.	4 WVC	7/6/63–3/15/64
Etzler, Martin Pvt.	17 OHI	4/22/61–8/15/61
also Sgt.	170 OHI	5/2/64–9/10/64
also Pvt.	15 OHI	3/27/65–11/21/65
Faith, Isaac Pvt.	1 WVI	5/16/61–8/16/61
Farley, Patrick Sgt.	1 WVC	8/28/61 8/28/64
Farrall, Samuel B. Pvt.	43 OHI	10/13/61–11/28/64
Farris, Joseph A. Capt.	6 WVI	10/1/61–11/17/64
Farrnes?, Charles Pvt.	18 PAC	62/65
Fay, Ferdinand Pvt.	1 WVC	2/15/64–7/20/65
Feller, Henry J.	US NF	
Ferrell, James W.	US NF	
Fette, Wm. Pvt.	6 WVI	2/18/65–6/10/65
Ficher?, Henry Pvt.	24 VAC (CSA?)	NF
Fisher, John Pvt.	WVI "Exempts"	9/19/62–5/31/65
Fitzgerald, Wm.	NF (20 VAC CSA)	
Fleming, James Pvt.	1 VAC	2/64–7/6/65
Fleming, Samuel Pvt.	12 WVI	NF
Fletcher, Philip S. Pvt.	1 WVA	8/22/62–6/27/65
Florence, Sam J. Sgt.	6 WVI	10/1/61–11/17/64
Folitick, John Pvt.	3 WVC	2/21/65–6/30/65
Fonner, David Pvt.	18 PAC	9/18/62–7/10/65
Foreman, Wm. L. Pvt.	12 WVI	2/17/64–6/2/65
Foster, Henry A.	NF	
Foster, John A. Cpl.	1 WVI	9/9/61–11/25/64
Fox, Adam Pvt.	6 WVI	9/19/61–12/29/64
Fox, Arthur W. Pvt.	39 OHI	7/16/61–7/9/65
Frank, Valentine Pvt.	84 OHI	5/28/62–9/14/62
also	3 WVC	2/14/65–6/30/65
Frank, Wm. Pvt.	1 WVA	8/16/62–5/22/65
Franzell, Lewis	NF	
Frazier, Daniel G. Pvt.	12 WVI	8/14/62–6/16/65
Frazier, Joseph C. Pvt.	140 PAI	8/14/62–9/3/63
also Cpl.	178 PAI	2/23/65–9/11/65
Fremter, Edward Pvt.	6 WVI	NF

Fren, Alexander Cpl.	1 WVI	5/7/61–8/23/61
also Capt.	15 WVI	8/7/62–6/14/65
Frew, Robert T. Pvt.	1 WVI	10/17/61–11/26/64
Friedrich, F.C.	CSA NF	
Fritz, Adolph Cpl.	1 WVI	5/17/61–8/28/61
Fritz, Edward Pvt.	1 WVA	2/63–7/27/65
Frye, Isaac Cpl.	6 WVI	10/8/61–11/25/64
Fullerton, Wm. R.C. Pvt.	7 VAI	8/7/61–1/64
Fullmer, Milton Pvt.	3 WVC	2/65–7/65
Gallagher, Wm. J. Pvt.	9 PAI	6/10/61–5/11/64
also Sgt.	57 PAI	8/29/64–5/31/65
Gamison?, Hiram Pvt.	2 WVI	2/64–7/64
Gardner, John Pvt.	22 PAC	9/6/62–6/1/65
Gary, Wm. R.	NF	
Geotze, Charles Pvt.	6 WVI	9/28/61–12/1/64
Gewunger, Meinrad Pvt.	13 PAI	4/25/61–7/25/61
aka R. Binhart		
Giesey?, Valentine	NF	
Giffin, Daniel A. Pvt.	12 WVI	8/14/62–6/20/65
Giffin, Robert M. Pvt.	1 WVC	2/21/65–6/21/65
Gilbreath, Wm. L. Pvt.	12 WVI	8/19/62–2/24/63
Gillespie, Andrew Pvt.	1 WVI	9/20/61–10/1/62
Gillespie, Cornelius Sgt.	6 WVI	10/1/61–11/12/64
Gillispie, John Pvt.	1 WVI	61/61
Githens, Lafaett Pvt.	55 OHI	NF
Glistner, Adam Pvt.	5 VAC	5/21/61–1/4/64
also	6 WVC	6/5/64–5/22/66
Goetze, Henry Pvt.	5 VAC	6/61–6/64
Gomer, Wm. D. Pvt.	3 PAC	8/13/61–8/24/64
Gooding, Benj. D. Pvt.	1 WVI	5/10/61–8/27/61
Gosney, Richard Pvt.	1 WVI	10/1/61–6/2/62
Gould, George L. Pvt.	1 WVI	10/6/61–10/64
Grabe, Wm. F. Sgt.	5 WVC	5/10/61–6/14/64
Gradie?, Louis H. Pvt.	6 WVI	2/16/65–7/13/65
Graffe, John Pvt.	6 WVI	10/2/61–12/1/64
Gray, Hanimul Pvt.	15 WVI	NF
Gray, James T. Sgt.	3 WVC	65/65
Gray, John Pvt.	6 WVI	2/13/65–6/10/65
Greenwald, August Pvt.	— KYI	NF
Greer, David Pvt.	1 WVI	9/16/61–2/11/64
also	2 WVI	2/11/64–7/16/65
Greer, Joseph Pvt.	1 WVA	8/16/62–6/27/65
Griffin, Wm. Pvt.	1 OHA	6/63–8/65
Grimm, Fredrick Pvt.	NF	
Groves, John T. Pvt.	19 OHI	9/28/64–6/8/65
Gruber, Charles Pvt.	1 WVI	9/16/61–1/1/65
Gruber, Fred Musician	23 PAI	61/64

Gruber, Jacob Pvt.	1 WVC	3/64–7/65
Gump, James Pvt.	11 WVI	6/29/61–12/17/63
Gundling, Peter W. Pvt.	1 WVC	2/28/65–7/8/65
Guy, Robert A. Pvt.	1 WVI	5/15/61–7/19/65
Habig, Peter Pvt.	1 VAI	9/21/61–11/26/64
Habig, Rinehart Pvt.	1 WVA	9/3/64–6/1/65
Hagan, Wm. Sgt.	16 PAC	8/20/62–6/15/65
Haines, James E. Pvt.	6 WVI	9/27/61–11/25/64
Hall, James R. Pvt.	3 WVC	10/8/62–6/5/65
Hall, Jesse Pvt.	1 WVA	8/16/62–6/27/65
Hall, Jones P. Pvt.	126 OHI	8/27/62–7/3/65
Hall, Travis A. Pvt.	125 OHI	10/23/62–9/25/65
Hall, Wm. Pvt.	1 WVI	9/23/61–11/26/64
Halpin, John Pvt.	1 VAI	4/7/61–8/61
Halpin, Patrick Pvt.	1 WVI	5/61–8/61
Hamilton, Smith Cpl.	1 WVI	7/61–2/63
also Sgt.	2 WVI	2/63–7/65
Hamilton, Wm. J. Pvt.	6 WVI	12/1/61–12/5/64
Hamilton, Wm. Pvt.	15 WVI	8/15/62–8/13/65
Hammond, James Pvt.	77 OHI	10/18/61–11/62
Hanna, Thomas Engineer	Juliet (USN?)	8/18/64–6/17/65
Hanna, Wm. R. Pvt.	12 WVI	8/14/62–6/16/65
Hannon, Wm. Pvt.	5 WVC	6/1/61–6/14/64
Harpit, George Pvt.	2 MDI	2/2/62–2/2/65
Harrel, Artemus C. Pvt.	31 NCC CSA	NF
Harris, Alexander Pvt.	25 NYC	6/16/63–6/65
Harris, John	US NF	
Harris, Thomas Pvt.	NF	
Harrison, John W.	US NF	
Harry, Edwin C. Pvt.	34 INI	8/61–2/66
Hastings, James Pvt.	157 OHI	5/1/64–9/10/64
Hawkins, Hugh Pvt.	15 OHI	8/30/61–11/21/65
Hawkins, James Pvt.	1 WVI	2/8/64–7/8/65
Hayes, Henry Pvt.	Negro NF	
Haymaker, Charles E. Cpl.	1 VAI	5/61–5/25/65
Hazlet, Robert Cpl.	14 PAC	1/5/64–8/24/65
Hazlett, John A. Pvt.	1 WVA	9/28/64–6/6/65
Hazlett, Robert W. Dr.	2 WVI	6/15/61–6/15/65
Heil, Charles Pvt.	47 NYI	12/1/64–8/12/65
Heil, Nicholas Cpl.	6 WVI	9/19/61–12/29/64
Heller, Lawrence Pvt.	1 WVA	8/24/64–7/11/65
Henderson, J.P. Pvt.	1 WVA	6/63–1/18/65
Henning, Wm. H. Pvt.	6 TNC	9/2/62–7/2/65
Henry, James A. Pvt.	1 WVI	8/25/61–11/26/64
Henry, John L. Pvt.	3 WVC	2/21/65–6/30/65
Hercules, George W. Pvt.	15 WVI	8/7/62–7/5/65
Hercules, Wm. H. Pvt.	82 OHI	9/13/64–6/10/65

Herman, George Pvt.	5 WVI	NF
Hertzog, Samuel Pvt.	16 PAC	9/18/62–NF
Heston, Benj.	NF	
Heston, Benj. Pvt.	1 WVI	3/1/64–7/22/65
Hidinger, Joseph	Teamster	NF
Higgins, Tom N. Pvt.	148 OHI	5/10/64–9/64
Hill, George Cpl.	1 VAI	10/12/61–11/26/64
Hill, James W. Pvt.	2 WVC	2/29/64–7/16/65
Hill, James W. Pvt.	1 WVA	9/10/63–4/15/64
Hill, John W. Pvt.	1 WVI	5/61–6/20/65
Hine, Wm. D. Pvt.	6 WVI	10/13/61–12/27/64
Hines, Jonathan G. Pvt.	1 WVI	2/29/62–7/23/65
Hobbs, Marshall R. Pvt.	157 OHI	5/15/64–9/2/64
also	– PAA	10/6/64–6/15/65
Hoffer, Henry Pvt.	1 WVC	2/18/64–7/24/65
Holmes, Wm. H. Pvt.	11 PAI	9/20/64–7/27/66
Holt, John Pvt.	1 VAI	5/10/61–8/27/61
also Lt.	11 WVI	2/20/62–2/24/65
Honicker, Jacob Pvt.	1 WVA	8/22/62–6/17/65
Hoose, Julius Musician	NF	
Horner, Clark M. Pvt.	179 OHI	9/19/63–6/25/65
Horner, George W. Pvt.	5 OHC	1/13/63–6/5/65
Hosenfend, Frederick Pvt.	6 WVI	61/62
Hotchkis, Wm. Pvt.	1 WVI	8/28/64–7/11/65
Howelfield, Alexander Pvt	NF	
Howell, James W.	NF	
Hubbard, Wm. P. Lt.	1 WVI	NF
Hudson, E.H.	NF	
Hughs, Edward Cpl.	3 MDI	12/1/61–5/25/65
Humes Samuel Pvt.	6 WVI	10/14/61–6/10/65
Humes, David Pvt.	6 WVI	2/10/65–4/10/65
Humes, Franklin Pvt.	6 WVI	9/10/61–6/5/65
Humphy, Sam C. Pvt.	9 INC	1/7/64–3/14/65
Humrickhouse, Chas. W.	14 PAC (Scout)	NF
Hund, Henry Pvt.	6 WVI	10/2/61–12/1/64
Ichbad, Bessee Pvt.	18 MAI	NF
Ickler, John Pvt.	– VA –	6/61–7/64
Ikin, Benj. Pvt.	6 WVI	9/23/61–5/19/64
Imer, Henry Pvt.	1 —I	9/25/61–11/26/64
Imer, Wm. N. Pvt.	6 WVI	10/17/61–11/26/64
Inman, John Pvt.	5 PAA	6/12/64–7/30/65
Irwin, Clarence Sgt.	1 WVI	5/61–2/64
also Capt.	2 WVI	7/65–NF
Jack, Charles T. Pvt.	49 INI	9/30/61–2/2/64
Jacobs, Joseph Cpl.	13 OHC	3/21/65–7/4/65
Johnson, James Pvt.	15 WVI	8/11/62–6/14/65
Johnson, Stephen G "Fifer"	1 WVI	5/15/61–8/29/61

Name	Unit	Dates
Johnson, Willis Cpl.	USI (Negro)	64/65
Johnston, Wm. Sgt.	2 MDI	7/26/61–2/14/64
Jones, Andrew Sgt.	3 CAI	10/10/61–7/27/66
Jones, Griffith B. Pvt.	102 PAI	8/19/61–6/5/65
Jones, Henry Pvt.	1 WVI	8/31/62–6/27/65
Jones, John Y. Pvt.	45 USC	3/29/65–11/4/65
Jones, Oliver Pvt.	1 VAI	9/16/61–NF
Jones, Vestuf Pvt.	USC	1856/1862
Junkins, Robert Pvt.	15 WVC	2/18/64–7/8/65
Kappler, George F. Pvt.	6 WVI	9/19/61–12/29/64
Kasley, Sam L. Pvt.	43 OHI	1/62–9/65
Keeney, Benj. F. Pvt.	22 INI	NF
Keifer, David W. Pvt.	14 WVI	8/8/62–7/3/65
Keller, James M. Pvt.	12 WVI	8/13/62–6/16/65
Kemp, Wm. G. Pvt.	7 VAI	9/20/61–11/26/64
Kemp, Wm. Musician	1 WVI	4/61–6/63
Kenedy, Wilson G.	3 WVC	2/14/65–6/30/65
Kistler, Jacob Pvt.	6 PAA	8/31/64–6/13/65
Klaproth, Wm. Pvt.	3 WVM	4/63–3/4/64
Klein, John Pvt.	55 OHI	9/28/64–6/10/65
Kleives, Theodore Pvt.	——	62/63
Kleproth, Charles Cpl.	6 WVI	9/19/61–12/29/64
Klevis. Charles F. Pvt.	NF	
Knight, Samuel Pvt.	6 WVI	62/65
Knout, Frederick Pvt.	6 WVI	10/7/61–12/1/64
Koch, Warren Pvt.	200 PAI	8/15/64–5/30/65
Kolb, Andrew R.	—MAI?	8/9/62–6/17/65
Kraft, Louis Pvt.	6 VAI	6/61–1865
Kraus, Samuel Capt.	7 WVI	8/7/61–10/7/64
Laflam, Napolean Teamster	27 NJI	9/3/62–7/2/63
Lang, Wm. Pvt.	41 NYI	NF
Laurell, John Pvt.	15 WVI	8/11/62–6/14/65
Leach, Ambrose Pvt.	2 WVI	2/22/64–7/16/65
Leach, Wm. Pvt.	2 WVI	2/29/64–7/16/65
Leanhast, Conrad	NF	
Leasure, James A. Cpl.	1 VAI	6/61–8/65
Lemon, Wm. M. Pvt.	15 ——	8/11/62–6/14/65
Lewellen, John Pvt.	188 PAI	3/7/64–12/14/65
Lewis, David A. Pvt.	5 PAA	8/16/64–6/15/65
Lewis, Frank Pvt.	4 WVC	7/63–3/64
also	11 WVI	4/64–9/65
Lewis, Wharton Pvt.	1 WVI	9/25/61–11/26/64
Liston, Scott Pvt.	15 OHI	5/4/61–8/27/61
also Sgt.	1 VAC	12/2/61–7/18/65
Long, David A. Pvt.	1 WVC	10/1/61–11/26/64
Long, John J. Pvt.	17 WVI	8/12/64–6/30/65
Long, John Pvt.	1 VAI	5/15/61–8/27/61

Lucas, John C. Pvt.	1 WVC	2/28/63–7/65
Lukins, Abraham Pvt.	1 VAA	8/16/62–6/27/65
Lunan, Henry Pvt.	15 WVI	8/22/62–6/21/65
Lydick, Oliver H. Pvt.	3 WVI	7/1/61–6/30/64
Lyons, James E. Pvt.	1 WVA	8/20/62–6/22/65
Lytle, Wm. Pvt.	1 WVI	3/13/64–7/21/65
Maheny, Patrick Sgt.	6 WVC	1861–NF
Manamon, Martin Pvt.	6 WVI	NF
Mangus, Isaac Pvt.	21 PAC	NF
Manley, Ellison Pvt.	43 OHI	4/64–9/64
Manning, Samuel	NF	
Marsh, Mathew	NF	
Marsh, Wm. C. Pvt.	7 WVI	9/2/61–11/5/64
Marshal, George H. Pvt.	1 OHI	4/15/61–8/1/61
also	122 OHI	11/6/62–6/26/65
Marshall, Andrew Cpl.	2 VAI	2/61–7/15/65
Marshall, Emanuel Pvt.	1 VAI	5/1/61–8/61
Marshall, George Cpl.	1 VAC	8/31/61–7/8/65
Marshall, Wm. H. Pvt.	2 WVI	2/10/62–7/16/65
Martin, Charles Pvt.	25 OHI	5/25/64–6/15/66
Martin, David Pvt.	6 WVI	9/23/61–11/23/64
Martin, George W.	Ohio River Gunboat	5/61–10/61
Martin, Jacob Pvt.	1 WVA	8/14/62–8/14/65
Martin, John Pvt.	6 VAI	10/10/61–6/18/65
Martin, Joseph H. Pvt.	1 WVI	5/21/61–11/27/64
Mathews, George Pvt.	2 NYI	4/61–7/12/65
Mathews, George W. Pvt.	1 VAI	10/1/61–5/23/62
also	10 VAI	2/12/64–8/9/65
Mathews, John Pvt.	1 WVI	10/1/61–5/23/62
Mathews, Wm. Pvt.	1 WVI	9/19/61–9/12/62
Maxwell, Daniel Sgt.	12 WVI	8/18/62–6/16/65
Maxwell, James C. Sgt.	1 MDC	9/3/61–9/3/64
Maxwell, Wm. D. Pvt.	12 WVI	NF
Mayer, Henry P. Pvt.	1 VAI	9/10/61–10/10/64
McAdams, James	CSA NF	
McAdams, John T. Pvt.	1 WVI	9/23/61–2/28/64
also	2 WVI	2/28/64–7/16/65
McAdams, Wm. Pvt.	1 WVC	9/14/61–12/28/64
McCandel, John T. Pvt.	1 WVC	2/18/62–7/8/65
McCauslin, Joseph Pvt.	12 WVI	8/25/62–6/20/65
McChesney, Thomas "Cook"	76 PAI	9/2/61–1/18/65
McConneha, Alexander Cpl.	12 WVI	8/8/62–6/16/65
McCoullough, Paxton	USN	5/1/62–10/1/62
McCoy, Wm. A. Cpl.	12 PAI	4/19/61–NF
also Capt.	1 WVC	8/23/61–11/11/64
McCready, James T. Pvt.	6 WVI	9/25/61–11/30/64
McDermott, John Pvt.	1 WVI	5/10/61–8/28/61

McDonald, Wm. Pvt.	5 PAC	8/23/64–6/30/65
McFarland?, Ed Pvt.	CSA NF	
McGee, James Pvt.	104 OHI	2/2/64–7/16/65
McGhumphy, Wm. Pvt.	1 PAC	3/20/64–8/25/65
McGinley, Daniel	NF	
McGinnis, Dorance Cpl.	17 IAI	3/13/62–6/8/64
McGivern, H.J. Pvt.	4 USA	5/3/63–8/28/65
McKenney, Patrick Pvt.	19 MAI	1/12/62–6/22/65
McKinley, Daniel F. Pvt.	1 WVI	5/11/61–8/28/61
also Sgt.	4 WVC	7/16/63–3/18/64
McKown, Joseph Pvt.	6 WVI	63/65
McLain, John C. Pvt.	84 OHI	1862–NF
McLauchlin, James T.	NF	
McMorris, John Pvt.	55 OHI	11/3/61–11/9/63
McNash, Andrew J. Pvt.	3 WVC	2/14/65–6/30/65
McVay, Samuel Sgt.	1 WVC	10/22/61–11/30/63
McVenes, James Pvt.	NF	
Meder, Louis Pvt.	2 WVI	4/5/65–7/18/65
Meek, Wm. S. Musician	43 OHI	12/24/63–7/18/65
Meissner, John G. Pvt.	2 WVI	2/11/64–7/16/65
Melaney, Thomas Pvt.	1 PAA	5/26/64–9/3/64
Mercer, Charles N. Pvt.	28 ILI	8/8/61–8/2/62
Mercer, Jesse Pvt. & Cook	1 WVC	8/8/61–7/8/65
Merrifield, Wm. M. Pvt.	14 WVI	9/25/62–7/25/65
Metzer, Louis Pvt.	6 WVI	10/2/61–11/25/64
aka Lewis Mexicar		
Metzgar, Bernard Pvt.	4 MOI	8/18/64–7/11/65
Miller, Charles F. Pvt.	1 WVC	2/15/64–7/8/65
Miller, John Pvt.	6 WVI	9/28/61–12/1/64
Miller, Joshua Pvt.	6 WVI	61/65
Miller, Michael Pvt.	1 WVI	9/24/61–9/30/62
Miller, Nick	NF	
Miller, Orloff C. Cpl.	1 VAI	9/21/61–10/15/62
Millett, John W. Pvt.	129 OHI	7/63–2/64
also	161–OHI	6/64–9/64
Montgomery, George Cpl.	1 WVI	5/11/61–2/8/64
also Cpl.	2 WVI	2/8/64–7/16/65
Montgomery, James	NF	
Mooney, John Pvt.	6 WVI	10/1/61–9/4/64
Mooney, Richard Pvt.	52 VAI CSA	8/1/62–NF
Mooney, Wm. Pvt.	52 VAI CSA	6/61–5/62
Moore, John E. Pvt.	3 NJI	1/8/62–2/27/64
Moore, John H. Pvt.	3 WVC	7/21/61–8/27/64
Moore, Shadrak Pvt.	77 OHI	NF
Morgan, David G. Pvt.	6 WVI	10/2/61–11/25/64
Morgan, Wm. M. Pvt.	6 WVI	9/27/61–1862
also	1 WVA	62/65

Morrison, Giffin Pvt.	12 WVI	8/14/62–7/19/65
Mossburg, Wm. H. Pvt.	NF	
Murdoch, Godfrey G. Pvt.	- WVI	8/11/63–4/23/64
Murphy, Martin Pvt.	1 USC	11/11/62–11/11/65
Murrin, George A. Sgt.	1 VAI	5/17/61–11/26/64
Myers, Ross M. Engineer	USN	6/10/63–1/65
Myles, John J. Pvt.	3 WVI	2/65–8/65
Myrtle, Wm. R. Pvt.	52 VAI CSA	4/10/61–5/30/64
Narey, John	NF	
Neidhardt, John Pvt.	2 WVI	6/1/61–6/64
Neitzel, Paul Pvt.	178 NYI	6/4/63–5/8/65
Nesbitt, David Blksmith	——	1863–NF
Nestline, Joshua Pvt.	178 OHI	9/8/64–6/29/65
Newman, Thomas Pvt.	1 VAI	9/28/61–7/16/65
Nickerson, David Pvt.	12 WVI	8/13/62–6/16/65
Nickerson, Nehamiah Pvt.	12 WVI	8/13/62–7/65
Nightengale, George R. Pvt	——	61/65
Niron, James Pvt.	43 OHI	NF
Nixon, Wm. Pvt.	NF (62–VAI CSA?)	
Nolte, Frank Pvt.	6 WVI	61/65
Norman, John W. Pvt.	1 WVC	2/8/64–7/8/65
Norton, Thomas H. Major	USA NF	
Nowvisck, Louis H. Pvt.	42 PAI	5/63–1866
Ocker, Wm. Lt.	100 PAI	8/29/61–11/26/62
Orr, Thomas J. Pvt.	12 WVI	8/14/62–6/26/65
Osteman, Anthony Pvt.	1 VAC	9/8/61–12/31/63
Osterman, Anthony Cpl.	1 WVC	12/23/63–7/8/65
Pappert, Ignatz Pvt.	6 WVI	9/28/61–12/1/64
Paradise, Louis Pvt.	27 NJI	NF
Pastoris, John Pvt.	14 PAC	11/5/62–8/24/65
Patterson, John W. Pvt.	170 OHI	5/13/64–9/10/64
Patton, Wm. D. Pvt.	77 OHI	10/8/62–1/3/65
Paulus, George Pvt.	1 WVI	10/18/61–3/23/63
Pebler?, Henry Pvt.	1 WVA	8/20/62–6/27/65
Petner, George W. Pvt.	53 PAC	10/20/63–1/30/65
Peyton, Howard Pvt.	2 VAI	2/20/65–7/20/65
Phipps, Samuel Pvt.	1 WVA	10/1/61–10/22/64
Pierce, Joseph S. Cpl.	1 WVC	6/61–12/28/65
Piper, John H. Pvt.	4 WVC	7/63–3/64
Plant, John J. Sgt.	1 MDI CSA	5/21/61–7/62
Plante, George W. Pvt.	8 PAI	4/15/61–5/24/64
Platt, Charles H. Pvt.	55 OHI	NF
Plaukey, Frank Pvt.	2 WVI	6/1/62–5/18/63
Plues, Edward Pvt.	15 WVI	8/12/62–6/14/65
Porter, George A. Pvt.	17 WVI	NF
Porter, Joseph Pvt.	1 WVI	10/1/61–3/25/65
Powell, John Pvt.	3 WVC	3/7/65–6/30/65

Name	Unit	Dates
Powes?, John Pvt.	1 WVI	8/22/64–7/11/65
Prager, George Pvt.	1 WVI	11/5/61–11/26/64
Pratt, Charles E.	HQ Clerk	64/65
Prettyman, Robert Pvt.	1 WVI	9/17/61–9/18/64
Prichard, James N. Pvt.	6 WVI	4/5/62–4/5/65
Puriton, Thomas Pvt.	6 WVI	8/29/61–6/10/65
Queell, Andrew Pvt.	6 WVI	9/19/61–12/28/64
Rauch, Jacob Cpl.	6 WVI	10/20/61–12/29/64
Rawling, Charles J. Pvt.	1 WVI	11/5/61–4/14/63
Ray, Andrew Pvt.	4 WVC	7/6/63–3/15/64
Reaman, Albert Cpl.	1 WVA	8/16/62–6/22/65
Reed?, Oliver Pvt.	—I	10/1/63–7/22/64
Rhodenbaugh, George Pvt.	1 USC	10/13/62–10/13/65
Rice, George L. Cpl.	15 WVI	8/14/62–6/14/65
Rice, John K. Pvt.	1 WVI	61/62
also	15 WVI	8/14/62–6/14/65
Riddle, Alexander Pvt.	6 WVI	9/27/61–11/25/64
Riddle, James H. Pvt.	17 WVI	2/16/65–5/20/65
Riester, Blasious Pvt.	5 WVC	6/1/61–6/14/64
Rihaldaffer, Wm. G. Pvt.	4 WVC	7/15/63–3/15/64
Riley, Charles W. Pvt.	1 VAI	9/17/61–2/8/64
also Sqt.	2 WVI	2/8/64–7/16/65
Riley, Hyder Pvt.	17 WVI	8/30/64–6/30/65
Ritz, Daniel Pvt.	2 WVI	6/7/63–6/7/65
Rizor, David Pvt.	22 PAC	8/21/62–6/1/65
Rlein, Jacob Pvt.	5 WVC	5/10/61–4/24/65
Roberts, Wm. Musician	NF	
Robertson, Edward Pvt.	5 ILC	4/11/65–10/16/65
Robertson, Richard Pvt.	4 WVC	6/10/63–3/10/64
also	1 WVA	3/24/64–7/11/65–
Robinson, John S.	NF (46 VAI CSA?)	
Roblinson, Thomas Pvt.	1 WVI	9/12/61–10/31/62
Rodenback, Wm. Pvt.	1 VAI	10/13/61–7/16/65
Rodgers, Wm. Pvt.	12 WVI	8/14/62–6/16/65
Rodgers, Wm. W. Capt.	2 KYC	NF
Rolf, August Lt.	2 VAI	6/10/61–9/20/62
Roller, Theodore Pvt.	1 WVA	8/20/62–6/27/65
Rose, Henry G. Pvt.	- WVI	NF
Rose, James T. Pvt.	1 WVI	9/23/61–7/16/65
Rose, John B. Cpl.	12 WVI	8/19/62–6/16/65
Rose, Wm. H. Pvt.	1 WVA	7/12/64–6/20/65
Roseberry, John T. Pvt.	15 WVI	8/8/62–5/65
Rouhan, John Pvt.	1 WVI	9/61–7/17/65
Russ?, Gosslab Pvt.	50 OHI	8/13/62–6/26/65
Russel, Eli W. Pvt.	27 VAI CSA	NF
Ryan, Thomas Pvt.	68 NYI	4/8/62–12/22/64
Ryner, Edwin D. Sgt.	175 OHI	9/3/64–6/16/65

Sadler, Isaac Pvt.	1 WVA	8/20/62–6/16/65
Sadler, James H. Surgeon	1 WVA	8/20/62–6/27/65
Salomon, David Pvt.	23 NYM	5/16/61–5/22/65
Salterbach, Louis P. Capt.	5 VAC	5/10/61–11/17/64
Sauber, John Pvt.	1 WVC	NF
Sauer, August Pvt.	16 ILC	7/7/61–7/16/64
Schan, Louis Pvt.	39 OHI	7/20/61–1/17/62
Scharf, Frederick W. Pvt. *aka* Fred Sharp	83 PAI	2/25/65–6/28/65
Schatzinger, John Pvt.	6 WVI	9/19/61–12/29/64
Schlatter, Anton Sgt.	6 WVI	9/19/61–12/29/64
Schnider, Jacob H. Pvt. *aka* Jacob Vetter	1 VAC	7/12/62–7/25/65
Schultze, Henry Lt.	5 WVC	6/1/61–12/9/63
Schultze, John W. Pvt.	1 WVI	5/11/61–8/28/61
Schwanenberger, George Pvt	6 VAI	9/9/61–1864
Schwartz, Ferdinand	NF	
Scott, James	US NF	
Scott, N.B. QM/Sgt.	— OHI	63/65
Seabright, Frederick Pvt.	6 WVI	10/14/61–12/14/64
Seamon, August Pvt.	WVI "Exempts"	9/19/62–5/31/65
Seamon, Henry Pvt.	1 WVA	8/20/62–5/27/65
Seemeye, Frank Pvt.	15 NYI	NF
Seiler, Adam Pvt.	67 PAI	11/16/64–7/14/65
SeileY/ Oscar	NF	
Senseney, Charles H. Pvt.	1 WVA	8/2/62–6/27/65
Sentlinger, Jacob Pvt.	5 PAA	9/1/64–6/30/65
Serig, Louis Pvt.	6 VAI	10/1/61–11/17/64
Shaffer, Edward C. Pvt.	6 WVI	8/12/61–8/12/64
Shanley, Frank Pvt.	1 VAI	9/20/61–11/26/64
Sheekey, John S. Steward	USN	5/1/61–7/30/61
Sheets, John A. Pvt.	16 INC?	6/24/61–6/30/64
Sheridan, James Sgt.	6 WVI	9/23/61–6/11/65
Shipman, Chrisitan Pvt.	1 WVI	10/1/61–11/26/64
Shoekey, Wm. Capt.	6 WVI	9/28/61–6/10/65
Shook, Isra Pvt.	12 WVI	8/10/62–6/27/65
Shorts, Samuel Pvt.	Ohio Guards	5/13/64–9/10/64
Skeid, Frederick Pvt.	45 NYI	9/61–10/6/62
Smith, Gabriel Pvt.	6 WVI	NF
Smith, James D. Pvt.	1 WVI	5/11/61–8/28/61
Smith, John W. Pvt.	1 WVI	5/17/61–11/26/64
Smith, Levi Pvt.	12 WVI	6/18/61–6/10/65
Smith, Porter Sgt.	1 WVI	6/61–9/61
Smith, Reuben R. Pvt.	61 ILI	4/29/64–9/5/65
Snyder, Henry Pvt.	148 OHI	5/2/64–9/14/64
Soldan, Andrew Pvt.	1 WVC	9/18/61–11/16/64
Soles, Jacob Pvt.	1 VAI	9/23/61–11/26/64

Speers, Thomas	NF	
Spidel, Nicholas Pvt.	6 WVI	2/10/65–4/10/65
Spitzl, Otto Pvt.	7 OHI	4/13/63–8/17/66
Springer, John Pvt.	194 OHI	3/7/65–NF
Springer, Jonas H. Pvt.	4 WVC	7/25/63–3/8/64
also	187 OHC	3/2/65–7/20/66
Spure?, Henry Sgt.	12 WVI	8/9/62–6/23/65
Stamen, John L. Pvt.	12 WVI	8/12/62–6/16/65
Stanton, James D.	NF	
Stathers, Walter E. Cpl.	6 WVI	9/8/64–6/10/65
Stephens, Benj. Pvt.	61–PAI	6/6/63–7/1/65
Sterling, Hugh Pvt.	12 PAI	4/18/61–7/18/61
also	23 PAI	9/6/61–9/6/64
Stevens, Ernest Pvt.	32 OHI	9/22/64–5/29/65
Stevens, Ernest Pvt.	NF	
Stevenson, Andrew M. Cpl.	52 OHI	8/22/62–12/13/62
Stewart, Henry Pvt.	1 WVA	8/15/62–6/22/65
Stewart, Isaac Sgt.	6 PAA	8/27/64–6/13/65
Stollert, Henry Pvt.	2 WVI	1/4/65–7/6/65
aka Wm. H. Hornes		
Stotsberg, Wilham L.	US NF	
Straub, Joseph Sgt.	6 WVI	5/31/62–6/10/65
Stroble, Robert W. Cpl.	1 WVI	10/5/61–11/29/64
Stump, Albert Pvt.	12 WVI	8/23/62–6/16/65
Sullivan, John Pvt.	14 VAC CSA	4/20/61–6/11/64
Sullivan, Owen Pvt.	5 WVC	6/1/61–12/31/64
Sunman, Robert	CSA NF	
Sutton, Carter Pvt.	1 WVC	2/6/64–7/8/65
Sykes, Wm. C. Pvt.	78 PAI	9/17/61–11/2/64
Sylvis, Caleb Pvt.	1 WVC	5/17/61–7/8/65
also	1 WVI	NF
Tanner, James M. Pvt.	12 WVI	8/14/62–6/26/65
Tates, David Pvt.	NF	
Taylor, Frank Pvt.	1 VAI	5/11/61–8/28/61
Taylor, Jacob Pvt.	6 WVI	10/12/61–11/25/64
Taylor, James M. Pvt.	1 WVI	5/15/61–8/29/61
Taylor, Robert S. Pvt.	4 WVI	6/10/61–7/5/65
Teasdale, Robert T. Pvt.	4 PAI	3/7/65–7/24/65
Telomann, Henry C. Pvt.	13 PAI	NF
also	102 PAI	5/17/61–NF
Thomas, James B. Pvt.	18 VAC CSA	63/65
Thompson, Hershel Pvt.	1 VAI	9/15/61–1865
Thompson, Isaac S. Pvt.	6 WVI	8/12/61–6/13/64
Throckmorten, Joseph Pvt.	101 PAI	7/16/63–5/3/65
Thurber, Delaware A. Cpl.	3 VAI	5/61–6/66
Thurlow, Charles W. Pvt.	1 MEI	4/61–7/61
Tolbert, John R. Pvt.	12 WVI	8/62–6/65

Tracy, George W.	NF	
Tracy, Stephen	NF	
Travis, Wm. H. Cpl.	1 WVI	5/11/61–8/30/61
also Lt.	4 WVC	7/16/63–3/15/64
Troy, John	NF	
Truax, Wm. Pvt.	1 WVC	3/7/65–7/8/65
Turner, Wm. H. Pvt.	8 MII	10/18/62–7/18/63
Ulrich, Charles F. Dr.	1 KYI	4/10/64–8/10/65
Uselton, Daniel Pvt.	77 OHI	10/25/61–1/30/65
Vanaman, Nathan Pvt.	12 VAI	8/25/62–7/65
Vanaman, Richard L. Pvt.	90 OHI	7/62–1865
Vanburgh, Tobius Cpl.	108 NYI	7/29/62–5/28/65
Vermillion, Richard J. Pvt	14 WVI	8/14/62–6/16/65
Vierheller, Chrisitan Lt.	2 WVI	5/10/61–4/11/63
Walkenhauser, Henrich Pvt.	6 WVI	61/65
Wallace, Rather Pvt.	16 PAC	2/65–8/65
Wallace, Wm. M. Pvt.	6 WVI	10/1/61–11/25/64
Walter, Frank Sgt.	1 WVI	1861–NF
Walters, Robert Pvt.	NF	
Walton, John Lt.	25 OHI	4/29/61–6/19/66
Walton, Thomas	NF	
Warfful, George Pvt.	15 WVI	8/15/62–6/14/65
Washington, George W. Cpl.	1 USI	5/63–10/65
Watier, James Pvt.	21 NYC	12/3/63–11/18/65
Watkins, Charles Pvt.	1 VAA	8/16/62–8/27/65
Watson, Jacob Pvt.	3 WVC	64/65
Watt, David M. Pvt.	1 PAA	7/13/63–1/20/64
Webb, Joseph Pvt.	1 MDC	8/2/61–11/8/62
also	2 WVI	2/12/65–7/15/65
Webb, Zachariah	US NF	
Weishar, Joseph Pvt.	13 KSI	9/5/61–1/65
Welling, Edward M. Pvt.	2 WVI	3/17/64–7/16/65
Wells, Albert L. Pvt.	15 WVI	10/1/62–6/23/64
also Lt.	15 WVI	7/2/64–9/23/65
Wells, Jesse H. Pvt.	1 WVA	3/29/64–7/11/65
Wells, Robert M. Pvt.	1 VAI	5/11/61–8/28/61
Wells, Theodore F. Pvt.	15 WVI	8/8/62–6/14/65
Wentzberger, Henry Pvt.	1 WVC	63/65
Werner, George Pvt.	9 PAI	4/15/61–7/3/65
West, John E. Cpl.	7 WVI	8/7/61–2/63
West, John Pvt.	NF	
Westlake, Benj. F. Sgt.	43 OHI	10/1/61–7/13/65
Westwood, John T. Pvt.	4 VAC	63/64
Wharton, Wm. Pvt.	1 WVI	NF
Wheeler, Joseph Pvt.	1 WVA	8/22/64–6/27/65
While, Wm. H. Pvt.	15 WVI	62/65
White, John H. Pvt.	— WVA?	NF

White, Robert Col.	21 BTN VAC CSA	62/65	
Whitecotton, Nathaniel Pvt	10 WVI	7/1/62–6/13/65	
Whitham, Wm. F. Pvt.	12 WVI	8/25/62–6/20/65	
Wilbert, Charles Pvt.	3 WVC	2/17/65–6/30/65	
Wilcox, Stephen	US NF		
Wilkey, Andrew F. Pvt.	7 VAI	3/65–7/10/65	
Williams, Bynard Pvt.	50 OHI	8/15/62–4/10/65	
Williams, Peter Pvt.	22 PAI	8/3/62–5/63	
Williams, Wm. H. Pvt.	12 WVI	8/18/62–5/23/65	
Williamson, Robert T. Pvt.	6 WVI	9/23/61–11/20/64	
Wilson, George D. Pvt.	1 VAI	9/25/61–11/26/64	
Wilson, John B. Pvt.	1 WVA	9/64–6/65	
Wilson, Thomas P.	NF		
Wincher, Wm. Pvt.	1 VAI	9/23/61–10/4/64	
Winesburg, Robert W. Pvt.	13 WVI	9/16/63–4/23/65	
Winters, Oscar Pvt.	USI (Negro)	NF	
Winzenreid, Godfrey Cpl.	1 VAC	9/20/61–1864	
Wise, John L. Pvt.	13 PAI	4/15/61–7/27/61	
Wohnhas, John Pvt.	28 OHI	6/13/61–7/23/64	
Wolf, Andrew	NF		
Woods, Daniel A. Pvt.	1 WVC	2/11/64–7/8/65	
Work, Alfred D. Pvt.	1 WVI	5/11/61–8/28/61	
also	1 WVC	2/13/65–NF	
Worls, George W. Pvt.	5 PAA	8/26/64–6/30/65	
Yahrling, Charles F. Capt.	6 WVI	61/65	
Young, Wm. Teamster	— WV	5/12/61–6/20/64	
Zimmerman, Frederick Pvt.	6 WVI	10/9/61–4/28/64	

Ohio County Remarks

Adams, T.—RH
Albinger, H.—rupture, thrown from horse
Armbruster, F.F.—RH
Armbruster, J.—RH
Babcock, H.M.—rupture
Backer, L.—broken down in health all over
Baggs, G.W.—papers at pension office D.C.
Bailey, J.B.W.—shot through legs
Baker, G.—HD from exposure
Barber, H.M.—wounded left leg
Barr, J.A.—ruptured
Barriss, E.—bronchitis
Bartholomaus, W.—UFL
Baukard, A.M.—wounded in foot 1863

Biggs, B.—POW Andersonville, CDR, piles & disease of rectum
Biggs, J.H.—POW Libby prison & Belle Isle 6 weeks, UFL, HD
Billick, J.G.—DSC
Bistel, S.—asthma since 1864, hernia right side, pensioned
Blan, W.H.—RH
Blayney, D.M.—bronchitis, throat trouble, HD & CDR 26 years
Bliss, I.M.—suffering from sword cut wound on head
Blowers, J.Q.—CDR
Boice, G.—RH
Bonar, J.—WIA, breast, battle of Ft. Hudson, Louisiana (negro)
Bowers, G.—shot in shoulder
Boyd, A.—LD
Boyd, M.—RH
Boylan, T.—sick in hospital 18 months
Brimer, G.—renmatism health not good
Broest, D.—feeble
Brown, J.J.—deformaty of chest of spine
Brown, J.W.—discharge papers in the hands of a pension agent
Buey, Z.—index finger shot off left hand, pension $4 month
Burdatts, O.S.—has since lost right eye
Burdett, W.H.—POW 2 months Libby & POW 8 months Salisbury, N.C.
Burley, J.A.—RH
Bye, F.—ruptured from riding
Caldobaugh, P.—sore on left leg
Carroll, O.—disabled in right arm
Case, W.—HD
Chippy, S.W.—in Mexican War & Civil War
Church, M.W.—RH
Clark, G.W.—CDR
Clatterbuck, W.H.—gunshot wound left breast
Clifton, G.W.—RH
Coen, J.H.—ezemia, draws pension $8 per month
Condon, W.—health not very good
Connelly, B.—CDR & RH
Connelly, J.H.—POW Libby & Belle Island 2 months, HD
Conwell, J.—hearing impaired, epileptic fits 10 years
Cook, C.W.—broken down in health
Cook, L.—rupture, Nat Soldier Home Barracks 18 Dayton, Ohio
Cox, W.M.—disease of throught
Craft, J.—drummer
Craig, D.W.—WIA 3 times, piles
Culver, J.—injury of right hip
Culver, S.—POW
Curtis, W.B.—RH, CDR & deafness, UFL, no pension
Daugherty, J.H.—catarrh of kidneys, health not good
Davis, J.A.—ruptured
Davis, J.W.—WIA, head, Cedar Mountain, DSC, pensioned

Davis, S.P.—left shoulder crippled
Dean, A.—RH since 1864
Dean, J.M.—DSC
Defibaugh, A.—gunshot hip
Defibaugh, G.W.—health not very good
Defibaugh, S.—RH
Deiters, C.H.—POW at Richmond & Belle Island, UFL, RH & CDR
Donnelly, J.H.*—RH
Doyle, G.—POW Belle Island, dropsy of chest
Dunlap, B.F.—gunshot wound right shoulder, battle Pitts Landing
Echols, W.W.—catarrah & RH
Elliott, C.H.—HD
Engelhart, F.W.—asthma
Fleming, S.—right leg shot off
Fletcher, P.S.—disease of throught
Foreman, W.L.—injured by a horse stepping on breast while asleep
Foster, J.A.—RH
Frank, W.—RH 25 years
Frazier, D.G.—RH
Fren, A.—RH
Frew, R.T.—colarbone broken
Fullerton, W.R.C.—adhesion of lungs & piles
Gallagher, W.J.—WIA twice, UFL
Gardner, J.—asthma & bronchial trouble, UFL 1/2 the time
Giffin, D.A.—CDR 26 years
Giffin, R.M.—stomach & bowel trouble
Gillespie, C.—spinal disease, piles & weak breast
Glistner, A.—RH, discharged at Ft. Leavenworth, Kansas
Goetze, H.—CDR
Greer, D.—shot in left side flesh wound
Greer, J.—injury to abdominal walls, fell off caisson
Griffin, W.—ruptured
Groves, J.T.—dumb ague
Gruber, F.—papers lost in fire of 1876
Gundling, P.W.—weak lungs, consumption
Hagan, W.—lumbago, back
Halpin, J.—deaf & RH
Hamilton, S.—gunshot wound right elbow
Hamilton, W.—can not do much
Hammond, J.—shot in the back
Hannon, W.—health failing
Harpit, G.—rupture both sides, DSC
Harrel, A.C.*—health good
Hazlett, J.A.—POW 3 months Libby prison, piles & RH
Henderson, J.P.—blindness
Henry, J.A.—disease of throught
Henry, J.L.—RH

Herman, G.—discharge in hands of an agent
Hertzog, S.—HD
Heston, B.—CDR, member Co D 2nd Regiment
Hill, J.W.—deafness
Hill, J.W.—gunshot wound left knee, almost blind
Hine, W.D.—RH & neuralgia
Hines, J.G.—POW 109 days Belle Isle Va & RH
Holmes, W.H.—HD
Honicker, J.—lost right arm
Humes, F.—eyes affected
Humphy, S.C.—loss of sight & RH
Ichbad, B.—scurvy etc.
Ickler, J.—HD
Imer, H.—RH
Imer, W.N.—POW Libby prison 6 months
Inman, J.—necrocis
Irwin, C.—unable to give dates, papers in Washington D.C.
Jack, C.T.—cholera
Jones, A.—5 years in regular army in Mexican War
Jones, G.B.—WIA Cold Harbor 6/3/64 shot through left wrist
Keifer, D.W.—wounded in side & thigh
Kemp, W.G.—health broken down, hard hearing
Kenney, B.F.—WIA Pea Ridge
Koch, W.—injured by lifting timber
Kolb, A.R.—RH
Laflam, N.—ankle sprained on 1st enlistment
Laurell, J.—taken POW at Cedar Creek, RH & pyles
Leach, A.—HD & stomach trouble, RH 26 years, no pension
Lewellen, J.—gunshot right leg
Lewis, F.—gunshot right knee POW 9 months Andersonville,
   Florence & Charleston, S.C.
Lewis, W.—slight wound, asthma result of measles
Long, J.J.—liver complaint & RH
Lucas, J.C.—deaf in left ear & erisipelas
Lydick, O.H.—deafness & weak back
Lytle, W.—wounded by shell
Marshal, G.H.—POW 2 months Winchester, RH, health fair
Martin, G.W.—gunboat Hanibal City & Jotan (?) nervous disability
Mathews, G.W.—gunshot foot
Mathews, G.—WIA 3 times, POW
Mathews, J.—HD
Mathews, W.—HD
Maxwell, D.—skull cracked by gunshot
McAdams, W.—LD, POW Belle Island & Libby prison
McCauslin, J.—RH & gastritis 26 years, draws no pension
McCoy, W.A.—shot through left lung
McKown, J.—LD

McLauchlin, J.T.—insane from troubles, discharge lost 1884 flood
McVay, S.—piles
Mercer, C.N.—paralysis
Merrifield, W.M.—left leg shot off
Metzer, L.—hard of hearing since 1865
Miller, C.F.—POW Danville Va 7 months
Miller, M.—RH, pensioned
Miller, N.—RH, rupture & piles
Millett, J.W.—gunshot right thigh
Moore, S.—RH & HD
Morgan, D.G.—malarial fever since 1864, ague fever
Morrison, G.—crippled in back by being thrown from a horse
Murrin, G.A.—wounded right side
Myles, J.J.—ruptured
Myrtle, W.R.*—wounded in face, battle McCannicksville
Nestline, J.—piles & RH
Nickerson, N.—POW 10 1/2 months
Osterman, A.—health not very good
Paradise, L.—bronchitis, catarh etc.
Pastoris, J.—lost hearing in right ear
Platt, C.H.—wounded in chin
Plaukey, F.—ruptured
Plues, E.—lumbago
Porter, J.—POW 6 months, almost disabled
Powell, J.—CDR for 17 years
Prettyman, R.—blind
Rawling, C.J.—gunshot left arm, discharged order Sec. of War
Ray, A.—eyes affected
Rice, G.L.—shot in left forearm
Rice, J.K.—piles
Riddle, A.—RH
Riddle, J.H.—burn of right hand
Riester, B.—broken down
Riley, C.W.—catarrah
Roblinson, T.—loss of left arm from gunshot wound
Rodgers, W.—wound in the left arm
Rose, J.T.—piles & HD from Hunter's Rade
Rouhan, J.—HD from exposure
Salomon, D.—ruptured
Scharf, F.W.—RH since 1866
Schatzin~er, J.—dropsy
Schlatter, A.—left eye shot out
Schwartz, F.—RH & HD
Seabright, F.—lame hip
Seamon, H.—RH & exema, POW Andersonville, discharged Sec of War
Sentlinger, J.—frozen feet, hemorages & RH
Seriq, L.—RH

Sheets, J.A.—kidneys & piles
Shipman, C.—UFL
Shockey, W.—RH & VV
Shook, I.—CDR
Shorts, S.—CDR
Skeid, F.—RH, DSC
Smith, G.—VV caused in charging at Grafton, WV health fair
Smith, J.W.—WIA, left foot, battle of New Market
Smith, L.—POW 10 months
Smith, R.R.—RH, bronchitis & asthma
Springer, J.H.—loss of hearing in army
Springer, J.—POW Andersonville 6 mo. discharge lost 1884 flood
Stephens, B.—WIA three times left leg
Stewart, I.—DSC, RH
Straub, J.—throat disease & hearing, kidney disease
Stroble, R.W.—eye disease
Thompson, H.—has lost 1 eye and other almost useless
Thompson, I.S.—RH & HD
Throckmorten, J.—eyes affected
Turner, W.H.—gunshot foot
Vanaman, N.—rupture & dyspepsia
Vanaman, R.F.—VV left leg, stumbled carrying a log
Walkenhauser, H.—RH
Walters, R.—scalp cut, health not very good
Webb, J.—loss of eye
Welling, E.M.—lost 2 fingers, index & middle right hand
Wells, A.L.—loss of eye
Wells, R.M.—LD
Wells, T.F.—rupture
West, J.E.—DSC
Westlake, B.F.—RH
Westwood, J.T.—left leg injured
Wharton, W.—POW 14 months Belle Isle, chronic RH
Whitecotton, N.S.—RH
Wilbert, C.—RH
Wilkey, A.F.—breast sore at times
Williams, B.—paralysis of lower limbs
Williams, W.H.—RH
Wilson, G.D.—POW 6 months, RH & weak kidneys
Work, A.D.—first private soldier injured, WIA Philippi
Yahrling, C.F.A.—CDR

Pendleton County

*CS Service
NC—not found on 1860 Census
[1] Additional information found in *A History of Pendleton County* by Oren F. Morten, 1910

Ault, Isaac Capt.* age 49, farmer, first served the 46th VAM CSA, subsequently served 46 VAM USA 7/1/63–7/1/64.
Ault, Jacob Pvt.* age 21, laborer, 46 VAM CS & US, 7/1/63–7/1/64.
Ault, Michael Pvt. NC, 46 VAM US 7/1/63–7/1/64.[1]
Bennett, Elijah Pvt.* age 20, laborer, served first the 25th and 31st VAI CSA from 1861-63, deserted, sent as POW to Camp Chase, Ohio and subsequently joined the Swamp Dragons, WVA scouts of US service.
Boggs, John Capt. age 44, farmer, served WVA US scouts beginning on or about 3/10/63, subsequently formed his own company of US scouts and was elected captain on 4/28/64. Company received final discharge 5/31/65.
Bond, John S. Capt. NC, a justice of the Pendleton County, court 1852-59, during the war he formed a company of WVA scouts composed mostly of men from Hardy County.[1]
Borror, Simon Cpl. age 26, farmer, joined Captain Michael Mallow's company WVA scouts 7/1/63 to discharge of company on 3/30/65.
Burns, Sylvester Pvt. age 14, joined 10 WVI 7/10/62–6/28/65 was WIA near Winchester, Va 9/19/64.
Burns, Kennison Pvt. NC, joined Capt. Boggs' company WV scouts 12/1/64–5/31/65.[1]
Carr, John Pvt. age 16, laborer, joined Captain Boggs' company WVA scouts 3/24/63–5/31/65.
Champ, Amos Pvt.* age 18, laborer, served first the 46 VAM CSA subsequently joined Captain Boggs' WVA scouts 5/24/63–5/31/65 was absent sick part of 1864.
Champ, Thomas Pvt. age 22, laborer, joined Captain Boggs' WVA scouts 4/14/63–5/31/65.
Cook, Nicholas L. Sgt. age 36, farmer, joined Captain Mallow's company WVA scouts 7/1/63 captured 2/7/65.
Cunningham, Thomas Pvt.* age 43, laborer, may have served the 62 VAI CSA from 8/20/62 POW 10/4/62 exchanged and POW 9/19/64 paroled 5/16/65.
Davis, Jethro Pvt. age 37, laborer, joined Captain Boggs' company WVA scouts 3/24/63–5/31/65.
Davis, Job Pvt. age 16, laborer, joined Captain Boggs' comapny WVA scouts 3/24/63–5/31/65.
Day, Aaron H. Sgt. age 26, laborer, joined 7 WVI 11/22/61 subsequently served Captain Boggs' company WVA scouts 5/1/64–5/31/65.

Dean, Hiram Pvt.* age 13, served first the 46 VAM CSA and subsequently joined Captain Mallow's company WVA scouts 7/1/63–3/30/65.

Dolly, Isaac J. Pvt.* age 19, laborer, served first the 46 VAM CSA and subsequently joined Captain Boggs' company WVA scouts 3/24/63–5/31/65.

Dolly, John R. Sgt. NC, age 20 on service record, joined 7 WVI 1862-65.

Dice, Daniel Pvt. age 16, laborer, joined Captain BoggsI, company WVA scouts 3/24/63 taken POW and released 10/17/64.

Graham, Kenison Pvt.* NC, age 25, served first the 25 VAI CSA and subsequently joined the 46 VAM US 7/1/63–7/1/64. A prewar resident of Randolph Co., WVA.

Greenwalt, Jacob Pvt. age 23, farmer, joined Captain E.C. Harper's company 46 VAM US 6/1/63–7/1/64.

Greenwalt, Noah Pvt. age 15, laborer, joined Captain Mallow's company WVA scouts 7/1/63–3/30/65.

Harman, Cyrus Pvt. age 14, joined Captain Boggs' company WVA scouts 4/1/64–5/31/65.

Harman, David H. Pvt.* age 18, laborer, served first the 46 VAM CSA and subsequently joined the 2 VAI US 4/62–4/65.

Harman, Elijah Pvt.* age 27, farmer, served first the 46 VAM CSA and subsequently joined Captain Boggs' company WVA scouts 3/24/63–5/31/65.

Harman, Henry Pvt. age 35, laborer, joined Captain Boggs' company WVA scouts 6/1/64–5/31/65, sick part of 1864.

Harman, Jacob Sgt.* age 17, laborer, served first the 46 VAM CSA and subsequently joined Captain Boggs' company WVA scouts 3/24/63–5/31/65 was absent sick part of 1864.

Harman, John H. Pvt.* age 26, farmer, served first the 46 VAM CSA and subsequently joined Captain Boggs' company WVA scouts 6/1/64–5/31/65.

Harman, Joseph Pvt. age 18, laborer, joined Captain Boggs' company WVA scouts 3/24/63 WIA and POW 1/31/65.

Harman, Moab Pvt. age 37, farmer, joined Captain Mallow's company WVA scouts 7/1/63–3/30/65.

Harper, James D. Pvt. age 21, laborer, served 46 VAM US 1862-65.

Harper, John A. Sgt. age 17, laborer, joined Captain Boggs' company WVA scouts 3/24/63–5/31/65.

Harper, John W. Pvt. age 21, laborer, joined Captain John S. Bond's company WVA scouts 1863-65.

Harper, Martin Pvt. NC, served 149 OHI 1864-65.

Harper, Wm. P. Pvt. age 38, laborer, joined Captain Boggs' company WVA scouts 3/24/63–5/31/65 absent sick 1864.

Hedricks, Adam J. Pvt.* age 16, laborer, served first the 46 VAM CSA and may have served 62–VAI CSA, subsequently joined, Captain Boggs' company WVA scouts 6/1/64 captured and POW 2/24/65.

Hedrick, Henry C. Pvt.* age 19, laborer, served both the 46 VAM CSA and 62 VAI CSA 1861-63, subsequently joined Captain Mallow's company WVA scouts 7/1/63–3/30/65.

Hedrick, John Pvt. NC, served 7 WVI 2/26/62–2/26/65.

Helmick, Benj. F. Pvt. NC, served 22 PAC 11/63–6/65.

Helmick, Matthias Pvt.* age 27, farmer, served first the 46 VAM CSA and the WVA scouts of Captain John S. Bond's company US. Subsequently joined the 7 WVI 12/3/61–1/1/63.

Helmick, Noah C. Sgt. age 22, laborer, joined Captain Boggs' company WVA scouts 3/24/63–5/31/65.

Holmes, George W. Pvt. NC, served 73 OHI 1864–5/1/65.

Huffman, Soloman Pvt.* age 50, farmer, may have served first the 58 VAM CSA and subsequently joined Captain Boggs' company WVA scouts 3/24/63 and deserted.

Judy, Noah Pvt. NC, 1890 census indicates service 46 VAM US 7/1/63–7/1/64. Name not found in militia records.

Kesner, Jacob Cpl. NC, served first the 7 WVI from 11/23/61, subsequently joined Captain Mallow's company WVA scouts, 7/1/63–3/30/65 promoted 4th Cpl. 7/1/64[1]

Kesner, John H. Pvt. NC, joined Captain Mallow's company WVA scouts 7/1/63–3/30/65.[1]

Kesner, Van B. Pvt. NC, served first the 7 WVI 11/23/61–6/29/63 subsequently joined Captain Mallow's company WVA scouts 7/1/64–3/30/65.[1]

Kesner, Wm. Pvt. NC, joined Captain Mallow's company WVA scouts 7/1/63–3/30/65.[1]

Ketterman, Wm. W. Sgt.* age 28, laborer, served first the 46 VAM CSA and subsequently joined Captain Boggs' company WVA scouts 3/24/63–5/31/65.

Kile, George W. Pvt.* age 29, farmer, served first the 46 VAM CSA and subsequently joined Captain Mallow's company WVA scouts 7/1/63–3/30/65.

Kimble, Abraham Pvt.* age 39, laborer, served first the 46 VAM CSA and subsequently joined Captain Mallow's company WVA scouts 7/1/63–3/30/65.

Kimble, Adam Pvt.* age 34, farmer, served first the 46 VAM CSA and subsequently joined Captain Mallow's company WVA scouts 7/1/63–3/30/65.

Kimble, Alfred Pvt. age 32, farmer, joined Captain Mallow's company WVA scouts 7/1/63–3/30/65.

Kimble, Wm. R. Pvt. NC, 1890 census says 46 VAM US 7/1/63–7/1/64. Name not found on Pendleton Co. militia records.

Kimble, Wm. W. Pvt. NC, the only Wm. W. Kimble on the 1860 census is listed as being 9 years old. Pendleton Co. militia records indicate member of Captain Mallow's company WVA scouts 7/1/63–3/30/65.[1]

Kisamore, Adam J. Cpl.* NC, served first the 46 VAM CSA and subsequently joined Captain Boggs' company WVA scouts 3/24/63–5/31/65. Name is Kysemore on militia records.[1]

Kisamore, Jonas Pvt.* NC, served first the 46 VAM CSA and subsequently joined Captain Boggs' company WVA scouts 3/24/63–5/31/65. POW from enlistment to 10/17/63.[1]

Lambert, Albert Pvt. NC, served 11 OHC 6/3/63–1866.

Lewis, Jacob Pvt. NC, joined Captain Boggs' company WVA scouts 3/24/63–5/31/65.

Long, Wm. Pvt. age 32, farmer, served 7 WVI 11/22/61–3/21/63.

Lough, Daniel Sgt.* age 28, farmer, served first the 46 VAM CSA as sergeant, subsequently served Captain Mallow's company WVA scouts as corporal 7/1/63–3/30/65.

Lough, George A. Pvt.* age 41, farmer, 1890 census says 7 WVI 12/4/61–NF. Records of 62 VAI CSA say enlisted 9/27/63 and POW 8/15/64 sent to Camp Chase and Pt. Lookout prisons. Date of birth 8/30/20 died 3/2/95. A justice of the Pendleton Co. court 1852-1861.

Lough, George Pvt. age 34, laborer, joined Captain Mallow's company WVA scouts 7/1/63–3/30/65. WIA NF.

Lough, Josiah Pvt. age 25, laborer, joined Captain Mallow's company WVA scouts 7/1/63–3/30/65.

Lough, Soloman H. Pvt.* age 27, farmer, served first the 46 VAM CSA and subsequently joined Captain Harper's company 46 VAM US 7/1/63–7/1/64.

Mallow, Abraham Cpl.* age 18, laborer, served first the 46 VAM CSA and subsequently joined Captain Boggs' company WVA scouts 3/24/63–5/31/65.

Mallow, George W. Pvt. age 45, farmer, joined Captain Boggs' company WVA scouts 3/24/63–5/31/65.

Mallow, Jacob Pvt. age 31, laborer, served 7 WVI 11/23/63 until 7/1/64 when joined Captain Mallow's company WVA scouts.

Mallow, Moses Cpl. NC, joined Captain Mallow's company WVA scouts 7/1/63–3/30/65.[1]

Middleton, John A. Cpl.* age 14, may have served first the 62 VAI CSA from 7/20/62 deserted 5/11/64 subsequently joined Captain Boggs' company WVA scouts and was dishonorably discharged.

Miller, Isaac P. Pvt. age 20, laborer, served 7 WVI 11/22/61–NF.

Miller, Jacob Pvt.* age 32, served first the 46 VAM CSA and subsequently joined Captain Harper's company 46 VAM US 7/1/63–7/1/64.

Miller, John H. Sgt. age 45, farmer, served first the 7 WVI 11/22/61–9/7/63 and subsequently joined Captain Boggs' company WVA scouts 6/1/64–5/31/65.

Miller, Sam H. Pvt. NC, served first the 7 WVI 11/22/61 Boggs' company WVA scouts 3/24/63–2/14/65.[1]

Morrell, Amos Pvt. age 21, laborer, served 7 WVI 11/22/61–8/24/65.

Payne, John D. Sgt.* age 28, saddler, may have served first the 67 VAM CSA and subsequently joined Captain Boggs' company WVA scouts 3/24/63–5/31/65.

Phares, Wm. Lt.* NC, served first as lieutenant 46 VAM CSA and subsequently joined Captain Boggs' company WVA scouts also as lieutenant 3/24/63 and POW 1/15/64, escaped 2/14/64 at Charleston S.C. back home 4/16/65.[1]

Poole, Lewis R. NC, served as blacksmith 14 PAC 9/18/62–5/30/65.

Rexrode, Hezakiah Pvt.* age 31, farmer, may have served first the 14 VAM CSA. Information he supplied on 1890 census indicates service with 46 VAM US, however name does not appear, in militia records.

Riggleman, Hiram Pvt. NC, joined Captain Harper's company 46 VAM US 7/1/63–7/1/64.[1]

Riggleman, Jeremiah Pvt. NC, listed as veteran 1890 census however name does not appear in US or CS records.

Riggleman, John Pvt. NC, joined Captain Mallow's company WVA scouts 7/1/63–3/30/65.[1]

Ritchie, George W. Pvt.* NC, may have served first the 58 VAM CSA and subsequently joined Captain Boggs' company WVA scouts 3/24/63–5/31/65.[1]

Shirk, Amos Pvt.* NC, served first the 46 VAM CSA and subsequently joined Captain Harper's company 46 VAM US 7/1/63–7/1/64.[1]

Shreve, Nicodemus Pvt.* age 18, laborer, served first the 46 VAM CSA. Information he supplied on 1890 census indicates service with 46 VAM US, however name not found in records.

Shreve, Daniel G. Sgt. NC, joined Captain Mallow's company WVA scouts 7/1/63–7/1/64.[1]

Simmons, Henry Pvt. age 23, farmer, served 7 WVI 11/25/61–2/17/63.

Simmons, Jonas Pvt.* age 30, laborer, served first the 46 VAM CSA and subsequently joined Captain Mallow's company WVA scouts 7/1/63–3/30/65.

Teter, David K. Pvt.* age 17, laborer, served first the 46 VAM CSA and may have served the 62 VAI CSA briefly from 7/3/62. Subsequently joined Captain Boggs' company WVA scouts 3/24/63–5/31/65.

Teter, George Pvt. age 15, laborer, joined Captain Boggs' company WVA scouts 3/24/63–5/31/65.

Teter, Isaac Jr. Cpl.* age 16, laborer, served first the 62 VAI CSA and deserted 8/11/63 in Pendleton County. POW at Camp Chase, Ohio. Agreed to enlist 168 OHI and released, served 5/2/64–9/8/64.

Vance, John A. Sgt.* NC, served first the 46 VAM CSA and subsequently joined the 7 WVI 12/4/61–2/3/63. Joined Captain Boggs' company WVA scouts 3/24/63–5/31/65.[1]

Vance, Reuben Cpl.* age 34, farmer, served first the 46 VAM CSA and subsequently joined the 7 WVI 11/25/61–1863. Joined Captain Boggs' company WVA scouts 3/24/63–5/31/65.

Vanmeter, George S. Cpl. NC, served the 7 WVI 2/26/62–2/26/65.

Watts, Bethuel Pvt. NC, information he supplied on 1890 census indicates service with WVA scouts though name not found in militia records.

Westfall, John Pvt.* NC, may have served the 60 VAI CSA, NF.

Wilfong, Abel Pvt.* NC, served first the 46 VAM CSA and subsequently served the 7 WVI 11/26/61–2/26/62.[1]

Pendleton County Remarks

Bennett, E.—badly broken down
Boggs, J.—RH & now nearly blind
Burns, S.—shot in thigh
Day, A.H.—LD from measles, ¼ disabled at present
Harman, D.H.*—rupture artery, reinlisted Snyder's Scout
Harman, E.*—POW at Richmond
Harman, H.—served another year, has no discharge for
Harman, J.—shot in thigh
Harman, J.—shot through right arm
Harper, J.A.—served a short time, has no discharge for
Harper, J.D.—shot left hip & right fore finger
Harper, W.P.—served another year, has no discharge for
Hedrick, A.C.—POW in Richmond
Helmick, M.—shot through middle of body
Holmes, G.W.—shot through foot
Kesner, W.—shot through hand
Kisamore, J.—POW Richmond 9 months
Lambert, A.—general disability
Long, W.—shot right arm
Lough, G.—disabled left leg by fever, 1/4 disabled(7WVI)
Lough, G.—sent home sick
Malow, M.—measles & catarrah
Miller, I.P.—injured by mumps
Miller, J.H.—headache, MS, weak eyes & KD, reinlisted
Miller, S.H.—KD, LD, reinlisted WV Scouts for protection, served 1 yr 10 mos & 21 days
Morral, A.—shot in left arm
Phares, W.—shot right shoulder & left thigh, POW at Richmond & other places 16 months
Poole, L.R.—disease of stomach, bowells & heart
Ritchie, G.W.*—shot through right arm, now crippled
Teter, I. Jr.—broken veins in leg
Watts, B.—POW

Pendleton Co. Statistics

No. veterans 1890 census	99
United States veterans	58 or 58.6%
Confederate veterans	41 or 41.4%
No. veterans enlisted U.S. & C.S.	39 or 39.3%
No. of veterans who were prewar residents of Pendleton County	85 or 85.8%
No. prewar residents U.S. veteran	45 or 52.9%
No. prewar residents C.S. veteran	40 or 47.1%
No. veterans age identified by 1860 census	67
age of youngest veteran (1860)	13
age of oldest veteran (1860).	50
average age for all veterans	25.8
Distribution by rank: Private	73
Corporal	09
Sergeant	12
Lieutenant	01
Captain	03
Total:	98
(one blacksmith)	
No. veterans occupation identified:	61
Distribution by occupation: farmer	22
laborer	36
judge	02
saddler	01
No. veterans claiming service related disability:	24 or 24.2%
No. veterans wounded in action:	11 or 11.1%
No. veterans held prisoner of war:	05 or 5.0%

Pleasants County

NAME/RANK	REGIMENT	WHEN SERVED
Adams, Henry A. Pvt.	25 OHI	7/8/61–7/8/64
Adams, Jacob Pvt.	4 VAC	8/63–2/64
Adams, Joseph Pvt.	7 WVI	7/4/61–7/4/65
Arn, Frederick Pvt.	14 WVI	2/65–7/3/65
Barcy, Alexander Pvt.	5 OHA	8/14/63–2/15/65
also	186 OHI	2/14/65–9/18/65
Barnes, Wm. H. Pvt.	77 OHI	2/24/64–3/8/66
Bennett, Samuel	NF	
Bier, Wm. E. Sgt.	15 WVI	8/13/62–4/8/65
Blouir, Hiram A. Pvt.	77 OHI	11/3/61–3/12/65
Boley, John Pvt.	1 WVI	11/1/61–12/26/64
Bonar, James C. Pvt.	17 WVI	8/30/64–6/30/65
Brown, Elijah Pvt.	14 WVI	2/20/64–6/27/65
Brown, George W. Pvt.	7 OHI	61/65
Buchanan, Louis S. Pvt.	15 WVI	1/18/64–8/19/65
Butcher, Jehu H. Pvt.	14 WVI	8/9/62–6/27/65
Camron, John R. Pvt.	77 OHI	NF
Carr, Thomas H. Sgt.	1 OHA	9/1/61–7/18/65
Clovis, Theodore Pvt.	10 WVI	1/62–8/10/65
Cole, Alfred H. Cpl.	15 WVI	8/11/62–6/24/65
Coleman, Trickett Pvt.	4 VAC	7/30/63–3/11/64
Cooper, Wm. H. Pvt.	11 WVI	7/12/63–8/9/65
Cornell, Amos Pvt.	17 WVI	NF
Cotton, Abram M. Pvt.	14 WVI	7/12/62–7/24/65
Cronon, John Pvt.	15 WVI	8/10/62–1/20/65
Cross, Albert M. Cpl.	1 OHA	9/1/61–NF
Davis, Kins Cpl.	25 OHI	6/14/61–6/8/66
Davis, Thomas C. Pvt.	77 OHI	2/18/62–7/31/65
Dennis, Joseph A. Pvt.	55 OHI	10/21/64–7/11/65
Deviese, Henry Pvt. Seaman	(Ship) Dafadel	6/64–6/65
Dobins, Henry Pvt.	2 OHA	NF
Dunn, Daniel R. Pvt.	11 WVI	5/13/63–7/4/65
Earley, John M. Pvt.	77 OHI	11/11/61–3/28/66
Earley, Thomas Pvt.	27 OHI	8/61–6/65
Fletcher, Albert Pvt.	10 WVI	3/4/62–8/5/65
Flowers, John H. Pvt.	17 VAI	6/64–7/65
Gardiner, Joseph Sgt.	92 OHI	8/8/62–12/6/64
Garrison, Nathaniel Pvt.	14 WVI	8/12/62–8/14/65
Gatrell, Norman A. Pvt.	11 WVI	7/22/62–2/16/63
also	7 WVI	2/26/64–7/1/65
Gault, Andrew Pvt.	2 WVI	9/61–6/65
Gault, Peter Pvt.	NF	
Giboney, Lewis C. Pvt.	CSA NF (46 BTN VAC)	

Gilmore, Jonathan Pvt.	27 OHI	2/13/64–7/11/65
Glover, Sylvester Pvt.	92 OHI	8/6/62–6/12/65
Goins, Samuel Pvt.	7 WVC	63/65
Gorrell, Archemeds W. Pvt.	14 WVI	8/14/62–3/25/63
Gray, Merriman Pvt.	116 OHI	8/13/62–7/14/65
Greenwalt, Peter R. Pvt.	10 WVI	4/5/62–5/13/65
Hamilton, Samuel	US NF	
Hanes, Theodore W. Cpl.	7 WVI	10/16/61–1/11/65
Hanes, Wm. Pvt.	9 OHC	11/27/63–7/20/65
Harris, John Pvt.	77 OHI	8/10/64–8/10/65
Hashman, Hezekiah Pvt.	36 OHI	2/9/65–7/27/65
Haught, Enos Pvt.	14 WVI	8/14/62–6/27/65
Hays, Wm. L. Pvt.	184 OHI	1/30/65–9/20/65
Hays, Wm. Pvt.	7 WVI	8/7/61–6/9/62
Hendershot, Amos Pvt.	180 OHI	9/26/64–6/7/65
Hernsworth, Lorenzo D. Pvt	14 WVI	8/9/62–7/3/65
Higgans, Wm. Pvt.	15 WVI	7/22/62–5/15/65
Hinds, John M. Pvt.	25 OHI	4/29/61–12/31/66
Hobbs, Enoch N. Pvt.	12 VAI	8/14/62–4/4/63
Hoff, James L. Pvt.	26 IAI	NF
Howell, Benj. F. Pvt.	180 OHI	10/2/64–8/12/65
Howell, Henry Pvt.	154 OHI	2/28/65–6/3/65
Howell, Isaac Pvt.	116 OHI	8/18/62–6/14/65
Hoy, James Pvt.	1 WVC	4/61–3/63
Ingram, John Pvt.	77 OHI	10/8/61–11/64
Ingram, Randall Pvt.	36 OHI	8/17/62–8/17/65
Ingram, Thomas M. Pvt.	129 OHI	7/63–3/64
also	148 OHI	5/2/64–9/14/64
also Sgt.	32 OHI	1/21/65–5/11/65
Jarvis, George H. Pvt.	—WVI	9/61–3/65
Jewell, Samuel Pvt.	77 OHI	8/2/61–3/8/66
Justice, John Pvt.	1 WVI	10/61–10/62
Justice, John W. Cpl.	1 OHI	11/15/61–7/8/65
Kelley, Wm. W. Pvt.	1 OHA	7/4/61–NF
Kerns, John Pvt.	77 OHI	NF
Kidder, Erastus Pvt.	148 OHI	5/1/64–9/14/64
also	195 OHI	2/28/65–12/18/65
Kidder, Rufus Cpl.	188 OHI	5/1/64–9/14/64
also Pvt.	32 OHI	10/12/64–5/11/65
Kincaid, Isaac	NF	
Kincaid, James Pvt.	2 WVC	9/25/61–11/28/64
King, Shepard R. Pvt.	36 OHI	8/61–2/63
Knight, John H. Pvt.	184 OHI	2/1/65–9/20/65
Knight, John L. Sgt.	184 OHI	2/3/65–9/20/65
Little, Thomas J. Pvt.	43 OHC	2/24/65–7/13/65
Marple, John H. Cpl.	17 WVI	8/64–7/65
Marple, Thomas Cpl.	12 WVI	8/14/62–6/16/65

Marsh, Wm. Pvt.	11 WVI	NF
Martin, Calvin B. Pvt.	5 WVC	6/16/61–6/16/64
Mason, James B. Pvt.	11 WVI	3/20/62–3/22/64
also	10 WVI	3/22/64–8/9/65
Mason, John R. Pvt.	7 WVI	8/7/61–8/25/64
McClelland, Tom W. Pvt.	5 WVC	4/25/61–8/20/64
also	7 WVI	3/28/65–7/1/65
McEldowney, James H.	Teamster NF	
McFadden, Enos M. Pvt.	92 OHI	8/13/62–6/11/65
McHenry, James S. Pvt.	10 WVI	1/13/62–8/9/65
McKineY, Robert D. Pvt.	174 OHI	9/13/64–1865
McKnight, James 8. Pvt.	77 OHI	11/61–3/66
McKnight, Wm. S. Pvt.	71 OHI	9/30/64–6/12/65
Meanor, George M. Pvt.	78 PAI	2/24/65–5/27/65
Menges, James Pvt.	66 OHI	9/14/64–7/14/65
Metze, Jacob Pvt.	10 WVI	5/19/62–8/9/65
Miller, Franklin Pvt.	62 OHI	64/65
Miller, George Pvt.	7 WVI	11/18/61–11/17/64
Miller, Greenbery Pvt.	39 OHI	3/65–7/3/65
Miller, James H. Pvt.	187 OHI	2/14/65–1/20/66
Minor, Alexander Pvt.	12 WVI	8/7/62–6/16/65
Morehead, John T. Pvt.	1 OHA	9/11/61–11/12/64
Morgan, Charles W. Pvt.	10 WVI	3/7/62–7/25/65
Morgan, Francis M. Pvt.	3 WVI	7/4/61–8/16/64
Morgan, John S. Pvt.	4 VAC	9/16/64–10/16/65
Myer, Jacob Pvt.	7 WVI	8/7/61–8/1/65
Myers, Henry	NF	
Newland, Andrew Sgt.	6 WVC	6/25/61–8/15/64
Oldfield, John B. Pvt.	14 WVI	8/12/62–7/3/65
Oldfield, Thadeus B. Pvt.	1 WVI	11/1/61–7/16/65
Oliver, John W. Pvt.	187 OHI	2/15/65–1/66
Peterson, Thomas Pvt.	116 OHI	8/22/62–8/8/65
Pickens, John F.	NF	
Pitcher, Wm. Pvt.	43 OHI	2/16/65–6/10/65
Pool, James L. Pvt.	77 OHI	10/61–3/4/66
Pool, Richard Pvt.	180 OHI	8/22/64–7/12/65
Racer, Prescot Pvt.	OHNG	NF
Raiguel, Augustus J.	NF	
Reed, Vincent A. Pvt.	20 VAC CSA	5/62–4/65
Rice, Isaac Pvt.	NF	
Rice, Moses Sgt.	12 PAC	2/28/64–8/10/65
Riggs, Andrew J. Pvt.	14 WVI	8/11/62–6/27/65
Roby, Godfrey C. Pvt.	10 WVI	2/22/64–8/9/65
Ross, Cornelius P. Pvt.	CSA NF (51 VAI?)	
Scott, Esan P. Pvt.	94 ILI	8/7/62–7/17/65
Scott, Westly S. Sgt.	7 WVI	8/7/61–8/18/62
Scott, Wm. Pvt.	168 PAI	10/16/62–7/15/63

Sharp, Spencer J. Pvt.	26 VAI CSA	7/11/63–6/65
Shepherdson, Wm. R. Pvt.	1 WVI	4/5/64–7/19/65
Smith, Joseph S. Pvt.	11 WVI	7/12/63–8/9/65
Smith, Josiah R. Pvt.	2 WVI	6/29/61–1/8/64
Snively, James N. Pvt.	77 OHI	9/15/62–7/19/65
Steel, Henry Pvt.	14 WVI	8/2/62–6/27/65
Stetson, George H. Sgt.	180 OHI	10/4/64–7/26/65
Stine, Jesse M. Pvt.	116 OHI	8/16/62–6/14/65
Stuart, David Pvt.	7 WVI	NF
Thrasher, George B. Pvt.	15 WVI	9/18/62–6/14/65
Tice, Noah Pvt.	77 OHI	11/4/61–10/27/63
also	182 OHI	9/64–7/7/65
Tompson, James F. Pvt.	77 OHI	8/13/61–7/5/65
Villars, Albert Pvt.	11 WVI	6/14/61–8/29/65
Virden, Absalon Cpl.	11 WVI	7/17/62–6/17/65
Wagner, Isaac Sgt.	14 WVI	8/14/62–7/3/65
Watson, George Pvt.	14 WVI	7/14/62–7/3/65
Wells, Christopher Pvt.	39 OHI	3/65–7/65
Wells, Eli D. Pvt.	10 WVI	5/7/63–5/1/65
Wells, Sam W. Pvt.	39 OHI	3/25/65–7/9/65
Westbrook, Westly J. Pvt.	116 OHI	8/62–5/65
Westbrook, Wm. S. Pvt.	180 OHI	9/27/64–7/12/65
Whaley, Tom H. Pvt.	14 WVI	8/9/62–7/3/65
White, Samuel Pvt.	25 OHI	4/30/61–10/62
Williams, George H. Pvt.	22 ILI	6/15/64–9/1/64
Williamson, George W. Pvt.	14 WVI	8/14/62–6/27/65
Williamson, Joshua	NF	
Willis, James Pvt.	37 OHI	10/64–7/65
Wines, Edward	NF	
Wingrove, John Cpl.	77 OHI	11/15/61–3/8/66
Wright, James G. Pvt.	4 WVC	6/63–3/28/64
Wright, John A. Pvt.	4 WVC	7/27/63–3/8/64

Pleasants Co. Remarks

Adams, J.—RH & HD
Adams, J.—shot through leg & measles
Arn, F.—RH
Blouir, H.A.—RH & HD
Boley, J.—gunshot wound in left hand
Bonar, J.C.—HD & KD
Brown, E.—rupture in side
Buchanan, L.S.—RH & CDR
Butcher, J.H.—gunshot in left hip
Carr, T.H.—HD & RH
Cross, A.M.—toes cut off
Davis, K.—piles, RH, HD, affection of eyes

Davis, T.C.—RH & CDR, POW 10 months
Dennis, J.A.—paralisis nerves, KD, POW Tyler TX 10 mo.
Dobins, H.—mashed foot
Dunn, D.R.—CDR
Fletcher, A.—rupture & CDR, drawing pension
Flowers, J.H.—disease of eye, neuralgia head & shoulder
Gardiner, J.—spinal meingitis, rupture of left side
Garrison, N.—CDR, RH & weak eyes
Gatrell, N.A.—LD
Gault, A.—wound right shoulder, disease of eye, HD
Gault, P.—shot in left rist
Gilmore, J.—RH
Glover, S.—CDR
Gorrell, A.W.—RH & HD
Gray, M.—disease of legs
Greenwalt, P.R.—gunshot wounds
Hanes, T.W.—HD Sept 1862, transfered vet reserve core
Harris, J.—RH
Hashman, H.—mashed breast
Haught, E.—RH & HD
Hays, W.—RH & partial deafness both ears
Hays, W.L.—disease of brain & HD
Hendershot, A.—TYF & RH
Higgans, W.—bronchitis & piles
Hinds, J.M.—gunshot in shoulder
Hobbs, E.N.—HD, LD, UFL
Hoff, J.L.—left leg & ankle
Howell, B.F.—CDR
Howell, H.—KD & liver complaint, deafness right ear
Hoy, J.—arsiphlus fever
Ingram, J.—asma
Ingram, R.—loss of hand
Jarvis, G.H.—deafness, wounds & etc.
Jewell, S.—CDR & liver complaint, UFL
Justice, J.—crippled hand
Justice, J.W.—near total deafness right ear & VV
Kelley, W.W.—rupture, totally disabled
Kidder, E.—piles, spinal affection, catarrh in head
Kidder, R.—KD
Kincaid, I.—eyes & lungs affected
Kincaid, J.—injury to spine, total blindness left eye
King, S.P.—dispepsia & liver
Knight, J.H.—RH
Little, T.J.—eyes damaged
Marple, J.H.—bronchitis, "I enlisted in Aug 1862 Com C discharged Feb. of 1863"
Marsh, W.—head, throat, lung & heart disabled
Martin, C.B.—shot right shoulder, shoulder paralyzed

McKiney, R.D.—bronchitis
McKnight, J.B.—disease of stomach
McKnight, W.S.—general disability
Metze, J.—HD
Miller, F.—bronchitis & RH, discharged at Ft Monroe
Miller, G.—scrofla
Miller, G.—weak eyes & lame back, resulting from MS
Minor, A.—CDR, totally disabled
Morehead, J.T.—HD, CDR, LD
Morgan, C.W.—gunshot wound in hand
Morgan, F.M.—RH & HD
Morgan, J.S.—RH & HD, able to do light work
Myer, J.—gunshot wound & HD
Newland, A.—asma
Oldfield, J.B.—wounded in head & shoulder
Oliver, J.W.—CDR, works all the time
Peterson, T.—gunshot left foot, POW Andersonville 5 mo
Pitcher, W.—neuralgia of throat & KD, partial deafnes
Pool, J.L.—general disability by smallpox & malaria
Racer, P.—catarrh 26 years
Reed, V.A.*—harty & sound, only Reb. Sol. in district
Roby, G.C.—RH & HD, able to work if he had too
Ross, C.P.*—LD, discharged by close of war
Scott, E.P.—RH
Scott, W.—rupture, CDR & piles
Shepherdson, W.R.—piles & gunshot wound on left hand
Smith, J.R.—RH, works whenever he can get job
Snively, J.M.—CDR, piles & disease of back
Steel, H.—CDR, piles & disease of rectum
Stetson, G.H.—HD & piles
Stine, J.M.—neurstrophy & nervous sibility
Stuart, D.—fractured right elbow joint, RH & HD
Thrasher, G.B.—RH & piles
Tice, N.—CDR
Trickett, C.—RH, reasonable health
Villars, A.—gunshot wound
Virden, A.—total deafness of left ear
Wagner, T.—breast weak from MS, in 13 engagements
Westbrook, W.J.—RH, HD & piles
Whaley, T.H.—CDR
White, S.—three—fourths disabled, gunshot
Williams, G.H.—wrecked physically, UFL
Williamson, G.M.—MS & LD
Willis, J.—RH back, leg, arm, now feet suffering
Wingrove, J.—bronchitis, lungs & back
Wright, J.G.—loss of palate & LD, this soldier deserves a pension for he is seeing hard times

Pocahontas County

NAME/RANK	REGIMENT	WHEN SERVED
Allen, Isaac W. Capt.	—WV	4/4/64–6/1/65
Apperson, James R. Capt.	31 VAI CSA	61/65
Arbogast, George W. Pvt.	1 WVA	6/15/63–6/27/65
Arbogast, McHenry B. Pvt.	3 WVC	3/15/64–6/30/65
Armstrong, John H. Pvt.	—WV	5/63–4/65
Baslow, Wesley Pvt.	3 VAC	4/62–4/65
Beverage, Jacob M. Pvt.	62–VAI CSA	2/13/63–6/15/65
Beverage, Levi Pvt.	62–VAI CSA	6/1/61–6/1/65
Bishop, David Pvt.	1 WVC	11/20/62–3/20/65
Blair, John W. Pvt.	39 KYI	61/65
Boggs, Madison	NF	
Bright, John E. Pvt.	18 VAC CSA	4/61–4/65
Buzzard, Armenius Pvt.	10 WVI	6/10/62–6/29/65
Collins, Hamilton Pvt.	1 TNC CSA	4/61–6/65
Combs, Armsted Pvt.	11 VAC CSA	4/61–4/65
Cook, Charles Sgt.	3 KYC CSA	8/61–4/65
Courtney, Thomas Pvt.	18 VAC CSA	5/62–6/65
Cullip, Abraham E. Pvt.	3 VAC	6/20/62–7/4/65
Curry, Amos C. Pvt.	31 VAI CSA	NF
Dilley, Jeremiah Pvt.	(19 VAC CSA)	4/4/64–4/6/65
Dilley, Martin C. Pvt.	1 WVA	6/15/63–6/27/65
Duffield, Henry W. Pvt.	6 VAC	3/16/65–7/16/65
Duncan, James H. Pvt.	3 VAC	2/63–6/30/65
Flemer, Henry Pvt.	55 PAA	NF
Flemer, John C. Pvt.	55 PAA	NF
Fleming, James G. Pvt.	1 VAC	5/62–6/64
Foreman, Charles H. Pvt.	39 MOI	3/19/64–3/13/65
Friel, James T. Pvt.	62 VAI CSA	4/62–4/65
Galford, Thomas Pvt.	19 VAC CSA	4/62–6/65
Gatewood, Andrew C. Lt.	11 VAC CSA	4/61–4/65
Gay, Hamilton B. Pvt.	20 VAC CSA	4/1/62–6/1/65
Gay, Joseph C. Lt.	62 VAI CSA	10/62–4/65
Gay, Levi Pvt.	31 VAI CSA	3/62–6/65
Gay, Samuel M? Pvt.	CSA NF (31 VAI)	
Gay, Wm. A. Pvt.	—WVI	5/64–4/65
Geiger, Godfrey Pvt.	62 VAI CSA	1863–4/65
Gordon, Mitchel W. Pvt.	42 VAC CSA	4/64–4/65
Grimes, Zanie B. Pvt.	3 WVC	6/25/63–6/30/65
Hannah, Sheldon C. Pvt.	CSA	62/65
Hannah, Wm. B. Sgt.	—WV	5/63–6/10/65
Hefner, Alexander G. Pvt.	26 VAI CSA	9/63–3/65

Higgins, Samuel C. Pvt.	31 VAI CSA	5/61–6/65
Huggins, Wm. H. Pvt.	36 VAI CSA	NF
Hull, Wm. C. Pvt.	60 VAI CSA	4/62–4/65
Inglow, Solomon Pvt.	39 —	NF
Irvine, George R. Pvt.	CSA (19 VAC)	6/62–6/65
Irvine, John W. Pvt.	18 VAC CSA	9/62–6/65
Jack, Wm. O. Pvt.	31 VAI CSA	63/65
Jackson, John Pvt.	4 VAI CSA	61/65
Jordan, Wm. D. Pvt.	11 VAC CSA	6/61–5/65
Kee, Aaron M. Pvt.	— WV	4/64–4/65
Kee, George M. Pvt.	36 VAC CSA	8/62–4/65
Kelley, Calvin Pvt.	3 WVC	3/1/63–6/19/65
Kelley, Wm. A. Pvt.	3 WVC	3/1/63–6/30/65
Kellison, Clark Pvt.	6 WVC	8/63–5/66
Kellison, Jacob S. Pvt.	—	3/4/62–5/25/62
Kramer, Philip Pvt.	18 VAC CSA	12/1/62–3/1/65
Lakin, James C. Ltc.	27 NYI	9/18/63–7/20/65
Liggon, John Sgt/Ast. Srgn	19 VAC CSA	4/61–6/65
Louk, John E. Pvt.	52 VAI CSA	4/62–4/65
McAlpin, James W? Pvt.	19 VAC CSA	12/63–6/65
McCarty, Peter	NF	
McClintic, Wm. H. Pvt.	19 VAC CSA	63/65
McCormick, Robert H.	NF	
McElwee, Divers B. Pvt.	77 OHI	2/23/64–11/26/65
McGlaughlin, Andrew Sgt.	19 VAC CSA	12/1/62–6/65
McGlaughlin, George H.	CSA NF (19 VAC)	
McKeever, George W. Lt.	— WV	62/65
McNeil, James M. Capt.	22 VAI CSA	6/61–6/65
McNeill, Claiborne Pvt.	31 VAI CSA	3/62–8/62
Miller, John M. Pvt.	52 VAI CSA	4/62–4/65
Moore, David Pvt.	10 WVI	5/29/62–6/28/65
Moore, Jacob S. Pvt.	19 VAC CSA	11/64–6/65
Moore, John R. Pvt.	— WV	10/62–6/65
Moore, Joseph F. Pvt.	10 WVI	5/17/62–6/28/65
Moore, Mathias L. Pvt.	31 VAI CSA	3/62–4/65
Moore, Samuel A. Pvt.	19 VAC CSA	4/62–4/65
Moore, Thomas M. Pvt.	19 VAC CSA	4/62–4/65
Ovesholt, Ruben E. Pvt.	36 VAC CSA	4/61–6/65
Price, James H. Pvt.	19 VAC CSA	1/63–3/65
Price, John C. Sgt.	19 VAC CSA	10/62–6/12/65
Price, Josiah W. Lt.	19 VAC CSA	4/62–6/65
Ratliff, James A. Pvt.	VAC CSA (34?)	3/63–6/65
Ratliff, John M. Pvt.	5 VAI CSA	10/63–6/16/65
Rhea, Charles A. Pvt.	31 VAI CSA	5/62–8/63
Rhea, James B. Pvt.	18 VAC CSA	7/64–6/65
Rider, James Pvt.	6 WVC	6/17/61–8/12/64
Rogers, James L. Pvt.	WV State Guard	1863–4/65

Name	Unit	Dates
Rogers, Wm. B. Pvt.	3 WVI	3/19/62–8/28/62
Saddler, Wm. T. Pvt.	22 VAI CSA	5/62–10/64
Sharp, Abreham Pvt.	3 WVC	3/1/63–6/30/65
Sharp, Charles O. W. Cpl.	3 WVC	6/9/63–6/30/65
Sharp, Henry D. Pvt.	CSA (59 VAI?)	4/64–4/65
Sharp, Morris Pvt.	18 VAI CSA	9/62–1865
Shearer, Henry B. Sgt.	4 VAC CSA	5/61–10/61
Shears, David C. Pvt.	3 MDI	1/15/63–5/29/65
Showalter, Jacob W. Pvt.	5 VAI CSA	4/62–6/65
Silva, Christopher C. Pvt.	—WV	4/64–4/65
Simmons, Jacob Lt.	19 VAC CSA	6/61–6/65
Simons, John Pvt.	31 VAI CSA	4/61–4/65
Slavin, John W.	NF	
Taylor, Andrew N. Pvt.	81 VA (VAM CSA)	1862–4/65
Tracy, John C. Pvt.	VAC CSA (19?)	6/61–4/65
Tyler, John W. Pvt.	3 WVC	3/63–7/65
Varns?, John W. Pvt.	19 VAC CSA	5/61–4/65
Wade, Anderson	NF (26 BTN VAI CSA?)	
Wade, George W. Pvt.	26 BTN (VAI CS)	1862–NF
Wanless, John F. Capt.	4 WVC	8/14/63–NF
Wanless, Stephen H. Pvt.	6 WVI	9/9/64–6/10/65
Ward, Nathaniel Pvt.	39 KYI	12/6/62–9/15/65
Waugh, Beverly Sgt.	3 WVC	2/20/63–6/30/65
Waugh, Levi Pvt.	20 VAC CSA	NF
Wauless, Andrew	NF	
Weiford, John W. Pvt.	6 WVC	3/62–7/65
Wilfong, Benj.	NF	

Pocahontas Co. Remarks

Arbogast, M.B.—LD, bronchial tubes defected
Armstrong, J.H.—shot through left arm (WV State Troops)
Blair, J.W.—fever
Buzzard, A.—gunshot in left hip
Cullip, A.—deafness
Dilley, J.*—RH (served also WV State Scouts U.S.)
Flemer, H.—WIA
Flemer, J.C.—POW 13 months
Gay, L.*—wounded left leg
Grimes, Z.B.—injury to right forearm
Kelley, C.—phltisic
Kelley, W.A.—three ribs broken & leg injured fall from horse
Kramer, P.*—POW Pt. Lookout 16 months
Lakin, J.C.—RH
McElwee, D.B.—ruptured
McNeil, J.M.*—POW Ft. Delaware 19 months
Moore, D.—CDR
Moore, J.F.—gunshot left shoulder & RH
Ratliff, J.A.*—left shot off
Rider, J.—RH & gunshot wound of right arm
Rogers, J.L.—WIA at Duncan's Lane
Sharp, A.—CDR
Sharp, C.O.W.—HD
Shears, D.C.—ruptured at Eliesville
Showalter, J.W.*—POW Ft. Delaware 12 mont h s
Taylor, A.N.*—shot through right leg
Wade, G.W.*—no discharge was home sick at close of war
Wanless, S.H.—asthma
Ward, N.—loss of right eye

Preston County

NAME/RANK	REGIMENT	WHEN SERVED
Adams, George	USN? Wabush?	1861–10/11/64
Adey, Wm. H. Pvt.	3 MDI	5/10/61–5/26/62
Albright, Daniel Sgt.	17 WVI	8/18/64–7/65
Albright, Henry B. Pvt.	6 WVC	3/4/64–5/22/66
Albright, Marcellus Sgt.	6 WVC	3/10/64–6/66
Albright, Samuel Pvt.	17 WVI	64/65
Allen, Joseph M.	2 WVI	NF
Anderson, Eli (C)	NF (63 VAI CSA?)	
Annan, Joseph A. Lt.	6 WVI	9/5/61–6/10/65
Anthony, David Pvt.	45 OHI	8/19/62–6/65
Ashby, Erasmus B. Pvt.	10 WVI	1/23/64–8/9/65
Ashby, George W. Pvt.	3 WVC	10/10/62–7/13/65
Ashby, James F. Pvt.	6 WVC	6/7/61–1/31/64
Atkinson, Charles T.	NF (18 VAI CSA)	
Awnom, Benj. Pvt.	3 WVI	10/9/61–1/5/65
Ayersman, Philip Pvt.	6 WVI	8/29/61–6/10/65
Balyard, John M. Pvt.	7 WVI	4/5/65–8/1/65
Barb, Reuben M. Pvt.	6 WVI	8/12/61–6/10/65
Baugh, Wm. H. Pvt.	4 WVC	8/1/63–3/7/64
also	6 WVI	8/22/64–6/10/65
Bayles, Thomas Pvt.	7 WVI	7/3/61–9/1/62
Bean, John Pvt.	6 WVC	11/63–4/65
Beavers, David R. Sgt.	6 PAI	1/9/63–6/10/65
Beavers, George W. Pvt.	6 WVI	9/3/64–6/10/65
Beavers, Moses C. Pvt.	6 WVI	8/24/64–6/10/65
Bennett, Joshua G.	CSA NF (11 VAC)	
Benson, E. D. Cpl.	6 WVC	6/61–8/65
Benson, James D.	NF (41 VAI CSA?)	
Bickford, Albert Pvt.	2 MDI	9/18/61–10/31/64
Binns, James Cpl.	104 OHI	8/14/62–6/17/65
Bishoff, David D. Pvt.	14 WVI	8/20/62–5/20/65
Bishoff, Elisha Pvt.	17 WVI	2/17/65–6/31/65
Bishoff, Henry Cpl.	—WVI	8/19/61–6/12/65
Bishoff, John H. Pvt.	14 WVI	8/13/62–6/21/65
Bishopp, John A. Pvt.	—WVI	8/19/61–6/12/65
Blake, Hiram Pvt.	6 WVI	1861–6/65
Blaney, John E. Pvt.	3 WVI	6/4/61–6/66
Blaney, Lawrence S. Pvt.	14 WVI	8/12/62–7/3/65
Blanney, Isaac J. Pvt.	7 WVI	12/63–NF
Bolner, John Pvt.	15 WVI	8/22/62–6/14/65
Bolyard, Chrisitan Pvt.	6 WVI	NF

Name	Unit	Dates
Bolyard, Frederick Pvt.	17 WVI	2/7/65–6/13/65
Bolyard, Henry Pvt.	12 WVI	2/25/64–8/9/65
Bolyard, James H. Pvt.	3 WVI	NF
Bolyard, John A. Pvt.	15 WVI	8/22/62–6/14/65
Bolyard, Wm. H. Pvt.	3 WVI	6/23/63–8/8/65
Bomar, Wm.	NF	
Boogher, Alfred Pvt.	17 WVI	1/65–6/65
Bower, Jacob Pvt.	17 WVI	2/23/65–7/5/65
Bowman, Jacob Pvt.	67 PAI	10/64–7/20/65
Braham, Thomas Pvt.	6 WVI	8/30/64–6/10/65
Braham, Wm. J. Pvt.	6 WVI	8/30/64–6/10/65
Brain, John W. Pvt.	NF	
Brand, James F. Cpl.	1 WVC	2/26/64–7/8/65
Brand, Wm. H. QM/Sgt.	1 WVC	8/8/61–7/8/65
Breakeron, Joshua Pvt.	2 MDI	8/16/61–9/28/64
Britton, John W. Pvt.	15 WVI	8/22/62–8/5/65
Broomhall, Wm.	17 WVI	NF
Brown, Lyurgus Pvt.	15 WVI	1862–7/65
Brown, Wm. B. Pvt.	17 WVI	8/64–6/65
Bryte, Milton S. Lt.	3 MDI	3/64–6/65
Buckland, John C. Pvt.	6 WVI	10/19/64–6/10/65
Bucklew, Eugenius Pvt.	6 WVI	3/10/63–6/14/65
Bucklew, John A. Pvt.	6 WVI	4/61–6/65
Bucklew, John E. Pvt.	6 WVI	3/2/62–1865
Bucklew, Wm. J. Pvt.	4 WVC	11/27/63–6/23/64
Butler, John V. Pvt.	17 WVI	9/5/64–6/30/65
Cale, Asreal Sgt.	3 MDI	10/23/61–5/29/65
Cale, Christopher Pvt.	3 MDI	8/17/63–5/29/65
Cale, Elijah Sgt.	7 WVI	7/4/61–9/3/63
Cale, Jacob Pvt.	6 WVI	12/4/61–6/10/65
Calhoun, Reuben C. Pvt.	6 WVI	10/61–6/62
Callens, James Pvt.	6 WVI	6/1/61–6/10/65
Calvert, Enoch Pvt.	6 WVI	10/19/64–6/10/65
Calvert, Josiah Cpl.	6 WVC	5/22/61–6/2/66
Caredy, James Pvt.	6 WVI	2/11/65–6/10/65
Carico, James A. Sgt.	6 WVI	9/5/61–6/10/65
Carr, John Pvt.	12 WII	12/23/63–7/16/65
Carrico, John H. Lt.	6 WVI	9/25/61–6/10/65
Carson, James A. Pvt.	NF (62 VAI CSA?)	
Casady, George Pvt.	6 WVI	5/15/63–6/10/65
Case, Edward W. Pvt.	11 WVC	8/15/61–8/15/64
Cassady, Isaac G.	NF	
Casseday, James Cpl.	10 WVI	2/9/64–8/9/65
Casteel, Soloman Cpl.	7 WVI	7/4/61–6/27/65
Casteel, Thomas Pvt.	3 MDI	5/62–1865
Casteel, Wm. A. Pvt.	7 WVI	7/4/61–2/28/63
Casteel, Wm. H. Pvt.	14 WVI	62/65

Cathell, Plat M.	——	8/23/64–5/1/65
aka Nan M. Fierman		
Caton, George Pvt.	6 WVC	3/4/65–5/2/66
Chidester, Alpheus W. Pvt.	17 WVI	2/28/65–6/30/65
Chidester, Amazial	17 WVI	2/14/65–NF
Chidester, James M. Pvt.	3 WVI	6/28/61–3/1/64
Chidester, Wm. Pvt.	3 MDI	NF
Chidister, George W. Pvt.	6 WVI	NF
Childs, Esiah L. Pvt.	6 WVI	2/10/65–6/10/65
Childs, Jesse A. Pvt.	14 WVI	NF
Chiles, Salathiel H. Pvt.	47 OHNG	5/20/65–5/1/66
Clark, James Pvt.	17 VAI	2/3/64–NF
Clingan, James Pvt.	6 WVC	3/28/64–5/28/66
Cloth, George Pvt.	27 PAI	1861–4/65
Cobern, Davis S. Cpl.	4 WVC	7/9/63–3/7/64
Cobert, John Pvt.	50 PAI	9/28/64–6/2/65
Coburn, Wm. S. Pvt.	6 WVC	3/4/64–10/24/65
Cole, Wm. Pvt.	3 MDI	3/29/62–2/17/63
Collins, Andrew F. Pvt.	3 MDI	3/29/64–6/11/65
Collins, George Pvt.	6 WVC	2/29/64–7/15/65
Collins, George W.	NF	
Collins, John M. Drummer	17 WVI	9/64–7/65
Combs, Henry Pvt.	15 WVI	8/22/62–6/14/65
Combs, John W. Pvt.	6 WVC	6/21/61–8/15/64
Conley, Benj. F. Pvt.	2 PAA	1/3/62–1/28/65
Conner, Michael Pvt.	3 WVI	6/22/61–8/17/64
Copeman, Henry F.A. Cpl.	17 WVI	2/15/65–6/30/65
Corbin, Benj. "Artificer"	1 IAA?	8/17/61–6/16/63
Corbin, Wm. B. Pvt.	17 WVI	9/5/64–6/30/65
Core, Wm. K. Pvt.	6 WVI	1/2/62–5/20/63
Corrils, John M. Pvt.	6 WVI	2/11/65–6/10/65
Costolo, Edward M. Pvt.	17 WVI	2/14/65–6/30/65
Cramer, Wm. H. Pvt.	17 WVI	2/24/65–6/30/65
Crane, Elliott Sgt.	6 WVC	3/4/64–5/22/66
Crane, John C. Sgt.	14 WVI	8/25/62–7/3/65
Crane, Martin L. Cpl.	14 WVI	NF
Crawford, Charles R. Pvt.	37 MAI	7/1/62–6/21/65
Criss, Isaac W. Pvt.	3 WVI	6/61–8/64
Cunningham, Thadeus Pvt.	142 PAI	8/13/62–3/6/63
Cupp, Jacob Sgt.	3 MDI	4/17/62–5/29/65
Cupp, John Pvt.	3 MDI	3/4/62–6/1/65
Cupp, Lewis J. Pvt.	17 WVI	NF
Cupp, Wm. H. Pvt.	3 WVI	8/26/61–8/16/64
Cuppeth, George A. Pvt.	6 PAA	64/65
Dailey, James Pvt.	146 —	9/62–6/65
Davis, Benj. Pvt.	6 WVI	8/22/64–6/10/65
Davis, Joseph W. Pvt.	6 WVI	2/10/65–6/10/65

Davis, Robert S. Cpl.	6 WVI	8/29/61–6/10/65
Dawson, James W. Pvt.	14 WVI	8/62–1865
Deakins, Leonard Pvt.	6 WVI	8/64–6/15/65
Deal, John H. Cpl.	3 MDI	3/30/64–5/29/65
Deavers, Warner W. Pvt.	3 WVI	6/61–7/65
Deavers, Wm. H. Pvt.	6 WVC	6/25/63–5/22/66
Devall, Alpheus Sgt.	6 WVC	3/4/64–7/14/65
Dewitt, Ed P. Pvt.	6 WVI	3/24/63–6/10/65
Dewitt, Richard Pvt.	6 WVI	3/26/63–6/10/65
Dille, John Pvt.	14 WVI	8/62–7/3/65
Dille, Sam A. Sgt.	6 WVC	6/22/61–10/15/65
Dudley, Elias A. Sgt.	1 WVC	7/18/61–7/16/65
Dulin, James M. Pvt.	7 VAI CSA	5/61–1865
Dunbar, John H. Pvt.	96 PAI	6/62–7/65
Edmond, Samuel	—WV	11/5/64–9/21/65
Eichelberger, James D Pvt.	10 WVI	2/16/64–8/9/65
Eliason, Zeri Pvt.	3 WVI	6/21/61–8/64
Elliot, Sam P. Pvt.	7 WVI	7/16/61–2/63
Elliott, Wm. Capt.	NF	
Elsey, Jacob Pvt.	6 WVI	2/11/65–6/11/65
Emerson, James A. Pvt.	6 WVI	6/23/63–6/10/65
Eugle, Wm. Cpl.	6 WVI	10/23/61–6/10/65
Everly, Absalom W. Pvt.	3 WVI	6/22/61–NF
Everly, Adam Pvt.	7 WVI	6/61–7/1/65
Everly, Elijah S. Pvt.	6 WVI	2/29/64–6/10/65
Everly, George H. Pvt.	7 WVI	7/4/61–7/1/65
Everly, John G. Pvt.	4 WVC	7/13/63–3/7/64
Everly, John L. Pvt.	7 WVI	7/4/61–8/7/64
Everly, Joseph H. Pvt.	6 WVI	2/29/64–6/10/65
Everly, Leonard J. Pvt.	4 WVC	7/11/63–3/10/64
also	6 WVC	3/10/64–5/29/66
Everly, Leonard P. Pvt.	3 MDI	7/29/62–5/29/65
Everly, Peter Pvt.	3 MDI	NF
Everly, Wm. H. Pvt.	6 WVC	1/64–NF
Everts, Adam F. Pvt.	17 WVI	2/21/65–6/30/65
Everts, Wm. D. Pvt.	3 WVC	9/62–7/65
Farley, George W. Pvt.	NF (CSA?)	
Father, Jacob W. Cpl.	17 WVI	2/65–6/65
Father, Joseph C. Pvt.	6 PAA	9/64–6/13/65
Faulkner, Tom R. Pvt.	5 WVI	8/9/61–7/26/65
Fawcett, Daniel F. Pvt.	17 WVI	2/20/65–6/30/65
Feather, Abraham Pvt.	6 PAA	9/15/64–6/15/65
Feather, Daniel C. Pvt.	14 WVI	8/15/62–4/11/65
Feather, David S. Pvt.	222 PAA	8/23/64–6/15/65
Feather, Isaac B. Sgt.	7 WVI	7/4/61–2/6/63
Feather, John H. Sgt.	17 WVI	2/14/65–6/30/65
Felton, Henry M. Sgt.	17 WVI	8/64–6/30/65

Field, A.D. Pvt.	3 MDI	8/17/63–5/29/65
Field, Barton Pvt.	6 WVI	9/27/61–11/25/64
Field, George W. Pvt.	6 WVI	9/27/61–11/25/64
Field, Israel B. Pvt.	6 WVC	6/22/61–4/24/65
Field, Richard F. Pvt.	17 WVI	2/22/65–6/30/65
Field, Wm. P. Pvt.	14 WVI	8/15/62–6/27/65
Fike, Wm. H. Pvt.	3 MDI	62/64
Finger, Ephraim J. Drummer	14 ILI	2/18/65–9/16/65
Fiser, James P. Pvt.	NF	
Fisher, Silvester Pvt.	6 WVI	8/22/64–6/10/65
Fogle, Robert B. Pvt.	45 ILI	12/28/61–11/6/62
Fogle, James B. Lt.	14 WVI	8/20/62–6/65
Ford, Benj. F. Pvt.	17 WVI	2/17/65–6/30/65
Ford, Fred G.W. Capt.	15 WVI	8/27/62–6/65
Fortney, Charles S. Cpl.	15 WVI	8/15/62–6/23/65
Fortney, David H. Pvt.	6 WVI	6/25/63–5/25/66
Fortney, Francis A. Pvt.	3 MDI	6/22/61–1/21/65
Fortney, Jacob W. Pvt.	17 WVI	2/11/65–6/30/65
Fortney, John A. Pvt.	6 WVI	3/18/63–5/10/65
Fortney, Wm. F. Pvt.	4 WVC	7/16/63–4/7/64
Fraley, Burbridge F. Pvt.	6 WVC	6/22/63–5/22/66
Francis, Wm. Pvt.	NF	
Frankhose, Martin Pvt.	3 MDI	9/5/61–5/29/65
Frankhouser, Daniel H. Pvt	6 WVC	3/9/64–11/3/65
Freeland, James A. Pvt.	6 WVI	9/27/61–11/25/64
Freeland, John M. Pvt.	17 WVI	2/14/65–6/30/65
Freeland, Samuel Pvt.	7 WVI	2/10/65–6/10/65
Friend, D.A. Pvt.	3 MDI	3/29/64–5/29/65
Froley, John F. Pvt.	— WV	2/62–6/65
Funk, Samuel M. Pvt.	6 WVI	8/29/61–6/10/65
Funk, Wm. M. Pvt.	12 WVI	8/16/62–6/16/65
Galkran, Wm. B. Pvt.	15 WVI	8/22/62–6/14/65
Gandy, Amos F. Pvt.	5 WVC	5/18/61–6/15/64
Gandy, Cornelius Capt.	15 WVI	8/22/62–6/14/65
Gapp, Larkin P. Pvt.	6 WVC	9/25/64–5/19/65
Gibson, Edgar C. Pvt.	NF	
Gidley, Clark Pvt.	1 WVC	6/18/64–6/1/65
Gillis, Hamilton L. Pvt.	3 WVI	61/62
Glover, Andrew Pvt.	3 MDI	5/8/62–4/20/65
Glover, Preston Pvt.	6 WVC	6/28/61–5/22/66
Glover, Wm. H. Pvt.	NF (2 VAC CSA?)	
Glover, Wm. H. Pvt.	3 MDI	2/64–5/29/65
Godwin, Joseph M. Cpl.	6 WVI	11/14/61–12/19/64
Goff, George W. Sgt.	3 WVI	6/28/61–5/22/66
Goff, Hiram M. Pvt.	6 WVC	1/22/64–7/15/65
Goff, Martin N.B. Pvt.	6 WVI	9/5/64–6/11/65
Gooding, Elias Pvt.	3 MDI	3/8/64–5/29/65

Name	Unit	Dates
Gooding, Wm. Pvt.	3 MDI	3/64–6/1/65
Graham, David Sgt.	3 MDI	64/64
Graham, James Pvt.	14 WVI	63/65
Graham, Lee J. Pvt.	45 USC	2/18/65–6/12/65
Greathouse, John C. Pvt.	14 WVI	NF
Greathouse, Reuben Pvt.	3 MDI	8/63–7/65
Greenleaf, Charles H.	USN NF	
Greser, Frank Pvt.	NF	
Griffith, Henry Teamster	6 WVI	9/28/61–6/65
Grim, Henry Pvt.	6 WVI	8/24/61–6/10/65
Grim, Wm. H. Pvt.	NF	
Grimes, Hiram S. Pvt.	6 WVI	10/1/61–6/10/65
Grimes, Wm. M. Pvt.	12 WVI	NF
also	10 WVI	2/25/64–8/9/65
Grimm, George M. Pvt.	87 OHI	NF
also	129 OHI	NF
also	161 OHI	NF
also	185 OHI	1/25/65–9/26/65
Grimm, Harrison Lt.	3 WVI?	61/64
Grimm, Hiram A. Pvt.	NF	
Grimm, Paul Pvt.	15 WVI	8/22/62–6/14/65
Gross, Imanuel Pvt.	7 WVI	7/16/61–12/27/61
Gross, Noah Pvt.	3 WVI	6/22/61–5/22/66
Groves, Sam E. Pvt.	3 MDI	3/27/62–1863
Groves, Wm. H. Pvt.	17 WVI	NF
Guseman, Jacob J. Sgt.	6 WVC	3/4/64–5/22/66
Hagans, H.C. Capt.	3 WVI	6/26/61–3/62
Halbritter, Fred M. Pvt.	15 WVI	2/26/64–8/9/65
Halbritter, Lewis M. Capt.	6 WVC	6/21/61–9/15/64
Hamilton, James M. Sgt.	6 WVC	6/24/63–8/8/65
Hardsty, John Sgt.	7 WVI	10/21/61–6/14/65
Harrington, Francis M. Pvt	4 WVC	7/13/63–3/7/64
Harrington, Thomas Cpl.	15 WVI	8/22/62–6/29/65
Harrington, Wm. J. Pvt.	4 WVC	7/13/63–3/7/64
Harrison, James G. Pvt.	10 WVI	1862–5/65
Hart, Nathaniel Pvt.	202 PAI	NF
also	— PA	NF
also	207 PAI	NF
Hartley, Henry A. Sgt.	14 WVI	8/15/62–6/27/65
Hartman, Elisha Pvt.	4 WVI	NF
Hartman, George W. Cpl.	6 WVI	9/61–6/65
Hartman, Lucian A. Pvt.	3 WVI	5/22/61–8/17/64
Hartman, Michael Pvt.	6 WVI	12/11/61–2/23/64
Hartsell, George W. Sgt.	14 WVI	8/15/62–7/3/65
Hartsell, Jacob Pvt.	NF	
Hartsell, Robert A. Pvt.	17 WVI	2/14/65–6/13/65
Hass, John J. Pvt.	6 WVI	2/23/64–6/10/65

Name	Unit	Dates
Hass, John J. Sgt.	NF	
Hauger, John A. Pvt.	6 PAA	8/16/64–6/13/65
Hawker, Tom D. Pvt.	1 WVC	7/18/61–1864
Hawkins, John W. Pvt.	6 WVI	9/3/62–6/10/65
Hawley, Elisha Pvt.	17 WVI	2/22/65–5/17/65
Hawley, Solomon P. Pvt.	3 WVI	6/22/61–8/64
Hayden, C. J. Pvt.	85 PAI	11/21/61–12/1/64
Hayden, Henry M. Cpl.	85 PAI	12/22/61–5/30/65
Heaten, James Cpl.	6 WVI	8/4/61–10/24/64
Hedron, Samuel Pvt.	3 MDI	8/62–6/65
Hell, Robert H. Pvt.	6 WVI	9/25/61–6/10/65
Helm, Elijah J.	NF	
Helms, George W. Pvt.	3 WVI	6/22/61–NF
Hennry, Thomas Pvt.	85 PAI	64/64
Herndon, James M. Sgt.	6 WVI	10/5/61–12/19/64
Hewitt, John Pvt.	6 WVC	3/4/64–8/12/65
Hey, Henry Pvt.	6 WVI	8/29/61–6/10/65
Hileman, Bartholomew Pvt.	14 WVI	8/15/62–7/3/65
Hileman, John Pvt.	133 PAI	8/6/62–12/15/62
Hileman, Sam J. Pvt.	6 WVI	3/4/64–5/29/65
Hill, John W. Pvt.	17 WVI	1865–7/9/65
Hill, Tom H. Pvt.	14 PAC	64/66
Hinarck, Alexander Pvt.	17 WVI	2/65–7/15/65
Hinebaugh, John Lt.	6 WVC	6/21/61–8/24/64
Hoffman, George F. Pvt.	3 WVI	NF
Hoffman, James A. Pvt.	1 MDI	8/21/61–9/6/64
Hollis, James W. Lt.	3 WVI	5/61–11/7/64
Homer, Wm. H.	US NF	
Hooton, Charles M. Pvt.	6 WVI	8/22/64–6/10/65
Hose, Samuel Pvt.	6 WVC	3/64–8/8/65
Hoveatter, Henry	Wagonmaster	NF
Howard, Cornelius S. Sgt.	4 WVC	7/13/63–3/7/64
Hudson, John M. Pvt.	20 INI	8/62–6/9/65
Huff, Ralph T. Cpl.	6 WVC	2/21/64–5/22/66
Huffman, Elijah S. Pvt.	4 WVC	7/13/63–3/7/64
Huffman, Francis M. Cpl.	3 WVI	6/21/61–2/13/63
Huggins, Albert "Fifer"	3 WVI	6/21/61–8/15/64
Huggins, Eugene Sgt.	6 WVC	1/21/61–8/15/64
Huggins, Linsey Pvt.	6 WVC	6/22/61–1~65
Hunt, Aguilla Pvt.	1 WVC	2/10/65–7/8/65
Jackson, Andrew Pvt.	6 WVI	NF
Jackson, Daniel R. Pvt.	14 WVI	4/5/63–7/3/65
Jackson, George B. Pvt.	1 WVA	9/27/61–1/18/65
Jackson, Henry C. Pvt.	1 MDI	NF
Jackson, James V. Pvt.	1 WVA	9/27/61–1/18/65
Jackson, Sam J. Pvt.	6 WVI	8/29/61–6/10/65
Jefferys, Richard Pvt.	6 WVI	10/5/61–6/5/65

Name	Unit	Dates
Jeffreys, Elisha Pvt.	3 MDI	3/23/64–5/19/65
Jeffreys, Jackson Pvt.	6 WVC	6/26/61–8/16/64
Jenkins, Andrew J. Pvt.	85 PAI	10/22/61–11/22/64
Jenkins, Elisha Pvt.	7 WVI	8/4/61–7/1/65
Jenkins, Eugenius Pvt.	14 WVI	8/14/62–7/3/65
Jenkins, Francis Pvt.	15 WVI	8/22/62–6/9/65
Jenkins, Henry E. Pvt.	17 WVI	2/24/65–6/30/65
Jenkins, Levi H. Pvt.	17 WVI	11/28/62–7/7/65
Jenkins, Wm. H. Lt.	3 MDI	9/22/61–4/12/65
Jenkins, Wm. H. Sgt.	2 WVC	5/20/61–6/14/64
Jenkins, Wm. M. Pvt.	7 WVI	7/4/61–8/7/64
Jessop, Charles Sgt.	33 NJI	6/22/61–6/22/63
Johnson, James W. Pvt.	3 WVI	6/22/61–10/65
Johnson, Jesse M. Cpl.	3 WVI	6/22/61–1/65
Jones, Edwin C. Pvt.	27 INI	8/12/61–1/31/63
Jones, John M. Pvt.	6 WVI	8/22/64–6/10/65
Jones, Wm. Pvt.	3 WVI	11/7/63–9/15/64
Keefover, David L. Pvt.	3 WVI	6/22/61–5/22/66
Kelly, Elias Pvt.	3 WVI	6/21/61–8/27/64
Kelly, John Pvt.	17 WVI	9/64–7/9/65
Kelly, Joseph M.A. Cpl.	4 WVC	7/11/63–3/7/64
Kemp, Milton Pvt.	133 PAI	8/16/62–5/26/63
also	6 WVC	5/63–5/22/66
Kendall, Wm. C. Pvt.	8 OHC	1/5/64–7/30/65
Kenney, Israel Pvt.	6 WVI	12/17/61–12/20/64
King, Eugenus B. Pvt.	17 WVI	2/14/65–6/27/65
King, George H. Lt.	1 WVC	7/15/61–11/15/61
Kirk, Isaiah Capt.	3 WVI	6/61–9/62
Kirk, Richard A. Pvt.	17 WVI	8/26/64–7/7/65
Kirk, Samuel B. Sgt.	17 WVI	2/8/65–6/30/65
Kisner, Sam R. Pvt.	7 WVI	4/9/65–7/65
Knisell, Wm. F. Pvt.	6 WVI	2/18/65–6/10/65
Knott, Philip E. Pvt.	3 WVI	6/20/61–1/25/64
also Sgt.	6 WVC	1/25/64–5/22/66
Knotts, Andrew J. Pvt.	15 WVI	8/22/62–6/14/65
Knotts, James H. Pvt.	15 WVI	2/22/64–2/25/65
Knotts, Lewis Pvt.	3 WVI	6/28/61–8/15/64
Knotts, Robert A. Pvt.	15 WVI	8/22/62–6/14/65
Knotts, Wm. Pvt.	7 WVI	7/4/61–7/8/62
Lampbert, Peter Pvt.	3 MDI	3/1/61–6/2/64
Lanham, Eugeneus Sgt.	14 WVI	8/14/62–6/27/65
Lanham, Zadoc Pvt.	7 WVI	9/1/61–1/7/63
Lantz, David Pvt.	15 WVI	4/22/64–1865
Lantz, Washington Cpl.	15 WVI	8/62–1/65
Laub, George Cpl.	3 MDI	3/21/64–5/28/65
Laughery, David Pvt.	14 PAC	NF
Lautz, Luther L. Pvt.	17 WVI	2/62–7/3/65

Lee, Christopher C. Capt.	7 WVI	NF
Lee, Samuel B. Pvt.	3 MDI	3/2/62–5/29/65
Lemon, Jacob J. Sgt.	3 WVC	9/1/62–6/65
Lenhart, Aaron Pvt.	14 WVI	8/13/62–7/3/65
Lewis, Henry Pvt.	3 MDI	7/22/62–5/29/65
Lewis, Joseph A. Pvt.	NF	
Lictwell, Noah Pvt.	7 WVI	7/4/61–6/30/65
Linton, Cyrus Pvt.	4 WVC	3/13/63–3/7/64
Linton, Sam P. Cpl.	15 WVI	8/22/62–6/14/65
Lipcomb, John H. Pvt.	6 WVI	9/4/64–6/10/65
Lipcomb, Sylvester Pvt.	6 WVI	8/29/61–6/11/65
Lipscomb, David Pvt.	6 WVI	8/29/61–12/31/63
Lipscomb, Joshua Pvt.	6 WVI	9/15/64–6/65
Liston, Abner Pvt.	6 WVI	12/3/61–6/11/65
Liston, Alexander Pvt.	17 WVI	2/14/65–6/30/65
Liston, Henson Pvt.	7 WVI	7/21/61–7/24/64
Liston, John A. Pvt.	6 WVI	12/1/61–12/19/64
Liston, John L. Pvt.	14 WVI	8/14/62–6/27/65
Litchnell, Andrew C. Cpl.	3 MDI	3/62–6/8/64
Longster, Thomas J. Pvt.	7 WVI	9/18/61–2/2/63
Loughridge, Wm. Pvt.	15 WVI	8/22/62–3/27/65
Luois, Wm. Pvt.	3 MDI	2/28/64–5/31/65
Lyons, Aaron J. Chaplain	11 WVI	10/10/63–4/ll/67
Lyons, Henry Pvt.	4 WVC	7/4/63–3/7/64
MaCombs, John M.	US NF	
Magill, George Pvt.	14 WVI	2/63–7/65
Manear, Cornelius W. Pvt.	3 WVI	6/22/61–12/20/64
Manown, James H. Surgeon	14 WVI	2/6/64–7/1/65
Martin, Daniel H. Musician	3 MDI	9/27/64–5/29/65
Martin, Edgar C. Pvt.	6 WVI	3/23/63–6/14/65
Martin, Isaac P. Sgt.	3 WVC	8/22/62–7/10/65
Martin, James K. Sgt.	3 MDI	5/62–5/29/65
Martin, Nathan G. Pvt.	3 MDI	3/29/64–5/29/65
Martin, Rolly F. Musician	7 WVI	7/4/61–7/1/65
Martin, Sam J. Pvt.	—WVI	61/64
Martin, Sam M. Pvt.	15 WVI	8/22/62–6/17/65
Martin, Samuel Musician	17 WVI	2/14/65–7/7/65
Martin, Simon R. Cpl.	3 MDI	3/5/62–5/29/65
Martin, Sylvester Pvt.	3 WVI	6/61–7/65
Martin, Wm. T.D. Pvt.	6 WVI	8/12/64–6/12/65
Massey, Hiram M. Blksmith	4 WVC	7/13/63–3/7/64
Matheny, Silas Pvt.	3 MDI	2/64–3/29/65
Matheny, Elisha M. Pvt.	3 WVI	6/28/61–8/17/64
Matheny, George Pvt.	14 WVI	8/15/62–1865
Matheny, Perry Pvt.	4 WVC	64/64
Matthews, Wm. Cpl.	3 WVI	6/28/61–1862
Maust, Abraham Pvt.	14 PAC	NF

Name	Unit	Dates
Mays, John W. Cpl.	6 WVC	8/7/61–5/15/66
McCauley, James Pvt.	14 WVI	8/15/62–6/29/65
McElroy, John M. Pvt.	116 OHI	8/14/62–6/15/65
McGinnis, John W. Pvt.	6 WVC	6/21/61–5/22/66
McGinnis, Joseph B. Cpl.	3 WVI	6/22/61–2/15/65
McGinnis, Van Y. Pvt.	6 WVI	11/29/61–12/19/64
McGinnis, Wm. A. Cpl.	4 WVC	7/15/63–3/8/64
McKinney, Elisha Cpl.	14 WVI	8/15/62–6/29/65
McKinney, Gouch? Pvt.	13 WVI	8/22/62–6/10/65
McKinney, Samuel Pvt.	7 WVI	7/61–1/63
McKinney, Sansom W. Pvt.	17 WVI	3/64–7/65
McKinney, Joseph J. Cpl.	14 WVI	8/15/62–6/29/65
McMillen, Benj. V. Pvt.	17 WVI	7/10/63–NF
also	4 WVC	2/20/65–7/65
McMillen, James C. Pvt.	3 MDI	NF
McNare, Perry Pvt.	3 MDI	2/14/65–7/7/65
McPeck, Wm. Pvt.	3 WVI	6/7/61–6/66
McSolie, Henry C. Pvt.	3 WVC	11/1/62–4/8/63
McTire, George W. Pvt.	6 WVI	6/22/62–6/10/65
McWilliams, John Pvt.	4 WVC	7/14/63–3/9/64
Means, Isaac Pvt.	17 WVI	8/28/64–7/7/65
Menear, Wm. F. Cpl.	3 WVI	6/22/61–5/22/66
Menen, Jacob L. Pvt.	2 PAA	6/26/63–1/29/66
Meredith, Ennix Pvt.	85 PAI	NF
Messenger, Edmund Cpl.	17 WVI	2/65–NF
Messenger, Elijah Pvt.	17 WVI	2/18/65–7/8/65
Messenger, Marcellus Pvt.	6 WVI	2/10/65–6/10/65
Messenger, Samuel Pvt.	6 WVI	10/12/61–12/18/64
Messenger, Solomon W. Pvt	6 WVI	9/18/61–6/12/65
Methany, George W.	NF	
Metheny, Joseph M. Cpl.	17 WVI	2/17/64–6/30/65
Metheny, Silas M. Pvt.	3 MDI	2/64–5/65
Metheny, Wm. H. Cpl.	3 MDI	1/64–6/65
Michael, Joseph W.	NF	
Michaels, John F. Cpl.	17 WVI	NF
Miller, George W. Pvt.	17 WVI	8/64–7/65
Miller, Hesacire Pvt.	6 WVI	11/21/62–6/10/65
Miller, Israel Pvt.	17 WVI	2/28/65–7/6/65
Miller, James G. Pvt.	6 WVI	4/21/62–4/30/65
Miller, John M. Pvt.	6 WVC	7/21/61–3/7/64
Miller, John Pvt.	17 WVI	9/1/64–6/13/65
Miller, Joseph A. Pvt.	3 MDI	5/27/62–5/29/65
Miller, Levi G. Cpl.	3 WVC	NF
Miller, Wm. H. Pvt.	3 WVI	NF
Minear, Amos J. Pvt.	14 WVI	8/62–7/65
Minear, Benj. F. Pvt.	3 WVI	6/22/61–8/27/65
Minear, Hiram Pvt.	3 WVI	6/61–8/64

Minear, Wm. C. Pvt.	14 WVI	61/64
Minifee, James T. Bugler	4 WVC	7/14/63–3/7/64
Mitchnell?, John Pvt.	3 MDI	3/8/62–6/8/65
Modespaugh, James Pvt.	NF	
Moon, George W. Pvt.	6 WVI	12/9/61–12/14/64
Moran, John Pvt.	23 ILI	6/1/62–6/1/65
Morris, David Y. Pvt.	14 WVI	NF
Murdock, James E. Lt.	7 WVI	7/4/61–11/24/64
Murphy, Warren Pvt.	3 WVC	9/3/62–6/6/65
Myers, James S. Pvt.	6 WVI	9/14/61–6/8/65
Myers, Wm. C. Pvt.	3 WVI	9/12/61–1/21/65
Neal, Daniel W.O. Pvt.	54 PAI	9/17/61–12/16/64
Neff, John T.	NF	
Neff, Wm. W. Pvt.	6 WVC	3/4/64–6/1/66
Nine, John W. Pvt.	6 WVI	2/11/65–6/10/65
Nose, Eli Pvt.	12 WVI	2/19/64–6/28/65
Nose, Samuel Pvt.	12 WVI	2/19/64–7/28/65
O'Conor, John Pvt.	NF	
Obrien, Thomas Pvt.	36 NYI	NF
Orr, Ami Pvt.	4 WVC	7/14/63–3/30/64
also	17 WVI	9/1/64–6/30/65
Orr, Miles H. Pvt.	14 WVI	8/15/62–6/27/65
Orr, Uriah N. Sgt.	6 WVI	1861–NF
Paling, Peter M. Pvt.	2 PAA	1/29/62–2/12/65
Paul, —— Capt.	15 WVI	8/22/62–1864
Paul, Amody?	NF	
Paul, George Pvt.	3 WVC	9/30/62–6/30/65
Peaslee, John K. Pvt.	6 WVI	8/29/61–6/21/65
Pell, Thomas A. Pvt.	11 WVI	2/5/65–6/30/65
Pell, Wm. F. Pvt.	2 WVI	5/20/61–5/14/64
Perkins, John G. Pvt.	6 WVI	2/7/64–6/10/65
Perrill, James I. Pvt.	3 WVI	6/22/61–8/17/64
Perrill, John A. Pvt.	3 WVI	6/22/61–7/8/64
Peters, John A.	NF (2 BTN MDI CSA?)	
Phillips, Oliver Cpl.	1 WVC	5/20/61–7/17/65
Pifer, Andrew J. Pvt.	6 WVI	1/64–7/65
Pifer, Joshua Pvt.	6 WVI	10/64–6/65
Piles, Caleb Pvt.	6 WVI	2/14/65–6/14/65
Piles, Charles W. Pvt.	17 WVI	2/9/65–6/30/65
Piles, Cornelious Pvt.	3 WVC	6/22/61–7/15/65
Piles, John C. Pvt.	6 WVI	2/14/65–6/14/65
Plum, James Pvt.	15 WVI	8/22/62–6/14/65
Plum, John C. Pvt.	6 WVI	8/29/61–6/10/65
Plum, Wm. J. Pvt.	15 WVI	8/22/62–6/14/65
Posten, Nicholas Pvt.	14 WVI	8/15/62–6/27/65
Pratt, John W. Pvt.	6 WVC	8/26/64–5/19/65
Pratt, Richard Pvt.	3 WVI	61/62

Price, Grandison T. Pvt.	6 WVI	9/64–6/65
Pugh, Alpheus Pvt.	17 WVI	9/11/64–6/30/65
Pulliam, James Pvt.	3 MDI	12/61–5/27/64
Purinton, John R. Pvt.	9 MIC	6/19/63–6/22/65
Radabaugh, John A. Pvt.	14 WVI	7/62–4/64
Radabaugh, John H. Pvt.	WVI	
Radihour?, George H. Pvt.	6 WVI	3/1/64–3/26/66
Radihour?, Wm. B. Pvt.	6 WVI	3/1/64–2/6/65
Ratliff, Colbert Pvt.	39 KYI	3/19/62–9/15/65
Reckard, Joseph Pvt.	168 PAI	10/16/62–5/63
Reedy, Eli Pvt.	10 WVI	2/28/65–8/9/65
Reid, Robert B. Pvt.	14 WVI	4/5/63–6/27/65
Renshaw, Aaron E. Pvt.	6 WVI	9/21/61–11/25/64
Rhino, Fromhart Pvt.	NF	
Rhodes, Joseph T. Pvt.	6 WVI	9/5/61–6/10/65
Richards, Anthony F. Pvt.	4 WVC	8/1/63–3/12/64
Richter, Fred J. Pvt.	6 WVI	11/25/61–6/10/65
Rickard, Henry L. Pvt.	7 WVI	7/4/61–8/11/64
Rickard, Jacob Pvt.	17 WVI	9/3/64–6/30/65
Riddle, Wm. C. Pvt.	1 WVC	7/18/61–9/22/64
Ridenour, Wm. M. Pvt.	14 WVI	8/15/63–7/4/65
Rigg, John D. Sgt.	7 WVI	7/4/61–6/19/62
Riley, David Pvt.	6 WVC	3/64–4/66
Riley, Mark Pvt.	15 WVI	7/62–6/65
Riley, Mark M. Pvt.	4 WVC	6/63–1864
Ringer, Andrew J. Pvt.	4 WVC	7/11/63–10/7/64
also	6 WVC	3/10/64–6/14/65
Ringer, Jacob H. Pvt.	168 PAI	10/17/62–7/24/63
also	6 WVC	9/18/64–5/65
Ringer, Preston Cpl.	3 WVI	6/28/61–8/15/64
Robinson, Cyrus Pvt.	6 MDI	NF
Robinson, James M. Pvt.	12 WVI	8/16/62–6/16/65
Romesburg, Samuel Pvt.	12 OHC	10/9/63–11/2/65
Rowe, Alpheus E. Pvt.	CSA NF (46 BTN VAC?)	
Roy, Wm.	Teamster NF	
Rude, George Pvt.	3 WVC	12/31/61–2/12/63
Runner, John Pvt.	15 WVI	8/22/62–6/14/65
Rush, Jacob W. Pvt.	212 PAA	8/64–6/65
Sanders, John S. Pvt.	6 WVI	5/61–10/63
Sanders, Thomas W. Pvt.	6 WVI	8/28/64–6/10/65
Sapp, Benj. F. Lt.	1 WVC	6/22/61–1865
Sauders, Andrew J. Pvt.	3 MDI	3/20/64–5/29/65
Scott, Amos C. Sgt.	15 WVI	8/22/62–6/14/65
Seece, Andrew J. Pvt.	NF	
Seth?, Daniel W. Pvt.	6 WVI	10/1/64–6/3/65
Shafer, Cyrus Pvt.	4 WVC	8/2/63–3/7/64
also	6 WVC	NF

Shaffer, Alpheus F. Cpl.	6 WVC	2/29/64–5/29/66
Shaffer, David Pvt.	6 WVC	8/22/64–5/19/65
Shaffer, Draper C. Sgt.	10 WVI	3/20/62–5/7/65
Shaffer, George M. Pvt.	6 WVC	NF
Shaffer, John R. Pvt.	6 WVI	64/65
Shaffer, Wm. A. Pvt.	3 MDI	3/29/62–5/29/65
Shahan, Abraham Pvt.	17 WVI	2/20/65–6/30/65
Shahan, Allen Pvt.	15 WVI	1/26/64–8/9/65
Shahan, Hiram Pvt.	6 WVC	6/19/61–8/12/64
Shahan, Martin L. Pvt.	6 WVC	6/21/61–8/15/64
Shahan, Rawley Pvt.	6 WVC	6/21/61–8/15/64
Shahan, Richard Pvt.	6 WVI	9/13/61–10/20/64
Shahen, Miner Pvt.	6 WVI	8/15/61–8/15/64
Sharps, Allen Pvt.	5 WVC	1863–5/22/66
Sharps, James P. Pvt.	3 WVI	61/65
Shaw, John Pvt.	NF	
Shaw, Joseph M. Sgt.	6 WVI	8/61–10/8/65
Shaw, Leroy Cpl.	7 WVI	7/4/61–5/22/66
Shaw, Thomas J. Pvt.	15 WVI	8/22/62–6/14/65
Shay, Benj. Blksmith	6 WVC	6/28/63–5/22/66
Sheets, Luther W. Pvt.	3 WVC	2/10/64–1865
Showalter, Tom J. Pvt.	6 WVI	9/6/64–1/13/65
Shrout, Andy J. Pvt.	3 WVC	10/30/61–6/30/65
Shrout, Charles W. Pvt.	NF	
Shrout, James W. Pvt.	6 WVI	11/30/64–6/10/65
Shutteworth, Benj. Pvt.	4 WVC	7/14/63–3/7/64
also	17 WVI	2/10/64–6/30/65
Sigley, Wm. F. Pvt.	15 WVI	8/22/62–6/22/65
Sinclair, Alexander Pvt.	6 WVI	9/61–6/65
Sinclair, George Pvt.	NF	
Sinclair, Silas Pvt.	17 WVI	8/29/64–6/13/65
Sinclair, Wm. Pvt.	6 WVI	NF
Sisler, Alfred Cpl.	3 WVC	9/23/62–6/30/65
Sisler, Andrew S. Pvt.	4 WVC	7/25/63–3/7/64
also	7 WVI	9/5/64–6/30/65
Sisler, Sam A. Pvt.	7 WVI	NF
Sisler, Samuel B. Pvt.	NF	
Smalley, Sanson W. Cpl.	6 WVI	12/61–1864
Smallwood, Robert M. Pvt.	14 WVI	6/5/62–7/5/65
Smith, Henry A. Pvt.	4 WVC	7/63–7/65
Smith, Isaac H.	17 WVI	NF
Smith, James W. Pvt.	4 WVC	7/20/63–3/7/64
Smith, John H. Pvt.	110 PAI	3/20/63–7/17/65
Smith, John Pvt.	4 PAC	11/30/63–7/25/65
aka Charles Smith		
Smith, John Teamster	6 WVI	8/29/61–10/18/64
Smith, John W. Pvt.	— OH	7/21/63–11/1/65

Smith, L.H. Pvt.	3 MDI	8/13/62–5/25/63
Smith, Lewis Pvt.	3 MDI	2/10/62–5/29/65
Smith, Mathias B. Pvt.	3 WVC	9/28/62–6/63
Smith, Wm. H. Pvt.	17 WVI	2/22/65–6/8/65
Smith, Wm. H. Pvt.	4 WVC	7/14/63–3/27/64
Smith, Wm. M. Pvt.	17 WVI	2/14/65–6/27/65
Smouse, Edward Pvt.	2 MDI	4/15/65–6/29/65
Snider, Wm. D. Drummer	6 WVI	NF
Snyder, Albert J. Pvt.	17 WVI	2/28/65–6/28/65
Snyder, Simon Pvt.	6 WVI	10/5/61–5/63
Sommers, Tom M. Pvt.	3 USI	6/21/61–11/6/62
Spears, Sam J. Pvt.	29 MEI	12/31/63–6/21/66
Spenser, John Pvt.	3 MDI	2/27/64–5/29/65
Spielman, John P. Pvt.	3 MDI	2/21/64–5/29/65
Spiker, John J. Pvt.	6 WVC	3/4/64–4/14/66
Spiker, Robert R. Pvt.	3 WVI	6/26/61–8/16/65
Spurgeon, George B. Cpl.	3 WVI	6/61–1863
Squires, John H. Cpl.	3 WVI	6/21/61–8/15/64
Squires, Thomas S. Pvt.	4 WVC	7/20/63–7/8/65
Stafford, Seth D.L. Pvt.	3 WVI	NF
also	6 WVC	6/22/61–5/15/65
Stafford, Wm. E. Pvt.	6 WVC	5/20/61–11/26/64
Stafford, Wm. H. Pvt.	14 WVI	4/13/64–6/27/65
Stemple, Louis S. Pvt.	17 MAI?	2/24/65–7/65
Stone, John C. Pvt.	17 WVI	64/65
Stonebraker, James Pvt.	6 WVI	1861–6/10/65
Stonebraker, Volentine Pvt	3 MDI	4/12/62–2/26/65
Strawser, Wm. Pvt.	6 WVI	6/62–6/65
Street, Wm. J. Pvt.	3 WVC	5/61–6/65
Stuck, Edgar C. Pvt.	3 WVI	6/61–8/64
Stuck, Mathias F. Pvt.	6 WVI	63/64
Sutton, Eugene K. Pvt.	3 PAA	12/29/63–11/14/65
Swearengen, Marmaduke Pvt.	1 WVA	8/62–1865
Sypolt, Clark Cpl.	3 WVC	8/28/62–7/9/65
Sypolt, Eugenius Pvt.	NF	
Talbott, James Pvt.	3 WVC	9/25/62–6/30/65
Taylor, Caleb Pvt.	17 WVI	2/24/65–6/30/65
Taylor, George W. Pvt.	3 MDI	7/29/62–5/29/65
Taylor, James C. Pvt.	6 WVI	9/23/61–6/10/65
Taylor, Joseph Pvt.	3 MDI	8/62–5/29/65
Taylor, Sam N. Pvt.	6 WVI	2/14/65–6/14/65
Taylor, Wm. B.	NF	
Taylor, Zachariah Pvt.	3 MDI	8/17/63–6/3/65
Teats, Isaac Pvt.	3 WVI	6/22/61–3/22/65
Teats, Lewis Pvt.	7 WVI	7/4/61–2/7/63
Teets, Albert Lt.	3 WVC	10/12/61–6/30/65
Teets, Elisha Pvt.	3 WVI	9/17/61–6/1/65

Teets, George H. Pvt.	17 WVI	9/5/64–6/30/65
Teets, Levi Pvt.	11 WVC	NF
Thomas, Abraham	US NF	
Thomas, Andrew J. Pvt.	17 WVI	2/17/65–6/13/65
Thomas, Jacob Pvt.	17 WVI	2/17/65–6/10/65
Titchewell, Simon B. Cpl.	14 WVI	8/15/62–7/3/65
Titchnell, Jack Pvt.	17 WVI	2/14/65–7/7/65
Titchnell, Peter Pvt.	3 MDI	5/8/61–5/29/65
Titchwell, Silas Pvt.	3 MDI	3/63–6/9/65
Trickett, Harmon Pvt.	NF	
Trippitt, Caleb J. Cpl.	19 VAI CSA	9/61–NF
Trisle, Samuel Pvt.	3 WVC	9/20/62–7/13/65
Trotter, James Pvt.	168 OHI	5/21/64–9/14/64
Trowbridge, John W. Pvt.	3 WVI	6/22/61–8/17/64
Tucker, Horace	NF	
Turner, John W. Fvt.	4 WVC	1863–3/10/64
Turner, Thomas A. Pvt.	3 WVI	6/22/61–9/18/62
also	4 WVC	3/7/64–NF
Uphold, James Pvt.	2 MDI	61/65
Uphold, Norman Pvt.	2 WVI	2/1/62–3/18/63
Uppole, David E. Pvt.	1 MDI	9/13/61–6/16/65
Vansickle, Elias Pvt.	6 WVC	9/1/64–5/22/66
Vanwert, Chrisitan F. Pvt.	6 WVI	10/4/61–12/19/64
Waddle, Richard B. Sgt.	6 WVC	3/4/64–5/28/66
Walker, John T. Pvt.	12 WVI	1/4/64–8/9/65
Walles, James Pvt.	12 PAC	2/5/62–7/20/65
Walls, Solomon C. Pvt.	6 WVI	61/65
Walls, John M. Pvt.	4 WVC	7/13/63–3/7/64
Walls, Sam G. Pvt.	4 WVC	7/14/63–7/64
Walls, Soloman Cpl.	3 MDI	8/15/62–5/29/65
Walters, Wm. Pvt.	15 WVI	8/22/62–6/14/65
Watkens, John C.R. Pvt.	6 WVI	8/29/61–10/18/64
Watkins, Raese Pvt.	3 PAI	4/17/61–7/30/61
Watson, George W. Pvt.	17 WVI	9/2/64–6/65
Watson, James W. Pvt.	14 WVI	8/14/62–6/27/65
Watson, Joseph	NF (26 BTN VAI CSA?)	
Watson, Santford Sgt.	3 WVI	6/20/61–7/64
Watson, Thomas J. Sgt.	20 OHI	8/18/61–8/27/65
Watson, Wm. S. Pvt.	3 MDI	2/64–6/65
Watts, Alexander Cpl.	2 WVI	9/9/61–NF
also Pvt.	5 WVC	6/64–10/30/64
Weaver, Jacob D.	NF	
Welburn, Ralph T. Pvt.	3 MDI	11/1/61–9/30/62
Welch, Jacob H. Sgt.	7 WVI	7/4/61–9/17/63
Welsh, Joseph J. Pvt.	6 WVI	9/28/61–6/11/65
Wheeler, Henry H. Sgt.	6 WVI	8/29/61–10/18/64
Whetsell, Wm. H. Cpl.	17 WVI	8/1/63–7/1/65

Name	Unit	Dates
White, Joseph Pvt.	4 IAI	7/1/63–12/31/63
also Cpl.	11 IAI	1/1/64–7/25/65
Whitehair, Edmond Pvt.	17 WVI	2/65–6/65
Whiting, Isaac E. Pvt.	NF	
Wilbern, Albert P. Pvt.	78 OHI	10/18/64–7/5/65
Wile, Leonard Pvt.	15 WVI	8/22/62–6/19/65
Wilhelm, Christian Pvt.	NF	
Wilhelm, David Pvt.	3 MDI	5/10/62–6/27/65
Wilkin, Isaac Pvt.	4 WVC	7/13/63–3/7/64
Williams, Andrew J. Pvt.	1 WVI	5/21/61–8/24/61
also	1 WVA	8/20/63–4/15/64
Williams, George Cpl.	10 WVI	4/21/62–5/7/65
Williams, John Cpl.	14 WVI	1862–7/3/65
Wilson, George W. Pvt.	6 WVI	1/4/64–6/11/65
Wilson, Wm. Cpl.	17 WVI	2/14/65–7/7/65
Wilt, David S. Sgt.	6 WVC	3/2/64–5/66
With?, H.K. Pvt.	13 WVI?	2/24/65–7/7/65
Wolf, George W. Pvt.	17 WVI	2/15/65–6/30/65
Wolf, Wm. Pvt.	1 WVC	10/1/61–7/8/65
Wolring, Samuel Pvt.	6 WVC	3/4/64–5/22/66
Wolring, Henry G. Pvt.	6 WVI	NF
Wolring, Wm. J. Cpl.	12 WVI	8/16/62–6/16/65
Worthington, Eugene A. Pvt	NF	
Wright, Henry C. Pvt.	6 WVI	12/1/61–12/2/64
Wright, James P. Pvt.	7 WVI	1/30/62–6/30/65
Yeast, Wm. Pvt.	6 WVC	3/1/64–NF
Zinn, Alexander W. Cpl.	4 WVC	7/5/63–1865
Zinn, George H. Pvt.	4 WVC	7/13/63–3/7/64
Zinn, George P. Pvt.	4 WVC	7/13/63–3/7/64
Zinn, George W. Pvt.	107 PAI	9/64–6/65
Zinn, Oliver Pvt.	4 WVC	7/63–3/64
Zinn, Wm. H. Pvt.	4 WVC	7/13/63–3/7/64

Preston County Remarks

Adey, W.H.—RH, crippled knee, stricture of urethra
Albright, D.—RH
Albright, H.B.—RH
Albright, M.—CDR & piles
Albright, S.—CDR & RH
Anderson, E.—ruptured
Ashby, E.E.—RH & HD
Ashby, G.W.—RH 26 years, asthma 10 years
Ashby, J.F.—KD
Awnom, B.—LD
Balyard, J.M.—MS, LD & epilected
Barb, R.M.—gunshot wound
Baugh, W.H.—RH
Bayles, T.—CDR 28 years
Bean, J.—RH & asthma
Beavers, D.R.—partial blindness from smallpox
Beavers, G.W.—catarrh in head
Beavers, M.C.—catarah & RH
Bennett, J.G.★—diserted the rebel army
Bickford, A.—CDR, fever, ague
Binns, J.—gunshot wound, scurvy & piles 25 years
Bishoff, D.D.—HD
Bishoff, E.—RH
Bishoff, H.—bilious colic
Bishoff, J.H.—shot in head
Bishopp, J.A.—RH
Blaney, J.E.—RH & LD
Blaney, L.S.—LD
Blanney, I.J.—MS, MP, soreness in back
Bolner, J.—WIA left breast
Bolyard, H.—HD, KD, eyes affected
Bolyard, W.H.—CDR
Bomas, W.—RH & hearing
Bower, J.—RH & KD
Brain, J.W.—RH
Brand, J.F.—ague & RH
Brand, W.H.—asthma, MS, WIA left thigh
Breakeron, J.—piles 27 years
Britton, J.W.—WIA right hip joint
Brown, L.—asthma, CDR, deafness
Brown, W.B.—RH & LD
Bryte, M.S.—double hernia
Buckland, J.C.—RH & HD
Bucklew, E.—TYF

Bucklew, J.E.—RH, rupture
Bucklew, W.J.—KD & HD
Cale, C.—RH & piles
Cale, E.—HD & LD
Cale, J.—RH
Calvert, J.—RH & LD
Combs, H.—RH & CDR 27 years
Carr, J.—RH
Carrico, J.H.—LD & RH
Carson, J.A.*—ruptured
Cassady, I.G.—ruptured & neuralgia of stomach
Casseday, J.—LD & brest disease
Casteel, T.—CDR 27 years
Casteel, W.A.—liver disease
Casteel, W.H.—POW Andersonville 7 months, HD & RH
Cathell, P.M.—LD, DSC
Caton, G.—RH, crippled knee
Chidester, A.W.—RH, KD, liver disease
Chidester, J.M.—lost left arm at elbow, taken POW
Chidister, G.W.—VV
Childs, J.A.—shot in the thigh
Chiles, S.H.—catarrh
Clark, J.—piles, CDR, RH came home got sick
Cobern, D.S.—blindness & RH
Cole, W.—piles
Collins, A.F.—SS & malary poison
Collins, G.W.—WIA right elbow
Collins, J.M.—bronchitis, LD & throat disease
Conley, B.F.—scarlet fever
Corbin, B.—HD, eye trouble, DSC
Corbin, W.B.—atrophy right side, draws a pension
Core, W.K.—asthma
Costolo, E.M.—piles
Cramer, W.H.—ruptured
Crane, E.—RH
Crane, J.C.—chronic neuralgia
Crawford, C.R.—shell wound resulting deafness
Criss, I.W.—liver disease result of jaundice
Cunningham, T.—lost left arm at shoulder
Cupp, J.—HD
Cupp, J.—RH & CDR
Cupp, L.J.—piles & scurvy
Cupp, W.H.—wound in right thigh
Dailey, J.—POW Andersonville, HD, CDR
Davis, J.W.—CDR
Deavers, W.H.—disabled from scurvy & RH
Deavers, W.W.—almost blind

Devall, A.—RH
Dille, J.—RH & LD
Dille, S.A.—CDR & piles
Dulin, J.M.*—WIA left leg at 7 pines
Eichelberger, J.—WIA head & eyes by shell
Eliason, Z.—CDR
Elliott, S.P.—CDR
Elliott, W.—brigade quartermaster served 14 months
Emerson, J.A.—3 ribs broken in servis
Eugle, W.—RH
Everly, A.—wound in neck
Everly, E.S.—scarlet fever settling in head
Everly, J.G.—RH & piles
Everly, J.H.—back hurt, privates
Everly, J.L.—RH claims to have killed Stonewall Jacksn
Everly, P.—RH
Everly, W.H.—mashed back, scurvy, KD
Everts, A.F.—CDR & RH
Everts, W.D.—KD
Father, J.C.—LD
Father, J.W.—RH & eyes affected
Faulkner, T.R.—WIA left arm, chronic nervousness
Fawcett, D.F.—RH & HD
Feather, D.C.—wound
Feather, I.B.—HD & LD
Feather, J.H.—asthma & RH
Field, A.D.—CDR, disease of back & kidneys
Field, B.—LD
Field, G.W.—KD
Field, I.B.—gunshot wound
Field, R.F.—wounded in thigh
Field, W.P.—LD
Fisher, S.—RH
Fogle, J.B.—deafness for 26 years
Fogle, R.B.—piles, CDR, hearing
Ford, F.G.W.—CDR, rupture, sprained ankle
Fortney, C.S.—WIA right leg, contracted CDR in 1865
Fortney, D.H.—RH 25 years, frozen feet in service
Fortney, F.A.—POW Andersonville 4 months, RH & CDR
Fortney, J.A.—fever & ague, causing enlarged spleen
Fraley, B.F.—liver & kidney disease
Frankhose, M.—spine disease contracted
Frankhouser, DH—MS & LD
Freeland, J.A.—malaria poison
Friend, D.A.—RH & bladder disease
Gandy, A.F.—CDR & RH
Gandy, C.—catarrh in head from exposure, near deaf

Gapp, L.P.—RH
Gillis, H.L.—epilepsy
Glover, A.—RH & LD
Glover, P.—RH & dyspepsia
Godwin, J.M.—RH & HD
Goff, G.W.—POW Libby prison
Goff, H.M.—sight impaired 26 years
Gooding, E.—HD, LD, RH, KD & liver disease
Graham, D.—stomach disease & dysentary
Graham, J.—wounded twice in back by gunshot
Graham, L.J.—SS, wounded little finger
Greathouse, J.C.—bloody piles
Greathouse, R.—consumption
Griffith, H.—RH & piles
Grim, H.—throat & LD
Grimes, H.S.—POW in pemberton 3 months
Grimes, W.M.—HD & partial blindness
Grimm, H.A.—HD
Grimm, P.—RH & piles
Gross, I.—hip hurt drilling
Gross, N.—RH
Groves, S.E.—fits pain in stomach 25 years
Groves, W.H.—TYF
Guseman, J.J.—skurvy, piles & liver disease
Halbritter, F.M.—lungs & bak rupture
Hamilton, J.M.—hernia & defective sight
Hardsty, J.—WIA 5 times
Harrington, F.M.—stomach trouble
Harrington, T.—shell wound left hand, finger amputated
Harrinqton, W.J.—RH & bronchitis
Hartley, H.A.—catarrh, LD, piles, deafness
Hartman, G.W.—TYF & dispepsia
Hartman, L.A.—CDR, head trouble, sight affected
Hartman, M.—partial loss of sight right eye
Hartsell, G.W.—gunshot wound left arm
Hauger, J.A.—RH
Hawker, T.D.—gunshot neck, rupture, teeth knocked out
Hawkins, J.W.—ruptured
Hawley, E.—disease of head & eyes
Hawley, S.P.—HD & LD
Hayden, H.M.—RH & HD
Hedron, S.—RH & HD
Hell, R.H.—RH
Helms, G.W.—RH & eresyphelas
Hennry, T.—SS
Herndon, J.M.—fistula
Hewitt, J.—POW at Libby

Hey, H.—coler bone broken
Hileman, B.—CDR
Hileman, J.—throat & lungs
Hill, J.W.—constipation, bowels, arm sprained, eyes
Hill, T.H.—erysipelas, TYF, RH, wounded with ax
Hinebaugh, J.—RH & CDR
Hoffman, G.F.—CDR & piles, reinlisted 1864
Hoffman, J.A.—HD, LD, served 3 mo prior to above enlist
Hollis, J.W.—RH & piles
Hooton, C.M.—muskler RH
Hose, S.—POW 2 months & 7 days, LD & RH
Hoveatter h.—defective in mind
Howard, C.S.—RH, catarrh in head
Hudson, J.M.—WIA leg & arm, previously in 2 OHI
Huffman, E.S.—disease of spine, injury to eyesight
Huffman, F.M.—CDR & loss of left leg
Huggins, A.—piles, also in 6 WVC
Huggins, E.—shot in right arm
Hunt, A.—MP, HD, stomach trouble 25 years
Jackson, D.R.—WIA right leg, deaf right ear from cannon
Jackson, G.B.—RH, MP & piles
Jackson, H.C.—RH
Jackson, J.V.—dropsical sores & RH
Jackson, S.J.—LD & throat disease
Jeffreys, E.—RH
Jeffreys, J.—disabled left ankle
Jenkins, A.J.—piles, CDR, inflamation of bowels 27 yr
Jenkins, E.—CDR, piles, hemorhage of lungs, 26 years
Jenkins, E.—deafness
Jenkins, F.—VV
Jenkins, H.E.—catarrh, side plurisy & nervous disease
Jenkins, L.H.—RH
Jenkins, W.H.—deafness
Jenkins, W.H.—rupture right arm, WIA left foot
Jenkins, W.M.—RH, piles, neumonia
Johnson, J.M.—POW Andersonville 5 months
Johnson, J.W.—gunshot left foot, reinlisted Co B 6 INC
Jones, E.C.—RH & HD since 1862
Jones, W.—catarrh, bronchitis, state troops under Capt. Yaqer & Cap Haller
Keefover, D.L.—CDR & disease of testicles
Kelly, E.—CDR, RH & constipation
Kelly, J.M.A.—hernia right side
Kelly, J.—RH
Kemp, M.—LD, loss of right lung
Kendall, W.C.—RH 26 years
Kenney, I.—RH & neuralgia

King, G.H.—RH & HD
Kirk, I.—KD, back disease caused from cold
Kirk, R.A.—RH & sore eyes 26 years
Kirk, S.B.—RH
Kisner, S.R.—RH
Knisell, W.F.—RH & catarah
Knott, P.E.—RH
Knotts, A.J.—affection of back & chest
Knotts, J.H.—cronic disease, eyesight, no pension
Knotts, L.—wounded in leg by shell
Knotts, R.A.—diseased liver
Lampbert, P.—defective hearing both ears
Lanham, E.—RH & tonsiletis
Lanham, Z.—measles caused partial deafness
Lantz, D.—CDR
Laub, G.—effects of SS
Laughery, D.—RH
Lee, C.C.—RH & HD 27 years
Lee, S.B.—liver & kidney disease
Lemon, J.J.—RH & throat trouble
Lenhart, A.—HD
Lewis, H.—ruptured since 1862
Lictwell, N.—RH
Linton, C.—RH, deafness, catarrh head, erysipelas
Linton, S.P.—blood poison, RH, sight impaired
Liston, A.—LD
Liston, J.A.—blood poison & HD
Liston, J.L.—piles & RH
Longster, T.J.—WIA left forearm
Loughridge, W.—CDR, pensioned
Luois, W.—shoulder hurt
Lyons, A.J.—KD, RH & liver disease
Lyons, H.—quinsy
MaCombs, J.M.—ruptured
Magill, G.—RH & LD
Manear, C.W.—CDR, frozen feet
Manown, J.H.—KD, deafness, liver disease
Martin, E.C.—CDR & HD
Martin, I.P.—HD
Martin, N.G.—rupture, liver disease, piles & CDR
Martin, R.F.—CDR & piles
Martin, S.—disease of chest
Martin, S.J.—wounds & rupture
Martin, S.M.—piles & HD
Martin, S.M.—POW 4 months Libby prison, scurvy & HD
Martin, S.R.—VV & back injury
Martin, W.T.D.—RH, KD, liver disease

Massey, H.M.—CDR
Matheny, E.M.—RH
Matheny, G.—dyspepsia & HD 26 years
Matheny, P.—RH
Matheny, S.—CDR, RH & piles
Matthews, W.—TYF
Maust, A.—injury to head, fits & etc.
Mays, J.W.—RH 25 years
McCauley, J.—HD, KD, RH
McGinnis, J.B.—POW Andersonville, MS, TYF, scurvy
McGinnis, J.W.—MS & RH
McGinnis, V.Y.—rupture
McGinnis, W.A.—piles, CDR
McKinney, E.—KD, weak back
McKinney, J.J.—KD, eyesight, hearing
McKinney, S.—RH & piles
McMillen, B.V.—HD, LD, throat trouble
McNare, P.—wounded leg
McNear, D.—HD
McPeck, W.—plurisy
Menear, W.F.—RH, CDR & dyspepsia
Menen, J.L.—erysipelis & ague
Messenger, Ed.—RH, catarrh, CDR
Messenger, S.—POW
Messenger, S.W.—ruptured 27 years
Metheny, J.M.—HD & RH
Metheny, S.M.—injury to ears
Metheny, W.H.—diseased liver, VV, HD, pain in head
Miller, I.—RH & LD
Miller, J.G.—smallpox in eyes blood right eye
Miller, Jn.—HD & RH
Miller, L.G.—catarrh
Minear, A.J.—hip & rist
Minear, B.F.—throat & lung disease, rupture
Minear, H.—CDR & RH
Minear, W.C.—RH, HD, gunshot wound right thigh
Minifee, J.T.—CDR
Mitchnell, J.—CDR & piles
Modespaugh, J.—RH, reinlisted veteran
Moon, G.W.—chills & fever & effects of mumps
Moran, J.—RH
Morris, D.Y.—piles & rupture
Murdock, J.E.—scrofula
Murphy, W.—piles, RH, gravel (?) 26 years
Myers, W.C.—injured hip, back & right shoulder
Neff, W.W.—CDR & lumbago
Nose, E.—WIA right leg below knee

Orr, A.—RH, KD, piles, scurvy, quinsy, sore eyes
Orr, M.H.—dislocated ankle, KD & LD
Orr, U.N.—RH, deafness
Paling, P.M.—LD
Paul, G.—crippled in left hip
Pell, T.A.—RH
Pell, W.F.—HD 27 years
Perkins, J.G.—KD
Perrill, J.I.—LD & RH
Phillips, O.—hearing injured by measles
Piles, C.—deafness in both ears
Piles, C.—RH & bronchitis
Piles, J.C.—RH
Plum, J.C.—LD, MP, sight & hearing
Plum, J.—catarh head & liver disease
Plum, W.J.—hearing affected, wounded in legg
Posten, N.—piles, disentary, RH
Pratt, J.W.—CDR & piles
Price, G.—RH & HD
Purinton, J.R.—MS & CDR 26 years, nervous disability
Radabaugh, J.A.—RH
Radihour, W.B.—shoulder broken
Ratliff, C.—growth on abdomen, had smallpox
Reckard, J.—RH & DSC
Reedy, E.—WIA right thigh, RH & piles
Reid, R.B.—CDR 26 years
Renshaw, A.E.—malarial poisoning liver & spleen disease
Rhodes, J.T.—RH
Richards, A.F.—blind in right eye
Richter, F.J.—HD & piles
Rickard, H.L.—RH
Rickard, J.—CDR & piles
Riddle, W.C.—HD
Ridenour, W.M.—WIA left foot, right leg amputated @ knee
Rigg, J.D.—TYF
Riley, D.—RH & HD
Riley, M.—RH & defective eyesight
Ringer, P.—MS, piles, HD 26 years
Robinson, J.M.—asthma
Romesburg, S.—RH, transferred to invalid corp
Rowe, A.E.*—shot in right leg 27 years, bullet remain in leg 16 years 2 m. amputated 1888
Rude, G.—RH, HD, injured testicles
Runner, J.—RH & spine disease
Sapp, B.F.—POW 9 months
Sauders, A.J.—sight injured
Seece, A.J.—WIA head & side

Shafer, C.—RH, CDR, catarrh, weak back
Shaffer, A.F.—RH, piles & scurvy
Shaffer, D.C.—RH, sight injured
Shaffer, G.M.—vertigo, loss of sight
Shaffer, W.A.—KD
Shahan, A.—CDR
Shahan, Ab.—KD
Shahan, H.—dysentery & RH
Shahan, R.—breast diseased, crippled left leg
Shahan, R.—WIA left hip, piles & RH
Shahen, M.—CDR, eyes affected
Sharps, A.—scurvy, RH & CDR
Shaw, J.M.—wound
Shaw, L.—shot right thumb subsequently 4 & 6 WVC
Shaw, T.J.—RH from MS
Shay, B.—gunshot wound, DSC
Shrout, A.J.—ruPture & RH
Shrout, C.W.—crippled from measles
Shutteworth, B.—asthma & piles
Sigley, W.F.—eyes bad, cronic disease, POW Andersonvil
Sinclair, A.—MS
Sinclair, W.—partial loss of eyesight
Sisler, A.—POW Libby prison, shot in breast
Sisler, S.A.—RH
Smalley, S.W.—Varicocle, RH & HD
Smith, I.H.—RH & piles
Smith, J.—crippled elbow, atrophied arm
Smith, Jm.W.—asthma, catarrh in stomach, lumbago 26 yr
Smith, L.H.—discharged, being only support of mother
Smith, L.—TYF
Smith, M.B.—deserted at Charleston, WV
Smith, W.H.—RH, HD, KD, LD & piles
Snider, W.D.—RH, CDR, stomach trouble
Snyder, A.J.—HD & RH
Snyder, S.—dropsy & KD
Sommers, T.M.—hernia, DSC
Spears, S.J.—SS, chills & fever & jaundice
Spenser, J.—KD & MS
Spielman, J.P.—RH
Spiker, J.J.—ribs broken & MS
Spiker, R.R.—LD & RH
Spurgeon, G.B.—LD
Squires, J.H.—RH & HD
Squires, T.S.—stomach trouble, RH, reinlisted 1 WVC
Stafford, S.D.L.—POW 17 months, scurvy, chills, F & wounds
Stafford, W.E.—RH & CDR POW Andersnvill
Stafford, W.H.—catarh & deafness

Stone, J.C.—RH
Street, W.J.—wounded in write hip
Stuck, E.C.—cold on mumps & measles
Sutton, E.K.—RH & bronchitis
Swearenqen, M.D.—KD & RH
Sypolt, C.—horse kick ruptured side in hospital 3 mo
Sypolt, E.—chronic liver complaint
Talbott, J.—rupture 27 years
Taylor, C.—RH
Taylor, G.W.—SS & rupture
Teats, L.—dropsy feet & legs
Teets, A.—left eye blind, back hurt
Teets, G.H.—RH
Thomas, A.J.—RH
Thomas, J.—weak eyes, defective sight
Titchewell, S.B.—gunshot wound right jaw
Titchnell, J.—RH & MP
Titchnell, P.—RH
Titchwell, S.—gunshot wound in hip
Trisle, S.—RH & CDR 26 years
Turner, J.W.—RH & HD, reinlisted 17 WVI
Turner, T.A.—general disability
Uphold, J.—right arm shot off
Uphold, N.—spine trouble
Uppole, D.E.—CDR, HD, piles
Vansickle, E.—RH, general disability
Vanwert, C.F.—bronchitis, asthma, LD
Waddle, R.B.—CDR, piles, weak eyes
Walker, J.T.—spinal disease
Walles, J.—eyesight & piles
Walls, J.M.—HD, mustered as cavalry never got horses
Walls, S.—aneurism inside left knee
Walls, S.G.—rupture, sprined ankle, RH 29 years, pile
Walters, W.—RH
Watkens, J.C.R.—ruptured
Watkins, R.—RH
Watson, J.★—CDR & catarrh 26 years
Watson, J.W.—RH, HD & piles
Watson, S.—WIA right leg
Watson, T.J.—loss of riqht arm
Watson, W.S.—LD & KD
Watts, A.—hernia right side & mashed
Weaver, J.D.—wound of left forearm & right knee
Welburn, R.T.—RH & piles
Welch, J.H.—POW Libby prison, left leg shot off
Wheeler, H.H.—shoulder broken
Whiting, I.E.—piles, scurvy, KD

Wilhelm, D.—heart & liver disease
Wilkin, I.—CDR & catarrh, reinlisted 2/6/65
Williams, A.J.—legg broken
Williams, G.—RH & hemorrhoids
Williams, J.—deafness from artillery at Cross Keys
Wilson, G.W.—left arm mashed & CDR
Wilson, W.—LD
Wolf, G.W.—RH, kicked by mule
Wolf, W.—LD & HD, pensioned
Wolring, W.J.—head hurt by concussion of shell, HD
Wright, H.C.—WIA right hip & left hand, RH
Yeast, W.—LD
Zinn, A.W.—RH
Zinn, G.H.—CDR & piles
Zinn, G.P.—CDR & piles
Zinn, G.W.—gunshot wound stomach & head, RH
Zinn, O.—HD & LD
Zinn, W.H.—CDR

Putnam County

NAME/RANK	REGIMENT	WHEN SERVED
Adkins, Floyd Pvt.	11 VAI	NF
Adkins, Hiram Pvt.	11 WVI	61/65
Alexander, Wm. T.	NF	
Allen, Charles Pvt.	11 VAI	NF
Allison, John W. Pvt.	8 VAI	10/1/61–8/1/65
Anderson, Benj. Pvt.	NF	
Anderson, George T. Pvt.	171 OHI	63/63
Arthur, Edward J. Pvt.	7 WVC	9/4/61–8/1/65
Bancroft, Thomas B. Lt.	27 PAI	6/20/64–9/64
Barr, John W. Pvt.	134 PAI	8/6/62–5/26/63
Barrett, Samuel Pvt.	116 OHI	7/18/62–6/6/65
Benner, John H. Pvt.	91 OHI	7/25/62–6/13/65
Bess, John A. Pvt.	11 WVI	8/22/62–6/11/65
Bias, Wm. A. Pvt.	36 VAC CSA	12/62–1865
Blake, Clyde S. Sgt.	22 VAI CSA	5/1/61–6/19/65
Blake, James F. Pvt.	4 WVI	6/19/61–7/18/65
Blankenship, Washington	NF	
Boggess, A.J.B. Pvt.	NF	
Boice, Lemeul Pvt.	7 OHC	9/62–4/65
Bowling, John Pvt.	73 OHI	10/61–12/64
Bowls, James W. Pvt.	24 VAI CSA	1861–NF
Bowman, Henry Pvt.	91 OHI	8/12/62–8/65
Bowyer, John L. Pvt.	7 WVI	3/4/65–6/65
Bronough, Edwin Pvt.	CSA (36 VAI)	NF
Brown, Henry C. Sgt.	7 WVC	10/30/61–6/28/65
Brown, Henry Pvt.	4 PAC	8/25/64–7/1/65
Bryan, Rees Pvt.	36 VAI CSA	5/13/61–4/12/65
Bryan, W.L. Pvt.	36 VAI CSA	5/13/61–4/12/65
Burdett, John Jr. Pvt.	NF (22 VAI CSA?)	
Burford, A.J. Capt.	36 VAI CSA	5/13/61–6/14/65
Byne, Bennett	NF	
Caldwell, Caleb	NF	
Cantrell, Abraham Pvt.	10 VAC CSA	8/10/61–6/20/65
Carson, Thomas Pvt.	8 VAI	6/20/61–1/64
also	7 WVC	2/1/64–8/1/65
Cartwright, Wm. Pvt.	7 WVI	9/61–2/64
Cash, Marsellius Pvt.	7 WVI	2/2/65–7/1/65
Casto, Enoch Pvt.	NF	
Chealey, John M.	NF	
Chere?, Wm. Pvt.	1 WVC	2/63–8/65
Clinton, Charles B. Pvt.	—WVI	62/65

Coalman, N. Pvt.	8 VAI	6/27/61–6/21/65
Collins, James H. Cpl.	12 OHI	4/22/61–7/23/64
Coplen, John Pvt.	NF	
Corhnill, James Pvt.	13 WVI	8/15/62–6/22/65
Cothern, Andrew J. Pvt.	174 OHI	8/16/64–5/26/65
Coulter, Abraham Pvt.	116 OHI	8/16/62–6/66
Cox, Henry Pvt.	15 VAI	8/10/62–1865
Coy, Columbus M. Pvt.	36 OHI	NF
Crago, George R. Pvt.	4 WVI	6/17/61–5/25/64
Crago, Harrison Pvt.	11 WVI	9/18/62–7/5/65
Crago, Madison Pvt.	7 WVI	61/65
Crago, Wm. H. Pvt.	11 WVI	9/17/62–6/27/65
Crandall, Richard H.	NF	
Cunningham, Mortimer Sgt.	174 OHI	8/17/64–6/28/65
Daniels, Christopher C. Pvt.	173 OHI	9/1/64–6/26/65
Dartte, Chauncy M. Pvt.	187 OHI	2/20/64–2/65
Daughtery, Stephen Pvt.	62 OHI	9/62–7/63
also	68 OHI	3/64–6/65
Davis, John W. Blksmith	8 WVI	12/61–2/63
also	7 WVC	2/63–8/65
Deal, Martin V.B.	NF (129 VAM CSA)	
Delabrange, Bemabas Pvt.	1 WVC	8/7/61–7/8/65
Dillon, George P.	NF	
Downlain, James G. Sgt.	5 WVI	4/5/64–8/12/65
Duncan, James W. Pvt.	7 WVC	10/25/64–8/11/65
Dunfield, Alphonso Pvt.	77 OHI	3/1/64–8/1/65
Earlywine, Dunfee Pvt.	5 OHI	8/10/61–7/5/65
Eckard, John W. Pvt.	7 WVC	3/28/64–8/10/65
Edwards, Thomas	NF (8 VAC CSA?)	
Enicks, Wm. H. Pvt.	11 WVI	8/25/62–7/5/65
Escue, George Pvt.	13 WVI	7/62–7/65
Eskins, Henry A. Pvt.	7 WVC	2/16/65–8/1/65
Evans, John Pvt.	4 WVI	6/5/61–7/4/64
Fickle, John Sgt.	6 WVI	2/20/63–2/8/65
Fife, James F. Pvt.	36 VAI CSA	4/61–4/65
Fife, W.E. Ltc.	36 VAI CSA	5/13/61–6/17/65
Fish, W.V. Pvt.	7 WVI	2/18/65–6/17/65
Fisher, Henry F. Pvt.	8 VAI	1861–NF
Fowler, James Pvt.	7 WVC	2/24/64–8/9/65
Fowler, John W. Pvt.	7 WVC	10/29/61–6/15/65
Fowler, Thomas Pvt.	7 WVC	3/31/64–8/9/65
Frantz, Joseph Pvt.	WV Scouts	8/63–8/65
Furgeson, A.L. Pvt.	13 WVI	12/23/63–7/5/65
Gardner, Andrew Pvt.	92 OHI	8/6/62–6/65
Geary, Francis L. Sgt.	7 WVC	10/13/62–8/4/65
George, Beverly Pvt.	36 VAI CSA	5/15/61–3/1/62
also	8 VAC CSA	12/28/62–4/13/65

Gibson, James J. Sgt.	2 KYR	2/25/64–8/23/65
Gibson, Jeremiah Pvt.	—WVI	8/63–NF
Gibson, John H.	NF (45 BTN VAI CSA)	
Gibson, Thomas Pvt.	8 OHI	9/61–NF
Gillespie, Sampson Pvt.	7 WVC	3/23/64–8/1/65
Gillespie, Wm. M. Pvt.	12 OHC	10/18/64–10/18/65
Glenn, George Pvt.	13 VAI	63/65
Grant, John W. Pvt.	7 WVC	64/65
Gwin, Ahas S. Sgt.	4 WVI	6/4/61–7/5/64
Haden, Frank	CSA (7 LAI)	
Hall, Thomas Pvt.	4 VAI	8/30/61–7/16/65
Harge, G. W. Pvt.	13 VAI	1/3/64–5/15/65
Harmon, Thomas F. Pvt.	4 WVI	7/61–7/65
Harper, Alfred Pvt.	18 OHI	9/61–8/62
Harrison, Abner Pvt.	8 WVI	7/27/61–1/27/63
Harrison, John Pvt.	13 WVI	63/65
Harrison, Joseph Pvt.	13 WVI	12/28/63–6/22/65
Harrison, Madison Pvt.	——	1861–NF
Harrison, Reuben Lt.	7 WVC	NF
Hartman, David S. Cpl.	28 PAI	6/61–1864
Heartney, Michael Pvt.	28 PAI	5/64–8/65
Hedrick, Robert Pvt.	7 WVC	2/15/62–NF
Hemmings, Wm. H. Pvt.	7 WVC	9/2/61–1/25/65
Henderson, John C. Pvt.	14 KYI	12/20/61–3/20/64
Hennings, Elizah Sgt.	13 VAI	8/62–8/65
Henson, Alexander Pvt.	11 VAI	NF
Henson, Hesakiah Pvt.	11 VAI	NF
Higginbotham, James T. Pvt.	13 WVI	10/3/63–5/29/65
Higginbotham, John D. Cpl.	7 WVC	3/28/64–8/1/65
Higginbotham, L. Pvt.	11 VAI	9/18/62–7/4/64
Hill, Isaac	NF (8 VAC CSA?)	
Hill, John W. Pvt.	13 WVI	63/65
Holley, Joseph Pvt.	175 OHI	2/22/65–2/3/66
Holstein, Albert J. Sgt.	8 WVI	9/2/61–2/1/64
also	7 WVC	2/1/64–8/9/65
Holstein, Daliver Pvt.	7 VAC	3/64–8/9/65
Holstein, L. M. Pvt.	7 WVI	9/2/63–8/1/65
Howell, Augustus Pvt.	29 OHI	11/64–6/65
Hull, Oscar D. Pvt.	—OHI	2/23/65–8/65
Hummion, Elias Pvt.	13 WVI	12/23/63–6/22/65
Humphrey, Lewis Pvt.	13 VAI	8/13/62–6/22/65
Jeffers, Samuel Pvt.	3 WVC	9/16/63–7/65
Jeffers, Wm. H. Pvt.	3 WVC	8/20/63–6/30/65
Johnson, Edward Pvt.	Gunboat Allice	NF
Jones, G. W. Pvt.	8 VAI	9/61–2/1/64
also	7 WVC	2/1/64–8/7/65
Jones, John G. Pvt.	5 OHI	10/15/61–11/19/64

Joseph, Evan Cpl.	187 OHI	2/11/65–6/20/65
Kane, Henry Pvt.	——	1864–NF
Keaton, John L. Pvt.	36 VAC CSA	62/65
Keith, Wm. A. Pvt.	4 MDI	6/61–7/64
Kelly, Joseph Pvt.	7 WVC	9/61–1/65
King, James M. Pvt.	11 WVI	8/14/62–6/17/65
King, James W. Pvt.	7 WVC	2/1/64–8/1/65
King, Nathaniel Pvt.	13 WVI	2/25/65–6/20/65
Kingry, Abner Pvt.	22 OHI	11/64–7/15/65
Kitchen, Wm.	NF	
Knapp, John Pvt.	8 WVI	10/61–1864
Kollins?, Jack Pvt.	18 OHI	9/3/61–11/9/64
Kollins, Wm. K. Pvt.	73 OHI	9/12/61–2/14/63
Kunshaw, John A. Pvt.	7 WVC	3/1/64–8/1/65
Landers, Samuel Pvt.	11 WVI	12/63–8/65
Larabee, Samuel P. Pvt.	23 OHI	6/1/61–6/30/64
Lawhorn, James M. Pvt.	14 VAC CSA	62/65
Laynell, Malindy M.	NF	
Leadman, James	NF	
Leadman, Ruben Pvt.	7 OHC	8/62–6/7/65
Lee, Wm. Pvt.	13 VAI	8/13/62–6/22/65
Leonard, John C. Pvt.	91 OHI	2/24/64–6/24/65
Logue, Wm. W. Pvt.	— OHI	62/65
Love, Samuel C. Sgt.	13 WVI	6/61–6/22/65
Mabe, Martin	NF (53 NCI CSA?)	
Markham, Thomas H. Pvt.	1 VAI CSA	1863–2/65
Mason, Theo Sgt.	36 VAC CSA	62/65
Mattox, Alias G. Pvt.	16 VAC CSA	62/64
Maxwell, John T. Pvt.	39 OHI	NF
McClean, James L. Cpl.	31 NYI	7/62–4/63
McCoy, David Lt.	22 VAI CSA	7/1/61–7/17/65
McCoy, Samuel Pvt.	36 VAI CSA	5/61–4/65
McDewell, James D. Pvt.	2 VAI CSA	8/62–1865
McDowell, Eli L. Pvt.	11 VAI	7/62–7/65
McGrew, Jasper Pvt.	8 VAI	9/18/61–2/1/64
also	7 WVC	2/1/64–8/1/65
McGrew, Wm. Pvt.	2 VAC	8/17/62–6/30/65
McLaughlin, Noah Pvt.	7 VAC (CSA)	9/29/61–6/3/64
McLean, Mahlon Pvt.	3 WVC	62/65
Meadows, Alford Pvt.	7 WVC	9/2/61–8/13/65
Means, Wm.	NF	
Miels, Isaac Lt.	7 WVC	8/4/61–2/13/65
Mitchell, John Pvt.	193 OHI	3/9/65–8/4/65
Moore, Thomas Sgt.	13 WVI	8/15/62–6/23/65
Morrison, Alonzo Pvt.	13 WVI	8/21/62–6/22/65
Moses, Wm. H. Pvt.	11 WVI	8/23/63–6/14/65
Myres, John W. Pvt.	11 VAI	NF

Name	Unit	Dates
Narret, Rhad F. Surgeon	——	NF
Nicholas, Andrew J. Sgt.	11 WVI	2/11/62–5/15/65
Nichols, W.F.	NF	
Null, Henry Pvt.	13 WVI	NF
Nye, John W. Pvt.	Jack Bat	63/65
Ohlinger, Conrad Pvt.	187 OHI	2/14/65–1/20/66
Oldaker, Levi W. Pvt.	8 WVI	12/16/61–2/29/64
also	7 WVI	3/1/64–8/1/65
Patchell, Wm.	Mury Cook?	6/61–1865
Phelps, Rayal Pvt.	116 OHI	8/16/62–6/1/65
Phelps, Samuel Pvt.	4 VAI	NF
Piles, John	NF	
Piles, Oliver	NF	
Pohner, Robert M. Pvt.	23 KYI	4/7/60 4/65
Priddy, Mathew Pvt.	8 WVI	61/65
Queen, Wm. H. Pvt.	7 WVC	3/64–8/9/65
Racer, John S. Pvt.	11 WVI	10/62–6/65
Ray, Edward A. Sgt.	7 WVC	9/17/61–4/65
Rayner, Allen	CSA (24 NCI?)	
Reed, James E. Pvt.	7 WVC	7/27/61–8/15/65
Rider, John T. Pvt.	——	62/65
Roberts, Samuel Pvt.	8 VAI	9/22/64–9/26/65
Ross, Hugh S.C.	NF	
Rowley, Calvin W.	NF	
Runner, John L. Pvt.	44 OHI	8/21/62–5/31/65
Rupe, Mathias Pvt.	NF	
Russell, Alvin Cpl.	13 WVI	10/62–6/65
Rutherford, Charles Pvt.	7 WVC	8/15/61–7/64
Sanders, Steven E. Pvt.	117 OHI	60/64
Schwarz, Frederick	37 OHI	8/9/61–9/9/64
Scott, George Pvt.	107 OHI	62/65
Scott, James Pvt.	107 PAI	9/64–6/6/65
Scott, M.C. Cpl.	CS ART. 12 VAA	61/63
Sharp, Thomas Pvt.	NF	
Shoemaker, Chas. V.	NF (8 VAC CSA)	
Shuebery, Shue Pvt.	73 OHI	2/4/64–12/6/64
Silmon, Garnett Pvt.	7 WVC	7/27/61–2/23/63
Simmons, Henry Pvt.	8 WVI	10/15/61–9/8/62
Sloan, George W. Pvt.	NF	
Smallridge, James H. Pvt.	9 VAI	12/26/61–7/26/65
Smith, George W. Pvt.	13 WVI	1/1/64–6/28/65
Smith, John R. Pvt.	7 WVC	62/65
Smith, Joshua	NF (19 VAC CSA)	
Smith, Joshua Pvt.	45 KYI	5/64–2/15/65
Smith, Wm. M. Pvt.	7 VAI	3/16/65–7/1/65
Smith, Zachariah P. Pvt.	63 OHI	9/30/61–7/8/65
Sowers, Mathew Pvt.	1 VAC	9/8/61–11/17/64

Name	Unit	Dates
Spradling, Andrew J. Pvt.	7 WVC	7/61–1/25/65
Spurlock, Jackson Pvt.	NF	
Staneart, Philip Pvt.	55 OHI	8/7/62–8/65
Steel, James	NF	
Steele, Thomas W. Sgt.	3 VAC	8/5/62–7/22/65
Steell, Arthur J. Pvt.	8 WVI	63/65
Stewart, Henry H. Pvt.	1 MNI	9/23/62–10/4/65
Summers, James Pvt.	11 WVI	62/65
Tackett, James Pvt.	11 VAI	NF
Tackett, W.P. Pvt.	11 WVI	10/62–8/65
Taylor, Samuel Pvt.	78 PAI	2/29/65–5/23/65
Tewell, Charles W. Pvt.	7 WVC	11/10/62–8/1/65
Thacker, Alexander Capt.	45 KYI	6/3/63–3/25/64
Thacker, Elihu Chaplain	45 KYI	9/63–12/64
Thomas, Henry Pvt.	27 OHI	6/25/61–7/65
Thomas, Lemeul C. Pvt.	9 WVI	12/10/61–7/21/65
Thomas, Robert H.	NF (46 VAI CSA?)	
Thumm, John M. Pvt.	75 OHI	9/10/61–7/18/65
Tinis, L.J. Cpl.	36 VAI CSA	5/28/61–6/13/65
Tucker, J.M. Pvt.	7 WVC	9/15/64–6/65
Tucker, Thomas J. Sgt.	8 WVI	9/61–NF
Turley, Thomas B. Pvt.	22 VAI CSA	62/65
Turner, Samuel Pvt.	NF (36 VAC CSA?)	
Wagner, John	NF (10 VAC CSA?)	
Wallace, Ludwell Pvt.	7 WVC	3/28/64–8/1/65
Ward, Alexander Sgt.	141 OHI	5/2/64–9/3/64
also	193 OHI	3/9/65–8/4/65
Warmer, Allen B. Pvt.	13 WVI	61/63
Wartenberg, Alexander Lt.	4 WVI	6/17/61–7/5/64
Weale, George W. Pvt.	8 VAC CSA	10/62–4/65
Whitesiels, John F. Pvt.	17 WVI	8/30/64–6/19/65
Whittington, Allen Pvt.	NF	
Whittington, John Pvt.	8 VAI	61/63
also	7 WVC	2/1/64–8/1/65
Wilson, J.A.	NF (62 VAI CSA?)	
Withrow, Francis M. Pvt.	7 WVC	2/16/65–8/1/65
Withrow, Wm. A. Pvt.	13 WVI	8/15/62–6/22/65
Wood, Chauncy T. Pvt.	— OHI	62/65
Workman, Benj. F. Pvt.	82 PAI	12/63–8/65
Wright, Wm.	———	5/61–4/65
Wright, Wm. Pvt.	12 WVI	8/16/62–6/16/65
Young, John Pvt.	7 WVC	2/65–8/65

Putnam County Remarks

Adkins, H.—shot in the hip
Alexander, W.T.—catarrh & RH
Allison, J.W.—horse thrown injured breast
Arthur, E.J.—RH & SS
Barrett, S.—wound right ankle, horseness from MS & MP
Benner, J.H.—throat, bronchitis, HD
Bess, J.A.—shot in left hand
Bias, W.A.*—thumb shot off
Blake, J.F.—LD & RH
Boice, L.—RH & eyes affected
Bowling, J.—RH & HD
Bowman, H.—HD & pleurisy, feet injured
Bowyer, J.L.—dysentary
Brown, H.C.—foot mashed by fall of horse
Brown, H.—dysentary
Bryan, R.*—wounded in left hand
Burford, A.J.*—went in service Lieut came out Captain
Cantrell, A.*—thrown from horse, hernia
Carson, T.—gunshot wound left breast
Cartwright, W.—ankle & wrist displaced
Chere, W.—RH
Coalman, N.—SS, piles, scurvy
Collins, J.H.—result of fevers, HD, hurt spine
Cothern, A.J.—RH
Coulter, A.—gone down weakness
Coy, C.M.—gunshot left foot, RH
Crago, G.R.—DSC 1864 chronic hiptitus, gunshot right hand
Crago, W.H.—crippled right shoulder & breast by gunshot 1864
Cunningham, M.—RH 26 years from exposure
Daniels, C.C.—CDR
Daughtery, S.—chronic pleurisy
DeLabrange, B.—lame back from falling off horse, granulated eyes
Duncan, J.W.—CDR
Dunfield, A.—injured right leg, left jaw, chest, bowels ruptured
Eckard, J.W.—kicked by horse in breast
Edwards, T.*—RH
Enicks, W.H.—wounded left hip
Evans, J.—gunshot neck
Fickle, J.—crippled hand
Fife, W.E.*—shot through right hip
Fish, W.~.—injury to abdomen
Fisher, H.F.—cold on measles
Fowler, J.—RH, maybe lumbago of back
Fowler, J.W.—wounded by fall from horse, 2 ulcers & back hurt
Gardner, A.—gunshot in right side

Geary, F.L.—RH & HD
Gibson, J.—formerly in the Confederate army
Gibson, J.J.—RH
Gibson, T.—hearing affected
Gillespie, W.M.—SS
Glenn, G.—hernia & catarrh
Gwin, A.S.—CDR
Hall, T.—eyesight & hearing, LD
Harge, G.W.—bronchitis
Harmon, T.F.—wounded in left knee
Harper, A.—eye disease, substitute
Harrison, A.—ruptured
Harrison, R.—CDR
Hartman, D.S.—shot in the right wrist
Heartney, M.—lame left hip, piles
Hedrick, R.—loss of eyesight
Hemmings, E.—gunshot, stiff arm
Hemmings, W.H.—RH, broken veins, piles
Henderson, J.C.—KD, promoted to Lt. transferred to 45 KY as major
Higginbotham, J.T.—sore breast from being run over by horse in army
Higginbotham, L.—gunshot in right hand, left foot, right leg
Hill, J.W.—SS
Hiqqinbotham, J.D.—heart & stomach disease
Holley, J.—RH
Holstein, A.J.—nervous debility pain in left side
Holstein, D.—general disability
Howell, A.—catarrh
Hummion, E.—lame back
Humphrey, L.—eyes & head affected
Jeffers, S.—RH & LD
Jones, G.W.—injured right shoulder & hip, left testicle mashed
Jones, J.G.—general disability
Joseph, E.—CDR & RH
Kane, H.—wounded in side
Kane, H.—wounded in side
King, J.M.—liver complaint
King, J.W.—malarial poison & stomach trouble
King, N.—back & breast injured by exposure
Kingry, A.—LD from measles
Kollins, J.—back & stomach
Kollins, W.K.—KD
Kunshaw, J.A.—RH
Landers, S.—wounded left knee joint, injured by exposure
Larabee, S.P.—gunshot right forearm
Leadman, R.—gunshot right breast
Lee, W.—bronchitis
Leonard, J.C.—RH

Mabe, M.*—shot through wrist badly injured
Markham, T.H.*—VV
Mason, T.*—kicked on leg by horse
Maxwell, J.T.—KD
McDowell, E.L.—catarrh head
McGrew, J.—TYF & MS
McLaughlin, N.*—gunshot wound
Meadows, A.—sore back crippled by horse, left testicle by mumps
Miels, I.—RH
Mitchell, J.—HD & piles, chills & fever
Moore, T.—injured eyes & RH
Moses, W.H.—chronic bronchitis
Nye, J.W.—RH & piles
Patchell, W.—CDR, Mury Cook & 7 others
Phelps, R.—KD
Piles, O.—HD
Pohner, R.M.—lost right leg
Queen, W.H.—thrown from horse
Racer, J.S.—hernia
Ray, E.A.—CDR
Roberts, S.—piles from flux (?) & palpitutios heart
Runner, J.L.—RH
Russell, A.—CDR
Rutherford, C.—RH
Sanders, S.E.—eyes slightly affected
Schwarz, F.—hernia
Scott, G.—general debility
Scott, J.—pulmonary consumption
Shuebery, S.—chronic spinal minengitis from injury, DSC
Silmon, G.—piles, catarrh head, bronchitis, part deaf right
Simmons, H.—RH from exposure ever since the war
Smallridge, J.H.—hernia
Smith, G.W.—CDR & lumbago
Smith, J.—rupture neuralgia & RH
Smith, Z.P.—RH & deafness
Souers, M.—RH
Staneart, P.—hearing
Steele, T.W.—deaf left ear, pleurisy riqht side
Summers, J.—shot in the head
Tackett, W.P.—RH & neuralgia
Taylor, S.—RH
Tewell, C.W.—bronchitis & hearing
Thacker, A.—RH & piles
Thacker, E.—gunshot arm & leg
Thomas, L.C.—RH hips & back from exposure on Linchburg raid
Thumm, J.M.—maimed in right arm
Tucker, J.M.—pneumonia from gunshot

Tucker, T.J.—CDR, neuralgia of head, lumbago, sore eyes
Wallace, L.—RH
Ward, A.—SS
Warmer, A.B.—HD
Wartenburg, A.—eyesight affected
Whitesiels, J.F.—LD from measles
Withrow, F.M.—neuralgia & RH
Withrow, W.A.—RH
Young, J.—dislocated collarbone & injury to arm

NOTE: George R. Crago and Madison Crago were first in the 22 VAI CSA and subsequently joined the 4th WVI and 7th WVI. Noah McLaughlin was also in the 22 VAI CSA then served the 7th VAC U.S.

Raleigh County

NAME/RANK	REGIMENT	WHEN SERVED
Abbott, Wm. H. Pvt.	7 WVC	11/5/61–8/1/65
Adkins, Henry	—(17 VAC CSA?)	61/62
Adkins, Stephen Pvt.	NF (30 BTN VASS CSA)	
Arnold, Jackson Pvt.	WV Guards	NF
Adkins, Peter Pvt.	NF (19 VAC CSA)	
Adkins, Robert Pvt.	NF (45 BTN VAI CSA?)	
Barr, Edwin V. Pvt.	——	63/65
Berry, Wm. Pvt.	7 VAC	61/64
Bradford, John A. Pvt.	22 OHI	NF
Bragg, Alexander Pvt.	135 ILI	5/63–11/1/63
also	34 ILI	11/1/63–11/27/65
Bragg, Francis M. Pvt.	135 ILI	5/64–10/64
also	34 ILI	10/64–5/65
Burnett, Archibal Pvt.	——	6/1/61–1864
Burnside, Andrew S. Pvt.	7 WVI	10/62–8/1/65
Burnside, Joseph C. Pvt.	7 WVI	3/13/64–8/1/65
Burnside, Wesley M. Pvt.	7 WVC	4/30/64–8/1/65
Cales, Ephraim	NF	
Cantley, George Pvt.	7 WVC	11/8/62–8/1/65
Clay, George A. Pvt.	1 WVC	9/61–9/64
Clay, James M. Pvt.	7 WVC	11/2/61–4/12/65
Clay, Masten G. Pvt.	—WVI	3/1/62–4/1/65
Clay, Ralph S. Sgt.	7 WVC	2/11/64–2/1/65
Collins, David Pvt.	7 WVC	2/22/65–8/1/65
Conner, Simon	NF	

Cook, George P. Pvt.	7 WVC	10/64–8/1/65
Cook, Leonidas H. Pvt.	7 WVC	12/61–NF
Daniel, John Pvt.	1 WVC	9/61–9/64
Daniel R. Pvt.	NF	
Daniel, Wm. C. Pvt.	13 WVI	9/13/62–6/24/65
Daniel, Wm. Pvt.	13 WVI	9/13/62–5/65
Davis, Samuel L. Pvt.	7 WVC	2/62–8/1/65
Dekins, Daniel Pvt.	7 WVC	10/10/61–6/23/65
Dekins, Eperham J. Pvt.	7 WVC	11/61–8/1/65
Dickins, James Pvt.	7 WVC	10/10/61–6/23/65
Diller, Abner Pvt.	7 VAI	9/61–1866
Dunbar, Wm. S. Lt.	7 WVC	9/1/61–6/22/62
Edmands, Joel Pvt.	7 WVC	3/25/64–8/1/65
Goins, Thomas F. Pvt.	7 VA—	12/63–1865
Graham, James Pvt.	7 VAC	2/63–7/8/65
Graham, Lewis Pvt.	7 VAC	2/63–7/8/65
Harless, Benj. F. Cpl.	7 WVC	9/8/61–8/8/65
Harper, Hamilton Sgt.	WV Guards	12/25/63–2/22/65
Hensley, Stephen H. Pvt.	7 WVC	9/61–2/62
Hodges, Allen Pvt.	8 WVI	2/62–8/62
Horrow, Thomas Pvt.	NF	
Hunt, Lewis F. Pvt.	7 WVC	3/63–8/1/65
Jackson, Jacob Cpl.	7 WVC	5/2/63–5/12/65
Jarrell, Lemeul Blksmith	7 WVC	10/10/61–1/23/65
Johnson, W.R. Pvt.	112 PAA	12/18/61–12/18/64
Kidd, John E. Pvt.	7 WVC	9/13/61–1/23/64
Laverty, John Pvt.	7 WVC	10/12/62–8/1/65
Livertiy, Marion Pvt.	7 WVC	6/5/63–8/9/65
Maynor, George W. Cpl.	7 WVC	2/23/61–8/1/65
Maynor, Wm. Pvt.	7 WVC	10/1/61–8/1/65
McClaver, John W. Sgt.	9 VA—	61/65
McGinnis, Achiles Lt.	7 WVC	10/10/61–8/1/65
McGinnis, Thomas J. Pvt.	7 WVC	10/13/61–6/23/65
Metcham, Jacob S. Pvt.	1 MDI	1/16/64–1/18/66
Milam, Reece A. Pvt.	7 WVC	NF
Miller, Henry F. Pvt.	13 WVI	9/13/62–6/23/64
Mitchum, James A. Cpl.	——	2/63–7/8/65
Moles, James Pvt.	7 WVC	9/1/61–9/12/62
Parker, Benj. F. Pvt.	——	7/64–5/65
Peter Pvt.	NF (19 VAC CSA?)	
Pettery, John Pvt.	7 WVC	12/62–8/1/65
Price, David Pvt.	2 WVC	4/20/63–6/18/65
Redden, Wm. "Spy"	9 VA (60 VAI CSA?)	62/64
Richmond, Samuel L. Pvt.	—WVC	6/62–6/64
Riffle, Robert Pvt	NF(45 BTN VAI CSA?)	
Ruble, Charles Pvt.	1 WVC	10/1/61–6/26/65
Scott, Moses Pvt.	7 VAC	NF

Scott, Oliver Cpl.	7 VAC	11/64–1865
Short, Skelton Pvt.	7 WVC	1/25/62–6/3/65
Shrewsberry, George W. Lt.	7 VAC	2/63–7/8/65
Stover, Harrison Pvt.	7 WVC	NF
Stover, Tollison Pvt.	7 WVC	NF
Turner, Wm. Pvt.	7 WVC	12/31/61–3/15/63
Weaver, Jonathan Cpl.	7 WVC	9/61–1865
Webb, James M. Pvt.	—WVI	3/62–4/64
Webb, John W. Pvt.	61 NYI	64/65
Webb, Wm. R. Pvt.	8 WVC	NF
Williams, Andrew J. Pvt.	7 WVC	12/30/61–9/4/63
Williams, Ballard Pvt.	WV Guards	2/15/64–2/22/65
Williams, Henry	NF (36 VAI CSA?)	
Williams, Stephen Pvt.	WV Guards	2/15/64–2/22/65
Wiseman, George L. Pvt.	2 WVC	8/27/64–6/7/65
Workman, Joseph H. Pvt.	7 WVC	9/1/61–1/21/63
Workman, Wm. F. Pvt.	7 WVC	8/10/61–10/16/64
Wriston, James Cpl.	7 WVC	9/1/61–1/23/65
Young, Josepn F. Pvt.	NF (17 VAC CSA)	

Raleigh County Remarks

Berry, W.—very poor
Bragg, A.—bayonet wound in legs
Bragg, F.M.—LD
Cantley, G.—VV & headache contracted in service 1864
Clay, M.G.—thigh & arm broken
Collins, D.—RH & partial deaf
Daniel, J.—RH
Daniel, W.—bayonet wound left hand, result cancer & amputation
Daniel, W.C.—contracted erysiphelas in arm winter of 1862—63
Davis, S.L.—eyes injured & TYF
Diller, A.—living by days work
Dunbar, W.S.—KD & gen paralysis result exposure 1862
Edmands, J.—CDR & HD
Goins, T.F.—thrown from horse hip dislocated hearing impaired
Harless, B.F.—piles & lumbago since 1862
Harper, H.—piles
Hodges, A.—enlisted 2/1862 deserted 8/1862
Horrow, T.—very poor
Jarrell, L.—crippled in back while horse shoeing July 1863
Kidd, J.E.—LD & VV
Laverty, J.—injury of left wrist
Maynor, G.W.—ruptured
Maynor, W.—mumps & piles

McGinnis, T.J.—VV
Metcham, J.S.—blind, caused by overheat & cold
Miller, H.F.—falling mumps injury to back since winter 62–63
Moles, J.—LD since July 1862
Price, D.—shot in left shoulder
Richmond, S.L.—RH from exposure
Riffle, D.R.—shot in arm, POW Richmond
Ruble, C.—RH, POW Andersonville
Scott, M.—spinal affection
Short, S.—LD since 1864
Shrewsberry, G.W.—shot in left arm
Stover, H.—gunshot left hand, middle finger off thumb stiff
Stover, T.—RH & KD since 1864
Turner, W.—gunshot right shoulder, partial paralysis
Weaver, J.—scurvy, UFL
Webb, J.W.—catarrh
Williams, A.J.—hernia & stricture of orsophagus since July 1862
Williams, S.—gen debility from exposure Md State Troops & 2 WV
Wiseman, G.L.—gunshot wound right shoulder
Workman, J.H.—hernia & VV left leg since June 1862
Workman, W.F.—testicle disease & KD result mumps spring 1862
Wriston, J.—LD, right hand partially shot off in June 1864

Randolph County

NAME/RANK	REGIMENT	WHEN SERVED
Allen, Joseph M. Pvt.	5 WVC	3/18/61–6/14/64
Antill, Jesse Pvt.	11 OHI	8/14/62–6/6/65
Arbogast, George W. Pvt.	(25 VAI CSA)	1863–4/15/65
Bart, Peter B. Pvt.	46 VC CSA	6/63–4/14/65
Bean, George Pvt.	10 WVI	9/8/61–2/27/64
Bennett, Daniel Pvt.	WV SCOUT	NF
Bennett, Martin V. Sgt.	(25 VAI CSA)	2/29/64–4/15/65
Bing, John E. Pvt.	56 OHI	11/2/61–4/23/66
Bodkin, Henry B. Pvt.	62 VAI (CSA)	4/61–4/65
Bodkin, Michael Pvt.	62 VAI CSA	61–65
Bosley, William H. Pvt.	6 WVC	3/20/64–6/19/65
Bouer, Columbus C. Pvt.	WV GUARDS	1/64–5/30/65
Browning, James H. Cpl.	10 WVI	10/18/61–8/9/65
Buzzell, Frank H. Pvt.	NF	
Collens, Archibald Pvt.	10 WVI NF	
Collier, William H. Pvt.	25 OHI	6/15/61–6/29/64
Cooper, Daniel Pvt.	WV GUARDS	2/64–2/65
Cooper, Elijah Pvt.	WV GUARDS	7/63–4/65
Courtney, John N. Pvt.	20 VAC CSA	6/63–4/19/65
Crawford, Emmet Pvt.	31 VAC CSA	12/63–6/65
Cunnigham, Henry Pvt.	18 VAC CSA	62–65
Currence, Jacob Capt.	31 VAI CSA	5/24/61–2/13/62
Curtis, David B. Pvt.	2 WVI	4/21/63–5/22/66
Custis, Thomas C. Cpl.	10 WVI	7/1/62–7/3/65
Cutright, Gideon M. Pvt.	1 WVA	8/15/62–6/28/65
Cutright, Jacob W. Pvt.	1 WVA	8/14/63–6/28/65
Cutright, Watson W. Surgeon	3 WVC	3/1/63–6/30/65
Day, John A.	US NF	
Dolly, Amoy H. Pvt.	WV GUARDS	7/2/63–6/1/65
Ehard, William Pvt.	68 NYI	8/61–8/20/64
Elkins, Stephen B. Capt.	6 WVC	6/62–9/63
Fahrion, Lewis Sgt.	1 OHA	4/20/61–7/22/65
Fahrner, Gotlieb Pvt.	15 MOI	9/1/61–4/13/64
Fay, Alfred Pvt.	2 MIC	1/4/64–8/14/65
Fincham, Charles H. Pvt.	6 WVI	9/64–7/65
Gabbert, Joseph H. Sgt.	1 WVC	6/26/61–8/15/65
Garton, James W. Pvt.	6 VAI	8/31/64–6/10/65
Geyer, Michael Pvt.	10 WVI	9/8/61–2/11/63
Gibson, David N.	SCOUT NF	
Glass, James W. Pvt.	6 MDI	7/15/63–4/5/65
Graves, Dennis	US NF	
Hammons, Mark Pvt.	BRAXTON HOME GUARD CSA	62/65

Name	Unit	Dates
Haney, Wm F. Pvt.	1 WVA	8/15/62–6/28/65
Hardsock, George W. Pvt.	NF	
Harman, Jesse Cpl.	WV GUARDS	3/14/64–4/15/65
Harman, Solomon Pvt.	WV GUARDS	2/29/64–4/15/65
Harper, John D. Pvt.	WV GUARDS	3/13/64–4/15/65
Hart, Alexander P. Cpl.	4 WVC	7/7/63–3/6/64
Hart, Squire B. Pvt.	1 WVA	8/12/62–6/28/65
Haymond, Daniel S. Pvt.	12 WVI	8/16/62–3/63
Hinchman, Joseph	10 WVI	3/5/62–5/5/65
Holland, John A. Pvt.	14 WVI	8/14/62–6/27/65
Johnston, Mortimer Pvt.	25 VAI CSA	5/28/61–4/9/65
Jordan, Adanijah N. Pvt.	WV GUARDS	6/7/64–4/15/65
Joyce, Thomas Pvt.	12 KYI	9/14/64–6/14/65
Joyce, Wm Pvt.	23 ILI	5/19/62–5/12/65
Judy, Zebulon Pvt.	46 VAM (CSA)	7/63–7/1/64
Ketterman, Mordecai N. Cpl.	WV GUARDS	1/7/64–5/30/65
Kile, Isaac Pvt.	18 VAC CSA	NF
Kittle, Andrew J. Pvt.	7 WVC	4/18/63–6/13/65
Kittle, John J. Pvt.	168 OHI	5/2/64–9/8/64
Kittle, Smith Pvt.	3 WVC	3/22/65–6/65
Kittle, Squire B. Sgt.	62 VAI CSA	5/61–5/23/65
Lambert, John G. Pvt.	25 VAI CSA	5/61–4/65
Lappen, Wellington Pvt.	7 VAI	11/22/61–9/7/63
Lewis, Albert G. Pvt.	79 OHI	8/11/62–6/30/65
Lewis, Henry H. Lt.	10 WVI	9/8/61–12/29/64
Lewis, William Pvt.	10 WVI	9/26/61–1863
Long, Absalom Pvt.	WV GUARDS	12/23/63–4/23/64
Long, Samuel B. Pvt.	WV GUARDS	3/13/64–4/15/65
Madden, Eward Pvt.	7 WVI	3/14/65–7/1/65
Madden, William Pvt.	3 VAI	6/27/61–8/9/62
Mallow, Abraham W. Pvt.	7 VAI	11/15/61–4/15/65
Mallow, William H. Pvt.	WV GUARDS	7/1/64–4/15/65
Marti, Mathias Pvt.	78 NYI	3/4/62–3/30/65
McCallister, John W. Pvt.	10 VAI (CSA)	61–64
McElwee, Francis L. Pvt.	20 VAC CSA	5/62–5/65
Meeks, John W. Sgt.	22 VAI CSA	8/61–4/65
Mehnoler, John Pvt.	37 OHI	9/1/61–10/8/62
Morgan, Charles Lt.	10 WVI	9/8/61–10/2/62
Mullins, Marshall Pvt.	19 VAC CSA	8/61–3/65
Nelson, Thomas Pvt.	WV GUARDS	9/63–10/64
Northcraft, John W. Pvt.	21 PAC	63–64
Oxier, Lorenzo Pvt.	22 VAI CSA	10/61–4/28/65
Parsons, Job W. Capt.	18 VAC CSA	62–65
Phillips, Asher M. Pvt.	2 WVI	1/7/62–6/9/65
Pickens, James Pvt.	10 WVI	9/25/61–3/12/65
Pritt, Homan (S) Pvt.	31 VAI CSA	5/62–5/65
Rader, Claude G. Capt.	20 VAC CSA	12/62–7/5/65

Name	Unit	Dates
Ray, Chancey R. Pvt.	11 PAC	61/65
Roy, Isaac J. Pvt.	WV GUARDS	2/29/64–4/15/65
Roy, Jacob Pvt.	WV GUARDS	1/30/65–5/30/65
Roy, Jelson B. Pvt.	WV GUARDS	2/20/64–5/30/65
Roy, John P. Pvt.	WV GUARDS	2/24/64–4/15/65
Roy, Solomon A. Pvt.	WV GUARDS	2/64–4/65
Roy, Washington Pvt.	WV GUARDS	2/29/64–4/15/65
Rutherford, John E. Pvt.	31 VAI CSA	6/61–3/65
Rutherford, Marcus S. Pvt.	31 VAI CSA	5/61–6/65
Sawyers, Jeremiah M. Sgt.	3 WVC	9/15/62–6/30/65
Scott, Jefferson Pvt.	10 WVI	8/28/62–7/3/65
Schloo, Herman Musician	4 USI	10/21/61–1865
Shannon, Martin Pvt.	20 VAC CSA	7/7/63–6/22/65
Shannon, Michael Sgt.	25 VAI CSA	1861–5/65
Shiflet, William M.	SCOUT	NF
Shobe, Wm H. Pvt.	18 VAC CSA	10/62–4/5/65
Shockey, Henry Sgt.	16 KYI	2/11/62–7/15/65
Sidwell, Henry Pvt.	WVI	NF
Simmons, Jonas J. Pvt.	10 WVI	NF
Simmons, William M. Cpl.	4 WVC	7/10/63–3/6/64
Skidmore, James S. Pvt.	10 WVI	7/1/62–7/3/65
Smith, Abraham Pvt.	WV GUARDS	2/24/63–5/1/64
Smith, Dennis O. Pvt.	3 MDI	NF
Smith, Laban V. Pvt.	WV GUARDS	7/62–4/65
Snider, Sampson Pvt.	32 OHI	12/27/61–4/15/65
Stalnaker, Adam Lt.	20 VAC CSA	5/7/63–4/20/65
Stalnaker, Alfred Pvt.	10 WVI	62–65
Stalnaker, Solomon Lt.	107 VAM (CSA)	4/63–2/65
Strader, Lorenzo D. Pvt.	1 WVC	5/4/62–5/4/65
Sturm, Jacob Pvt.	6 WVI	6/62–6/65
Summerfield, Abraham	NF	
Summerfield, Andrew J. Cpl.	WV GUARDS	11/63–4/8/65
Summerfield, John Pvt.	10 WVI	6/9/63–8/9/65
Summerfield, John W. Pvt.	10 WVI	7/3/63–9/14/64
Taylor, Eli Pvt.	18 VAC CSA	61/65
Taylor, Judson Pvt.	18 VAC CSA	5/62–4/65
Teter, Cyrus Cpl.	62 VAI (CSA)	63–64
Teter, John A. Sgt.	46 VAI (CSA)	3/64–4/9/65
Thomason, John N. Pvt.	3 WVC	3/21/65–6/30/65
Thompson, John Pvt.	18 VAC CSA	9/62–6/11/65
Tingler, Miles Pvt.	VAI CSA	5/62–NF
Tricket, Ezekiel Pvt.	14 WVI	8/14/62–3/13/65
Truax, William Pvt.	5 WVC	3/18/61–6/14/64
Tyre, John M. Pvt.	1 WVA NF	
Vandevender, Isaac Pvt.	25 VAI (CSA)	61–65
Vaughan, James A. Sgt.	7 WVI	9/1/61–12 8/62
Vogel, Bernhard Pvt.	9 ILI	8/10/61–7/9/65

Waelchby, Frederick Pvt.	77 OHI	10/6/62–7/31/63
Wamsley, William H. Pvt.	31 VAI CSA	5/61–6/65
Westfall, Lorenzo D. Pvt.	31 VAI CSA	5/61–4/9/65
White, William	US NF	
Whitmire, Nathan C. Cpl.	2 MDI	7/25/61–5/29/65
Wilfong, Hugh A. Pvt.	WV GUARDS	9/27/62–8/1/64
Williams, Thomas R. Cpl.	2 WVI	6/10/61–6/29/64
Workman, Andrew Pvt.	10 USI	3/27/38 3/27/63
Workman, Joseph	5 WVC	6/10/61–6/29/64
Yeager, Daniel M. Pvt.	15 VAI	7/26/62–6/14/65
Yoakum, Adam Sgt.	7 VAI (CSA)	11/22/61–9/7/63

Randolph County Remarks

Allen, J.M.—blood poison
Antill, J.—injured by a horse in fall from a wagon
Arbogast, G.W.*—made deaf in one ear by blow (deserted to WV Guards)
Bean, G.—RH & rupture
Bennett, D.—LD, ribs broken & RH, (Capt. Snyder's WV Scouts)
Bennett, M.V.*—shot through lung (deserted & served WV Guards US)
Browning, J.H.—KD & HD
Collier, W.H.—RH contracted on Salem raid
Curtis, D.B.—bronchitis, asthma, RH, 6 WVC 5/1864 Martinsburg
Curtis, T.C.—catarrahal affection
Cutright, J.W.—RH, injured eyesight
Cutright, W.W.—fever & ague
Ehard, W.—reinlisted Co G 75 PAI
Fahrion, L.—RH, shot in left leg
Fahrner, G.—shot in spine through lung & in thigh & head, RH, SS
Fay, A.—hernia contracted at Franklin, Tennessee
Fincham, C.H.—RH & bronchitis
Garton, J.W.—KD
Geyer, M.—rupture & eresypelas
Glass, J.W.—wounded at battle of Bull Run in left leg & hand
Haney, W.F.—RH, right side & lower extremities paralyzed
Harper, J.D.—contracted disease in service
Haymond, D.S.—falling back measles, not drawing pension
Johnston, M.*—left leg shot off
Joyce, T.—partial loss of sight & partial deafness
Joyce, W.—deafness & RH
Kittle, A.J.—broken leg

Kittle, S.—RH, MP & phthisic
Lappen, W.—shot through testicles
Lewis, A.G.—pneumonia, RH, smallpox, DSC at Nashville, Tenn.
Lewis, H.H.—RH & rupture
Lewis, W.—rupture
Madden, W.—falling of mumps
Marti, M.—RH
McCallister, J.W.*—arm broken in charge
Mehnoler, J.—RH
Morgan, C.—RH
Mullins, M.*—broken left arm by being thrown off horse
Oxier, L.*—shot across abdomen
Pickens, J.—shot in left leg
Pritt, H.*—eyes injured
Ray, C.R.—RH
Rutherford, M.S.*—shot in right thigh & across top of head
Sawyers, J.M.—bruised testicles
Schloo, H.—shot in left rist, reinlisted 14 years
Scott, J.—piles & gunshot
Shockey, H.—RH, HD, vision, rupture of bowels
Sidwell, H.—RH
Simmons, W.M.—dyspepsia & nervousness
Skidmore, J.S.—wounded at Carneysville, WV applied for pension
Smith, D.O.—chronic dysentery, drawing pension $8 per month
Snider, S.—tibia on shin bone broken
Strader, L.D.—right arm injured
Summerfield, J.—VV
Summerfield, J.W.—shot through left hand & left knee
Thomason, J.N.—RH & piles
Tinqler, M.*—shot through left shoulder (deserted)
Tricket, E.—gunshot wound at Cedar Creek, Va
Vaughan, J.A.—gunshot wound left leg & diseases contracted in army
Vogel, B.—shot left thigh & right rist
Waelchby, F.—RH, reinlisted 3/24/65
Westfall, L.D.*—shot in left arm
Williams, T.R.—gunshot right hip, grapeshot right shoulder
Workman, J.—chronic sore eyes contracted at Beverly, WV
Yeager, D.M.—crippled back & hips
Yoakum, A.*—shot through left ear

Ritchie County

NAME/RANK	REGIMENT	WHEN SERVED
Adams, Harvey H. Pvt.	36 OHI	2/14/64–7/27/65
Alkier, Wm. Pvt.	14 WVI	8/14/62–6/27/65
Alkire, Marion Pvt.	14 VAI	8/9/62–7/3/65
Ambble?, James B. Cpl.	14 WVI	8/15/62–7/3/65
Ankrom, David Pvt.	2 WVC	9/12/61–12/20/64
Archbold, Adam T. Pvt.	16 INI	4/21/61–12/16/61
Arnett, James Cpl.	10 WVI	2/12/62–5/65
Atkinson, George Pvt.	36 OHI	2/27/64–7/27/65
Ayers, Daniel Sgt.	15 WVI	9/10/62–6/14/65
Ayers, Michael A. Major	11 WVI	12/22/61–6/17/65
Ayrie, John F. Pvt.	10 WVI	62/65
Barker, Levi Pvt.	77 OHI	2/13/64–3/8/66
Barker, Oliver Pvt.	10 WVI	61/65
Barr, Alfred Musician	11 WVI	12/22/61–12/24/64
Bartlett, Lorenzo D. Pvt.	17 WVI	2/16/65–6/13/65
Batten, Hezekial Pvt.	7 WVI	9/21/61–8/4/65
Beagle, Edgar J. Pvt.	17 WVI	7/64–6/65
Beard, John C. Pvt.	18 OHI	8/15/61–11/9/64
BeBruear, John M. Pvt.	6 WVI	8/20/61–6/10/65
Bee, Azariah Pvt.	6 WVI	9/20/64–6/10/65
Bee, Obadiah Pvt.	6 WVI	11/15/61–6/10/65
Bircher, Jeremiah F. Pvt.	17 WVI	7/64–6/65
Bird, Davis Pvt.	NF	
Black, George P. Sgt.	6 WVI	8/6/61–8/16/64
Black, Wm. Pvt.	6 VAI	8/20/61–11/10/64
Bond, Richard E. Pvt.	6 WVC	3/29/64–5/22/66
Boner, Ferrel D. Pvt.	11 WVI	12/10/61–12/24/65
Boner, James Pvt.	11 WVI	11/10/61–12/24/64
Boner, Valentine Pvt.	11 WVI	11/61–NF
Border, John Pvt.	91 OHI	8/12/62–6/30/65
Boston, Michael Pvt.	77 OHI	NF
Bowie, Eli Pvt.	36 OHI	1861–8/65
Bowie, Harvey Pvt.	36 OHI	8/25/64–6/27/65
Brake, James R. Sgt.	14 WVI	9/7/62–6/27/65
Brinker, C.C. Pvt.	11 PAI	4/19/61–8/5/61
Britton, John W. Pvt.	17 WVI	8/21/64–6/30/65
Broadwater, Marcus Pvt.	6 WVI	2/26/64–6/10/65
Brooks?, John	CSA NF (19 VAC?)	
Brooks, Nicholas	NF	
Brown, Edward M. Pvt.	6 WVI	9/20/64–6/10/65
Brown, John W. Pvt.	6 WVI	8/15/62–6/5/65
Buckhannon, Thomas Pvt.	10 WVI	6/15/62–7/65
Bumgardner, Samuel Sgt.	14 VAI	8/9/62–3/5/65

Name	Unit	Dates
Bumgarner, Daniel C. Pvt.	6 VAI	8/20/61–8/27/64
Burris?, Wm. M. Sgt.	2 DEI?	9/61–1865
Bush, Daniel C. Sgt.	6 WVI	8/18/61–12/20/64
also Lt.	6 WVI	3/29/65–6/10/65
Bush, Daniel D. Pvt.	10 WVI	4/3/62–3/12/63
Butcher, Ephram Pvt.	14 VAI	8/62–7/2/65
Calhoun, Eugenius Pvt.	14 WVI	9/13/62–7/3/65
Campbell, Daniel Pvt.	11 WVI	8/14/62–6/23/65
Carder, Thomas Pvt.	6 WVI	8/6/61–7/13/65
Carpenter, Reason Pvt.	116 OHI	8/62–8/65
Caton, Alfred T. Pvt.	6 WVI	8/12/61–6/10/65
Champ, Jackson Pvt.	15 WVI	8/21/62–6/12/65
Chapman, Vivian B. Pvt.	92 OHI	8/11/62–6/30/65
Ciders, Jesse M. Pvt.	6 WVI	9/4/61–6/10/65
Clammer, Jacob Capt.	11 WVI	11/10/61–12/24/64
Clark, George W. Pvt.	194 OHI	2/18/64–10/24/65
Clark, John Pvt.	22 OHI	4/20/61–8/19/61
also Capt.	6 WVI	9/23/61–6/10/65
Clark, John Pvt.	46 OHI	NF
Clark, Wm. J. Pvt.	11 WVI	10/26/61–4/22/63
Clayton, John S. Cpl.	4 WVC	8/10/63–3/8/64
Clevenger, Sam L. Pvt.	62–VAI CSA	8/62–4/18/65
Colegate, John C. Pvt.	6 WVI	8/15/61–9/10/64
Collins, Isaac S. Cpl.	11 WVI	10/21/61–2/3/65
Collins, Sedgwick C. Pvt.	11 WVI	7/62–7/65
Collins, Shadrach?	NF (3 SCI CSA?)	
Constable, Wm. Pvt.	6 WVI	NF
Cowan, M.D. Pvt.	10 VAI	2/20/64–8/9/65
Cox, Daniel W. Pvt.	6 WVI	8/31/61–NF
Cox, Grafton J. Pvt.	WV Scouts	10/14/64–4/13/65
Cox, John M. Pvt.	3 WVI	7/4/61–9/12/62
Crawford, Wm. P. Pvt.	106 PAI	NF
Criss, Eugenius Pvt.	14 WVI	9/12/62–6/27/65
Criss, Newton Pvt.	6 WVC	9/26/64–5/19/65
Crites, Isaac N.G. Pvt.	10 WVI	10/18/61–12/29/64
Cross, George W. Pvt.	14 WVI	8/15/62–7/3/65
Cross, John A. Pvt.	14 WVI	8/15/62–7/3/65
Cross, Thomas F. Pvt.	1 WVC	2/64–7/13/65
Crow, Wm. Sgt.	4 WVC	7/2/63–3/10/64
Crown, Andrew Pvt.	96 OHI	8/14/62–7/4/65
Crumrine, James B. Pvt.	58 PAI	7/7/63–9/15/63
Culp, James M. Pvt.	11 WVI	8/8/62–6/16/65
Cummins, Ashbury Sgt.	4 WVC	7/2/63–3/10/64
also	17 WVI	2/17/65–6/13/65
Cunningham, Benj. F. Pvt.	4 WVC	7/25/63–3/8/64
Cunningham, John R. Pvt.	11 WVI	12/22/61–12/24/64
Cunningham, Moses Pvt.	6 WVI	7/16/62–6/10/65

Name	Unit	Dates
Cunningham, Wilson Pvt.	77 OHI	NF
Cunningham, Wm. J. Pvt.	6 WVI	8/20/61–6/10/65
Daily, Smith J. Pvt.	7 WVI	6/61–9/62
Davidson, Jasper W. Cpl.	6 WVI	9/23/61–12/3/64
Davis, Benj. F. Pvt.	14 WVI	8/11/62–6/27/65
Davis, James M. Pvt.	3 WVI	7/4/61–10/28/62
Davis, Wm. R. Pvt.	17 WVI	7/28/62–7/18/65
Deem, David Capt.	11 WVI	8/23/62–6/1/65
Deem, John Pvt.	11 WVI	NF
Delancey, James M. Pvt.	92 OHI	9/17/62–7/23/64
Delony, John W. Pvt.	92 OHI	6/62–6/63
also	23 OHI	7/27/64–6/30/65
Doe, Frederick Pvt.	140 NYI	9/2/62–6/18/65
Dolan, James T. Pvt.	NF (1 VAI CSA?)	
Dotson, Clinton Pvt.	6 WVI	8/18/61–9/10/64
Dotson, Hiram Pvt.	6 WVC	5/17/63–5/66
Dotson, Hiram S. Pvt.	14 WVI	8/2/62–11/15/63
Dougherty, George W. Pvt.	6 WVI	8/18/61–6/10/65
Douglas, George B. Pvt.	6 VAI	8/20/61–8/27/64
Douglas, Jeremiah R. Pvt.	6 VAI	8/20/62–6/10/65
Drake, Thomas Pvt.	2 WVC	7/61–7/65
Dunn, Wm. Pvt.	7 WVI	3/21/65–9/6/65
Dye, Wm. H. Pvt.	116 OHI	8/14/62–6/14/65
Earnest, Martin L. Sgt.	1 DEC	64/65
Echols, Wm. W. Lt.	6 WVI	9/15/61–6/18/65
Elder, Robert L. B. Pvt.	NF	
Elefril, Enoch F. Pvt.	14 WVI	7/28/62–6/27/65
Elliott, Henry S. Pvt.	3 WVC	62/65
Elliott, Nashville	11 WVI	NF
Elliott, Thomas J. Pvt.	6 WVI	1/13/65–6/18/65
Elliott, Washington Pvt.	3 WVC	62/65
Emery, Wilford Cpl.	1 WVI	5/9/61–8/61
Evans, Andrew J. Pvt.	11 WVI	12/22/61–12/24/64
Exlisre?, Abraham Cpl.	6 WVI	8/18/61–9/10/64
Feassel, James A. Pvt.	3 WVC	9/15/63–6/30/65
Ferrell, Robert Pvt.	NF	
Flanagan, James H. Pvt.	36 OHI	1/15/65–7/27/65
Flesher, Adam Pvt.	7 OHC	9/1/62–6/29/65
Flesher, John Pvt.	13 OHI	NF
Fordham, Thomas	6 WVI	64/65
Frederick, W. T. Pvt.	10 WVI	1/3/64–8/65
Frier, Romeo H. Pvt.	86 OHI	7/14/62–12/27/64
Fultz, Silas G. Cpl.	53 OHI	10/26/61–10/30/62
Gabbert, John W. Pvt.	12 WVI	8/13/62–6/11/65
Garrell, Parker C. Pvt.	3 WVI	7/4/61–1/22/64
also	6 WVC	1/22/64–10/14/65
Garrison, Daniel Pvt.	14 WVI	8/8/62–6/9/65

Garrison, Wm. G. Pvt.	6 WVI	8/20/61–6/10/65
Gary, Samuel R. Pvt.	1 WVI	61/61
also	17 WVI	7/1/64–1865
Gary, Simon Pvt.	NF	
Giebell, Conrad Pvt.	155 PAI	8/6/64–5/30/65
Gilmore, John T. Pvt.	174 OHI	8/18/64–6/28/65
Gitchell, Joseph H. Pvt.	148 OHI	5/1/64–9/18/64
Givens, Daniel W. Pvt.	77 OHI	2/26/64–3/8/66
Glover, Robert E. Pvt.	11 WVI	7/11/63–8/20/65
Gluck, Joseph C. Sgt.	10 WVI	3/62–8/9/65
Goff, Elijah C. Sgt.	6 WVI	7/62–6/10/65
Gorrell, Martin L. Pvt.	17 WVI	2/28/65–6/14/66
Gray, D. W. Pvt.	184 OHI	NF
Gregg, Samuel Pvt.	7 WVI	61/64
Gregory, John Pvt.	179 OHI	9/64–6/65
Gribble, Thomas N. Pvt.	6 WVI	8/14/62–6/27/65
Griffin, Ebenezer B. Pvt.	3 VAI	7/4/61–1/28/64
also Cpl.	6 VAC	1/27/64–5/22/66
Gulley, Czreneus Pvt.	9 OHC	9/62–7/17/65
Haddox, Cincinnatus P. Pvt	23 NYA	12/19/63–7/14/65
Hague, David B. Pvt.	1 WVA	8/26/61–9/14/64
Hall, John A. Pvt.	6 WVI	9/10/64–6/10/65
Hall, Moses S. Ltc.	10 WVI	7/4/61–3/20/65
Hamerick, Wm. Pvt.	11 WVI	11/10/61–12/24/64
Hamilton, Henry E. Pvt.	7 WVI	61/65
Hammer, Lewis Pvt.	10 WVI	2/23/64–8/9/65
Hamrick, Thomas Pvt.	14 WVI	8/12/62–6/28/65
Haney, Chesman Pvt.	116 OHI	8/10/62–6/20/65
Hardesty, James H. Pvt.	6 WVI	6/26/63–6/9/65
Hardin, George W. Pvt.	14 VAI	8/18/62–6/27/65
Hardman, James S. Pvt.	11 WVI	12/63–8/65
Harper, Mordecai Pvt.	186 OHI	2/20/65–9/18/65
Harris, Thomas M. Gen.	10 WVI	3/10/62–4/30/66
Harter, Wm. M. Pvt.	3 VAC	2/17/65–6/28/65
Hartleben, Robert Sgt.	6 VAI	9/12/62–6/10/65
Hartley, Joseph Pvt.	3 WVC	8/25/62–6/27/65
Hashman, Thomas Pvt.	77 OHI	NF
Hatfield, Samuel Cpl.	6 WVI	8/20/61–8/27/64
Haught, Archelus J. Pvt.	7 WVI	1862–7/9/65
Hemselman, Chrisitan Cpl.	75 OHI	10/23/61–12/22/64
Hess, Thomas Lt.	10 WVI	6/10/62–10/23/64
Hewitt, Charles Lt.	3 WVI	7/4/61–2/11/62
also Sgt.	6 WVI	9/19/64–6/11/65
Hickman, Bassel (H?)	CSA NF (25 VAI?)	
Hinton, Samuel P. Cpl.	77 OHI	11/6/61–3/8/66
Hinton, Tom J. Pvt.	36 OHI	8/12/61–3/7/65
Hodge, John A. Pvt.	10 WVI	12/17/61–4/1/63

Hoff, Wm. J. Pvt.	3 WVC	3/30/65–6/30/65
Holstein, Wm. A. Pvt.	13 WVI	4/12/62–7/23/65
Hooper, Isaac Pvt.	62–OHI	10/4/61–8/31/62
Huey, James Pvt.	36 OHI	NF
Hyson, Benj. F. Pvt.	19 VAC CSA	62/64
Ireland, George M. Capt.	6 WVI	8/31/61–6/10/65
Isner, Washington Pvt.	6 WVC	6/25/61–7/1/65
Jamison, James M. Pvt.	92 OHI	8/11/62–6/5/65
Jenkins, Asa Pvt.	10 WVI	8/20/62–7/65
Jett, Sylvester Pvt.	6 WVI	8/27/64–6/10/65
Johnson, Amos N. Pvt.	Lurty's VAA CSA	6/63–5/11/65
Johnson, John H. Pvt.	11 WVI	9/5/61–8/2/65
Jones, Francis M. Pvt.	14 WVI	8/15/62–6/27/65
Jones, Jacob C. Sgt.	14 WVI	8/14/62–4/1/63
Jones, Joshua Pvt.	12 WVI	8/27/62–6/16/65
Jordan, John H. Pvt.	3 VAI	7/61–NF
Jordan, Wm. A. Pvt.	14 WVI	62/65
Jordan, Wm. H. Pvt.	6 WVI	1/3/62–5/15/62
also	1 OHA	8/18/64–7/65
Joy, Harvey Pvt.	62 OHI	12/9/61–7/13/65
Keener, David Pvt.	11 WVI	6/8/63–8/65
Kelley, John H. Pvt.	10 VAI	6/11/62–6/27/65
Kelly, John O. Pvt.	6 WVI	8/31/61–6/10/65
Kennedy, John P. Pvt.	6 WVI	9/14/61–6/13/65
Kershner, David Pvt.	17 WVI	2/14/65–6/30/65
Kilden, F. M. Pvt.	3 WVC	9/15/62–6/30/65
Kirby, Wm. H. Pvt.	14 WVI	8/15/62–6/27/65
Kirkpatrick, Ephraim Pvt.	3 WVI	7/4/61–8/16/64
Kirkpatrick, Levi Pvt.	3 WVI	7/4/61–9/25/65
Knight, Hiram J. Pvt.	6 WVC	9/20/63–5/20/65
Lafaye, John A.	S.C. CSA (Manigault's SCA)	
Lee, Asbury Pvt.	6 WVI	9/21/64–6/10/65
Lee, Marvin Pvt.	18 OHI	9/23/61–11/19/64
Lee, Peter Pvt.	6 WVI	9/20/64–6/10/65
Lewellyn, Wm. Pvt.	2 KSC	6/22/62–6/22/65
Lewis, Wm. A. Pvt.	11 WVI	10/15/62–8/9/65
Lipscomb, Christopher Pvt.	6 WVC	1/31/65–5/22/66
Longfellow, John H. Pvt.	43 OHI	2/15/63–7/7/65
Lough, Nimrod Pvt.	11 WVI	11/24/61–12/24/64
Lowe, Walker M. Pvt.	— VAI	NF
Lowther, Wm. G. Lt.	14 WVI	8/11/62–6/17/65
Lucas, Abraham F. Pvt.	20 VAC CSA	6/63–1865
Luke, John Pvt.	36 OHI	8/12/62–7/8/65
Lydick, Wm. H. Pvt.	17 WVI	2/15/65–6/30/65
Mallory, Johnson B. Pvt.	1 KSI	5/30/61–12/16/62
Mapel, David Pvt.	1 PAC	9/16/64–8/7/65
Marsh, James	NF	

Marshall, Benj. P. Pvt.	11 WVI	7/22/62–6/17/65
Marshall, Joseph H. Pvt.	27 OHI	7/61–8/25/65
Martin, Joab Pvt.	14 VAI	8/14/62–6/14/65
Martin, John F. Pvt.	6 WVI	8/61–6/10/65
Martin, Marcus E. Pvt.	6 WVC	9/64–5/19/65
Mason, Eber Pvt.	14 VAI	8/15/62–6/27/65
Mason, Eli Pvt.	6 WVI	9/30/64–6/10/65
Mason, Jacob A. QM/Sgt.	4 VAC	7/25/63–3/8/64
Mason, Philip Pvt.	NF	
Matheny, Archbold Pvt.	11 OHC	6/3/63–5/1/66
Mathers, Joseph Pvt.	1 OHC	1/18/64–10/65
Mathews, Waitman T. Sgt.	4 WVC	7/26/63–3/7/64
Maulsby, John W. Pvt.	6 VAI	1/2/62–1/2/65
Maxwell, Lamar Pvt.	6 WVI	64/65
McBee, Zadoc Pvt.	17 WVI	9/64–7/65
McClain, Eugenius Pvt.	6 WVI	6/27/61–9/7/64
McClead, Eli Pvt.	179 OHI	9/1/64–6/8/65
McDonald, Mack Pvt.	10 WVI	5/63–8/9/65
McDonald, Wesley Pvt.	6 WVI	8/18/61–6/10/65
McDougal, Charles W. Pvt.	WVI	8/63–7/65
McGinnis, Benj. Pvt.	6 WVC	7/10/61–8/17/64
McGregor, Silas Pvt.	3 VAI	7/4/61–8/13/64
McGregor, Spencer B. Cpl.	4 WVC	6/25/62–4/1/63
also Pvt.	17 WVI	2/28/65–6/13/65
McIntire, Archibald Pvt.	5 CAI	61/66
McKinley, Wm. P. Pvt.	7 WVI	3/22/65–6/21/65
McMillen, Wm. Pvt.	1 PAA	5/27/64–9/12/64
McMullen, Richard Pvt.	9 OHC	63/65
McMullen, Wm. Pvt.	30 OHI	8/27/61–8/13/65
McMullin, Gregory Pvt.	14 WVI	8/12/62–7/3/65
McMullin, John Sgt.	14 WVI	8/15/62–7/3/65
Metz, Wm. F. Pvt.	7 WVI	10/16/61–1/7/63
Miller, Wm. G. Pvt.	74 PAI	10/61–10/64
Miller, Wm. S.	NF	
Miracle, Wm. B. Pvt.	174 OHI	8/26/64–7/22/65
Mitchell, Aaron Pvt.	10 WVI	NF
Mitchell, Robert Pvt.	6 WVI	8/18/61–6/10/65
Moats, Andrew Pvt.	2 WVC	6/16/61–6/16/64
Moats, Benj. Lt.	10 WVI	2/1/62–2/21/65
Moats, Cornelius Pvt.	11 WVI	8/8/62–6/17/65
Monroe, John R. Pvt.	179 OHI	9/3/64–6/17/65
Moore, Thomas Pvt.	92 OHI	8/7/62–6/10/65
More, James B. Pvt.	6 WVC	9/26/64–5/19/65
More, John Pvt.	3 WVI	7/4/61–8/16/64
Morris, Wm. Pvt.	14 WVI	3/8/65–7/3/65
Mortin, Wm. Pvt.	14 WVI	7/12/62–6/65
Mowry, John Pvt.	1 OHA	7/25/61–7/27/65

Mulinax, Washington J. Pvt	10 VAI	6/10/61–8/27/64
Mulnax, Owen Pvt.	78 OHI	11/23/61–7/4/64
Murdock, James Pvt.	179 OHI	9/8/64–6/17/65
Musgrave, Job Pvt.	12 WVI	8/14/62–6/16/65
Nalley, Levi Pvt.	92 OHI	8/8/62–6/10/65
Nash, Martin Pvt.	1 OHA	61/65
Nay, Daniel Sgt.	WV Scouts	4/23/64–4/30/65
Nay, James A. Pvt.	6 WVI	65/65
Neptune, Wm. W. Cpl.	92 OHI	8/62–5/65
Norman, James E. Pvt.	10 WVI	4/5/62–5/6/65
Norris, Wm. W. Pvt.	6 WVI	1/3/64–6/10/65
Nutter, Benj. W. Pvt.	3 WVI	6/25/61–6/7/62
Nutter, Christopher B. Pvt	11 WVI	7/17/62–6/17/65
Nutter, Tom E. Pvt.	6 WVI	8/18/61–9/14/64
Overton, John P. Pvt.	3 MDC	9/18/63–9/7/65
Palmer, Elisha Pvt.	1 OHA	9/1/61–7/65
Park, Sam C. Cpl.	14 WVI	7/28/62–6/15/65
Parks, Eli Pvt.	7 WVI	12/61–4/2/63
Parks, John C. Sgt.	14 WVI	8/11/62–6/27/65
Parks, Wm. H. Pvt.	6 WVI	8/20/61–6/10/65
Payne, Daniel G. Pvt.	92 OHI	1/3/63–7/4/65
Payne, James M. Pvt.	34 OHI	1/28/63–7/20/65
Pearl, Uriah Sgt.	6 WVI	9/27/64–5/19/65
Peck, Jacob Pvt.	31 VAI (CSA)	6/62–1865
Peck, Tarlton Pvt.	6 WVI	8/20/61–8/27/64
Perrin, Amos Pvt.	11 WVI	8/4/62–6/6/65
Pickering, Jasper Pvt.	53 OHI	2/64–8/65
Pierpoint, Larkin Ltc.	6 WVI	9/2/61–6/10/65
Poynter, Hynson C. Pvt.	6 WVI	8/15/62–2/12/64
Pratt, Hira Pvt.	14 WVI	8/2/62–6/27/65
Pratt, James E. Pvt.	4 WVC	7/25/63–3/8/64
also	17 WVI	2/28/65–6/30/65
Price, John Pvt.	14 WVI	8/9/62–6/9/65
Pringle, John C. Pvt.	1 WVA	8/24/62–6/23/65
Pritchard, Jasper W. Pvt.	10 WVI	3/62–9/65
Prunty, Alex Sgt.	4 WVC	8/63–3/64
Prunty, Elmore Cpl.	6 WVI	8/18/61–9/10/64
Prunty, Fenton Pvt.	3 WVC	3/1/63–6/30/65
Rexroad, Zachariah P.	6 WVI	8/20/61–6/10/65
Riddle, David C. Pvt.	6 WVI	8/18/61–9/10/64
Riddle, George W. Pvt.	10 WVI	8/19/62–6/29/65
Rieves, Peachy H. Pvt.	3 MDC	61/64
Riggs, Allen Pvt.	10 VAI	2/23/62–5/65
Riggs, Eli B. Pvt.	10 WVI	1/16/62–7/7/65
Riggs, Isaac B. Pvt.	14 WVI	8/11/62–3/29/65
Riggs, John Pvt.	10 WVI	5/10/61–2/23/63
Rivve, Israel L.	US NF	

Roach, Warren W. Pvt.	6 WVI	8/7/62–6/10/65
Rodgers, Sanderson H. Pvt.	36 OHI	7/31/61–10/24/64
Rogers, John H. Pvt.	77 OHI	11/18/61–3/2/66
Rogers, Lewis Pvt.	6 WVI	NF
Rollins, Benj. F. Pvt.	6 WVI	8/18/61–9/10/64
Rollins, Edward Pvt.	6 WVI	9/2/61–9/10/64
Rollins, George W. Pvt.	15 WVI	9/28/64–5/23/65
Rush, Joseph Pvt.	21 WVC	9/1/61–11/28/65
Russell, James O. Pvt.	6 WVC	8/26/64–5/19/65
Rutz, Lewis P. Sgt.	14 WVI	9/62–6/65
Rymer, James D. Pvt.	6 WVI	9/4/64–6/13/65
Satterfield, Elias L. Capt	14 VAI	8/22/62–1863
Satterfield, S.J. Pvt.	6 WVI	8/20/61–6/10/65
Satterfield, Sanford C Pvt	6 WVC	NF
also	5 WVI	7/4/61–2/64
Sayer, Cornelious Pvt.	27 OHI	8/18/61–8/65
Scott, James B. Pvt.	125 OHI	10/22/62–9/25/65
Selby, ——? Pvt.	186 OHI	2/14/65–9/18/65
Shannon, Murrey Pvt.	30 OHI	8/22/61–8/29/64
Sharpnack, Anthony Pvt.	6 VAI	8/27/61–6/10/65
Sharpnack, D.M. Cpl.	6 VAI	6/7/62–6/10/65
Sharpnack, Elias H. Pvt.	6 VAI	7/22/62–1/17/65
Shephera, Charles C. Pvt.	6 VAI	8/20/61–6/10/65
Shepherd, Ezekial Lt.	6 WVI	8/20/61–8/17/64
Shilling, John W. Pvt.	92 OHI	62/63
Shrader, John Pvt.	77 OHI	10/17/61–3/8/66
Shrader, Uriah Pvt.	6 VAI	8/20/61–6/10/65
Simmons, Alfred Pvt.	3 VAI	6/10/61–8/2/64
Simmons, John W. Pvt.	10 WVI	8/6/62–3/7/65
Simmons, Louis Pvt.	14 WVI	8/22/62–6/27/65
Simonton, Wm. Pvt.	4 WVC	7/25/63–3/8/64
also	17 WVI	2/28/65–6/14/65
Sinnett, John P. Pvt.	10 WVI	2/20/62–5/2/65
Skidmore, James Pvt.	6 WVI	8/1/61–5/1/64
Slack, Enoch Pvt.	80 OHI	1/30/65–8/13/65
Smith, Barnes Pvt.	CSA NF (19 VAC)	
Smith, Daniel M. Pvt.	3 WVI	7/1/61–NF
also Sgt.	6 WVC	3/63–5/30/66
Smith, Enoch H. Pvt.	22 OHI	4/17/61–11/19/65
Smith, Gilbert Pvt.	6 WVI	62/65
Smith, Henry M. Pvt.	NF (62–VAI CSA?)	
Smith, Isaac S. Sgt.	1 OHA	9/1/61–1/16/65
Smith, James T. Pvt.	14 WVI	8/22/62–6/27/65
Smith, John B. Pvt.	18 OHI	4/19/61–8/28/61
also	1 WVA	9/20/61–8/22/62
Smith, Martin Pvt.	11 WVI	12/22/61–12/24/64
Snider, Edgar Sgt.	— PAI	NF

Snider, Stephen Pvt.	14 WVI	3/3/65–7/5/65
Snodgrass, Clyde C. Pvt.	6 WVI	8/18/61–9/10/64
Snodgrass, Jeremiah Sgt.	14 WVI	8/13/62–6/27/65
Snodgrass, John Pvt.	6 WVI	2/16/65–6/10/65
Sommerville, John Capt.	6 WVC	6/27/61–6/17/65
Speer, Earnest Pvt.	6 WVC	6/9/61–8/15/64
Spilson, Jasper	NF	
Springston, Josiah B. Pvt.	3 VAC	8/14/62–7/10/65
Stanley, Eli M. Pvt.	10 WVI	1/1/64–5/28/65
Stanly, Wm. B.	19 VAC CSA	62/65
Stasell, John T. Pvt.	10 WVI	12/61–3/17/65
Stewart, Nathan H. Pvt.	14 WVI	8/14/62–6/27/65
Stewart, Peter Cpl.	7 WVI	8/7/61–1/31/65
Stewart, Robert W. Pvt.	6 WVI	8/31/61–9/1/64
Stock, Wm. Pvt.	36 OHI	8/12/61–8/26/64
Stone, Cornelious Cpl.	7 WVI	9/25/61–6/18/65
Stonestreet, Wm. Pvt.	3 WVC	10/16/61–7/15/65
Summers, Thomas M. Pvt.	4 WVC	7/8/63–3/8/64
Summers, Tom M. Pvt.	5 WVI	2/64–8/65
Taitt, John A. Pvt.	— OHI	64/65
Thomas, John J. Pvt.	6 VAI	62/65
Thomas, Pimm T.	— OHI	NF
Tibbs, Edwin R. Pvt.	14 WVI	8/22/62–6/27/65
Tichner, George Sgt.	6 WVI	8/10/61–6/10/65
Tichner, John Pvt.	6 WVI	8/12/61–8/20/64
Tingler, Granville Pvt.	11 WVI	12/22/61–12/24/64
Toothman, John H. Pvt.	6 WVC	2/29/64–5/22/66
Trainer, Edgar Pvt.	6 WVI	9/1/64–6/10/65
Vincent, David Pvt.	6 WVI	8/31/64–6/10/65
Vincent, Francis M. Pvt.	31 VAI CSA	61/62
Vincent, Isaac L. Pvt.	5 WVC	8/20/61–6/14/64
also	12 WVI	9/5/64–6/15/65
Vore, Ellis Pvt.	92 OHI	8/9/62–4/23/63
Wade, Andrew M. Pvt.	4 WVC	8/1/63–3/8/64
Wade, Selby Pvt.	4 WVC	8/1/63–3/8/64
Wake, Thomas Cpl.	2 — I (Negro)	8/18/63–6/20/66
Waller, Benj. F. Pvt.	12 WVI	1862–6/65
Wanlass, Richard Pvt.	4 WVC	NF
Ward, George Pvt.	77 OHI	11/21/61–3/20/65
Warder, Thomby Pvt.	14 WVI	2/11/65–6/30/65
Washburn, Cyrus Pvt.	5 WVI	6/10/61–1/31/64
also	6 WVC	1/31/64–8/8/65
Wass, Harrison Pvt.	6 WVI	9/61–9/64
Watson, Morgan B. Pvt.	6 WVI	8/27/64–6/22/65
Watson, Wilson Pvt.	14 WVI	8/14/62–6/27/65
Weaver, Elam Pvt.	17 WVI	2/65–7/65
Webb, Nathan C. B. Pvt.	3 WVI	6/25/61–7/17/62

Webster, Paul Pvt.	20 KYI	10/24/61–9/6/65
Weekly, George W. Pvt.	6 WVI	1/31/62–2/5/65
Weinrich, Charles Pvt.	6 WVI	62/65
Weinrich, Lewis Sgt.	10 WVI	2/1/62–5/2/65
Wells, Benj. Pvt.	6 WVC	9/26/64–5/19/65
Wells, George M.D. Pvt.	10 WVI	2/22/64–8/9/65
West, George W. Pvt.	3 WVC	9/3/62–9/65
West, George W. Pvt.	77 OHI	11/23/61–12/19/63
West, Joshue W. Pvt.	176 OHI	9/19/64–6/14/65
Westfall, Wm. A. Cpl.	10 WVI	2/20/62–8/9/65
Whaley, Josiah M. Sgt.	10 VAI	NF
Whitehair, John P. Pvt.	6 WVI	9/4/64–6/10/65
Whiteman, David C. Cpl.	6 VAI	8/27/61–6/10/65
Whiteman, Robert R. Pvt.	6 VAI	6/30/63–6/10/65
Whitzel, Jonathan Pvt.	6 WVI	9/14/61–6/13/65
Wigner, Robert H.	NF	
Wildman, John P. Pvt.	3 VAI	8/10/61–6/10/65
Williams, Chester Pvt.	6 WVI	9/4/64–6/12/65
Williams, Hiram Pvt.	6 WVI	8/18/61–6/10/65
Williams, Jacob Pvt.	6 WVI	10/16/61–12/64
Williamson, Silas G. Pvt.	10 VAI	1/4/62–8/9/65
Wilson, Abraham Pvt.	14 WVI	8/9/62–7/3/65
Wilson, Arter Pvt.	6 WVI	8/1/61–6/13/65
Wilson, Daniel Pvt.	11 WVI	12/22/61–12/24/64
Wilson, Edgar C. Sgt.	9 WVI	3/31/62–5/3/65
Wilson, Joshua Pvt.	6 WVI	8/10/62–9/16/65
Wilson, Lemuel Pvt.	6 WVC	8/64–5/65
Wilson, Thomas Pvt.	6 WVI	2/4/64–6/10/65
Wolf, John W.	NF (12 VAC CSA)	
Woofton, Thomas J.	US NF	
Wright, Zachariah Pvt.	20 VAC CSA	6/63–6/64
Wright, Loyd Pvt.	20 VAC CSA	6/62–4/65
Wright, Nathan Pvt.	92 OHI	8/6/62–3/19/64
Wylie, Daniel Pvt.	- OHI	1861–NF
also	176 OHI	NF
Yockey, Jacob Pvt.	142 PAI	8/15/62–6/2/65
Young, John A. Sgt.	77 OHI	10/11/61–3/18/66
Zickifoose, A.W. Sgt.	10 WVI	2/2/62–5/2/65
Zinn, Granville P. Pvt.	6 WVI	8/18/61–9/10/64
Zinn, Henry C. Pvt.	6 WVI	9/20/64–6/10/65
Zinn, Thomas G. Pvt.	6 WVI	9/64–6/10/65
Zinn, Wm. B. Pvt.	6 WVI	8/18/61–9/10/64

Ritchie County Remarks

Adams, H.H.—catarrh & LD
Alkier, W.—disease of stomach & piles
Alkire, M.—piles, RH & dyspepsia
Ankrom, D.—gunshot wound left shoulder, pensioner
Archbold, A.T.—hemorhage of lungs
Arnett, J.—hurt in knee
Atkinson, G.—WIA 8/12/6
Ayers, M.A.—throat & stomach disease, AFP
Ayrie, J.F.—wounded in finger
Bailey, J.H.—gunshot wounds, pensioner
Barker, L.—RH
Barker, O.—pensioner
Barr, A.—gunshot left side & arm, RH, pensioner
Batten, H.—injury to left knee & eye disease, pensioner
Beagle, E.J.—LD & RH, pensioner
Beard, J.C.—2 gunshot wounds, pneumonia, W , disease of throat
Bee, O.—RH & KD, AFP
Bircher, J.F.—eyesight impaired, AFP
Bird, D.—pensioner
Black, G.P.—loss of an eye
Boner, F.D.—HD & palsey
Boner, J.—shell wound & disease of eye
Boner, V.—LD & RH
Border, J.—pensioner
Bowie, E.—RH
Bowie, H.—RH & KD
Brake, J.R.—KD & jaundice
Brinker, C.C.—SS
Brown, J.W.—eye disease & injury to left arm
Buckhannon, T.—TYF & CDR
Bumgardner, S.—loss of both feet
Bumgarner, D.C.—RH & HD
Burris?, W.M.—RH
Butcher, E.—gunshot wound
Calhoun, E.—RH
Campbell, D.—RH & chest disease, pensioner
Carder, T.—dyspepsia
Carpenter, R.—defective sight both eyes, pensioner
Caton, A.T.—RH & general disability
Clammer, J.—stomach & liver disease, pensioner
Clark, G.W.—RH & general disability
Clark, J.—CDR
Clark, W.J.—nicrosis tarsal bones right foot, AFP
Collins, S.C.—disease of head & eyes, pensioner
Cox, D.W.—weak lungs from lung fever
Cox, J.M.—AFP

Crawford, W.P.—lost use of right hand, drafted & DSC
Criss, E.—W
Criss, N.—gunshot wound
Cross, G.W.—crippled through loins by shell
Cross, T.F.—sawer eyes & deaf one ear
Crow, W.—cold on measles
Crown, A.—CDR & RH
Cunningham, B.F.—AFP
Cunningham, J.R.—deaf left ear, RH & dyspepsia, pensioner
Cunningham, W.J.—disease of back, kidneys & bladder, pensloner
Daily, S.J.—gunshot face & head resulting epilepsy, pensioner
Davidson, J.W.—HD & RH
Davis, B.F.—gunshot of hips & scurvy, pensioner
Davis, J.M.—right arm shot off
Davis, W.R.—lung fever left his lungs weak
Deem, D.—gunshot great toe left foot, bronchitis, pensioner
Deem, J.—AFP
DeLancey, J.M.—HD
Delony, J.W.—pulmonary & cardiac disease resulting hemiplegia
Doe, F.—POW Andersonville, eyes badly defective
Dolan, J.T.—gunshot wound, pensioner
Dotson, C.—LD
Dotson, H.S.—throat disease
Dotson, H.—wound & other disabilities
Dougherty, G.W.—disease of testicles, pensioner
Douglas, G.B.—hernia right side
Drake, T.—breast injury from fall from horse
Dunn, W.—KD
Dye, W.H.—CDR, pensioner
Earnest, M.L.—CDR & piles
Echols, W.W.—dyspepsia & other matters
Elder, R.L.B.—pensioner
Elliott, H.S.—RH, pensioner
Elliott, W.—bronchitis, pensioner
Emery, W.—left leg broken, AFP
Evans, A.J.—piles, hydrocele & RH 25 years, pensioner
Flanagan, J.H.—TYF & RH
Flesher, J.—sworn soldier but always detached, personal service
Frederick, W.T.—hernia left side, AFP
Frier, R.H.—catarrh from cold at Cumberland Gap Ky 63—64
Fultz, S.G.—injury of back
Garrell, P.C.—LD & piles
Garrison, D.—thumb shot off left hand & shot in neck
Garrison, W.G.—catarah in head
Gary, S.R.—pensioner
Giebell, C.—RH
Gilmore, J.T.—lumbago & other disease
Gitchell, J.H.—rupture in bowells

Givens, D.W.—effects of measles
Glover, R.E.—HD, pensioner
Goff, E.C.—RH & HD, pensioner
Gray, D.W.—hurt in breast & SS
Gregg, S.—thumb off right hand & RH
Gregory, J.—CDR
Griffin, E.B.—scurvy
Gulley, C.—RH from fever, POW 9 months Andersonville
Hague, D.B.—CDR
Hall, J.A.—piles
Hall, M.S.—gunshot wound in side, was Capt. Co K 3rd—6th WVC
Hamerick, W.—CDR & RH
Hamilton, H.E.—HD, pensioner
Haney, C.—LD, catarrh, throat disease
Hardman, J.S.—RH & LD, hernia both sides 8 years, AFP
Harper, M.—RH
Harris, T.M.—Lt. Col. recruited a regt & brevet Brig General
Harter, W.M.—hernia
Hartleben, R.—hip & back injured by a skid (?) striking him
Hartley, J.—qunshot wound, pensioner
Haught, A.J.—WIA, CDR, piles
Hess, T.—resigned 10/23/64
Hinton, S.P.—POW Tyler Texas 10 months 1 day, scurvey
Hinton, T.J.—RH & scurvy
Holstein, W.A.—RH, AFP
Huey, J.—chronic sore eyes, WIA left leg
Hyson, B.F.*—WIA & DSC
Isner, W.—RH & LD, pensioner
Jamison, J.M.—catarrh & HD
Jenkins, A.—AFP
Johnson, J.H.—shot in right thigh & finger shot off
Jones, F.M.—RH, CDR, eyes
Jones, J.C.—CDR & bronchitis
Jones, J.—disease of resperatory organs
Jordan, J.H.—spinal disease
Jordan, W.A.—scurvy, pensioner
Jordan, W.H.—paralysis
Joy, H.—CDR & other ailments
Keener, D.—gunshot wound right knee, pensioner
Kelley, J.K.—disease of stomach & eyes
Kelly, J.O.—general break down
Kirkpatrick, L.—gunshot wound right leg & right shoulder
Lafaye, J.A.*—WIA
Lee, A.—RH & piles since 1864, AFP
Lee, P.—RH
Lewellyn, W.—AFP
Lewis, W.A.—AFP
Lowe, W.M.—LD

Lowther, W.G.—RH, piles, HD, pensioner
Luke, J.—CDR
Mallory, J.B.—injury to right eye, pensioned
Marshall, J.H.—liver & kidney complaint
Martin, J.F.—TYF & HD
Mason, E.—fever resulting in pleurisy & deafness
Mason, J.A.—RH, piles & TYF
Mason, P.—pensioner
Maulsby, J.W.—RH, HD, KD
Maxwell, L.—LD, KD, stomach disease
McBee, Z.—catarrh in head & lameness right arm, pensioner
McClain, E.—RH
McClead, E.—measles settled in his back
McDougal, C.W.—RH
McGill, J.W.—eyesight affected, pensioner
McGregor, S.B.—HD & KD
McGregor, S.—frozen feet & HD
McIntire, A.—rupture
McMullen, R.—trouble in left side, ague from measles
McMullen, W.—malarial poison resulting in general disability
McMullin, G.—gunshot wound
McMullin, J.—injury to eyes, nearly blind
Metz, W.F.—KD, LD, liver disease
Miller, W.G.—lost his papers dont remember dates
Miracle, W.B.—RH in back
Mitchell, A.—RH, AFP
Moats, A.—gunshot wound in right thigh
Moats, B.—gunshot wound right leg
Moats, C.—disease of stomach & heart
Monroe, J.R.—MS & RH
Moore, T.—CDR, dislocated ankle joint
More, J.—broken leg, POW 9 months Richmond & Andersonville
Morris, W.—partial deafness, defective eyesight, RH, AFP
Mortin, W.—RH & HD
Mowry, J.—wounded in head by shell
Murdock, J.—HD
Nalley, L.—RH & HD
Nash, M.—lumbago
Neptune, W.W.—RH, shell wound & paralysis
Nutter, B.W.—hemorages of lungs
Nutter, C.B.—defective sight, pensioner
Overton, J.P.—AFP
Palmer, E.—CDR & appoplexy, pensioner
Parks, E.—CDR & RH, pensioner
Parks, J.C.—piles & RH, leg broken recently
Parks, W.H.—RH & disease of eyes
Payne, D.G.—CDR
Payne, J.M.—CDR

Pearl, U.—LD
Pickering, J.—gunshot wound
Pierpoint, L.—LD from winter 61/62, heart trouble from gunshot
Poynter, H.C.—hernia
Pratt, H.—rupture & W
Pratt, J.E.—kidney stones & RH
Price, J.—injury to left shoulder & head
Pritchard, J.W.—bronchitis & CDR, pensioner
Prunty, E.—LD & HD
Prunty, F.—right wrist dislocated, pensioner
Rexroad, Z.P.—RH & eyes affected
Rieves, P.H.—sabre cut of right hand, pensioner
Riggs, A.—gunshot wound, CDR & HD
Riggs, E.B.—hand badly crippled
Riggs, I.B.—gunshot wound & RH
Roach, W.W.—RH & neuralgia
Rodgers, S.H.—gunshot wound left foot, pensioner
Rogers, J.H.—HD
Rogers, L.—pensioner
Rollins, E.—RH
Rollins, G.W.—AFP
Rush, J.—disease of stomach 25 years, pensioner
Russell, J.O.—asthma & HD
Rymer, J.D.—RH
Satterfield, E.L.—CDR & piles
Satterfield, S.C.—HD, RH, dyspepsia
Satterfield, S.J.—RH & LD
Sayer, C.—MS, LD, eyes affected
Scott, J.B.—piles, RH, HD
Selby,—?—CDR
Shannon, M.—bronchitis
Shephera, C.C.—RH & HD
Shepherd, E.—disease of heart & back
Shilling, J.W.—CDR & lame
Shrader, J.—CDR, RH, HD, dyspepsia, scurvy, general disability
Shrader, U.—POW 1 month
Simmons, J.W.—HD
Slack, E.—RH, ague, weak breast & lungs
Smith, B.*—hip disabled
Smith, D.M.—scurvy
Smith, E.H.—wound in foot, HD, general disability
Smith, G.—AFP
Smith, I.S.—RH & HD
Smith, J.B.—general disability
Smith, J.T.—defective sight both eyes, pensioner
Smith, Martin—affection of eyes caused by measles in army
Snider, E.—not home, 2nd wife knows nothing about discharge
Snodgrass, C.C.—wounded in right foot, pensioner

Snodgrass, J.—gunshot wound
Snodgrass, J.—left ankle dislocated
Speer, E.—WIA right hand
Stanly, W.B.*—bronchitis
Stewart, N.H.—sprained back
Stewart, P.—gunshot wound at Andersonville (POW)
Stewart, R.W.—dyspepsia contracted in army, pensioner
Stock, W.—gunshot wound & scurvy
Stone, C.—LD & gunshot
Stonestreet, W.—iniured in spine by the bustinq of a shell
Summers, T.M.—AFP
Thomas, T.J.—LD & HD
Tichner, G.—blood poison from vaccination
Tingler, G.—piles & CDR, pensioner
Valentine, H.—catarrh
Valentine, W.A.—AFP
Vancourt, T.D.—RH
Vincent, I.L.—strained in hip & back
Vore, E.—CDR, LD, HD
Waller, B.F.—AFP
Ward, G.—CDR
Washburn, C.—RH, CDR, HD, MS
Wass, H.—piles, pensioner
Webb, N.C.B.—RH & dispepsia, UFL
Webster, P.—gunshot right foot, finger off left hand, AFP
Weekly, G.W.—CDR
Weinrich, C.—disease of throat & neck, pensioner
Weinrich, L.—RH & HD, pensioner
Wells, G.M.D.—shell wound
West, G.W.—CDR
West, G.W.—pistol shot of right groin 25 years, pensioner
Whaley, J.M.—asthma
Whiteman, D.C.—throat & lung disease
Whitzel, J.—pensioner
Williams, H.—CDR & throat disease
Williamson, S.G.—gunshot wound
Wilson, A.—RH, piles, defective eyesight, AFP
Wilson, A.—right shoulder broke & stomach disease
Wilson, D.—pensioner
Wilson, L.—loss of left eye, pensioner
Wolf, J.W.*—RH
Wright, N.—CDR & piles
Wylie, D.—RH
Young, J.A.—wounded in right leg
Zickifoose, A.W.—2 gunshot wounds, one in each leg

Roane County

NAME/RANK	REGIMENT	WHEN SERVED
Ableins, Abraham	NF	
Allen, Isaac Pvt.	9 WVI	3/13/65–7/8/65
Anderson, Alexander Pvt.	1 WVI	11/21/61–7/21/65
Anderson, Ezra L. Pvt.	11 WVI	11/63–8/65
Argabright, George L. Cpl.	11 WVI	8/22/62–7/10/65
Argabrite, Jacob H. Pvt.	9 WVI	2/19/62–2/19/65
Armsted, James A. Pvt.	4 VAI	64/65
Arnott, Wm. T. Cpl.	9 WVI	2/15/62–7/21/65
Arnotte, Henry M.	NF	
Ashley, John T. Pvt.	7 VAI	8/61–10/65
Askins, Henry S. Pvt.	126 OHI	5/18/63–6/22/65
Atkinson, Charles Pvt.	30 OHI	8/23/64–6/23/65
Bailey, Benj. Pvt.	1 WVA	12/62–6/65
Barnt, Thomas Pvt.	45 PAI	11/11/61–11/11/64
Beach, Wm. Pvt.	25 OHI	7/12/61–7/64
Bee, Joel G. Pvt.	1 VAA	9/61–6/65
Bee, Stinnett Sgt.	6 WVI	2/15/65–6/10/65
Belcher, John Pvt.	2 KYI	62/62
Bell, Hedgman Sgt.	15 WVI	8/26/62–6/14/65
Bishop, John Pvt.	13 WVI	7/62–4/65
Bissell, Alden S. Pvt.	60 OHI	2/22/64–7/28/65
Blackburn, Kelly Pvt.	1 WVI	3/9/62–3/29/65
Board, Thomas J. Pvt.	11 WVI	8/62–NF
Boggs, John R. Pvt.	11 WVI	8/30/62–6/17/65
Boggs, Thadeus	NF (19 VAC CSA)	
Bower, Daniel Pvt.	9 WVI	1/23/62–1/23/65
Boyer, A. J. Pvt.	9 WVI	2/62–2/29/64
also	1 WVI	2/29/64–7/21/65
Branan, John S.	NF (19 VAC CSA)	
Brown, Carr B. Pvt.	9 WVI	9/16/61–3/30/64
Butcher, Nicholas F. Pvt.	4 WVC	7/14/63–3/9/64
Byce, Francis Pvt.	6 VAI	10/61–11/64
Carpenter, Hezekiah Pvt.	4 WVC	NF
Carper, Alkanah W. Pvt.	9 WVI	2/19/62–2/19/65
Carper, Calahan C. Pvt.	9 WVI	12/2/61–5/16/65
Carr, Nicholas Pvt.	15 WVI	8/62–6/14/65
Casto, Edwon Pvt.	13 WVI	9/1/63–5/25/65
Casto, John B. Pvt.	9 WVI	9/16/61–10/5/64
Casto, Pelly P. Pvt.	9 WVI	10/20/61–2/28/64
Casto, Washington Pvt.	9 WVI	9/10/61–10/9/62
Chancey, Andrew Pvt.	10 WVI	2/24/64–8/9/65
Cheuvrout, Aaron Pvt.	11 VAI	8/63–1/65

Name	Unit	Dates
Cleavenqer, James M. Pvt.	7 WVC	2/20/65–8/10/65
Cobb, Henry F. Pvt.	13 WVI	3/20/63–6/22/65
Coff, Wm. H. Pvt.	13 VAI	8/15/62–6/28/65
Coff, Wm. Pvt.	4 WVI	6/61–1863
Collins, Alexander Pvt.	4 WVC	7/25/63–3/24/64
also	6 WVI	9/26/64–6/10/65
Conley, John N. Pvt.	11 WVI	62/65
Cook, Barnabas S. Pvt.	—WVI	4/4/62–9/1/64
Cook, Joseph L. Pvt.	8 VAI	9/1/62–8/18/65
Cook, Wm. Pvt.	37 KYI	62/65
Coon, Jacob S. Pvt.	4 VAI	7/22/61–7/27/65
Cooper, Clifton H. Pvt.	9 WVI	11/1/61–11/1/64
Cummings, Hiram Pvt.	NF	
Cunningham, Jacob M. Pvt.	11 WVI	9/29/62–5/10/64
Damewood, Michael	Home Guard	NF
Davis, James S. Pvt.	9 WVI	10/18/61–10/18/64
Dix?, Wm.	NF	
Dobbins, Uriah Sgt.	9 WVI	7/16/61–7/18/65
Dodson, Lee	NF	
Douglas, James C. Pvt.	7 WVC	9/2/61–3/25/65
Drake, Charley Pvt.	9 WVI	10/62–7/65
Drake, Harvey Pvt.	9 WVI	61/63
Drake, Isaac Pvt.	1 WVI	9/9/61–6/20/65
Drake, Sutton Pvt.	9 WVI	12/10/——7/21/65
Drennen, Andrew C. Pvt.	9 WVI	9/16/61–5/18/65
Eaton, John Y. Cpl.	11 WVI	8/12/62–6/27/65
Ellmore, Joel B.	NF	
Engle, Joseph F. Pvt.	11 WVI	8/12/62–7/65
Epiling, Lenard Pvt.	9 WVI	3/1/62–5/1/63
Evilsizer, Samuel H. Pvt.	92 OHI	8/5/62–6/20/65
Ferrell, Major A. Pvt.	4 VAI	7/1/61–8/1/64
Fowler, James Pvt.	63–OHI	10/14/61–1/26/62
Gandee, Wm. Pvt.	9 VAI	9/16/61–10/5/64
Garrett, Wm. W. Cpl.	7 WVC	11/12/61–8/9/65
Gibson, Izaah Pvt.	39 KYI	12/26/63–9/13/65
Giles, Wm. Pvt.	9 WVI	2/29/64–7/21/65
Glaze, Isaac M. Drummer	13 WVI	9/1/63–6/65
Goad, James H. Pvt.	13 WVI	12/6/62–6/22/65
Goardee, Fredrick Pvt.	9 WVI	10/14/61–10/14/64
Graves, Wm. M.	NF (26 VAC CSA?)	
Greathouse, Wm. D. Pvt.	11 WVI	4/6/62–6/17/65
Gross, George W. Musician	8 WVI	9/15/61–6/21/65
Hall, James Pvt.	9 WVI	62/65
Hardman, Joseph F. Pvt.	11 WVI	8/23/62–7/10/65
Harper, James W. Pvt.	NF	
Harper, Jordan Pvt.	13 WVI	8/1/63–6/17/65
Harper, Robert Pvt.	13 WVI	9/1/62–6/22/65

Name	Unit	Dates
Harrold, Daniel Pvt.	9 WVI	10/19/63–6/13/65
Harrold, Jesse Pvt.	—WVI	63/65
Hawkins, Benj. F. Sgt.	13 WVI	7/25/63–6/25/65
Hearns, Alfred M. Pvt.	11 WVI	5/2/63–5/25/65
Heckman, James O. Pvt.	11 WVI	10/26/61–10/26/64
Heckman, Samuel Cpl.	153 INI	1/13/65–9/4/65
Hefs, Ephraim Pvt.	7 WVC	8/1/64–8/1/65
Hickle, Salathiel S. Pvt.	9 WVI	2/28/62–7/27/65
Hiles, David Pvt.	114 OHI	10/22/62–2/3/64
Hill, David A. Pvt.	13 WVI	1/3/63–5/17/65
Hively, James Pvt.	NF (62 VAI CSA?)	
Hively, Madison	NF	
Hoff, John A. Pvt.	3 WVC	1/18/63–6/30/65
Hornbeck, Isaac Pvt.	15 VAI	8/11/62–4/11/65
House, John Pvt.	48 OHI	5/2/64–9/14/64
Hunt, Eraspus P. Pvt.	7 WVC	12/26/61–8/1/65
Hunt, John H. Pvt.	13 WVI	1/1/64–6/3/65
Hunt, Oliver B. Pvt.	13 WVI	/25/63–5/30/65
Hunt, Wm. H. Pvt.	11 WVI	2/11/62–5/29/65
Hunt, Wm. M. Pvt.	13 WVI	8/1/63–6/22/65
Husk, John Pvt.	6 WVI	11/26/61–6/10/65
Huston, John Pvt.	NF (28 VAI CSA?)	
Icard, Isaiah Pvt.	12 WVI	8/61–8/63
also	17 WVI	8/27/63–7/4/65
Jackson, Nithaniel M. Pvt.	13 WVI	12/24/62–6/7/65
Jaratt, Melvin Pvt.	NF	
Jenkins, Levi H. Pvt.	10 WVI	8/62–6/65
Jett, Jacob Pvt.	14 WVI	8/15/62–7/27/65
Jones, Asa Pvt.	13 WVI	2/20/64–6/17/64
Jones, Daniel Pvt.	NF (10 VAC CSA?)	
Jones, Emanuel Pvt.	2 WVC	5/1/64–6/30/65
Jones, Granville A. Pvt.	7 WVC	2/65–8/65
Jones, Nathaniel	Home Guard	NF
Kelly, John N. Pvt.	9 WVI	1/31/62–1/31/65
Lawson, George P. Cpl.	13 WVI	8/2/62–6/2/65
Lewis, Asbury Capt.	20 VAC CSA	4/20/61–4/10/65
Lewis, Wm. H. Pvt.	11 CTI	3/25/64–9/1/65
Lloyd, Joseph Pvt.	4 WVI	6/24/63–3/12/65
Lowe, Nimrod Pvt.	14 WVI	8/5/62–6/27/65
Lowery, John A. Pvt.	1 WVC	3/11/64–7/8/65
Mahan, John P. Pvt.	13 WVI	8/22/62–6/22/65
Marks, Cornelius J. Pvt.	9 WVI	11/30/63–5/29/65
Marks, John W. Pvt.	9 VAI	10/15/63–7/21/65
Marks, Thomas C. Pvt.	9 WVI	9/16/61–2/5/65
Mayne, Samuel Pvt.	14 WVI	NF
McCan, Patrick Pvt.	7 OHC	7/9/62–9/9/65
McCan, Solomon Cpl.	9 VAI	9/16/61–2/28/64

Name	Unit	Dates
McCoy, Samuel Pvt.	9 WVI	2/20/62–2/22/65
McCroskey, Wm. Pvt.	9 WVI	9/15/61–7/24/65
McDonald, Nathaniel Pvt.	——	5/22/63–8/9/65
McKown, Ephaim Sgt.	11 WVI	8/14/62–6/17/65
McKown, Norman T. Pvt.	9 WVI	9/16/61–10/5/64
McWilliams, John F. Pvt.	11 WVI	6/29/61–5/29/65
Merrill, Benj. F.	NF	
Montong, Charles Pvt.	NF	
Moore, James M. Pvt.	7 WVC	1/1/65–8/13/65
Moore, John G. Pvt.	13 WVI	8/15/62–6/5/65
More, John Pvt.	—(19 VAC CS?)	62/64
Naylor, Wm. Pvt.	1 WVI	63/65
Newton, Salathiel Pvt.	2 WVI	5/21/61–6/14/64
Nicholas, Isaac Pvt.	NF	
Nicholson, Edmond Pvt.	6 WVI	1/8/63–6/9/65
O'Brian, John Pvt.	8 VAI	64/65
Palmer, Elias Pvt.	4 WVC	6/24/63–3/11/64
also	7 WVC	2/23/65–8/1/65
Parks, Thomas J. Sgt.	77 OHI	62/63
Parsons, John R. Pvt.	7 WVC	2/7/65–8/1/65
Patterson, Joseph Pvt.	37 MOI	61/65
Patton, John H.	NF	
Payne, Wm. W.	NF	
Powell, Lorenzo Sgt.	30 OHI	8/23/61–4/23/63
Price, Thomas Pvt.	4 USA	63/65
Prichard, Elias R. Pvt.	6 WVC	9/26/64–5/19/65
Pringle, Jacob Pvt.	11 VAI	9/1/62–5/29/65
Quick, Sarshfield Pvt.	15 WVI	8/10/62–6/14/65
Radabaugh, James E. Pvt.	9 WVI	2/22/62–2/22/65
Rader, John H. Pvt.	13 WVI	9/15/62–6/27/65
Rader, Lewis A. Cpl.	13 WVI	3/20/63–6/22/65
Raines, Joseph M. Pvt.	13 WVI	9/1/63–6/23/65
Ray, Wm. Pvt.	9 WVI	9/16/61–3/30/64
Reger, Henry Pvt.	1 WVA	7/62–6/29/65
Reynolds, Benj. Pvt.	—WVI	12/31/63–8/9/65
Reynolds, Wm. L. Pvt.	9 WVI	9/16/61–2/29/64
also	1 WVI	2/29/64–7/21/65
Rhodes, Joseph Pvt.	13 WVI	63/64
Rhodes, Preston Pvt.	1 WVI	11/21/61–7/21/65
Riddle, Elijah M. Cpl.	1 VAI	12/6/61–7/21/65
Roberts, Daniel Pvt.	11 WVI	8/28/62–6/29/65
Roberts, James M. Pvt.	7 WVI	8/7/61–7/1/65
Roberts, Nelson Pvt.	3 WVC	3/21/65–6/30/65
Roberts, Simon Pvt.	11 WVI	8/29/62–6/29/65
Roberts, Thomas A. Adj.	11 WVI	11/61–1863
Robinson, David L. Pvt.	NF	
Robinson, David M. Pvt.	15 VAI	10/24/62–10/24/65

Name	Unit	Dates
Rodgers, Eli Pvt.	11 WVI	11/20/61–11/21/64
Romine, Benj. F. Pvt.	9 VAI	2/18/62–2/18/65
Romine, John M. Pvt.	9 WVI	9/16/61–10/7/64
Rood, Charles H. Pvt.	11 WVC	62/64
Runnion, Alfred A. Pvt.	NF	
Ryne, Charlie F. Pvt.	25 OHI	6/4/61–3/18/66
Sarver, Barnibas Pvt.	5 USI	4/15/65–10/15/66
Schilling, John "Chaplain"	1 MDI	64/65
Schoolcraft, Aaron Pvt.	9 WVI	12/23/63–7/21/65
Schoolcraft, John A. Pvt.	1 WVI	12/12/63–7/21/65
Schoolcraft, Samuel Pvt.	7 WVC	61/65
Scott, Henry L. Pvt.	3 WVI	6/1/61–1/63
Scott, Thomas Pvt.	15 OHI	8/62–6/63
Settle, Abner Pvt.	11 WVI	8/30/62–5/16/65
Shafer, David Pvt.	9 VAI	9/16/61–10/5/64
Shafer, John Pvt.	13 WVI	11/63–6/7/65
Shafer, John S. Pvt.	7 VAI	2/1/65–7/1/65
Shaffer, Perry G. Pvt.	7 WVI	3/1/64–6/23/65
Sherman, Thomas C. Pvt.	10 WVI	8/13/62–6/31/65
Short, David Pvt.	9 WVI	12/11/61–12/17/65
Short, Hiram Pvt.	9 WVI	12/21/61–7/25/65
Short, Jacob Pvt.	9 WVI	11/1/63–6/10/65
Sleath, Adam C. Pvt.	15 WVI	8/14/62–3/20/65
Smith, Isaac N. Pvt.	6 WVI	2/6/65–6/10/65
Smith, John H. Cpl.	7 WVC	1/6/61–8/1/65
Smith, Linzey E. Pvt.	9 WVI	12/61–7/65
Smith, Martin V. Pvt.	5 WVI	7/19/63–6/14/65
Smith, Robert Pvt.	5 VAI	8/20/61–9/20/64
Smith, Samuel F. Pvt.	40 OHI	10/19/61–11/19/64
Smith, Samuel H. Pvt.	11 WVI	8/26/62–6/21/65
Smith, Wm. G. Pvt.	(Smiths VAI CS)	61/63
Snyder, Nimrod Pvt.	9 VAI	61/65
Spencer, John Capt.	9 WVI	12/15/61–12/15/63
Spencer, Othey H. Pvt.	12 WVI	8/62–6/65
States, T.S. Pvt.	6 WVI	9/64–6/65
Stricklan, Wm. L. Pvt.	13 VAI	12/17/63–6/22/65
Striclan, Sutton M. Pvt.	13 VAI	12/17/64–6/22/65
Stump, Henry Capt.	13 WVI	3/62–10/18/64
Stutler, John D. Pvt.	179 OHI	7/64–6/65
Summers, Andrew Sgt.	34 IAI	8/11/62–6/11/63
Tanner, Wm. Pvt.	192 OHI	2/21/65–7/29/65
Taugh, Andrew J. Pvt.	1 WVC	3/8/65–6/5/65
Tawney, John Pvt.	9 WVI	10/63–7/21/65
Taylor, Alexander G.	NF	
Taylor, Elijah J. Pvt.	7 WVC	9/5/61–1/26/65
Taylor, James H. Pvt.	13 WVI	8/1/63–6/22/65
Taylor, John Pvt.	9 WVI	9/16/61–9/16/64

Taylor, Joseph J. Pvt.	16 PAC	9/12/62–7/12/65
Thomas, Cornelious Pvt.	6 WVI	1/24/65–6/12/65
Tibble, James Lt.	175 OHI	12/62–2/63
Timnel, Ferdinand G. Pvt.	9 WVI	NF
Truman, Elijah Pvt.	9 WVI	1861–NF
Upton, Alphus H. Pvt.	8 WVI	12/6/61–8/1/65
Valentine, Amos E. Pvt.	6 WVC	9/26/64–6/26/65
Vance, Calom Pvt.	13 WVI	8/14/62–5/29/65
Waggoner, Elijah Pvt.	11 WVI	9/25/62–6/29/65
Walker, Benj. F. Pvt.	2 MNC	12/10/63–11/30/65
Walker, Daniel M. Cpl.	13 WVI	9/1/63–6/22/65
Walker, David L. Pvt.	13 WVI	8/7/63–6/22/65
Walker, Wm. E. Pvt.	15 WVI	3/28/64–8/19/65
Ward, Jobey A. Pvt.	9 WVI	9/16/61–9/17/63
Warner, Adison N. Pvt.	4 WVC	7/18/63–2/6/64
also	3 WVC	3/21/65–6/3/65
Watson, Jacob Pvt.	6 WVC	7/14/61–5/22/66
Watson, Othey G. Pvt.	6 WVI	9/2/61–9/10/64
West, Granville W. Pvt.	10 WVI	9/23/61–6/7/65
Westfall, Clark Pvt.	13 WVI	12/21/63–6/26/65
Westfall, Nathan Pvt.	13 WVI	9/1/63–6/2/65
Westfall, Noah Pvt.	7 VAI	9/8/61–10/9/62
Whetsel?, Jacob Pvt.	4 WVI	8/5/63–3/11/64
also	7 WVC	2/25/65–8/1/65
White, Andrew E. Pvt.	10 WVI	12/25/61–1865
White, Burwell S. Pvt.	1 VAI	2/24/62–3/1/65
White, Henderson Pvt.	13 WVI	8/1/63–6/22/65
Willard, Francis M. Pvt.	4 VAI	7/16/61–7/18/65
Willson, Wm. A. Pvt.	NF (22 VAI CSA?)	
Wilson, Arariah F. Pvt.	9 WVI	10/18/61–10/18/64
Wilson, John Pvt.	9 WVI	9/16/61–10/5/64
Wilson, Wesley Pvt.	9 WVI	9/16/61–10/5/64
Wine, Samuel Pvt.	1 WVI	3/26/64–7/21/65
Wine, Thomas	NF	
Wolf, Isaac Pvt.	4 WVI	11/7/61–12/17/64
Wright, Bassel B. Pvt.	11 WVI	9/21/62–6/7/65
Wyatt, John W. Pvt.	1 WVC	2/28/65–7/28/65

Roane County Remarks

Anderson, A.—SS
Argabright, G.L.—disease of testicles from mumps
Armsted, J.A.—CDR
Ashley, J.T.—DSC for white swelling
Askins, H.S.—gunshot in back, shoulder, breast & thigh
Bailey, B.—WIA neck & left knee
Beach, W.—RH & head hurt
Bee, S.—suffering from rupture of hart
Bishop, J.—gunshot wound in head
Bissell, A.S.—piles, KD, general disability, AFP
Blackburn, K.—wounded in left thigh
Board, T.J.—gunshot in leg, loss of health
Byce, F.—HD, eyesight affected
Carpenter, H.—reinlisted in Co F 7 WVC
Carr, N.—left eye nearly gone, was a drummer, AFP
Casto, E.—HD & RH
Casto, J.B.—worn out constitution
Casto, P.P.—gunshot in hand
Casto, W.—VV
Chancey, A.—eyes injured & HD
Cheuvrout, A.—nervousness, DSC
Coff, W.H.—shell wound head, hernia
Collins, A.—piles
Cook, J.L.—RH
Coon, J.S.—piles, gunshot wound, falling of mumps
Cunningham, J.M.—wounded in arm
Davis, J.S.—HD result of SS
Douglas, J.C.—piles
Eaton, J.Y.—RH
Evilsizer, S.H.—POW Libby & other prisons 7 months 12 days, RH
Ferrell, M.A.—wounded right shoulder
Gandee, W.—RH
Garrett, W.W.—almost blind
Gibson, I.—eyes
Hardman, J.F.—piles, disease of liver & kidney
Harper, J.W.—hearing
Hawkins, B.F.—breast
Hearns, A.M.—wounded left arm
Heckman, J.O.—RH & HD
Heckman, S.—blind one eye
Hefs, E.—shot thru left breast in WVA, reenlisted regular Army 6/20/70 to 7/9/80, shot in left arm in Idaho
Hickle, S.S.—dispepsia
Hiles, D.—chills & fever
Hill, D.A.—blind in one eye

Hornbeck, I.—paralysis of left side & HD
House, J.—RH & HD
Hunt, E.P.—feet
Hunt, J.H.—small arm result of measles
Hunt, O.B.—rupture & HD
Hunt, W.M.—abdomen affected
Icard, I.—dropsy, disabled breast & back, RH, pensioner
Jackson, N.M.—nose broken
Jenkins, L.H.—KD
Jett, J.—catarrh & deafness 26 years ago
Jones, A.—measles
Jones, D.*—RH
Jones, E.—LD
Kelly, J.N.—diseased testicles result of mumps
Lawson, G.P.—gunshot left hand
Lewis, A.*—nasal catarrh
Lewis, W.H.—general disability
Mahan, J.P.—HD & CDR
Marks, C.J.—bronchitis
McCan, S.—RH
McCoy, S.—KD from measles
McWilliams, J.F.—loss little finger injury 3rd finger Cedar Creek
Merrill, B.F.—sore eyes
Moore, J.G.—epilepsy
Moore, J.M.—leg hurt
O'Brian, J.—wound left side breast by horse, almost destitute
Parks, T.J.—gunshot left thigh at Pittsburgh Landing
Parsons, J.R.—left knee & foot dislocated, horse fell on him
Patterson, J.—palpitation of heart
Powell, L.—piles, CDR, stomach disease
Price, T.—disabled back, rupture left side incurred Bermuda Hundred 1864, AFP
Pringle, J.—WIA right arm
Radabaugh, J.E.—spinal affection result of SS
Rader, J.H.—chills & fever, eyesight affected
Raines, J.M.—eyes affected
Ray, W.—frost bitten feet
Rhodes, J.—LD
Rhodes, P.—LD
Riddle, E.M.—wounded left foot
Roberts, J.M.—RH, piles, eye disease, shot in right arm at the battle of Gettysburg Penn.
Roberts, S.—gunshot wound right groin at New Creek
Roberts, T.A.—CDR
Robinson, D.M.—bronchitis
Romine, J.M.—bronchitis
Rood, C.H.—wounded in privates by gunshot, disbeptic

Scott, T.—bronchitis
Settle, A.—CDR, pensioner
Shafer, J.—foot mashed
Shafer, J.S.—cold settled on lungs
Shaffer, P.G.—foot mashed
Sleath, A.C.—disease of back & catarrh
Smith, I.N.—HD
Smith, J.H.—eye out
Smith, R.—RH, 1st shot off left hand
Smith, S.H.—RH & pain in side
Snyder, N.—RH
States, T.S.—defect in hearing, disabled in back
Stricklan, W.L.—hearing affected
Striclan, S.M.—cold settled in hip
Stutler, J.D.—RH & sight injured
Summers, A.—dropsy heart
Taylor, E.J.—frozen feet
Taylor, J.H.—breast disease
Taylor, J.—right forefinger shot off
Timnel, F.G.—CDR
Valentine, A.E.—RH, is drawing pension
Vance, C.—gunshot wound left foot at Cedar Creek Va
Waggoner, E.—loss index finger, RH 27 years
Walker, W.E.—gunshot wound hip & abdomen KD & liver disease
Westfall, C.—piles
Westfall, N.—eyes
Westfall, No.—blind right eye
Whetsel, J.—disease of head & kidneys
White, H.—gunshot in thigh, eyes affected
Wilson, A.F.—deaf right ear, brain injury, partial paralysis of both legs caused by shell concussion
Wilson, J.—shot through left leg
Wolf, I.—wounded in hand at Vicksburg, pension $6 per month
Wyatt, J.W.—eyesight

Summers County

NAME/RANK	REGIMENT	WHEN SERVED
Adkins, James C. Pvt.	WV Guards	4/1/65–6/20/65
Adkins, John Pvt.	NF (30 BTN VASS CSA?)	
Adkins, Parker Pvt.	8 WVI	1862–NF
Adkins, Ryley A. Pvt.	23 OHI	12/61–NF
also	21 OHI	NF
Adkins, Wm. Pvt.	7 WVC	64/65
Allen, George Pvt.	12 OHI	1862–4/64
Bancroft, Simond B. Pvt.	20 NYC	8/63–1865
Beasley, James F.M. Pvt.	12 OHI	7/10/62–2/15/64
Bowden, Jovan H. Pvt.	12 ILI	4/28/61–7/10/65
Boyer, Andrew L. Pvt.	1 NYI	11/9/64–5/1/65
Bragg, Rufus Pvt.	33 OHI	12/62–7/65
Buckland, Joseph S.	NF	
Cales, Isaac Pvt.	——	12/61–NF
Cales, James Pvt.	7 WVC	3/1/65–8/2/65
Cales, Peter Pvt.	7 WVC	3/1/65–8/2/65
Cales, Wm. H. Cpl.	——	12/2/61–NF
Coby, Wm. Pvt.	7 PAC	6/1/61–4/4/65
Coleman, Isaac Pvt.	62 OHI	9/1/61–1/63
Cooper, John Pvt.	4 WVC	6/63–8/65
Coverston, Wilson Pvt.	1 OHC	9/12/61–10/16/64
Crook, Wm. D. Pvt.	9 WVI	9/62–NF
Fink, Harvey N. Pvt.	13 WVI	3/30/64–7/7/65
Garvey, John B. Pvt.	1 WVC	5/62–NF
James, John C. Pvt.	4 PAM	NF
Jones, Alexander A. Pvt.	140 INI	12/63–11/64
Knapp, Wm. T. Pvt.	NF	
Lee, John H.	NF (49 VAI CSA?)	
Light, James Pvt.	1 WVI	3/8/65–8/15/65
Lilly, George W. Pvt.	2 WVC	63/65
Lilly, Pleasant H.	WV Guards	9/18/62–6/20/65
Lively, Leroy A. Pvt.	WV Guards	9/4/64–4/15/65
Longfellow, John D.	NF	
Martin, Ephraim Pvt.	47 OHI	1861–NF
McCormick, John T. Pvt.	23 OHI	6/10/61–8/1/65
Meadows, Francis Pvt.	—WV	4/1/65–6/20/65
Meadows, Wm. M. Pvt.	2 WVC	8/63–1864
Prince, James Pvt.	125 OHI	9/21/64–6/24/65
Ratliff, Thomas M.	NF (17 VAC CSA?)	
Richmond, Daniel Pvt.	—WV	4/1/65–6/20/65
Richmond, Thomas L. Pvt.	WV Guards	4/1/61–6/20/65

Shanklin, Riley C. Pvt.	WV Guards	4/64–6/65
Thomas, Charles A. Pvt.	140 OHI	NF
Tripp, Lewis Pvt.	18 OHI	9/21/61–8/17/65
Waddle, Robert G. Pvt.	10 WVI	11/62–NF
Ward, Robert Jr. Pvt.	173 ILI	8/9/64–NF
Willey, Eber Pvt.	2 WVC	8/18/64–6/7/65

Summers County Remarks

Adkins, P.—health tolerable good, receives a pension
Adkins, W.—loss of health, poor
Bancroft, S.B.—suffers effects of disease from service
Beasley, J.F.M.—crippled hand from gunshot, RH
Bowden, J.H.—WIA right leg, not suffering from it now
Cales, W.H.—RH
Coleman, I.—wounded in arm, weak eyes
Crook, W.D.—general health gone, in bad condition
Fink, H.N.—partial deafness right ear
Garvey, J.B.—WIA left arm, RH, detailed as teamster then wagon master, acting Q.M. & etc.
Lilly, G.W.—health very fair, receives a pension
Lilly, P.H.—bad health from war
Lively, L.A.—disabled from fall, did U.S. service in WVA Meadows,
W.M.—health entirely gone, bad condition
Tripp, L.—RH, bronchitis, liver disease
Waddle, R.G.—health some injured

Taylor County

NAME/RANK	REGIMENT	WHEN SERVED
Allen, Joseph M. Pvt.	4 WVC	7/14/63–3/9/64
Allen, Thomas B. Pvt.	6 WVC	8/13/62–5/19/65
Allender, Mathias Pvt.	1 ILA	12/27/62–6/13/65
Annagarn, Harmon Sgt.	5 OHI	4/19/61–7/26/65
Arble, David U. Pvt.	12 PAI	9/63–7/65
Atherton, Benj. Pvt.	17 WVI	8/26/64–6/13/65
Atherton, Wm. H. Pvt.	38 OHI	9/63–6/65
Ayer, Samuel B. Pvt.	1 MEA	7/10/62–5/11/65
Bailey, Cornelius H. Cpl.	12 WVI	8/16/62–6/16/65
Bailey, Martin Pvt.	2 VAI	5/20/61–6/14/64
Bailey, Thornsbery Pvt.	12 WVI	8/62–6/65
Barnhouse, Alpheus N. Pvt.	6 WVI	2/10/65–6/10/65
Bartlett, Fred J. Pvt.	3 WVC	10/63–6/65
Bartlett, George W. Pvt.	6 WVI	5/25/61–8/15/64
Bartlett, Samuel C. Pvt.	5 WVC	5/20/61–3/16/63
Batson, Calvin E. Pvt.	1 WVI	2/15/65–6/30/65
Baylor, Andrew J. Pvt.	52 VAI CSA	61/65
Beall, Vernon Musician	17 WVI	8/31/61–6/30/65
Behen, Wm. E. Pvt.	17 WVI	NF
Binnegar, Jesse H. Pvt.	17 WVI	9/2/64–6/30/65
Bishop, Wm. H. Pvt.	6 WVI	12/27/63–6/10/65
Blue, Bruce T. Pvt.	17 WVI	9/64–7/65
Bolinger, Jacob Pvt.	15 WVI	9/10/62–1865
Bolyard, Alexander Pvt.	3 WVI	1861–8/15/64
also	6 WVC	NF
Bosley, Robert L. Pvt.	1 WVA	8/14/62–6/28/65
Boyd, Wm. A.	NF	
Boyles, Lloyd M. Pvt.	15 WVI	8/27/62–6/14/65
Brohard, Gideon C. Pvt.	17 WVI	2/28/65–6/13/65
Brohard, Humphrey T. Sgt.	2 WVI	5/20/61–6/14/64
Brown, Christopher C. Pvt.	4 WVC	63/64
Brown, Thomas J. Pvt.	17 WVI	9/26/64–6/13/65
Bush, Theodore Pvt.	6 WVI	1/64–6/65
Butcher, Edgar Pvt.	17 WVI	8/16/64–6/30/65
Butler, George H. Pvt.	17 WVI	8/26/64–6/30/65
Campbell, Wm. H. Pvt.	15 WVI	8/18/62–6/14/65
Carder, Cornelius H. Pvt.	38 OHI	10/6/64–7/12/65
Carpenter, David 0. Pvt.	2 WVI	5/25/61–9/63
also	5 WVI & 6 MDC	NF
Casseday, Moses Pvt.	6 WVI	9/12/61–10/18/64
Cassell, John Pvt.	12 WVI	8/16/62–6/16/65
Cassell, Peter Pvt.	12 WVI	8/16/62–6/16/65

Cather, Robert G. Sgt.	3 WVI	6/25/61–9/14/63
Chambers, George W. Pvt.	7 WVI	4/61–7/65
Channell, Wesley Pvt.	4 VAC	NF
Cole, Thomas Pvt.	17 WVI	8/29/64–6/30/65
Collins, Robert A. Pvt.	2 MDI	10/1/62–5/29/65
Cottrill, Calvin Pvt.	14 WVI	3/16/61–6/27/65
Cox, Lindsley Pvt.	14 WVI	2/25/64–6/27/65
Craig, Milton L.	1 WVA	8/19/62–7/21/65
Crawford, John W. Pvt.	45 —	8/9/64–8/15/65
Crayton, Robert Sgt.	4 WVC	7/14/63–3/9/64
Crouse, Anthony Pvt.	18 VAI	1/22/62–6/28/65
Curtin, George W. Lt.	7 PAI	61/65
Davidson, Claudius Pvt.	17 WVI	2/28/65–6/30/65
Davidson, Curtis Lt.	3 WVI	6/25/61–NF
Davis, George W. Pvt.	17 WVI	8/64–7/7/65
Davis, Thomas E. Lt.	17 WVI	8/17/64–7/6/65
Dawson, Francis M. Pvt.	17 WVI	2/21/65–6/30/65
Dawson, George W. Pvt.	6 WVC	6/26/61–8/15/64
Dean, Jesse Pvt.	17 WVI	8/27/64–1865
Dearing, John C. Pvt.	3 VAI	6/25/61–6/7/62
Demoss, Cyrus E. Pvt.	6 WVI	9/27/61–11/25/64
Demoss, Samuel U. Pvt.	17 WVI	2/65–7/65
Demoss, Upton L. Pvt.	28 OHI	6/6/64–1/6/65
Demoss, Wm. M. Sgt.	12 WVI	10/16/62–6/16/65
Dillon, Reuben H. Pvt.	9 OHC	5/17/61–6/1/66
also served in	2, 5, & 6, WVC	NF
Dillon, Wm. Pvt.	4 WVC	7/14/63–3/9/64
Dix, Christopher Pvt.	3 WVC	4/1/65–6/30/65
Donohoe, John Capt.	6 WVI	9/24/61–6/10/65
Donohue, Michael Capt.	6 WVC	8/29/63–4/7/66
Eichelberger, John C. Pvt.	17 WVI	8/21/64–6/30/65
Fauley, Jacob Pvt.	12 WVI	8/17/62–3/16/63
Flanagan, James Cpl.	15 WVI	8/62–7/65
Fleming, Henry F. Pvt.	6 WVI	8/6/61–8/15/64
Fleming, James B. Cpl.	3 WVI	6/25/61–8/16/64
Ford, Wm. H. Cpl.	17 WVI	8/29/64–6/30/65
Foreman, Upton Pvt.	17 WVI	8/31/64–6/30/65
Fowler, Noah C. Pvt.	11 WVI	3/61–5/65
also	62 MNC	NF
Frazier, Lattimer	NF	
Frum, Porter Cpl.	6 WVC	6/25/61–7/10/64
Fry, Samuel Pvt.	6 WVI	1864–6/12/65
Fryer, Robert W. Pvt.	52 NYI	8/23/64–7/24/65
Furner, James W. Pvt.	6 WVI	12/13/63–6/15/65
Gallaher, John S. Pvt.	17 WVI	2/20/65–6/30/65
Garlow, Samuel E. Pvt.	1 WVI	3/27/65–7/21/65
Glen, Elias J. Pvt.	2 WVI	12/18/61–6/5/64

also	6 WVC	6/5/64–5/25/65
Gooding, Isaac S. Pvt.	185 OHI	2/13/65–6/28/65
Goodnoe, Jason S. Pvt.	10 MEI	9/10/61–2/18/65
Goodwin, Wm. S. Pvt.	14 WVI	3/14/65–6/27/65
Gowers, Isaac Pvt.	17 WVI	2/13/65–7/65
Gragg, Henry H. Pvt.	17 WVI	7/64–7/12/65
Graham, Wm. Pvt.	17 WVI	3/1/65–6/30/65
Graham, Wm. Pvt.	7 WVI	8/7/61–4/17/63
Gramm, Samuel H. Pvt.	127 PAI	8/29/62–5/29/63
Grant, Wm. L. Surgeon	9 WVI	2/62–10/62
Gray, Samuel Pvt.	14 WVI	3/13/65–6/27/65
Grow, Adam Lt.	6 WVI	8/15/61–6/10/65
Guseman, Henry H. Sgt.	6 WVC	2/22/63–8/65
Haddix, Jonathan Pvt.	17 WVI	2/16/65–6/30/65
Hamvay, James Cpl.	10 WVI	6/25/64–8/9/65
Hannan, James Pvt.	102 PAI	9/15/61–7/5/65
Hardie, Wm. D. Pvt.	17 WVI	2/16/65–7/12/65
Hargett, George W. Pvt.	1 MDI	3/62–3/65
Harr, John M. Pvt.	2 WVI	12/12/62–NF
also	5 MDC	1863–NF
Harris, Winfield S. Pvt.	41 USI (Negro)	9/7/64–9/30/65
Harter, Scott A. Lt.	4 WVC	5/1/63–NF
also Capt.	17 WVI	2/65–7/65
Hawkins, John A. Pvt.	38 —I	8/27/61–7/15/65
Hawkins, Wm. Pvt.	6 WVI	9/12/64–6/10/65
Hebb, John Pvt.	3 WVI	6/21/61–7/15/65
Hedrick, Henry Pvt.	6 WVI	10/4/61–12/1/64
Hefner, Nathaniel Pvt.	10 VAI	3/62–6/5/65
Henderson, Alexander M Pvt.	15 WVI	9/15/62–6/15/65
Hendrickson, James T. Pvt.	7 WVI	61/65
Henry, David L. Pvt.	6 WVC	6/16/64–6/16/65
Herbert, John H "Messenger"	U.S. Allegheny	1849/1865
Herr, John S.S. Lt.	1 WVA	9/27/61–9/12/63
Hill, Benj.	NF	
Hill, Minchel Pvt.	12 WVI	8/20/62–6/15/65
Hose, Andrew W. Pvt.	17 WVI	2/28/65–6/13/65
Hoskins, Elza T. Cpl.	—WVI	6/20/61–8/21/62
Hovey, Franklin Pvt.	13 OHC	1862–NF
Huuk, Israel B. Pvt.	12 WVI	8/16/62–6/16/65
Hyman, Joyce Pvt.	2 WVI	62/63
Isner, Hamilton Pvt.	15 WVI	8/27/62–6/14/65
Jackson, John C. Pvt.	17 WVI	2/15/65–7/16/65
Jaco, Job Pvt.	17 WVI	8/30/64–6/30/65
Jefferys, Melker M. Pvt.	15 WVI	8/22/62–9/11/65
Jenkins, John D. Pvt.	3 WVI	6/7/61–8/14/64
Jones, John J. Pvt.	7 WVC	3/25/64–8/1/65
Jones, Sanford Pvt.	6 WVI	12/11/61–6/10/65

Jones, Spencer	US NF	
Jones, Uriah Pvt.	17 WVI	8/31/64–6/30/65
Keener, Harman Pvt.	17 WVI	8/31/64–6/30/65
Keller, Lafayette	NF	
Kerns, Francis M. Pvt.	4 WVC	7/14/63–3/64
Kidwell, Thomas E. Pvt.	12 WVI	NF
King, James Pvt.	2 MDI	NF
Kinter, Wilson P. Pvt.	53 PAI	2/17/64–6/30/65
Knaggs, John Pvt.	17 WVI	9/1/64–1/15/65
Lambert, James W. Pvt.	14 WVI	3/14/65–7/3/65
Lambert, Joseph H. Pvt.	6 WVI	7/1/62–1/5/65
Lambert, Wm. P. Pvt.	14 WVI	4/1/65–6/27/65
Laundress, Edward Pvt.	CSA NF	
Layman, Elias E. Pvt.	17 WVI	9/3/64–6/30/65
Leeds, Alexander Lt.	6 MDI	NF
Legg, John T. Musician	3 MDI	7/15/62–5/20/65
Lewellen, John C. Pvt.	17 WVI	8/29/64–6/30/65
Lewin, Francis M. Pvt.	6 WVI	8/29/64–6/10/65
Lewis, Wm. H. Pvt.	3 WVC	2/63–6/65
Lilly, Thomas P. Pvt.	85 PAI	1861–NF
Lipscomb, Abraham R. Pvt.	15 WVI	8/22/62–6/14/65
Litinger, Dennis A. Capt.	2 WVI	62/63
Lobe, Simion S. Pvt.	17 WVI	2/21/65–6/13/65
Logue, Wm. H. Pvt.	7 PAI	7/16/61–6/16/64
Luyadda, Abraham Pvt.	12 WVI	8/62–6/65
Magill, John L. Pvt.	NF	
Male, Jonathan Pvt.	17 WVI	2/23/65–7/5/65
Manuel, John J. Pvt.	6 WVI	12/2/61–12/1/64
Marple, Ezekial Pvt.	14 WVI	8/25/62–6/27/65
Marqueys, Quguilla Pvt.	12 WVI	8/62–6/65
Marthen, Frank A. Lt.	6 WVI	8/21/61–3/20/66
Martin, Samuel Pvt.	36 INI	8/26/61–12/12/62
Mason, Elisha Pvt.	6 WVI	11/25/61–6/10/65
Maxwell, James P. Pvt.	14 WVI	65/65
McAtee, Samuel Pvt.	3 WVI	6/10/61–2/1/64
also	6 WVC	NF
McCafferty, Charles H.	NF	
McCartney, Isaac Pvt.	6 WVI	9/1/64–6/10/65
McConkey, Robert Cpl.	17 WVI	2/13/65–6/30/65
McDaniel, Abraham Pvt.	13 WVI	6/25/61–8/15/64
also	6 WVC	NF
McDaniel, Alpheus Pvt.	12 VAI	8/1/62–6/65
McDaniel, Chafeu Pvt.	6 WVC	6/25/61–8/15/64
McDaniel, Samuel Pvt.	12 WVI	8/16/62–6/16/65
McDaniel, Samuel Pvt.	17 WVI	2/65–7/65
McDonall, John W. Pvt.	6 WVI	12/27/62–6/10/65
McElfresh, Joshua Pvt.	——	3/5/65–6/12/65

McGee, George W. Pvt.	—	62/65
McGlumphry, Tom B. Sgt.	1 WVC	8/6/61–7/8/65
McVeigh, Patrick Pvt.	206 PAI	7/64–6/65
McVicker, Joseph Pvt.	2 VAI	NF
McWilliams, Abner Pvt.	15 WVI	8/10/62–6/14/65
McWilliams, Robert W. Pvt.	12 WVI	8/10/62–8/10/65
Means, James K. Sgt.	12 WVI	8/16/62–6/16/65
Miller, John Pvt.	45 NYI	64/65
Miller, Joseph J. Sgt.	17 WVI	2/65–7/65
Minard, Henry Pvt.	17 WVI	2/15/65–6/13/65
Moats, James Pvt.	NF (62 VAI CSA?)	
Moorehead, Elijah Pvt.	41 PAI	64/65
Moran, Alpheus Pvt.	12 WVI	8/16/62–6/16/65
Morgan, Wm. H. Sgt.	6 WVI	8/61–9/64
Morris, Calvin H. Pvt.	6 WVI	4/6/63–6/10/65
Murphy, Josiah M. Cpl.	12 WVI	12/25/63–8/9/65
Myers, Andrew J. Pvt.	6 WVI	9/61–3/64
Neal, James A. Pvt.	1 WVC	7/18/61–9/15/64
also	100 PAI	3/9/65–7/24/65
Nestor, Andrew M. Pvt.	WV Guards	1/27/64–5/30/65
Nestor, Sanford M.	WV Guards	NF
Newcomb, Leroy M. Pvt.	15 WVI	8/22/62–6/20/65
Newlon, John Pvt.	12 WVI	8/16/62–6/16/65
Newlow, Alfred Pvt.	6 WVC	6/23/63–5/22/66
Newlow, Nathan E. Pvt.	NF	
Nixon, Robert P. Pvt.	6 WVI	3/6/65–6/10/65
Norris, Wm. Pvt.	73 OHI	12/61–NF
Nortring, John W. Pvt.	17 WVI	8/11/64–7/30/65
Nuzum, Andrew J. Lt.	17 WVI	9/7/64–6/30/65
Nuzum, Charles A. Pvt.	17 WVI	2/22/65–6/30/65
Nuzum, Theophilus C. Pvt.	2 WVI	8/29/62–6/64
Nuzum, Thomas Pvt.	17 WVI	8/17/64–7/65
Osburn, James H.	NF	
Parnell, Isaac Pvt.	17 WVI	65/65
Parsons, Marshall J. Pvt.	— WVI	1/65–5/65
Patton, John B. Pvt.	13 WVI	8/24/62–6/65
Patton, Milton M. Cpl.	6 WVI	2/29/64–6/10/65
Payne, Charles H. Pvt.	3 WVI	6/25/61–5/5/63
Peden, Thomas E. Pvt.	173 OHI	8/28/64–7/5/65
Peters, Henry Pvt.	30 MAI	9/1/64–3/10/66
Phillips, Eli Sgt.	6 WVI	8/16/62–6/15/65
Phillips, Raben E. Pvt.	7 WVI	3/1/62–3/1/65
Pilson, John T. Cpl.	Bruce's MDA	6/26/63–1/19/64
Poe, Edgar M. Pvt.	6 WVC	1/1/62–1/23/65
Poe, Wm. L. Pvt.	4 WVC	9/63–6/64
Pool, James W. Pvt.	12 WVI	8/16/62–6/16/65
Powell, Daniel D. Pvt.	6 VAI	1864–6/10/65

Powell, David Sgt.	3 WVI	6/25/61–9/5/62
also Lt.	12 WVI	9/5/62–2/5/65
Powell, James Pvt.	6 WVC	6/25/61–8/17/64
Powell, Jasper C. Pvt.	1 WVC	64/65
Pryor, Wesley C. Pvt.	NF	
Redehare, Henry Sgt.	6 WVI	9/27/64–6/10/65
Reed, Alexander H. Pvt.	17 WVI	8/19/64–6/10/65
Reed, Rufus	NF	
Reese, James W. Pvt.	12 WVI	12/24/64–8/21/65
Reese, Samuel L.	NF	
Renneman, Charles	NF	
Ridenour, David Cpl.	1 WVI	3/17/63–6/5/65
Ridenour, Wm. H. Pvt.	6 VAI	8/29/61–6/16/62
Riley, John W. Pvt.	12 WVI	3/6/64–5/28/65
Ringler, Cyrus E. Cpl.	5 WVC	NF
Roach, Thomas P. Pvt.	6 WVI	8/7/62–6/10/65
Roach, Wm. A. Pvt.	191 PAI	NF
also	6 WVI	8/7/62–6/10/65
Robins, Washington A. Pvt.	NF (26 VAI CSA?)	
Robinson, Hezekiah Pvt.	NF	
Roe, Joseph A. Sgt.	3 WVI	6/25/61–6/7/62
Rogers, James Pvt.	12 WVI	8/16/62–6/16/65
Rogers, John W. Pvt.	6 WVC	8/9/64–5/25/65
Rogers, Wm. (L.)	NF (62 VAI CSA?)	
Rosier, Edgar Pvt.	12 WVI	8/16/62–8/28/65
Rosier, Lemeul C. Cpl.	12 WVI	8/16/62–6/16/65
Ross, Justice F. Pvt.	3 WVI	6/7/61–8/13/64
Saffel, Elias Pvt.	3 WVC	4/3/65–6/30/65
Sandy, John B. Pvt.	6 VAI	12/28/61–6/10/65
Satterfield, Benj Pvt.	7 WVI	4/5/65–7/1/65
Scott, Sandy M. Pvt.	17 WVI	10/5/64–9/5/65
Shaferman, John C. Pvt.	17 WVI	8/31/64–6/30/65
Shahan, George W. Pvt.	15 GAI CSA	7/10/61–1/10/62
Shaw, A. W. Pvt.	4 WVC	6/63–1864
Shrayer, Lewis M. Pvt.	4 WVC	7/29/63–3/1/64
Shroyer, Tyler M. Pvt.	12 WVI	8/16/62–1863
Simonton, Damiel M. Pvt.	14 PAC	9/27/62–5/30/65
Sinclair, James E. Pvt.	6 VAI	2/11/65–6/10/66
Smallwood, James T. Pvt.	4 WVC	7/27/63–3/9/64
also	17 WVI	9/28/64–6/30/65
Smedley, John R. Pvt.	15 WVI	8/22/62–6/14/65
Snider, Jacob Pvt.	12 WVI	8/15/62–6/65
Snider, Joseph Pvt.	12 WVI	8/16/62–8/18/63
also	6 WVC	8/18/64–5/19/65
Spencer, Caleb D. Pvt.	14 WVI	8/14/62–6/27/65
Spencer, Jackson V. Pvt.	6 WVI	8/26/61–10/30/64
Spencer, Joseph C. Pvt.	193 PAI	7/19/64–11/9/64

Name	Unit	Dates
Spies, Henry A. Cpl.	54 PAI	9/4/61–7/15/65
Spring, Wm. Pvt.	12 WVI	8/19/62–6/27/65
Springer, Alpheus Pvt.	3 WVC	9/3/62–6/6/65
Stamfofle, Jacob Pvt.	NF	
Stephens, Evan Pvt.	15 WVI	8/22/62–1/14/65
Sterride?, Orlando	NF	
Stewart, John W. Pvt.	17 WVI	2/28/65–6/30/65
Straub, John Pvt.	1 WVC	4/23/61–6/26/62
Stuck, Squire H. Cpl.	15 WVI	4/8/62–5/30/65
Thayer, Abel H. Surgeon	6 WVC	8/26/62–5/23/66
Thomas, Doctor A. Pvt.	12 WVI	63/65
Thomas, Wm. A. Pvt.	12 WVI	8/19/62–6/27/65
Travis, Robert Pvt.	15 WVI	8/3/62–4/16/63
Triplett, Anthony Pvt.	18 VAC (CSA)	4/1/63–1865
Waller, Georhe H. Pvt.	6 WVC	6/25/61–8/15/64
Waller, Thomas J. Pvt.	6 WVC	6/25/61–8/16/64
also	17 WVI	2/28/65–6/30/65
Walter, Henry QM/Sgt.	15 WVI	8/22/62–6/14/65
Warlhen, Francis A. Pvt.	15 WVI	2/23/64–5/30/65
Warther, John Q. Cpl.	3 PAC	9/19/62–7/65
Wehn, Henry Pvt.	17 WVI	9/2/64–1865
Wells, Thomas "Fireman"	Iron Clad Reno	5/15/65–12/10/65
Wells, Thomas V. Sgt.	14 WVI	8/8/62–7/3/65
Wenzum, Benj. Pvt.	NF	
West, John M. Pvt.	2 WVI	5/20/61–1/4/64
also	6 WVC	1/5/64–5/22/66
Wheeler, Wm. Pvt.	1 WVI	3/27/65–7/21/65
Wheler, John Pvt.	3 WVC	8/1/62–7/1/65
White, Charles Pvt.	—WVC	3/65–6/16/65
White, Wm. Pvt.	NF	
Whithair, Conrad Pvt.	14 WVI	3/18/65–6/27/65
Whithair, George W. Pvt.	17 WVI	8/15/64–6/30/65
Whithair, James Pvt.	2 WVI	5/20/61–4/17/63
Whithair, Jonathan Pvt.	17 WVI	9/2/64–6/13/65
Willhide, John W.	NF	
Willhide, Singleton J. Pvt	5 WVC	5/20/61–6/14/64
Willhide, Wm. Pvt.	NF	
Williams, Wm. Pvt.	17 WVI	8/30/64–6/30/65
Williams, Wm. Pvt.	6 WVI	9/27/61–11/25/64
Wilson, Hezekiah	NF (31 VAI CSA?)	
Wilson, Josiah F. Pvt.	6 WVC	2/27/64–8/8/65
Windle, Lewis Pvt.	6 WVC	6/1/61–10/1/64
Wonnycott, Wm. J. Pvt.	15 WVI	9/13/62–6/14/65
Wright, Johnathan Pvt.	6 WVC	6/1/61–1863
Wyant, Henry M. Pvt.	6 WVI	1864–6/12/65
Wyckoff, Harmon Pvt.	3 WVI	2/2/65–6/12/65
Young, Hiram Pvt.	200 PAI	8/11/64–5/13/65

Taylor County Remarks

Allen, T.B.—gunshot wound
Allender, M.—enlisted Co B 36 Regt US Inf 11/22/65 to 12/29/68
Annagarn, H.—gunshot wounds POW
Arble, D.U.—rupture
Bailey, C.H.—liver complaint
Bailey, M.—piles & rupture
Bartlett, F.J.—epileptic fits & RH, totally disabled requires constant care fell in fire April 9 burned hand & nerves
Bartlett, S.C.—dropsy & mumps, lost his discharge
Bishop, W.H.—shot through right arm near shoulder
Bosley, R.L.—bronchitis
Brown, C.C.—loss forefinger
Cather, R.G.—gunshot wound, dyspepsia, HD, DSC
Craig, M.L.—CDR, RH, conjunctivitis
Crawford, J.W.—kicked by mule in right groin
Dawson, G.W.—RH
Dearing, J.C.—palpitation of heart, dispepsia
Demoss, C.E.—partially deaf from stroke in head with a gun
Dix, C.—RH
Fauley, J.—DSC
Fowler, N.C.—shot right leg
Frum, P.—leg shot off
Grow, A.—catarrh in head
Haddix, J.—CDR, piles, pleurisy
Harr, J.M.—hernia, CDR, piles
Hawkins, J.A.—chills, fever, RH
Hebb, J.—knee injured
Hoskins, E.T.—fever at Ft. McHenry
Hovey, F.—CDR 25 years
Jefferys, M.M.—lost right arm, Linchburg Va June 18, 1864
Jenkins, J.D.—gunshot wound & frost bite
Kinter, W.P.—throat trouble & RH
Lilly, T.P.—ruptured
Lipscomb, A.R.—now totally disabled from active work of any kind
Litinger, D.A.—CDR
Mason, E.—blindness
McAtee, S.—gunshot wound in left side, neuralgia of heart
McCartney, I.—liver & kidney disease
McDaniel, A.—shot through hip
McDaniel, S.—shot through shoulder
McWilliams, A.—catarrh & hearing
Moran, A.—RH
Morris, C.H.—CDR, piles, premature aging
Peters, H.—now suffering from lungs & lumbago
Phillips, E.—throat & lung trouble, catarrh head, stomach trouble

Poe, E.M.—CDR & piles
Pool, J.W.—RH & neuralgia, KD, HD, rectum
Powell, D.—RI I
Powell, J.—brights disease, LD, neuralgia, dates from memory
Ridenour, W.H.—RH
Riley, J.W.—brights disease
Roach, W.A.—RH
Roe, J.A.—neuralgia of face, neurosis of jaw bone
Rogers, J.—asma
Rogers, J.W.—sabre cut in head, deaf right ear, CDR, blind, piles, chronic inflamation right ear
Simonton, D.M.—gunshot wound
Springer, A.—ankle joint disabled, ulcer leg & general disability
Stenitt?, O.—draws a pension
Stephens, E.—gunshot wound
Stewart, J.W.—asthma
Triplett, A.*—POW 8 months
Waller, G.H.—cold on measles resulting in catarrh
Waller, T.J.—gunshot wound, deafness left ear
Wells, T.V.—injury to back
West, J.M.—KD, RH, intestinal tumor
Wheeler, W.—left thigh broken, hernia left
Whithair, G.W.—RH & KD
Whithair, J.—KD, LD, piles, bladder, 25 years
Whithair, Jm.—gunshot wound, LD, RH 28 years
Windle, L.—piles
Wright, J.—RH of heart
Wyckoff, H.—RH

Tucker County

NAME/RANK	REGIMENT	WHEN SERVED
Awbrey, Wilson M.	NF	
Barney, John H. Sgt.	3 MDI	11/9/61–5/29/65
Beckner, (Oliver) C. Pvt.	28 VAI CSA	12/61–6/65
Bergoyne, Henry H. Pvt.	15 WVI	8/22/62–6/14/65
Bevens, J.F.P. Pvt.	6 WVI	8/29/61–6/11/65
Black, Joseph M. Fifer	140 OHI	5/2/64–9/19/64
Blackhart, John W. Pvt.	22 PAC	2/23/64–10/31/65
Blarshard, Frank	NF	
Bohon, Peter Pvt.	6 WVI	12/4/61–11/4/64
Bohone, Mathias	NF	
Bolyard, Isaac	NF	
Bolyard, James H.	NF	
Bunger, Thomas	US NF	
Burke, Thomas G.	NF (8 VAC CSA?)	
Canfield, Marshall Pvt.	10 WVI	1863–6/23/65
Channel, Cylvester	NF	
Cline, John J. Pvt.	4 WVC	8/1/63–3/65
Coffman, Benj. Pvt.	15 WVI	10/30/62–6/65
Colbert, George W. Sgt.	3 MDI	9/61–5/65
Cropland, George T. Pvt.	1 ILA	6/62–5/65
Davis, John M.	NF	
Davis, Timothy Pvt.	NF	
Deets, John H. Pvt.	NF	
Dumire, John W. Pvt.	6 WVI	10/5/64–5/21/65
Dunnoe, Andrew L. Pvt.	6 WVI	2/26/64–6/10/65
Echard, John	NF (27 VAI CSA?)	
Esham, George	NF	
Felton, John C. Capt.	7 WVI	7/4/61–7/1/65
Fisher, Bernard W. Cpl.	7 WVI	9/2/61–7/1/65
Fortney, Jacob W. Pvt.	6 WVI	9/27/61–11/25/64
Fortney, John H.	——	63/64
Frederick, Frank B. Pvt.	NF	
Frumhart, Peter Pvt.	——	62/65
Garrison, Lorensia Pvt.	NF	
Gebb, Wm. P.	NF	
George, Gings Pvt.	NF	
George, Wm. Pvt.	7 WVI	NF
Gilpin, Lorenzo D. Pvt.	195 PAI	8/14/62–6/17/65
Gladwell, Lewis Pvt.	15 WVI	8/62–5/63
Goff, Elisha	——	64/65–NF
Goff, Wm. H. Pvt.	6 WVI	2/2/65–5/21/65

Haddix, Adam	NF	
Haddix, Enoch	NF	
Hady, Fred	NF	
Haller, Herman	NF	
Ham, Jacob Pvt.	NF	
Harner, Henry Pvt.	4 WVC	1862–3/64
Harsh, David Pvt.	6 WVI	NF
Hebb, John C. Pvt.	6 WVI	6/14/63–6/10/65
Hebb, Thomas F. Pvt.	6 WVI	11/4/61–6/10/65
Hebb, Thornton F. Lt.	6 WVI	9/1/61–10/25/64
Helmick, Abe	NF (62 VAI CSA)	
Helmick, Mathias	NF (62 VAI CSA)	
Hill, Aaron B.	NF (14 VAC CSA)	
Hill, Wm. Pvt.	6 USA	8/26/64–NF
Himebrick, Henry Pvt.	6 WVI	9/25/61–11/17/64
House, David Bugler	3 MDI	NF
Jones, G.W. Pvt.	6 WVI	9/64–6/11/65
Jordan, Noah	NF	
Lambert, James H. Capt.	——	1/1/65–5/65
Lavelle, Thomas Pvt.	—VAC	2/65–7/65
Lipscomb, Jacob	NF	
Losh, Wm.	NF	
Loughry, John R. Pvt.	6 WVI	2/25/64–7/10/65
Loughry, Nathan A. Pvt.	6 WVI	2/2/65–6/10/65
Loujien, Wm. Pvt.	84 PAI	2/62–10/65
Mason, Joshua J. Pvt.	3 MDI	7/13/61–1865
McDaniel, John Pvt.	12 WVI	8/62–6/14/63
Merill?, James H. Pvt.	CSA	61/64
Messenger, Joshua Pvt.	17 WVI	2/65–7/65
Millens, Joseph Pvt.	NF	
Miller, A.M.	NF	
Muler, M.V. Pvt	3 MDI	1861–5/28/65
Neall, Harry B.	NF	
Nine, John Pvt.	15 WVI	8/22/62–6/20/65
Palmer, Thomas E. Pvt.	76 PAI	64/65
Pennington, Jesse Pvt.	NF	
Phillips, Albert (G.)	CSA NF (31 VAI CSA)	
Phillips, Isaac N. Pvt.	1 WVC	7/18/64–2/23/65
Plumb, Eugene Pvt.	6 WVI	9/1/61–10/25/64
Powell, Amassa	NF	
Refran, Francis Pvt.	6 WVI	6/21/61–5/22/66
Richards, Jacob L. Pvt.	11 WVI	4/14/62–6/17/65
Shaffer, John A. Pvt.	6 WVI	7/29/61–6/10/65
Shaffer, John	CSA NF (19 VAC)	
Showalters, Henry Pvt.	191 PAI	8/23/61–10/25/64
Siler, John R. Pvt.	28 PAI	6/63–7/63
Sowers, Benj. Pvt.	6 WVI	12/2/61–6/10/65

Sowers, John Pvt.	3 MDI	4/27/62–5/29/65
Spangler, George	US NF	
Spring, John H. Cpl.	69 PAI	62/65
Springs, George T. Pvt.	3 WVC	NF
Steringer, Jacob A.	NF	
Stevens, James Pvt.	——	63/65
Stull, Jefferson Pvt.	3 WVI	1/62–2/6/64
Swanner, Samuel	NF	
Talbott, Wm. E. Pvt.	28 VAI CSA	63/65
Thomas, Spencer	NF	
Wamesly, Samuel B. Pvt.	CSA (19 VAC)	62/64
Wamsley, Adam H.	CSA NF (19 VAC)	
West, John R. Pvt.	1 WVC	NF
Williams, George W. Pvt.	15 WVI	2/62–10/65
Williams, Samuel F.	NF	
Woodruff, Jacob	NF	

Tucker County Remarks

Barney, J.H.—RH & piles
Bergoyne, H.H.—hernia of left side
Bohon, P.—right wrist broken
Bolyard, J.H.—POW Andersonville 6 months, generally disabled
Cline, J.J.—disease of rectum
Colbert, G.W.—shot left leg
Cropland, G.T.—POW Libby 3 months, RH, papers burned
Deets, J.H.—broken foot & bad hearing
Dumire, J.W.—RH
Fisher, B.W.—shot through right leg, disabled by RH
Frederick, F.B.—shot in left shoulder
Garrison, L.—hearing
Gebb, W.P.—generally disabled
George, W.—RH, served 6 months 7 WVI & 1 year Home Guards
Gladwell, L.—shot left leg below knee
Goff, E.—mumps
Harsh, D.—hart disease
Hebb, T.F.—strained knee
Hebb, T.F.—TYF
Helmick, A.*—deserter
Helmick, M.*—deserter
Jones, G.W.—disease of breast, RH, rupture right side
Lambert, J.H.—general disability, served 1 year as Sgt. 4 mo Capt.

Loujien, W.—shot through left knee
Miller, A.M.—shot through both lungs
Muler, M.V.—piles, wound in neck
Nine, J.—dispepsia & RH, POW Libby
Phillips, I.N.—cut on head with saber
Refran, F.—RH
Shaffer, J.A.—RH & bad hearing
Showalters, H.—POW Libby 3 months, fourth finger left hand shot off deaf in left ear bursting of shell
Talbott, W.E.*—deserted
Thomas, S.—shot through left foot

Tyler County

NAME/RANK	REGIMENT	WHEN SERVED
Adams, George W. Pvt.	36 OHI	9/17/61–5/23/65
Adams, Joseph M. Pvt.	77 OHI	2/3/64–3/8/66
Alkire, Jennison P. Pvt.	4 WVC	8/63–8/64
Alkire, Oliver D. Pvt.	14 WVI	8/14/62–5/29/65
Allen, Joel T. Pvt.	92 OHI	7/63–7/65
Alvis, Joseph H. Pvt.	7 WVI	8/61–1/63
Ankrom, Andrew Pvt.	2 WVC	9/12/61–10/17/62
Ankrom, Jonathan Sgt.	14 WVI	8/62–7/3/65
Arnett, Norman Pvt.	15 WVI	8/15/62–6/20/65
Arthur, Wm. D. Pvt.	77 OHI	11/17/61–10/12/62
also	77 OHI	1/4/64–3/28/66
Ash, Adam Pvt.	14 WVI	7/4/62–6/27/65
Ash, Amos Pvt.	3 WVI	6/17/61–3/9/64
also Cpl.	6 WVC	3/10/64–7/17/65
Ash, James	NF	
Ash, John L. Cpl.	14 WVI	7/62–NF
Atchison, George W. Pvt.	31 VAI (CSA)	6/61–5/12/65
Baker, Dickson Pvt.	14 WVI	8/11/62–7/27/65
Baker, Elijah Pvt.	20 OHI	12/61–1864
Baker, George M. Pvt.	7 WVI	8/1/61–8/7/64
Barnes, John H. Pvt.	15 VRC?	12/25/61–8/23/65
Beagle, Wm. A. Capt.	7 WVI	10/61–7/65
Beaty, John A. Pvt.	6 WVI	1864–7/3/65
Beckett, Wm. B. Pvt.	2 WVC	9/10/64–6/7/65
Bell, Henry Pvt.	14 WVI	7/19/62–6/30/65
Bellville, George W. Pvt.	14 WVI	7/63–7/3/65
Bellville, James Pvt.	5 OHI	4/5/64–6/29/65
Bennett, Daniel Pvt.	116 OHI	8/14/62–6/26/65
Bennett, James C. Pvt.	15 WVI	2/1/64–6/1/65
Bennett, Simeon S. Pvt.	39 OHI	3/17/65–7/17/65
Boner, Martin P. Capt.	12 WVI	7/25/62–2/23/63
Booher, Noah Pvt.	10 WVI	3/7/62–5/2/65
Bright, Jacob Pvt.	77 OHI	11/61–7/65
Britton, Jarret Pvt.	6 WVI	9/4/64–6/10/65
Brohard, Nimrod Pvt.	3 WVI	61/65
Buck, Alexander Pvt.	104 OHI	2/65–5/65
Bumfell, Thomas Pvt.	19 OHI	3/7/65–9/11/65
Burgess, Thomas Pvt.	11 WVI	9/7/62–3/1/63
Burrows, George W. Pvt.	7 WVI	2/64–7/65
Byers, Charles H.	US NF	
Calvert, Washington Pvt.	63 OHI	10/61–8/63

Carney, Michael Pvt.	17 WVI	2/6/65–6/13/65
Carpenter, Alexander Pvt.	77 OHI	12/7/61–2/28/66
Carrick, George Pvt.	88 OI II	7/20/63–7/4/65
Chapman, Alfred A.	NF	
Clark, Isaac T. Pvt.	78 OHI	1/9/62–1/9/65
Coe, Peter Pvt.	92 OHI	8/6/62–6/10/65
Condray, Martin Pvt.	15 WVI	8/15/62–6/23/65
Cooper, Abram C. Pvt.	4 WVC	8/1/63–3/8/64
Corrall, Jacob Pvt.	7 WVI	8/7/61–7/19/62
Cox, John W. Pvt.	77 OHI	10/61–1863
Cox, Wm. T. Pvt.	2 WVC	6/16/61–6/20/64
Craig, Sylvester M. Pvt.	92 OHI	8/64–8/65
Craven, Joseph F. Pvt.	22 PAC	8/19/62–5/24/65
Cumberledge, Ellis Pvt.	6 WVI	9/4/64–6/10/65
Cumberledge, George F. Pvt	7 WVI	9/61–7/65
Cumberledge, Sam D. Pvt.	6 WVI	12/61–12/65
Davis, Bowers Cpl.	14 WVI	8/8/62–6/28/65
Davis, Charles W. Pvt.	14 WVI	8/14/62–6/27/65
Davis, David Pvt.	6 WVI	NF
Davis, Isaac N. Pvt.	196 OHI	3/7/65–6/11/65
Davis, Levi Pvt.	4 WVC	8/63–3/64
also Sgt.	6 WVI	9/1/64–6/65
Davis, Robert Pvt.	14 WVI	8/8/62–5/10/65
Dawson, James H. Pvt.	15 WVI	2/24/64–8/65
Delor, John H. Pvt.	7 PAA	8/10/63–12/20/63
Detwiller, Wm. M. Sgt.	116 OHI	8/15/62–6/14/65
Dillen, Jacob Pvt.	116 OHI	8/13/62–8/13/65
Doak, Davis Pvt.	1 WVA	8/15/62–8/15/65
Doak, Robert Pvt.	4 WVC	9/63–3/8/64
Duty, Andrew W. Sgt.	14 WVI	8/11/62–7/3/65
Eddy, Eli J. Pvt.	7 WVI	10/17/61–12/9/62
also	10 WVI	3/23/64–8/9/65
Edgell, John Pvt.	77 OHI	8/61–3/66
Edy, James P. Pvt.	6 WVI	9/24/64–6/10/65
Elder, Ross Pvt.	14 WVI	8/22/62–6/29/65
Enochs, Joseph Pvt.	92 OHI	8/13/61–10/4/66
Evans, Alfred C. Pvt.	12 WVI	8/16/62–6/15/65
Fasester, Christian Pvt.	——	11/18/61–11/64
Felton, Conrad Pvt.	1 OHA	11/12/61–11/12/64
Fetty, John P. Pvt.	1 WVI	4/15/64–8/24/65
Fish, Henry Pvt.	7 WVI	8/7/61–8/7/64
Fletcher, Daniel M. Pvt.	7 WVI	4/5/65–7/6/65
Fordyce, James Pvt.	2 WVI	6/12/61–6/12/64
also	6 WVC	6/12/64–6/5/65
Forester, Harrison Pvt.	10 WVI	2/18/62–8/18/65
Forester, James Pvt.	10 WVI	2/18/62–5/2/66
Founds, David B. Pvt.	17 WVI	8/13/64–6/13/65

Fox, Ambrose Pvt.	14 WVI	8/11/62–7/4/65
Fox, Barnet W. Pvt.	NF	
Franks, Michael Cpl.	7 WVI	7/61–2/63
Frum, Hamilton G. Pvt.	14 WVI	8/15/62–7/65
Fulmer, James Pvt.	71 OHI	9/28/64–6/12/65
Garrison, Irad Pvt.	14 WVI	8/16/62–6/27/65
Garrison, John W. Pvt.	1 WVI	10/25/61–11/26/64
Gatewood, Jesse L.D. Cpl.	1 WVI	5/15/61–8/19/61
also Pvt.	1 WVA	8/24/61–6/27/65
Glendening, George W. Pvt.	6 WVI	2/13/65–6/13/65
Glendening, Washington Pvt	6 WVI	NF
Goodrich, John W. Pvt.	1 OHA	9/10/61–7/12/65
Gorby, Alexander Pvt.	13 WVI	12/22/63–6/22/65
Gorrell, John B. Pvt.	3 WVI	7/4/61–3/4/64
also QM/Sgt.	6 WVC	3/4/64–5/30/66
Gorrell, Thomas Pvt.	14 WVI	8/13/62–6/27/65
Grey, James Pvt.	17 WVI	9/24/64–7/8/65
Griffin, Wm. E.	NF	
Grim, Salem Lt.	15 WVI	8/62–6/65
Hanline, Tarleton Pvt.	10 WVI	3/8/62–8/14/65
Hawkins, Joshua F.A. Pvt.	14 WVI	8/12/62–7/3/65
Hays, Oliver P. Pvt.	2 WVC	NF
Hayse, Christopher Pvt.	2 WVC	9/7/61–6/30/65
Hendershot, Isaac N. Pvt.	9 WVI	NF
Henderson, John Pvt.	25 OHI	3/22/63–7/64
Henderson, Martin P. Pvt.	14 WVI	8/8/62–6/27/65
Henderson, Silas Pvt.	3 WVC	3/26/64–6/30/65
Henderson, Wm. H. Pvt.	7 WVI	7/61–2/63
Henthom, Jacob Pvt.	63–OHI	3/28/65–7/25/65
Henthom, Richard Pvt.	1 WVI	10/14/61–1862
Hill, Thomas Pvt.	6 WVI	9/10/64–6/10/65
Hissom, Samuel Pvt.	10 WVI	8/62–7/65
Hitchcock, Lewis H. Pvt.	1 OHA	10/12/61–4/18/63
Horner, Peter Pvt.	17 WVI	2/11/65–6/5/65
Howell, Freeman	NF	
Hughes, Henry Pvt.	34 INI	9/61–6/16/65
Ice, John Pvt.	1 WVI	NF
Ireland, Nathan Cpl.	7 WVI	8/7/61–7/12/65
Johnson, Daniel D. Col.	14 WVI	8/62–6/65
Johnson, Moses W. Pvt.	7 WVI	9/61–7/6/65
Johnston, Henry F. Pvt.	4 WVC	8/63–3/64
Johnston, Joseph Pvt.	14 WVI	8/16/62–7/3/65
Joseph, Nathan Pvt.	4 WVC	9/1/63–3/8/64
Kearns, Eli Pvt.	14 WVI	8/11/62–6/27/65
Kearns, Felix E. Pvt.	7 VAI	3/64–7/7/65
Keck, George Pvt.	11 WVI	12/19/61–6/17/65
Keener, Wm. Pvt.	6 OHI	1/63–7/65

Kellar, John M. Pvt.	19 VAC CSA	1862–8/63
also	3 MDC CSA	8/63–9/65
Keller, Charles Pvt.	7 WVI	10/12/61–10/12/64
Keller, David Pvt.	7 WVI	8/7/61–8/10/64
Keller, Martin Pvt.	18 WVI	12/20/61–12/20/64
Kernes, Francis A. Pvt.	15 WVI	8/24/62–6/30/65
Kile, John W. Pvt.	10 WVI	3/9/62–5/9/65
Kimball, Joseph Pvt.	NF	
King, Daniel Pvt.	140 PAI	8/1/62–7/3/65
Lamberson, Dennis Pvt.	14 WVI	8/14/62–6/27/65
Lazear, Wm. Pvt.	194 OHI	3/65–11/65
Leach, Benj. T. Pvt.	179 OHI	9/18/64–6/17/65
Lemley, Isaac S. Sgt.	14 WVI	8/62–7/65
Lemley, John M. Pvt.	7 WVI	3/31/64–7/1/65
Lewis, Abraham Pvt.	6 WVI	8/28/64–6/11/65
Loneberger, John W. Pvt.	10 WVI	6/15/62–7/9/65
Long, Bradford	NF	
Long, Eli B. Pvt.	14 WVI	8/14/62–7/3/65
Long, Jefferson Pvt.	77 OHI	10/24/61–3/26/66
Long, Johnson G. Pvt.	14 WVI	1/64–7/65
Long, Lehaven Pvt.	11 WVI	2/14/63–8/9/65
Luringston, Jeremiah D Pvt	2 WVC	2/64–5/25/65
Marshall, Thomas J. Pvt.	77 OHI	12/12/61–12/25/62
Martin, Jeremiah M. Pvt.	14 WVI	8/15/62–7/3/65
Martin, Reuben D. Pvt.	7 WVI	10/16/61–12/20/64
Martin, Robert B. Sgt.	7 WVI	NF
Massey, Richard C. Pvt.	59 OHI	10/61–3/63
Mathews, Andrew Pvt.	7 WVI	NF
Maxton, James L. Lt.	— PAI	62/63
Maxwell, Wm. Pvt.	116 OHI	8/16/62–6/23/65
Mayfield, James M. Cpl.	15 WVI	9/19/62–7/5/65
Mayfield, Robert Pvt.	15 WVI	8/24/62–6/22/65
McCarty, Boyd G. Pvt.	160 PAI	8/22/62–6/8/63
McCullough, George Cpl.	14 WVI	8/14/62–5/6/65
McCullough, James R. Pvt.	NF	
McElfresh, Samuel W. Pvt.	92 OHI	11/10/63–7/20/65
McGeorge, Griffith J. Pvt.	5 OHC	2/14/65–11/16/65
McMullen, John Pvt.	———	12/61–8/62
McNeely, Richard Pvt.	18 OHI	3/15/65–10/30/65
Mead, George Pvt.	174 OHI	8/64–7/65
Meeker, Edwin D.	NF	
Mercer, John W. Pvt.	15 WVI	8/19/62–6/14/65
Mercer, Lebann F. Pvt.	1 WVI	3/1/64–8/30/65
Michael, James Pvt.	7 WVI	2/25/64–7/1/65
Mikes, Andrew J. Pvt.	NF	
Miller, Mahlon Pvt.	70 OHI	7/29/64–5/29/65
Mires, Oscar P. Pvt.	6 WVI	9/17/61–10/8/64

Mires, Thomas P. Pvt.	7 WVI	3/19/65–NF
Mitchell, Jacoh J. Pvt.	1 PAC	8/62–5/29/65
Moffett, Eldridge Pvt.	116 OHI	NF
Montgomery, Wm. Pvt.	6 WVI	8/19/64–6/10/65
Moore, Andrew J. Pvt.	10 WVI	12/15/62–8/15/65
Moore, Israel Sgt.	7 WVI	10/16/61–7/1/65
Moore, John M. Pvt.	113 OHI	11/64–1865
Moore, Levi Pvt.	6 WVI	9/1/64–6/10/65
Moore, Marion Pvt.	7 WVI	NF
Moore, Wm. M. Pvt.	——	10/61–12/61
Moore, Wm. Pvt.	7 WVI	8/61–7/7/65
Moores, Levi Pvt.	4 WVC	7/27/63–3/8/64
Morgan, Levi Pvt.	10 WVI	8/1/62–8/10/65
Murphy, Samuel C. Pvt.	11 PAI	9/20/64–7/27/65
Myers, Enos J. Pvt.	17 WVI	9/8/64–6/30/65
Nichols, Samuel C. Sgt.	15 WVI	NF
Osborn, Ezra J. Pvt.	18 OHI	9/61–2/28/64
Parks, Wm. H. Pvt.	6 WVI	9/24/64–6/3/65
Patterson, David Lt.	10 WVI	1/16/62–6/3/65
Peggs, Preston Pvt.	1 WVI	10/13/61–10/20/64
Pemer, Charles Pvt.	116 OHI	6/1/62–12/7/64
Phillips, David Pvt.	7 WVI	9/61–10/64
Phillips, Richard Pvt.	2 WVC	10/61–6/63
Pitts, Elijah Pvt.	2 WVI	6/15/61–6/15/64
Pitts, George W. Pvt.	10 WVI	2/2/62–5/9/64
Pitts, Stephen Pvt.	6 WVI	2/28/65–5/28/65
Poe, James L. Pvt.	20 VAC CSA	63/65
Powell, Wm. M. Capt.	14 WVI	8/11/62–6/27/65
Pratt, John E. Pvt.	6 WVI	9/10/64–6/10/65
Pratt, John W. Pvt.	6 WVI	10/12/61
also	— WVA	1/18/62–1/18/65
Railing, Solomon Pvt.	116 OHI	8/12/62–6/27/65
Rice, John K. Pvt.	57 OHI	9/23/61–7/65
Richmond, Charles Cpl.	6 WVI	10/12/61–11/12/64
Richmond, Silas Pvt.	6 WVI	10/12/61–11/12/64
Richmond, Wm. M. Pvt.	4 WVC	8/12/63–3/10/64
Riggs, James S. Pvt.	——	8/14/62–7/65
Roberts, Eli Pvt.	14 WVI	7/15/62–7/4/65
Roberts, Elias Pvt.	14 WVI	8/22/62–6/27/65
Roberts, Jacob J. Pvt.	12 WVI	8/16/62–8/15/65
Robinson, Justice Pvt.	2 WVC	11/7/61–6/13/65
Robinson, Levi Pvt.	1 WVC	2/15/65–7/15/65
Rockwell, Lowry G. Lt.	22 NYC	1862–12/15/63
Rose, Ellis N. Pvt.	60 ILI	5/61–5/28/64
Sebolt, Nicholas Pvt.	7 WVI	10/16/61–12/23/64
Shafer, Daniel W. Pvt.	25 OHI	6/61–1863
Shepherd, John Sgt.	7 WVI	8/7/61–7/8/65

Sheves, Isaac Pvt.	14 WVI	8/62–7/65
Shine, Evander Pvt.	77 OHI	1/25/63–3/11/66
Simons, Thomas Pvt.	116 OHI	8/62–7/15/65
Smith, Anthony Pvt.	14 WVI	8/14/62–6/20/65
Smith, Jackson Pvt.	14 WVI	8/13/62–7/3/65
Smith, Jacob Pvt.	6 WVC	10/9/62–11/13/65
Smith, James B. Pvt.	2 WVI	6/24/61–1/13/65
also Capt.	6 WVC	1/24/65–5/22/66
Smith, John M. Cpl.	14 WVI	8/10/62–7/1/65
Smith, Riley H. Pvt.	3 WVC	9/11/62–7/22/64
Smith, Silas Cpl.	2 WVC	10/61–6/65
Snodgras, John D. Cpl.	6 WVI	2/18/65–6/11/65
Spencer, Elijah Pvt.	7 WVI	NF
Spencer, Henry L. Pvt.	7 WVI	9/61–12/64
Statler, Andrew J.	NF	
Statler, Robert Pvt.	6 WVI	9/11/64–6/10/65
Steele, Thomas S. Pvt.	14 WVI	8/62–6/65
Stevens, James Pvt.	7 WVI	9/1/61–1/3/64
also	1 WVI	1/4/64–7/1/65
Stewart, Alexander Cpl.	7 WVI	3/64–7/65
Stewart, Solomon Drummer	14 WVI	6/62–6/27/65
Stidd, Elizabeth Pvt.	60 OHI	2/26/64–7/23/65
Stidd, John R. Pvt.	77 OHI	2/11/64–3/8/66
Stonking, Samuel Pvt.	14 WVI	8/16/62–11/18/64
Straight, Wm. M. Pvt.	197 OHI	3/25/65–7/31/65
Stringer, Joseph W.	US NF	
Sturm, Joshua L. Pvt.	6 WVI	8/13/61–8/15/64
Summers, Nathan Pvt.	1 OHA	1861–7/65
Sweeney, John L. Surgeon	14 WVI	8/62–3/63
Talkington, Levi Pvt.	14 WVI	1/23/64–6/27/65
Thomas, Elias Cpl.	14 WVI	9/9/62–7/3/65
Thompson, George Pvt.	10 WVI	2/8/62–8/26/65
Thompson, James Cpl.	10 WVI	2/28/62–8/19/65
Tuttle, Jesse Fifer	10 WVI	3/62–3/3/65
Twyman, Joseph W. Pvt.	2 WVC	5/10/61–10/19/62
Twyman, Wm. B. Pvt.	14 WVI	3/3/65–6/27/65
Underwood, Casssy A. Pvt.	14 WVI	8/62–NF
Underwood, Ellis Pvt.	6 WVI	8/30/64–6/10/65
Underwood, Holly W. Pvt.	14 WVI	8/8/62–7/1/65
Underwood, James C. Pvt.	14 WVI	8/14/62–7/15/65
Underwood, Joseph F. Pvt.	6 WVI	10/4/61–12/10/64
also	14 WVI	3/4/65–6/28/65
Underwood, Joseph W. Cpl.	14 WVI	8/8/62–6/27/65
Vansickle, Alonzo Cpl.	2 WVC	10/61–7/4/65
Villers, James Pvt.	7 WVI	8/7/61–6/15/65
Virden, David W. Pvt.	14 WVI	8/62–7/65
Virden, Thornton Pvt.	14 WVI	8/62–6/65

Watkins, Thomas B. Pvt.	14 WVI	8/15/62–7/3/65
Watson, Charles D. Pvt.	116 OHI	8/11/62–6/14/65
Watts, Felix Pvt.	6 WVI	9/23/64–6/10/65
Week, Isaac Pvt.	7 WVI	3/24/64–7/1/65
Weekley, Daniel Pvt.	14 WVI	8/14/62–6/12/65
Weekley, Isaiah Sgt.	14 WVI	8/12/62–7/1/65
Weekly, Elmore W. Pvt.	7 WVI	8/7/61–8/1/65
Weekly, James H. Pvt.	14 WVI	8/8/62–6/27/65
Weekly, Levi Pvt.	10 WVI	3/10/62–5/7/65
Weekly, Wm. W. Pvt.	7 WVI	3/15/64–7/15/65
Weekly, Zane Cpl.	14 WVI	8/8/62–6/27/65
Wells, Clinton M.	US NF	
Wetzel, Wm. H.	US NF	
White, Benj. F. Musician	6 WVI	10/19/61–6/11/65
White, Francis W. Pvt.	NF	
White, Zachariah T. Pvt.	6 WVI	9/64–6/65
Whitzel, John Pvt.	14 WVI	8/13/62–6/27/65
Williamson, George Pvt.	14 WVI	2/64–6/65
Williamson, Joseph A. Pvt.	11 WVI	3/63–3/65
Willison, Samuel T. Pvt.	7 WVI	10/16/61–8/8/62
Wilson, Alexander Cpl.	4 WVC	8/63–5/70
Wilson, George Pvt.	1 OHA	8/61–7/15/65
Wilson, Newton Pvt.	10 WVI	1/16/62–3/14/63
Woodbonne, John Pvt.	14 WVI	8/13/62–6/13/65
Workman, Remus A. Pvt.	7 WVI	10/16/61–7/1/65
Wright, Josiah Pvt.	NF	
Wright, Major F. Pvt.	3 WVI	6/15/61–1/28/64
also Cpl.	6 WVC	1/28/64–5/65
Wright, Major W. Pvt.	15 WVI	9/8/62–1865
Yost, Aaron Pvt.	1 WVI	10/61–1865
Yost, Lemuel Pvt.	20 VAC CSA	4/64–10/64

Tyler County Remarks

Adams, J.M.— disability from mumps
Alkire, J.P.—RH, HD, liver disease
Allen, J.T.—shell wound right shoulder
Alvis, J.H.—KD, HD & bladder disease
Arnett, N.—left hip & side ciatic result
Arthur, W.D.—TYF
Ash, A.—eyes & rupture
Ash, Adam—fever sore on right
Ash, J.L.—aritable heart & RH
Atchison, G.W.*—POW Ft. Delaware
Baker, D.—bronchitis & HD
Baker, G.M.—qunshot wound through shoulder
Bauseman, J.—headache & nervousness caused by TYF
Beagle, W.A.—CDR, piles, malarial fever, eye disease, RH
Bennett, J.C.—liver complaint
Boner, M.P.—rupture, resigned on surgeons certificate
Booher, N.—lungs & atrophy
Bright, J.—wounded right leg & left shoulder
Burgess, T.—loss use of legs
Burrows, G.W.—shot in left breast
Calvert, W.—paralysis of eyes from shell, eczema also
Campbell, J.—HD, piles, RH, catarrh, deafness
Campbell, R.W.—CDR, DSC
Carney, M.—right arm broken & wrist out of place
Carpenter, A.—RH
Carrick, G.—nervous RH
Clark, I.T.—gunshot in left leg
Coe, P.—CDR
Cooper, A.C.—DSC
Cox, J.W.—ruptured
Cox, W.T.—piles
Craig, S.M.—CDR
Cumberledge, S.D.—defective in eyes & lungs
Cumberledqe, G.F.—RH, qunshot wound in breast
Cumherledge, E.—disability eyes, hearing & RH
Cutright, C.—hernia
Davis, B.—CDR, disease of left leg
Davis, C.W.—disease of eyes
Dean, G.H.—asthma
Delor, J.H.—rupture, DSC
Detwiller, W.M.—CDR
Dillen, J.—RH
Dillworth, J.J.—hurt by being thrown from a horse
Doak, R.—KD
Duty, A.W.—wounded left leg, deafness & scurvy

Eddy, E.J.—POW Andersonville, buckshot in leg, DSC
Edgell, J.—ague & fever 1863 resulting KD, piles, neuralgia
Elder, R.—RH
Felton, C.—gunshot in both arms, LD & RH
Fordyce, J.—WIA at Bullrun, ague & fever
Forester, H.—finger shot off
Fox, A.—asthma, atrophy of testicle
Franks, M.—KD, CDR, HD
Fulmer, J.—head wounded with shell
Gatewood, J.L.D.—wounded in small of back
Glendening, W.—fistula in arm
Goodrich, J.W.—bronchitis, LD & RH
Gorrell, J.B.—scurvy
Gorrell, T.—foot mashed by wagon
Grim, S.—disease of the eyes
Groves, C.M.—disease of throat & breast
Hanline, T.—leg off below knee
Hayse, C.—stomach, head & left ankle
Henderson, J.—gun shot arm off, DSC
Henderson, S.—pain in head
Henderson, W.H.—RH 27 years, HD
Henthom, R.—fingers shot off
Hess, N.—WIA Droop Mountain, gunshot left knee
Hinkle, C.—CDR & RH
Hissom, S.—disease of eyes & deafness
Hitchcock, L.H.—MS, TYF, piles
Horner, P.—disease of chest & lungs
Jack, J.W.—relapse on measles, DSC
Jackson, M.O.—RH & CDR
Johnson, D.D.—gunshot right forearm, com. 2 brig. 2 div. of WVA
Johnston, H.F.—RH, LD, dyspepsia, spinal
Kearns, E.—piles
Kearns, F.E.—eyes, back & lungs
Keener, W.—chronic sore eyes & loss of left eye, nearly blind
Keller, C.—shot in left leg
Kile, J.W.—RH & disease of eyes
King, D.—gunshot on head, DSC
Lanham, G.—HD, RH, urinary disorder
Leach, B.T.—wounded left leg below knee, crushed breast
Lemley, I.S.—listless 25 years, never applied for pension
Long, J.—POW hurt in prison by bag (?) falling, shot in knee
Long, L.—RH
Marshal, T.J.—CDR & RH
Marteny, J.N.—piles
Martin, J.M.—RH
Martin, R.D.—wounded in right forearm
Massey, R.C.—RH 28 years, piles & HD

Maxson, J.C.—wounded in hip causing sciatia
Maxwell, W.—gunshot left shoulder
Mayfield, J.M.—gunshot wound
McCullough, G.—RH, gunshot wound in hip
McElfresh, S.W.—RH
McGeorge, G.J.—deficient in back & shoulder cause thrown from horse
McMullen, J.—DSC
McNeely, R.—piles, ruptured
Mead, G.—disease of shoulder & back
Mercer, J.W.—veriacel, DSC
Miller, M.—RH 26 years, neuralgia
Mires, O.P.—rupture
Mitchell, J.J.—RH 27 years, UFL
Moffett, E.—POW Libby, gunshot wound hand
Moore, A.J.—disease of stomach & liver
Moore, I.—LD
Moreland, W.S.—LD, DSC
Morgan, L.—right eye out
Murphy, S.C.—lungs liver & stomach
Nay, J.—shot through right knee
Osborn, E.J.—right leg off 8 in. from knee, WIA Chickamauga 9/63
Painter, E.—hernia, hearing lost in right ear, RH & MP
Parks, W.H.—SS
Peggs, P.—W left leg
Pemer, C.—POW Saulsbury NC, HD & RH
Pitts, E.—CDR & RH
Pratt, J.E.—laryngitis
Pratt, J.W.—catarrh on bowels
Rice, J.K.—CDR 28 years, KD
Richmond, C.—ruptured
Richmond, W.M.—KD
Riggs, J.S.—frozen testicle
Roberts, J.J.—ruptured
Rocwell, L.G.—shot through right leg, enlisted in Rebel army
Rodabaugh, A.—catarrh
Rose, E.N.—wounded in face & shoulder
Rucker, A.—lost left leg, RH, CDR, piles
Sandridge, S.J.—fistula & piles
Sebolt, N.—SS
Shafer, D.W.—quinsy
Shepherd, J.—deafness right ear, wounded right shoulder
Shreves, I.—broken leg & back, RH
Smith, A.—POW Andersonville 1 year
Smith, J.B.—RH
Smith, J.M.—gunshot left shoulder
Smith, Jacob—RH
Smith, Silas—lumbago & KD

Smith, W.B.—TYF & pneumonia
Snodgrass, J.D.—lost sight of eye
Spencer, H.L.—lump on right hip
Steele, T.S.—CDR 26 years
Stevens, Jm.—gunshot wound leg
Stewart, A.—RH
Stewart, S.—disease of right thigh & leg
Stidd, J.R.—deafness in left ear
Stonking, S.—spinal affection caused by fever
Sturm, J.L.—HD
Summers, N.—RH & HD, disabled 2/3 of year
Sweeney, J.L.—CDR 27 years, LD from measles
Talkington, L.—disease of head
Thomas, E.—hernia
Thompson, G.—bayonet wound at Petersburg
Thompson, J.—gunshot wound 3 times
Trussler, J.—bronchitis
Tuttle, J.—shoulder j. knee j. & pleurisy, AFP 1871
Underwood, J.F.—RH
Vansickle, A.—RH, HD, piles
Virden, D.W.—piles & falling of bowels 27 years
Virden, T.—disease of rectum 27 years, also pain right side
Watts, F.—rheumatic neuralge
Week, I.—paralysed in left arm & shoulder
Weekley, D.—bronchitis, hernia, RH
Weekley, I.—gunshot right thigh
Weekly, E.W.—gunshot in right hand
Weekly, J.H.—deafness, LD, HD, RH
Weekly, W.W.—wound in left heel, DSC
Wentz, D.M.—RH
Wentz, J.D.—MS & piles
Westfall, H.—shot through hip
White, B.F.—lung trouble & disease of left leg
Whitzel, J.—2 fingers shot off
Williams, D.M.—neuralgia, RH & HD
Williams, Jn.—CDR, tumor on back & chest,
Williamson, G.—local paralysis left side, general disability
Williamson, J.A.—gunshot forearm
Willison, S.T.—DSC
Wilson, G.—mashed ankle, cut head, colarbone broke, 2 ribs brk
Wilson, N.—DSC
Woodbonne, J.—disabled by fall
Wright, M.F.—HD, L
Wyman, J.W.—DSC
Yost, A.—LD, can't work ¼ time

Upshur County

NAME/RANK	REGIMENT	WHEN SERVED
Allen, Edward Pvt.	— MAI (Negro)	NF
Antney, Wm. Pvt.	10 WVI	64/65
Arbogast, James Pvt.	4 WVC	7/25/63–3/6/64
Bailey, J.C. Pvt.	3 WVC	9/15/64–6/30/65
Bailey, Wm. H. Pvt.	10 WVI	3/4/64–8/9/65
Barton, James Pvt.	12 WVI	8/12/62–5/11/65
Bauseman, Jonathan Pvt.	1 WVC	8/5/63–7/8/65
Bean, Gabriel Pvt.	1 WVA	9/62–6/65
Beer, George W.	US NF	
Bennett, Abram Pvt.	1 WVA	2/11/64–6/28/65
Bennett, Elias Pvt.	1 WVA	NF
Bennett, Moses H. Pvt.	10 WVI	6/1/62–6/26/65
Bennett, Solomon S. Pvt.	3 WVC	3/65–NF
Bennett, Walter F. Capt.	3 NJC	4/26/61–8/17/65
Black, Andrew Pvt.	1 WVA	8/14/62–5/18/65
Black, L.D. Pvt.	3 WVC	3/21/65–6/30/65
Blagg, Henry M. Pvt.	116 OHI	8/24/62–6/24/65
Blagg, Wm. Pvt.	1 WVA	7/62–6/22/65
Blair, Jonathan P. Surgeon	10 WVI	7/1/62–6/2/65
Boyles, Michah Pvt.	1 WVA	8/14/62–6/28/65
Brady, Caswell E. Pvt.	1 WVC	3/3/65–7/16/65
Brain, Rufus Pvt.	3 WVC	8/11/61–6/15/65
Bready, C.E. Pvt.	NF	
Bronson, Elias Ast/Surgeon	———	9/10/63–3/19/65
Brooks, Luke P. Pvt.	10 WVI	3/11/65–8/9/65
Brown, Frederic W. Pvt.	178 OHI	9/28/64–6/27/65
Brown, Henry P. Musician	212 PAI	9/3/64–6/10/65
Brown, Sam I. Pvt.	10 WVI	1/20/62–8/14/65
Brown, Wm. I. Pvt.	3 WVI	6/61–NF
Brubaker, Daniel Pvt.	70 NYI	6/12/61–2/20/62
Bryan, Wm. F. Pvt.	1 WVA	7/9/62–7/3/65
Buchanan, Andrew C. Pvt.	10 WVI	4/13/62–8/5/63
Buckhannon, Renic Pvt.	3 WVC	NF
Burke, Walter Pvt.	NF	
Burner, George W. Lt.	1 WVA	8/13/62–10/8/64
Campbell, Jacob Pvt.	15 WVI	8/7/62–6/14/65
Campbell, Reuben W. Pvt.	10 WVI	8/15/62–3/63
Carpenter, Ethan Pvt.	———	62/65
Carr, Amos F. Cpl.	3 WVC	7/62–6/30/65
Carter, T.A. Pvt.	10 WVI	2/1/62–8/15/65
Casker, Daniel J. Pvt.	1 WVC	9/19/64–7/8/65
Champ, John L. Pvt.	15 WVI	9/64–6/14/65

Name	Unit	Dates
Cherry, Theron R. Cpl.	122 NYI	8/2/62–12/27/62
Childers, Daniel Pvt.	NF	
Claypoole, George W. Pvt.	10 WVI	10/61–3/65
Colender, Wm. L. Pvt.	1 WVA	8/1/62–7/1/65
Conley, Jeremiah C. Pvt.	1 WVA	8/4/62–6/28/65
Cotter, Conrad C. Pvt.	1 WVC	7/8/61–7/8/65
Crites, Abram L. Pvt.	10 WVI	10/61–10/64
Crites, George L. Pvt.	4 WVC	8/1/63–3/6/64
also	1 WVC	3/3/65–7/8/65
Crites, Homer Cpl.	3 WVC	62/65
Crites, John D. Sgt.	10 WVI	3/12/62–6/65
Crites, Joseph Pvt.	10 WVI	NF
Crites, Wm. M. Pvt.	10 WVI	9/8/61–11/10/65
Cutright, Amos C. Pvt.	1 WVA	8/14/62–6/28/65
Cutright, Berry Pvt.	10 WVI	9/8/61 8/9/65
Cutright, Clark Pvt.	3 WVC	3/31/65–7/13/65
Cutright, Clayton P. Pvt.	1 WVA	8/14/62–6/30/65
Cutright, L.D. Pvt.	3 WVC	1863–6/30/65
Cutright, Daniel Pvt.	1 WVA	8/14/62–6/28/65
Cutright, Granville H.	3 WVI	1/11/62–6/66
Cutright, Granville Pvt.	1 WVA	8/20/62–6/25/65
Cutright, Isaac Pvt.	15 WVI	62/65
Cutright, Jacob E. Pvt.	3 WVC	3/1/63–6/30/65
Cutright, Lemeul R. Pvt.	3 WVC	3/27/65–7/9/65
Cutright, Mason W. Pvt.	3 WVI?	6/22/61–2/28/64
also	6 WVC?	2/29/64–8/8/65
Cutright, Thomas Pvt.	4 WVC	7/16/63–1865
Davis, Caleb P. Pvt.	3 WVI	6/10/61–1/31/64
Davis, Edward Sgt.	9 WVI	9/16/61–9/64
Davis, Wm. Pvt.	10 WVI	61/65
Dawson, T.J. Pvt.	Ambulance Corp	4/63–5/65
Dean, Granville H. Pvt.	—WVI	63/65
DeBarr, James W. Pvt.	6 WVC	1863–5/66
DeBarr, Lafayette Pvt.	4 WVC	8/25/63–3/6/64
Demoss, Dennis Pvt.	10 WVI	2/1/62–3/16/65
DeMoss, James S. Pvt.	4 WVC	1865–NF
Depoy, Joseph Pvt.	4 WVC	7/25/63–3/6/64
Dillworth, John J. Pvt.	1 WVC	9/10/64–7/8/65
Dooley, Elam Pvt.	4 WVC	8/25/63–7/8/65
Dranien, Alexander S. Pvt.	1 WVC	2/22/62–6/10/65
Eskew, Lewis A. Pvt.	1 WVA	2/4/64–6/28/65
Farnsworth, F.L. Pvt.	2 MOC CSA	6/61–2/24/65
Findlay, Wm. K. Pvt.	142 PAI	8/16/62–5/24/65
Fitzgerald, James L. Pvt.	1 WVA	1862–NF
Fletcher, Gilmore C. Pvt.	1 WVA	8/15/62–6/28/65
Flowers, E.	US NF	
Flowers, Seldon Musician	12 WVI	8/11/62–6/16/65

Fogg, Mandeville J. Pvt.	1 WVA	NF
Foster, John A. Pvt.	1 WVA	8/62–6/20/65
Fox, John W. Pvt.	15 WVI	3/23/64–8/9/65
Freeman, Homer Pvt.	10 WVI	8/11/62–3/29/65
Friend, Henry Pvt.	3 MDI	8/8/62–5/29/65
Fround?, Amos? Pvt.	3 WVC	3/10/64–6/30/65
Frousman, Nelson J. Pvt.	3 WVC	3/5/64–6/30/65
Gaunt, Joshua Pvt.	1 R. Ashby?	8/5/61–6/5/65
Gawthrop, Richard Pvt.	4 WVC	NF
Geyer, Henry Pvt.	3 WVI	6/22/61–5/22/66
Gillum, Alfred A. Cpl.	3 WVI	61/65
Gladwell, Andrew J. Pvt.	NF	
Goose, John A. Sgt.	10 WVI	9/8/61–8/9/65
Gould, Chandeller D. Pvt.	3 WVI	6/22/61–1/28/64
also	6 WVC	1/28/64–5/22/66
Gould, Jonathan Cpl.	10 WVI	9/8/61–1/3/65
Gould, Marshal Lt.	3 WVI	6/61–11/64
Gould, Watson Pvt.	3 WVI	NF
Greathouse, Moses C.	NF	
Groves, Charles M. Lt.	15 WVI	8/27/62–6/14/65
Gum, George W. Pvt.	4 WVC	7/17/63–3/6/64
Haddock, Ebea Pvt.	4 WVC	8/63–4/64
Hamner, Edward A. Pvt.	NF	
Hannah, Thomas H. Pvt.	3 WVC	4/2/63–6/30/65
Hansen, James T. Sgt.	125 OHI	10/1/62–6/22/65
Harman, Enos Pvt.	47 VAI (CSA)	7/20/64–11/30/64
Harper, Peter Pvt.	3 WVC	2/64–7/65
Harris, John D. Pvt.	11 WVI	6/30/62–6/17/65
Hart, Creek W. Pvt.	1 WVA	8/15/62–6/28/65
Haskins, John T. Cpl.	3 WVI	6/5/61–1/28/64
also Sgt.	6 WVC	1/29/64–5/22/66
Hawkins, Leroy H. Pvt.	6 WVI	10/20/64–6/10/65
Heavner, George M. Pvt.	1 WVA	2/14/62–6/28/65
Heavner, Jacob W. Capt.	3 WVC	4/8/64–6/30/65
Helmick, Absalom Pvt.	1 WVA	8/13/62–6/25/65
Henderson, Jacob Pvt.	17 WVI	2/12/65–7/12/65
Henline, Asa C. Pvt.	3 WVC	3/21/65–6/25/65
Henline, Jacoh B. Pvt.	1 WVA	8/22/62–6/30/65
Hess, Javan Pvt.	10 WVI	11/11/62–8/9/65
Hess, Newton Pvt.	10 WVI	7/28/62–6/28/65
Hinkle, Abram A. Pvt.	3 WVC	9/15/62–6/5/65
Hinkle, Cyrus Pvt.	3 WVC	4/1/65–7/1/65
Hinkle, Foster Pvt.	3 WVC	4/1/65–6/30/65
Hinkle, Isaac Pvt.	3 WVC	4/1/65–6/30/65
Hinkle, Ithiel Pvt.	3 WVC	3/21/65–6/30/65
Hinkle, Minter J. Pvt.	1 WVC	4/1/65–6/20/65
Hoasflook, Andrew Blksmith	4 WVC	7/18/63–3/6/64

Name	Unit	Dates
Hoover, George Pvt.	4 WVC	9/63–1864
Hornbec, Benj. C. Pvt.	4 WVC	6/64–3/65
Hosaflock, Wm. A. Pvt.	4 WVC	NF
Howell, Fountain H. Pvt.	10 WVI	4/1/62–6/28/65
Howes, Andrew Pvt.	3 WVI	6/27/61–5/66
Huffman, Wm. R. Pvt.	3 WVC	1/14/62–1/14/65
Hupps?, George Pvt.	10 WVI	10/18/61–12/29/64
Hurst, John L. Major?	3 WVC	8/24/63–6/30/65
Hyre, Elijah W. Pvt.	3 WVC	3/21/65–6/13/65
Hyre, Stewart Pvt.	1 WVA	7/17/63–3/6/64
Hyre, Wm. J. Pvt.	4 WVC	7/18/63–3/6/64
Jack, John W. Pvt.	10 WVI	3/8/62–9/1/62
Jackson, M.O. Pvt.	3 WVC	3/21/65–6/30/65
Jackson, Samuel D. Pvt.	3 WVC	6/1/64–6/30/65
Jordon, Lewis H.	NF	
Karickhoff, Henry N. Pvt.	3 WVC	3/21/65–6/30/65
Kelley, Nathan C. Pvt.	1 WVC	3/3/65–7/8/65
Kerns, Adam M. Pvt.	3 WVC	62/65
King, J.J. Pvt.	17 WVI	12/4/62–6/30/65
Koon, J.K.P. Pvt.	10 WVI	9/8/61–7/12/65
Lamb, Alexander Pvt.	11 WVI	10/26/61–2/26/64
Lane, Samuel A. Pvt.	3 WVI	9/1/61–3/12/63
Lanham, Ephraim Pvt.	10 WVI	9/8/61–8/14/65
Lanham, Granville Pvt.	3 WVC	3/5/64–6/19/65
Lanham, Samuel T. Pvt.	10 WVI	10/8/61–8/9/65
Lee, Daniel C. Cpl.	10 WVI	10/61–12/64
Lee, Wm. Pvt.	56 PAI	9/2/61–7/1/65
Lemons, John J. Pvt.	1 WVA	8/14/62–12/63
Lemons, Wm. H.H. Pvt.	3 WVI	6/22/61–NF
Lewis, Jacob Cpl.	10 WVI	3/3/62–3/12/65
Lewis, John Pvt.	10 WVI	9/26/61–12/27/64
Lewis, Marcellus Pvt.	3 WVC	3/1/64–6/30/65
Lorentz, Jasper N. Pvt.	1 WVA	8/14/62–6/28/65
Lorentz, Lafayette L. Pvt.	1 WVA	8/1/62–6/28/65
Loudin, John L. Cpl.	10 WVI	8/14/62–6/30/65
Lowe, Wm. R. Pvt.	1 WVA	8/12/62–6/28/65
Luddarth, James Pvt.	3 WVI	6/27/61–5/22/66
Marley, Charles Pvt.	3 WVC	4/6/65–7/2/65
Marple, Minter F. Sgt.	10 WVI	1/22/62–5/7/65
Marteny, Jasper N. Pvt.	10 WVI	7/1/63–8/9/65
Martin, George W. Pvt.	1 WVC	4/5/65–7/8/65
Martin, Josiah Pvt.	10 WVI	8/8/61–9/1/62
Martin, Obadiah W. Pvt.	10 WVI	8/20/62–6/30/65
Mathers, Joseph R. Pvt.	3 WVI	6/7/61–7/6/64
Maxson, Jacob C. Pvt.	10 WVI	1/2/62–8/18/65
Mayo, Wm. T. Pvt.	62 VAI CSA	10/62–5/20/65
McCauley, Garret L. Pvt.	1 WVC	8/15/63–5/5/65

McClean, Wm. P. Pvt.	3 WVI	6/61–6/63
McCoy, Chapman Sgt.	3 WVI	6/22/61–8/15/64
McKeever, Alfred L. Cpl.	3 WVI	3/19/62–3/19/64
also Sgt.	6 WVC	3/19/64–5/22/66
McLaughlin, John B. Pvt.	10 WVI	3/17/62–8/22/65
McNeal, Anthony	NF	
McNulty, Wm. A. Lt.	1 WVA	NF
Messman, John H. Pvt.	10 WVI	3/15/62–8/16/65
Miller, James H. Pvt.	1 WVA	8/15/62–6~28/65
Miller, John Pvt.	3 WVC	4/11/64–1865
Miller, Joseph Pvt.	1 WVC	2/22/62–7/8/65
Miller, Phillip Pvt.	4 WVC	7/25/63–3/6/64
Moreland, Wm. S. Pvt.	Upshur Battery	9/13/62–4/4/63
Morgan, David C. Pvt.	10 WVI	9/8/61–8/12/65
Morgan, Joseph J. Pvt.	6 WVI	8/6/61–8/15/64
Morgan, Littleton T. Sgt.	6 WVC	6/10/61–5/22/65
Morgan, Stephen Cpl.	6 WVI	8/5/61–8/18/64
Morris?, Morgan Pvt.	10 WVI?	61/64
Morrison, David Pvt.	10 WVI	10/61–6/65
Munday, Nimrod G. Pvt.	1 WVC	4/3/65–7/8/65
Napier, James P. Pvt.	10 WVI	8/62–6/1/65
Nay, Jezeniah Pvt.	1 WVI	10/10/61–11/26/64
Neely, Alvy Pvt.	1 WVA	8/16/62–6/30/65
Neely, Anthony Pvt.	3 WVC	3/1/65–6/30/65
Neff, Thomas H.B. Pvt.	3 WVC	3/1/63–7/9/65
Nethken, Meshack A. Pvt.	7 PAI	2/25/64–9/5/65
Ogden, Joshua C. Pvt.	17 WVI	9/26/64–6/30/65
Ordaker, David Pvt.	NF	
Ours, Jacob Pvt.	4 WVC	7/25/63–3/6/64
Ours, Mearbec Pvt.	1 WVA	8/15/62–12/24/63
Ours, Nicholas Pvt.	1 WVA	8/15/62–6/28/65
Owens, Silas Pvt.	186 OHI	10/3/62–9/25/65
Painter, Eli Sgt.	15 WVI	8/28/62–6/14/65
Paugh, John C. Pvt.	1 WVC	3/1/65–7/8/65
Peck, Thomas Pvt.	6 WVI	10/8/61–6/10/65
Perry, John Pvt.	1 WVA	6/62–6/29/65
Peters, Joshua G. Pvt.	1 WVA	8/12/62–6/28/65
Phillips, Burton Pvt.	1 WVA	7/15/62–5/30/65
Phillips, David Pvt.	10 WVI	8/14/62–7/1/65
Phillips, Franklin Sgt.	3 WVI	1861–8/15/64
Phillips, George Sgt.	3 WVI	6/22/61–5/22/66
Phillips, John E. Pvt.	1 WVC	8/10/63–7/8/65
Phillips, Lafayette Pvt.	3 WVI	61/65
Phillips, Lothrop Pvt.	1 WVA	NF
Phillips, Simeon Pvt.	3 WVI	6/27/61–4/14/66
Phillips, Spencer Musician	3 WVI	5/13/61–2/28/64
also	6 WVC	2/28/64–10/15/65

Name	Unit	Dates
Phillips, Sylvester Capt.	3 WVI	6/22/61–11/8/62
also Capt.	19—	11/19/63–11/64
Phillips, Wallace R. Pvt.	4 WVC	NF
Phillips, Walter Musician	3 WVI	NF
Phillips, Wirt Pvt.	10 WVI	6/19/62–6/29/65
Piles, Hiram Pvt.	1 WVC	7/4/61–7/8/65
Powell, Joseph A. Pvt.	136 INI	5/15/63–9/7/64
Powers, Elmore Sgt.	10 WVI	10/1/61–8/19/65
Pringle, Richard H. W. Pvt.	1 WVI	65/65
Quin?, Granville Pvt.	1 WVA	8/14/62–6/28/65
Radabaugh, Isaac Pvt.	1 WVA	8/14/62–6/28/65
Ratcliff, George W. Pvt.	1 WVC	4/5/65–7/8/65
Ray, Wm. Pvt.	2 WVI	5/20/61–6/4/64
Reger?, John N. Chaplain/Grafton Hospital		3/64–8/65
Rexroad, Miranda H. Cpl.	10 WVI	9/25/61–3/12/65
Richards, James Pvt.	14 WVI	7/28/62–6/27/65
Riggs, Theodore J. Pvt.	10 WVI	8/12/62–7/1/65
Robinson, Andrew Pvt.	1 WVA	8/12/62–6/28/65
Robinson, Noah O. Cpl.	6 WVC	11/61–6/66
Roby, Elmack H. Cpl.	10 WVI	9/22/61–2/27/65
Rodabaugh, Adam Pvt.	WV Scouts	62/65
Rohrbough, John W. Sgt.	1 WVA	8/9/62–6/28/65
Rollins, Abram S. Cpl.	1 WVA	8/13/62–6/25/65
Rollins, Albert G. Pvt.	6 WVC	7/30/61–5/22/66
Ross, James Pvt.	7 WVI	3/15/65–7/2/65
Roundstone, Alexander Capt	62 OHI	10/14/61–12/25/62
also Capt.	5 USI	8/20/63–9/20/65
Rucker, Abram Pvt.	10 WVI	9/8/61–5/14/65
Rucker, Samuel Pvt.	10 WVI	11/1/61–8/9/65
Russell, John R. Sailor/Frigate Congress		5/61–9/62
Russell, Patrick H. Pvt.	3 WVC	3/21/65–6/30/65
Sandridge, Suther J. Pvt.	15 WVI	8/23/62–6/14/65
Savely, James W. Cpl.	63 OHI	1/2/62–7/8/65
Sellar, Henry Col.	OHIO	61/65–NF
Sexton, George A. Capt.	3 WVC	5/16/62–6/30/65
Shahan, James Pvt.	6 WVI	8/6/61–8/6/64
Shamburg, Francis Capt.	1 MDC	4/26/62–8/18/65
Shanabarger, Sam A. Pvt.	1 WVA	9/27/61–6/24/65
Shaw, Thomas Pvt.	10 WVI	9/8/61–1865
Sheets, Jacob Pvt.	1 WVC	5/20/64–7/8/65
Shingleton, Anderson Pvt.	14 WVI	3/17/65–6/27/65
Shipman, George Pvt.	3 WVC	63/65
Shipman, John B.	Guide US	NF
Shipman, Sam W. Pvt.	3 WVC	3/1/63–7/9/65
Shocks, James M. Pvt.	17 WVI	2/14/65–6/30/65
Shreve, N. G. Cpl.	3 WVC	1/1/64–6/30/65
Simmons, Charles S. Pvt.	3 WVC	NF

Name	Unit	Dates
Simon, Chrisitan Pvt.	4 WVC	8/27/63–3/12/64
Simons, George W. Pvt.	1 WVA	8/12/62–3/6/64
Simons, James D. Pvt.	3 WVI	8/19/61–5/22/66
Simons, Seymour Pvt.	1 WVA	8/62–6/65
Sive, David Pvt.	3 MDI	4/17/62–5/29/65
Sive, Wm. Pvt.	3 MDI	8/62–5/29/65
Smallridge, Jacob J. Pvt.	3 WVC	3/6/65–6/30/65
Smallridge, James A. Pvt.	3 WVC	3/1/64–3/30/65
Smallridge, Samuel D. Pvt.	1 WVA	8/13/62–1865
Smallridge, Wm. B. Pvt.	3 WVI	61/63
Smallridge, Wm. E. Pvt.	1 WVA	8/15/62–6/28/65
Smith, Peter J. Pvt.	3 WVC	3/12/65–7/12/65
Smith, Wm. B. Pvt.	1 WVA	6/62–6/65
Snider, Ephram Pvt.	10 WVI	7/9/61–7/64
Snyder, Frederic Pvt.	10 WVI	9/8/61–8/9/65
Snyder, Thomas W. Pvt.	4 WVC	7/18/63–3/6/64
Spiker, John Pvt.	2 MDI	12/22/64–7/24/65
Strader, Granville Pvt.	3 WVC	3/1/65–6/30/65
Strader, Salathiel Cpl.	10 WVI	61/64
Strather, Solomon L. Pvt.	3 WVC	3/21/65–6/13/65
Stuart, George W. Cpl.	8 OHC	6/5/64–7/30/65
Tenney, James B. Pvt.	6 WVC	7/4/61–7/16/65
Tenney, Jonathan Pvt.	1 WVA	8/14/62–7/1/65
Tenney, Josiah Pvt.	1 WVA	8/12/62–7/1/65
Thompson, James M. Pvt.	6 WVI	8/13/61–8/15/64
Thorne, John N. Drummer	6 WVI	8/12/61–6/15/65
Totten, W.G.L. Sgt.	169 PAI	10/16/62–7/26/63
Trussler, James Pvt.	WV Scouts	1863–4/10/65
Vangilder, Frederic Pvt.	3 WVA	8/61–6/65
VanTroup, John A. Pvt.	4 WVI	1861–NF
Wagoner, Wm. Pvt.	NF	
Waid, Chauncy W. Pvt.	10 PAI	61/62
Wamsley, Lloyd Pvt.	10 WVI	6/7/62–7/3/65
Warner, Marshall L. Pvt.	10 WVI	8/18/62–6/29/65
Warner, Wm. W. Pvt.	3 WVC	3/21/65–6/30/65
Waugh, Brom Pvt.	1 WVC	3/16/65–7/16/65
Waugh, Evan S. Pvt.	1 WVA	8/12/62–6/25/65
Wentz, David M. Sgt.	WV Scouts	62/64
Wentz, John D. Pvt.	WV Scouts	62/65
Westfall, Henderson Pvt.	10 WVI	61/65
Westfall, Thomas Pvt.	11 WVI	NF
Wilder, Thomas J. Pvt.	150 PAI	3/31/64–6/30/65
Wilfong, Daniel Pvt.	3 WVC	3/10/65–6/30/65
Wilfong, George Pvt.	10 WVI	4/2/62–6/28/65
Wilfong, John Pvt.	3 WVC	1863–7/9/65
Willfong, Ashley Pvt.	17 WVI	9/7/63–7/7/65
Williams, D.M. Pvt.	15 WVI	8/23/62–11/21/64

Williams, John Pvt.	4 USA	8/1/61–2/12/67
Williams, Lemeul Pvt.	6 WVI	10/64–6/65
Williams, Solomon Cpl.	1 WVA	8/13/62–6/29/65
Wolf, James A. Pvt.	10 WVI	9/8/61–8/9/65
Young, James G. Pvt.	1 WVA	8/15/62–6/28/65
Young, Richard P. Pvt.	1 WVA	8/15/62–6/28/65
Young, Stittman Pvt.	1 WVA	8/13/62–6/28/65
Zickafoose, H. Pvt.	3 WVC	5/23/63–6/30/65
Zickefoose, Elias	NF	

Upshur County Remarks

Arbogast, J.—WIA near New Creek, gunshot left leg, injury to right testicle, constant loss of urine
Bailey, J.C.—ruptured & deaf in left ear
Bailey, W.H.—shell wound left hip, back hurt by a fall
Barton, J.—RH & CDR
Bauseman, J.—headache & nervousness caused by TYF
Bean, G.—quinsy (?)
Bennett, A.—disabled in back & left hip, hurt by horse falling
Bennett, E.—hemorage & lumbago
Bennett, M.H.—tumor in stomach & piles, was in 18 engagements
Bennett, S.S.—RH & HD, went home on visit for a few days, reg was discharged before his return he was marked deserter
Bennett, W.F.—RH
Black, A.—WIA Buckhannon, shot in testicle
Black, L.D.—CDR, not pensioned
Blagg, W.—disability caused by CDR
Boyles, M.—RH
Brain, R.—ruptured
Bronson, E.—CDR & malarial poisoning
Brown, S.I.—consumption catarrh of lungs 25 yr badly affected
Brubaker, D.—disease of respiratory organs & RH
Bryan, W.F.—LD & HD, old & feeble
Buckhannon, R.—RH
Burner, G.W.—CDR
Campbell, J.—HD, piles, RH, catarrh, deafness
CamPbell, R.W.—CDR, DSC
Carpenter, E.—gunshot wound in leg
Carr, A.F.—shoulders dislocated, CDR, piles, double hernia, shot on the breast, broken jaw
Carter, T.A.—wounded twice
Casker, D.J.—RH, slight gunshot wound in side
Cherry, T.R.—rupture
Claypoole, G.W.—mashed arm & disease in body from fever in army
Colender, W.L.—VV right leg

Crites, A.L.—discharge papers in pension office
Crites, G.L.—asthma
Crites, I I.—loss of health
Crites, J.D.—effects of fever & mumps
Crites, W.M.—lost right arm
Curtight, B.—piles, CDR, HD
Cutright, C.—hernia
Cutright, C.P.—general disability
Cutright, G.H.—gunshot wound left side, RH, ague
Cutright, I.—RH
Cutright, L.D.—lumbago, piles, CDR
Cutright, L.R.—CDR
Cutright, T.—general disability
Davis, C.P.—RH right hip & leg
Davis, E.—RH & gunshot wound left arm
Dawson, T.J.—mumps fell on scrotum & injured right testicle
Dean, G.H.—asthma
DeBarr, J.W.—LD
Demoss, D.—deafness, weak eyes, breast & back
DeMoss, J.S.—general disability, not pensioned
Depoy, J.—sciatic RH
Dillworth, J.J.—hurt by being thrown from a horse
Dooley, E.—piles & disease of eyes
Eskew, L.A.—piles, disabled
Findlay, W.K.—slight wound in head
Fitzgerald, J.L.—left arm broken below elbow
Fletcher, G.C.—suffering with RH
Flowers, S.—POW a short time
Foster, J.A.—LD
Fox, J.W.—disease of eyes, defective hearing
Freeman, H.—RH, bronchitis, asthma, throat disease, fistula anus
Friend, H.—RH
Frousman, N.J.—hemorrhoids
Gaunt, J.—rupture left side
Geyer, H.—neurotrophy, broken veins in legs etc.
Gladwell, A.J.—gunshot wound both hips
Goose, J.A.—VV right leg
Gould, J.—WIA, hip, 7/24/63 RH, POW Libby prison
Gould, M.—catarrh of head
Gould, W.—stomach disease
Groves, C.M.—disease of throat & breast
Gum, G.W.—RH
Haddock, E.—LD
Hannah, T.H.—stomach disease
Hansen, J.T.—POW 5 months Belle Island
Harman, E.—LD, had cough
Harper, P.—KD & CDR
Haskins, J.T.—POW Libby prison 5 months, on western plains 1 year

Hawkins, L.H.—sprained ankle & CDR
Heavner, G.M.—eyes injured & slight deafness, POW
Henderson, J.D.—RH & catarrh
Henline, A.C.—rupture & SS
Hess, J.—piles & RH
Hess, N.—WIA Droop Mountain, gunshot left knee
Hinkle, C.—CDR & RH
Hinkle, F.—CDR
Hinkle, I.—RH & CDR
Hinkle, M.J.—CDR
Hoasflook, A.—CDR, general disability
Howell, F.H.—CDR
Howes, A.—VV in leg
Hupps, G.—CDR
Hurst, J.L.—wounded in heel
Hyre, S.—tumor right leg & piles
Jack, J.W.—relapse on measles, DSC
Jackson, M.O.—RH & CDR
Jackson, S.D.—RH & HD
Karickhoff, H.N.—RH & CDR
Kerns, A.M.—lumbago
King, J.J.—RH
Koon, J.K.P.—left arm shot off close shoulder joint
Lamb, A.—ruptured, neuralgia caused arm to shrivel, DSC
Lane, S.A.—LD, HD, CDR, dyspepsia
Lanham, E.—SS & RH
Lanham, G.—HD, RH, urinary disorder
Lanham, S.T.—general disability from measles, partial deafness
Lee, D.C.—piles & general disability
Lee, W.—RH
Lemons, J.J.—paralysis left side
Lemons, W.H.H.—gunshot wound knee cap
Lewis, J.—hearing & piles
Lewis, Ja.—disease of eyes & lungs from measles
Lewis, M.—RH & deafness
Loudin, J.L.—KD
Lowe, W.R.—varicele of left side
Marple, M.F.—gunshot wound in thigh, shell wound in back, results disease of kidney, spine, liver & stomach. In all engageaments of the regt except one
Marteny, J.N.—piles
Martin, J.—broken veins & general disability
Martin, O.W.—injury to eye sight
Maxson, J.C.—wounded in hip causing sciatia
Mayo, W.T.*—parolled
McCauley, G.L.—discharge in hands of pension office
McCoy, C.—2 gunshot wounds 1 shoulder joint 1 shoulder blade
McLaughlin, J.B.—catarrh, not pensioned

McNulty, W.A.—WIA right thigh & hand, 2/5/64
Messman, J.H.—sciatic RH
Miller, J.H.—CDR
Miller, J.—piles & CDR
Miller, Jn.—injury to back
Miller, P.—RH & piles
Moreland, W.S.—LD, DSC
Morgan, D.C.—malarial poison
Morgan, L.T.—gunshot wound left hand
Morgan, S.—RH
Morris, M.—SS
Morrison, D.—ruptured & blind of an eye
Napier, J.P.—ague, shot in right leg & head, frozen feet
Nay, J.—shot through right knee
Neff, T.H.B.—RH & HD
Ours, M.—LD
Ours, N.—neuralgia, hearing slightly affected
Owens, S.—mashed left testicle, struck by shell on ankle bone
Painter, E.—hernia, hearing lost in riqht ear, RH & MP
Peck, T.—broken do~n in health
Perry, J.—LD
Peters, J.G.—CDR
Phillips, B.—chest & hip injury
Phillips, D.—rupture testacle
Phillips, F.—severe gunshot wound both thighs partially paralyzed
Phillips, J.E.—RH & LD
Phillips, L.—general disability
Phillips, Lo.—LD
Phillips, S.—VV both legs
Phillips, W.—disabled in hips result of TYF
Powell, J.A.—RH & HD
Powers, E.—chills & fever
Quin, G.—injured left side & chest
Radabaugh, I.—piles, had smallpox in army
Ratcliff, G.W.—soldier 1812
Ray, W.—RH 26 years
Richards, J.—gunshot wound left foot
Riggs, T.J.—general disability of the system
Robinson, A.—RH
Roby, E.H.—gunshot wound left leg
Rodabaugh, A.—catarrh
Rohinson, N.O.—general disability 25 years
Rollins, A.G.—measles
Ross, J.—bronchitis
Rucker, A.—lost left leg, RH, CDR, piles
Rucker, S.—hearing partially destroyed by explosion of shell
Russell, J.R.—injury to right hip 3/8/62 in action with ram merrimac, captured at Newrport News Va 3/8/62

Russell, P.H.—piles & RH
Sandridge, S.J.—fistula & piles
Sellar, H.—wound
Shahan, J.—suffers from back & kidney disease
Shanabarger, S.A.—POW Richmond Belle Island, 3 months
Shaw, T.—gunshot through lungs
Shipman, G.—gunshot wound right hip
Shipman, S.W.—blood poison & RH, hands almost disabled broken rist
Shreve, N.G.—RH
Simmons, C.S.—hearing affected by lightning injury to back
Simons, G.W.—spinal affection
Simons, S.—stomach disease
Sive, D.—VV both legs & deaft in one ear
Sive, W.—RH
Smallridge, J.J.—SS & LD
Smallridge, W.E.—measles settled on lungs caused general disability
Smallridqe, W.B.—shot throuqh left shoulder & lung
Smith, W.B.—TYF & pneumonia
Snider, E.—wound in leg
Snyder, F.—stiff legs & hurt in breast, struck by shell piece
Strader, S.—CDR & disease of rectum
Tenney, J.B.—hip pain from injury, captured once
Tenney, Jn.—effects of measles
Tenney, Jo.—catarrh from fever & RH, crippled in back
Thompson, J.M.—asthma & right knee injured by a fall
Thorne, J.N.—kidney trouble 2 yr & stomach trouble 10 yr
Trussler, J.—bronchitis
Vangilder, F.—asthma & general disability
Waid, C.W.—HD & general disability
Wamsley, L.—catarrh in head
Warner, M.L.—RH, pensioned
Warner, W.W.—catarrh in head
Waugh, E.S.—disease of side, stomach & lungs
Wentz, D.M.—RH
Wentz, J.D.—MS & piles
Westfall, H.—shot through hip
Westfall, T.—mumps, very ill 2 or 3 days ago
Wilder, T.J.—asthma, gunshot wound & tumor on side
Wilfong, G.—catarrh in head, back & throat, old & feeble
Wilfong, J.—lumbago & malarial poison
Willfong, A.—CDR & disease of rectum
Williams, D.M.—neuralgia, RH & HD
Williams, Jn.—CDR, tumor on back & chest,
Williams, S.—general disability
Young, J.G.—liver & stomach disease
Young, R.P.—loss of left testicle, injury left knee

Wayne County

NAME/RANK	REGIMENT	WHEN SERVED
Adkins, Alexander Pvt.	45 VAI BTN CSA	63/64
Adkins, David Pvt.	7 WVC	62/65
Adkins, Harmon Sgt.	45 KYI	8/8/62–12/24/64
Adkins, Jesse	NF (34 BTN VAC CSA)	
Adkins, Pleasant A. Cpl.	5 VAI	10/12/61–6/15/64
Adkins, Wm. R. Pvt.	14 KYI	NF
Adkins, Wyatt E. Pvt.	62 VAI (CSA)	8/15/61–8/63
Akers, Burwell Pvt.	14 WVI	11/19/61–1/31/65
Akers, Burwell Pvt.	53 KYI	4/15/65–9/15/65
Akers, James Pvt.	14 KYI	8/1/63–6/1/65
Akers, Lewis Pvt.	39 OHI	8/62–7/7/65
Atkins, J.D. Pvt.	34 KYI	3/64–9/65
Babbus, James N. Pvt.	5 VAI	9/1/62–9/1/63
Bailey, Lemeul Pvt.	14 KYC	9/62–9/12/63
Baker, Samuel Pvt.	45 KYI	8/63–12/24/64
Baker, Thomas Pvt.	45 KYI	8/63–12/24/64
Ball, Silas Pvt.	16 VAI	62/63
Banlvan, Elisha Pvt.	5 WVI	10/61–10/63
Barnell, Charles Pvt.	NF	
Bartram, John Pvt.	68 KYI	5/61–7/64
Bartram, Samuel Pvt.	53 KYI	4/11/65–9/15/65
Bellomey, Marshal Pvt.	14 KYI	8/14/63–9/15/65
Bench, Lewis Pvt.	NF	
Bentley, John L. Pvt.	39 KYI	12/15/62–9/15/65
Birt, Michael Pvt.	1 KYI?	NF
Blair, James C. Pvt.	13 VAI	8/14/62–6/22/65
Blake, Henry T. Pvt.	7 WVC	64/65
Blankenship, Jesse Pvt.	34 VAC CSA	NF
Blankenship, John Cpl.	5 VAI	9/61–9/64
Bloss, Harvey Pvt.	45 KYI	8/15/63–12/28/64
Booth, Francis M. Sgt.	8 VAC CSA	5/61–1865
Boothe, Francis M.	16 VAC CSA	NF
Bowe, John Pvt.	NF	
Bowen, David M. Pvt.	8 VAC CSA	NF
Boyd, Arthur Sgt.	39 KYI	9/13/62–9/15/65
Bradshaw, Thomas Pvt.	1 KYI	63/65
Bradshaw, Wm. T. Pvt.	9 WVI	2/20/62–2/28/64
Brock, Aaron Pvt.	39 KYI	65/65
Burris, Wm. H. Pvt.	39 KYI	11/22/62–9/15/65
Burt, Charles Pvt.	6 KYI	6/16/64–NF
Canterbury, George W. Pvt.	7 OHC	NF
Canterbury, Joel Pvt.	13 VAI	8/12/62–6/22/65
Carey, Henry Pvt.	45 KYI	8/2/63–12/16/64

Carls, James Pvt.	9 VAI	1/10/63–12/31/65
Carver, Wiley Pvt.	39 KYI	9/10/63–9/15/65
Castle, David Pvt.	39 KYI	9/62–9/65
Chadwick, Hiram Pvt.	5 WVI	8/20/61–10/3/64
Chaffin, Wm. Pvt.	14 KYI?	NF
Chapman, George E. Sgt.	173 OHI	8/4/64–7/8/65
Chapman, Martin V. Pvt.	3 WVC	1/3/64–7/13/65
Chrisitan, Allan Pvt.	1 WVI	7/18/63–7/31/65
Chrisitan, Daniel Pvt.	39 KYI	64/65
Clark, John Pvt.	45 KYI	8/1/63–12/1/64
Collins, Isaac Pvt.	5 VAI	6/61–3/64
Cooper, Hiram C.B. Pvt.	10— C	6/2/61–6/62
also	34 ILI	4/2/63–7/14/65
Copley, Benj. F. Pvt.	14 KYI	8/8/63–12/24/64
Copley, Cyrus Pvt.	5 WVI	8/10/61–9/3/62
Copley, Edward H. Cpl.	45 KYI	1863–2/15/65
Copley, Henry H. Pvt.	5 VAI	5/61–1862
Copley, Ira G. Lt.	5 VAI	9/14/61–3/20/62
Copley, Johnson Pvt.	14 KYI	NF
Copley, Nicholas Pvt.	5 VAI	8/10/61–9/23/64
Copley, Stanley Pvt.	14 KYI	9/17/63–9/15/65
Copley, Thomas D. Pvt.	5 WVI	61/65
Copley, Thomas J. Pvt.	5 WVI	61/65
Copley, Willy Pvt.	NF	
Copley, Wm. Lt.	———	62/64
Cordell, Samuel Pvt.	5 WVI	NF
Crum?, Leonard Sgt.	5 VAI	8/10/61–9/23/64
Cunningham, Jesse C. Sgt.	9 WVI	11/2/61–12/31/63
Damron, Samuel D.	NF (8 VAC CSA)	
Darling, James A. Sgt.	5 WVI	7/13/61–9/20/64
Dass, John	NF	
Davis, James Pvt.	45 VAC CSA	8/63–12/64
Davis, Lewis Pvt.	45 VAI CSA	7/24/63–12/24/64
Davis, Wm. Pvt.	45 VAI CSA	8/14/63–12/24/64
Dean, Joseph Pvt.	14 KYI	NF
Defoe, Wm. A. Pvt.	NF (34 BTN VAC CSA)	
Dishman, Samuel R. Pvt.	13 WVI	NF
Dishman, Wm. Pvt.	5 WVI	7/13/61–7/28/65
Dixon, George B. Sgt.	45 KYI	10/1/63–2/14/65
Dixon, Hugh B. Pvt.	5 WVI	8/15/62–6/28/65
Dixon, Wm. J. Capt.	5 WVI	7/21/61–10/4/64
Duncan, Andrew J. Cpl.	1 OHA	12/3/61–12/3/64
Duncan, Henry C. Pvt.	18 OHI	4/19/61–8/19/61
also	9 WVI	1/6/62–10/31/64
also Capt.	1 WVI	12/12/64–7/21/65
Eaves, James F. Pvt.	5 WVI	7/18/61–9/26/64
Elexander, Lewis Pvt.	67 WV (VAM CS?)	62/63

Elkins, Milton Pvt.	5 WVI	NF
Estep, John W. Sgt.	28 WVC	10/13/61–8/1/65
Evick, Wm. Pvt.	5 VAI	6/11/61–9/24/64
Fane, James	NF	
Fell, Jacob H. Cpl.	13 VAI	62/65
Ferguson, James H.	NF (10 VAC CSA?)	
Ferguson, Samuel J. Lt.	8 VAC CSA	6/61–4/65
Ferguson, Samuel Pvt.	8 VAC CSA	10/15/61–12/18/64
Ferguson, Wm. V. Pvt.	35 KYI	3/63–9/63
Findley, Samuel Pvt.	39 KYI	9/15/62–9/15/65
Flinn, George Pvt.	6 KYC	5/9/63–6/1/65
Fortune, Charles L.	NF	
Foster, Robert C. Pvt.	7 WVC	3/1/65–8/1/65
Frasher, David K. Lt.	167 VAM	7/2/62–NF
Frasher, James Pvt.	167 VAM	7/2/62–NF
Frasher, Wm. H. Pvt.	8 VAC CSA	1862–NF
Fry, Van Buren B. Sgt.	45 BTN VAI CSA	62/65
Fuller, Hiram Pvt.	13 WVI	8/14/62–6/22/65
Fuller, Sylvester B. Pvt.	5 VAI	7/13/61–9/24/64
Galloway, John H. Pvt.	149 OHNG	5/2/64–8/13/64
Garrett, Alonzo	NF	
Gibson, Henderson R. Pvt.	39 KYI	9/15/62–5/1/65
Gilkerson, Henry Pvt.	14 KYI	60/65
Gilmore, Wm. Pvt.	45 KYI	7/14/63–4/26/64
Goodman, Pleasant Pvt.	39 KYI	1863–9/22/65
Goodwin, Preston Sgt.	8 VAC CSA	5/10/61–4/27/65
Granville, Robert Pvt.	1 KYI	NF
Green, John W. Pvt.	53 KYI	63/64
Gum, Charles R. Pvt.	— WVA	9/20/61–10/24/64
Halbs, James M.	NF	
Hale, Andrew Pvt.	45 KYI	62/64
Halley, Edmond Pvt.	40 KYI	63/65
Hampton, Autrey Pvt.	45 KYI	8/8/63–12/24/64
Hams, Samuel Cpl.	39 KYI	9/15/62–9/15/65
Hankin, Wm. Pvt.	9 WVI	4/5/62–4/30/65
Hankins, Wm. D. Pvt.	69 INI	8/1/62–11/24/62
Hanshaw, David H. Pvt.	NF	
Harmon, Wm. H. Pvt.	5 WVI	7/13/61–12/23/63
also	1 WVI	12/23/63–7/21/65
Hart, Joseph H. Sgt.	18 KYI	0/8/61–7/18/65
Harvey, Samuel Pvt.	14 KYC	8/25/62–4/65
Hazel, John Pvt.	13 VAI	8/11/62–1865
Hensley, James W. Pvt.	53 KYI	3/65–9/65
Hite, Andrew J. Pvt.	14 KYI	9/5/61–2/10/65
Hodson, David W. Pvt.	13 MEI	12/28/61–1/31/64
also	30 MEI	2/1/64–8/20/65
Hooker, George H. Major	Asst/AG.	1861–9/14/65

Hooser, John W. Pvt.	39 OHI	12/22/63–7/9/65
Hooser, Wm. Pvt.	39 OHI	12/22/63–7/9/65
Hughes, John W. Pvt.	7 WVC	3/28/64–8/1/65
Hunt, Thomas Pvt.	14 KYI	1/62–12/65
Hunter, Joseph Cpl.	10 KYC	7/15/63–9/15/65
Hunter, Wm. Pvt.	26 VAI (BTN)CS	NF
Hurley, John W. Pvt.	39 KYI	10/21/62–9/16/65
Hutchinson, Joseph Pvt.	13 WVI	NF
Hutchinson, Peter D. Pvt.	13 WVI	8/2/62–6/24/65
Hutchinson, Wm.	NF (36 VAI CSA?)	
Hutchison, David N. Pvt.	5 WVI	8/20/61–10/3/64
Hylton, Jefferson Pvt.	14 KYI	1/21/62–7/21/65
Irby, George W. Pvt.	13 WVI	8/14/62–6/22/65
Irons, Solomon Pvt.	5 WVI	8/20/62–12/7/64
James, Smith Pvt.	8 VAC CSA	5/10/61–4/65
Johnson, Clatus Pvt.	34 KYI	11/1/63–6/24/65
Johnson, James Pvt.	34 VAC (CSA)	4/15/61–3/15/65
Justice, George T. Pvt.	39 KYI	11/19/62–9/65
Kelley, Wm. Pvt.	1 VAA	8/61–8/62
Kimbler, Joseph Pvt.	14 KYI	11/29/62–9/15/65
King, Eliphas H. Pvt.	32 INI	NF
Koontz, Elihu P. Sgt.	4 WVI	7/61–7/65
Lafferty, Steel Sgt.	Raleigh Guards	6/1/64–6/1/65
Lamasters, Samuel Pvt.	45 KYI	9/18/63–12/26/64
Layne, Henry Pvt.	2 VAC	9/1/61–5/1/65
Lear?, Henry Pvt.	45 KYI	9/6/63–12/14/64
Lett, Alexander Pvt.	1 VAC CSA?	4/1/64–4/9/65
Lett, Joseph Pvt.	9 VAI	3/13/62–1865
Lewes, Allen Pvt.	14 KYI	11/19/61–1/31/65
Louis, Thompson	WV Guards	NF
Lowe, Samuel F. Pvt.	5 VAI	7/3/61–12/22/63
also	1 WVI	12/63–8/1/65
Lucky, Thomas Pvt.	45 KYC	5/62–12/62
Luther, David H. Pvt.	3 WVI	7/13/61–8/27/64
Lykens, Moses D. Pvt.	39 KYI	1862–9/15/65
Lynch, Homer Pvt.	22 KYI	10/21/61–1/20/65
Marcum, John Pvt.	39 KYI	5/15/62–9/15/65
Marcum, Joseph M. Sgt.	45 VAI CSA	8/8/62–8/8/64
Marran, James H. Pvt.	3 OHI	NF
Marschall, John D. Pvt.	39 KYI	4/18/64–9/15/65
Martin, Simeon Pvt.	7 OHC	8/30/62–7/8/65
Mayhan, Wm. H. Pvt.	45 KYC	62/63
Maynard, Aaron Pvt.	45 KYI	8/8/63–12/24/64
Maynard, John F. Sgt.	NF	
Maynard, John J. Pvt.	45 KYC	8/8/63–12/28/65
Maynard, Lewis Pvt.	5 VAI	10/1/61–3/26/62
Maynard, Marcus Pvt.	39 KYI	10/63–10/65

Maynard, Samuel Pvt.	5 VAI	10/1/61–3/26/62
Mays, John Y. Pvt.	13 VAI	12/10/63–6/22/65
Mays, Julius R. Pvt.	13 WVI	12/10/63–6/22/65
McCalister, James Pvt.	5 VAI	61/65
McCannon, Sampson Pvt.	5 VAI	64/65
McCloud, Bonaparte Pvt.	7 VAC	9/1/61–8/9/65
McCloud, Elijah Pvt.	53 KYI	5/64–5/65
McCloud, Jonathan Pvt.	14 KYI	61/65
McClure, Stephen R. Pvt.	1 KYC	63/64
McCormas, Dick Pvt.	NF	
McCormick, James Pvt.	14 KYI	9/20/61–2/10/65
McIntosh, Pleasant B. Pvt.	NF	
McMullen, Jesse Pvt.	5 WVI	4/10/61–8/22/65
Mead, Arnold Pvt.	45 KYI	8/8/63–12/24/64
Mead, Rhodes Pvt.	45 KYI	8/8/63–12/24/64
Millender, John H. Lt.	4 MDI	9/16/62–5/10/64
Miller, Sylvester B. Sgt.	39 KYI	12/2/62–2/2/65
also	150 ILI	2/20/65–5/15/65
Mills, Wm. C. Pvt.	45 KYC	6/23/63–9/13/65
Mitchel, Andrew J. Pvt.	— VAI	5/7/62–9/62
Moore, Alexander Pvt.	9 VAI	6/1/61–7/20/65
Moore, Amos L. Pvt.	173 OHI	8/64–5/65
Moore, George W. Pvt.	VAC CSA (34?)	NF
Moore?, Stephen Pvt.	NF	
More, Calvin Pvt.	29 VAI CSA	4/62–NF
More, Gilbert Pvt.	4 VAI	10/1/61–3/26/62
Morrison, James Pvt.	53 KYI	3/13/65–9/13/65
Mott, Frank Capt.	10 KYC	8/9/62–9/17/63
also	45 KYC	2/29/64–12/24/64
Muck, James W. Pvt.	5 WVI	7/18/61–9/24/64
Muncy, Samuel Pvt.	5 WVI	9/1/61–11/20/62
Murray, Drewary Pvt.	45 KYI	12/8/63–2/14/65
Music, James K. Pvt.	5 WVI	61/64
Myers, Martin F. Pvt.	14 KYI	62/63
Myres, James H. Pvt.	11? TNC	7/27/63–4/6/65
Nance, Clemon C. Pvt.	1 VA-	8/17/61–8/23/63
Neece, James Pvt.	3 VAI	6/61–1865
Nelson, Greenville Pvt.	5 VAI	62/62
also	45 KYI	8/63–12/24/64
Nelson, Wm.	NF	
Newman, Peyton Pvt.	9 WVI	4/15/62–1/25/65
Newton, Hanley Pvt.	4 OHI	5/13/64–7/12/65
Nicholas, Willis W. Pvt.	4 VAI	3/62–3/64
also	2 VAI	3/30/64–7/10/65
Nixon, Robert Pvt.	3 VAC	12/21/62–6/30/65
Osborne, Samuel Pvt.	16 VAC CSA	63/63
Osbourn, Samuel Pvt.	115 KYI	8/7/63–11/64

Name	Unit	Dates
Owens, Henry T. Pvt.	13 WVI	8/14/62–6/22/65
Owens, James M. Pvt.	13 WVI	8/14/62–6/22/65
Pack, Andrew J. Pvt.	39 KYI	6/22/63–9/15/65
Pack, David Pvt.	5 VAI	9/14/61–8/28/63
Pack, George Pvt.	5 VAI	8/10/61–8/30/63
Pack, John W. Pvt.	5 VAI	8/10/61–9/25/64
Parsons, George W. Pvt.	45 VAI (BTN) CSA	
Patterson, Berry Pvt.	189 OHI	2/14/65–9/8/65
Patterson, Robert Pvt.	— KYI	7/1/64–3/11/65
Perry, Andrew Pvt.	45 KYI	8/8/63–12/24/64
Perry, Nathaniel Pvt.	8 VAC CSA	10/15/61–12/18/64
Pinson, John Pvt.	4 KYI	NF
Powell, Washington Pvt.	12 KYC	5/22/61–9/14/65
Powers, Jonas Pvt.	39 KYI	3/8/62–9/15/65
Preston, Dennis Pvt.	8 VAC CSA	5/10/62–4/15/65
Price, Charles Pvt.	7 KYC	11/1/62–9/6/65
Price, James W. Pvt.	34 KYI	63/65
Price, John B. QM	Vessel Lexington	5/3/63–7/3/64
Queen, Jesse Pvt.	—VA	10/1/61–3/26/62
Queen, Lewis C. Pvt.	5 VAI	10/1/61–3/26/62
Rakes, Peter Pvt.	39 KYI	9/14/62–9/15/65
Ramsey?, Stephen Pvt.	24 VAI CSA	62/65
Ratliff, Ephraim Pvt.	9 VAI	1/8/62–12/10/62
Ratliff, George F. Lt.	45 KYI	5/6/64–10/3/64
Ratliff, George F. Sgt.	45 KYC	64/65
Ratliff, Jeremiah Pvt.	1 USI	4/4/64–5/21/66
Ray, Albert Pvt.	13 VAI	8/1/62–6/17/65
Reed, Ed G. Pvt.	14 KYI	10/10/61–2/15/65
Rigg, Jaret F. Pvt.	13 VAI	8/11/62–6/22/65
Rowe, Stephen Pvt.	39 KYI	10/12/62–8/18/65
Roberts, James T. Pvt.	9 VAI	10/10/62–7/22/65
Robinson, Wm. Pvt.	14 KYI	62/65
Ross, John M.W. Pvt.	14 VAI	8/1/62–2/2/64
Rowe, Solomon Pvt.	39 KYI	62/65
Backus, Jesse Pvt.	4 WVC	8/63–NF
Rowe, Uriah Cpl.	5 WVI	7/13/61–12/23/63
also	1 WVI	12/23/63–7/24/65
Runyon, Harry Pvt.	14 KYI	NF
Rutherford, Spencer Pvt.	13 VA-	8/63–1865
Salmon, Flurry Pvt.	14 KYI	6/63–9/65
Salmons, Wm. Pvt.	14 KYI	3/12/63–9/15/65
Sanborn, Andrew Pvt.	16 VAC CSA	62/65
Saul, Aaron T. Pvt.	42 VAI CSA	NF
Saunders, Jacob Pvt.	39 KYI	62/65
Schakelberry, John H.	NF	
Schoop, Peyton D. Pvt.	5 WVI	8/20/61–10/3/64
Shannon, Wm. Lt.	13 VAI	62/65

Shean, Thomas Pvt.	39 KYI	11/7/63–9/15/65
Shuff, Smith Pvt.	14 KYI	10/25/61–10/20/64
Simmons, Nathaniel Pvt.	13 WVI	8/4/62 6/20/65
Skeens, Archibald Sgt.	5 VAI	8/10/61–9/23/64
Skeens, Henry A. Pvt.	39 KYI	9/22/63–9/5/65
Smith, Gilbert Pvt.	3 AKI CSA	6/61–4/15/65
Smith, John B. Pvt.	5 WVI	8/10/61–6/12/62
Smith, Matison Pvt.	45 KYC	2/10/65–NF
Smith, Samuel Pvt.	14 KYI	10/28/63–9/15/65
Spears, Wm. Pvt.	173 OHI	62/65
Spradling, John Pvt.	3 VAI	7/63–7/65
Stableton, Iseral	NF	
Stuck, Henry Pvt.	5 WVI	7/24/61–9/24/64
Stump, Michael Pvt.	13 WVI	8/12/62–6/22/65
Swanson, James Pvt.	5 WVI	7/13/61–2/14/64
also Cpl.	1 WVI	2/14/64–7/21/65
Teel, Wm. T. Pvt.	1 VAI	10/24/61–1/10/65
Thacker, John Pvt.	45 KYI	7/14/63–12/14/64
Thacker, Stephen	NF	
Thall, Homer Capt.	17 OHI	4/28/61–8/15/61
also Ltc.	22 OHI	9/2/61–11/18/64
Thomas, Wm. Pvt.	9 OHC	6/13/63–8/4/65
Thompson, Aaron Pvt.	9 WVI	11/28/61–3/18/63
Tillman, Ferguson Pvt.	8 VAC CSA	NF
Toppin, John Pvt.	65–ILI	1861–NF
Toppin, Wm. Pvt.	45 KYI	NF
Travis, Wm. Pvt.	14 KYI	61/65
Turner, George W. Pvt.	13 WVI	9/1/63–6/22/65
Turner, Wm. Capt.	9 VAI	1861–NF
Tyer, John Pvt.	45 KYI	1863–NF
Tyler, David Pvt.	12 TNI	1863–NF
Walker, Wm. Pvt.	CSA NF (8 VAC)	
Wallace, Solomon Pvt.	14 KYI	10/25/61–2/2/63
Ward, Allen Pvt.	6 VAI	9/27/64–7/21/65
Ward, Daniel Pvt.	9 VAI	11/3/61–7/21/65
Ward, James Pvt.	3 VAI	9/61–6/65
Warden, George W. Pvt.	24? VAI CSA	5/10/61–4/13/65
Waymer, James P. Major	1 WVI	8/12/61–7/21/65
Webb, Francis Pvt.	5 WVI	NF
Webb, Samuel Pvt.	5 VAI	9/62–9/64
Weddington, Henry Pvt.	39 KYI	9/6/63–9/15/65
Welch, Peter S. Pvt.	39 KYI	9/6/62–9/27/65
Wharton, John Ast/Srgn	6 WVI	8/27/61–12/14/64
Wiley, Wm. Pvt.	3 VAI	62/63
Williams, Lawson Pvt.	22 KYI	10/61–10/64
also	7 KYI	10/64–3/66
Williamson, John Pvt.	91 OHI	2/11/65–7/1/65

Willis, Hamilton M. Sgt.	5 WVI	8/20/61–NF
also Capt.	5 WVI	9/29/63–7/24/65
Willson, Morris Pvt.	1 OHC	9/22/61–1/16/62
Willson, Parrot Pvt.	5 VAI	NF
Woklar?, Martin Pvt.	5 VAI	61/63
Workman, James K.P. Pvt.	3 WVC	2/24/64–9/1/65

Wayne County Remarks

Adkins, D.—catarrh head 27 years
Adkins, H.—upper abdomen broke by thrown from horse in battle
Adkins, P.A.—shot in left ankle causing bad wound
Adkins, W.E.*—POW at Richmond 5 months, now blind in right eye (apparently served US and CS army)
Akers, J.—blind in one eye
Akers, L.—blind
Babbus, J.N.—cut on nose with bullet, Damrons Indpt Co to 5th Virginia
Bailey, L.—ruptured, the old man is in a bad fix
Baker, S.—RH
Baker, T.—KD
Ball, S.—eyes injured
Banlvan, E.—CDR 28 years & LD
Bartram, S.—nervous disease
Bellomey, M.—HD & sore eyes 15 years
Blankenship, J.*—wounded in right thigh
Bloss, H.—measles & weak voice, AFP
Booth, F.M.*—gunshot mouth & head
Bowe, J.—bronchitis
Boyd, A.—shot in left groin
Burris, W.H.—lost right testicle mumps, $6 month pension
Carls, J.—lost right eye from TYF
Carver, W.—yellow janders (?)
Castle, D.—frost bit hands & feet
Chaffin, W.—measles settled on lungs
Chapman, G.E.—deafness
Collins, I.—right scrotal hernia
Cooper, H.C.B.—saber cut on left hand
Copley, E.H.—liver disease
Copley, H.H.—RH, discharge at Washington in hands of atty.
Copley, N.—RH
Copley, S.—back trouble
Copley, T.D.—sore throat & bronchitis
Copley, T.J.—disease of the spine
Copley, W.—HD

Cunningham, J.C.—mumps & SS, UFL outdoors because of SS
Dean, J.—fever in war
Defoe, W.A.*—RH
Eaves, J.F.—shot through left lung, POW Libby
Elexander, L.*—RH
Estep, J.W.—SS
Fell, J.H.—shot both legs crippled in right leg, $18 pension
Ferguson, W.V.—catarrh of head
Findley, S.—back injured by horse falling
Frasher, D.K.—CDR, in volunteer company attached to 167 regt 22 brigade & 5th division Virginia Militia
Fry, V.B.*—rupture
Fuller, S.B.—RH & rupture
Gibson, H.B.—dyspepsia & HD, draws $10 pension
Gilkerson, H.—LD
Goodman, P.—chills & LD
Goodwin, P.*—shot in riqht side
Hampton, A.—hurt in right lung
Hams, S.—shot in left arm, hernia & injury, fistula
Hankins, W.D.—fracture left humonous
Hite, A.J.—TYF caused liver & kidney disease 28 years, UFL
Hooker, G.H.—shot in shoulder, wounds growing worse
Hunt, T.—injured breast by horse falling
Hurley, J.W.—HD, abscess on left knee
Hutchinson, J.—shot in right arm
James, S.*—POW Camp Chase 2 months
King, E.H.—blind
Lafferty, S.—WVA State Troops for Raleigh Co.
Lamasters, S.—horse thrown & hip hurt
Lett, J.—gunshot wound
Lowe, S.F.—crippled arm by horse falling
Lucky, T.—pauper in Wayne Co poor house
Luther, D.H.—disease, draws $6 pension
Lykens, M.D.—head trouble & KD, DSC
Lynch, H.—gunshot wound
Marcum, J.M.*—soar eyes, not able to see to labor well
Marcum, J.—WIA left thigh, now has piles & KD (drummer 39 KYI)
Marschall, J.D.—ruptured
Mayhan, W.H.—general disability
Maynard, J.J.—POW 1 month
Maynard, M.—carbuncle by riding & disability
Maynard, S.—RH
Mays, J.Y.—RH & HD, bad nerves
McCalister, J.—WIA & lungs affected, draws $12 pension
McCloud, B.—frozen feet
McCloud, J.—MS & LD, AFP
McCormick, J.—hearing affected by measles

McIntosh, P.B.—HD & foot broke
Mitchel, A.J.—now suffering with bronchitis
Moore, A.L.—measles on lungs, $4 pension
More, G.—KD
Morrison, J.—TYF
Muncy, S.—gunshot wound, deafness, POW
Myers, M.F.—piles & RH 26 years
Myres, J.H.—shot in left side
Nance, C.C.—trouble in back
Neece, J.—shot in left arm
Nelson, G.—left arm broke
Newman, P.—RH & HD, AFP
Nixon, R.—RH
Osbourn, S.—thumm shot off
Owens, J.M.—sight & hearing
Pack, D.—RH
Pack, J.W.—RH in worst form
Powers, J.—eresyphelas, RH, $10 pension
Preston, D.—RH 15 years
Price, J.B.—diabetis, KD, blader
Rakes, P.—RH
Ramsey, S.*—WIA right hand, UFL
Ratliff, E.—mumps settled in back 1/2 time, UFL
Ray, A.—mumps, HD, malarial poison, draws $8 pension
Reed, E.G.—RH 25 years
Rigg, J.F.—HD & RH, pensioned
Roberts, J.T.—gunshot wound index finger left hand, disabled UFL
Robinson, W.—KD
Rowe, S.—ruptured
Rowe, S.—shot in shoulder & breast, drawing pension
Rowe, U.—shot under right arm, shot in left arm
Rutherford, S.—2 fingers shot off
Salmon, F.—right shoulder dislocated
Salmons, W.—RH, now suffering with soar eyes
Saunders, J.—shot in leg
Shean, T.—POW Pemberton 2 months & 3 days
Skeens, H.A.—hernia, ruptured
Smith, G.*—wounded in head
Smith, J.B.—nervous debility, HD, LD, bronchitis
Smith, M.—ruptured 5 years
Smith, S.—RH, UFL
Spears, W.—shot in right leg
Spradling, J.—general disability, MS
Stableton, I.—fever fell in left leg
Swanson, J.—shot through thighs
Teel, W.T.—shot in left leg, POW Libby & Salsbury
Tillman, F.*—WIA shot

Toppin, J.—sore eyes
Turner, G.W.—bleeding piles 28 years
Turner, W.—ruptured, POW & bonded, got no discharge
Tyer, J.—neuralgia & RH
Wallace, S.—bronchitis
Ward, A.—TYF
Ward, J.—measles & LD
Warden, G.W.*—HD, UFL 1/2 time
Weddington, H.—paralized 4 years & dimness of sight 6 years
Williams, L.—injured in back
Woklar, M.—WIA
Workman, J.K.P.—wounded left hand, draws $2 per month pension

Webster County

NAME/RANK	REGIMENT	WHEN SERVED
Arbogast, Benj. A. Pvt.	14? WVI	7/63–3/64
Bennett, Samuel Pvt.	3 PAC	8/60 8/64
Blankenship, Conley Pvt.	68 KYI	62/64
Boyd, Eli L. Pvt.	7 WVC	64/65
Buchanan, John W.	NF	
Collins, Wm. R. Pvt.	15 WVI	3/17/64–8/65
Cutter, James W. Pvt.	29 USI	9/63–6/20/66
Duke, Wm. F. Pvt.	8 VAC?	2/22/64–7/2/65
Elliott, Thomas I. Lt.	75 PAI	4/25/61–8/30/62
Farley, Charles H. Pvt.	10 VA—	61/65
Fisher, Allison Mc. Pvt.	10 WVI	1/9/64–8/15/65
Hammock, Martin Pvt.	—	63/65
Hamrick, Wm. G. Cpl.	10 VA	6/12/62–6/26/65
Harsner?, Wm. Pvt.	—WVI	NF
Hart, Kelly S. Cpl.	1 WVI	9/16/61–7/25/65
Hutchinson, Wm. W. Pvt.	—	9/61–4/65
Jeffries, Wm. Pvt.	9 WVI	6/16/62–6/16/65
Jones, John E. Pvt.	7 WVC	9/4/64–6/9/65
Kelley, Peyton Pvt.	9 WVI	9/62–7/65
Light, John Pvt.	—WVC	6/27/63–6/27/65
Little, Robert A. T. Pvt.	1 WV—	1862–6/65
Lunceford, Theophilus Pvt.	—WVC	9/15/63–8/1/65
Mason, Riley Sgt.	6 WVI	8/18/61–6/15/65
Newberry, Simon Pvt.	18 OHI	8/14/61–11/64
Norman, Henry Pvt.	6 WVI	10/26/61–11/11/64

Norman, Philip Cpl.	11 WVI	9/26/61–11/11/64
Phillips, Beecher Pvt.	3 WVI	6/12/61–7/12/62
also	3 WVC	7/13/63–6/30/65
Randolph, Samuel T. Pvt.	6 WV—	7/61–12/64
Russle, Absalom Pvt.	16 KYI	3/62–6/65
Sandy, Wm. H. H. Cpl.	6 WV—	9/61–6/65
Sills, Samuel Pvt.	15 VAI	63/65
Steel, George I. Pvt.	3 WVC	3/1/65–6/16/65
Stout?, Zedoc Pvt.	14 WVI	8/12/62–6/12/65
Thomas, George Pvt.	6 WVC	3/10/64–1865

Webster County Remarks

Bennett, S.—RH
Blankenship, C.—RH
Collins, W.R.—hernia
Duke, W.F.—malarial disease
Hammock, M.—cripple
Harsner, W.—RH
Hart, K.S.—loss of eye
Hutchison, W.W.—injured
Jeffries, W.—RH
Jones, J.E.—dyspepsia, nervous debility, neuralgia
Lunceford, T.—loss of sight left eye
Mason, R.—RH, disease of head, physical wreck
Norman, H.—piles
Norman, P.—spinal affection, RH, piles
Phillips, B.—shell wound of leg
Russle, A.—injury of eyes
Sills, S.—wounded
Steel, G.I.—piles

Wetzel County

NAME/RANK	REGIMENT	WHEN SERVED
Abaugh, George Pvt.	14 WVI	8/20/62–6/26/65
Adams, Henry P. Pvt.	1 WVC	6/4/64–7/8/65
Allbright, Levi Pvt.	2 WVI	3/30/64–7/16/65
Allen, Wm. B. Cpl.	7 WVI	3/13/65–7/8/65
Amos, Enos Pvt.	9 WVI	3/1/62–7/1/65
Anderson, Charles Pvt.	15 WVI	62/64
Arnett, John C. Pvt.	10 WVI	3/1/62–2/1/64
Arnett, Wm. Pvt.	15 WVI	1863–8/9/65
Ashby, George W. Pvt.	6 WVI	11/17/61–6/10/65
Ashcraft, James M. Pvt.	6 WVC	3/10/64–9/29/65
Ashcroft, Zacharius Pvt.	WV Exempts	5/1/62–5/1/65
Barker, John Pvt.	6 WVI	NF
Barker, Wm. Pvt.	7 WVI	3/13/65–7/1/65
Barnhart, Benj. Pvt.	18 PAC	62/64
Barnhouse, Shephard Cpl.	116 OHI	8/18/62–6/17/65
Barr, Rolland Pvt.	—I	10/7/61–3/27/64
also Cpl.	6 WVI	3/28/64–6/10/65
Barr, Thornton Pvt.	2 WVI	3/14/64–7/16/65
Barr, Wm. Pvt.	2 WVI	61/65
Batson, Elias Pvt.	6 WVI	2/3/65–6/5/65
Beck, Charles	US NF	
Bell, Allen Pvt.	10 WVI	12/9/62–8/9/65
Bell, Wm. Pvt.	14 WVI	8/20/62–6/27/65
Bennett, John Pvt.	17 WVI	NF
Berdin, Levi Pvt.	3 WVC	NF
Bissett, Reason Sgt.	14 WVI	9/16/62–6/27/65
Bissett, Andrew J. Sgt.	8 PAI	7/15/61–2/28/64
also	191 PAI	2/29/64–6/28/65
Black, Conrad	63 OHI	4/11/65–5/15/65
Black, Frank J. Pvt.	20 VAC (CSA)	NF
Blair, James T. Pvt.	63 OHI	3/24/65–5/15/65
Blake, Isaac Jr. Pvt.	1 WVI	12/61–6/63
Blake, Jeremiah Pvt.	1 WVI	3/1/64–7/16/65
Blake, Joseph Pvt.	12 WVI	8/11/62–6/65
Booth, James A. Cpl.	11 WVI	9/7/64–6/30/65
Booth, John J. Pvt.	12 WVI	8/13/62–5/15/65
Borliman, Herman Pvt.	25 OHI	4/61–2/63
Bowers, Basil T. Lt.	2 WVI	6/16/61–12/10/61
also Pvt.	Signal Corp	3/64–10/20/64
also Lt.	12 OHA	4/1/62–9/2/62
also Lt.	23 USCT?	10/22/64–11/30/65
also Lt. and aid to General R. H. Milroy		1/1/62–6/6/62

Name	Unit	Dates
Brock, Isaac Cpl.	15 WVI	8/11/62–6/20/65
Broclc, Jacob R. Pvt.	2 WVI	2/24/65–7/12/65
Brookover, Jacob Pvt.	1 WVA	1864–7/21/65
Brost, Louis Sgt.	6 WVI	9/19/61–5/26/64
Brown, Samuel Pvt.	12 VAI	8/9/62–6/16/65
Bumaye, Jacob Pvt.	—WVI	9/3/64–6/4/65
Burrow, Richard A. Pvt.	6 WVI	10/10/64–6/10/65
aka Michael Burrows		
Butcher, George W.	NF	
Butcher, George W. Pvt.	14 WVI	2/14/65–6/30/65
Butcher, Hunnun Pvt.	6 WVI	7/14/62–6/10/65
Butcher, Nimrod J. Pvt.	6 WVI	9/25/61–11/10/64
Butler, Henry Pvt.	7 VAI	8/7/61–8/7/64
Butler, Robert Pvt.	17 WVI	65/65
Cain, Ansom Pvt.	17 WVI	8/17/64–6/13/65
Cain, Jacob Pvt.	1 WVC	3/8/65–7/8/65
Carney, Hiram Pvt.	4 WVC	7/8/63–3/10/64
also	17 WVI	2/15/65–6/30/65
Carney, Matthew Pvt.	4 WVC	7/8/63–3/10/64
Carney, Wm. Pvt.	4 WVC	11/63–3/64
Carpenter, Sam B. Pvt.	116 OHI	8/22/62–6/65
Carr, Edward Pvt.	1 WVI	4/61–7/61
also	12 WVI	8/13/62–6/16/65
Carrell, Sam J. Pvt.	1 VAI	1/1/62–6/20/62
Carson, Benj. E. Pvt.	5 WVC	7/23/64–6/30/65
Cears, John Pvt.	12 WVI	8/11/62–5/13/65
Cecil, George W. Pvt.	12 VAI	8/20/62–6/15/65
Church, Wm. Pvt.	6 WVI	8/14/62–6/10/65
Coal, Wm. Pvt.	18 PAC	9/11/62–7/11/65
Coen, John Pvt.	113 OHI	7/15/64–7/15/65
Conelly, James Pvt.	NF	
Connelly, Jacob A. Pvt.	17 WVI	9/19/64–6/30/65
Conner, Samuel N. Pvt.	7 WVI	2/11/—7/7/65
Conrey, Joseph D. Pvt.	3 MDI	9/11/61–9/13/64
Cook, George W. Pvt.	3 WVC	3/7/65–6/30/65
Cook, Irad Pvt.	3 WVC	3/7/65–6/18/65
Cosgray, John Pvt.	2 WVI	12/16/63–7/16/65
Couchiever, Joseph Cpl.	62 PAI	7/4/61–6/24/63
Coulter, John D. Pvt.	63 OHI	3/24/65–5/15/65
Craig, Abraham P. Pvt.	6 WVI	2/17/65–6/10/65
Crawford, Isaac N. Sgt.	11 WVI	10/4/61–11/14/64
Crist, Alexander C. Pvt.	52 OHI	8/13/62–6/12/65
Criswell, John W. Pvt.	6 WVI	12/25/63–6/10/65
Cross, John T. Pvt.	14 WVI	8/20/62–5/27/65
Cross, Samuel Pvt.	15 WVI	8/20/62–6/2/65
Crow, Simon P. Pvt.	1 MOI	61/64
Crunbrage, Joseph Pvt.	17 WVI	10/26/64–6/30/65

Name	Unit	Dates
Cunningham, George W.	NF (36 BTN VAC CSA?)	
Curmon, John L. Pvt.	6 WVI	2/16/65–6/13/65
Dacen, John Sgt.	7 WVI	8/12/61 9/12/63
Darling, Elijah Pvt.	14 WVI	8/31/62–6/25/65
Daugherty, Robert H. Pvt.	17 WVI	10/30/64–6/30/65
Davis, Samuel Pvt.	7 WVI	10/10/61–3/11/65
Dean, Stephen Pvt.	23 NYI	5/16/61–6/13/65
Debolt, Benj. Cpl.	6 WVI	10/4/61–10/13/64
Dent, Morman D. Pvt.	—WVC	61/65
Dillon, Lloyd Pvt.	9 WVI	8/14/62–7/65
Dulany, John Pvt.	7 VAI	3/16/64–7/9/65
Earl, Elias Pvt.	6 VAI	10/1/61–11/12/64
Edge, Frederic Pvt.	116 OHI	8/16/62–6/14/65
Edgell, James G. Pvt.	6 WVI	2/18/65–5/10/65
Edgell, James Pvt.	1 WVI	6/1/62–6/1/65
Edgell, Pinkney Pvt.	WV Exempts	12/3/62–4/23/64
also	6 WVI	2/18/65–6/10/65
Edgell, Wm. Pvt.	6 WVI	8/1/61–4/1/64
Eisunbarth, C. Sgt.	77 OHI	11/61–8/8/62
Ernest, John Pvt.	85 PAI	1/20/64–8/28/65
Estep, George W.	US NF	
Evans, Francis M. Pvt.	1 WVI	8/15/62–6/17/65
Evans, John H. Pvt.	15 WVI	8/15/62–6/17/65
Evins, Francis N. Pvt.	11 WVI	3/15/64–8/9/65
Farmer, Garah Pvt.	1 OHA	10/25/61–10/24/64
Ferguson, Remembrance Pvt.	6 WVI	11/14/— 6/10/65
Fisher, Jacob Pvt.	1 WVC	8/6/61–6/23/62
Fisher, John PVt.	140 PAI	8/18/62–7/8/65
Fisher, Samuel Pvt.	61 PAI	7/16/63–7/12/65
Fluharty, Charles G. Pvt.	1 WVI	9/6/61–7/18/65
Fluharty, David Pvt.	1 WVI	10/17/61–7/17/65
Fluharty, David Pvt.	2 WVI	3/24/64–6/2/65
Fowler, Wm. Pvt.	137 PAI	63/64
Fox, Frederick Pvt.	15 WVI	8/15/62–6/17/65
Fraeys, Jacob Pvt.	12 WVI	2/27/64–8/9/65
Francis, James M. Pvt.	61 OHI	2/17/62–8/15/65
Francis, Z. T. Pvt.	15 OHI	3/11/64–11/21/65
Frankhauser, John C. Pvt.	2 WVI	6/19/61–6/19/64
Freeland, James J. Pvt.	5 PAA	9/3/64–6/30/65
Furbee, Jacob Pvt.	20 (VAC CSA)	62/65
Galentine, Wm. Pvt.	2 WVI	2/18/64–7/16/65
Gamble, David W. Pvt.	15 WVI	8/15/62–6/14/65
Garrison, Adam Lt.	WV Exempts	10/4/62–6/14/65
Garrison, Silas Pvt.	85 PAI	2/6/64–12/14/65
Gehring, Henry Pvt.	5 WVC	6/24/61–6/24/64
Gilbert, Aguila Pvt.	17 WVI	64/65
Gilbert, Michael	NF	

Glendenning, James Cpl.	WV Exempts	10/4/62–6/65
Godard, David Pvt.	15 WVI	9/62–6/14/65
Goodrich, James D. Pvt.	NF	
Gorby, Ira Pvt.	1 WVI	6/21/61–10/10/64
Gorby, Jesse Pvt.	2 WVI	2/23/65–7/18/65
Greathouse, Hiram Pvt.	12 WVI	8/15/62–6/16/65
Greathouse, John Pvt.	12 WVI	8/14/62–6/16/65
Greathouse, Thomas Pvt.	12 WVI	3/5/64–8/9/65
Griffith, Amos Pvt.	12 WVI	8/15/62–6/16/65
Grim, Joseph Pvt.	14 WVI	8/18/62–8/25/63
Groves, Henry Pvt.	123 PAI	8/3/62–5/13/63
also Sgt.	6 PAA	8/23/64–6/13/65
Gump, Daniel S. Pvt.	11 WVI	9/3/63–8/9/65
Gump, Philip Pvt.	18 PAC	9/3/62–3/63
Gump, Philip Pvt.	7 WVI	2/29/64–7/1/65
Haney, John Pvt.	6 PAA	8/31/64–6/13/65
Harman, Joseph S. Pvt.	77 OHI	10/16/61–8/8/62
Harris, James Pvt.	11 WVI	8/12/62–6/23/65
Harris, Leander B. Pvt.	17 WVI	2/18/65–6/30/65
Harris, Uriah Pvt.	6 WVI	12/1/61–6/10/65
Hart, Joseph E. Pvt.	6 INI	4/15/61–8/2/61
also	7 INI	8/2/61–6/28/62
also Lt.	12 INI	7/17/62–6/9/65
Harvey, Charles W. Pvt.	42 OHI	9/17/61–11/15/65
Harvey, Franklin C. Pvt.	5 OHI	NF
Haughtn, Wm. Pvt.	17 WVI	9/3/64–6/30/65
Hawkins, Samuel Pvt.	15 WVI	8/15/62–5/29/65
Hayes, Edmond J. Pvt.	6 WVI	8/15/62–6/15/65
Hays, John P. Pvt.	14 WVI	8/8/62–6/25/65
Headle, Anthony Pvt.	15 WVI	8/24/62–6/30/65
Henderson, Abner Pvt.	18 PAC	9/15/62–7/10/65
Henderson, Wm. Cpl.	188 PAI	6/20/64–12/14/65
Henry, James Cpl.	17 WVI	8/30/64–6/30/65
Heslep, John D. Pvt.	7 WVI	10/16/61–7/1/65
Hexenbaugh, Abraham Pvt.	6 WVI	7/6/62–8/10/65
Hickman, George Pvt.	1 WVI	12/24/62–4/23/64
Higgins, Jacob Pvt.	11 WVI	2/28/64–5/28/65
Higgins, John L. Pvt.	17 WVI	3/13/65–7/1/65
Higgins, Joshua Pvt.	14 WVI	8/20/62–6/27/65
Higgins, Stephen Pvt.	17 WVI	2/28/65–7/8/65
Hill, Thomas W. Cpl.	15 WVI	8/11/62–6/14/65
Himelick, Francis Pvt.	17 WVI	2/8/65–7/30/65
Himelick, Wm. Pvt.	6 WVI	8/7/62–6/10/65
Himelrick, John M. Pvt.	6 WVI	8/7/62–6/10/65
Hitchcock, George W. Pvt.	1 WVI	10/61–8/5/62
Hitchcock, Walter H. Cpl.	1 WVI	11/14/61–11/26/64
Hixenbaugh, Henry Pvt.	6 WVI	9/25/61–11/17/64

Name	Unit	Dates
Hixenbaugh, John Pvt.	18 PAC	2/29/64–6/19/65
Hoge, John A. Sgt.	16 WVI	9/25/61–11/17/64
Hohman, George Pvt.	7 WVI	3/65–7/65
Holland, James Pvt.	52 OHI	8/22/62–6/3/65
Horner, Charles Pvt.	6 WVI	9/25/61–11/17/64
Horner, Josiah Pvt.	17 WVI	2/16/65–6/30/65
Hostetler, Abraham Pvt.	6 WVI	3/15/62–6/20/65
Hostetler, Jackson Pvt.	17 WVI	2/14/65–6/30/65
Hostetler, Robinson Pvt.	6 WVI	3/15/62–6/10/65
Hostetlet, David Pvt.	17 WVI	2/13/65–6/30/65
Howard, John Cpl.	1 WVI	5/21/61–8/27/61
Howelt, Thomas Pvt.	77 OHI	10/29/61–2/20/66
Hudson, John Pvt.	4 WVC	7/20/63–3/7/64
Huff, Isaac Cpl.	15 WVI	8/16/62–6/14/65
Huff, James Pvt.	180 OHI	9/22/64–1/65
Hull, Archabeld Pvt.	91 PAI	3/16/65–7/10/65
Hunter, Charles W.	NF (44 VAI CSA?)	
Hussig, Henry Pvt.	1 WVA	10/12/61–3/9/63
Ice, Ellum Pvt.	NF	
Ingold, John Pvt.	77 OHI	12/64–NF
Jackson, Caleb Cpl.	4 WVC	7/22/63–3/7/64
Jackson, Franklin Pvt.	14 WVI	8/8/62–6/27/65
Jackson, John L. Pvt.	4 WVC	7/22/63–3/7/64
Johnson, Ezra Pvt.	98 OHI	8/12/62–6/2/65
Johnston, Isaac M. Pvt.	6 WVI	9/5/64–6/10/65
Johnston, J. W. Pvt.	12 WVI	8/61–9/65
Johnston, Jacob Pvt.	6 WVI	8/15/61–1863
Judge, John W. Pvt.	4 WVC	63/64
also	180 OHI	64/65
Kaufman, John Pvt.	77 OHI	10/5/62–7/29/63
Kelley, Hamilton N. Pvt.	4 WVC	7/8/63–3/10/64
Keltch, Robert D. Pvt.	2 WVI	5/61–1865
Kerns, James M. Pvt.	6 WVI	8/12/61–8/12/64
Kidder, Coralus Pvt.	195 OHI	2/28/65–12/21/65
Kimble, Abraham D. Pvt.	17 WVI	9/27/64–6/30/65
King, Henry Pvt.	76 PAI	7/14/63–7/12/65
King, Wm. M.	US NF	
Kirkman, John Pvt.	15 WVI	8/16/62–6/14/65
Kirkpatrick, Erastus Pvt.	NF	
Kirkpatrick, Isaac L. Pvt.	17 WVI	2/15/65–6/20/65
Kirkpatrick, Isaac Pvt.	1 WVI	9/15/61–4/62
Kirkpatrick, John Pvt.	7 WVI	3/13/65–7/1/65
Kirkpatrick, Sam K. Capt.	11 WVI	10/20/61–7/10/65
Knapp, Wm. Pvt.	17 WVI	2/16/65–6/30/65
Knox, Summerville A.	CSA NF (8 MSC)	
Kocher, John Pvt.	77 OHI	3/8/64–3/24/66
Kuhnes, Daniel Pvt.	11 WVI	9/5/61–8/9/65

Kuhnes, Henry Pvt.	17 WVI	NF
Laman, Moses Pvt.	6 WVI	8/11/61–6/10/65
Lancaster, David Pvt.	7 WVI	3/10/55 7/1/65
Lancaster, Isaac Pvt.	1 WVC	3/8/65–7/8/65
Lancaster, Thomas M. Pvt.	17 WVI	2/22/65–6/30/65
Langwell, Robert Pvt.	25 OHI	5/24/61–5/24/62
Lauck, Edgar W. Pvt.	15 WVI	8/10/62–6/10/65
Laughlin, John J. Pvt.	2 WV Exempts	10/1/62–3/23/63
Laughlin, Wm. M. Pvt.	1 WVC	3/8/65–7/8/65
Leasure, Ephram Pvt.	14 WVI	8/62–5/8/65
Leasure, Wm. Pvt.	1 WVI	NF
Lee, Aaron Pvt.	1 VAI	1/1/62–7/1/62
Lemaster, Albert W. Lt.	11 WVI	6/10/61–6/17/65
Lemasters, Isaac W. Pvt.	7 WVI	3/13/65–7/1/65
Lemasters, James A. Pvt.	17 WVI	2/21/65–7/7/65
Lemasters, Levi Pvt.	11 WVI	9/13/61–11/26/64
Lemasters, Wm. Cpl.	11 WVI	9/5/61–11/14/64
Lemasters, Wm. Pvt.	1 VAI	10/9/61–5/19/62
Lemates, James D. Pvt.	— WVI	12/4/62–4/23/64
Leonard, Garrison Pvt.	61 PAI	NF
Leonard, Glover? Pvt.	1 VAC CSA	11/12/61–3/65
Lewis, James Pvt.	17 WVI	2/17/65–6/30/65
Lieuts, Francis D. Pvt.	1 VAI	9/18/61–11/1/62
Liston, Allen Pvt.	15 WVI	NF
Liston, John G. Pvt.	15 WVI	8/12/62–4/13/63
Long, Jeremiah Pvt.	1 WVC	3/2/65–7/8/65
Long, Wm. Pvt.	116 OHI	8/22/62–6/14/65
Lovell, Anthony Pvt.	14 WVI	9/62–7/24/65
Lowe, David Pvt.	6 WVI	10/1/61–6/10/65
Mabley, Andrew Pvt.	116 OHI	NF
Magee, John Pvt.	85 PAI	9/8/61–11/24/64
Main, Steveson Pvt.	17 WVI	2/13/65–6/30/65
Marshall, Tom T. Pvt.	6 WVI	2/22/64–6/10/65
Martin, Nelson Cpl.	14 WVI	7/20/62–7/3/65
Mason, Wm. Pvt.	17 WVI	8/20/61–6/65
Matthews, Jacob Pvt.	14 WVI	8/16/62–6/27/65
Mayfield, Ashbury Pvt.	6 WVI	2/3/65–6/10/65
McAlister, James C. Pvt.	6 WVI	9/1/64–6/5/65
McAlister, Robert Pvt.	WV Exempts	10/1/62–5/31/65
McCams, Wm. A. Musician	6 WVI	9/25/61–6/10/65
McCann, Moses Pvt.	6 WVI	NF
McCarr, John Pvt.	18 PAC	10/25/62–8/2/65
McCloud, Thomas Pvt.	7 VAI	9/2/61–11/5/64
McCollough, Joseph T. Pvt.	1 WVI	9/12/61–11/26/64
McCullough, Wm. Pvt.	1 WVI	3/3/65–7/8/65
McDonald, James A. Pvt.	12 WVI	8/13/62–4/1/63
McFann, John Pvt.	17 WVI	2/16/65–6/30/65

McGill, Reese Pvt.	7 WVI	NF
McLaughlin, John Pvt.	1 WVC	3/8/64–7/8/64
McReynolds, Wm. Pvt.	11 WVI	6/29/61–11/22/64
Meighan, Thomas H. Pvt.	7 WVI	8/31/61–3/16/63
Meldowney, Wm. H. Pvt.	15 WVI	8/5/62–6/14/65
Melott, Gilbert Pvt.	7 WVI	11/19/61–11/19/64
Melott, Henry Pvt.	7 WVI	8/12/61–12/23/62
Merrifield, John M. Pvt.	17 WVI	9/3/64–6/30/65
Merrifield, Z.A. Pvt.	1 WVI	12/61–1862
Merrines, George M. Pvt.	140 PAI	8/18/62–7/18/65
Metz, Samuel Pvt.	14 WVI	NF
Midcap, Walter Pvt.	17 WVI	2/20/65–6/30/65
Mike, Curtis Pvt.	7 WVI	11/61–11/62
Miller, Jenkins Pvt.	1 WVI	8/12/62–6/28/65
Miller, Samuel Pvt.	7 WVI	8/7/61–7/1/65
Miller, Wm. Pvt.	17 WVI	2/15/65–6/30/65
Mills, John J. Pvt.	15 OHI	9/6/61–4/18/65
Mills, Robert Pvt.	3 WVC	11/19/61–6/25/65
Mills, Thomas Pvt.	103 PAI	7/64–7/17/65
Mine, Tabeus Pvt.	6 WVI	3/24/62–6/10/65
Miner, Abner Pvt.	14 WVI	9/61–9/64
Money, Andy L. Pvt.	———	2/61–6/10/65
Moore, Anthony C. Pvt.	7 WVI	3/9/65–7/1/65
Moore, Henry Pvt.	116 OHI	8/62–6/14/65
Moore, Washington J. Cpl.	6 WVI	9/25/61–11/17/64
Morris, Anthony T. Pvt.	6 WVI	8/63–6/65
Morris, Moses R. Pvt.	4 WVC	7/63–3/64
also	82 OHI	12/64–6/10/65
Morris, W.P. Pvt.	17 WVI	8/16/64–6/30/65
Moser, John Pvt.	1 WVI	10/61–7/62
Murphy, Jeremiah Pvt.	6 WVI	10/12/61–6/3/62
Murphy, John Pvt.	15 WVI	8/7/62–6/14/65
Murphy, Wm. H. Pvt.	11 WVI	2/25/62–2/25/64
also	10 WVI	1/20/64–8/9/65
Neer, Milton Pvt.	14 WVI	8/12/62–9/10/64
Newman, Wm. A. Cpl.	7 WVI	2/20/63–7/7/65
Nontgomery, Andrew J. Pvt.	3 WVC	NF
Norris, J.W. Pvt.	6 VAI	8/12/61–8/20/64
Null, John M. Pvt.	136 PAI	6/27/64–9/27/65–
Ott, Ezra Pvt.	188 PAI	1/20/64–12/14/65
Ott, Salem Pvt.	85 PAI	3/31/64–12/14/65
Palmer, John W. Pvt.	1 VAI	10/4/61–11/20/64
Park, James Pvt.	WV Exempts	10/3/62–5/3/63
Parks, John Pvt.	6 WVI	1/18/65–6/14/65
Pasco, Emanuel Pvt.	7 WVI	11/17/61–11/17/64
Pegg, Thomas Pvt.	2 WVI	2/26/64–7/16/65
Pemberton, Robert Pvt.	45 PAI	6/29/63–8/29/63

Name	Unit	Dates
Pettit, Henry Pvt.	85 PAI	10/20/61–11/22/64
Pfau, Alfred Pvt.	17 WVI	9/13/64–6/13/65
Pierson, Alpheus Pvt.	6 WVI	2/15/62–6/10/65
Pierson, Nicholas Pvt.	6 WVI	2/15/65–6/15/65
Pogue, Thomas C. Pvt.	114 OHI	6/21/63–3/4/64
Polton, Marion Pvt.	42 OHI	9/17/61–9/30/64
Postelthwait, Nelson Pvt.	11 WVI	3/3/64–8/19/65
Poulston, Elmore Pvt.	1 WVC?	8/5/62–5/16/65
Powers, Jacob Pvt.	1 WVC	2/19/64–7/8/65
Price, John Pvt.	17 WVI	9/1/64–6/5/65
Price, Lewis Pvt.	17 WVI	8/17/64–6/13/65
Price, Wm. Pvt.	14 WVI	8/14/62–6/7/65
Provmer, J.P. Pvt.	8 PAI	8/26/62–2/12/63
also	——	5/27/64–5/8/65
Pyles, Eli Pvt.	1 WVI	NF
Pyles, Felix Pvt.	1 WVC	3/8/65–7/65
Pyles, Michael Pvt.	15 WVI	8/20/62–6/65
Reger, John H. Pvt.	62 OHI	1862–NF
Rice, John T. Pvt.	1 WVC	1/1/64–7/21/65
Richardson, Ruben J. Pvt.	1 WVC	2/63–7/65
Richman, Isaac Pvt.	6 WVI	10/1/61–11/12/64
Riggs, Cimeon A. Pvt.	6 WVI	2/3/65–6/10/65
Riggs, James J. Pvt.	11 WVI	6/29/61–12/22/64
Roberts, Eli Pvt.	14 WVI	11/1/62–6/27/65
Robeson, James C. Pvt.	NF	
Robinson, John J. Pvt.	11 WVI	10/15/61–10/17/65
Rockwell, Joshua Pvt.	85 PAI	11/15/61–12/15/61
Rohrbough, J.T. Pvt.	1 WVC	2/22/62–2/22/65
Row, Jerome Pvt.	6 WVI	9/18/64–6/10/65
Rurch, Thomas M. Pvt.	12 WVI	8/13/62–6/16/65
Rush, Isaiah Pvt.	18 PAC	9/28/62–11/10/64
Sayre, Harvey Pvt.	6 WVI	2/9/65–6/15/65
Sayre, Wm. W. Pvt.	7 WVI	8/61–7/1/65
Schamp, Jacob S. Pvt.	NF	
Schining, Theodore Pvt.	180 OHI	8/24/64–7/12/65
Shepard, David Pvt.	15 WVI	8/15/62–6/17/65
Shepherd, Michael Pvt.	42 OHI	1861–10/64
Showalter, Edward H. Pvt.	11 WVI	1/11/63–8/10/65
Showalter, John J. Sgt.	14 WVI	8/20/62–6/27/65
Shreve, John B. Pvt.	WV Exempts	62/63
Shreve, Wm. J. Pvt.	WV Exempts	12/4/62–3/14/64
also	7 WVI	3/14/64–7/5/65
Shriver, James Pvt.	1 WVI	9/10/61–7/26/62
Shummer, Nimrod Pvt.	15 WVI	8/20/62–12/19/64
Siers, Wm. H. Pvt.	NF (14 VAC CSA?)	
Six, Emanuel Pvt.	6 WVI	9/15/61–6/10/65
Skinner, Wm. J. Pvt.	63 OHI	3/65–6/65

Name	Unit	Dates
Sloan, Mordecai Pvt.	6 WVI	10/1/61–6/10/65
Smith, Wm. T. Pvt.	77 OHI	12/10/61–3/9/66
Snider, Hugh Pvt.	6 WVI	9/25/61–6/10/65
Snider, Noah Pvt.	18 PAC	1/16/64–6/15/65
Snider, Samuel Pvt.	6 WVI	2/18/65–6/10/65
Snodgrass, Aaron Pvt.	—WVI	12/4/62–4/25/64
Snodgrass, Freldon S. Pvt.	6 WVI	2/13/65–6/12/65
Snodgrass, James C. Pvt.	17 WVI	12/4/62–6/30/65
Snodgrass, James T. Pvt.	7 WVI	3/29/65–7/1/65
Sole, David Pvt.	14 WVI	8/20/62–6/27/65
South, Wm. A. Pvt.	52 OHI	8/22/62–6/3/65
Sprankler, Nathan P. Pvt.	165 PAI	8/61–1864
Springer, Sam C. Pvt.	1 WVI	3/5/62–10/25/62
Starkey, John T. Pvt.	WV Exempts	12/30/62–3/25/64
also	7 WVI	3/27/64–6/15/65
Starkey, John W. Cpl.	6 WVI	10/1/61–11/12/64
Starkey, Levi Pvt.	14 WVI	8/62–6/65
Starkey, Sam P. Pvt.	NF	
Starkey, Samuel Jr. Cpl.	WV Exempts	12/3/62–6/23/63
Starkey, Wm. Cpl.	WV Exempts	12/3/62–4/23/64
also	6 WVI	2/18/65–6/10/65
Steel, Alphred B. Sgt.	3 WVC	3/1/65–6/30/65
Steel, Fredric G. Pvt.	3 WVC	3/8/65–6/30/65
Steight, Uris M. Pvt.	NF	
Stephens, John Pvt.	11 WVI	61/64
Stookhouse, Joshua Pvt.	170 OHI	5/64–9/64
Stout, Samuel Pvt.	6 WVI	10/1/61–7/10/65
Street, H.E. Pvt.	3 WVC	2/3/65–7/3/65
Stump, Adam Pvt.	17 WVI	2/15/65–6/30/65
Swann, Wm. S. Sgt.	52 OHI	8/22/62–6/3/65
Swiger, Wm. E. Pvt.	6 WVI	2/18/65–6/10/65
Taylor, Chrisitan J. Pvt.	6 WVI	10/14/61–11/14/64
Taylor, Francis Pvt.	7 WVI	8/30/61–1/7/63
Taylor, Francis Pvt.	7 WVI	NF
Taylor, Henry Pvt.	6 WVI	9/25/61–6/10/65
Taylor, Thomas W. Pvt.	10 WVI	5/4/63–8/9/65
Thomas, George W. Pvt.	6 WVI	9/25/61–11/17/64
Thompson, John D. Pvt.	1 WVI	10/16/61–11/28/64
Toothman, Jesse Pvt.	14 WVI	2/28/64–6/27/65
Travis, Wm. Pvt.	180 OHI	8/64–5/11/65
Truex, Asa Pvt.	116 OHI	8/20/62–8/20/65
Tuttle, Richard L. Cpl.	14 WVI	8/20/62–6/27/65
Ullum, Hiram Pvt.	6 WVI	9/25/61–11/17/64
Utt, Henry Pvt.	1 WVI	10/62–6/65
Vancamp, John M. Pvt.	15 WVI	8/15/62–7/13/65
VanCamp, John W.	US NF	
VanCamp, Melvin	US NF	

Vandine, John W. Pvt.	15 WVI	8/11/62–6/14/65
Vandyue, Johnithan Pvt.	—OH	NF
Vanhorn, Alexander Pvt.	6 WVI	2/10/65–6/18/65
Vanhorn, James Pvt.	14 WVI	8/20/62–6/2/65
Vellers, Abraham Pvt.	14 WVI	8/20/62–6/27/65
Villers, Alexander Pvt.	14 WVI	9/14/62–7/4/64
Villers, Alvin Pvt.	14 WVI	9/14/62–6/27/65
Villers, Elias Pvt.	14 WVI	8/29/62–7/3/65
Walters, Jacob Pvt.	—PAI	62/63
Ward, Lemeul Pvt.	11 WVI	6/5/63–8/9/65
Waters, Levi Pvt.	1 WVC	6/16/61–6/16/64
Watson, Benj. F. Pvt.	3 WVC	9/14/62–6/13/65
Waytt, Andrew J. Pvt.	15 WVI	8/20/62–6/14/65
Wells, R.S. Pvt.	3 WVI	7/6/61–10/8/64
West, Isaac Pvt.	17 WVI	2/65–1865
Wetzel, Eli Pvt.	14 WVI	8/14/62–6/27/65
Wetzel, George Pvt.	1 WVI	12/24/62–4/23/64
White, Charles Pvt.	17 WVI	2/17/65–6/23/65
White, Richard M.	NF	
Whiteman, Marshall Sgt.	1 WVI	9/10/61–11/25/64
Whittatch, Wm. C. Cpl.	6 WVI	9/25/61–11/17/64
Wilkinson, Alfred Pvt.	1 WVI	10/4/61–11/28/64
Willey, Isaac Pvt.	7 WVI	8/7/61–2/12/63
Williams, Isaac Pvt.	14 WVI	7/28/62–5/30/65
Willson, John A. Pvt.	WV Exempts	6/63–1864
Wingrove, John Sgt.	2 WVI	10/11/61–7/22/65
Witchie, Jacob Pvt.	1 WVI	9/21/61–11/25/64
Wood, James A. Cpl.	11 WVI	9/5/61–NF
also Sgt.	10 WVI	8/9/65–NF
Wood, Sanford T. Pvt.	17 WVI	2/18/65–6/24/65
Woodcock, George B. Pvt.	31 OHI	3/4/64–3/65
Workman, Alexander Pvt.	130 INI	1/64–NF
Wright, George W. Pvt.	—OH	1861–NF
Wright, Nathan Pvt.	17 WVI	2/16/65–6/30/65
Wright, Wm. Pvt.	NF (36 VAI CSA?)	
Wyatt, Lewis Pvt.	WV Exempts	12/4/62–4/23/64
Wyckoff, Wm. Pvt.	17 WVI	2/25/65–6/30/65
Yost, Chrisitan Cpl.	77 OHI	12/61–3/66
Yost, Elias Pvt.	4 WVC	8/29/63–3/15/64
Youst, Aaron Pvt.	CSA NF (20 VAC)	
Yuyer, Charles L. Pvt.	Pierpont Guards	90 days' service
also Cpl.	6 WVI	NF
also Pvt.	179 OHI	NF

Wetzel County Remarks

Abauqh, G.—spine & head injured on Lynchburg raid
Allen, W.B.—CDR & RH
Amos, E.—HD
Arnett, J.C.—heart & eye disease
Arnett, W.—RH
Ashby, G.W.—lungs & bronchitis
Ashcraft, J.M.—CDR, KD, piles
Barker, J.—MP & MS
Barker, W.—loss of right eye
Barr, R.—RH
Barr, T.—asthma
Barr, W.—disability in leg
Beck, C.—crippled right ankle
Bell, A.—CDR
Bell, W.—RH, catarrh, bronchitis
Bennett, J.—deserter
Bisset, A.J.—wounded in leg, CDR, captured 8/19/64 with regiment POW 6 months 20 days in Belle Island & Saulsbury SC also scurvy, RH & impaired eyesight
Bissett, R.—gunshot wound, deafness
Blake, J.—CDR
Blake, J.—CDR
Booth, J.A.—both thighs broke
Booth, J.J.—right foot amputated in the army
Borliman, H.—RH
Bowers, B.T.—malarial poisoning & fracture of right shoulder
Brock, I.—rupture
Brookover, J.—spinal affection, kicked by a horse
Brost, L.—hernia & CDR
Burrow, R.A.—CDR
Butcher, G.W.—MS, KD, LD, eyes
Butcher, H.—RH & stomach trouble
Butcher, N.J.—broken bone in breast
Butler, H.—HD
Cain, A.—gunshot wound
Cain, J.—RH
Carpenter, S.B.—disease of head & loss of memory
Carr, E.—also belonged to independent scouts 3 months
Carson, B.E.—RH
Cears, J.—rupture privates
Church, W.—sciofula
Connelly, J.A.—neuralgia, spinal affection
Conner, S.N.—ulcers & affection of eyes
Cook, G.W.—lung & liver disease
Couchiever, J.—gunshot wound, RH & HD
Crawford, I.N.—rupture & KD

Crist, A.C.—gunshot wound right breast
Cross, J.T.—gunshot wound left shoulder, TYF
Cross, S.—stomach trouble, mashed shoulder
Crow, S.P.—cramps in side
Cunnina,ham, G.W.—chills & fever
Curmon, J.L.—CDR
Dacen, J.—mustered out by reason of consolidation
Darling, E.—CDR & piles POW Andersonville 7 months 21 days
Davis, S.—CDR & wounded left leg below knee
Debolt, B.—rupture right side
Earl, E.—ruptured
Edge, F.—HD & RH
Edgell, J.—lungs & back
Edgell, W.—LD
Edqell, J.G.—fever & eyes
Eisunbarth, C.—gunshot through right hand & left shoulder
Ernest, J.—discharged from Mower hos.
Evans, F.M.—gunshot wound right rist & hand
Evins, F.M.—RH, HD, weak eyes, discharge is lost
Ferguson, R.—pulmonare ca—tarrah cause TYF
Fisher, J.—HD
Fisher, Jn.—gunshot wound
Fisher, S.—gunshot left leg
Fluharty, C.G.—top of left hip shot
Fluharty, D.—gunshot left arm
Fox, F.—RH 25 years
Frankhauser, J.C.—piles & LD, mustered out 5th WVC
Freeland, J.J.—neuralgia
Galentine, W.—RH causing loss of use left leg, fever & ague
Gamble, D.W.—HD & liver disease
Garrison, A.—absess in side
Garrison, S.—broken arm, lungs defective
Gehring, H.—RH & KD
Glendenning, J.—TYF, RH & HD
Godard, D.—ruptured privates
Gorby, I.—disease of breast
Greathouse, T.—hernia left side
Griffith, A.—broke down generally
Grim, J.—paralasus left leg, HD
Groves, H.—CDR & terminated in fistula
Gump, D.S.—CDR & piles, mustered out in Co E 10 W~TI
Gump, P.—DSC
Harman, J.S.—RH & gunshot wound
Harris, L.B.—MS & CDR
Harris, U.—disabled right leg
Hart. J.E.—CDR, mustered out as CaPt. Co H 12 INI
Hawkins, S.—piles
Hays, J.P.—WIA

Henderson, A.—CDR
Henry, J.—SS
Heslep, J.D.—LD & KD, mustered out Co E 7WVI
Hexenbaugh, A.—cararrh & lung trouble
Hickman, G.—loss of finger
Higgins, J.—piles
Higgins, J.—RH
Higgins, S.—RH
Hill, T.W.—back & kidneys
Himelick, W.—RH right leg, deafness left ear
Hitchcock, J.W.—piles
Hixenbaugh, J.—HD, LD, back trouble
Holland, J.—WIA by piece of shell, RH
Hostetler, D.—RH & piles
Hostetler, J.—measles affecting the eyes
Hostetler, R.—piles
Howard, J.—LD, HD, KD
Howelt, T.—left shoulder dislocated
Hudson, J.—RH, liver disease, general disability
Huff, I.—lameness
Hull, A.—catarrh in head
Hunter, C.W.★—hearing
Hussig, H.—LD
Ice, E.—piles 28 years
Jackson, C.—RH & general disability, this old soldier is 71
Jackson, F.—RH
Jackson, J.L.—right testicle mashed
Johnson, E.—gunshot wound right thigh, hernia both sides, was in Mexican War
Judge, J.W.—piles & catarrh head
Kerns, J.M.—MP
Kimble, A.D.—RH, KD, liver disease
King, H.—HD
Kirkman, J.—disability
Kirkpatrick, I.—fits & catarrh head
Kirkpatrick, I.L.—LD
Kirkpatrick, J.—RH
Kirkpatrick, S.K.—gunshot wound left hand, broke down constitution
Kuhnes, D.—blind left eye, deaf left ear
Kuhnes, H.—a deserter no discharge
Laman, M.—paralasus of right leg
Lancaster, I.—neuralgia, deaf left ear
Lang~ell, R.—wounded in left temple, KD
Lauck, E.W.—gunshot wound left foot
Laughlin, J.J.—LD
Leasure, E.—shot in left thigh
Lee, A.—frozen feet & LD, HD
Lemasters, A.W.—smallpox, blind left eye, right eye defective

Lemasters, I.W.—piles & HD
Lemasters, J.A.—liver disease
Lemasters, L.—bone erysipelas ad fits
Lemasters, W.—disabled in shoulder lVAl
Lemasters, W.—HD, eyes & lungs
Leonard, G.—drafted, special bill for his relief 51st Con
Leonard, G.*—gunshot wound
Lewis, J.—RH & HD
Liston, A.—CDR
Liston, J.G.—DSC
Long, J.—LD
Lowe, D.—deafness
Magee, J.—liver & stomach, piles, only six days in hospital
Main, S.—liver & kidney disease
Main, T.—liver & kidney
Marshall, T.T.—lost forefinger right hand, gunshot wound left arm
Matthews, J.—neuralgia in face
Mayfield, A.—piles
McAlister, J.C.—catarrah
McAlister, R.—RH
McCarr, J.—gravel, piles, rupture
McCloud, T.—RH
McCullough, W.—CDR
McDonald, J.A.—liver complaint resulting in dropsy, DSC
McFann, J.—CDR & piles
McLaughlin, J.—chills
McReynolds, W.—CDR
Meighan, T.H.—CDR, foot injured by horse 10/26/61
Melott, G.—eyesight affected
Melott, H.—yellow jaundice, TYF, CDR
Merrifield, Z.A.—RH
Merrines, G.M.—piles, ague, strained back
Metz, S.—WIA right ankle
Miller, J.—lumbago
Miller, S.—gunshot wound, loss of an eye, loss of hearing
Miller, W.—RH
Mills, J.J.—POW 17 months 4 days, defective eyesight
Mills, R.—POW 3 months & 20 days at parole camp
Moore, A.C.—walked out without a discharge
Moore, H.—HD
Moore, W.J.—RH both legs
Morris, A.T.—HD
Morris, M.R.—RH & HD, dispepsia
Morris, W.P.—asthma
Murphy, J.—CDR & SS
Murphy, J.—chronic hipititus resulting in indegestion
Murphy, W.H.—sore gums, scurvy, frozen feet
Neer, M.—left arm off below elbow, under jaw broken

Norris, J.W.—deaf left ear
Null, J.M.—mustered out Co A 15 PAC
Park, J.—cold on cough & mumps
Parks, J.—KD sight impaired
Pegg, T.—effected in hearing
Pfau, A.—stomach cramps
Pogue, T.C.—KD
Polton, M.—WIA right side, also HD
Postelthwait, N.—erysipelas
Poulston, E.—RH, eye disease, has no discharge
Price, J.—lung & back trouble
Price, W.—back & heart affected
Provmer, J.P.—weakness in back & lungs
Pyles, M.—CDR & rupture
Riggs, C.A.—piles & rupture
Riggs, J.J.—CDR, lungs, sight of right eye gone
Roberts, E.—HD
Robinson, J.J.—MS, stomach disease, resulting iratable heart
Rockwell, J.—lumbago & eye disease
Rohrbough, J.T.—KD
Row, J.—HD, liver disease
Rush, I.—HD
Sayre, W.W.—HD, catarrh causing deafness left ear, spinal injury carrying sand bags
Schining, T.—deafness
Shepherd, M.—deafness
Showalter, E.H.—RH terminating in HD
Showalter, J.J.—hip (?) disease & neuralgia
Shriver, J.—injury in back
Six, E.—RH & piles
Skinner, W.J.—loss of eyesight
Sloan, M.—RH & weak eyes
Smith, W.T.—lumbago
Snider, H.—liver complaint
Snider, N.—MS
Snider, S.—LD, HD, bronchitis
Snodgrass, F.S.—deafness
Snodgrass, J.C.—RH
Snodgrass, J.T.—throat disease
Sole, D.—eyes affected
South, W.A.—CDR
Sprankler, N.P.—shot in left jaw
Starkey, J.T.—totally disabled
Starkey, J.W.—eyes affected from fall
Starkey, S.—MP
Starkey, W.—liver & kidney complaint
Stephens, J.—disabled in leg
Stookhouse, J.—lame back

Street, H.E.—piles, bloody
Stump, A.—RH
Swann, W.S.—RH
Swiger, W.E.—disease of throat & eyes
Taylor, C.J.—catarrh in head
Taylor, F.—CDR, nervous affection all over
Taylor, H.—RH & HD
Taylor, T.W.—TYF at New Creek Va & never been able bodied since
Thomas, G.W.—HD, stomach trouble
Thompson, J.D.—bronchitis, RH, rupture, POW 184 days
Toothman, J.—piles & KD
Travis, W.—pain in breast & head, DSC
Truex, A.—RH
Tuttle, R.L.—HD, gunshot wound right wrist & right leg
Ullum, H.—liver & kidney disease
Utt, H.—deaf riqht ear, loss of siqht left eye
Vancamp, J.M.—concussion caused by explosion of shell
VanCamp, J.W.—disabled hand
VanCamp, M.—gunshot in shoulder
Vandine, J.W.—HD & results therefrom
Vanhorn, A.—CDR, KD, stomach trouble
Vanhorn, J.—wounded in hand, ruptured, eyes frosted (?)
Vellers, A.—gunshot wound right leg below knee
Villers, A.—defective hearing caused by heavy artillery
Villers, A.—WIA left breast by ball, lung trouble from shot
Villers, E.—17 months in hospital
Walters, J.—gunshot wound
Ward, L.—piles, bronchitis, weak eyes caused by measles
Waters, L.—ruptured
Watson, B.F.—CDR & HD
Waytt, A.J.—CDR
Wells, R.S.—gunshot wound in side
Wetzel, G.—catarrh in head
White, R.M.—KD, MS, LD, liver disease, partial loss of sight
Whiteman, M.—HD
Whittatch, W.C.—RH & catarrh of head
Wilkinson, A.—disease of rectum
Williams, I.—gunshot wound both legs
Willson, J.A.—RH & neuralgia in head
Wingrove, J.—bullet shot in hand
Wood, J.A.—gunshot wound left thigh, sore eyes, LD
Woodcock, G.B.—CDR & general disability
Workman, A.—deserter
Yost, C.—sore eyes contracted in service
Yost, E.—eye disease from MS, one eye blind, deaf one ear
Youst, A.★—he was a Confederate, no papers
Yuyer, C.L.—pneumonia

Wirt County

NAME/RANK	REGIMENT	WHEN SERVED
Amos, Fredric T. Pvt.	17 WVI	8/9/64–6/30/65
Arnold, David D. Pvt.	11 WVI	12/1/62–5/24/63
Backus, Jesse Pvt.	4 WVC	8/63–NF
Baker, Henry W. Pvt.	11 WVI	3/64–8/65
Baker, Benj. Pvt.	17 PAC	8/25/62–7/5/65
Bayley, Isaac S. Pvt.	1 WVC	8/61–2/62
Benington, H.H. Sgt.	2 WVC	7/61–12/64
Bennett, Lorenzo (Lt.)	NF (27 NCI CSA?)	
Bennett, Sylvester Pvt.	15 WVI	3/17/62–8/2/65
Beylor, Thornton W. Pvt.	1 USI	5/64–5/20/66
Bidwell, Leonard Pvt.	NF	
Bigley, Sylvester Pvt.	124 OHI	6/28/63–NF
Blane, Henry Pvt.	63 OHI	11/1/61–7/8/65
Board, James Cpl.	11 WVI	10/26/61–11/12/64
Boice, Samuel Pvt.	9 WVI	10/26/61–10/27/64
Bomes, Robert H. Pvt.	1 WVI	10/26/61–1/11/65
Bonet, Samuel H. Sgt.	11 WVI	10/16/61–11/11/64
Bonnet, Elias Pvt.	11 WVI	9/63–12/63
Boyles, Charles H. Pvt.	7 WVI	8/9/61–7/9/65
Britton, Gustavus S. Pvt.	6 WVI	8/64–6/16/65
Brown, James Pvt.	6 WVC	6/10/61–8/16/64
Brown, Wm. J. Pvt.	6 WVI	8/8/61–6/10/65
Brown, Wm. Pvt.	7 PAI	4/61–NF
Burton, Richard Capt.	7 WVI	9/2/61–7/1/65
Cain, George W. Pvt.	11 WVI	10/26/61–11/11/64
Cain, Granville Pvt.	6 WVI	8/20/61–8/27/64
Cain, David Pvt.	6 WVI	8/27/61–6/10/65
Campbell, Hiram Pvt.	11 WVI	12/15/61–12/15/64
Caplinger, Elias Pvt.	14 WVI	8/13/62–6/27/65
Carpenter, Wm. Pvt.	1 WVI	5/23/62–5/23/65
Chadock, George W. Pvt.	11 WVI	NF
Channel, Levi Pvt.	6 WVI	8/20/62–6/10/65
Chemvrout, Wm. M. Pvt.	4 WVC	7/8/63–1/15/64
Clark, Adolphus P. Pvt.	11 WVI	12/61–6/65
Cline, Martin V. Pvt.	7 WVI	7/9/61–2/3/63
Cline, Samuel Pvt.	1 OHA	10/10/61–4/22/64
Collum, John W. "Drafted"	—	9/22/64–10/8/64
Conley, Cornelius M. Capt.	9 WVI	10/7/61–7/25/65
Copen, George W. Cpl.	7 WVI	8/15/61–12/11/63
Corbit, Mathew Pvt.	11 WVI	61/65
Cothern, James E. Cpl.	3 WVC	9/2/62–6/30/65

Courtney, Saub S. Pvt.	161 OHI	64/64
Courtney, Wm. Pvt.	9 WVI	10/61–3/63
Crowser, George W. Pvt.	1 WVC	12/3/63–7/8/65
Culver, John J. Pvt.	62 OHI	11/62–1863
Davis, Charles W. Pvt.	11 WVI	8/1/62–3/14/65
Davis, Joseph A.	NF	
Davis, Robert H. Cpl.	15 WVI	8/10/62–6/14/65
Day, Smith Pvt.	92 OHI	8/9/62–6/30/65
Deem, John Pvt.	6 WVI	8/20/61–6/10/65
Deem, Peter Pvt.	11 WVI	8/11/62–6/17/65
Done, Richard Sgt.	2 WVC	12/64–NF
Dovener, Robert G. Surgeon	15 WVI	11/4/62–9/18/63
Dwees, Benj. C. Pvt.	11 WVI	8/18/62–6/17/65
Enoch, Martin V. Pvt.	6 WVI	9/63–10/63
Evans, Edward Sgt.	141 OHNG	5/5/64–9/15/64
Evans, Thomas W. Pvt.	88 OHI	5/29/62–6/26/62
Finch, Wm. M. Pvt.	11 WVI	8/15/62–6/17/65
Fluharty, Lewis Pvt.	15 WVI	8/14/62–6/14/65
Forthofer, Charles	NF	
Fortney, Isiah Pvt.	6 WVI	11/26/61–6/10/65
Fouty, James F. Pvt.	11 WVI	6/20/62–1864
Fox, Mathias Pvt.	197 OHI	3/25/65–7/30/65
Frazier, James Pvt.	11 WVI	8/11/62–6/17/65
Fulkerth, David S. Pvt.	15 PAC	8/14/62–6/21/65
Gant, Samuel Pvt.	161 OHI	5/2/64–9/2/64
Gillaspie, Wellington Pvt.	52 —	8/22/62–6/3/65
Gilmore, Augustine Pvt.	77 OHI	9/16/62–7/19/65
Grass, Martin	US NF	
Grier, Otho B. Cpl.	97 OHI	NF
Guthrie, Edwin Pvt.	1 WVC	10/61–6/22/65
Hall, Benj. H. Pvt.	11 WVI	10/26/61–6/15/65
Hall, James M. Musician	11 WVI	9/62–6/65
Hall, Peter Pvt.	6 WVI	9/64–6/2/65
Hardway, George W. Pvt.	11 WVI	2/62–1/63
Harper, John G. Pvt.	22 KYI	10/10/61–3/13/66
Harper, Wm. Pvt.	77 OHI	11/15/61–12/19/63
Harris, Samuel R. Pvt.	6 WVI	63/64
Harris, Thomas J. Pvt.	18 MII	7/16/62–7/65
Hayes, Charles P. Pvt.	22 OHI	4/17/61–7/15/65
Hendershot, Aaron Pvt.	11 WVI	10/26/61–11/11/64
Henderson, James R. Pvt.	22 PAI?	9/61–7/4/65
Hickman, Abraham Pvt.	11 WVI	10/61–1863
Hickman, Eliab Pvt.	92 OHI	7/30/62–6/13/65
Hickman, Zachariah Pvt.	11 WVI	10/61–12/61
Hill, Elijah Pvt.	4 WVC	7/64–3/15/65
Howard, Jacob Cpl.	1 WVI	9/61–6/62
Howley, Martin Pvt.	NF	

Hoy, Elijah Pvt.	— 6 WVI	1/20/62–6/10/65
Hupp, David Pvt.	176 OHI	8/27/64–2/11/65
Hutchinson, Thomas L. Pvt.	11 WVI	1/3/62–5/29/65
James, John E. Pvt.	6 VAI	9/61–1/10/63
Jefferies, Edwin A. Pvt.	122 PAI	7/61–1862
Jewell, Thomas Pvt.	78 PAI	9/61–1864
Justis, Aaron J. Pvt.	9 WVI	10/15/63–7/65
Kerr, Alexander	US NF	
Kiger, Wm. P. Pvt.	3 WVC	3/1/65–6/30/65
King, James I. Pvt.	11 WVI	3/24/64–8/9/65
Kirkendall, John A. Pvt.	12 WVI	8/62–4/3/63
Kirklin, David	US NF	
Laird, Milton Pvt.	5 PAI	6/1/61–6/17/64
Leason, Richard Pvt.	11 WVI	8/11/62–6/17/65
Leasure, Comadore Pvt.	6 WVI	9/26/61–6/10/63
Lediam, Wm. H. Pvt.	11 WVI	10/61–9/64
Lee, Jesse Pvt.	1 WVC	6/10/61–5/17/62
Lemon, George H.	———	9/22/64–10/8/64
Life, Draper C. Cpl.	11 WVI	11/1/61–8/9/65
Lockhart, Franklin T. Pvt.	17 WVI	8/30/64–6/30/65
Lockhart, George W. Pvt.	1 WVC	2/64–3/64
Lockhart, Isiah Pvt.	4 WVI	7/63–NF
Logston, Leander Pvt.	9 WVI	10/19/61–10/26/64
Longsworth, James T. Pvt.	31 INI	9/10/61–9/15/64
Lott, Caleb A. Pvt.	11 WVI	12/15/61–12/15/64
Lynch, Francis M. Pvt.	7 WVI	1/16/62–3/29/65
Lyons, Wm. W. Pvt.	11 WVI	9/21/62–6/17/65
Madden, Nelson D. Pvt.	15 OHI	9/6/61–10/16/64
Marshal, Thomas H. Cpl.	1 WVC	1/1/64–6/21/65
Martin, Wm. J. Pvt.	11 WVI	12/18/61–8/20/65
Mason, Gideon Pvt.	92 OHI	8/10/62–6/28/65
Mason, Lewis G. Pvt.	25 OHI	4/29/61–8/2/65
Maygold, Henry Pvt.	9 NYA	5/24/— NF
AKA Henry H. Leavenworth	NF	
McCoy, Wm. A. Lt.	11 WVI	8/14/62–6/21/65
McDonald, Alexander Pvt.	6 WVI	8/18/61–9/10/64
McFee, Louis Pvt.	11 WVI	10/26/61–11/11/64
McKitrick, Abraham Pvt.	26 ILI	6/23/61–4/28/62
also	116 ILI	8/14/62–6/7/65
McKitrick, Mahlon L. Pvt.	4 WVI	6/29/61–7/8/64
McMillion, Robert A. Lt.	11 WVI	8/14/62–6/21/65
Mercer, David B. Sgt.	78 OHI	12/8/61–7/11/65
Merell, Jackson Pvt.	11 WVI	10/26/61–11/11/64
Merill, Richard Pvt.	11 WVI	10/26/61–11/11/64
Metz, Henry Pvt.	12 WVI	8/16/62–12/12/65
Miller, John W. Pvt.	6 WVI	12/11/61–12/11/64
Mills, Wesley Pvt.	7 WVI	8/1/61–1/8/64

Name	Unit	Dates
Moffitt, Isaac "Wagoneer"	11 WVI	10/26/61–8/9/65
Mooney, Samuel Pvt.	39 OHI	7/9/61–7/13/65
Newman, Henry Capt.	15 WVI	6/61–1864
Nigh, Jacob G. Cpl.	39 OHI	7/16/61–11/62
Nolf, Augustus Pvt.	105 PAI	8/5/61–8/5/64
Norehead, Thomas J. Pvt.	11 WVI	9/1/64–6/17/65
Nugum, Theopholus S. Pvt.	2 WVI	3/20/65–6/65
Park, Martin Lt.	11 WVI	10/26/61–12/64
Parks, Wilavy M. Pvt.	1 WVC	7/61–10/61
Parsons, Robert Pvt.	43 OHI	2/13/63–7/15/65
Patterson, Samuel Pvt.	85 PAI	8/15/61–1864
Pell, Wm. F. Capt.	11 WVI	8/27/62–3/4/63
Petty, W.J. Pvt.	11 WVI	10/26/61–10/1/62
Philips, John Pvt.	7 VAI	9/61–11/28/62
Phillips, Alexander Pvt.	11 WVI	11/28/61–12/26/64
Phillips, George W. Pvt.	55 OHI	9/22/64–6/25/65
Pierce, Wm. Pvt.	1 WVI	2/29/64–7/16/65
Pierson, James M. Pvt.	4 WVC	8/7/61–7/18/65
Piggott, James T. Pvt.	116 OHI	NF
Plate, Wm. F. Pvt.	1 WVI	1861–7/16/65
Porter, John W. Pvt.	30 OHI	8/13/62–5/31/65
Price, Moses Pvt.	11 WVI	10/3/62–8/1/65
Price, Warner P. Pvt.	15 WVI	8/10/62–6/20/65
Provance, John W. Pvt.	189 OHI	2/22/65–9/28/65
Provance, Simeon Pvt.	11 WVI	8/15/62–6/17/65
Pyles, Daniel M.	US NF	
Rathbone, Sam B. Capt.	22 OHI	61/63
also Ranger	17 INI	NF
Ratliff, Eli Pvt.	5 WVI	5/1/61–5/1/65
Reed, Solomon Cpl.	15 WVI	8/10/62–6/14/65
Reeder, Charles L. Sgt.	15 OHI	8/9/61–10/21/65
Reynolds, Vincent D. Pvt.	11 WVI	10/26/61–10/1/62
Riddle, George M. Pvt.	3 WVC	5/29/63–5/30/65
Roberts, Francis M.	US NF	
Roberts, Samuel C. Cpl.	3 WVC	12/16/61–6/10/65
Robinson, Francis M. Cpl.	15 WVI	8/14/62–6/14/65
Rockhold, Charles A.	NF	
Ross, Milton Pvt.	123 PAI	8/9/62–5/12/63
Ruble, Abraham Pvt.	15 WVI	NF
Ryan, Jerry L. Pvt.	56 OHI	10/8/62–7/8/63
Sharpnack, Wm. H. Pvt.	6 WVI	1/1/62–6/10/65
Shears, Solomon Pvt.	9 WVI	10/19/61–7/21/65
Shettleworth, Jerome Pvt.	11 WVI	6/10/61–7/65
Shiflett, Edward Pvt.	10 WVI	4/22/62–1865
Showalters, Henry H. Pvt.	7 WVI	3/13/65–7/1/65
Simpson, Wm. Pvt.	2 OHI	8/19/61–10/10/64
Sink, George Pvt.	11 WVI	8/2/62–6/20/65

Slater, Wm. Pvt.	—WVI	61/64
Smith, Edmond J. Pvt.	12 WVI	8/16/62–6/29/65
Smith, Henry B. Pvt.	6 PAI	7/27/61–3/21/62
Snider, Daniel Pvt.	9 WVI	11/12/61–11/16/64
Sommerville, Samuel Pvt.	7 WVC	2/23/65–8/9/65
Stallings, Joseph R. Pvt.	33 OHI	9/28/64–6/5/65
Summner, Kosolam Pvt.	11 WVI	NF
Tarrance, Colgan Pvt.	11 WVI	11/5/61–6/17/65
Teel, Wm. Pvt.	7 WVC	61/65
Thompson, George W. Pvt.	1 OHA	6/16/62–6/20/65
Tichenor, Wm. R. Pvt.	6 WVI	8/12/61–8/15/64
Townsend, Commodore Pvt.	10 WVI	10/10/61–3/12/65
Townsend, George W. Pvt.	4 WVI	1/20/64–7/16/65
Trader, John N. Pvt.	NF	
Tucker, James R. Pvt.	91 OHI	8/62–9/63
Tuell, Francis Pvt.	1 OHA	11/5/61–2/7/64
Tufts, Eli L. Sgt.	17 OHI	9/15/61–8/20/65
Umstead, James W. Cpl.	2 WVI	6/16/61–6/16/64
Vandyke, Peter Pvt.	78 OHI	8/20/62–6/1/65
Vaught, Stephen Pvt.	17 WVI	8/30/64–6/30/65
Vernon, Martin V. B. Sgt.	1 WVC	8/30/61–7/8/65
Watson, Adam Pvt.	3 WVC	11/28/62–6/30/65
Wayne, Leroy Pvt.	9 WVI	2/8/62–2/28/64
Weaver, Edward Pvt.	7 WVC	8/12/61–8/65
Weaver, John Pvt.	11 WVI	8/14/62–6/17/65
Weaver, Rufus E. Pvt.	1 WVC	9/9/61–7/20/65
Weaver, Wm. Pvt.	1 WVC	8/30/61–12/31/65
Weekley, Wm. Cpl.	62 OHI	10/28/61–8/23/65
Welsh, Thomas Pvt.	Washington Cav.	8/12/61–10/64
also Ast/Surgeon	USS Camellia	3/65–7/65
Wever, Blackburn Cpl.	1 WVC	6/61–7/8/65
Wheatcroft, Malichi Pvt.	160 OHNG	64/64
Willets, Martin P. Pvt.	63 PAI	7/63–3/30/65
Williams, Joshua Pvt.	11 WVI	9/20/64–6/15/65
Wilson, James H. Sgt.	1 WVC	8/30/61–7/8/65
Wilson, John Pvt.	92 OHI	8/4/62–8/16/64
Wilson, Van C. Pvt.	10 WVI	63/65
Wilson, Wm. Cpl.	14 WVI	8/15/62–6/27/65
Wine, Robert Pvt.	NF (27 VAI CSA?)	
Wiseman, Joseph P. Cpl.	11 WVI	8/15/62–6/17/65
Woodyard, Taylor Pvt.	4 WVC	7/31/63–7/31/65
Yoho, Jacob L. Cpl.	78 OHI	8/20/62–6/1/65
Yonkings, George W. Pvt.	11 PAI	9/20/64–5/31/65

Wirt County Remarks

Arnold, D.D.—scarred with a ball
Baker, B.—strain in back, blind
Bayley, I.S.—LD, RH, MS
Benington, H.H.—hurt knee in line of duty
Bennett, S.—RH 25 years
Blane, H.—RH 15 years
Board, J.—RH & dropsy
Boice, S.—RH 27 years
Bomes, R.H.—wound in riqht arm at Fishers Hill
Bonet, S.H.—catarrh
Boyles, C.H.—gunshot wound right thigh
Britton, G.S.—catarrh of head, discharge burnt up
Brown, J.—RH & KD
Brown, W.—asthma
Brown, W.J.—CDR
Burton, R.—RH 25 years
Cain, D.—flux
Cain, G.—throat & lung disease
Cain, G.W.—HD
Campbell, H.—RH in May 186
Caplinger, E.—nearly deaf
Carpenter, W.—wounded in head, pension $8 per month
Clark, A.P.—RH
Cline, M.V.—throat & lung disease, DSC
Cline, S.—gunshot right knee
Conley, C.M.—gunshot wound left hand
Copen, G.W.—wound in left arm
Corbit, M.—RH
Cothern, J.E.—lumbago & HD
Courtney, W.—bronchitis 28 years
Crowser, G.W.—cold on measles, result bronchitis
Culver, J.J.—spine & kidney, discharge in Ohio
Davis, C.W.—spinal disease & piles 25 years
Davis, J.A.—arm taken off in the war
Davis, R.H.—RH 25 years
Day, S.—sciatic RH & HD
Deem, J.—RH
Dwees, B.C.—gunshot right side, SS
Evans, T.W.—varicose ulcer, discharged by reason of ulcer
Fluharty, L.—VV
Fortney, I.—deafness, RH
Fouty, J.F.—fistula
Fox, M.—spinal disease effects of fever
Frazier, J.—tumor
Gillaspie, W.—catarrh in head 25 years

Gilmore, A.—neuralgia 25 years, blind in one eye
Guthrie, E.—nervousness, RH
Hall, B.H.—RH & HD, detailed as head nurse in hospital
Hall, J.M.—RH 27 years
Hall, P.—RH
Hardway, G.W.—RH, scurvy, inconstansy of urine
Harper, J.G.—LD, wrist cut with axe
Harper, W.—RH 7 years
Harris, S.R.—LD
Hayes, C.P.—wounded right leg below knee, reinlisted Co F 1 WVC
Hickman, E.—disability incurred 2/63 by MS & CDR
Hickman, Z.—RH
Howard, J.—RH
Hoy, E.—injury to back
Hupp, D.—broken leg caused by war
Hutchinson, T.L.—lame in wrist, stiff hand
James, J.E.—rupture
Jefferies, E.A.—bronchitis, hearing & sight defective
Justice, A.C.—eye disease
Kiger, W.P.—RH 27 years
King, J.I.—wounded right ankle, discharged by order War Dept.
Laird, M.—POW Libby prison, stomach trouble, TYF 62 & 63, KD
Leasure, C.—HD
Lediam, W.H.—weakness in breast, UFL
Life, D.C.—RH 26 years
Lockhart, I.—POW captured within 2 months, never got discharge
Logston, L.—RH
Longsworth, J.T.—RH
Lynch, F.M.—gunshot of right thigh
Madden, N.D.—gunshot wound
Martin, W.J.—neuralgia of stomach 21 years
Mason, G.—CDR & RH 26 years
Mason, L.G.—POW Libby & Belle Isle, CDR & HD
McCoy, W.A.—RH & piles, promoted 11/2/6
McDonald, A.—RH, HD, nervous prostration
McFee, L.—RH, deafness, pneumonia fever in service
McKitrick, A.—gunshot of neck
McKitrick, M.L.—partial paralysis left side & arm, stomach disease
Merill, R.—RH 1863
Metz, H.—chronic sore leg caused by fever 26 years
Miller, J.W.—HD, spinal affection, stomach disease
Moffitt, I.—RH
Mooney, S.—RH
Morehead, T.J.—bleeding of lungs & gunshot wound
Newman, H.—weak eyes
Nolf, A.—HD
Park, M.—RH in 1863

Parks, W.M.—DSC
Parsons, R.—loss of left eye
Pell, W.F.—hernia
Petty, W.J.—RH & stomach disease contracted 1862
Philips, J.—gunshot wound, UFL
Phillips, G.W.—RH
Pierce, W.—RH
Plate, W.F.—catarrh, bronchitis, partial deafness both ears
Porter, J.W.—piles & rupture
Price, M.—WIA at Cedar Creek Va
Price, W.P.—gunshot left leg & hand
Provance, J.W.—RH 10 years
Provance, S.—hard of hearing
Rathbone, S.B.—RH & HD, soldier & marine, has lost discharge
Ratliff, E.—gunshot wound
Reed, S.—gunshot of hip
Reynolds, V.D.—RH
Riddle, G.M.—gunshot wound left shoulder
Robinson, F.M.—CDR & RH
Ruble, A.—RH
Ryan, J.L.—catarrh & piles 25 years
Sharpnack, W.H.—piles
Shettleworth, J.—hearing, UFL
Shiflett, E.—CDR
Showalters, H.H.—ruptured
Simpson, W.—general disability
Sink, G.—HD, RH, smallpox
Slater, W.—RH, supported by county
Smith, E.J.—liver complaint
Summner, A.—served only about 2 weeks & discharged
Tarrance, C.—RH, WIA at Hatchers Run 1865
Teel, W.—injured by fall from horse
Thompson, G.W.—loss of right eye
Tichenor, W.R.—hearing & shortness of breath
Townsend, C.—LD, gunshot wound left foot
Townsend, G.W.—wounded right shoulder, veteran served about 4 yrs
Tucker, J.R.—side injured on march
Tuell, F.—granulated sore eyes 27 years
Tufts, E.L.—RH
Umstead, J.W.—injury to right eye by shell explosion 8/25/62
Vandyke, P.—gunshot of neck
Vaught, S.—asthma 25 years
Weaver, J.—spinal neuralgia
Weaver, R.E.—gunshot wound left leg & stomach disease
Weaver, W.—SS
Weekley, W.—malarial poisoning
Welsh, T.—wounded in upper maxileary bone

Wever, B.—hemorrhoids, UFL
Wheatcroft, M.—catarrh & indigestion
Willets, M.P.—gunshot wound right foot
Williams, J.—RH 25 years
Wilson, J.H.—RH & stomach disease
Wilson, Jn.—general dibility 27 years
Wilson, V.C.—CDR & RH
Wilson, W.—RH & leg hurt by shell
Wine, R.—HD 26 years
Woodyard, T.—RH & general dibility

Wood County

NAME/RANK	REGIMENT	WHEN SERVED
Adams, Alsynus H. Pvt.	148 OHNG	9/10/64–12/15/64
Affolter, Jacob Pvt.	74 PAI	8/27/62–6/22/65
Alleman, Wm. H.	NF	
Allen, Wm. A. Pvt.	11 MDI	5/27/64–9/29/64
Ambler, Samuel Pvt.	2 WVI	6/15/61–12/3/62
Amos, David C. Pvt.	9 WVI	2/10/62–2/28/64
also	1 WVI	2/29/64–7/21/65
Amos, Robert H. Pvt.	9 WVI	10/19/61–7/22/65
Anders, Chrisitan Pvt.	1 WVA	8/28/62–6/28/65
Anderson, Grovend C. Pvt.	11 WVI	9/16/63–8/9/65
Anderson, James A. Pvt.	NF	
Anderson, Nathaniel Pvt.	3 VAC	12/10/61–2/10/64
Anderson, Otis B. Pvt.	17 WVI	8/64–6/30/65
Anderson, Robert A. Pvt.	7 VAI	9/7/61–2/13/63
Angus, Richard Cpl.	15 VAI	3/11/64–9/20/65
Archball, Charles W. Pvt.	87 OHI	5/27/62–10/1/62
Armstrong, Samuel Pvt.	1 WVC	12/23/61–7/8/65
Arnold, George S. Pvt.	13 WVI	3/29/64–6/23/65
Atkinson, James B. Pvt.	15 VAI	8/19/62–6/14/65
Atkinson, Mathew Pvt.	10 WVI	2/26/64–8/9/65
Aumiller, Henry Pvt.	193 OHI	2/6/65–8/4/65
Ayers, Wm. Pvt.	10 WVI	9/10/63–8/9/65
Backus, Joseph Pvt.	6 WVI	12/28/61–6/10/65
Badgley, Drure Cpl.	1 WVC	9/16/61–11/20/64
Bailey, A.P. Pvt.	11 —	8/62–6/27/65
Bailey, James E. Pvt.	14 WVI	8/6/62–6/27/65
Baily, George H. Pvt.	5 OHI	6/29/63–7/27/64

Baker, Caleb A. Pvt.	116 OHI	NF
Baker, John A. Pvt.	82 OHI	61/65
Baldwin, James Pvt.	193 OHI	3/9/65–8/4/65
Balentine, Wm. E. Pvt.	——	8/28/61–1864
Ball, Wm. H. Pvt.	20 VAC CSA	7/4/63–4/9/65
Balsley, Samuel K. Pvt.	14 WVI	8/62–6/65
Baltin, Samuel Capt.	7 WVI	8/1/61–7/13/65
Barnes, Alexander Pvt.	11 WVI	8/11/62–6/65
Barnes, James M. Pvt.	Signal Corp	7/22/61–7/27/64
Barrett, James R. Pvt.	15 WVI	8/62–6/65
Barrett, Samuel Pvt.	15 WVI	8/12/62–6/20/65
Barringer, Martin L. Pvt.	4 WVI	4/28/61–6/22/64
Barron, Joseph Pvt.	1 WVA	10/1/61–3/30/65
Bartlett, Marion B. Cpl.	2 WVC	8/18/62–1865
Bartlett, Silas B. Pvt.	6 WVI	9/16/61–6/10/65
Barton, Bennett Pvt.	75 OHI	12/61–7/11/65
Basetar, Thornton Pvt.	11 WVI	5/61–7/65
Batten, Thomas Cpl.	25 OHI	4/29/61–9/17/63
Battese, Hearnes Cpl.	25 OHI	4/29/61–9/17/63
Batton, Clarence L. Pvt.	6 WVI	10/20/61–6/10/65
Bauer, Jacob Pvt.	18 OHI	4/1/61–7/15/61
also	1 OHC	12/4/63–10/6/65
Bauer, Mathew Pvt.	194 OHI	2/13/65–10/4/65
Baughman, Samuel Pvt.	13 PAC	3/10/62–3/10/63
Bauman, Martin Pvt.	9 WVI	10/19/61–7/25/65
Baxter, John A. Pvt.	11 WVI	8/11/62–6/7/65
Beabout, Wm. Pvt.	170 OHI	5/2/64–9/10/65
Beasure, John H. Pvt.	6 WVI	5/14/62–6/10/65
Beckwith, Lewis Pvt.	14 WVI	8/15/62–6/17/65
Beebe, John W. Pvt.	148 OHNG	5/2/64–9/14/64
Bekens, Charles Pvt.	7 PAI	4/61–7/61
Bell, Wm. Lt.	174 OHI	8/25/64–6/28/65
Benny, Benj. T. Pvt.	11 WVI	8/8/62–6/17/65
Beorn, George Pvt.	11 WVI	7/2/62–NF
Bibbee, Franklin H. Pvt.	6 WVI	1864–6/13/65
Birch, John Pvt.	4 WVI	6/6/61–7/18/65
Black, Joseph Sgt.	5 WVC	5/30/61–6/30/64
Black, Samuel N. Pvt.	14 WVI	62/65
Black, Thomas A. Pvt.	1 WVC	9/28/61–11/27/64
Blevins, Jesse Pvt.	10 WVI	8/19/62–6/29/65
Bogue, Lyman D. Pvt.	114 NYI	9/1/64–6/8/65
Bolen, Jeptha J. Pvt.	36 OHI	9/4/62–9/4/65
Bond, E.D.J. Surgeon	11 WVI	NF
Bonnett, Henry Pvt.	17 WVI?	11/1/61–12/26/64
Boone, Jesse T. Pvt.	3 WVC	9/11/62–6/30/65
Boso, John R. Pvt.	17 WVI	8/4/64–6/30/65
Boso, Kinsman Pvt.	9 WVI	10/25/61–7/21/65

Bowersook, Adam L. Pvt.	1 VAA	8/25/61–11/6/62
Bowery, Richard Pvt.	1 —	8/61–7/65
Bowyer, Washington Pvt.	3 WVC	5/2/63–6/3/65
Bracy, Nathan Pvt.	— OHA	2/11/64–8/11/65
Braden, Peter T.	NF	
Bradford, Abraham Pvt.	15 WVI	8/14/62–NF
Bradley, John Sgt.	3 KYC	6/26/64–7/15/65
Bradley, Mickel Pvt.	15 VAI	8/62–6/65
Bradley, Oliver Pvt.	14 WVI	6/62–1865
Brafford, George S. Pvt.	15 WVI	8/22/62–6/14/65
Brahan, Edward Pvt.	11 WVI	8/28/62–6/17/65
Brahm, Leonard T. Pvt.	9 PAC	9/61–1863
also	184 PAC	5/12/64–1/14/65
Brand, John F. Pvt.	3 WVC	9/3/62–6/6/65
Broom, James Pvt.	196 OHI	2/65–9/65
Brown, Coleby W. Pvt.	1 WVC	12/2/61–7/8/65
Brown, George W. Pvt.	NF (25 VAI CSA?)	
Brown, Isaac Pvt.	1 WVA	7/2/62–7/5/65
Brown, James F. Pvt.	7 USI	NF
Brown, Jesse B. Pvt.	17 WVI	2/25/65–6/30/65
Brown, John C. Pvt.	1 MDC	9/21/— 6/26/65
Brown, John Pvt.	116 OHI	8/62–3/30/63
Brown, Samuel A. Pvt.	1 MDC	9/23/62–6/28/65
Brown, Thomas W. Pvt.	11 WVI	8/12/62–6/17/65
Brownfield, Enos J. Pvt.	1 WVC	10/61–7/65
Bruny, Christian Pvt.	180 OHI	10/4/64–7/12/65
Buckley, J. L. Pvt.	1 VAC	9/9/61–7/8/65
Bukey, Van H.	NF	
Bumgarner, Joseph W. Pvt.	18 WVI	7/61–1864
Burdett, Alexander Pvt.	17 WVI	8/13/64–6/30/65
Burdett, Peter A. Pvt.	17 WVI	2/28/65–6/30/65
Burdette, Wm. Sgt.	92 OHI	7/26/62–6/17/65
Burns, Nathaniel Pvt.	3 OHI	4/14/61–6/22/65
Bushong, Joseph S. Capt.	5 USC	4/61–4/64
Butcher, Thomas P. Lt.	15 WVI	63/65
Butler, Wm. O. Pvt.	62–OHI	10/5/61–8/25/65
Buzzard, John Pvt.	— PAA	2/13/64–6/26/65
Byers, Jacob Pvt.	116 OHI	8/13/62–6/14/65
Cade, Wm. Pvt.	11 VAI	8/16/63–8/65
Cage, Samuel Pvt.	17 WVI	2/18/65–6/14/65
Cain, Albert W. Pvt.	6 WVI	8/20/61–6/10/65
Cain, Charles S. Pvt.	20 OHI	4/14/64–NF
Cain, Charles S. Pvt.	26 OHI	4/18/64–7/65
Caldwell, Charles T. Pvt.	23 OHI	2/15/65–5/15/65
Cale, Andrew Pvt.	6 WVI	8/29/62–6/10/65
Cale, Isaac Cpl.	6 WVI	8/29/62–6/10/65
Cale, Martin V. Pvt.	3 WVC	1/65–6/65

Name	Unit	Dates
Cales, Lewis M. Pvt.	141 OHI	5/2/64–9/12/64
Caltrider, George T. Sgt.	11 WVI	8/14/62–6/17/65
Campbell, Levi	NF (60 VAI CSA?)	
Caplinger, David Pvt.	15 WVI	NF
Caplinger, John W. Pvt.	10 WVI	2/19/64–8/9/65
Carder, James W. Pvt.	6 VAI	8/61–6/10/65
Carothers, James J. Sgt.	25 OHI	4/25/61–1/11/62
also Lt.	78 OHI	1/11/62–1/28/65
Carr, Wm. H.	NF	
Casteel, George W. Pvt.	15 WVI	9/15/63–5/25/65
Cecil, John L. Pvt.	148 OHNG	5/22/64–9/14/64
Chandler, John D. Pvt.	NF (52 VAI CSA?)	
Chivalier, Arthur H. Capt.	——	1861–6/66
Christopher, Clark D. Pvt.	6 PAA	64/65
Clark, Abeslva Pvt.	6 WVI	9/30/61–6/10/65
Clark, Jaco Pvt.	11 WVI	8/11/62–6/17/65
Clark, James L.	Legislative?	7/26/63–7/31/63
Clay, Benj. F. Pvt.	6 WVI	10/15/62–6/10/65
Clay, John F. Sgt.	22 OHI	9/6/61–11/18/64
Clemence, O. M. Capt.	NF	
Clous, Theodore J. Pvt.	7 WVI	9/2/61–6/16/63
Coffman, Adam Pvt.	12 WVI	8/62–6/65
Coffman, Henry	NF	
Cokeley, Daniel R. Pvt.	15 WVI	8/10/62–6/14/65
Cole, Lucius A. Seaman	Naid?	2/18/64–10/18/65
Cole, Wm. H. Pvt.	7 OHC	8/30/62–7/3/65
Collins, Henry S. Pvt.	23 OHI	12/4/63–8/3/65
Collins, Loman P. Pvt.	14 WVI	8/13/62–7/17/65
Collins, Martin V. Pvt.	77 OHI	63/65
Combs, James B. Pvt.	NF	
Congleton, Burris Pvt.	39 OHI	3/23/65–7/9/65
Congleton, Joseph Cpl.	92 OHI	8/18/62–6/20/65
Congo, Charles Pvt.	3 WVC	7/62–7/65
Congrove, Isaac Pvt.	174 OHI	8/29/64–6/28/65
Conkle, Jacob Pvt.	4 WVC	63/64
also	7 WVI	3/64–7/65
Cook, Wm. Pvt.	14 WVI	9/2/64–7/3/65
Cooper, Rece Cpl.	36 OHI	8/26/61–7/27/65
Cooper, Thomas J. Pvt.	14 WVI	8/13/62–7/3/65
Corbin, Imiah J. Pvt.	NF	
Cornell, George W. Pvt.	11 WVI	12/22/61–1/15/65
Cothern, Thomas C. Pvt.	3 WVC	9/12/62–6/30/65
Cottrill, John L. Pvt.	19 OHI	10/4/64–10/17/65
Coull, Ogelen Pvt.	3 WVC	9/11/62–7/30/65
Covert, Ralph Pvt.	63–PAI	9/20/61–1862
Crippin, John H. Pvt.	5 OHI	4/19/61–8/63
Crist, Wm. Pvt.	CSA NF (Jackson's VAA?)	

Crista, Fredric W. Pvt.	14 WVI	3/13/65–6/27/65
Croft, Wm. M. Pvt.	190 PAI	9/3/62–2/25/65
Cronin, Wm. Pvt.	—WSA	3/6/62–4/20/65
Crook, A.K. Pvt.	NF	
Cross, Ephram W. Pvt.	62–VAI CSA	1862–10/22/63
Cross, Joseph Pvt.	170 OHI	NF
Cross, Monroe Pvt.	2 WVC	3/61–11/28/64
Cross, Robert B. Pvt.	1 OHA	9/1/61–7/13/65
Crossom, James Pvt.	NF (26 VAC CSA)	
Crouse, James P. Pvt.	78 OHI	12/16/61–12/16/64
Crow, Wm. Pvt.	11 WVI	9/27/61–8/16/65
Cullett, Eugene Pvt.	15 WVI	62/65
Cunningham, Benj. S. Pvt.	6 WVI	8/18/61–4/17/65
Cunningham, John W. Pvt.	6 WVI	7/23/62–6/9/65
Curtis, John P. Pvt.	NF (20 VAC CSA?)	
Curtis, Theodore Pvt.	92 OHI	8/15/62–8/22/64
Daggett, Derastus P. Cpl.	7 WVI	9/29/61–9/30/64
Daily, John H. Pvt.	161 OHNG	5/2/64–9/2/64
Daily, Wm. Cpl.	161 OHNG	5/2/64–9/2/64
Daugherty, Patrick	Teamster NF	
Davis, Henry C. Pvt.	9 WVI	10/26/61–7/1/65
Davis, Isiah Pvt.	1 OHA	3/23/64–6/14/65
Davis, John W. Pvt.	22 PAC	2/24/64–10/31/65
Davis, Morgan D. Pvt.	3 WVC	2/65/ 7/65
Dayhuff, Martin Pvt.	35 OHI	8/22/61–8/6/64
Dearing, Wm. M. Pvt.	3 VAI	6/25/61–8/15/64
Deaton, James M. Pvt.	4 MDA	1864–6/18/65
Deem, Derastus Pvt.	15 WVI	8/10/62–7/6/65
Deem, Isa Pvt.	6 VAI CSA	8/61–6/6/65
Deem, Michael Pvt.	11 WVI	8/5/62–6/17/65
Deem, Washington Sgt.	15 WVI	8/10/64–6/4/65
Delancey, Levi Pvt.	NF	
Demoss, Nathaniel D. Pvt.	19 VAC CSA	7/61–4/65
Denham, Andrew J. Pvt.	12 WVI	8/15/61–6/15/65
Devaughn, Elmore Pvt.	6 WVI	10/11/61–10/13/64
Devaugnh, Cornelius Pvt.	1 VAC	9/61–12/3/64
Devers, Wm. H. Cpl.	6 WVC	8/62–5/66
Dickerson, Elijah Pvt.	92 OHI	8/14/61–NF
Dickson, John Pvt.	14 WVI	8/15/62–6/27/65
Dickson, Wm. Pvt.	14 WVI	8/15/62–6/27/65
Dillon, James M. Pvt.	12 WVI	6/9/62–8/9/65
Dils, Charles Pvt.	6 WVI	8/26/61–10/13/64
Dollman, Charles M. Pvt.	77 OHI	2/4/64–3/25/66
Donahue, James H. Pvt.	61—	8/61–2/63
Dotson, Michael Pvt.	148 OHI	5/2/64–9/14/64
Drennen, George A. Pvt.	1 WVC	NF
Drum, James K.	NF	

Dugan, James (W.) Pvt.	2 VAI CSA	4/18/61–5/3/63
Dunhum, Wm. Pvt.	2 MDI	NF
Dunlap, Robert Pvt.	77 OHI	2/23/64–3/8/66
Dunn, Granville D. Pvt.	6 VAI	61/64
Dye, Henry Pvt.	11 WVI	8/14/62–6/17/65
Dye, Iven E. Pvt.	15 WVI	8/30/62–6/14/65
Dye, Wm. S. Pvt.	116 OHI	62/65
Dyke, Alonzo S. Pvt.	3 WVC	9/18/62–7/10/65
Eaton, Elijah Pvt.	17 WVI	9/8/64–6/30/65
Edmonds, Wm. Cpl.	4 WVI	6/12/61–2/25/65
Edmonson, George Pvt.	— USI	8/22/64–9/8/65
Elbert, Charles Pvt.	12 WVI	8/11/62–6/16/65
Elliott, John W.	NF	
Elliott, Peter F. Pvt.	204 PAA	8/20/64–7/8/65
Elliott, Robert	NF	
Emrick, Camden Pvt.	17 VAC CSA	11/62–1865
Emrick, Charles L. Pvt.	17 VAC CSA	9/28/62–11/1/64
Eskey, Samuel Pvt.	148 OHNG	5/22/64–9/14/64
Evans, Robert F. Pvt.	11 WVI	8/8/62–7/17/65
Evans, Wm. Cpl.	1 MDI	5/23/61–6/25/64
Evilsizer, Josiah Pvt.	36 OHI	2/63–7/31/65
Faling, George E. Pvt.	71 NYI	5/1/61–7/13/64
Farnsworth, Dan B. Pvt.	4 VAC	63/64
Farnsworth, John J. Pvt.	15 WVI	10/61–5/65
Farr, John A. Pvt.	NF (18 MSI CSA?)	
Farron?, George	NF	
Farrow, Hiram Pvt.	14 NYI	12/28/63–8/29/65
Feldner, Henry Pvt.	63 OHI	11/7/61–7/8/65
Fellows, Louis C. Pvt.	8 KYC	8/62–9/63
Feltner, Robert H. Cpl.	3 WVI	6/22/61–8/15/64
Fischer, Charles L. Pvt.	1 NYC	6/19/61–2/8/63
Fisher, John W. Cpl.	25 OHI	4/29/61–12/5/62
Fleek, Parker Cpl.	11 WVI	11/30/61–12/24/64
Fleming, John J. Pvt.	NF	
Fleming, Edward J. Pvt.	3 VAI	6/24/61–8/15/64
Fletsher, Porter Lt.	6 VAC	7/61–6/66
Flinn, Barney D. Pvt.	11 WVI	11/1/61–12/27/65
Flinn, John C. Sgt.	11 WVI	11/1/61–12/27/64
Flinn, Nelson C. Sgt.	13 WVI	7/62–1865
Florence, Loring Pvt.	14 WVI	8/28/62–7/2/65
Fluharty, John J. Pvt.	6 WVI	4/29/61–10/22/61
Folwell, Foittel J. Pvt.	1 PAC	1/5/64–7/15/65
Fortner, Isaac Pvt.	14 WVI	8/15/62–6/27/65
Fouse, Fredric Pvt.	9 OHC	10/24/62–7/13/65
Frazier, Wm. Pvt.	140 PAI	6/14/62–6/27/65
Freeland, Solomon Pvt.	10 WVI	1/19/62–6/17/65
Freeman, Wm. L. Pvt.	NF (23 BTN VAI CSA?)	

Frost, Harvey Pvt.	192 OHI	3/1/65–9/7/65
Frost, John F. Pvt.	Walkers Art.	4/15/61–4/9/65
Fry, Alexander Cpl.	17 WVI	2/15/65–6/30/65
Fry, Rueben Pvt.	3 VAI	4/17/61–1865
Fuld?, Thomas G. Pvt.	18 OHI	4/17/61–5/3/65
Full, Zebedee (E.) Pvt.	19 VAC CSA	8/62–4/65
Fulton, James J. Capt.	NF	
Garrett, Thomas Pvt.	36 OHI	8/10/62–7/65
Garrison, Jacob Pvt.	15 WVI	8/14/62–6/29/65
Garrison, Rodney G. Pvt.	39 OHI	7/22/61–10/62
also Cpl.	148 OHNG	64/64
Gearhart, George T. Pvt.	4 WVC	62/64
also	175 OHI	64/65
Gible, Louis Pvt.	1 WVA	8/12/62–6/28/65
Gilchrist, Daniel Pvt.	148 OHI	5/2/64–9/14/64
Gillman, Fredric Pvt.	5 OHI	4/20/61–6/5/65
Gilmore, Charles Pvt.	77 OHI	9/15/62–7/19/65
Givens, James H. Pvt.	174 OHI	9/64–5/65
Gladwell, George W. Pvt.	3 WVI	6/27/61–2/62
Goowin, Richard Pvt.	10 WVI	3/19/62–5/2/65
Gorden, John W. Pvt.	CS Artly. (20 BTN VAA?)	61/65
Gordon, Wm. C.	US NF	
Gossett, Miles	NF	
Grable, Samuel B. Pvt.	10 PA–	61/64
Graham, James A. Pvt.	11 WVI	6/8/63–8/10/65
Graham, Justice A. Pvt.	12 OHC	NF
Graves, George W.	NAVY	61/63
Gribble, Alexander Pvt.	6 VAI	9/61–1864
Griffin, Lemeul Pvt.	116 OHI	8/22/62–7/7/65
Grimm, John W. Pvt.	17 WVI	2/28/65–6/30/65
Grimm, Stephen S. Pvt.	11 WVI	2/27/64–8/9/65
Grimm, Thomas Pvt.	77 OHI	10/13/63–10/12/65
Guinn, John Pvt.	1 WVI	9/28/61–5/29/65
Guinn, Thomas Pvt.	11 WVI	2/25/64–3/4/65
Haddex, Isaac Pvt.	4 WVC	8/63–3/64
Haddox, Wm. B. Pvt.	NF	
Haddox, Edward S. Pvt.	NF	
Hall, Benj. F.	USS Victory #33	6/12/62–7/65
Hall, Elitia T. Pvt.	140 OHI	5/13/64–9/65
Hall, Francis M.	NF (14 VAC CSA)	
Hall, Wm. F. Pvt.	102 PAI	8/13/63–7/5/65
Hall, Wm. H.H. Pvt.	15 WVI	8/7/62–6/14/65
Hamilton, George R. Sgt.	4 WVC	9/21/63–6/23/64
Hamilton, Patrick	NF	
Hammat, Giles R. Pvt.	26 VAC CSA	7/63–4/65
Hammat, John W. Capt.	CSA (26 VAC?)	7/63–4/65

Hardin, Enos D. Sgt.	77 OHI	2/62–1/65
Harper, Wm. Pvt.	NF	
Harrass, Thomas G. Pvt.	1 WVC	10/29/61–12/62
Harrison, Wm. H. Pvt.	15 WVI	8/62–6/14/65
Haught, Jackson Pvt.	1 VAA	62/65
Haynes, Crawford Pvt.	36 OHI	2/64–NF
Hays, George B. Pvt.	4 PAC	8/22/62–6/25/65
Headley, Henry Pvt.	15 WVI	8/62–8/65
Headley, James Pvt.	11 WVI	61/65
Heath, Franklin Pvt.	20 MAI	8/8/61–7/15/65
Heatherby, Elam T. Pvt.	11 VAI	7/20/62–6/30/63
Heaton, Hewitt C. Pvt.	2 WVI	7/5/61–10/24/62
Hedrick, Isaac Y. Pvt.	62 VAI CSA	8/12/61–4/9/65
Hefling, James (L.) Pvt.	47 VAI CSA	4/20/62–NF
Henderson, Isaac M. Pvt.	11 WVI	6/27/63–8/9/65
Henderson, J.R. Pvt.	15 WVI	8/23/62–6/15/65
Hendrickson, James Pvt.	15 WVI	6/13/62–12/12/64
Henthorne, Andrew W. Pvt.	116 OHI	8/16/62–6/14/65
Henthorne, Leason Pvt.	NF	
Herdman, John W. Pvt.	11 WVI	12/16/62–8/9/65
Hewett, Wm. A. Cpl.	1 OHC	9/3/61–7/3/64
Hewett, Wm. A. Cpl.	1 OHC	9/3/61–9/20/65
Hickman, Thomas P. Pvt.	11 WVI	8/20/62–6/17/65
Higgins, Perry Pvt.	15 WVI	8/62–NF
Hilfinger, Jacob Pvt.	134 PAI	8/7/62–5/26/63
Hill, Joseph G. Cpl.	77 OHI	11/61–10/62
Hillard, James W. Pvt.	6 WVI	8/8/62–6/10/65
Hine, George W. Pvt.	143 PAI	63/65
Hinman, Isaac K. Pvt.	3 WVC	12/63–7/25/65
Hoce, Oscar L. Pvt.	NF	
Hodgkins, Joseph Sgt.	NF	
Hogan, John Pvt.	1 VAI	9/61–1864
Holbert, Michael Pvt.	11 WVI	8/15/62–8/20/65
Holland, Levi W. Pvt.	45 KYI	NF
also	7 WVI	9/2/61–9/7/63
Holman, Richard P. Pvt.	11 KYC	8/3/63–5/21/65
Holmes, Thomas Pvt.	3 WVC	1/7/63–6/13/65
Holtz, Lewis Cpl.	14 WVI	8/15/62–6/27/65
Hombeck, Benj. Pvt.	11 WVI	8/15/62–5/24/65
Horr, Josiah T. Pvt.	97 OHI	8/62–12/23/62
also	13 OHC	3/64–8/65
Houser, George B. Pvt.	14 WVI	8/13/62–7/20/65
Hoy, Amos Pvt.	3 WVC	3/11/64–6/20/65
Huggins, John J. Pvt.	15 WVI	8/14/62–5/28/65
Hughes, navid A. Pvt.	4 WVC	7/24/63–3/19/64
Hull, James F. Pvt.	14 WVI	8/13/62–6/27/65
Hunt, L.O. Pvt.	12 WVI	2/24/64–8/65

Hurst, Lemeul J. Pvt.	3 MDI	5/62–7/63
Huzen, S.S. Cpl.	2 OHA	6/24/61–6/24/65
Jackson, Edward H.	NF	
Jacobs, James H. Pvt.	5 OHI	8/2/61–7/26/65
James, Daniel (C.) Surgeon	17 VAC CSA	8/12/62–1865
Jenkins, James Pvt.	NF	
Jenkins, Samuel Pvt.	10 WVI	7/4/61–7/7/65
Jenne, Stephen A. Cpl.	92 OHI	8/20/62–6/10/65
Johnson, Benj. B. Pvt.	32 WSI	8/15/62–6/12/65
Johnson, Elza Pvt.	15 VAI	8/12/62–6/11/65
Johnson, Joseph B. Pvt.	6 WVI	2/26/61–6/10/65
Johnson, Marion Pvt.	4 WVC	8/63–9/65
Johnson, Wm.	Morgan's Raid CSA	NF
Jones, Martin L. Pvt.	12 WVI	8/16/62–6/16/65
Jones, Oliver S. Sgt.	3 WVI	6/4/61–8/16/64
Jones, Wm. H. Pvt.	7 OHI	6/21/61–12/20/62
Jordan, Thomas W. Pvt.	2 OHC	4/15/61–11/27/65
Justice, Elijah Pvt.	10 WVI	8/28/62–8/9/65
Kaufman, George Pvt.	1 WVA	8/62–6/30/65
Keefer, John J. Pvt.	15 WVI	8/14/62–6/14/65
Keeper, Henry 0. Pvt.	14 WVI	8/30/62–6/27/65
Kelley, Amos Cpl.	11 WVI	8/20/62–6/17/65
Kelly, Dawson J.		
Kendall, James Ast/Srgn	11 WVI	NF
Kennedy, Alexander R. Pvt.	13 PAI	5/12/61–9/64
Kenney, George W. Pvt.	6 VAI	61/65
Kester, James A. Pvt.	11 WVI	6/11/63–8/9/65
Kesterson, G.W. Pvt.	14 WVI	8/12/62–6/17/65
Kesterson, John G. Cpl.	3 VAC	10/20/62–6/29/65
Kesterson, Wm. H. Pvt.	14 WVI	8/12/62–7/3/65
Kimes, John A. Pvt.	13 WVI	8/15/62–6/24/65
Kinkead, David	NF	
Kirk, Wm. Sgt.	46 PAI	7/21/63–7/23/65
Kirkpatrick, Patrick Pvt.	7 WVI	9/4/61–1/31/64
Knels?, Winfield S. Pvt.	NF	
Knight, Samuel D.	NF	
Kraft, Lewis D. Pvt.	6 WVI	2/16/64–6/25/65
Krass, Antony Pvt.	194 OHI	2/28/65–10/24/65
Lamb, Noah Pvt.	7 WVI	65/65
Lang, Augustus H. Capt.	1 WVI	5/11/61–8/11/61
also	6 WVI	9/28/61–6/10/65
Leach, David E. Pvt.	33 OHI	8/28/61–10/21/64
Leach, James A. Pvt.	10 WVI	1/5/64–8/9/65
Leasure, Jacob Pvt.	NF	
Leavitt, Charles R. Pvt.	3 WVC	1/7/63–6/30/65
Leavitt, George E. Pvt.	1 WVC	3/4/64–7/8/65
Lee, Alexander Pvt.	6 WVI	10/15/61–10/21/64

Lester, James Pvt.	9 WVI	62/65
Lidelle, Wm. W. Pvt.	148 OHI	5/2/64–9/14/64
Locker, Walter W. Pvt.	11 WVI	8/9/62–6/18/65
Lott, Andrew J. Pvt.	17 WVI	8/13/64–6/13/65
Lott, Bartholomew Pvt.	17 WVI	8/30/64–6/30/65
Lowers, Thomas J. Pvt.	19 VAC CSA	8/13/62–3/28/65
Lowers, Wm. (H.) Pvt.	19 VAC CSA	8/13/62–3/28/65
Loyd, James Pvt.	3 WVC	10/18/62–6/30/65
LoYers, Henry Pvt.	19 VAC CSA	8/62–2/65
Luthringer, Joseph A. Pvt.	148 OHI	5/2/64–9/14/64
Lutz, Balsor Cpl.	6 WVI	8/27/61–11/4/64
Luzader, James Pvt.	12 WVI	8/16/62–5/23/65
Lynch, Wm. A. Pvt.	15 WVI	8/14/62–6/29/65
Lyons, John Pvt.	1 OHI	9/10/61–2/16/65
Lyons, Zachary L. Pvt.	NF	
Madins, John Pvt.	2 WVI	7/61–5/12/66
Mahke, Francis J.H. Lt.	3 WVC	9/62–6/65
Mallory, George K. Pvt.	6 WVI	8/6/61–8/15/64
Mamel, Henry Pvt.	14 ILC	10/62–7/3/65
Manning, George Pvt.	4 WVC	7/6/63–3/7/64
Mariet, Benj. F. Pvt.	15 WVI	8/22/62–6/29/65
Marlough, Levi Cpl.	CSA (19 VAC)	1861–NF
Marne, Joseph P. Pvt.	1 WVC	9/9/61–12/3/64
Marquis, Samuel B. Pvt.	14 ILI	6/61–8/5/62
Marshal, John Pvt.	15 WVI	62/65
Martin, David Pvt.	NF	
Martin, Presley Cpl.	12 WVI	8/16/62–6/19/65
Marttin, Wm. C. Pvt.	11 VAI	12/28/63–NF
Marty, Jacob Pvt.	11 WVI	8/18/62–6/17/65
Masters, John	NF	
Matthews, Bayne Sgt.	1 WVC	61/65
May, Chrisitan Pvt.	52 OHI	7/12/62–10/23/64
McClain, Hannibal Pvt.	1 WVC	8/13/61–7/8/65
McClure, George W. Pvt.	7 WVI	2/29/64–7/1/65
McConaughy, Daniel Pvt.	78 OHI	12/16/61–9/16/62
McCulley, James Sgt.	4 PAC	8/61–8/65
McCullick, Anthony Pvt.	NF	63/65
McFarland, George F.	NF	
McGonigal, Wm. H. Sgt.	87 PAI?	7/26/61–7/3/65
McGuire, Charles E. Pvt.	36 VAI CSA	5/61–6/65
McGuire, John S. Capt.	36 VAI CSA	5/61–6/65
McHaley, Henry Pvt.	11 MOI	2/62–5/65
McHenry, Samuel Pvt.	1 OHA	10/10/61–7/3/65
McHenry, Winchester Sgt.	1 OHA	9/10/61–7/19/65
McIntire, Isaac Pvt.	5 AKI (CSA)	5/61–NF
McKee, Jordan Cpl.	123 PAI	8/61–10/63
McKinney, H.B. Pvt.	—WV	8/61–6/28/65

Name	Unit	Dates
McKusick, Ike Pvt.	11 PAC	4/27/63–8/64
McKusick, John F. Lt.	1 DEC	1/1/63–4/7/65
McMerry, Allen Pvt.	9 OHC	9/63–8/65
McMullin, Richard Pvt.	2 WVC	9/61–1864
McMullin, Uriah Pvt.	18 OHI	NF
McPeek, Allen Pvt.	— OHI	NF
McPeek, Philip Pvt.	31 OHI	2/4/65–6/23/65
McPherson, Monroe Sgt.	11 WVI	11/16/61–6/5/65
McPherson, Wm. Pvt.	11 WVI	8/9/62–6/26/65
McTaggart, Archie H. Lt.	17 WVI	63/65
Medlen, Wm. Pvt.	16 PAC	9/19/62–6/17/65
Meek, Benj. F. Pvt.	2 WVI	6/29/61–1/4/64
also	6 WVC	1/5/64–5/22/65
Mehl, Andrew Pvt.	77 OHI	11/21/61–10/62
Mellinger, Marcus B.	US NF	
Melrose, Samuel Pvt.	—WVI	8/12/62–3/13/63
Melrose, Wm. H. Pvt.	11 WVI	8/12/62–6/9/65
Metcalf, Eli W. Pvt.	6 WVI	61/64
Metz, Wm. M. Pvt.	NF	
Meyers, John R. Pvt.	1 WVC	3/8/64–7/8/65
Miles, Wm. H. Pvt.	176 OHI	8/29/64–6/14/65
Miller, Charles T. Pvt.	3 WVC	1/64–7/65
Mills, James Pvt.	17 VAC CSA	5/62–5/65
Mills, John Pvt.	6 WVI	9/12/63–6/12/65
Milstead, Isaac Pvt.	2 VAI	6/16/61–4/63
Minings, George Pvt.	2 WVC	9/18/64–6/7/65
Miracle, John Pvt.	63–OHI	9/10/61–7/65
Moeck, Peter Pvt.	193 PAI	7/12/63–11/12/63
Montgomery, John H. Pvt.	NF (11 VAI CSA?)	
Moore, Joseph Pvt.	11 WVI	8/12/62–6/17/65
Moore, Peter Pvt.	2 WVI	6/13/61–7/14/64
Moore, R. T. Pvt.	78 OHI	2/26/64–6/16/65
Moore, Wm. W. Pvt.	52 OHI	NF
Morgan, Stephen E.	NF (20 VAC CSA)	
Morris, Theodore Pvt.	180 OHI	9/9/64–7/12/65
Morris, Wm. H. Pvt.	92 OHI	2/20/64–8/20/65
Morrison, Wm. H. Pvt.	NF (12 VAI CSA?)	
Morrow, Alexander Pvt.	—WVI	2/18/65–6/30/65
Mosena, Frank Pvt.	77 OHI	NF
Mulinex, John Pvt.	37 OHI	64/65
Mullen, John J. Cpl.	1 WVC	9/9/61–7/8/65
Murphy, James W. Pvt.	6 VAI CSA	NF
Musser, Joseph Pvt.	6 WVI	8/26/61–6/9/65
Musser, Stanley Pvt.	10 WVI	8/1/63–8/9/65
Myers, Madison Pvt.	10 WVI	7/15/64–8/9/65
Neece, John Pvt.	2 OHI	61/65
Neill, Arthur O. Pvt.	NF	

Name	Unit	Dates
Nelson, David Pvt.	NF (36 BTN VAC CSA?)	
Nelson, Frank Pvt.	——	1/5/64–9/5/65
Neuber, George Lt.	12 PAI	7/11/61–6/11/64
also	200 PAI	9/1/64–5/30/65
Newbanks, Levi Pvt.	6 WVI	8/26/61–10/13/64
Newbanks, Wm. D. Pvt.	11 WVI	7/19/62–6/17/65
Newhart, George J. Pvt.	10 WVI	NF
Newlands, John H. Cpl.	1 OHA	7/61–7/65
Nixon, Wilson Pvt.	6? VAI CSA	61/65
Noice, Wm. Pvt.	12 WVI	8/12/62–7/12/65
Noland, Rubin	NF	
Noland, Wm. A. Pvt.	18 OHI	10/19/61–5/29/62
Nowery, John D. Pvt.	11 WVI	8/19/63–8/19/65
Nowery, Thomas Pvt.	11 WVI	8/19/63–8/19/65
Nowery, Wm. R. Pvt.	101 PAI	61/65
Nugent, Wilson S. Pvt.	2 OHA	6/16/63–9/65
O'hare, John Pvt.	3 VTC?	2/7/65–6/66
Offlighter, Wm. H. Pvt.	52 VAI CSA	5/7/61–11/63
Ogden, Elias Pvt.	11 WVI	8/20/62–6/17/65
Oliver, Wm. L. Pvt.	44 VAI CSA	6/61–4/65
Osburn, Lafayette Pvt.	2 OHC	11/15/62–11/15/65
Owings, Wm. Sgt.	43 OHI	12/15/61–7/25/65
Padgett, James Pvt.	12 WVI	8/22/62–6/16/65
Palmer, Michael Pvt.	116 OHI	8/14/62–7/1/65
Palmer, Wm. Pvt.	NF	
Parson, John Pvt.	12 ILI	7/61–7/65
Paul, Charles E. Pvt.	17 WVI	1/65–6/65
Pease, Francis G. Pvt.	20 VAC CSA	7/63–4/65
Pennybacker, Benj. Y. Pvt.	CSA (20 VAC)	7/28/62–2/4/65
Pennybacker, Hiram H. Lt.	20 VAC CSA	6/23/63–4/16/65
Pennybacker, John B. Lt.	20 VAC CSA	6/1/63–12/18/65
Pennybaker, Ben R. Pvt.	17 VAC CSA	
Peppler, John H.	NF	
Perry, Henry W. Pvt.	104 NYI	1861–8/7/65
Petit, Joseph L. Pvt.	11 WVI	8/14/62–6/14/65
Petty, George L. Pvt.	NF	
Phillips, George W. Pvt.	NF (19 VAC CSA)	
Pickett, Edward Pvt.	17 WVI	2/17/65–7/65
Pierce, Caleb Sgt.	77 OHI	11/19/61–1/19/66
Pifer, George Pvt.	116 OHI	8/8/62–3/6/63
Pilcher, George Pvt.	3 WVC	4/64–7/65
Pilcher, Moses Sgt.	3 WVC	10/62–6/30/65
Pilear, Henry Pvt.	6 WVI	9/17/64–6/19/65
Piles, Thomas Cpl.	92 OHI	8/9/62–6/10/65
Poetlewait, Uriah Pvt.	6 WVI	8/30/61–6/10/65
Pollock, Robert S. Pvt.	6 WVI	8/4/61–6/7/65
Porter, David R. Pvt.	8 PAI	7/29/61–8/27/61

also Pvt.	105 PAI	8/28/61–12/16/62
also Cpl.	18 PAI	12/20/62–6/18/65
Porter, George W. Pvt.	NF	
Postlethwait, John N. Pvt.	11 WVI	7/19/63–8/19/65
Postlewait, Wm. Pvt.	6 WVI	8/20/61–12/26/65
Powell, Banna Pvt.	25 OHI	4/29/61–7/5/62
Powell, Joseph Pvt.	NF	
Prettyman, J.J. Pvt.	11 WVI	6/24/63–6/14/65
Prettyman, Leven T. Pvt.	11 WVI	8/27/63–8/19/65
Price, Wm. S. Pvt.	18 USI	7/27/61–7/24/66
Prince, Lawrence B. Sgt.	14 VAI	8/6/62–6/27/65
Pritchard, Andrew J. Pvt.	10 WVI	2/8/65–8/9/65
Proffitt, Samuel N. Pvt.	13 WVI	10/15/63–6/25/65
Province, Jasper Pvt.	17 WVI	8/30/64–6/30/65
Putnam, George W. Lt.	36 OHI	7/61–12/64
Rapp, John D. Pvt.	1 VAC	4/4/62–1/5/65
Redford, Horace H.	NF	
Reed, Amaziah Pvt.	6 WVI	8/25/62–1/10/65
Reed, Colon M. Pvt.	NF	
Reeves, Abram Cpl.	92 OHI	8/9/62–5/26/65
Reynolds, John K. Pvt.	1 WVA	9/1/61–11/7/62
Rice, John B. Sgt.	6 WVI	12/10/61–12/29/64
Richardson, Wm. M. Pvt.	1 OHA	3/10/62–3/10/65
Riel, David Pvt.	15 WVI	8/22/62–4/65
Riffey, Jacob	NF (35 BTN VAC CSA?)	
Rilley, Silas Pvt.	11 WVI	12/26/61–12/30/63
Riser, Henry Cpl.	4 WVC	6/1/63–3/4/64
Roach, James A. Pvt.	1 WVC	1/1/62–7/8/65
Robbins, Lewis Pvt.	14 WVI	8/15/62–6/27/65
Roberts, Isaac Pvt.	2 USI	5/20/61–11/6/62
Roberts, Jacob T. Pvt.	100 PAI	4/8/64–7/27/65
Roberts, Wm. Cpl.	15 WVI	NF
Roberts, Wm. H?	CSA NF (19 VAC?)	
Robinson, David Pvt.	11 WVI	8/22/62–4/65
Robinson, Henry Pvt.	16 WVI	2/18/65–2/23/66
Roby, James H. Pvt.	4 WVC	4/63–12/63
Rodgers, George W. Cpl.	2 WVC	8/30/61–6/30/65
Roles, Daniel P. Sgt.	21 VAI?	6/29/61–8/16/64
Rollins, Wm. Pvt.	19 VAC CSA	6/62–11/62
Ronnine, Maleleel O. Cpl.	14 WVI	8/15/62–6/27/65
Rose, James H. Pvt.	4 VAC	63/63
also	3 VAI	64/65
Ross, Joseph G. Pvt.	4 WVI	6/5/61–7/5/64
Ross, Thomas W. Pvt.	144 PAI	1862–NF
Rost, George Pvt.	67 PAI	4/6/65–7/27/65
Rost, John Pvt.	6 PAA	8/10/64–6/13/65
Rouch, James A. Pvt.	1 WVC	1/1/62–7/8/65

Name	Unit	Dates
Rouse, George Pvt.	77 OHI	12/9/61–5/20/65
Rowell, Thomas Pvt.	1 WVA?	9/62–9/64
Rowley, Thomas Pvt.	116 OHI	8/62–6/65
Royers, James T. Pvt.	92 OHI	NF
also	31 OHI	NF
Ruble, Arthur Pvt.	15 WVI	8/20/62–6/14/65
Ruble, Henry H. Pvt.	11 WVI	8/13/62–6/17/65
Ruble, Iand Pvt.	7 WVI	9/4/61–11/5/64
Ruble, James A. Pvt.	15 WVI	8/10/62–7/6/65
Ruble, John Pvt.	3 WVC	3/65–8/65
Ruble, Palsen Cpl.	3 WVC	3/1/65–6/30/65
Ruder, James R. Pvt.	1 WVC	8/7/61–7/8/65
Runion, Samuel C. Pvt.	15 WVI	8/16/62–6/13/65
Rurton, Lorenzo Pvt.	92 OHI	NF
Safford, Joseph H. Cpl.	42 MAI	NF
Saik, Wm. Pvt.	37 OHI	9/20/61–9/18/63
Salow, Wm. E. Pvt.	1 WVC	8/29/64–7/8/65
Sams, Alexander Pvt.	14 WVI	8/12/62–6/23/65
Sams, David Pvt.	17 WVI	8/64–6/65
Sams, Frank W. Pvt.	14 WVI	8/18/62–6/27/65
Sams, George W. Pvt.	14 WVC	NF
Sams, John W. Pvt.	1 WVC	2/18/63–7/18/65
Sams, Samuel A. Pvt.	2 VAI	7/27/62–7/15/65
Sams, Wm. H. Pvt.	11 WVI	7/22/62–6/17/65
Sattow, Carel A. Pvt.	1 WVC	11/22/61–7/8/65
Sattow, Fredric Sgt.	1 WVC	9/9/61–7/15/65
Saxton, James Pvt.	6 ALI CSA	6/61–8/18/62
Schafer, John Pvt.	10 WVI	1/13/62–3/16/65
Schrader, Albert F. Pvt.	14 WVI	8/26/62–7/5/65
Schultz, Otto Cpl.	14 WVI	8/15/62–6/27/65
Scott, Jackson Sgt.	75 INI	8/6/62–6/8/65
Scott, Wm. T. Pvt.	82 OHI	9/24/64–6/10/65
Seevers, Joseph J. Pvt.	33 OHI	9/7/61–4/5/65
Seleg, Jacob Pvt.	34 NJI	1/17/64–1/16/65
Sexton, Lindsey Pvt.	2 VAI CSA	6/61–4/16/65
Shafer, George W. Pvt.	25 OHI	6/26/61–7/26/64
Shafer, James R. Pvt.	36 OHI	2/26/64–7/3/65
Sharp, J.P. Ast/Surgeon	US Army	NF
Shaver, Francis R.	NF	
Shaw, Sidney S. Pvt.	15 WVI	NF
Sheehy, John	NF	
Sheets, James A. Pvt.	3 WVC	3/2/65–6/30/65
Sheets, Neslon Pvt.	11 WVI	7/22/62–6/16/65
Sheets, Wm. H. Pvt.	17 WVI	8/9/64–7/8/65
Shingleton, Absalom Pvt.	——	4/65–6/65
Shingleton, James R. Pvt.	14 WVI	8/9/62–6/27/65
Shinn, Elbert R. Pvt.	2 WVC	9/6/64–6/20/65

Shook, Alfred Pvt.	177 PAI	10/63–8/64
Showalter, James D. Pvt.	CSA (58 VAM?)	61/65
Shriner, Adam Pvt.	6 WVI	NF
Shuespring, John A. Pvt.	6 WVI	9/24/61–6/10/65
Simms, George W. Pvt.	14 WVI	62/65
Simpson, James L. Pvt.	11 WVI	12/21/61–1/65
Sims, Ebenezer Pvt.	1 WVC	65/65
Sines, Jacob Pvt.	13 WVI	11/3/63–6/22/65
Skinner, Adolph Pvt.	18 WVC?	3/24/64–7/25/65
Smith, Barnes B. Pvt.	11 WVI	11/63–8/10/65
Smith, Edward T. Pvt.	1 WVC	9/61–6/5/65
Smith, George B. Pvt.	17 PAC	8/62–6/65
Smith, James A. Pvt.	11 WVI	10/8/63–8/9/65
Smith, James Cpl.	9 WVI	10/20/61–7/21/65
Smith, James D. Pvt.	3 WVI	7/4/61–8/12/61
also	6 WVI	8/12/61–6/12/65
Smith, James W. Pvt.	4 MDI	3/1/65–5/4/66
Smith, John H. Cpl.	193 PAI	7/15/64–11/9/64
Smith, Joseph Pvt.	11 WVI	NF
Smith, Phillip M. Pvt.	2 WVC	NF
Smith, Samuel Pvt.	1 WVI	3/25/65–7/21/65
Smith, Solomon Pvt.	17 WVI	8/9/64–6/30/65
Snider, Alfred Pvt.	63 WVI?	11/4/63–9/4/64
South, John L. Pvt.	11 WVI	2/62–6/25/65
South, Joseph Pvt.	15 WVI	8/12/62–6/29/65
Spague, Thomas J. Pvt.	2 WVC	9/1/62–8/28/63
also	4 WVC	8/28/63–3/8/64
Spencer, Jacob E. Pvt.	2 WVC	9/17/64–6/7/65
Spencer, Wm. P. Pvt.	66 OHI	8/10/64–6/25/65
Sprouse, Woodard Pvt.	10 WVI	1862–5/8/65
Stafford, James Pvt.	15 WVI	8/10/62–6/14/65
Stagg, Jerry	NF	
Stahley, Andrew J. Pvt.	15 WVI	8/62–8/65
Stallings, Wm. Pvt.	51 OHI	9/27/64–6/65
Stalnaker, Salathiel Pvt.	11 WVI	11/29/61–6/10/65
Stanley, Henry F. Cpl.	10 WVI	3/10/62–5/19/65
Starkey, Minor Pvt.	116 OHI	2/1/64–8/23/65
Starr, Richard Pvt.	15 WVI	NF
Staton, George W. Cpl.	10 WVI	4/4/62–5/6/65
Stayton, Walker A. Pvt.	14 VAI	8/20/64–7/3/65
Steel, Abraham Pvt.	CSA NF (Cutshaw's VAA)	
Steel, Cornelius B. Pvt.	7 WVI	8/1/61–7/1/65
Steel, Jonas M. Pvt.	14 WVI	62/65
Steers, Thomas J.	NF	
Stephens, James Pvt.	15 VAI	8/13/62–5/10/65
Stephens, Wm. H. Pvt.	24 NYC	5/64–NF
Stevens, Louis Pvt.	36 OHI	2/14/65–7/27/65

Stewart, David Pvt.	11 WVI	8/62–4/65
Stiele, George Pvt.	11 WVI	8/14/62–6/17/65
Still, James L. Pvt.	31 OHI	3/23/65–7/9/65
Still, John Pvt.	30 OHI	8/22/61–4/28/62
also	2 OHA	7/18/63–5/24/65
Stoneking, John Pvt.	14 WVI	NF
Stukey, Jacob Pvt.	3 WVC	3/2/65–6/7/65
Stukey, Joseph Pvt.	77 OHI	12/25/61–3/8/66
Stutler, Arthur Pvt.	10 VAI	62/65
Suell, George C. Pvt.	11 WVI	11/22/61–8/19/65
Swain, Wm. Pvt.	13 WVI	8/22/62–6/23/65
Swarts, Napolean B. Pvt.	194 OHI	2/23/65–10/24/65
Swearengin, Albian Pvt.	6 WVI	8/28/64–6/10/65
Swesey, John Pvt.	148 OHI	5/3/61–9/15/65
Taggert, George W. Ltc.	7 WVI	7/15/61–6/24/62
also	14 WVI	8/21/62–7/3/65
Taylor, John Pvt.	NF	
Taylor, Reuben B. Lt.	14 WVI	8/14/62–6/1/65
Taylor, Thomas Pvt.	11 WVI	8/62–6/17/65
Tebay, James M. Pvt.	9 OHC	2/27/64–7/20/65
Terry, Thomas Pvt.	18 OHI	64/64
Thomas, Francis M. Pvt.	77 OHI	2/1/64–3/8/66
Thomas, Richard H. Cpl.	47 PAI	7/1/63–8/13/63
Thompson, Abraham Pvt.	78 OHI	12/25/61–7/11/65
Thompson, Andrew J. Pvt.	12 OHC	9/26/63–7/24/65
Tice, John Pvt.	148 OHNG	9/10/64–12/15/64
Tichnell, Samuel Cpl.	3 WVC	10/61–6/31/65
Tippens, Edward Pvt.	77 OHI	11/4/61–1/28/63
Todd, George B. Pvt.	2 WVC	5/16/61–6/16/65
Tornash, Charles Pvt.	15 WVI	8/18/61–1865
Townsand, Paul Pvt.	1 WVC	3/15/64–7/8/65
Trader, Arther Pvt.	11 WVI	62/65
Traughn, Martin V. Sgt.	14 WVI	8/14/62–6/27/65
Tucker, James K. Pvt.	6 WVI?	9/29/64–6/4/65
Tucker, Jeremiah M. Pvt.	12 WVI	8/17/62–6/29/65
Turner, Duncan Pvt.	148 OHI	10/64–10/65
Turner, George Pvt.	36 OHI	10/64–10/65
Turner, Lemeul H. Pvt.	4 WVC	7/13/63–3/7/64
Twyman, Sam P. Pvt.	2 VAC	12/19/62–9/65
Tylor, Benj.	NF	
Uhl, Heber J. Pvt.	15 VAI	6/62–6/65
Upsen, Norton L. Pvt.	2 OHC	64/65
Vancamp, Samuel Pvt.	194 OHI	3/1/64–6/12/65
Vanney, Joseph O. Pvt.	39 OHI	3/27/65–7/9/65
Vanney, Robert L. Pvt.	77 OHI	10/61–3/66
Varner, Oliver Pvt.	6 WVI	6/63–5/65
Vaught, George W. Pvt.	34 ILI	1861–7/22/62

Vincent, Wm. H. Pvt.	10 WVI	2/26/64–8/9/65
Vrooman, Welington	Paymaster	4/22/63–2/1/69
Walker, James G. Pvt.	6 WVI	9/10/62–6/10/65
Wallace, John A.	Army Clerk	NF
Walther, Daniel G. Pvt.	97 PAI	11/23/64–10/28/65
Ward, Isaac Cpl.	77 OHI	11/26/61–11/19/63
Ward, Thomas Pvt.	4 OHC	6/25/64–11/12/64
Ware, Charles A. Cpl.	140 OHI	5/1/64–9/5/64
Warman, Frank Pvt.	18 OHI	4/23/61–8/28/61
Warren, Ancil M. Pvt.	129 OHI	6/30/63–8/2/65
Warther, Eldridge S. Pvt.	8 MDI	8/27/62–1/29/64
Wash, Joseph A. Pvt.	7 OHC	8/30/62–6/8/65
Watkins, John J. Pvt.	3 WVC	9/62–6/30/65
Watson, Jacob Pvt.	129 OHI	8/63–3/64
Wauck, Emanuel Pvt.	4 WVI?	7/30/61–6/62
Weekley, Levi Cpl.	3 WVC	8/22/62–6/15/65
Weigel, Augustine Sgt.	62–OHI	10/16/61–7/11/65
Wells, Austin Sgt.	11 WVI	8/11/62–6/17/65
Wells, Philip Pvt.	36 VA CSA	9/4/62–4/20/65
Welsh, Daniel W. Lt.	62–PAI	NF
Weltis, Thomas Musician	18 —	9/9/61–9/9/64
West, Mikael Pvt.	1 OHI	4/1/65–8/9/65
West, Sylvester Pvt.	77 OHI	10/5/61–NF
Wetzel, Lewis Pvt.	7 WVC	8/5/63–6/30/65
Wharton, Isaac Pvt.	3 VAC	11/2/62–6/7/65
Wheaton, John Pvt.	NF	
Wheory, Madison Pvt.	6 WVI	NF
Whipkey, Freeman Pvt.	7 WVI	8/7/61–8/65
Whipkey, Josiah Pvt.	6 WVI	10/1/61–6/10/65
Whiston, Joseph Pvt.	——	5/64–9/64
White, Adam Sgt.	11 WVI	3/27/64–8/9/65
White, Francis M. Pvt.	CS Artly.	5/61–4/65
Whitehead, Jacob Pvt.	63–OHI	10/3/61–1/18/65
Whitlatch, Edward Pvt.	15 WVI	8/14/62–6/2/65
Whitlatch, Josephus Pvt.	15 WVI	8/12/62–6/29/65
Whitlatch, Wm. P. Cpl.	6 WVI	9/18/61–10/13/64
Wigal, Haram H. Pvt.	11 WVI	7/62–NF
Wigal, John M. Pvt.	CSA (20 VAC)	6/28/62–2/4/65
Wigal, Philip Pvt.	17 WVI	8/8/64–6/30/65
Wigal, Wm. Pvt.	17 WVI	8/9/64–6/30/65
Wiliamson, Sam B. Pvt.	13 WVI	2/18/64–6/23/65
Wilkinson, Elmer Sgt.	15 WVI	8/12/62–6/29/65
Williams, Calvin P. Pvt.	52 OHI	7/12/62–NF
Williams, Wm. H. Pvt.	7 ILI	1/64–7/9/65
Williamson, Horace Cpl.	7 OHI	12/6/61–6/6/65
Williamson, James Pvt.	13 WVI	NF
Williamson, Samuel Cpl.	11 WVI	10/21/63–8/4/65

Willis, Andrew J. Pvt.	19 INI	7/61–5/31/65
Willis, Andrew J. Pvt.	3 VAC	3/3/65–6/3/65
Willson, Flavus K. Pvt.	NF	
Wilson, James	NF (19 VAC CSA?)	
Wilson, John R. Pvt.	7 WVI	1861–2/17/63
Wilson, John R. Pvt.	169 PAI	10/62–7/26/63
Wingrove, Wm. H. Pvt.	15 OHI	9/16/62–7/11/63
Wise, John W. Pvt.	NF	
Wood, Wm. Pvt.	NF	
Woolard, John R. Cpl.	12 WVI	8/16/62–6/26/65
Worley, Asbury Cpl.	11 WVI	8/15/62–4/15/65
Wright, George Pvt.	113 OHI	8/17/62–8/9/65
Wright, George W. Pvt.	6 WVI	7/61–NF
also	1 WVA	5/63–8/65
Yates, Hamilton Pvt.	11 WVI	2/6/64–8/18/65
Yates, John Pvt.	1 WVC	8/30/61–12/11/63
also	1 WVI	12/25/63–7/8/65
Yates, Solomon Pvt.	7 WVI	9/26/61–11/5/64
Yocom, Thomas B. Pvt.	15 OHI	9/6/61–1/29/64
Zink, Andrew J. Pvt.	6 OHI	1862–7/65

Wood County Remarks

Adams, A.H.—MS
Ambler, S.—wounded right knee, paralyzed, deaf right ear
Amos, D.C.—gunshot wound both thighs
Amos, R.H.—blind, granulated eyelids from measles in Mrch 1862
Anders, C.—disabled from head & lung disease
Anderson, G.C.—RH
Anderson, J.A.—lumbago, HD
Anderson, O.B.—blind & parcial deaf
Anderson, R.A.—HD & weak back
Angus, R.—CDR
Armstrong, S.—LD
Arnold, G.S.—hernia of right side
Atkinson, J.B.—brain fever effected head & eyes
Aumiller, H.—hernia right side
Backus, J.—sight affected
Badgley, D.—spinal trouble & crippled hands
Bailey, A.P.—blindness
Bailey, J.E.—KD caused by cold exposure
Balentine, W.E.—RH, catarrah
Ball, W.H.*—feaver some
Balsley, S.K.—piles, RH & crippled finger

Baltin, S.—WIA left forearm, neuralgia left shoulder
Barnes, A.—broken arm
Barrett, S.—shot in left breast
Barron, J.—hearing injured
Bartlett, M.B.—lost sight of eye
Bartlett, S.B.—deafness
Barton, B.—RH, effected eyes & head
Batten, T.—lost right arm, shot through hand & leg
Battese, H.—lost right arm, shot through hand & legs
Bauer, J.—general disability
Bauer, M.—RH
Bauman, M.—KD & liver complaint
Baxter, J.A.—had measles never fully recovered
Beorn, G.—shot in head
Birch, J.—WIA
Blevins, J.—enrolled into 15 reg which consolidated into 10 reg
Bolen, J.J.—POW 4 months, LD
Bonnett, H.—hurt at Lynchburg WVA by shell
Boone, J.T.—injured in hips & body
Boso, J.R.—catarrh head, HD, throat trouble very much diseased
Boso, K.—HD, piles, parcial deafness
Bowersook, A.L.—RH & HD
Bowery, R.—gunshot in right leg
Bowyer, W.—gunshot right shoulder & arm
Bracy, N.—stomach & HD
Bradford, A.—deserted at Richmond has no discharge
Bradley, O.—neuralgia, lost an eye
Brahm, L.T.—gunshot right thigh
Brand, J.F.—disabled hy fall of horse, dyspepsia, LD
Brown, C.W.—TYF
Brown, J.F.—gunshot wound
Brown, Jn.—catarrh of head, partial deaf
Brownfield, E.J.—disease of back, heart, & eyes
Bumgarner, J.W.—shot through hand
Burdett, A.—RH
Burdett, P.A.—LD
Burdette, W.—spinal affection & HD
Butler, W.O.—collarbone broken
Byers, J.—RH 28 years
Cain, A.W.—RH & HD
Cale, A.—fractured right thigh
Cale, I.—asthma, also injured by a fall from a horse
Caplinger, D.—kidney & jaundice
Carder, J.W.—disease of left testicle caused by mumps
Carothers, J.J.—gunshot wound right hand at Cheat Mountain
Casteel, G.W.—CDR
Christopher, C.D.—piles

Clark, A.—LD
Clark, Jaco—general disability
Clay, B.F.—RH
Clay, J.F.—CDR
Clous, T.J.—ruptured
Coffman, A.—piles, HD
Coffman, H.—shot in left arm
Collins, L.P.—crippled, shot right leg
Combs, J.B.—two gunshots
Congleton, B.—eyes injured from measles
Congo, C.—thrown from horse, left side & breast broken
Congrove, 1.—RH & HD
Cooper, R.—bronchitis
Cooper, T.J.—one eye lost, accidental wound left foot
Cornell, G.W.—wounded left leg, pain in side, RH of heart
Cothern, T.C.—lumbago
Coull, O.—catarrah of head
Croft, W.M.—shot in rist of right arm
Cronin, W.—ruptured
Cross, M.—injury in head
Cross, R.B.—injured by baggage wagon running over him
Crouse, J.P.—liver & spleen affection
Crow, W.—general disability
Cullett, E.—asthma
Cunningham, J.W.—deafness & other diseases
Curtis, T.—epilepsy, HD, spinal affection
Daggett, D.P.—MP & RH, partial loss right eye
Davis, H.C.—general dibility
Davis, J.W.—limbs crippled by TYF
Dearing, W.M.—right eye out
Deem, D.—gunshot wound from left side into small back
Deem, M.—chronic disability
Deem, W.—struck with shell, indigestion of stomach
Devaughn, E.—ruptured
Devers, W.H.—partial deaf caused from catarrah
Dils, C.—chronic newralga & mumps
Donahue, J.H.—HD
Dugan, J.W.*—lost an arm
Dunn, G.D.—fell off block house hurt back
Dye, H.—crippled in left foot
Dye, W.S.—lumbago of back
Dyke, A.S.—throat & stomach disease
Eaton, E.—spinal irritation & neuralgia from TYF
Edmonds, W.—left arm shot off
Elliott, P.F.—affection of head resulting from mumps
Emrick, C.L.*—cold on measles, result lung trouble
Emrick, C.*—RH

Eskey, S.—WIA
Evans, R.F.—TYF
Evans, W.—CDR & piles, pensioner
Evilsizer, J.—mashed on left side by horse
Farnsworth, J.J.—RH & HD
Farron, G.—lumbago of back
Feldner, H.—WIA left hand
Fisher, J.W.—wounded in hips, CDR
Fleek, P.—weakness & CDR
Fleming, J.J.—CDR & bleeding piles 26 years
Flesher, P.—VV both legs & deafness
Flinn, B.D.—lumbago of back & HD, piles, blind, in bad position
Flinn, J.C.—partial deaf & HD
Fouse, F.—liver, stomach & breast
Frazier, W.—leg shot off at Gettysburg
Freeland, S.—CDR
Garrison, J.—RH, sense of smell
Garrison, R.G.—CDR & general disability
Gible, L.—parcial deefness
Gilchrist, D.—chronic indigestion
Gilmore, C.—POW 10 months Tyler Texas
Givens, J.H.—shot in foot
Gladwell, G.W.—RH
Gorden, J.W.★—spinal affection
Grable, S.B.—rupture
Graham, J.A.—POW Libby prison 3 months
Graham, J.A.—spinal injury, wounded left knee
Gribble, A.—RH also disease of head
Grimm, J.W.—HD & bleeding piles
Grimm, S.S.—piles
Grimm, T.—POW 10 months
Hall, B.F.—piles
Hall, E.T.—HD
Hall, F.M.—sciofula
Hall, W.F.—wounded in hand
Hamilton, P.—gunshot wound & general disability
Hammat, G.R.★—shot in the arm
Hardin, E.D.—piles
Harper, W.—head affected by shell in army
Haynes, C.—worsted by measles
Headley, H.—catarrah
Heath, F.—gunshot wound, gen disability, in bad condition
Heaton, H.C.—CDR & HD
Hedrick, I.Y.★—scurvy, lost all teeth
Henderson, I.M.—POW Andersonville, general disability 9 mo 19 days
Henthorne, A.W.—POW Libby prison
Herdman, J.W.—scrofula on shin bone

Hewett, W.A.—shot in right arm
Higgins, P.—loss of left eye, shot through hand
Hilfinger, J.—CDR & LD
Hill, J.G.—left hernie, concossion of head, par deffness
Hinman, I.K.—liver & stomach disease
Hogan, J.—gunshot left hip
Holbert, M.—RH & HD
Holland, L.W.—CDR
Holtz, L.—KD, broncal affection of throat
Hombeck, B.—disabled
Hopkins, T.B.—wounded left knee
Horr, J.T.—shot in left hand
Houser, G.B.—wounded right thigh & left knee
Huggins, J.J.—throat & lung trouble
Hughes, D.A.—lwmbago of back
Hull, J.F.—spinal disease
Hurst, L.J.—eyes effected badly
Huzen, S.S.—WIA
Jackson, E.H.—was in but a short time not over 1 year
Jacobs, J.H.—fracture left collarbone, gunshot right forearm
Johnson, E.—hearing gone
Johnson, M.—eyesight
Johnson, W.*—was with Gen. Morgan but could give no dates
Jones, W.H.—VV, DSC
Justice, E.—stranulated hernia 26 years
Kaufman, G.—RH
Keefer, J.J.—WIA right thigh, WIA twice left ankle
Kelley, A.—fistela in breast
Kesterson, G.W.—bronchitis
Kesterson, J.G.—injured testacle
Kimes, J.A.—wounded right leg
Kirk, W.—bone disease in ankle
Knels, W.S.—CDR & HD
Leach, J.A.—blind in one eye
Leavitt, C.P.—bleeding piles
Leavitt, G.E.—piles & RH
Lee, A.—enlargement of spleen & dispepsia
Lester, J.—POW 13 months, shot through right shoulder
Lidelle, W.W.—enlargement of veins
Locker, W.W.—shot in knee
Loers, T.J.*—neuralgia of the stomach
Lott, B.—VV from TYF
Lowers, H.*—gunshot wound in arm
Loyd, J.—consumption
Luthringer, J.A.—wounded in head
Lynch, W.A.—RH & eyesight, one eye entirely gone
Lyons, J.—ruptured

Lyons, Z.L.—liver complaint, RH
Mahke, F.J.H.—total disability
Mamel, H.—disabled by horse falling on him, lame breast
Mariet, B.F.—lame back from measles & weak eyes
Marquis, S.B.—RH
Matthews, B.—neuralgia & RH
May, C.—eyesight injured
McClain, H.—wounded right thigh
McClure, G.W.—pluracy of side, B shot wound
McConaughy, D.—injury to back
McCullick, A.—HD
McHaley, H.—gunshot wound in right breast
McKee, J.—RH
McKinney, H.B.—CDR, deaf right ear
McKusick, J.F.—POW Libby prison 3 months
McMullin, R.—HD, RH, piles
McMullin, U.—ague
McPeek, P.—CDR
McPherson, M.—lost my health caused by mumps
Medlen, W.—POW Libby, shot right side, ruptured
Meek, B.F.—POW 4 months Richmond Va ruptured
Mehl, A.—general disability
Melrose, S.—cold on measles
Melrose, W.H.—bronchitis
Metz, W.M.—struck by shell in back of neck
Miles, W.H.—blind for 20 years
Mills, J.*—lumbago of back
Miracle, J.—shot & other disability
Moore, J.—deafness & fall
Moore, R.T.—WIA at battle of Atlanta Georgia 7/22/64
Moore, W.W.—gunshot wounds in thigh, leg & knee
More, P.—CDR & skervy
Morris, W.H.—diseased eyes & kidneys
Mosena, F.—wounded in leg
Mulinex, J.—skirvy
Mullen, J.J.—HD & RH
Musser, S.D.—mind affected
Neece, J.—paralysis & scurvy
Nelson, D.—disability in back caused by mumps
Newlands, J.H.—MS
Noland, R.—moved to Frost Ohio
Nowery, J.D.—rupture
Nowery, W.R.—scurvy
Nugent, W.S.—SS
Offlighter, W.H.—spinal affection
Ogden, E.—rheumatic heart
Oliver, W.L.*—swelling of feet

Padgett, J.—RH
Parson, J.—partially blind
Pennybacker, J.B.*—lameness of back
Perry, H.W.—gunshot wound, rupture
Petit, J.L.—POW 4 months, general disability
Phillips, G.W.*—RH & skervy
Pierce, C.—struck by shell
Pifer, G.—partial deaf, breast & back pain
Piles, T.—asthma & catarrh
Pitman, J.—back injured
Poetlewait, U.—HD & verico ciel (?)
Pollock, R.S.—RH, hearing injured
Porter, D.R.—wounded in both legs
Postlethwait, J.N.—RH
Prettyman, J.J.—leg off
Prettyman, L.T.—stomach disease
Price, W.S.—wounds & CDR
Proffitt, S.N.—scrofala & HD, left shoulder badly affected
Province, J.—catarrh & neuralgia
Putnam, G.W.—gunshot wound & piles
Reed, A.—RH, stomach disease, liver complaint
Rice, J.B.—RH
Roberts, I.—ruptured left side, injured left hip
Roberts, J.T.—hearing injured
Robinson, D.—CDR
Roby, J.H.—POW Libby prison, wounded in head
Ross, J.G.—shot right leg
Rost, G.—enlargement of veins
Rouse, G.—POW 18 months
Rowell, T.—RH & HD
Rowley, T.—eyesight & kidney affection
Royers, J.T.—HD
Ruble, A.—HD
Ruble, H.H.—LD from measles
Ruble, J.A.—RH & weakness 27 years
Ruble, Jn.—injury of right hip caused by shoeing mule
Ruble, P.—RH
Ruder, J.R.—KD
Runion, S.C.—gunshot in back
Safford, J.H.—POW Houston Texas 3 months
Salow, W.E.—WIA left side
Sams, D.—piles
Sams, F.W.—weak eyes
Sams, J.W.—bronchitis
Sams, S.A.—crippled in knee
Sams, W.H.—piles & RH
Samw, G.W.—WIA right hip

Sattow, C.A.—hernia of left side
Sattow, F.—gunshot wound & other disabilities
Saxton, J.★—WIA right side, conscript
Schultz, O.—cramp colic that ended in flux & bloody piles
Scott, J.—hernia left side, lumbago
Seevers, J.J.—CDR & piles
Seleg, J.—CDR & crippled feet
Shafer, G.W.—lumbago of back & hips
Shaw, S.S.—gunshot right side & back
Sheets, J.A.—stomach disease & liver complaint
Sheets, N.—HD
Sheets, W.H.—RH
Sines, J.—CDR, complete fistula, piles
Smith, B.B.—parcial deafness & HD
Smith, J.A.—affection of eyes & asthma
Smith, J.D.—CDR & piles
Smith, J.H.—contracted ague leaving pain in side 2 years after
Smith, Jm.—deficient in sight 9 WVI
Smith, Joseph—partial blindness & HD
Smith, Sam—lumbago
Smith, So.—catarrh of head, affected eyes & hearing
Snider, A.—fever & ague
Spaque, T.J.—left leg badly fractured, concussion of brain
Spencer, J.E.—rupture
Spencer, W.P.—deff in left ear
Sprouse, W.—RH
Stafford, J.—third finger shot off
Stahley, A.J.—RH
Stalnaker, S.—POW 18 months, RH, stomach trouble, CDR
Stanley, H.F.—wound in left leg, RH from exposure
Staton, G.W.—CDR
Stayton, W.A.—RH
Steed, C.B.—shot through thigh & arm
Stephens, J.—RH, MS, in hospital 3 times
Stevens, L.—lumbago of back
Stewart, D.—neuralgia heart
Still, J.—piles, MS, rupture, thrown from a building (?)
Stukey, J.—POW Tyler Texas & one eye lost by scurvy
Suell, G.C.—HD
Swearengin, A.—RH
Tebay, J.M.—cancer on face
Thompson, A.J.—LD
Thompson, A.—sore eyes from measles, shot right leg & left hip
Tice, J.—HD
Tichnell, S.—total disability, veteran now crippled in bed
Tippens, E.—fever sore, catarrh
Townsand, P.—RH

Trader, A.—derangement of liver & piles
Traugh, M.V.—wounded in left hip
Tucker, J.K.—RH
Tucker, J.M.—catarrh & lung affection
Turner, L.H.—rupture & ribs mashed
Uhl, H.J.—RH
Vanney, J.O.—deafness & RH
Vanney, R.L.—eyes, RH & piles
Walker, J.G.—injured in right knee & side
Ware, C.A.—nasil catarrh
Warther, E.S.—WIA
Watkins, J.J.—piles & RH
Watson, J.—wounded right leg
Wauck, E.—hernia right side
Weekley, L.—POW Libby prison 1 month
Weigel, A.—wounded left foot
Wells, A.—right leg wounded by shell
Wells, P.*—CDR
West, S.—out on sick list
Wharton, I.—RH, lumbago, crippled left foot
Whipkey, F.—lumbago, HD, wound right knee
Whipkey, J.—loss of left leg at knee & RH
Whiston, J.—deafness
White, A.—urinary disease now totally disabled
Whitlatch, E.—eyesight injured, nearly blind
Whitlatch, W.P.—RH & spinal affection
Wigal, H.H.—blind & hernia both sides
Wigal, P.—lumbago of back & hip
Williams, C.P.—catarrh & throat disease, POW & parolled
Williams, W.H.—eye injured
Williamson, S.B.—catarrh of head
Williamson, S.—lumbago of back & invalid piles
Willis, A.J.—hernia & CDR
Willis, A.J.—LD from MS
Wingrove, W.H.—RH
Woolard, J.R.—POW 7 months Danville
Wright, G.W.—POW 29 days Bell Island
Yates, J.—RH 25 years
Yates, S.—liver complaint & KD, insanity, WIA at X—roads battle in right shoulder, WIA arm at Cold Harbor
Yocom, T.B.—CDR & HD

Wyoming County

NAME/RANK	REGIMENT	WHEN SERVED
Adams, James Pvt.	10 OHC	5/10/63–7/11/65
Barley, Theodore F. Lt.	22 VAI CSA	6/12/61–4/12/65
Bishop, Gotha Pvt.	14 KYA?	10/10/61–1/31/65
Bishop, Harvey Pvt.	7 WVC	9/64–7/65
Bishop, John	NF (31 VAI CSA?)	
Brooks, Andrew J. Sgt.	CS (45 BTN VAI)	9/22/62–12/63
Brown, Harvey C.	—(34 VAC CSA?)	62/65
Brown, James R. Cpl.	7 WVC	12/1/62–8/1/65
Brown, Wilson Pvt.	7 WVI	3/63–7/29/65
Browning, John W. Pvt.	7 WVC	12/19/61–8/1/65
Buchanan, Greenbury Pvt.	7 WVI	9/9/64–8/1/65
Cook, Ballard P. Pvt.	7 WVC	3/20/64–8/1/65
Cook, Daniel Pvt.	7 WVC	3/17/64–8/1/65
Cook, David J. Pvt.	7 WVC	9/3/64–8/1/65
Cook, Isaac E. Pvt.	(45 BTN VAI CS)	1861–NF
Cook, Lanes S. Pvt.	7 WVC	11/14/64–8/l/65
Cook, Pemberlon Pvt.	— WVC NF	
Cook, Perry L.	7 WVC	12/7/61–8/1/65
Cook, William B. Pvt.	7 WVC	12/7/61–8/1/65
Cook, Wm. H.H. Sgt.	4 WVC	6/15/63–7/10/64
also QM/Sgt	7 WVC	7/28/64–8/1/65
Cooper, Wm. H. Pvt.	7 WVC	12/19/61–8/1/65
Elkins, Wesley Pvt.	7 WVC	10/14/64–8/1/65
Farley, Wesley P.	NF (23 BTN VAI CSA)	
Goodman, Wm. C. Pvt.	39 KYI	62/65
Harper, Samuel Pvt.	8 VAI	62/65
Jones, Vasa B. Pvt.	23 OHI	6/25/64–5/25/65
Kirby, John H. Sgt.	4 NYA?	8/11/62–6/21/65
Lambert, Philip Pvt.	7 WVC	8/1/64–8/1/65
Lewis, Arglon Pvt.	CSA (30 VASS?)	62/65
Little, Thomas Pvt.	26 OHI?	4/20/62–8/20/62
Mangus, Joseph Pvt.	7 WVC	1/62–3/65
Miller, Anderson Pvt.	2 WVC	3/25/64–6/30/65
Milurn, Adison Pvt.	7 WVI	8/1/64–8/1/65
Peatt, Andrew J. Pvt.	91 OHI	8/11/62–6/20/65
Perdue, Nathaniel Pvt.	1 WVC	12/61–8/1/65
Perry, James M. Sgt.	7 WVC	12/4/62–8/1/65
Roby, Quinn? A. Sgt.	4 NY—	11/62–3/65
Rose, Edward Pvt.	8 VAI	2/1/62–8/15/65
Sarver, Wm. F. Pvt.	CSA (45 VAI)	NF
Sarver, Wm. T. Pvt.	CSA (45 VAI?)	
Shians?, Heinerm? Pvt.	16 VAC CSA	61/64

Sizemore, John Pvt.	7 WVC	12/15/61–8/1/65
Stewart, James C. Pvt.	7 WVC	11/17/61–8/1/65
Stewart, Wm. H. Pvt.	7 WVC	NF
Tiller, Wm. W.H. Pvt.	7 WVI	7/23/64–8/23/65
Walker, James B.	CSA (6 VARS)	NF
Walker, Thompson L.	23 BTN VAI CSA	62/65
Walker, Wm. Pvt.	8 WVI	1861–NF
Wanan?, Henry Pvt.	36 OHI	8/15/61–5/18/64
Wills, Enoch B. Pvt.	7 WVC	12/1/61–8/1/65
Workman, John A. Pvt.	45 VAI CSA	4/1/61–4/65

Wyoming County Remarks

Bishop, G.—piles, RH, eyesight impaired
Brown, W.—LD
Cook, B.P.—rupture
Cook, P.—weak back
Jones, V.B.—POW 7 months Libby & Danville
Kirby, J.H.—RH
Little, T.—catarrh, injured eyes (?)
Mangus, J.—SS, fully disabled (?)
Peatt, A.J.—HD
Perry, J.M.—LD, left side now paralyzed
Roby, Q.A.—at present 3/4 disabled
Rose, E.—disabled back from fever
Tiller, W.H.H.—KD, hearing is not good
Walker, T.L.*—POW Pt. Lookout

Index to Confederate Soldiers 1890 Veteran Census

(see county for complete citation)
abbreviations used:
UNK: unknown

County names:

Barbour: BR
Berkeley: BK
Boone: BN
Braxton: BX
Brooke: BO
Cabell: CB
Calhoun: CA
Clay: CL
Doddridge: DD
Fayette: FY
Gilmer: GL
Grant: GR
Greenbrier: GB
Hampshire: HP
Hancock: HK
Hardy: NONE
Harrison: HR
Jackson: JK
Jefferson: JF
Kanawha: KN
Lewis: LE
Lincoln: LC
Logan: LO
Marion: MR
Marshall: MS
Mason: MA
McDowell: Mc
Mercer: ME
Mineral: ML
Monongalia: MG
Monroe: MN

Morgan: MO
Nicholas: NC
Ohio: OH
Pendleton: PD
Pleasants: PL
Pocahontas: PO
Preston: PR
Putnam: PT
Raleigh: RA
Randolph: RD
Ritchie: RT
Roane: RO
Summers: SM
Taylor: TL
Tucker: TK
Tyler: TY
Upshur: UP
Wayne: WN
Webster: NONE
Wetzel: WT
Wirt: WI
Wood: WD
Wyoming: WY

Confederate

Adkins, A.	34VAC	LC
Adkins, A.	45VAI	CB
Adkins, A.	45VAI	WN
Adkins, B.	50TNI	BN
Adkins, B.	?VAI	LC
Adkins, E.	45VAI	LC
Adkins, H.	17VAC	RA
Adkins, J.	30VASS	SM
Adkins, J.	34VAC	WN
Adkins, J.H.	129VAM	LC
Adkins, P.	19VAC	RA
Adkins, P.	34VAC	ME
Adkins, R.	45VAI	RA
Adkins, S.	30VASS	RA
Adkins, W.E.	62VAI	WN
Agle, G.B.	UNK	BK
Aguire, C.E.	21VAI	MN
Akers, H.H.	Fry's VAA	ME
Akers, N.B.	60VAI	ME
Akers, W.T.	24VAI	KN
Alkire, D.M.	25VAI	GL
Allen, G.W.	60VAI	GL
Allen, G.W.	Bryan's VAA	GB
Allen, J.G.	Thurmonds VARG	ME
Allen, J.H.	13VAI	KN
Altopp, E.	19VAC	GL
Ambrose, C.B.	41VAC	BK
Ambrose, J.W.	2VAI	BK
Amick, J.	14VAC	NC
Amick, J.M.	60VAI	NC
Anderson, E.C.	63VAI	PR
Anderson, J.D.	UNK	BK
Anderson, S.M.	37VAC	KN
Anderson, W.L.	27VAI	BX
Ankrum, W.R.	22VAI	CL
Apperson, J.R.	31VAI	PO
Arbogast, G.W.	25VAI	RD
Armstrong, J.M.	Jone's VAA	KN
Armuntrout, S.	18VAC	GR
Asbury, J.H.	24VAI	Mc
Ashcraft, P.	19VAC	DD
Astep, M.	22VAI	KN
Atchison, G.W.	31VAI	TY

Atkinson, C.T.	18 VAI	PR
Aued, T.	UNK	BK
Ault, J.	46 VAM	PD
Ault, I.	46 VAM	PD
Bagnett, W.	UNK	BK
Baisden, J.	25 VAI	LC
Balford, W.H.H.	18 VAC	BX
Ball, J.W.	30 VASS	MA
Ball, W.H.	20 VAC	WD
Barker, J.	13 VAC	BN
Barley, T.F.	22 VAI	WY
Barnett, J.	8 VAC	MA
Bart, P.B.	46 VAC	RD
Basham, J.	60 VAI	ME
Baylor, A.J.	52 VAI	TL
Beall, J.T.	20 VAC	MR
Bean, G.	18 VAC	GR
Beck, J.	5 VAI	MN
Beckman, L.	1 VAI	HP
Beckner, O.C.	28 VAI	TK
Belcher, J.F.	26 VAI	Mc
Bell, J.W.	1 VAI	CA
Bennet, S.	31 NCI	BK
Bennett, E.	25 VAI	PD
Bennett, J.G.	11 VAC	PR
Bennett, L.L.	27 NCI	WI
Bennett, M.	4 VAI	OH
Bennett, M.V.	25 VAI	RD
Benson, J.D.	41 VAI	PR
Bergdall, H.	UNK	GR
Berkley, R.	11 VAI	MG
Berry, H.N.	14 VARS	ML
Berry, J.M.	25 VAI	BX
Berry, J.W.	62 VAI	BX
Berry, P.B.	62 VAI	BX
Berry, T.J.	25 VAI	BX
Beverage, J.M.	62 VAI	PO
Beverage, L.	62 VAI	PO
Bias, W.A.	36 VAC	PT
Bibby, R.	59 VAI	KN
Bicknele, A.	2 NCI	ME
Bird, C.W.	162 VAM	KN
Bird, J.N.	31 VAI	MO
Bird, J.W.	31 VAI	BX
Bishop, J.	31 VAI	WY
Black, F.J.	20 VAC	WT
Black, G.W.	27 VAI	JF

Blackwood, W.R.	45 VAI	KN
Blake, C.S.	22 VAI	PT
Blake, J.J.	62 VAI	BX
Blakemore, W.	6 WLA	MS
Blankenship, J.	22 VAI	GB
Blankenship, J.	34 VAC	WN
Blankinship, S.J.	31 VAI	BO
Bly, W.E.	7 VAA	ML
Bodin, T.	2 VAI	BK
Bodkin, H.B.	62 VAI	RD
Bodkin, M.	62 VAI	RD
Boggs, T.	19 VAC	RO
Boley, W.M.	36 VAI	NC
Boon, J.A.	26 VAI	GB
Booth, F.M.	16 VAC	WN
Booth, F.M.	8 VAC	WN
Bowen, D.M.	8 VAC	WN
Bowling, C.A.	60 VAI	ME
Bowls, J.W.	24 VAI	PT
Bowman, P.	37 VAI	HP
Bown, T.	7 VA-	BK
Bragg, E.S.	25 VAI	BX
Brammly, J.A.	6 VAI	GL
Branan, J.S.	19 VAC	RO
Brant, M.M.	26 VAI	GB
Bright, J.E.	18 VAC	PO
Browning, J.	34 VAC	LC
Brown, J.	8 VAC	NC
Brown, H.C.	34 VAC	WY
Browning, F.	129 VAM	LC
Brownning, M.	36 VAI	LC
Bronough, E.	36 VAI	PT
Brookman, D.	27 VAI	GB
Brooks, A.J.	45 VAI	WY
Brooks, D.	UNK	DD
Brooks, J.	19 VAC	RT
Broun, H.S.	9 LAI	HR
Brown, A.S.	17 VAC	BX
Brown, D.S.	34 VAI	ML
Brown, G.W.	25 VAI	WD
Brown, J.	14 VAC	MA
Brown, J.	8 VAC	NC
Brown, J.F.	2 VAI	JF
Browning, C.	36 VAC	LC
Browning, J.	36 VAC	LC
Browning, M.B.	39 KYC	LC
Brummage, I.	20 VAC	MR

Brumba, D.	UNK	BK
Brumfield, J.S.	?VAC	LC
Brumfield, P.	UNK	LC
Bryan, R.	36 VAI	PT
Bryan, W.L.	36 VAI	PT
Bryant, J.	129 VAM	LC
Buchanan, G.	23 VAI	ME
Buchanan, J.A.	45 VAI	LO
Buckner, J.M.	19 VAC	KN
Burdett, J.	22 VAI	PT
Burford, A.J.	36 VAI	PT
Burge, E.	46 VAC	MS
Burk, J.H.	7 VAI	GL
Burke, T.G.	8 VAC	TK
Burton, E.	60 VAI	ME
Burtram, S.	33 VAI	BK
Bush, G.A.	19 VAC	GL
Bush, G.S.	19 VAC	GL
Bush, S.L.	19 VAC	GL
Bussey, E.	20 VAC	HR
Butcher, M.	26 VAC	BX
Cage, J.D.	2 VAI	BK
Callaway, J.M.	34 VAC	BO
Callison, I.A.	60 VAI	GB
Callison, M.	60 VAI	GB
Camey, J.V.	17 VAC	BK
Campbell, L.	60 VAI	WD
Canterberry, S.H.	22 VAI	KN
Cantrell, A.	10 VAC	PT
Carlin, G.	18 VAC	BX
Carpenter, A.	60 VAI	JK
Carson, J.A.	62 VAI	PR
Cart, J.W.	22 VAI	KN
Carter, J.	22 VAI	MA
Caseboalt, G.M.	60 VAI	GB
Cash, G.W.	19 VAA	CB
Castard, G.W.	33 VAI	HR
Champ, A.	46 VAM	PD
Champion, C.H.	UNK	NC
Chandler, J.D.	52 VAI	WD
Chapman, J.W.	22 VAI	NC
Cheuvront, J.	36 VAI	CA
Chort, F.	7 VAC	OH
Clark, E.	34 VAC	ME
Clark, H.	23 VAI	ME
Clayton, E.B.	20 VAC	MR
Clayton, M.H.	31 VAI	ML

Clevenger, S.L.	62 VAI	RT
Cline, J.	34 VAC	KN
Coberly, A.M.	19 VAC	GL
Coger, J.	62 VAI	BX
Collins, H.	1 TNC	PO
Collins, J.O.	36 VAI	GL
Collins, L.	34 VAC	LC
Collins, S.	3 SCI	RT
Combs, A.	11 VAC	PO
Combs, J.L.E.	1 VAC	BK
Conaway, J.E.	31 VAI	MR
Coney, G.	22 VAI	KN
Conred, J.	62 NCI	HR
Cook, C.	3 KYC	PO
Cook, G.W.	17 VAC	ME
Cook, I.E.	45 VAI	WY
Cooper, J.L.	60 VAI	GL
Cooper, J.M.	60 VAI	GL
Copenhaver, J.D.	2 VAI	BK
Cordill, A.	63 VAI	KN
Cornelius, W.	55 VAI	MA
Correll, W.M.	14 VAC	GB
Cottrill, E.	14 VAC	GL
Courtney, T.	18 VAC	PO
Courtney, J.N.	20 VAC	RD
Crabtree, J.D.	63 VAI	HP
Craivford, E.	31 VAI	RD
Crane, C.L.	14 VAC	GB
Crawford, J.	45 VAI	MA
Cremeans, L.	22 VAI	MR
Crist, W.	Jackson's VAA	WD
Crites, D.	11 VAC	GR
Cross, D.W.	7 VAC	BK
Cross, E.W.	62 VAI	WD
Crossom, J.	26 VAC	WD
Croy, I.	36 VAI	ME
Crump, R.	UNK	BK
Cuff, S.J.	5 VAI	DD
Cummings, J.	27 VAI	CB
Cummings, W.	31 VAI	BX
Cunningham, W.L.	1 VAC	BK
Cunningham, B.	22 VAI	MR
Cunningham, G.W.	36 VAC	WT
Cunningham, H.G.	18 VAC	RD
Cunningham, J.A.	18 VAI	DD
Cunningham, J.N.	1 VAC	BK
Cunningham, J.W.	7 VAC	ML

Cunningham, T.B.	62 VAI	BX
Cunningham, T.	62 VAI	PD
Currence, J.	31 VAI	RD
Currence, L.D.	25 VAI	BX
Curry, A.C.	31 VAI	PO
Curtis, J.P.	20 VAC	WD
Dakins, M.C.	UNK	DD
Damron, S.D.	8 VAC	WN
Darn, S.S.	3 MSA	MR
Davidson, I.S.	19 VAC	GL
Davis, A.	17 VAC	BX
Davis, A.W.	18 VAC	GR
Davis, J.	36 VAI	BO
Davis, J.	31 VAI	CA
Davis, J.	36 VAC	LC
Davis, J.	36 VAI	CA
Davis, J.	45 VAI	WN
Davis, J.R.	10 VAC	MS
Davis, L.	45 VAI	WN
Davis, M.	17 VAC	JK
Davis, R.C.	22 VAI	NC
Davis, W.	45 VAI	WN
Davis, W.H.	17 VAC	DD
Davis, W.T.	17 VAC	KN
Deal, M.V.B.	129 VAM	PT
Dean, H.	46 VAM	PD
Deck, E.C.	2 VAI	BK
Deem, I.	6 VAI	WD
Defoe, W.A.	34 VAC	WN
Deitz, J.	79 VAI	GB
Delay, W.T.	18 VAC	GR
Demoss, N.D.	19 VAC	WD
Dempsey, J.H.	8 VAC	NC
Dennison, J.	19 VAC	GL
Depriest, J.	79 VAM	GB
Detter, J.L.	UNK	BK
Dewese, D.	19 VAC	GL
Dicken, T.	24 VAC	HP
Dilley, J.	19 VAC	PO
Dingess, H.	36 VAC	LC
Dodd, A.A.	8 VAC	ME
Dolan, J.T.	1 VAI	RT
Dolly, T.J.	46 VAM	PD
Donald, E.M.	UNK	BK
Donnelly, J.H.	2 VAI	OH
Dorsey, J.A.	16 VAI	JF
Downs, J.S.	6 VAC	MR

Doyle, W.	UNK	ML
Draggoo, E.W.	20 VAC	JK
Drew, H.	UNK	BK
Drummond, P.	19 VAI	BX
Duemagan, L.D.	UNK	ME
Dugan, J.F.	2 VAI	BK
Dugan, J.W.	2 VAI	WD
Dulin, J.M.	7 VAI	PR
Dunbar, J.M.	22 VAI	KN
Duncan, D.J.	26 VAI	MA
Duncan, G.W.	25 VAI	MA
Duncan, W.H.	8 VAC	MS
Dunn, J.	26 VAI	MA
Dunn, J.	27 VAC	MA
Duty, W.	36 VAI	LC
Dye, C.	19 VAC	KN
Dyer, J.J.	62 VAI	BX
Eads, J.H.	26 VAI	MN
Echard, J.	27 VAI	TK
Edifards, T.	8 VAC	PT
Edman, J.J.	UNK	GL
Elexander, L.	67 VAM	WN
Eliott, J.	Byrnes KYA	LC
Elkins, A.	34 VAC	LC
Ellis, J.H.	UNK	FY
Ellison, N.	19 VAC	CA
Ellyson, R.F.	62 VAC	GL
Emricilcl C.	17 VAC	WD
Emrick, C.L.	17 VAC	WD
Epling, L.A.	36 VAI	ME
Erving, L.	36 VAI	LC
Estep, J.	13 KYC	LO
Evans, J.	129 VAM	JK
Eye, C.	36 VAI	NC
Farley, W.P.	23 VAI	WY
Farnsworth, F.L.	2 MOC	UP
Farr, J.A.	18 MSI	WD
Faulkner, G.	17 VAC	ME
Ferguson, C.D.	57 VAI	KN
Ferguson, E.R.	34 VAC	ME
Ferguson, J.H.	10 VAC	WN
Ferguson, S.	8 VAC	WN
Ferguson, S.J.	8 VAC	WN
Ferrell, H.A.	46 VAC	CA
Ficher, H.	24 VAC	OH
Fife, J.F.	36 VAI	PT
Fife, W.E.	36 VAI	PT

Name	Unit	Code
Finnegan, J.H.	18 VAC	BX
Fisher, C.	22 VAI	GB
Fitzgerald, G.W.	50 VAI	GB
Fitzgerald, W.	20 VAC	OH
Fleshmn, V.R.	14 VAC	GB
Fletcher, B.E.	19 VAC	MR
Ford, M.	14 VAC	GB
Fortex, J.B.	UNK	BK
Fowler, J.P.	1 VAC	LC
Fowler, W.T.	129 VAM	LC
Frank, T.J.	UNK	GL
Frasher, W.H.	8 VAC	WN
Freeman, W.L.	23 VAI	WD
Freeze, A.J.	1 VAC	BK
Friedrich, F.C.	UNK	OH
Friel, J.T.	62 VAI	PO
Fry, L.	1 VAC	LC
Fry, V.B.	45 VAI	WN
Full, Z.E.	19 VAC	WD
Furbee, J.	20 VAC	WR
Furguson, P.S.	UNK	CB
Ga,Ahrop, J.W.	25 VAI	BR
Gabert, J.L.	14 VAC	GB
Gadd, A.P.	23 VAI	ME
Galford, T.	19 VAC	PO
Garlic, J.F.	4 TNC	ME
Garnette, J.E.	5 VAI	KN
Gasman, J.	2 VAC	BK
Gatewood, A.C.	11 VAC	PO
Gatrell, J.W.	25 VAI	DD
Gaughan, J.	— LAA	MR
Gawthrop, J.A.	119 VAM	HR
Gay, H.B.	20 VAC	PO
Gay, J.C.	62 VAI	PO
Gay, L.	31 VAI	PO
Gay, S.M.	31 VAI	PO
Geiger, G.	62 VAI	PO
George, B.	36 VAI	PT
Giboney, L.C.	46 VAC	PL
Gibson, J.H.	45 VAI	PT
Glover, W.H.	2 VAC	PR
Godby, J.	7 VAC	JK
Golden, R.W.	10 VAC	DD
Goodwin, P.	8 VAC	WN
Gorden, J.W.	20 VAA	WD
Gorden, T.G.	1 VAC	LC
Gordon, M.W.	42 VAC	PO

Gouldizen, W.W.	18 VAC	GR
Gragg, J.	20 VAC	GL
Graham, K.	25 VAI	PD
Grass, E.	1 VAI	DD
Graves, W.M.	26 VAC	RO
Greenway, J.	54 VAI	KN
Gregg, H.	62 VAI	CA
Gregory, A.B.	62 VAI	BX
Grinn, J.V.	2 VAI	BK
Gulley, J.N.	20 VAC	DD
Gwinn, J.	2 VAI	BK
Haden, F.	7 LAI	PT
Hall, F.M.	14 VAC	WD
Hall, T.A.	27 VAI	GB
Hall, W.J.	24 VAI	KN
Halpin, R.J.	12 VAC	MS
Halstead, W.A.	22 VAI	NC
Halthrop, A.J.	31 VAI	DD
Hamaker, J.P.	50 VAI	FY
Hamilton, J.M.	20 VAC	KN
Hammons, M.	BX Guard	RD
Hammt, J.W.	46 VAC	WD
Hanna, A.M.	14 VAC	GB
Hannah, S.C.	UNK	PO
Hanshaw, S.S.	22 VAI	KN
Harding, G.	41 VAI	HP
Harlow, E.B.	UNK	BK
Harlow, J.A.	12 VAA	MR
Harlow, M.	26 VAC	BK
Harman, D.H.	46 VAM	PD
Harman, E.	47 VAI	UP
Harman, E.	46 VAM	PD
Harman, J.	46 VAM	PD
Harman, J.H.	46 VAM	PD
Harmann, W.	2 VAI	BK
Harness, G.S.	McNeill's VARG	GR
Harness, H.C.	5 MOC	GR
Harrel, A.C.	31 NCC	OH
Harrffnat, G.R.	26 VAC	WD
Harris, E.S.	6 NCI	HK
Harris, G.	31 VAI	BK
Harris, J.	2 VAI	JF
Harris, J.D.	UNK	BK
Harris, Z.	17 VAC	GL
Harrison, S.P.	2 VAC	BK
Hatcher, E.H.	23 VAI	ME
Hawes, H.W.	27 VAI	FY

Hayes, B.	60 VAI	GB
Hays, J.F.	2 VAI	BK
Heavner, A.	62 VAC	GR
Heck, J.W.	UNK	BK
Heck, W.S.	25 VAI	BX
Hedges, B.S.	1 VAA	BK
Hedrick, H.C.	46 VAM	PD
Hedrick, I.Y.	62 VAI	WD
Hedricks, A.J.	46 VAM	PD
Hefling, J.L.	47 VAI	WD
Hefner, A.G.	26 VAI	PO
Helmick, A.	62 VAI	TK
Helmick, I.	20 VAC	MR
Helmick, M.	62 VAI	TK
Helmick, M.	46 VAM	PD
Henry, J.	31 VAI	GL
Henry, J.B.	12 VAI	BK
Hevitt, R.R.	UNK	GL
Hickle, J.W.	13 VAI	ML
Hicknan, B.	25 VAI	RT
Hicks, J.	UNK	BK
Higgins, S.C.	31 VAI	PO
Hight, A.J.	UNK	KN
Hilkey, W.I.	17 VAC	GR
Hill, A.B.	14 VAC	TK
Hill, A.J.	Chapman's VAA	MA
Hill, I.	8 VAC	PT
Hill, W.B.	18 VAC	GR
Hingle, J.	62 VAI	BK
Hinkle, A.S.	60 VAI	GB
Hiser, J.	62 VAI	GR
Hite, C.A.	12 VAC	BK
Hively, J.	62 VAI	RO
Hogbin, J.C.	18 VAC	GR
Hoke, C.C.	19 VAC	GB
Hollida, J.W.	1 VAC	BK
Hoover, G.	62 VAI	GL
Horner, J.D.	20 VAC	MR
Houchins, G.H.	30 VAI	ME
Hubbard, P.A.	23 VAI	ME
Huff, E.	5 VAC	KN
Huffman, S.	58 VAM	PD
Huggins, W.H.	36 VAI	PO
Hull, J.	2 VAI	BK
Hull, W.C.	60 VAI	PO
Hunter, C.W.	44 VAI	WT
Hunter, R.	1 VSL	BN

Hunter, W.	26 VAI	WN
Hurt, E.F.	3 VARS	KN
Huston, J.	28 VAI	RO
Hutchinson, W.	36 VAI	WN
Hutton, I.W.	18 VAC	GR
Hyson, B.F.	19 VAC	RT
Irvine, G.R.	19 VAC	PO
Irvine, J.W.	18 VAC	PO
Jack, W.O.	31 VAI	PO
Jackson, J.	4 VAI	PO
James, D.C.	17 VAC	WD
James, S.	8 VAC	WN
Jarrell, J.	36 VAC	BN
Jarvis, W.	108 VAM	CB
Jewel, J.G.	45 VAI	ME
Johns, W.L.	19 VAC	JK
Johnson, A.N.	Lurty's VAA	RT
Johnson, E.W.	64 VAI	JF
Johnson, G.A.	6 VAC	HR
Johnson, H.W.	45 VAI	MR
Johnson, J.	14 VAC	BX
Johnson, J.	34 VAC	WN
Johnson, W.	UNK	WD
Johnston, M.	25 VAI	RD
Jones, A.F.	22 VAI	CL
Jones, C.W.	25 VAI	BX
Jones, D.	10 VAC	RO
Jones, F.M.	62 VAI	BX
Jones, J.W.	44 VAI	BX
Jones, S.	1 VAC	JF
Jordan, S.J.	Pegram's VAA	MA
Jordan, W.D.	11 VAC	PO
Judy, J.	McNeill's VARG	GR
Judy, Z.	46 VAM	RD
Kanode, M.	UNK	MA
Keaton, J.L.	36 VAC	PT
Kee, G.M.	36 VAC	PO
Kellar, J.M.	19 VAC	TY
Kelley, A.J.	60 VAI	KN
Kelly, W.C.	64 VAI	Mc
Kerfoot, J.W.	2 VAI	BK
Ketterman, W.W.	46 VAM	PD
Keusel, J.J.	UNK	BK
Keyser, D.	11 VAC	KN
Keyser, H.	11 VAC	KN
Kile, G.W.	46 VAM	PD
Kile, I.	18 VAC	RD

Kilmer, N.D.	1 VAC	BK
Kimble, A.	46 VAM	PD
Kimble, Ad.	46 VAM	PD
Kimble, J.	62 VAI	GR
Kincaid, A.	10 VAC	GB
King, J.M.	54 VAI	ME
Kisamore, A.J.	46 VAM	PD
Kisamore, J.	46 VAM	PD
Kittle, S.B.	62 VAI	RD
Klaus, J.	1 TXA	MA
Knopp, H.	17 VAC	JK
Knopp, J.A.	10 VAC	FY
Knox, S.A.	8 MSC	WT
Kramer, P.	18 VAC	PO
Kreglow, G.T.	2 VAI	BK
Kuhl, C.	31 VAI	GL
Kusser, D.	1 VAC	LC
Lackey, S.	UNK	LO
Lafaye, J.A.	Manigault's SCA	RT
Lainy, L.	22 VAC	BK
Lake, V.	Hunshell's VAC	BX
Lambert, H.	36 VAI	LC
Lambert, J.G.	25 VAI	RD
Lancaster, J.J.	13 VAA	JF
Lanham, C.C.	36 VAC	KN
Lardon, M.	UNK	BK
Laundress, E.	UNK	TL
Lawhorn, J.M.	14 VAC	PT
Layton, D.M.	25 VAI	GB
Lee, J.H.	49 VAI	SM
Legg, J.W.	14 VAC	GB
Lewis, A.	30 VASS	WY
Lemen, W.	1 VAC	BK
Lemowith, W.N.	2 VAI	BK
Leonard, G.	1 VAC	WT
Lester, A.	54 VAI	Mc
Lett, A.	1 VAC	WN
Lewis, A.	20 VAC	RO
Lewis, G.H.	14 VAC	GB
Licklider, J.	12 VAC	BK
Lieberman, C.A.	1 LAZ	ML
Liggon, J.	19 VAC	PO
Lilly, J.	23 VAI	ME
Lilly, J.E.	23 VAI	ME
Lilly, J.W.	23 VAI	ME
Lilly, R.B.	23 VAI	ME
Lilly, W.H.	36 VAI	ME

Lilly, W.P.	17 VAC	ME
Livesay, G.W.	60 VAI	GB
Long, J.L.	25 VAI	MG
Lough, A.B.	25 VAI	BX
Lough, D.	46 VAM	PD
Lough, F.M.	25 VAI	BX
Lough, G.A.	62 VAI	PD
Lough, J.V.	25 VAI	BX
Lough, S.H.	46 VAM	PD
Louk, J.E.	52 VAI	PO
Lowers, H.	19 VAC	WD
Lowers, T.J.	19 VAC	WD
Lowers, T.J.	19 VAC	WD
Lowers, W.H.	19 VAC	WD
Lucas, A.F.	20 VAC	RT
Lucas, E.	10 VAC	BK
Lurty, R.D.	20 VAC	DD
Lynch, J.	22 VAI	KN
Lynch, J.	31 VAI	JK
Lynn, W.H.	26 VAI	KN
Lyon, J.D.	23 VAI	ME
Maag, H.	15 TNI	MR
Mabe, M.	53 NCI	PT
Mace, J.	McNeill's VARG	GR
Malcom, J.A.	36 VAI	NC
Mallow, A.	46 VAM	PD
Manor, C.W.	2 VAI	BK
Marcum, J.M.	45 VAI	WN
Markham, T.H.	1 VAI	PT
Marks, E.	19 VAC	GL
Marshall, G.W.	1 VAC	BK
Marshall, M.	1 VAC	BK
Martain, S.	58 VAI	KN
Martin, G.W.	26 VAI	BK
Martin, J.	36 VAI	NC
Martin, J.T.	12 VAI	MR
Maryman, V.C.	21 VAI	DD
Mason, J.S.	Hoole's MSA	KN
Mason, R.J.	19 VAC	MR
Mason, T.	36 VAC	PT
Mason, T.J.	10 VAC	KN
Matheny, J.A.	10 VAC	KN
Matthews, B.F.	46 VAI	BK
Mattox, A.G.	16 VAC	PT
Mayhue, G.	62 VAC	ML
Mayo, W.T.	62 VAI	UP
Mayse, J.H.	27 VAI	JK

Maze, A.C.	17 VAC	CA
Maze, G.W.	19 VAC	CA
McAdams, J.	UNK	OH
McAlpin, J.W.	19 VAC	PO
McBride, T.	60 VAI	ME
McBride, T.W.	34 VAC	ME
McBride, J.	57 VAI	ME
McCallester, P.	UNK	MA
McCallister, J.W.	10 VAI	RD
McCann, P.	26 VAI	FY
McClanahn, T.A.	36 VAI	FY
McClintic, W.H.	19 VAC	PO
McClung, A.J.	36 VAI	NC
McClung, A.P.	14 VAC	GB
McClung, C.	14 VAC	GB
McClung, C.R.	27 VAI	GB
McClung, W.W.	22 VAI	NC
McCoy, D.	22 VAI	PT
McCoy, S.	36 VAI	PT
McDewell, J.D.	2 VAI	PT
McDonald, E.	3 VAI	GL
McDowell, C.	2 VAC	BK
McElwee, F.L.	20 VAC	RD
McFarland, E.	UNK	OH
McGlaughlin, A.	19 VAC	PO
McGlaughlin, G.H.	19 VAC	PO
McGuire, C.E.	36 VAI	WD
McGuire, J.S.	36 VAI	WD
McIntire, I.	5 AKI	WD
McKendric, S.	16 VAC	CB
McLaughlin, N.	7 VAC	PT
McMillan, J.P.	UNK	DD
McMillion, J.W.	60 VAI	GB
McNeil, J.M.	22 VAI	PO
McNeill, C.	31 VAI	PO
McNemar, W.B.	18 VAC	LE
McNorman, C.	2 VAC	GL
Meadar, C.T.	2 VAC	ME
Meadar, G.W.	23 VAI	NE
Meadar, L.	23 VAI	ME
Meadows, S.D.	34 VAC	ME
Meek, W.	8 VAC	LC
Meeks, J.W.	22 VAI	RD
Merchant, J.	89 VAM	BK
Merill, J.H.	UNK	TK
Metheny, G.W.	Chapman's VAA	MA
Middleton, J.A.	62 VAI	PD

Milam, W.T.	36 VAC	KN
Miles, J.T.	— VAI	BK
Miller, H.	89 VAM	BK
Miller, H.A.	2 VAC	BK
Miller, J.	46 VAM	PD
Miller, J.A.	2 VAI	BK
Miller, J.M.	52 VAI	PO
Miller, J.T.	8 VAC	CB
Miller, L.	36 VAI	CB
Mills, H.G.	23 VAI	ME
Mills, J.	17 VAC	WD
Mills, J.A.	16 VAC	HR
Mills, R.	8 VAC	FY
Mitchell, E.	23 VAI	KN
Moats, J.	62 VAI	TL
Moller, R.V.	12 VAC	JF
Monroe, J.W.	UNK	HR
Montgomery, J.H.	11 VAI	WD
Mooney, R.	52 VAI	OH
Mooney, W.	52 VAI	OH
Moore, A.	62 VAI	GL
Moore, C.	18 VAC	JK
Moore, G.W.	34 VAC	WN
Moore, J.S.	19 VAC	PO
Moore, M.	22 VAI	CL
Moore, M.L.	31 VAI	PO
Moore, S.	2 VAI	JF
Moore, S.A.	19 VAC	PO
Moore, T.M.	19 VAC	PO
Moran, J.	62 VAI	MG
More, C.	29 VAI	WN
More, J.	19 VAC	RO
Morgan, J.	24 VAI	KN
Morgan, J.S.	20 VAC	MR
Morgan, S.E.	20 VAC	WD
Morris, G.S.	62 VAI	MR
Morris, W.H.	7 VAC	KN
Morrison, W.H.	12 VAI	WD
Morrow, D.M.	19 VAC	HR
Moss, O.C.	19 VAC	BX
Moten, J.W.	11 VAI	ME
Mounts, C.W.	45 BTN VAI	LO
Mounts, Wm. H.	45 BTN VAI	LO
Mulens, H.	34 VAC	TIC
Mulens, V.B.	Swann's VAC	LC
Mullins, M.	19 VAC	RD
Mulvy, M.	31 VAI	BX

Murdock, J.A.	34 VAC	KN
Murphey, H.	34 VAC	KN
Murphy, A.C.	62 VAI	BX
Murphy, J.	25 VAI	Mc
Murphy, J.W.	6 VAI	WD
Murphy, W.F.	42 VAI	FY
Mussells, P.	UNK	BK
Myers, J.S.	25 VAI	BK
Myers, S.B.	62 VAI	BX
Myers, W.H.	12 VAC	BK
Myles, R.C.	14 VAC	GB
Myrtle, W.R.	52 VAI	OH
Nelson, D.	36 VAC	WD
Nelson, S.H.	10 VAI	GR
Nichels, A.J.	28 VAI	KN
Nicholas, M.	60 VAI	GB
Nikon, T.	27 VAI	BK
Nipe, J.P.	2 VAI	BK
Nixon, W.	6 VAI	WD
Nixon, W.	62 VAI	OH
Nokner, J.C.	12 LA-	BK
Noll, W.T.	1 VAC	BK
Norris, J.	25 VAI	BX
Oaks, J.	9 VAI	ME
Oaks, W.	9 VAI	ME
Ochletree, W.	62 VAI	BX
Offlighter, W.H.	52 VAI	WD
Ogden, B.	49 VAI	FY
Oliver, W.L.	44 VAI	WD
Osborne, S.	16 VAC	WN
Ovesholt, R.E.	36 VAC	PO
Owens, J.W.	1 MDA	BK
Oxier, L.	22 VAI	RD
Pack, J.A.	Swann's VAC	LO
Padgett, J.J.	11 VAI	KN
Parker, T.J.	37 VAC	MO
Parsons, A.H.	11 VAC	GR
Parsons, G.W.	45 VAI	WN
Parsons, J.W.	18 VAC	RD
Pate, A.	58 VAI	MN
Patterson, J.A.	23 VAC	MA
Payne, G.	19 VAC	FY
Payne, J.D.	67 VAM	PD
Payne, T.	2 VAI	BK
Paynter, W.	36 VAC	KN
Pearcy, A.F.	20 VAC	GL
Pease, F.G.	20 VAC	WD

Peck, J.	31 VAI	RT
Pegram, P.	8 VAC	MA
Pennington, G.W.	7 VAC	ME
Pennybacker, B.Y.	20 VAC	WD
Pennybacker, H.H.	20 VAC	WD
Pennybacker, J.B.	20 VAC	WD
Pennybaker, B.R.	17 VAC	WD
Perkins, P.	26 VAC	GL
Perry, I.G.	36 VAI	LC
Perry, J.R.	26 VAI	FY
Perry, L.D.	36 VAI	FY
Perry, N.	8 VAC	WN
Persinger, J.L.	26 VAI	BX
Peters, J.A.	2 MDI	PR
Phares, W.	46 VAM	PD
Phillips, A.G.	31 VAI	TK
Phillips, G.	62 VAI	BR
Phillips, G.W.	19 VAC	WD
Phillips, G.W.	31 VAI	BX
Phillips, J.F.	22 VAI	MA
Pickering, J.	10 VAC	GB
Pickering, M.W.	54 VAI	KN
Pitzer, C.A.	60 VAI	KN
Pitzer, E.M.	12 VAC	BK
Plant, J.J.	1 MDI	OH
Poe, J.L.	20 VAC	TY
Porter, C.	25 TNI	MN
Porter, C.	7 VAI	JF
Post, A.	20 VAC	MO
Preston, D.	8 VAC	WN
Price, H.D.	4 VAI	ME
Price, J.B.	19 VAC	KN
Price, J.C.	19 VAC	PO
Price, J.H.	19 VAC	PO
Price, J.W.	19 VAC	PO
Price, J.W.	60 VAI	GB
Price, S.	19 VAC	KN
Prine, J.D.	19 VAC	HR
Pritt, H.S.	31 VAI	RD
Puse, R.R.	UNK	GB
Queen, A.A.M.	17 VAC	BX
Rader, A.C.	22 VAI	NC
Rader, C.G.	20 VAC	RD
Rader, C.H.	7 VAC	GB
Rader, M.	22 VAI	NC
Radford, W.	166 VAM	KN
Raitt, T.	36 VAI	LE

Ramsey, S.	24 VAI	WN
Ratliff, J.	24 VAI	LC
Ratliff, J.A.	34 VAC	PO
Ratliff, J.M.	5 VAI	PO
Ratliff, T.M.	17 VAC	SM
Raymond, E.	Ast/Sgn	GB
Rayner, A.	24 NCI	PT
Read, J.	UNK	
Reaser, J.	26 VAI	GL
Reaser, S.S.	26 VAI	GL
Redden, W.	60 VAI	RA
Reed, J.B.	58 VAI	ME
Reed, V.A.	20 VAC	PL
Regents, J.R.	UNK	MA
Reid, G.W.	27 VAI	KN
Rex, E.H.	31 VAI	MR
Rexrode, H.	14 VAM	PD
Reynolds, W.F.	27 VAI	ML
Rhea, C.A.	31 VAI	PO
Rhea, J.B.	18 VAC	PO
Riblett, G.J.	19 VAC	HR
Riddle, C.	UNK	BK
Riddleberger, W.	UNK	BK
Riffey, J.	35 VAC	WD
Riffle, I.	62 VAI	BX
Ritchardson, J.W.	UNK	KN
Ritchie, G.W.	58 VAM	PD
Ritenhour, J.	2 VAI	BK
Roberts, D.	37 VAC	MG
Roberts, J.	34 VAC	KN
Roberts, J.F.	39 VAC	BK
Roberts, W.H.	19 VAC	WD
Robins, W.A.	26 VAI	TL
Robinson, J.S.	46 VAI	OH
Robison, J.	UNK	BK
Rogers, A.	10 VAI	GR
Rogers, W.L.	62 VAI	TL
Rohrbaugh, W.H.	18 VAC	GR
Rollins, W.	19 VAC	WD
Roberts, A.	46 VAC	Mc
Roop, H.	UNK	BK
Rose, B.	51 VAI	ME
Rose, E.B.	34 VAC	Mc
Rose, J.E.	Carpenter's VAA	CA
Rose, W.	22 VAC	LE
Ross, C.P.	51 VAI	PL
Ross, S.H.	167 VAM	LC

Rowe, A.E.	46 VAC	PR
Rumburg, W.J.	23 VAI	ME
Russel, E.W.	27 VAI	OH
Rutherford, M.S.	31 VAI	RD
Rutlierford, J.E.	31 VAI	RD
Saddler, W.T.	22 VAI	PO
Samples, T.	19 VAC	CL
Sanborn, A.	16 VAC	WN
Sarver, W.T.	45 VAI	WY
Saul, A.T.	42 VAI	WN
Sawyers, J.	27 VAI	FY
Saxton, J.	6 ALI	WD
Sayles, W.T.	11 VAC	BK
Schmidt, A.	Graham's VAA	BK
Schoolcraft, G.A.	36 VAC	KN
Schoolcraft, J.	14 VAC	KN
Schoppart, A.	UNK	BK
Scott, M.C.	12 VAA	PT
Scudder, F.	27 VAI	GB
Seal, J.W.	Hunsell's VAC	GL
Seaman, W.F.	25 VAI	ML
Seargeant, W.J.	23 VAI	MG
Seay, M.W.	57 VAI	NC
Sexton, L.	2 VAI	WD
Shackelford, F.	36 VAI	NC
Shaffer, J.	19 VAC	TK
Shahan, G.W.	15 GAI	TL
Shaiqver, A.C.	27 VAI	GB
Shamblin, J.	22 VAI	KN
Shannon, M.	20 VAC	RD
Shannon, M.	25 VAI	RD
Sharp, H.D.	59 VAI	PO
Sharp, M.	18 VAI	PO
Sharp, S.J.	26 VAI	PL
Shaw, I.	62 VAI	BK
Shaw, W.A.	8 MSI	JF
Shawver, J.T.	27 VAI	GB
Shearer, H.B.	4 VAC	PO
Sheets, F.W.	50 VAI	ML
Sheppard, A.J.	51 VAI	MA
Sheppard, J.T.	8 VAC	MA
Shians, H.	16 VAC	WY
Shields, W.H.	60 VAI	GB
Shirk, A.	46 VAM	PD
Shobe, I.N.	18 VAC	GR
Shobe, M.H.C.	18 VAC	GR
Shobe, W.H.	18 VAC	RD

Name	Unit	Code
Shoemaker, C.V.	8 VAC	PT
Showalter, J.D.	58 VAM	WD
Showalter, J.W.	5 VAI	PO
Shreve, N.	46 VAM	PD
Shrewsberry, J.W.	151 VAM	ME
Shumate, J.	61 VAI	HP
Sias, A.L.	34 VAC	LC
Sibert, E.	1 VAC	BK
Siers, J.	14 VAC	CA
Siers, W.	36 VAC	GL
Siers, W.H.	14 VAC	WT
Simmons, J.	19 VAC	PO
Simmons, J.	46 VAM	PD
Simons, J.	31 VAI	PO
Sizemore, J.	37 VAC	GB
Skidmar, J.M.	17 VAC	BX
Sletzer, J.M.	5 VAI	HR
Small, A.	10 VAI	BK
Small, G.H.	1 VAC	BK
Small, J.B.	2 VAI	BK
Small, J.M.	2 VAI	BK
Small, J.N.	2 VAI	BK
Small, R.W.	2 VAC	BK
Smith, B.	19 VAC	RT
Smith, G.	3 AKI	WN
Smith, H.M.	62 VAI	RT
Smith, J.	19 VAC	PT
Smith, J.	27 VAI	GB
Smith, J.W.	8 VAC	MA
Smith, J.W.	8 VAC	BX
Smith, L.	18 VAC	GR
Smith, P.	7 VAI	BK
Smith, W.G.	Smith's VAI	RO
Smoot, T.A.	19 VAC	HR
Snyder, J.	20 VAC	CA
Spaur, A.	26 VAC	BX
Spounagle, G.	18 VAC	GL
Sprinkle, A.N.	UNK	BK
Srnall, D.H.	1 VAC	BK
Staff, A.	1 VAA	BK
Stalnaker, A.	20 VAC	RD
Stalnaker, N.C.	20 VAC	GL
Stalnaker, S.	107 VAM	RD
Stanley, S.K.	26 VAI	FY
Stanly, W.B.	19 VAC	RT
Staphera, A.	2 VA-?	JF
Steel, A.	Cutshaw's VAA	WD

Stout, M.	UNK	GL
Straight, W.G.	20 VAC	MR
Strickland, W.W.	36 VAC	KN
Strother, W.	18 VAC	GR
Struetaler, J.	5 VAA	HR
Stump, A.	19 VAC	GL
Stump, L.	31 VAI	GL
Sullivan, D.	41 VAI	BK
Sullivan, J.	14 VAC	OH
Surber, T.C.	14 VAC	GB
Surman, R.	UNK	OH
Surver, W.F.	UNK	WY
Sutton, J.	UNK	BK
Swader, D.	11 VARS	NE
Swiger, C.	19 VAC	HR
Swinney, W.R.	23 VAI	KN
Tabler, A.A.	67 VAM	BK
Tabler, L.	67 VAM	BK
Tabor, G.O.	59 VAI	ME
Talbott, W.E.	28 VAI	TK
Taylor, J.	18 VAC	RD
Taylor, A.N.	81 VAM	PO
Taylor, C.F.	14 VAC	BX
Taylor, E.	18 VAC	RD
Taylor, H.	McNeill's VARG	GR
Taylor, J.	62 VAI	KN
Taylor, J.C.	14 VAC	BX
Tebo, J.A.	52 VAI	BK
Teter, C.	62 VAI	RD
Teter, D.K.	46 VAM	PD
Teter, I.J.	62 VAI	PD
Teter, J.A.	46 VAI	RD
Thalaker, H.	18 VAC	GR
Thomas, J.B.	18 VAC	OH
Thomas, J.B.	19 VAC	GB
Thomas, R.H.	46 VAI	PT
Thomas, T.H.	2 VAI	CA
Thomas, W.	23 VAI	ME
Thompson, G.W.	20 VAC	CL
Thompson, H.	Swann's VAC	LO
Thompson, J.	18 VAC	RD
Tillman, F.	8 VAC	WN
Tingler, M.	UNK	RD
Tinis, L.J.	36 VAI	PT
Tomland, A.	16 VAI	LC
Tomlin, A.	UNK	LC
Tona, S.	? VAC	LC

Toney, A.	8 VAC	CB
Tracy, J.C.	19 VAC	PO
Trent, T.W.	26 VAI	NC
Triplett, A.	18 VAC	TL
Trippett, P.	19 VAC	CA
Trippitt, C.J.	19 VAI	PR
Tucker, B.F.	19 VAC	HR
Turley, T.B.	22 VAI	PT
Turner, S.	36 VAC	PT
Tygrett, J.A.	79 VAM	NC
Underdonk, N.	UNK	BK
Vameter, N.	UNK	BK
Vance, A.J.	34 VAC	LC
Vance, F.	34 VAC	LC
Vance, J.A.	46 VAM	PD
Vance, M.	36 VAI	LC
Vance, R.	46 VAM	PD
Vance, W.	27 VAI	LC
Vandall, J.D.	60 VAI	FY
Vandevender, I.	25 VAI	RD
Vanhorn, J.A.	20 VAI	HR
Vannatter, S.	1 VAI	LC
Vanover, E.	French's VAI	Mc
Varns, J.W.	19 VAC	PO
Varuneter, J.	2 VAC	BK
Vaught, D.H.	Lowry's VAA	KN
Via, J.T.	14 VAC	GB
Via, W.F.	25 VAI	GB
Vincent, O.	31 VAI	MR
Vincent, F.M.	31 VAI	RT
Vorhess, A.	— VAI	BK
Wade, A.	26 VAI	PO
Wade, G.W.	26 VAI	PO
Wagner, J.	10 VAC	PT
Walker, J.B.	6 VARS	WY
Walker, T.L.	23 VAI	WY
Walker, W.	8 VAC	WN
Wall, J.	36 VAI	LC
Walters, J.P.	29 VAI	ME
Wamesly, S.B.	19 VAC	TK
Wamsley, A.H.	19 VAC	TK
Wamsley, W.H.	31 VAI	RD
Warden, G.W.	24 VAI	WN
Warth, C.S.	19 VAC	MA
Washington, L.	9 VAC	JF
Watson, J.	26 VAI	PR
Watson, W.	22 VAI	KN

Waugh, L.	20 VAC	PO
Way, G.W.	10 VAI	BK
Weale, G.W.	8 VAC	PT
Webb, J.	45 VAI	FY
Webb, T.S.	24 VAI	FY
Webster, W.H.	1 MDC	MO
Welch, J.P.	McNeill's VAR G	ML
Welch, J.R.	19 VAC	CA
Welch, L.	7 VAC	ML
Welch, R.B.	7 VAC	ML
Welch, W.	36 VAI	MS
Wells, P.	36 VAC	WD
Welshans, J.W.	67 VAM	BK
Welton, A.S.	18 VAC	GR
Welton, I.S.	18 VAC	GR
West, C.A.	17 VAC	DD
Westfall, J.	60 VAI	PD
Westfall, L.D.	31 VAI	RD
Wheeler, W.L.	5 ALI	BK
White, B.F.	2 VAC	JF
White, B.W.	129 VAM	LO
White, F.M.	Hamilton's GAA	WD
White, G.W.P.	30 VASS	ME
White, J.W.	19 VAC	BX
White, R.	21 VAC	OH
Wigal, J.M.	20 VAC	WD
Wilfong, A.	46 VAM	PD
Williams, H.	36 VAI	RA
Williams, W.P.	22 VAI	KN
Williams, W.W.	17 VAC	JK
Willinghouse, J.W.	2 VAI	BK
Willson, W.	62 VAI	GL
Willson, W.A.	22 VAI	RO
Wilphong, J.	31 VAI	GB
Wilson, C.	2 VAI	BK
Wilson, E.R.	19 VAC	MA
Wilson, H.	31 VAI	TL
Wilson, H.I.	22 VAI	ML
Wilson, J.	19 VAC	WD
Wilson, J.A.	62 VAI	PT
Wine, R.	27 VAI	WT
Wiseman, H.B.	5 VAI	MA
Wiseman, J.	19 VAC	MR
Wiseman, J.N.	36 VAI	NC
Wolf, J.W.	12 VAC	RT
Wolf, L.C.	19 VAC	BX
Wood, C.	60 VAI	ME

Wood, G.	34 VAC	HE
Woodard, G.L.	11 MDI	JF
Woodward, J.R.	14 VAC	GB
Woriman, J.A.	45 VAI	WY
Workman, J.A.	38 VAI	LO
Workman, W.	34 VAC	LC
Wormiy, J.	12 VAC	BK
Wright, L.	20 VAC	RT
Wright, T.	22 VAI	MR
Wright, W.	36 VAI	WT
Wright, Z.	20 VAC	RT
Wyant, W.	26 VAI	FY
Wyers, B.F.	19 VAC	GL
Yerkey, T.	19 VAI	GL
Yoakum, A.	7 VAI	RD
Yomrey, D.	1 VAC	BK
Yost, L.	20 VAC	TY
Young, J.F.	17 VAC	RA
Young, S.M.	22 VAI	KN
Youst, A.	20 VAC	WT

Veteran Distribution by County of Residence

COUNTY	U.S.	C.S.	TOTAL	COUNTY	U.S.	C.S.	TOTAL
Barbour	173	2	175	Mineral	155	16	171
Berkeley	225	112	337	Monongalia	358	5	363
Boone	86	4	90	Monroe	12	5	17
Braxton	157	47	204	Morgan	115	5	120
Brooke	159	3	162	Nicholas	66	21	87
Cabell	415	9	424	Ohio	708	20	728
Calhoun	146	15	161	Pendleton	58	41	99
Clay	72	5	77	Pleasants	156	4	160
Doddridge	307	15	322	Pocahontas	50	65	115
Fayette	134	18	152	Preston	698	12	710
Gilmer	179	43	222	Putnam	223	38	261
Grant	56	30	86	Raleigh	80	7	87
Greenbrier	76	50	126	Randolph	107	40	147
Hampshire	55	6	61	Ritchie	434	17	451
Hancock	143	1	144	Roane	250	10	260
Hardy	4	0	4	Summers	43	3	46
Harrison	463	17	480	Taylor	300	8	308
Jackson	455	11	466	Tucker	92	12	104
Jefferson	67	15	82	Tyler	290	4	294
Kanawha	713	63	776	Upshur	323	3	326
Lewis	283	3	286	Wayne	277	38	315
Lincoln	194	44	238	Webster	34	0	34
Logan	41	9	50	Wetzel	428	9	437
Marion	543	24	567	Wirt	219	2	221
Marshall	601	6	607	Wood	720	57	777
Mason	624	26	650	Wyoming	38	13	51
McDowell	39	8	47				
Mercer	39	56	95	TOTAL:	12,683	1,097	13,780

West Virginia Civil War Service Medals

IN 1866 THE INFANT State of West Virginia decided to give its Union soldiers medals. There were three kinds of medals to be awarded: Class I—Honorably Discharged; Class II—Killed in Battle; and Class III—For Liberty (for soldiers who died of disease or wounds received in battle). The total number of medals made was 26,099. Despite numerous efforts by the State of West Virginia to locate surviving veterans or their spouses, there still remained in 1870 about 7,000 of the medals.

To this day (June 10, 1997) there yet remain several thousand unclaimed medals, and the West Virginia Department of Archives and History, is searching for descendants of these men in the hope that these medals can finally be distributed. To that end, the author has included here a list of more than seven hundred veterans whose names appear in the 1890 veteran census, and whose service medals are unclaimed. The West Virginia Department of Archives and History, under direction of Frederick Armstrong and staff, supplied the author with a complete list of all unclaimed medals. That list was then checked against the 1890 census roster. Positive identification is nearly impossible because soldiers would routinely serve in more than one military unit during the war, and the unit they identified themselves with in 1890, might not be the "unit of record," the veteran was identified with when the medals were issued.

If the reader locates an ancestor's name in this list, contact the West Virginia Department of Archives and History, The Cultural Center, 1900 Kanawha Blvd. E. Charleston, WV 25305.

NAME	COUNTY
Able, Wm.	LE
Adams, Isaac	JK
Adams, Jacob	PL
Adams, John	BO
Adams, Wm. S.	CB
Adkins, Anderson	LC
Adkins, Benton	BN
Adkins, Parker	SM
Adkins, Wm.	SM
Ailor, Andrew J.	FY
Alhright, Samuel	PR
Alien, George	FY
Alien, Isaac	RO
Alien, James	KN
Alien, Joseph	PR
Alien, Wm.	DD
Alien, Wm. A.	WD
Anderson, George	PT
Anderson, Joseph	BK
Anderson, Wm.	BO
Anderson, Wm. C.	JK
Andrew, C.C.	MA
Arbogast, George	BR
Armstrong, Henry H.	HK
Armstrong, Jonathan	BX
Arnold, James M.	FY
Ashcraft, James M.	WT
Atha, Wm. M.	MR
Atkinson, Wm.	BO
Austin, Jo. N.	MR
Bailey, James	WD
Baker, George	OH
Baker, Henry W.	WI
Baker, James	MR
Baker, James M.	CB
Baker, John	BX
Barker, John	WT
Barker, Wm. D.	DD
Barker, Wm. F.	WT
Barnes, Wm.	CA
Barnhart, Jacob	JK
Barnhouse, Alpheus N.	TL
Barnhouse, Wm.	ML
Barr, James	OH
Barr, John	PT
Bartholomew, Wm.	OH
Bartlett, Daniel	JK
Bartlett, Hiram L.	HR
Baxter, George	BO
Beagle, Edgar J.	RT
Bell, Henry	TY
Bell, Wm. H.	WD
Bennett, James C.	TY
Bennett, Martin	RD
Bennett, Nathan D.	LE
Bennett, Wm.	MS
Bennett, Wm. A.	MS
Bennett, Wm. O.	HR
Birch, John	WD
Bird, Francis M.	BO
Bisset, John	MG
Black, George	RT
Black, James	JK
Blake, George W.	MO
Blankenship, Hiram	GB
Blankenship, W.W.	PT
Bostick, Joseph	MN
Boyce, David	JK
Boyd, James	MG
Boyd, James	OH
Bradford, Abraham	WD
Bradley, John L.	WD
Bragg, David C.	LO
Brannon, Wm. H.	HP
Brison, Wm. E.	LE
Brookhover, Jacob	WT
Brooks, George	JK
Brooks, Wm.	JK
Brooks, Wm.	WD
Brown, C.W.	WD
Brown, Jesse	LE
Brown, Jesse	WD
Brown, John B.	HR
Brown, John W.	RT
Brown, John W.D.	RT
Brown, Samuel	WT
Brown, Thomas	WN
Browning, James Z.	LC
Buckalew, John W.	PR
Bunner, Presley	MR
Burge, Andrew J.	MS
Burge, Eli	MS
Burge, Elijah	MS

Burgess, Wm.	MS	Cobb, Wm. C.	KN
Burnes, James L.	GB	Coffman, Adam	WD
Burnside, Wm. H.	LE	Cogan, John W.	ML
Burt, Robert	MS	Cole, Martin V.	WD
Butcher, Edgar	TL	Cole, Wm. R.	PR
Butcher, George	WT	Collins, Alexander	RO
Butcher, Wm.	MA	Collins, George	PR
Butler, Julius	HR	Collins, Isaac N.	WN
Byard, Wm. J.	MS	Collins, James	PT
Cage, Samuel	WD	Combs, James	WD
Cain, Jacob	WT	Compston, John H.	JK
Calesr Wm. H.H.	SM	Conkle, Jacob	WD
Calvert, Josiah	PR	Connelly, Michael	OH
Campbell, Wm. H.	TL	Conrad, John M.	HR
Carder, Jacob H.	LE	Cooper, Archemides	JK
Cardwell, Manoah W.	CB	Cooper, George T.	MA
Carlile, Calvin	MA	Cooper, George W.	MA
Carney, Wm. W.	WT	Cooper, Josephus	MA
Carpenter, John C.	MR	Cooper, Samuel	OH
Carr, Anthony	TL	Cooper, Wm.	JK
Carr, Edward	WT	Cornell, Amos	PL
Carr, Francis M.	KN	Cottrill, Calvin J.	TL
Carr, John C.	PR	Courtney, Wm. F.	WI
Carr, John T.	BX	Cox, Jacob W.	BR
Carroll, Wm.	MG	Craig, Ahraham	WT
Carson, Robert	LE	Craig, James	NC
Carter, Jasper	BR	Craig, Samuel	JK
Cash, Marseilles	PT	Crawford, John W.	TL
Chambers, G.W.	TL	Cremear, Wm. H.	MA
Chambers, James	MS	Crim, Wm. H.	MR
Cheak, John	KN	Crites, John	UP
Chippie, Samuel W.	OH	Cronin, John	PL
Clark, George	RT	Cross, John A.	RT
Clark, George W.	OH	Cross, John T.	WT
Clark, James	PR	Cross, Samuel	WT
Clark, Levi	MA	Cullen, Matthew	HK
Clark, Samuel	LC	Culp, Amos	MR
Clark, Thomas B.	MS	Cumberledge, Isaac	MA
Clark, Wm.	CB	Cummings, Wm.	BX
Clay, Henry	RA	Cunningham, B.F.	RT
Clayton, John W.	MS	Cunningham, David	MR
Clayton, Wm. P.	MS	Cunningham, Francis	HR
Clemensr Ferguson	DD	Cunningham, Joseph	JK
Clemens, John	LE	Curry, George	LC
Clifton, Wm.	LE	Custer, George W.	HR
Cline, John W.	KN	Darrah, Wm.	MS
Clingan, James M.	PR	Daugherty, Daniel	BX

Davis, Christopher C.	DD		Edwards, Samuel	MA
Davis, David	TY		Elkins, Charles R.	LO
Davis, George	MR		Elliott, Charles H.	OH
Davis, George W.	TL		Elliott, Henry S.	RT
Davis, Henry	HR		Ellis, John W.	ML
Davis, Isaac	TY		Epling, Levi A.	KN
Davis, Isaiah	WD		Erskine, John M.	HK
Davis, Jacob	MR		Evans, Edward	WI
Davis, James M.	RT		Evans, George	MS
Davis, John C.	MG		Evans, John	PT
Davis, John W.	BK		Evans, Wm. H.	BR
Davis, Jonathan	MR		Evertt, Lewis	HP
Davis, Jos. A.	WI		Everly, John G.	PR
Davis, Joseph H.	FY		Ewing, Robert H.	BX
Davis, Morgan D.	WD		Ewingr Wm. W.	MS
Davis, Robert W.	TY		Farley, George	PR
Davis, Samuel B.	HR		Feazel, Wm. E.	WN
Davis, Samuel H.	CB		Ferguson, Sam W.	WN
Davis, Thomas	MA		Firestone, Ml.	GL
Davis, Tim K.	TK		Fisher, Isaac F.	BX
Davis, Wm. G.	MS		Fleming, Wm. W.	LE
Dawson, Marion L.	CR		Fletcher, Joseph	MA
Dawson, Noah D.	MR		Fluharty, James S.	MR
Dawson, Wm. T.	HR		Ford, Thomas L.	HR
Dean, Jesse	TL		Fortney, Joshua D.	HR
Delaney, John	JK		Foulk, Wm. H.	OH
Delaney, Wm. C.	JK		Fowler, Noah C.	TL
Denham, Andrew J.	WD		Fox, Washington	MS
Dever, Wm.	HK		Frank, John	BK
Dillon, Charles	CB		Frasheur, Kincheloe	DD
Dillon, George P.	PT		Frasier, Joseph	PR
Dillon, Wm. J.	CB		Frazier, Joseph	PR
Dixon, James R.	MS		Frederick, Wm. T.	RT
Dixon, Wm.	WN		Freeland, Emanuel	MR
Dodd, John	MR		Freeman, Wm.	WD
Dotson, John S.	DD		French, Sam	MS
Doyle, George	OH		Furgeson, James K.	CB
Drake, Samuel	MS		aither, John R.	MO
Drummonds, Wilford	HR		Gardner, Thomas	HK
Duffield, H. W.	PO		Gary, Sam	RT
Duncan, Alva W.	DD		Gibbs, Sheldon	MA
Dunn, James T.	MA		Gibson, Wm. L.	CB
Dunn, Wm. B.	RT		Gilbert, Ml.	GL
Dye, John	DD		Giles, Wm. H.	RO
Eaten, John	RO		Gilland, John W.	JK
Edgar, David	WT		Glass, James	RD
Edmundson, David	WD		Glover, Henry C.	CB

Glover, Vincent A.	DD	Harris, John C.	MS
Goodrich, Lewis	MA	Harris, John W.	MS
Gorby, Alexander	TY	Harris, Wm. P.	MG
Gorhy, Jesse J.	WT	Harrison, Reynolds	ML
Gore, John H.	WN	Harrison, Wm. H.	WD
Gorrell, John B.	TY	Hart, Josiah	DD
Gosney, Richard	OH	Harter, Wm. M.	RT
Graham, Lee	PR	Harvey, Marcena	DD
Graham, Wm.	TL	Haught, Wm. E.	WT
Grandstaff, John R.	MS	Hays, James	BK
Grant, Granville A.	BR	Headly, James	WD
Gray, James	OH	Heflin, John S.	DD
Greathouse, Thomas	WT	Helmick, Jacob	DD
Green, John	KN	Henderson, Eli	HR
Green, Jonathan	BX	Henderson, Leroy	DD
Green, Joseph	OH	Henry, James M.	MG
Green, Wm.	MA	Henry, James R.	WT
Griffin, Wm.	OH	Henry, Levi M.	MO
Griffith, Joseph	LC	Hewitt, Richard B.	HK
Grim, Abraham	MS	Hickman, George W.	WT
Grim, George N.	MS	Hickman, W. H.	WI
Grimes, John W.	MS	Hicks, Wm. B.	MS
Grimes, Joseph	FY	Hill, Elijah	WI
Groves, Samuel	BX	Hill, George W.	KN
Groves, Wm. F.	MS	Hill, James W.	OH
Grubb, John	UP	Hill, John E.	BK
Gump, Dan S.	WT	Hill, John W.	OH
Gump, Philip H.	MR	Hill, Wm. V.	TK
Gunn, John F.	LE	Hixenbaugh, Henry	WT
Gwinn, George W.	CB	Hoce, George W.	WD
Haddox, Abram	BR	Hoffman, George F.	PR
Hager, James S.	MS	Holbert, Hen P.	GL
Hager, Russel	LC	Holder, James T.	KN
Halfin, Joseph F.	MG	Holland, Wm. E.	MG
Hall, Basil	JK	Holmes, George W.	PD
Hall, Francis M.	WD	Holmes, Wm. T.	KN
Hall, George W.	MS	Householder, Henry C.	MO
Hall, Henry C.	JK	Howell, Isaac	PL
Hall, Isaac	BK	Howly, Martin	WI
Hall, Joseph M.V.	LE	Huggins, John A.	WD
Hall, Josiah	PR	Hughes, Fleming T.	CB
Hall, Robert B.	CA	Hughes, John W.	NC
Hall, Robert E.	GB	Hugill, Wm. M.	DD
Hall, Tom J.	PT	Hundley, James M.	KN
Hamilton, Henry E.	RT	Hunter, George W.	HK
Hardie, Wm. D.	TL	Hunter, John W.	CB
Harris, David E.	GB	Hutchinson, George W.	CB

Hutson, Peter F.	DD		Lewis, John J.	MA
Jackson, Andrew P.	PR		Lewis, John R.	UP
Jarret, John Y.	KN		Lewis, Wm. W.	WD
Jenkins, Elias	PR		Lipscomb, Joshua	PR
Jenkins, Thomas	BO		Listen, Henson	PR
Jennewine, Bartholomew	MG		Livingston, George	TY
Johnson, J. W.	CL		Lockhart, George	WI
Johnson, James W.	PR		Looman, Eugenius C.	MR
Johnson, Jesse	BX		Looman, James	HR
Johnson, Marion	WD		Loughry, John	TK
Johnson, Thomas J.	LC		Loy, Wm.	WT
Jones, Andrew J.	MR		Ludwick, Thomas	HP
Jones, Andrew P.	OH		Lyons, James H.	WI
Jones, David E.	FY		Lyons, Wm. A.	DD
Jones, Elias M.	RO		Mace, Jacob	KN
Jones, Francis M.	KN		Mackey, Horatio N.	MG
Jones, George W.	BX		Maffit, Isaac	WI
Jones, James E.	CA		Magill, George E.	PR
Jones, James M.	BO		Malone, James H.	RT
Jones, James W.	MN		Mann, Patrick	HR
Jones, John Y.	OH		Marsh, James M.	RT
Jones, Wm. D.	OH		Marshall, Andrew	OH
Jordan, Charles H.	CB		Marshall, Asbury	WT
Joseph, Nathan	TY		Marshall, George L.	OH
Joseph, Simon	OH		Marshall, James W.	MS
Justice, Sam	MC		Marshall, John W.	WD
Justice, Wm.	CB		Marshall, Tom L.	WT
Kearnes, Jesse	MA		Martin, James M.	PL
Kearney, Patrick	HR		Martin, John B.	CB
Keller, Felan	MR		Martin, John F.	RT
Keller, Lafayette	TL		Martin, John W.	MG
Kelley, Dyre	BR		Martin, Wm. D.	TL
Kelley, Oscar	CA		Mason, Peter	MR
Kester, James A.	WD		Matheny, Elias	PR
Kidd, John E.	RA		Maxwell, Wm.	TY
Kidder, Ira	CA		Mayes, Charles W.	MA
King, Henry H.	MS		McCann, Moses	WT
Kinkaid, David M.	MR		McCannon, Sampson	WN
Kirkendall, John A.	WI		McCloud, Thomas	WT
Knight, John A.	CA		McCormick, Robert	PO
Lacy, George	KN		McCoy, John L.	DD
Lamberson, Dennis	TY		McCrea, Robert	KN
Lancaster, David	WT		McElroy, Samuel	MG
Lee, Charles	JK		McGee, George W.	TL
Lee, John	SM		McGill, Thomas W.	RT
Lemasters, John H.	WT		McGinnis, Thomas	RA
Lewis, Ben F.	MA		McLaughlin, John	WT

McMillan, Sam	HR	Nichols, Wm. T.	KN
McMillan, Wm. J.	RT	Noble, Anson	MA
McMurray, Wm. B.	JK	Nose, Samuel	PR
McNeff, James	KN	O'Haro, John	WD
McNemar, B. A.	HR	Oliver, James B.	KN
McSmith, Daniel	RT	Osburn, George	JK
McVicker, Wm.	BR	Owens, James W.	BK
Meder, Lewis	OH	Parker, Ben F.	RA
Menafee, James F.	PR	Parker, Wm. H.	GB
Mercer, Wm. W.	MS	Parsons, Eleazer	MA
Metcalf, Eli W.	WD	Parsons, John R.	RO
Metheny, Joseph M.	PR	Patterson, David	TY
Miley, Joseph	HR	Patton, Milton M.	TL
Miller, David K.	KN	Paxton, Wm. H.	RO
Miller, Elijah	WT	Payne, Wm. A.	MC
Miller, Enos	MR	Peck, Andrew J.	MA
Miller, George W.	GL	Perkins, Jesse	GB
Miller, Morgan	CB	Persinger, John L.	BX
Miller, Zachariah	CL	Peters, John	KN
Mills, Anderson	ME	Pettitt, Matthias	BX
Mills, James D.	MS	Phelps, Elisha	JK
Mills, Wm. A.	OH	Philips, Wm. O.	MR
Mitchell, Andrew J.	WN	Phillips, Wm. H.	MG
Mitchell, Ellis B.	MG	Pifer, George	WD
Mitchell, Isaac	MA	Pilcher, George	WD
Mobley, John E.	MS	Pinnell, James	DD
Montgomery, Andrew J.	WT	Pipes, John H.	OH
Montgomery, George B.	OH	Polk, Gideon	MA
Montgomery, John F.	BX	Pool, Charles E.	WD
Moody, John	GL	Powell, John R.	CB
Mooney, Andrew L.	WT	Powell, Reuben	DD
Moore, Eli	HR	Pratt, Charles	OH
Moore, Isaac A.	CL	Pratt, Richard	PR
Moore, John H.	OH	Proctor, Nathan	FY
Moore, Marion	TY	Reed, Alexander D.	HR
Moore, Washington	WT	Reid, John	MS
Moore, Wm. H.	CL	Reynolds, John	MG
Moreland, Jobny	PL	Rice, Charles	ML
Morris, Levi	MR	Rice, Josephus	HR
Murdock, Wm.	MR	Riffle, John W.	CB
Murphy, Jeremiah	WT	Riley, John W.	TL
Murphy, Wm. H.	WT	Riley, Mark M.	PR
Myers, Benton	GL	Rittenhouse, Dan C.	MR
Nance, Aaron	CB	Roberts, Eli	TY
Nelson, Wm. L.	LC	Roberts, Enoch	CA
Newlon, Thomas	RT	Runyan, George	CB
Newman, Henry C.	WI	Russell, Thomas	RK

Name	Code	Name	Code
Sanders, Samuel	MG	Steel, Fred G.	WT
Satterfield, Ben N.	TL	Steele, Thomas G.	MR
Satterfield, Sidney W.	MR	Stephens, David E.	HR
Savage, Wm.	KN	Stephens, E.J.	TL
Shafer, David H.	RO	Stewart, Alexander J.	TY
Shell, Daniel	GR	Stiles, John	MA
Shipman, George	UP	Strobridge, John U.	MG
Shoemaker, Charles	PT	Stump, Adam	WT
Shoemaker, Joseph H.	CB	Sturm, Joshua L.	TY
Shriver, Wm.	MG	Sutton, Ben	MS
Silcott, Emanuel B.	HR	Sutton, Harrison	JK
Silcott, Lewis T.	HR	Swesey, John	WD
Simpson, Robert J.	HP	Swiger, Fred L.	HR
Simpson, Wm. S.	HP	Tanner, John	CL
Sims, Alfred	LE	Tasker, Ben	ML
Singer, John	TY	Taylor, Ben	CA
Skinner, Adolphus	WD	Taylor, Richard	BR
Slack, John W.	KN	Thomas, Abraham	PR
Sloan, Henry L.	MS	Thomas, Charles	SM
Smallwood, Elisha	HR	Thomas, Philip	MS
Smith, Charles A.	GL	Thomas, Sam	MA
Smith, Edmund J.	WI	Thompson, Dallas	ME
Smith, Elisha	MA	Thrasher, David	BR
Smith, Frederick	FY	Todd, George B.	WD
Smith, Gabriel	OH	Toothman, Sam	MR
Smith, Harrison	MO	Trout, James H.	ML
Smith, Henry A.	PR	Truax, Wm.	RD
Smith, James H.	HR	Tucker, Wm. E.	BO
Smith, Jesse	HK	Turner, John W.	PR
Smith, Jos. O.	LE	Turner, Lemeul H.	WD
Smith, Peter	TY	Tuttle, Jesse	TY
Smith, Thomas J.	DD	Utterback, John T.	RT
Smith, Wm. B.	UP	Vance, Chapman	KN
Smith, Wm. O.	LC	Vanscoy, Abel	DD
Smith, Zach. T.	PT	Varner, Oliver	WD
Snider, Edgar C.	RT	Vincent, Riley	MR
Snider, Isaac	DD	Vincent, Sanford	DD
Snider, Sam	WT	Wallace, John	WD
Snyder, Elias A.	MA	Wallace, Tom H.	ML
Snyder, John A.	JF	Walls, Archibald	MR
South, Joseph	WD	Walters, George T.	UP
Spencer, Elijah	TY	Ward, Alexander	PT
Spencer, John L.	TY	Ward, John	LE
Spencer, Thomas	TK	Watkins, John	WD
Springer, John	OH	Watkins, Wilford	MR
Stafford, James P	KN	Watson, James	MN
Stanley, John	BK	Watson, Thomas	PR

Watts, Felix	TY	Williams, George W.	GL
Waugh, Charles C.	CB	Williams, Lewis	FY
Weaver, David	GB	Williams, Lloyd	BN
Weaver, George	KN	Williams, Solomon	UP
Webb, Francis	WN	Williams, Walter	KN
Webb, John D.	FY	Williamson, George W.	PL
Webb, Wm.	RA	Willis, Andrew J.	WD
Weekly, John	TY	Willison, George W.	CB
Welch, James	ML	Wilson, Virginus	MG
Welch, Robert	ML	Winemiller, Henry	LE
Wells, John L.	LE	Winesburg, Rarney	MS
Wells, Richard A.	MR	Winters, Thomas	JF
Welsh, Tom E.	WI	Wires, Thomas	MA
West, Isaac	WT	Wiseman, Jos. N.	NC
West, John R.	TK	Wolf, Jos. S.	HP
West, Tom F.	CL	Woodfield, Joseph	HR
West, Wm. A.	WD	Woods, Lewis	KN
Westwood, John	OH	Wray, Isaac M.	CB
Whipkey, Freeman	WD	Wright, Gad	PT
White, Andrew	RO	Wright, Harrison	JK
White, Ben F.	JF	Wright, Henry H.	RO
White, Charles	GB	Wright, James G.	PL
White, Henry	MS	Wright, Major W.	TY
White, John W.	BX	Wyant, Henry M.	TL
White, Wm. P.	KN	Wycoff, Wm.	WT
Whitecotton, N.S.	OH	Young, Charles A.	KN
Whitehead, Jacob	WD	Young, Ed P.	KN
Whiteman, Wm.	MS	Young, Isaac	ME
Whitney, James G.	FY	Young, John C.	LE
Whitzel, John D.	TY	Young, Joseph	RA
Williams, Andrew J.	PR	Young, Robert	MA
Williams, Ed J.	CA	Zink, George W.	BO
Williams, Elijah	MR		

West Virginia Confederate Soldiers and Citizens Who Died in Federal Prisons or Military Hospitals

BECAUSE OF A GENERAL breakdown in prisoner exchanges late in the Civil War, many Confederate soldiers, sailors, and citizens ultimately died in Federal prisons or military hospitals. In 1866 Secretary of war Edwin M. Stanton reported that more than 26,000 deaths had occurred among Confederate prisoners of war.

For many years after the war little care was exercised in marking these graves, although the names of the interred were often preserved in burial registers. In an address delivered at Atlanta, Georgia, on December 14, 1898, President William McKinley, himself a Union veteran of the Civil War, advocated Federal responsibility in caring for Confederate graves in the North. Gradually, between 1900 and 1906 Congress introduced bills and appropriated funds for the purpose of "appropriate marking of the graves of the soldiers and sailors of the Confederate Army and Navy who died in Northern prisons and were buried near the prisons where they died."

Confederate veterans' organizations became active in this work as well, with the United Confederate Veterans calling for Federal action at a Memphis, Tennessee, meeting of the national organization, May 28–30, 1901. The first Office of Commissioner for Marking the Graves of Confederate Dead was formed in March 1906 and continued until October 1912, by which time the Office had completed comprehensive burial lists. These lists are generally arranged alphabetically by name of prison camp or other location where the deaths occurred. Names of the deceased are also arranged alphabetically, giving rank, company, regiment, date of death, and number and location of the grave. However, in a few instances this information is incomplete. A few entries are for private Confederate citizens interred in the various cemeteries and some are for unknown graves. Other entries contain notations such as "body taken home by friends," or "removed."

This burial register is available from the National Archives and Records Administration (NARA) as part of Record Group 92, micropublication M918 roll 1. The index presented here of 309 West Virginia Confederate soldiers and citizens found on this microfilm, was culled by the author from more than 26,000 entries. This was accomplished by checking the name of each soldier from Virginia or West Virginia against the roster of West Virginia

Confederate soldiers published in 1995 by Jack Dickinson as *Tattered Uniforms and Bright Bayonet's: West Virginia's Confederate Soldiers*. This publication includes the names of more than 15,000 men who enlisted into Confederate service from West Virginia. Also utilized to a lesser extent were numerous volumes of the *Virginia Regimental History Series,* being published by H.E. Howard, Inc. of Lynchburg, Va. Additional research will no doubt reveal the names of other Confederate soldiers from West Virginia, and this initial index of 309 names will certainly increase in size.

Alton, Illinois, Prison

NAME	REGIMENT	DATE DIED
Marks, Gideon	14VAC	4/1/63

Annapolis, Maryland Prison

NAME	REGIMENT	DATE DIED
Allen, John A.	22VAI	10/18/64
Ruckman, Charles B.	19VAC	7/7/65

New York Prison (non-specific)

NAME	REGIMENT	DATE DIED
Schrader, Sam E.	25VAI	8/9/63

Camp Chase, Ohio

NAME	REGIMENT	DATE DIED
Adkins, Manvill A.	16VAC	11/11/63
Adkins, William A.	34BTN VAC	11/25/64
Alford, J.C.	Barbour County	3/7/64
Armstead, Josiah	22VAC	3/6/65
Arters, Robert F.	19VAC	12/16/64
Barnes, Nathaniel	Harrison County	6/23/63
Basham, Davis	Swann's BTN VAC	10/30/64
Baumgardner, John	8VAC	2/14/65
Bishop, Moses L.	19VAC	4/7/65
Blackwood, R. A.	20VAC	9/15/64
Burns, Andrew	36BTN VAC	12/16/63
Calford, Thomas	Pocahontas County	6/19/63
Christian, Jacob	34BTN VAC	8/15/64
Clark, Stephen	Randolph County	10/13/62
Clifton, Henry	Webster County	9/29/64
Cline, Cincinnati	Ritchie County	11/14/62
Coger, Christopher	Webster County	10/21/64

Cook, David	36VAI	2/6/65
Cooper, George F.	Taylor County	11/4/62
Cooper, Thompson	Taylor County	11/28/63
Courtney, Andrew J.	31VAI	11/4/62
Cowell, Elias	20VAC	4/14/65
Crawford, John	36VAI	12/13/64
Cunningham, Silas	17VAC	12/27/64
Cutlip, Jackson	19VAC	3/4/65
Davis, George	20VAC	1/23/65
Dilly, Thomas	19VAC	4/25/65
Dimmitt, William	Mason County	6/16/62
Elliot, Samuel	Barbour County	6/16/63
Ellyson, Ed G.	62VAI	10/18/63
Evans, Evan	31VAI	4/1/62
Eye, William M.	62VAI	2/25/65
Fenton, Wm. E.	26BTN VAI	8/2/64
Fisher, W.H.	Fayette County	10/12/63
Foster, Aaron L.	Monongalia County	9/8/63
Godby, James H.	17VAC	10/24/64
Golden, Andrew J.	19VAC	4/8/65
Hanly, Henry C.	8VAC	1/28/65
Harrison, Thomas	7VAC	3/26/65
Hartman, George	36VAI	10/13/64
Hatcher, Henry F.	17VAC	11/11/64
Hill, George W.	166VA Militia	7/27/62
Hill, Wm. M.	14VAC	5/10/65
Howard, Lewis L.	26VAC	3/20/65
Hunt, Henry F.	22VAI	1/28/65
Jarrett, Abraham	22VAI	11/10/64
Johnson, R.M.	20VAC	3/16/65
Judy, St. Clair	62VAI	2/13/64
Keaton, Wm. J.	17VAC	10/28/64
Ketterman, Adam	Hardy County	12/14/62
Kittle, Benjamin	Barbour County	8/5/64
Lake, John R.	62VAI	3/18/65
Lee, William	19VAC	9/13/65
Lemley, Samuel	19VAC	9/17/63
Long, William	Ritchie County	11/1/62
McCallister, Henry	36BTN VAC	11/6/64
McKinney, Joseph	20VAC	11/27/64
Maddox, Matthew	Harrison County	10/5/63
Malot, Reisin	Marion County	10/29/62
Martin, John	36VAI	10/22/64
May, Robert S.	19VAC	3/18/65
Morrison, Columbus	20VAC	3/18/65
Morrow, John	Wood County	6/30/63
Myers, Michael	62VAI	3/15/65

Name	Regiment/Unit	Date
Patterson, Wm.	Greenbrier County	8/3/62
Paul, J.E.	Putnam County	12/25/62
Pinson, Wm.	"Bushwhacker" Wayne Co.	6/3/63
Powell, Henry C.	8VAC	10/22/64
Propst, Adam	19VAC	8/23/64
Pugh, John W.	7VAC	3/6/65
Rader, James B.	62VAI	3/25/65
Reece, John H.	60VAI	1/9/65
Reed, James M.	8VAC	11/4/64
Roberts, Wm. R.	Doddridge County	6/16/63
Robison, Israel	8VAC	10/12/64
Romine, John	17VAC	9/29/63
Rutherford, John	Taylor County	10/25/62
Selards, David	16VAC	11/23/63
Sharp, George B.	19VAC	9/25/63
Sharp, James L.	19VAC	1/9/65
Small, James	19VAC	5/23/65
Smith, C.C.	36BTN VAC	1/28/65
Smith, Charles M.	36VAI	2/24/65
Smith, Jonas	Lewis County	6/16/63
Smith, Wm. S.	36BTN VAC	2/25/64
Standeford, George	Marshall County	8/11/62
Talkington, W.P.	Marion County	11/22/62
Taylor, Wm. J.	22VAI	8/24/64
Tench, Clark W.	Raleigh County	7/15/62
Thompson, A.D.	8VAC	12/1/64
Thompson, Patterson	8VAC	2/21/65
Trickett, M.E.	20VAC	9/10/64
Valentine, George	Ritchie County	6/3/62
Walker, James	16VAC	5/3/63
Watson, James A.	Upshur County	10/4/63
Wees, Amos	Hardy County	9/23/64
Weese, Isaac	60VAI	10/30/64
Williams, John	19VAC	3/15/65
Williams, John D.	60VAI	10/27/64
Windsor, Isaac	Thurmond's VA Rangers	12/10/62

Camp Douglas, Illinois, Prison

NAME	REGIMENT	DATE DIED
Sartain, A.J.	36VAI	5/20/64
Sipples, L.J.	45BTN VAI	12/16/64

Camp Morton, Indiana, Prison

NAME	REGIMENT	DATE DIED
Averil, Jacob	36VAI	8/23/64
Bail, Johnathan	36VAI	1/17/65

Name	Regiment	Date Died
Bailey, Mathias	60VAI	9/19/64
Broughman, H.J.	60VAI	10/3/64
Browning, A.J.	45BTN VAI	10/30/64
Crawford, Uriah F.	60VAI	1/16/65
Dennison, Andrew J.	20VAC	1/25/65
Fisher, Henry J.	36VAI	12/12/64
Friend, Marshall T.	60VAI	2/13/65
Gray, Andrew G.	36VAI	8/10/64
Landers, John	60VAI	9/10/64
McClung, Thaddeus	36VAI	2/20/65
Morris, Ed R.	36VAI	2/26/65
Petts, Hosea	45BTN VAI	1/16/65
Smith, George W.	36VAI	12/5/64
Varney, M.B.	45BTN VAI	4/2/65
White, John H.	8VAC	12/10/64
Wickham, Robert L.	36VAI	10/26/64
Wilson, Jesse P.	60VAI	2/8/65
Woodyard, Joe G.	36VAI	8/6/64
Yerkey, Robert G.	36BTN VAC	5/28/65

Clarksburg, West Virginia, Prison

NAME	REGIMENT	DATE DIED
McPherson, Thomas	62VAI	1/18/64

Elmira, New York, Prison

NAME	REGIMENT	DATE DIED
Alderman, A.C.	25VAI	11/27/64
Anderson, G.W.	26BTN VAI	1/13/65
Ballard, Archibald	26BTN VAI	1/6/65
Barnhart, Benjamin	22VAI	5/31/65
Basham, Wm. H.	26BTN VAI	10/16/64
Baxter, George H.	25VAI	1/19/65
Berry, Charles W.	25VAI	7/8/65
Boggs, Wm. M.	26BTN VAI	12/19/64
Boone, Thomas E.	25VAI	9/20/64
Bostick, Adison H.	26BTN VAI	7/5/65
Brooks, Andrew T.	19VAC	1/31/65
Chewning, John S.	26BTN VAI	12/12/64
Clinebell, John	26BTN VAI	3/16/65
Crawford, Joseph H.	26BTN VAI	9/7/64
Deal, Peter W.	22VAI	2/15/65
Dooley, Jackson H.	25VAI	9/9/64
Ellis, Harrison G.	26BTN VAI	12/6/64
Eskew, Casey B.	36VAI	3/19/65
Flint, Esekial	26BTN VAI	9/12/64

Flythe, James F.	25VAI	11/27/64
Foley, Coleman	25VAI	11/18/64
Foster, Estly M.	26BTN VAI	9/4/64
Gardner, A.M.	26BTN VAI	8/2/64
Goff, George A.	19VAC	8/7/64
Haynes, Robert P.	26BTN VAI	7/15/64
Hazelwood, John W.	22VAI	10/7/64
Hendricks, George	Randolph County	10/28/64
Henning, Lorenzo	22VAI	1/24/65
Hicks, John	22VAI	9/2/64
Hinkle, Wm.	19VAC	11/22/64
Jones, Wm. A.	22VAI	7/15/64
Keys, Isaac	26BTN VAI	9/28/64
Kirby, James H.	26BTN VAI	9/12/64
Lantz, Daniel	25VAI	9/29/64
Martin, Daniel B.	24VAI	9/23/64
May, John R.	19VAC	11/29/64
Meadows, Allen P.	26BTN VAI	10/19/64
Moore, Isaac	36VAI	8/12/64
Murphy, Marshall M.	25VAI	10/3/64
Noble, Joe E.	26BTN VAI	2/11/65
Parks, J.C.	22VAI	7/15/64
Peck, Wm. H.	26BTN VAI	12/31/64
Peters, Joe B.	25VAI	12/22/64
Powell, John	60VAI	1/31/65
Ray, Charles A.	22VAI	8/4/64
Reaser, Philip	26BTN VAI	7/15/64
Reese, M.	22VAI	9/23/64
Riley, Timothy	Bryan's BTY VAA	3/4/65
Roach, Charles B.	26BTN VAI	9/29/64
Seebert, Lancelot	25VAI	11/11/64
Shireman, John	18VAC	10/3/64
Summers, John	25VAI	10/12/64
Swadley, James	25VAI	11/3/64
Sydenstricker, John	26BTN VAI	2/6/65
Tomlinson, Joseph	26BTN VAI	11/3/64
Tracey, James A.	31VAI	4/26/65
Underwood, Jesse	60VAI	2/4/65
Warrick, Wm.	8VAC	5/22/65
Webb, Wm. H.	26BTN VAI	12/9/64
White, John T.	26BTN VAI	1/12/65
White, Wm.	20VAC	10/2/64
Whitteker, Byrd	60VAI	4/23/65
Williams, Alexander	26BTN VAI	9/6/64
Williams, Rufus	26BTN VAI	10/19/64
Wilson, Obediah	19VAC	3/24/65

Ft. Delaware Prison

NAME	REGIMENT	DATE DIED
Adkins, B.F.T.	16VAC	9/11/64
Anderson, W.F.	8VAC	4/8/65
Bailey, Wm. H.	22VAI	5/2/65
Bausel, Joseph	62VAI	8/31/63
Bennett, John	22VAI	4/15/64
Bouier, M.A.	Upshur County	9/8/63
Boyers, James R.	Randolph County	9/13/63
Bradshaw, James	16VAC	3/22/65
Brown, D.	Jackson County	9/18/63
Cadle, Nathaniel	14VAC	4/26/64
Campbell, Levi	60VAI	6/1/65
Cavendish, James W.	22VAI	4/15/64
Coffindiffer, Smith	Harrison County	9/6/63
Comer, John	30BTNVASS	4/6/65
Crouch, Smith	Randolph County	8/19/63
Edward, W.J.	8VAC	4/18/65
Ellis, Marion F.	36VAI	5/1/65
Fogleman, D.	Randolph County	9/20/63
Green, James B.	Lewis County	8/21/63
Gwinn, Wm. A.	22VAI	7/2/64
Hamilton, Adam G.	25VAI	7/28/64
Heater, Henry	7VAC	3/18/65
Henderson, James P.	36VAI	5/21/65
Hopkins, Reuben	60VAI	3/31/65
Houghton, Jesse M.	31VAI	10/1/63
Hutcheson, G.W.	22VAI	6/10/65
Isner, Allen	Randolph County	8/22/63
Kirk, Jordan A.	16VAC	9/1/64
Kirks, Henry T.	60VAI	11/29/63
Landrum, Felix A.	60VAI	4/3/65
McClung, Wm. A.	22VAI	8/23/64
McQueen, Thomas	19VAC	7/22/64
Massey, Wm. L.	36BTNVAC	5/18/65
Mills, Oliver	16VAC	8/11/64
Neel, John K.	60VAI	4/13/65
Nutter, John L.	36BTNVAC	4/21/65
Phillips, Wm. T.	23BTNVAC	5/8/64
Riffle, G.W.	20VAC	6/15/64
Shaver, George T.	36VAI	5/28/65
Shepherd, John F.	36VAI	4/13/65
Short, Elza	16VAC	8/13/64
Skaggs, Joe B.	22VAI	7/6/64
Strickler, Allen	22VAI	9/3/64
Thompson, Wm.	16VAC	2/9/65

Name	Regiment	Date Died
Toney, Robert	8VAC	8/4/64
Ward, Wm. T.	18VAC	9/24/63
Washington, Robert J.	36VAI	4/3/65
Wilson, James Wood	31VAI	9/20/63

Frederick, Maryland, Prison

NAME	REGIMENT	DATE DIED
McClung, George A.	14VAC	8/11/64
Morris, Joe W.	16VAC	9/9/64
Peadro, Sam M.	16VAC	NONE
Preston, Thomas C.	14VAC	8/2/64
Wooldridge, James R.	60VAI	3/23/65

Gallipolis, Ohio

NAME	REGIMENT	DATE DIED
McKiney, James H.	22VAI	7/19/62
Wickline, Wm. Z.	26BTN VAI	6/16/62

Johnson's Island, Ohio, Prison

NAME	REGIMENT	DATE DIED
Ash, Samuel	Doddridge County	1/3/63
Cole, Peter	60VAI	11/22/62
Parks, James S.	16VAC	6/27/63

New Creek (Keyser), West Virginia

NAME	REGIMENT	DATE DIED
Campbell, John W.	17VAC	8/13/64

Pt. Lookout, Maryland, Prison

NAME	REGIMENT	DATE DIED
Andrews, Charles P.	Chapman's BTY VAA	4/19/65
Arbogast, Wm. S.	25VAI	1/31/65
Bailey, John S.	60VAI	11/7/64
Ballard, Overton H.	26BTN VAI	12/16/64
Blair, John H.	14VAC	1/20/65
Boley, John W.	22VAI	2/4/65
Bragg, Joseph	22VAI	2/4/65
Bragg, Wm.	22VAI	2/8/65
Bragg, Wm.	26BTN VAI	8/22/64
Cain, Isaac	62VAI	10/-/63
Cassell, Robert E.	62VAI	2/9/65
Clendenon, Arglen	22VAI	2/24/65

Name	Regiment	Date Died
Coulter, George J.	14VAC	4/23/65
Craft, John H.	60VAI	1/6/65
Dent, James	19VAC	11/20/63
Dunn, Wm. A.	22VAI	1/23/65
Estill, D.H.	22VAI	1/5/65
Farley, Andrew T.	60VAI	1/4/65
Grant, Thomas T.	22VAI	10/8/64
Gray, Solomon	36VAI	3/8/65
Halstead, James H.	36VAI	4/4/65
Hedge, George	14VAC	2/13/65
Hogan, John A.	22VAI	12/27/64
Ingles, George A.	22VAI	12/31/64
Jackson, Henry	16VAC	1/24/65
Jones, George M.	26BTN VAI	8/26/64
Lilly, J.	36VAI	3/2/65
Lough, Washington	25VAI	8/8/64
McClintoc, Robert M.	14VAC	12/16/64
Malcolm, J.	19VAC	3/12/64
Myers, Daniel	62VAI	12/4/63
Park, John	18VAC	4/13/64
Puffenbarger, Wm.	25VAI	11/9/63
Starcher, James	22VAI	11/4/64
Taylor, Reuben	26BTN VAI	1/14/65
Van Horn, Washington	31VAI	6/19/64
Workman, Francis	16VAC	2/28/65
Wylie, Thomas H.	26BTN VAI	8/22/64
Yerkey, George P.	36VAI	11/7/63
Zombro, James W.	12VAC	12/20/64

Rock Island, Illinois, Prison

NAME	REGIMENT	DATE DIED
Bowden, John H.	8VAC	4/15/64
Butcher, Warrick	19VAC	12/3/64
Campbell, George	8VAC	9/1/64
Carpenter, Lewis	8VAC	4/14/64
Frasher, Louis F.	16VAC	8/7/64
Helmick, Isaac	62VAI	12/23/64
Hudkins, John M.	20VAC	3/19/64
Jones, Wm. H.	8VAC	2/18/64
Kincaid, Sam	22VAI	9/19/64
McKenzie, James H.	17VAC	2/22/64
Sick, Harrison	16VAC	10/30/64
Westfall, James H.	19VAC	6/18/64
Wheeler, Joseph	8VAC	2/12/64
Wright, David S.	20VAC	6/15/64
Wright, Richard	17VAC	2/21/64

Wheeling, West Virginia, Prison

Two citizen's listed with no state/county I.D. were very likely West Virginians: Henry Patterson 9/10/64 and John Yost 8/6/64.

Statistical Review

Mortality rate by year: 1862: 21
1863: 42
1864: 144
1865: <u>102</u>
Total: 309

The first West Virginia Confederate Soldier to die in a Federal prison was Evan Evans, of the 31st Virginia Infantry. His death occurred at Camp Chase, Ohio, on April 1, 1862.

The last West Virginia Confederate soldier to die in a Federal prison was William Lee, of the 19 Virginia Cavalry. His death occurred on September 13, 1865, also at Camp Chase.

The first and last West Virginia civilians to die in a Federal prison, were, respectively: George Valentine of Ritchie County, who died on June 3, 1862, and Christopher Coger of Webster County, who died on October 21, 1864. These deaths were also at Camp Chase, Ohio.

The prison having the largest number of deaths among West Virginians was Camp Chase, Ohio, with 99; followed by Elmyra, New York, with 65.

Regiments with highest death rate among prisoners: Infantry: 22 Regiment, Virginia Infantry with 32 deaths; Cavalry: 19 Regiment, Virginia Cavalry with 24 deaths

The county with highest civilian death rate was Randolph at 6.

Civilian deaths came from citizens of the following 21 West Virginia counties: Barbour, Doddridge, Fayette, Greenbrierr Hardy, Harrison, Jackson, Lewis, Marion, Marshall, Mason, Monongalia, Pocahontas, Raleigh, Randolph, Ritchie, Taylor, Wayne, Webster, Wood and Upshur.

West Virginians perished in a total of 15 Northern prisons.

The Southern Claims Commission

ON MARCH 3, 1871, nearly six years after the end of the American Civil War, Congress authorized a commission to receive, examine, and consider the claims of "those citizens who remained loyal adherents to the cause and the government of the United States during the war, for stores or supplies taken or furnished during the rebellion for the use of the Army of the United States in states proclaimed as in insurrection against the United States."

According to the 1871 act, commissioners were appointed by the President with the advice and consent of the Senate. This commission was formed to allow pro-Union Southerners an opportunity to seek reimbursement for financial losses incurred during the war at the hands of the Union Army or Navy. This "Southern Claims Commission," a three-man board, was to accept claims only from those who held American citizenship; resided in a state that seceded; could prove loyalty to the Federal government throughout the war; and had suffered *official* confiscation of property.

The Commissioners of Claims met first in Washington, DC, on March 16, 1871. They were to review the submitted evidence of each claim and satisfy themselves as to the loyalty of each claimant. This was to be accomplished by taking additional testimony from a claimant's friends and neighbors. The commissioners had to certify the amount, nature, and value of the property taken or furnished, and report their judgment on each claim in writing to the House of Representatives at the beginning of each session of Congress. The House would then vote to allow or disallow the claim and to appropriate money for payment.

Response by southern citizens was overwhelming, with 22,298 claims pouring in by March 3, 1873, the last day on which new claims could be presented. Investigation and settlement of these claims continued until the commission was terminated by Congress on March 10, 1880. All claims combined totaled $60,258,150.44, of which only $4,636,920.69 was paid. Of the 22,298 claims, only 7,092 satisfied the rigid tests of sworn statement and cross examination in proving both the claimants sustained Union loyalty and the validity of his claim.

Southern Claims Commission case files can sometimes provide a treasure-trove of previously "lost" information to the historian and genealogist. A case file may contain any or all of the following types of documents:

claimant's petition, depositions of neighbors and others, notes of the agent investigating the claim, reports from the Treasury Department relative to its search of captured Confederate records for any proof of disloyalty, and the final summary and recommendation of the commissioners.

The National Archives and Records Administration (NARA) in Washington, DC, maintains these records in five record groups:

> RG 56: General Records of the Department of the Treasury, which include administrative records and correspondence files.
> RG 123: Records of the U.S. Court of Claims
> RG 205: Records of the Court of Claims Justice Section, which include case files of disallowed claims referred by the House for appeal.
> RG 217: Records of the Accounting Officers of the Department of the Treasury; case files for approved claims.
> RG 233: Records of the U.S. House; case files for barred or disallowed claims.

Of the 22,298 claims filed, the author has identified 202 claims as citizens of West Virginia. Those claims are indexed here, giving first the claimant's name, followed by his files commission number, office number, report number, year the claim was filed, and the amount and status of the claim.

Claim Status Codes

> A—Allowed claim
> B—Barred claim (those submitted after the deadline of March 3, 1873.)
> D—Disallowed claim

The researcher should be aware that not all case files are extant, and that those listed as paid were almost always settled for a sum less than the claimant sought.

Accessing Case Files of the Southern Claims Commission

Identify the West Virginia claimant from this index and send all data given to:

Allowed claims: Civil Reference Branch (NNRC); National Archives, 8th and Pennsylvania, NW; Washington, DC 20408

Claims barred or disallowed: Send for NARA's Descriptive Pamphlet M1407 which indexes fiche numbers on which these files are contained. There is no charge for the pamphlet. Disallowed claims are arranged by "office number" and appear as fiche 1-4272. Barred claims are arranged alphabetically on fiche 4273-4829.

For M1407 and other publications: Publication Services Branch, National Archives, 8th & Penn., NW; Washington, DC 20408

Related Records

The dissatisfaction of many claimants with the outcome of their cases, and objections to the barring of claims that were not submitted prior to March 3, 1873, led to the Bowman Act of 1883 and the Tucker Act of 1887. These acts authorized Congress to reconsider any of the claims previously handled by the SCC and forward them to the U.S. Court of Claims for further review and recommendation. Thus some case files for barred or disallowed claims of the SCC are in Records of the U.S. Court of Claims, Record Group 123. If a case file is missing it may be found in RG 123. The NARA will assist the researcher in this regard and can help with accessing those records.

This list of West Virginia claimants of the SCC was assembled from three sources as follows:

1. NARA's micropublication M87, *Records of the Commissioners of Claims (SCC) 1871–1880* (roll 13). This *Geographical List of Claimants* is part of RG 56 and arranges the names of claimants according to state and county, with each county's claimants arranged alphabetically. The serial number and amount of claimed loss is part of this record. In a few instances notes appear indicating the action taken on individual claims. This roll of microfilm is the most useful tool in researching claims of the Southern Claims Commission, and as of this writing it is available from the National Archives for $36.00.

2. *Annual Reports of the Commissioner of Claims, House Miscellaneous Documents,* 42nd Congress, 2d Session through 46th Congress, 2nd Session. Washington, DC: Government Printing Officer 1871–1880.

3. *Consolidated Index of Claims Reported by the Commissioners of Claims to the House of Representatives from 1871–1880.* Washington, DC: Government Printing Office, 1892. This index is rare and difficult to locate. The author did find a copy in the holdings of the West Virginia and Regional History Collection at West Virginia University (Colson Hall) Morgantown, WV. This is the only index providing all three of the file numbers assigned to each claim, and all file numbers are needed by the Archives personnel to locate available case files. It should be noted however that some files do not have the full set of numbers listed. Should that be the case with a claim you're researching, send all of the information that *is* available. It is quite likely the NARA will still be able to access the record.

A Review of West Virginia SCC Claims

Citizens of eleven West Virginia counties are represented in case files of the SCC. The smallest claim was $33.00 submitted by Joseph Detter of Berkeley County. The largest was $50,000 submitted by well-known West Virginia artist and correspondent David Hunter Strother of Jefferson County.

Jefferson Countians filed the most claims, at 126. Their total value was $274,121 with the average claim being $2,228.00. Only 31 Jefferson County claims were paid. This represents just 24.6% of total claims filed.

The author has included following this index two West Virginia SCC case files. These will offer the reader an opportunity to see the type and quality of information available. The files presented here are only partially transcribed and represent Greenbrier and Jefferson counties.

Southern Claims Commission File Index

Berkeley County

CLAIMANT	CMSN. #	OFFICE #	REPORT #	YEAR	AMT/STATUS
Bain, Robert M	14,998	—	—	—	$240. B
Beeson, Lewis R. est.	12,425	—	3	1873	$320. A
Boltz, John H.	14,534	—	5	1875	$1,508 A
Criswell, James	15,196	—	—	—	$160. B
Dalwick, John est.	21,378	—	6	1876	$880. A
Detter, Joseph	15,197	—	—	—	$33. B
Freese, John W.	13,212	1172	4	1874	$175. D
Hayslett, John	15,004	—	—	—	$150. B
Henson, George W.	15,005	—	—	—	$690. B
Herring, Ezra	5,093	—	—	—	$2,476. B
Hoffman, Joseph	15,006	—	—	—	$1,200. B
Keiter, Hamilton J.	15,008	—	8	1878	$425. A
Lamon, John W.	15,009	—	—	—	$1,950. B
Lemen, Robert	5,341	—	—	—	$2,252. B
Lindsey, Sam K.	13,213	892	7	1877	$250. D
Lloyd, James	14,369	893	7	1877	$400. D
Lock, Benjamin	17,314	—	8	1878	$2,472 A
Morrison, Amos	10,709	1343	3	1873	$1.088 D
Morrow, James W.	17,315	753	5	1875	$2,521 D
Myers, Aaron est.	18,208	—	—	—	$1,155 B
Pitzer, George J.	5,342	895	7	1877	$430. D
Pitzer, James S.	14,535	—	4	1874	$977. A
Roberts, Wm. H.	15,011	1703	9	1879	$421. D
Robinson, James H.	15,198	—	—	—	$300. B
Shepherd, Francis R.	14,536	1184	4	1874	$320. D
Snapp, Jacob H.	15,199	879	8	1878	$528. D
Thompson, David	13,519	—	4	1874	$568. A
Turner, Anthony	14,537	—	5	1875	$440. A
Turner, John est.	17,313	—	—	—	$1,158. B
Welshans, Henry C.	14,544	1347	3	1873	$ 300. D

Claimant	CMSN. #	OFFICE #	REPORT #	YEAR	AMT/STATUS
Welshans, Philip H.	13,208	—	6	1876	$880. A
West, Joseph	10,446	1709	9	1879	$1,274. D
Wright, Daniel	15,013	—	—	—	$194. B
Zepp, George W.	1,182	880	8	1878	$400. D
Zepp, Henry	14,546	1348	3	1873	$1,894. D

Grant County

CLAIMANT	CMSN. #	OFFICE #	REPORT #	YEAR	AMT/STATUS
Graham, Isaac	16,833	—	3	1873	$140. A
Judy, Zebulon	16,834	—	—	—	$80. B
Ours, Elizabeth	16,837	—	—	—	$140. B
Seymour, Jonathan	18,585	1707	9	1879	$3,200. D

Greenbrier County

CLAIMANT	CMSN. #	OFFICE #	REPORT #	YEAR	AMT/STATUS
Caldwell, Joseph F.	11,428	—	6	1876	$1,450. A

Hampshire County

CLAIMANT	CMSN. #	OFFICE #	REPORT #	YEAR	AMT/STATUS
Craigen, Jacob J.	8,607	—	2	1872	$22,974 A
Daniels, Eliza J.	13,501	—	—	—	$125. B
Johnson, Zachariah	8,462	—	3	1873	$125. A
Light, Wm.	9,933	891	7	1877	$1,661. D
Malcolm, James	8464	1341	3	1873	$172. D
Malcolm, Robert	8463	1342	3	1873	$150. D

Hancock County

CLAIMANT	CMSN. #	OFFICE #	REPORT #	YEAR	AMT/STATUS
Atkinson, John H.	8,617	—	4	1874	$2,468 A

Hardy County

CLAIMANT	CMSN. #	OFFICE #	REPORT #	YEAR	AMT/STATUS
Baker, Wm. C.	1,114	—	7	1877	$1,240 A
Frye, Henry W.	11,320	—	3	1873	$670. A
Kotz, Francis	11,321	1340	3	1873	$279. D
Laudaker, Jesse	10,707	—	3	1873	$1,792 A
Russell, Wm.	21,305	—	9	1879	$1,903 A
Williams, George T.	21,379	—	—	—	$8,079 B

Jefferson County

CLAIMANT	CMSN. #	OFFICE #	REPORT #	YEAR	AMT/STATUS
Aglionby, Charles	14,627	1165	4	1874	$2,936 D
Andrews, Linton N.	4,259	—	—	—	$883. D
Bane, Garrett W.	15,589	1166	4	1874	$600. D

Baylor, Moses	15,980	1167	4	1874	$2,958 D
Beck, John	17,007	—	—	—	$772. B
Bell, Hector	15,591	—	—	—	$923. B
Boyers, G. W.	15,534	1168	4	1874	$3,280 D
Brotherton, Lee G.	13,289	1689	9	1879	$247. D
Brown, Thomas	13,291	1335	3	1873	$560. D
Burns, Caleb	15,592	—	—	—	$1,945 B
Burns, Isaac V.	13,207	1336	3	1873	$657. D
Cain, Augustine	11,324	—	6	1876	$440. A
Chamberlain, John	13,025	—	—	—	$687. D
Coalman, Daniel	15,000	1169	4	1874	$690. D
Cockrell, George W.	14,308	1170	4	1874	$1,200 D
Cockrell, John G.	14,428	1337	3	1873	$224. D
Colbert, Hezekiah	17,008	—	—	—	$1,932 B
Cook, John	13,211	1171	4	1874	$1,050 D
Copeland, Nathan H.	13,530	—	—	—	$339. B
Crow, Wm. est.	12,740	—	7	1877	$725. A
Custer, Jacob est.	14,843	751	5	1875	$— D
Custer, Randolph	12,726	—	7	1877	$2,518. A
Daley, Patrick H.	21,976	—	—	—	$425. B
Dixon, Wm. A.	15,593	—	6	1876	$150. A
Dixon, Wm. H.	11,712	—	9	1879	$1,146 A
Dust, Isaac	15,594	—	7	1877	$260. A
Eckles, Benjamin	15,595	1690	9	1879	$1,040 D
Engle, Edwin C.	13,287	1338	3	1873	$300. D
Fulk, Frederick A.	12,664	—	7	1877	$1,372 A
Goen, John F.	12,727	1173	4	1874	$1,625 D
Gordon, Philip	15,319	1339	3	1873	$1,210 D
Green, Wm.	14,628	—	—	—	$384. B
Grove, Wm. est.	14,394	1692	9	1879	$2,000 D
Haines, Edward V.	5,092	—	2	1872	$2,089 A
Hamill, Alleria A.	13,020	1174	4	1874	$425. D
Hawk, Elijah	20,179	—	7	1877	9386. A
Hazelwood, James T.	17,013	—	8	1878	$150. A
Hill, John W.	14,395	—	5	1875	$475. A
Hooff, Francis R.	14,844	752	5	1875	$3,285 D
Hopkins, E.C.	20,076	889	7	1877	$306. D
Huff, Harrison	353	1005	2	1872	$130. D
Hurst, Wm. est.	15,590	1688	9	1879	$4,105 D
Jewett, Mary S.	14,437	—	9	1879	$2,700 A
Johnson, Andrew J.	13,018	—	7	1877	$190. A
Kanode, John H.	12,355	—	7	1877	$2,945 A
Kennedy, Anna	20,178	—	—	—	$1,500 B
Kerny, A.H. est.	12,665	1175	4	1874	$750. D
Kidwiler, Adam	21,676	—	—	—	$3,914 B
Kidwiler, Isaac	20,229	—	—	—	$1,025 B
Kirwin, Thomas	20,175	—	7	1877	$495. A

Langdon, Charles	14,629	—	—	—	$151. B
Lemen, Wm. M.	13,118	890	7	1877	$939. D
Lemen, Willoughby N.	12,545	—	—	—	$112. B
Lewis, Samuel	13,523	—	9	1879	$260. A
Licklider, Thomas	13,288	—	—	—	$407. B
Lloyd, Dangerfield	14,845	—	5	1875	$1,163 A
Lock, John J.	12,723	1182	4	1874	
Lock, Remington S.	15,984	—	8	1878	$950. A
Loyd, Wm.	13,481	1176	4	1.874	$4,146 D
McCloy, James W.	15,987	—	8	1878	$232. A
McCurdy, John W.	14,370	—	—	—	$798. B
McSherry, Wm.	13,532	1697	9	1879	$1,7/13 D
Melvin, Joseph est.	17,012	1695	9	1879	$583. D
Menifee, Joseph	15,536	—	—	—	$1,030 B
Merritt, Jacob	13,019	1698	9	1879	$2,386 D
Miles, Thomas H.	21,619	1611	9	1879	$11,749 D
Miller, Ed W.	17,507	—	4	1874	$11,661 A
Miller, Jacob J.	13,022	—	8	1878	$1,285 A
Miller, Lydia	14,309	1177	4	1874	$4,020 D
Miller, Robert M.	12,364	—	—	—	$2,631 B
Mock, George W.	12,191	—	3	1873	$200. A
Moler, Daniel	1,925	—	1	1871	$12,892 A
Moler, Philip R.	13,023	894	7	1877	$908. D
Moler, Wm. J.	15,537	1178	4	1874	$517. D
Moreland, Samuel	14,371	1179	4	1874	92,588 D
Myers, James W.	13,209	1344	3	1873	$1,663 D
Myers, Lucinda	17,316	1699	9	1879	$150. D
Neer, John W.	14,431	1700	9	1879	$665. D
Nisewaner, John	1,696	—	5	1875	$420. A
Osborne, Mary est.	15,538	—	5	1875	$278. A
Osburn, Logan	14,433	1701	9	1879	$1,185 D
Ott, Barney est.	15,185	—	—	—	$1,207 B
Ott, Daniel	14,310	—	—	—	$593. B
Ott, John W.	12,666	877	8	1878	$1,842 D
Packett, John B.	14,434	—	—	—	$2,076 B
Packett, John W. est.	17,317	—	—	—	$837. B
Pane, Wm.	14,435	—	—	—	$1,750 B
Pettit, John J.	17,318	1702	9	1879	$3,004 D
Pool, Richard N.	1,213	—	—	—	$11,637 B
Ramey, Wm. C.	13,531	1345	3	1873	$2,576 D
Ramsbury, John J.	13,024	—	4	1874	$190. A
Reed, Henry	14,543	833	6	1876	$311. D
Ridenour, Samuel	14,436	1180	4	1874	$5,425 D
Roberts, Joe L.	13,017	1181	4	1874	$495. D
Rockenbaugh, John	14,311	—	—	—.	$701. B
Roper, James est.	14,372	—	7	1877	$9,920 D
Ruckle, Samuel	13,117	—	7	1877	$711. D

Claimant	CMSN. #	OFFICE #	REPORT #	YEAR	AMT/STATUS
Rutherford, Mary est.	12,723	1182	9	1879	$— D
Rutherford, Uriah est.	12,723	617	9	1879	$2,996. D
Seaman, Mary B.	11,464	—	—	—	$4,881 B
Shaull, George E.	13,480	878	8	1878	$530. D
Shaull, John F.	13,522	1183	4	1874	$973. D
Shaull, Nicholas S.	13,482	—	7	1877	$1,043 A
Show, George	13,210	1346	3	1873	$1,025 D
Snyder, James W.	13,021	896	7	1877	$2,3/10 D
Spotts, George W.	14,438	1185	4	1874	$962. D
Staley, Jacob W.	15,539	754	5	1875	$838. D
Staley, Stephen	12,725	—	—	—	$1,702 B
Stipes, Anna	20,173	—	9	1879	$162. A
Straith, John J.	13,119	834	6	1876	$3,330. D
Strother, David H.	21,715	—	—	—	$50,000 B
Thompson, Carey	1959	1115	2	1872	$1,886 D
Turner, Wm. F.	14,843	751	5	1875	$— D
Urton, John	14,312	1710	9	1879	$1,108 D
Wageley, David A.	12,546	1186	4	1874	$1,488 D
Walker, James	13,520	1187	4	1874	$300. D
Ware, John W.	12,354	—	3	1873	$1,533 A
Welcome, John	14,630	1708	9	1879	$265. D
Welsh, Elizabeth B.	14,313	1188	4	1874	1,537 D
Welshans, Joseph	13,521	—	8	1878	$453. A
West, Thomas	15,596	1189	4	1874	$3,380 D
Whittington, Francis	141545	1190	4	1874	$880. D
Willis, Thomas H.	11,945	5286	10	1880	$14,050 D
Woodward, Tom E.	11,325	—	3	1873	$716. A
Yates, Francis	15,597	1191	4	1874	$3,099 D
Zombro, George P.	13,518	1192	4	1874	$1,277 D

Monroe County

CLAIMANT	CMSN. #	OFFICE #	REPORT #	YEAR	AMT/STATUS
Ballard, Beverly	16,145	749	5	1875	$361. D
Bickett, James H.	19,312	—	—	—	$162. B
Campbell, Allan	19,343	—	9	1879	$150. A
Clark, Sam M.	16,146	751	5	1875	$130. D
Hellms, Leonard W.	16,849	1694	9	1879	$218. D
Jackson, Thomas	16,144	1696	9	1879	$50. D
Sears, Wm.	191341	1706	9	1879	$130. D
Tingler, Henry	5,006	866	8	1878	$232 D

Morgan County

CLAIMANT	CMSN. #	OFFICE #	REPORT #	YEAR	AMT/STATUS
Largent, Benjamin	15,373	—	7	1877	$468. A
Larkin, Michael	15,374	—	7	1877	$360. A
Ziler, Jacob	15,375	—	7	1877	$600. A

Pendleton County

CLAIMANT	CMSN. #	OFFICE #	REPORT #	YEAR	AMT/STATUS
Bond, John S.	11,317	—	9	1879	$1,383 A
Borror, Simon	17,280	—	—	—	$50. B
Bowers, Christian S.	16,397	750	5	1875	$385. D
Day, Leonard	18,058	—	—	—	$125. B
Eagle, Julia A.	17,281	—	3	1873	$340. A
Full, Jacob	17,282	1691	9	1879	$120. D
Graham, James H.	16,836	1693	9	1879	$418. D
Judy, Mary Ann est.	16,838	—	—	—	$184. B
Mowery, Anthony	16,398	—	9	1879	$140. A
Teter, John A.	17,283	—	—	—	$353. B
Wise, Zebulon	16,835	—	3	1873	$143 A

Randolph County

CLAIMANT	CMSN. #	OFFICE #	REPORT #	YEAR	AMT/STATUS
Frank, Joshua	576	—	—	—	$250. D

SCC Case Files of
Joseph Caldwell and Logan Osburn

THE FOLLOWING TWO CASE FILES of the Southern Claims Commission are only partially transcribed. Claimants were asked a series of questions from a pre-printed "interrogation form," and in some cases, their answers to these questions, along with witness statements and other supporting documents, created a rather large claim file. Joseph Caldwell's SCC file is one such example, containing nearly 75 pages of material.

Wealthy or well-connected claimants would usually ask their influential friends or associates to give sworn statements supporting their claim. Others, such as Mr. Osburn, of Jefferson County, asked even his former slave to sign a statement supporting the validity of his SCC claim.

It should be noted that many claimants sought reimbursement for their losses well before the SCC was formed. Mr. Caldwell, for example, sought compensation during the war for some weapons that were taken by U.S. forces. He also sought reimbursement in 1864 for the items that would eventually become part of his SCC claim. Mr. Caldwell, and many others, eventually settled their SCC claims for less than the amount of their alleged losses.

The author attempted to obtain from the National Archives a copy of the SCC file of David Hunter Strother, of Jefferson County. Unfortunately, that file is among those lost or accidentally destroyed. Mr. Strother's claim, at $50,000, was by far the largest claim of any West Virginia resident.

In transcribing these records, the original spelling and punctuation has been retained, with exception only for clarity.

No. 11428
The Claim of Joseph F. Caldwell of

No. of Item	DESCRIPTION	AMOUNT CLAIMED		AMOUNT ALLOWED		AMOUNT DISALLOWED
		Dollars	Cts.	Dollars	Cts.	Dollars
1	2 Horses & other things	600	00	350	00	250
2	7000 fence Rails	150	00	150	00	
3	1000 pounds Bacon	250	00	70	00	180
4	12 Fine Sheep	150	00	36	00	114
5	25 Hogs	300	00			300
	Total	1450	00	606	00	844

The SCC Case File of Joseph Caldwell

United States
    To J.F. Caldwell of Lewisburg
    Greenbrier County, West Va.

1864
May & June—1000 lbs bacon .25¢ $250.00

2 horses (blooded with two saddles
bridles & 2 buffalo robes) $600.00

12 head sheep, improved stock $150.00

25 hogs $300.00

7000 rails destroyed $150.00

Dental case & instruments $500.00

Case of mathematical instruments $150.00

1 large map of Virginia $25.00

1 Telescope, 1 Microscope, a Quadrant
with other instruments books, maps,
papers, clothing & etc.   <u>$1000.00</u>

                       $3125.00

Greenbrier County, State of West Virginia

    J.F. Caldwell on his solemn oath says that the foregoing statement of account of property taken by the Federal Army is correct. that the same has not been or any part returned to him, nor has he received compensation for any portion or part of the above account.

                                     J.F. Caldwell

Sworn and subscribed before me in & for the county aforesaid this the 21st day of April 1869

                                     J.W. Sampson, Justice

State of West Virginia
Greenbrier Co.

I Joel McPherson, Recorder of Greenbrier Co. also a Notary Public for sd County, hereby certify, that I have known Dr. J. F. Caldwell for many years. The sd Dr. Caldwell was in April last appointed Justice & Supervisor for the township of Lewisburg by the Hen. N. Harrison, Judge of the 9th Judicial Circuit.

The sd Caldwell also acting as Master Commissioner for the Cir Court of this County, also a member of "the County Board of Registration," as such acting in these several positions he has been and is recognized as a decided *Loyal Union Man*. He is not only known to myself as such but is so considered and recognized by the Gov. of our State, and the entire community in which he lives, as a loyal Union man he was an avowed enemy to Secession having written for the press against it and in defence of the Union. Given under my hand this 11th day of June 1866.

         Joel McPherson
         Recorder of Greenbrier
         Co. also
         Notary Public

Dec 20 1871
J. F. Caldwell

Why those who participated in the Rebellion dislike and slander him

I am not prompted by egotism to allude to or enumerate the offices which I have held, or appointments of trust to which I have been elected, or which have been confided to me, but my motive is to show and explain why it is that those who participated in the Rebellion united against me, because of my deciding by my mite to preserve the union of our States, & to oppose the traitors who have rebelled against it, & had expatriated & made themselves outlaws in our State. They combined to injure & destroy me by resorting all manner of means with their most malignant hate

Beginning with 1861, I published several addresses to the people in opposition to their secession from the Union, some hundred of which I sent to the P. Office in Lewisburg for the people of Greenbrier, the Rebels took them by Mob force & burnt them in the street, I still have copies of them

By the men loyal to the Union, after the Rebellion I was elected by the Republican Party, as the President of the Central Committee of the Republican Party for the County of Greenbrier, & was elected every year since to the same position, & at this time hold it

I was a member of the Republican Convention before the close of the Rebellion which met at Parkersburg, which nominated the Hon A. I Boreman for Governor of West Virginia

I was by the Republican Party elected a member of the first Board of

Supervisors after the war, & was by that Board elected to be their President I am still a member of this Court.

I was Justice of the peace for the Township of Lewisburg

I was a Representative in our State Legislature, and I have been a Master Commissioner in Chancery ever since the establishment of this State I was one of the first Commissioners of the Board of Registration which elected me its President, & remained a member until the repeal of it by the Legislature

I was three times elected Mayor of the town of Lewisburg. I was the President or Chairman of all the County Conventions and meetings of the Republican Party from the beginning of the State to the last one.

I was nominated by the Republican Party to the last State Senate

I was elected by the Board of Supervisors as the Proxy to [represent?] the $250,000 stock of this County in the Chesapeak & Ohio Rail Road Company 1870. I have been a delegate in every Convention to nominate a Candidate for Congress or Governor of the State

I have been a School Commissioner ever since the establishment of the State. In the spring of 1861, I arranged to enlist more than 100 Scotchmen as Solders in the service of the U States, but the Secretary of War, Mr. Cammeron declined to employ them after I had proposed to conduct them to Washington without expense to the Government.

J.F. Caldwell

Joseph F. Caldwell the claimant after having been first duly sworn deposes and says in answer to the following questions as follows,

1. My name is Joseph F. Caldwell, my age is seventy-nine years 2nd May 1875. My occupation is that of a dentist my residence is Lewisburg Greenbrier Co. West Va where I have resided since 1824.

2. I am the claimant.

3. I was born in Frederick County State of Virginia near Brucetown

4. I was in Knoxville, Tennessee six months before the outbreak of rebellion following my profession. I was in Kentucky and Ohio, and this date at Wheeling and Charleston being upwards of three years during the rebellion in Charleston Kanawha Co. West Va. and came here from Charleston on 12 October 1864

5. My sympathies during the war were from beginning to end were on the side of the Union.

6. I never said or did anything against the Union cause. but all my saying and doings were in aid of the Union cause.

7. I was at all times during the war ready and willing to do what I could in aid of the Union cause

8. I wrote articles in the public papers in favor of the Union cause at intervals throughout the war at Sandusky, Wheeling, Point Pleasant Gallipolis and Charleston West Va.

9. I had a son in the US Navy a surgeon Hanson Clay Caldwell. Who

died about the beginning of the war. I had a grandson, William Wise in the US Navy during the war

10. I was about sixty-five years old when the war commenced and was not in the service or employment of the US Government at any time during the war.

11. I never contributed anything to the Union cause except my service in a general way writing for and otherwise aiding and encouraging that side

12. I was always on the side of the Union in 1860 and 1861 and throughout the whole war. In 1860 I published an article in a newspaper in Sandusky Ohio, head "The Union it must be preserved"

13. I adhered to the Union cause and went in with what was called the restored Government of Virginia and was a member of the convention which set on foot the foundation of the state of West Virginia

14. I rejoiced in all federal victories and was grieved at all efforts to destroy the Union though I was sensitive and frequently hurt at individual injury & deaths on both sides.

15. I was always recognized as a loyal man. The Union officers always recognized me as a Union man.

16. I have since the war as a member of the West Va. legislature in 1868 as a justice and supervisor taken what is called the "iron clad oath" and on other occasions.

17. There were here at Lewisburg none that I could call Unionists certainly. I was myself a refugee from my home or rather kept away from my home on account of my adherence to the cause of the Union.

18. I cannot say that I was to any extent I did not return within the rebellion lines until Oct 1864 and was at that time almost blind was not seriously disturbed during the rest of the war

19. I was never arrested by any Confederate soldier or authority on that side.

20. None of my property was taken by the Confederates beyond something to eat now and then, of no great value.

21. None of my property was confiscated

22. I never did anything for the Confederate cause, but the contrary.

24. I was never in any service or business of any kind for the Confederacy.

26. I never took any oath of any kind to the so called Confederate States.

27. I never had any stores in my care or charge of property of any kind. Nor had I any share or interest in any contracts nor did I have anything to do in any way directly or indirectly with the soldiers or Confederate States

29. I was never interested in any vessel of any kind

30. I never subscribed to any loan to the so called Confederate States never owned and Confederate bonds, nor sold any cotton, or produce of any kind to the rebel government or anyone in their employment.

31. I never contributed to raising equiping or supporting any troops or to hospital relief funds or in any manner whatever in aid of the rebellion.

32. I never gave any information to any person in aid of military or naval operations against United States.

33. I never was at any time a member of any society or organization for

equiping volunteers, conscripts or for aiding the rebellion in any manner.

34. I never took any oath of allegiance to the so called Confederate States.

35. I never received any pass from rebel authority but came home in 1864 under escort of federal troops.

36. I suppose from information I have received some of my grand children were in the rebel service, but who or where they served I do not know anything about none of them was in said service by my consent or persuasion.

37. I was under no disabilities imposed by the 14th Amendment to the Constitution

38. I was never pardoned by the President or had need to be. 39. I never took any amnesty oath or had need to take any 40. I was never a prisoner to the U.S. authorities.

41. While at Coalsmouth, Kanawha Co. West Va. in 1863, I was arrested by command of a federal captain whose name I cannot now recollect, yes I remember it was Young, for attempting to arrest my colored servant who was trying to escape and was released by order or Col. A.J. Lightburn

42. No fines or anything of that kind were levied upon me by authorities of United States for any cause or in any way.

43. None of my property was ever taken or sold by the U.S. authorities under any confiscation law.

44. After 1860 and since I have voted generally for candidates opposed to secession I voted for Lincoln at his second election and urged the people of Greenbrier to vote against the ordinance of secession, & I voted against it myself

45. I belonged to no committee or to anything of that sort, put down or stifle Union sentiment

46. I was not in the Confederate service nor did I furnish any substitute or aid of any kind but the contrary as above stated

47. I was never in any branch of the Confederate service civil or military.

48. I never had charge of any trains teams or wagons, or had anything to do with the Confederate service in any way.

49. I was never employed in any saltpeter works or in tanning or milling or in any service of any kind in a direct or indirect of the rebellion.

50. I was never engaged in holding in custody directly or indirectly any persons taken by the rebel government in any way time or place

51. I was never in the Union army though I was within their lines assisting them all I could.

66. I was the owner of the property charged in this claim when it was taken

67. The property was taken from my farm and the house of my son except one horse taken from my grandson. My farm is situated in Greenbrier Co. West Va. on Greenbrier River about 3½ miles east of Lewisburg. I had about 400 acres in my farm about fifty acres were cleared and cultivated. The residue is woodland, there is no waste land, that is none thrown out or unfit for use.

68. I have never at any time filed any petition in bankruptcy or been declared bankrupt.

The United States,

To Joseph F. Caldwell, of W. Va.

For the amount allowed *him* by Act of Congress, Private No. 70, approved *March 3*, 1877, entitled "An Act making appropriations for the payment of claims reported allowed by the Commissioners of Claims under the Act of Congress of March 3, 1871:"

Six hundred and six dollars $606.00

72. I was not present when any of the property charged in this claim was taken. but was at Charleston Kanawha Co. WVa nor did I see it actually taken, but when the army came back to Kanawha Valley I found my two horses charged in the claim and a number of my dental instruments and some of my own clothing pants vests & etc. & a fine uniform coat costing fifty-four dollars naval uniform left me by my deceased son Hanson C. Caldwell. Also a fine buffalo robe, one sadle perhaps the other bridle in the possession of the federal soldiers, also one fine saddle, worth some forty dollars also another saddle worth about thirty dollars. the horses were fine blooded horses matches in every way except color and were worth two hundred and fifty dollars each. the dental instruments were worth about five hundred dollars.

(Question number and part of answer missing) and made complaint who declined doing anything in the matter saying as the reason that he had given my son D.B.C. Caldwell a certificate for the property, which turned out to be a mistake, and I asked for no voucher on that account, being assured that one had been given.

76. No payment was ever made to me or to anyone that I know of for any of the property. Gen Crook had four or five guns sent me for guns taken.

77. This property was taken by troops camped on my farm aforesaid.

78. I was absent I saw none of the property actually taken, but saw what I have mentioned after it was taken, in the possession of the federal troops in 1863 as follows: one sorrel horse about six years old blooded in good condition worth two hundred and fifty dollars. One bay horse same age of blooded stock in good condition worth at least two hundred and fifty dollars. Two bridles worth five dollars each I saw where about 7000 rails were burnt worth at least one hundred fifty dollars. I learned from the troops that they had taken about one thousand pounds of bacon worth almost two hundred fifty dollars. The twelve head of sheep were worth one hundred fifty dollars being of pure catsuald blood. I know nothing about the hogs definitely but from information of soldiers judged that at least twenty five head had been taken worth about three hundred dollars.

J.F. Caldwell
[no date, apparently Jan. 1875]

Ann F. Caldwell a witness of lawful age after having been first duly sworn to tell the truth, the whole truth and nothing but the truth concerning the matters under examination answers and says to the questions numbered as follows

1. My name is Ann Tyler Caldwell, my age is seventy two. My residence is Lewisburg Greenbrier County State of West Va. and has been such for the past fifty years, and am the wife of Dr. J.F. Caldwell the claimant.

2. I am the wife of Dr. J.F. Caldwell the claimant.

72. I was not present at the taking of any of the property charged in this claim, nor did I see any actually taken. All I know about the matter is, that owing to the shooting of a federal soldier near the town of Lewisburg, there was a rumor that the town was going to be burned, and therefore I packed up in two large trunks and a large box, the clothing of Dr. J.F. Caldwell consisting of all his clothing, boots, shoes, shirts, vests, coats, pants, stationary generally, the large box contained all the clothing & many naval instruments & other articles pertaining to the profession of my deceased son, Dr. Hanson Clay Caldwell late a surgeon in the U.S. Navy who died in 1859 leaving his father J.F. Caldwell his heir. These trunks and box I sent to our farm on Greenbrier River five miles from this place and one mile up the river above the crossing of the James River & Kanawha Turnpike.

74. No complaint was made by me to any officers. My husband being then absent in Charleston Kanawha Co. West Va.

75. No voucher or receipt was asked or given as far as I know.

76. No payment has ever been made for said property or any part that I am aware of.

77. This property was taken by troops camped on our farm under command of Col. Oley just after the said battle of Lewisburg.

79. I know nothing further about any of the items in this claim.

Ann F. Caldwell
[no date, apparently Jan. 1875]

$ 606.00

Payable in care of James H. Embry esq.
Washington, D.C.

TREASURY DEPARTMENT,
Second Comptroller's Office,
March 21, 1877.
H. Spalding
Clerk.

TREASURY DEPARTMENT,
Third Auditor's Office,
March 19th, 187
A. Jackson
Cle

The SCC Case of Logan Osburn

Quantities and Articles

July 19th 1864

35 head fat sheep taken by Col. Hays command, killed at his headquarters by his orders for the use of his regiment estimated to weigh 80 lbs each, 12½ cts per lb. — $350.00

One fine cavalry horse valued at $200 which was taken to Sheridan's command.
$200.00

About 100 bushels of oats taken in sheaf supposed to be worth at the time .75 cts per bushel $75.00

30 head sheep carried from farm $10 $300.00

10 tons hay taken from barn $20 $200.00

Waggon gears for four horses $60.00

Total, $1185.00

Sworn and subscribed in my presence, the seventh day of June, 1872

Edward Cooke, Justice

Logan Osburn, the claimant, a witness of lawful age being duly sworn deposes and says

64 years of age — Jefferson Co. farmer, have lived here 35 years, born in Loudoun Co Va.

Was a farmer before and during the war. I never changed my business or residence during the war. I was elected as a Union delegate to the Va Convention of 1861—voted against the ordinance of secession there and against its ratification by the people.

I never did or said anything against the Union cause. I was ready and willing to do anything in aid of the Union cause that surrounding circumstances would admit of.

I hauled flour to the Federal army at Harper's Ferry. Had no relations that I know of in the Union army east of the Alleghany Mountains. There were some in the western country.

Was not in the service of the U.S. at any time during the war. I received no favor or privileges from the Union army during the war.

I took an oath at Harper's Ferry, don't know if it was since or during the war. Took it for the purpose of getting some goods out of H. Ferry.

Some of the known Union men of my neighborhood during the war, Hen. Philip Gordon, Nat Langlon, John W & C.H. McCreedy & David Johnston.

I was frequently threatened by parties of Confederate soldiers. Never was arrested by any Confederate officers. My horses were taken by the Rebel soldiers, 8 or 9 horses in number. Never had any property confiscated by the Confederate authorities.

I once contributed 500 bushels of bread corn to the Confederate government, and I gave the corn for what I conceived to be justifiable reasons. I did it for the purpose of having my property protected, as I was being robbed all the time & I thought a contribution would he the means of protecting my property to some extent, and it was so suggested by some of my warmest friends in the Confederacy.

From questions 23 to 36th inclusive my answer in the negative. Nearly every relation I had was in the Confederate army.

From questions 37 to 43rd, my answer is in the negative.

From 44th to 51 inclusive my answer in the negative.

66th to 68th question, I was the owner of the property charged in this claim. The 35 head of sheep was taken from a farm about 1 mile distant from my residence. The farm was about 150 acres in size, about 125 acres in cultivation & balance in woodland.

I have never filed any petition in bankruptcy.

72nd I saw the four sets of harness & the horse charged in my bill taken by Federal soldiers.

I complained to the officers. The officers in charge were not commissioned officers & refused to give me a voucher for the articles taken, but told me to come to headquarters, but I could not get through the pickets.

No payment has ever been made for any property charged in this claim. In answer to 2nd part of question 76. Payment has been made for other articles taken at the same time as articles charged in this claim.

The horse and gearing were taken by troops encamped about 6 miles west of where I lived.

The 35 head of sheep were taken for the use of soldiers stationed near Kabletown Church, in Jeff. Co. W.Va.

I don't know what regiment or troops took the harness & horse. They were taken by the troops that were moving hay, and taken to Genl. Sheridan's Hdqrs. No commissioned officers that I could see were present. There were about 25 wagons & a force of 200 or 300 men taking hay to the army h protecting the wagon train.

         Logan Osburn

The foregoing deposition taken, sworn to and subscribed before me this the 3rd day of February 1877.

         Cleon Moore
         Special Comm.

Harrison Smith (colored) being duly sworn deposes and says, my name is Harrison Smith 45 yrs of age, formerly a slave of claimant have lived in Jefferson County for tile last 25 years, am not interested in the success of claim of claimant. Live now on farm adjoining claimant hut not on his land. Am not now in his service or employment. Am not now in his debt, and am not to share in any way in this claim if allowed.

Witness states that during the war, a soldier of the Union army rode up to Mr. Osburn's barn, where I was engaged in hauling hay, and ordered me to unhitch one of the horses I had to the wagon. He told me that he belonged to the 6th Corps. I had to unhitch the horse and he took the gears off and went away with the horse. There was a large force of the Union army about 6 miles above towards Clarke County. The soldier came to Mr. Osburn's farm with a body of Union soldiers that came through hauling hay. This horse was of medium size a, of good action.

Witness
Cleon Moore
this the 3rd day of February 1877

                                                Harrison Smith
                                                          his
                                                           X
                                                         mark

REMARKS

Mr. Osburn is a prominent citizen of Kabletown, Jefferson Co. W.Va. Several of his witnesses testify in general terms that he was reputed to be a Union man and that he talked in favor of the Union and against the Confederacy. In passing upon the question of loyalty we invariably place more confidence in the conduct and acts of claimants than in proof of general reputation and their present professions of loyalty. Disloyal acts necessarily outweigh present professions and the opinion of claimants friendly neighbors. Mr. Osburn swears that he was elected a delegate to the secession convention, that he voted against the ordinance of secession and when it was submitted to the people, voted against its adoption. After the ordinance was passed by the convention he signed it. But one (ex-Senator Lewis) of all the delegates resisted the pressure of popular sentiment and refused his signature to that instrument. If after signing the ordinance Mr. Osburn opposed its ratification by the people we can only say that his actions were not consistent. He contributed 500 bushels of corn to the Confederate government. No satisfactory excuse is given for rendering this aid to the Confederacy.

    We cannot conclude this report without remarking that the claimants testimony is not full and is subject to severe criticism. The 14th interrogatory is not answered at all. Mr. Osburn says nearly all his near relatives were in the Confederate army. Yet he does not tell us whether any of them were his sons or whether he contributed to their outfit or support while in the army. The printed questions were before the claimant and special commissioner who took the testimony and must have been seen and read at the time as they are answered in their order excepting certain significant omissions of very pertinent and important interrogations.

Mr. Osburn must be judged by his conduct. When he affixed his signature to the ordinance of secession in the Virginia convention, although he had previously opposed its adoption, he committed an act entirely hostile to the Federal Union, and when he subsequently gave 500 bushels of corn to the Confederate government he gave direct aid to the Confederacy.

The claim is disallowed.

A.O. Aldis
I. Ferriss

Commissioners
of Claims

West Virginia Physicians in the Civil War

AT THE BEGINNING of the Civil War the regular Union Army had 30 surgeons and 83 assistant surgeons. In March 1861 the Confederate States Medical Department consisted of a surgeon general, four surgeons, and six assistant surgeons. By the war's end, more than 11,000 doctors had served in the Union Army, and more than 3,000 doctors aided the Confederate Army.

From the western Virginia counties which comprise the present state of West Virginia, at least 63 physicians enlisted into Confederate service, while 97 joined the effort to preserve the Union. Just as soldiers of the border states chose their sides according to their own strong beliefs, doctors went their different ways, and it was not uncommon for doctors from the same county or town to part company in favor of the Blue or Gray.

Becoming a military doctor was usually a simple matter. A physician would sign enlistment papers as a surgeon or assistant surgeon of a regiment being recruited or already formed from a particular area. He would then proceed with that unit to serve "in the field." If combat losses, termination of enlistment, or other reasons caused a regiment to be reorganized, the surgeon would sometimes be assigned to another unit or hospital. Some would take the opportunity to retire from service for a variety of reasons. Thus a physician might serve in more than one military unit during his career. Still others became contract surgeons, and served units stationed near their homes.

This list of 160 West Virginia doctors who served in the Civil War was compiled from the following sources:

Adjutant General of West Virginia, *Annual Report of 1864*. Wheeling, W.Va., 1865.
The 1890 Civil War Veteran Census
Dickinson, Jack L. *Tattered Uniforms and Bright Bayonets: West Virginia's Confederate Soldiers*. Marshall University Foundation, 1995.
Polk's Medical and Surgical Directory of the U.S. 1885. Detroit: P.L. Polk, 1886.
Roster of Regimental Surgeons, U.S. Pension Officer 1882. Washington, DC: N.A. Strait, 1882.

Physicians in Confederate Service

Sgn—Surgeon A/Sgn—Assistant Surgeon
★on 1890 census may not have been prewar resident

NAME/RANK	COUNTY	REGIMENT
Alexander, Cyrus Sgn.	Hampshire	62 VA Cavalry
Allen, Benj. W. Sgn.	Preston	General Hospital in VA
Armstrong, George A/Sgn.	Taylor	25 VA Infantry
Austin, Charles N. Sgn.	Jackson	22 VA Infantry
Austin, Samuel H. A/Sgn.	Jackson	20 VA Cavalry
Bailey, Arthur G. Sgn.	Roane	10 VA Cavalry
Barbee, Andrew R. Sgn.	Mason	22 VA Infantry
Barksdale, W.L. Sgn.	Greenbrier	19 VA Cavalry
Barnes, Wm. H. A/Sgn.	Hardy	25 VA Infantry
Bee, Isiah Sgn.	Harrison	17 VA Cavalry
Bell, R.H. Sgn.	Nicholas	General Hospital in VA
Black, Harvey Sgn.	Greenbrier	31 VA Infantry
Bland, Wm. J. Sgn.	Harrison	31 VA Infantry
Bond, John S. Sgn.★	Ohio	General & Staff
Bosworth, John W. Sgn.	Randolph	31 VA Infantry
Buttermore, Smith Sgn.	Lewis	31 VA Infantry
Campbell, William Sgn.	Monroe	22 VA Infantry
Cracraft, George A. Sgn.	Ohio	19 VA Cavalry
Creed, Isaac Sgn.	Greenbrier	22 VA Infantry
Creigh, Thomas Sgn.	Greenbrier	22 VA Infantry
Dailey, Robert W. Sgn.	Hampshire	Hospital/Lexington, VA
Egan, Charles Sgn.	Pocahontas	29 VA Cavalry
French, William Sgn.	Mason	General Hospital in VA
Gamble, H.M. A/Sgn.	Hardy	25 VA Infantry
Harris, Thomas A. Sgn.	Wood	General Hospital in VA
Hereford, Thomas A/Sgn.	Kanawha	14 VA Cavalry
Holliday, S.J. A/Sgn.	Monroe	27 VA Infantry
Houston, M.H. Sgn.	Ohio	General Hospital in VA
Huff, John T. Sgn.	Tucker	Inspecting Surgeon VA
James, Daniel C. Sgn.★	Wood	17 VA Cavalry
Jenkins, William Sgn.	Cabell	8 VA Cavalry
Johnson, John D. Sgn.	Pendleton	25 VA Infantry
Ligon, John Sgn.	Pocahontas	19 VA Cavalry
Lippitt, Charles A/Sgn.	Jefferson	2 VA Infantry
McDonald, George Sgn.	Greenbrier	22 VA Infantry
McGinnis, A.B. Sgn.	Cabell	17 VA Cavalry
McNemar, Martin R. Sgn.	Hardy	25 VA Infantry
McMahon, William B. Sgn.	Jackson	10 VA Cavalry
McSherry, James W. Sgn.	Berkeley	36 VA Infantry

Name/Rank	County	Regiment
Moss, V.R. Sgn.	Cabell	16 VA Cavalry
Noel, Henry Sgn.	Fayette	60 VA Infantry
Ogden, Presley B. Sgn.	Marion	General & Staff?
Patrick, Alfred S. Sgn.	Kanawha	22 VA Infantry
Ramsey, John W. A/Sgn.	Harrison	General & Staff
Stalnaker, J.W. Sgn.	Cabell	36 VA Cavalry
Starry, John D. Sgn.	Jefferson	7 VA Cavalry
Stites, John H. Sgn.	Fayette	22 VA Infantry
Swan, S.R. Sgn.	Kanawha	22 VA Cavalry
Tanner, Isaac S. Sgn.	Jefferson	21? NC Infantry
Templeton, James Sgn.	Jefferson	36 VA Cavalry
Thomas, Opie Sgn.	Randolph	25 VA Infantry
Thompson, Wm. J. Sgn.	Marion	19 VA Cavalry
Timms, C.W. A/Sgn.	Putnam	8 VA Cavalry
Waite, Anderson M. Sgn.	Monroe	Thurmond's VA Rangers
Walker, Harrison A/Sgn.	Wayne	16 VA Cavalry
Whiter Isaac Sgn.	Upshur	31 VA Infantry
Williams, Tom E. A/Sgn.	Jefferson	6 VA Cavalry
Wilson, B.F. Sgn.	Barbour	31 VA Infantry
Wilton, R.W. Sgn.	Lewis	36 VA Cavalry
Wily, John B. Sgn.	Berkeley	20 VA Infantry
Woodville, James L. Sgn.	Monroe	7 VA Infantry
Wright, M.F. Sgn.	Mineral	7 VA Infantry
Yost, Fielding H. Sgn.	Monongalia	Hospital, Monterey, VA

Physicians Who Served in the Union Army

NAME/RANK	COUNTY	REGIMENT
Ackley, D.R. Sgn.	Wayne	4 WV Infantry
Baguley, David Sgn.	Ohio	1 WV Infantry
Barlow, Charles A. Sgn.	Cabell	7 WV Cavalry
Barton, T.H. Sgn.	Kanawha	4 WV Infantry
Blair, Jonathan P. Sgn.	Upshur	10 WV Infantry
Bond, Erwin D.J. Sgn.	Wood	11 WV Infantry
Bouse, Isaac W. A/Sgn.	Upshur	10 WV Infantry
Brock, Hugh W. A/Sgn.	Monongalia	Hospital, Winchester, VA
Brownfield, James A/Sgn.	Marion	14 WV Infantry
Bryan, Sampson P. Sgn.	Pocahontas	12 WV Infantry
Bumgarner, James Sgn.	Harrison	15? WV Cavalry
Campbell, John C. A/Sgn.	Ohio	12 WV Infantry
Capehart, Henry Sgn.	Ohio	1 WV Cavalry
Carr, John D.M. Sgn.	Ohio	1 WV Infantry
Comstock, Lucius L. Sgn.	Kanawha	7 WV Cavalry

Cutright, Watson W.	Randolph	3 WV Cavalry
Dalley, Charles D. A/Sgn.	Wayne	5 WV Infantry
Davis, Aaron W. Sgn.	Jackson	3 WV Cavalry
Dorsey, Dennis B. Sgn.	Monongalia	6 WV Cavalry
Dovener, Robert G. A/Sgn.	Wirt	15 WV Infantry
English, John Sgn.	Ohio	1 WV Infantry
Enochs, Hiram D. A/Sgn.	Ohio	1 WV Cavalry
Fansler, Andrew Sgn.	Tucker	General Hospital in VA
Frissell, John Sgn.	Ohio	12 WV Infantry
Ford, Sample Sgn.	Ohio	5 WV Cavalry
Gans, George C. Sgn.	Webster	10 WV Infantry
Gardner, Perrin Sgn.	Wood	1 WV Cavalry
Gibson, Nicholas Sgn.	Braxton	General Hospital in VA
Gilliam, Ed. L. Sgn.	Mason	2 WV Cavalry
Gillespie, James A/Sgn.	Tyler	1 WV Infantry
Grant, William L. Sgn.	Taylor	9 WV Infantry
Hall, Moses S. Sgn.	Ritchie	10 WV Infantry
Hall, Silas W. Sgn.	Lewis	Harpers Ferry Hospital
Harris, Thomas M. Sgn.	Ritchie	10 WV Infantry
Hazlett, Robert W. Sgn.	Ohio	2 WV Infantry
Hicks, Wilson T. Sgn.	Marshall	7 WV Infantry
Hower James F. A/Sgn.	Pleasants	15 WV Infantry
Hysell, James H. A/Sgn.	Cabell	9 WV Infantry
Johnson, James J. A/Sgn.	Wirt	15 WV Infantry
Kendall, James E. A/Sgn.	Wood	11 WV Infantry
Kilmer, D. W. Sgn.	Marshall	16 WV Infantry
Kraft, A. W. D. Sgn.	Ohio	1 WV Infantry
Lallance, Jacoh Sgn.	Jackson	13 WV Infantry
Law, Galelma Sgn.	Lewis	6 WV Cavalry
Lazelle, James W. Sgn.	Monongalia	Camp Chase Hospital, Ohio
Love, Eli N. Sgn.	Pocahontas?	5 WV Cavalry
Manown, James H. Sgn.	Preston	14 WV Infantry
Mayer, Daniel A/Sgn,	Kanawha	5 WV Infantry
McEween, Matthew Sgn.	Harrison	2 WV Cavalry
Meers, Richard L. A/Sgn.	Wirt	1 WV Infantry
Millspaugh, Thee. A/Sgn.	Upshur	5 WV Cavalry
Morris, Jonathan Sgn.	Wayne	9 WV Infantry
Morton, Thomas Sgn.	Preston	3 WV Cavalry
Moss, John W. Sgn.	Braxton	11 WV Infantry
Neat, Thomas S. Sgn.	Ritchie	2 WV Cavalry
Neil, Alexander Sgn.	Hancock	12 WV Infantry
Nellis, Ozias Sgn.	Gilmer	10 WV Infantry
Nickel, John R. Sgn.	Wood	1 WV Cavalry
Osman, William Sgn.	Marion	16 WV Infantry
Parkinson, Benoni Sgn.	Monongalia	17 WV Infantry
Patton, Frederick Sgn.	Doddridge	12 WV Infantry
Philson, John R. Sgn.	Kanawha	4 WV Infantry

Pinnell, David S. Sgn.	Harrison	3 WV Cavalry
Putney, James Sgn.	Wood	7 WV Cavalry
Ramsey, James H. A/Sgn.	Brooke	17 WV Infantry
Randall, Peras R. A/Sgn.	Wayne	5 WV Infantry
Ross, Tim W. A/Sgn.	Monongalia	7 WV Infantry
Rouse, James H. A/Sgn.	Kanawha	7 WV Cavalry
Ruggles, Dwight A/Sgn.	Marion	12 WV Infantry
Sadler, James H. Sgn.	Ohio	1 WV Artillery
Safford, Erasmus A/Sgn.	Roane	6 WV Infantry
Scott, Isaac Sgn.	Wood	7 WV Infantry
Shanor, David Sgn.	Wood	6 WV Infantry
Sharp, J.P. A/Sgn.	Wood	General & Staff
Shaw, Samuel G. Sgn.	Mason	13 WV Infantry
Stanford, Louis V. Sgn.	Monongalia	7 WV Cavalry
Starr, David L. Sgn.	Wood	15 WV Infantry
Stewart, William A/Sgn.	Braxton	17 WV Infantry
Stidger, S.B. Sgn.	Marshall	1 WV Infantry
Summers, Edgar A. A/Sgn.	Kanawha	General & Staff
Sweeney, John L. Sgn.	Tyler	14 WV Infantry
Thacher, Charles A/Sgn.	Greenbrier	14 WV Infantry
Thayer, Abel H. Sgn.	Taylor	6 WV Cavalry
Thoburn, Joseph Sgn.	Ohio	1 WV Infantry
Thomas, Ebenezer C. Sgn.	Marshall	3 WV Infantry
Titus, Arthur Sgn.	Marshall	1 WV Cavalry
Trahern, John F. Sgn.	Barbour	4 WV Cavalry
Voorhies, Andrew D. Sgn.	Wood	11 WV Infantry
Waterman, Homer C. A/Sgn.	Logan	2 WV Infantry
Welch, Walter S. A/Sgn.	Brooke	14 WV Infantry
Welsh, Thomas A/Sgn.	Wirt	USS Camellia
Wharton, John T. Sgn.	Wayne	6 WV Infantry
Wheeler, Albert P. Sgn.	Wood	6 WV Infantry
White, Arthur Sgn.	Ohio	1 WV Cavalry
Williams, Abe D. A/Sgn.	Mason	13 WV Infantry
Williamson, James A. Sgn.	Wirt	11 WV Infantry
Worthington, William Sgn.	Braxton	10 WV Infantry

The Ft. Delaware Seventy-five

HUNDREDS OF CONFEDERATE soldiers were being held as prisoners of war when the conflict finally came to an end. In some instances their release was delayed for a variety of reasons, and this was the case with the former Confederate soldiers from West Virginia whose names are found in this roster. Having endured confinement and anxiety over their future for more than six weeks since General Lee's surrender at Appomattox, these men determined to ask the President of the United States to intervene on their behalf. By the end of June 1865 all of these men had been released. That fact, however, had nothing to do with the President, as their plea was not brought to his attention until July 15.

This material is found in National Archives Microcopy M1003 Roll 72 Target 2, Miscellaneous File: *Civil War Case Files of Applications From Confederate Soldiers For Presidential Pardon.*

Where the information could be found, the author has added first name and rank to this roster. Notes following the roster help further identify some of these men, whose roster entries do not match their available service records.

Prison Camp of Enlisted Men
Ft. Delaware, DE
May 31st 1865

To His Excellency
Andrew Johnson President U.S.A.
Sir,

We the undersigned are citizens of West Virginia now held at this place as prisoners of war. We have for some weeks been sincerely desirous to take the Oath of Allegiance and become again loyal and peaceable citizens of the United States. This desire was made known to the authorities here six weeks since. Being desirous of returning as speedily as possible to our homes and families we now most respectfully solicit your Excellency in your clemency to grant us a pardon and an order for our speedy release.

Most Respectfully
Your Obedient Servants

NAME/RANK	COMPANY	REGIMENT
Ezekiel Stone Sgt.	E	16VAC
Abram P. Ferguson Pvt.	E	16VAC
James M. Collins Pvt.	E	16VAC
Henry C. Ferguson Pvt.	E	16VAC
John Tassen Sgt.	K	16VAC
James A. West Pvt.	K	16VAC
Taswel O. Overstreet Cpl.	K	16VAC
Royal B. Childers Pvt.	K	16VAC
Ransom Templeton Cpl.	K	16VAC
Abraham Midkiff Pvt.	K	16VAC
Marin Plymale Pvt.	K	16VAC
Edward L. Ruby Pvt.	K	16VAC
Charles H. Gilkeson Sgt.	H	16VAC
Francis M. Wooten Pvt.	H	16VAC
Lemuel F. Scaggs Pvt.	H	16VAC
J.N. Russell Pvt.	E	8VAC
Edward S. Guthrie Pvt.	E	8VAC
William A. Perdew Pvt.	K	8VAC
George W. Grobe Pvt.	D	8VAC
D.J.H.? Smith (1)	G?	16VAC
Henry B. Saxton Pvt.	D	8VAC
J.M. Templeton Pvt.	D	8VAC
Jacob A. McPherson Pvt.	H	8VAC
Anthony Barnet Pvt.	I	8VAC
Henry S. Montgomery Pvt.	I	8VAC
John D. Kyer Sgt.	C	17VAC
Jacob P. McCally Pvt.	C	17VAC
Charles W. Trayler Cpl.	C	17VAC
Alfred Somerville Pvt.	F	17VAC
J.B. Robertson (2)	A	22VAI
John W. Hill Pvt.	A	22VAI
Robert T. Melton Sgt.	A	22VAI
William A. Gwinn Sgt.	F	22VAI
George L. Wood Musician	C	22VAI
Joseph Wheeler Pvt.	B	22VAI
James Elliott Pvt.	B	22VAI
John Carter Pvt.	B	22VAI
Vinsin Price Pvt.	E	22VAI
J.W. Mullan Sgt.	B	25VAI
James Fraizer Sgt.	D	36VAC
Preston Martin (3)	C	26VAC
Norman Belknap Pvt.	B	19VAC
Wilson Pugh Pvt.	A	19VAC
Eligah Heter Pvt. (4)	C	19VAC
Floyd S. Barker Pvt.	D	36VAI

Burwel Spurlock Pvt. (5)	A	22BTN
Stephen C. Combs Pvt.	C	8VAC
Thomas C. Bostick Pvt.	A	36VAC
John J. Johnson Pvt.	B	8VAC
Archibald Wheeler Sgt.	C	36VAC
Marcus T.C. Loving Pvt.	B	8VAC
James A. Collins Pvt.	B	8VAC
A. Long? (6)	B	8VAC
William J. Berry Sgt.	G	25VAI
William Paugh Sgt.	C	25VAI
Peter Pool Sgt.	G	60VAI
Green B. Foley Pvt.	A	36VAI
T.W. Brooks Pvt. (7)	A	36VAI
Gilbert Cottrell Pvt.	G	60VAI
Wm. F. Greathouse Pvt. (8)	F	30VAI
Hedrick Miller Pvt. (9)	F	30VAI
Frances M. Tibbs Pvt.	A	19VAC
Joseph E. Vaughan	B	37VAI
John B. Fogus Pvt.	A	36VAC
Henry Bennett (10)	A	18VAC
John N. Williams Pvt.	A	14VAC
Jacob L. Hypes Pvt.	D	22VAI
J.? P. Wilson (11)	K	22VAI
Joseph W. Dilworth Sgt.	B	22VAI
George Boggess Pvt.	G	10VAC
H.C. Ryan (12)	A	1VAA
W.S. Smith (13)	G	45VAI
Andrew J. Riptoe Pvt.	R	22VAI
John G. Cartmill Pvt.	R	22VAI
J.? F. Hamilton (14)	F	2BAT?

Notes

1. Name not found in CSR
2. This may be Joseph B. Roberts, Sgt. Co A 22VAI
3. In CSR as Presley Martin, 46VAC which in late 1864 became the 26VAC.
4. CSR gives name as Elijah Heater, Co B 19VAC with prior service 31VAI.
5. In CSR as 45BTNVAI. The 22BTNVAI, formerly the 2VAA, formed May, 1862 and disbanded 12/22/64.
6. Not found in CSR, may be Annel Lowe of Co C 8VAC, who was released from Ft. Delaware 6/20/65.
7. In history of 36VAI as Wm. Thomas Brook, who was released from Ft. Delaware 6/19/65.
8. Member 30th Virginia Sharpshooters.
9. Member 30th Virginia Sharpshooters.
10. In CSR as member of McNeill's Rangers, however the 18VAC absorbed part of McNeill's Rangers 1863.
11. Not found in CSR or history of the 22VAI, there was a J.P. Wilson in Co D 22VAC.
12. In CSR as member of Capt. Charles Griffin's Co. Virginia Light Artillery, which was attached to the 1VAA which later became the 1BTN VAA until disbanded January, 1865.
13. Not found in CSR or history of the 45VAI.
14. Not found in CSR as T.F. or J.F. Hamilton.

You Look Rather Hard

VERY LATE IN THE preparation of this book the letters of Lt. Jacob Gilbert Beaver and his brother, James A. Beaver, were brought to my attention by Tom Morgan of Gauley Bridge, WV. Realizing immediately the significance of these letters, and knowing Tom's desire to see his ancestors' story preserved, I determined to add another chapter to my Almanac.

Born at Millerstown, Pennsylvania on October 21, 1837, James A. Beaver entered Pine Grove Academy in Centre Co. Pennsylvania at age fourteen, and subsequently entered the junior class at Jefferson College. Graduating from college in 1856 he began to study law in the office of H.N. McAllister of Bellefonte, PA. Admitted to the bar in Centre Co. in January 1859, James Beaver joined McAllister as a partner.

Prior to the outbreak of the Civil War he joined the local militia company which was commanded by Captain Andrew G. Curtin, who later became Pennsylvania's war governor. Being keenly interested in drill and tactics, James Beaver was soon promoted to lieutenant of his company, the "Bellefonte Fencibles."

With the firing on Fort Sumter and President Lincoln's call for seventy-five thousand volunteers, the Fencibles entered the three months' service as Company H, 2nd Pennsylvania Volunteers. Serving with the 2nd Pennsylvania in western Maryland and at Harpers Ferry, Lt. Beaver was mustered out with his company on July 26, 1861, and subsequently received permission to recruit a regiment of infantry of which he would become the lieutenant colonel. On Beaver's twenty-fourth birthday, October 21, 1861, his 45th Regiment Pennsylvania Infantry mustered into service for three years. Between that time and September 1862 the 45th Pennsylvania served at Washington, Port Royal, South Carolina, and in Virginia with General Ambrose E. Burnside's IX Corps.

Responding to a request by the citizens of Centre County, Beaver traveled to Harrisburg, Pennsylvania where, on September 6, 1862, he accepted the position of colonel of the newly formed 148th Pennsylvania Infantry. Colonel Beaver's many talents for military training and discipline quickly manifest themselves as the 148th Regiment soon displayed such precision they were mistaken for a veteran regiment. Indeed, their energetic colonel prepared them well for the hardships they were soon to endure as one of the most fighting regiments of the Union army.

Colonel Beaver was wounded in the battle of Chancellorsville, Va., May 3, 1863; Cold Harbor, June 3, 1864; Petersburg, June 16, 1864, and he lost his right leg from wounds received at Ream's Station, Va., August 25, 1864. Once sufficiently recovered from the amputation of his leg, Colonel Beaver returned to Centre County Pennsylvania. Soon thereafter he was appointed brevet brigadier general for his meritorious conduct in the campaigns of

1864, especially while commanding a brigade at Cold Harbor. Discharged from the army on December 22, 1864 for disability resulting from his wounds, Beaver resumed his law practice. On December 26, 1865, he married Mary McAllister, daughter of his law partner.

Elected Governor of Pennsylvania in 1886, Beaver served one four-year term. He subsequently became president of a coal company and from 1895 until his death on January 31, 1914 he served as judge of the Pennsylvania Superior Court.

Jacob Gilbert Beaver was born March 6, 1840. His father died when "Gib" was five months old. Raised by his mother and stepfather, the Rev. Samuel H. MacDonald of Lewisburg, Pennsylvania, Gilbert Beaver became active in the mercantile trade at the age of sixteen. With the outbreak of the Civil War Gib obeyed the wishes of his mother and delayed entering the military until the course of the war could be determined. In early May 1861 Gib traveled to York, Pa., to visit his brother James A. Beaver, who was active training recruits at Camp Scott. Finally, in October 1861 Gilbert Beaver enlisted into the 51st Regiment Pennsylvania Infantry. He became lieutenant of Company H, serving conspicuously until his death at the battle of Antietam, Maryland Sept. 17, 1862. Lt. Beaver was shot through the neck in the final charge on Burnside Bridge.

Also included here are two war-period letters written by Abraham Addams MacDonald, half-brother of James A. and Jacob Gilbert Beaver. A.A. MacDonald enlisted into the 45th Regiment Pennsylvania Infantry, and served honorably throughout the war. He died at Covington, Va., on April 22, 1886.

FOR ADDITIONAL INFORMATION see: *Life and Achievements of James Addams Beaver*, by Frank A. Burr. Ferguson Bros. a Co. Philadelphia, 1882. This book contains excerpts from Beaver's Civil War diary as well as quotes from some of his war-period letters, other than those published here.

The Story of our Regiment: A History of the 148th Pennsylvania Volunteers, by Joseph W. Muffly. The Kenyon Printing & Mfg. Co. Des Moines, Iowa, 1904. Reprinted 1994 by Butternut and Blue, 3411 Northwind Rd. Baltimore, MD 21234. This book includes Beaver's role in the war written in his own words at the request of the publisher.

History of the Forty-Fifth Regiment Pennsylvania Veteran Volunteer Infantry, Allen D. Albert, ed., Williamsport, Pa., 1912.

History of the 51st Regiment of Pennsylvania Volunteers, by Thomas H. Parker. King & Baird, Philadelphia, 1869.

For genealogical information see: *Genealogical Record of the LeVan Family 1650 to 1927*, by Warren Fatten Coon. The Huguenot Society of New Jersey, 1927.

The Genealogy of the Beaver Family Vol. I, by Cora Beaver Home. Booklet, I. M. Beaver, Printer. Reading, Pa., 1930.

See also the index to the *War of the Rebellion: A Compilation of the Official Records of the Union and Confederate Armies*, 128 vols. U.S. War Dept. Washington, 1880–1901.

Col. James A. Beaver, 148th Pennsylvania Volunteer Infantry and postwar Governor of Pennsylvania.
PHOTO COURTESY TOM MORGAN, GAULEY BRIDGE, WV

The Letters of James A. Beaver

May 10th 1861 [Camp Scott, York, PA]

My dear Mother,

    My duties in camp are so varied and arduous that I have very little time to write. I have had some hoarseness and cold arising principally from commanding continually but syrup of tar has 'done me up' wonderfully. A member of our company has been detailed as telegraph operator in Baltimore. He telegraphs us today that 2,700 troops passed through Baltimore last night unmolested and cheered by the people. Baltimore is coming home to her allegiance. It is well that she is. I have little idea when we will leave here. Not until we are equipped though. The question of enlisting for 3 years is now ——— [?] in our Regiment, I scarcely know what to do. I like the service and will willingly stay in it as long as I am needed, but the thought of lying idle in a post of little or no consequence for the greater part of the time is scarcely to be thought of . . . . You cannot imagine how encouraging your letter has been to me . . .

Affectionately your son,
James A. Beaver

Camp Chambers
4 miles from Chambersburg
2nd June 1861

My dear Brother,

    The tented field has become a reality and we are now rejoicing in the enjoyment of pleasant army quarters in the country. We left York on Monday night last, came to Chambersburg Tuesday morning encamped at the fair grounds for two or three days and came out here on Friday morning. Our tents came Friday night. I assisted in putting up the mens tents and did not get my own up until 11 o clock at night. . . . There are a great number of small camps scattered around Chambersburg, each containing 2 or 3 regiments, and their are all together 11 or 12 regiments of infantry and 500 horseman within a circuit of 5 miles. All this force is of course destined for some point in Virginia, probably for Harpers Ferry. Our men are extremely anxious that our destination should be that point. If the rebels make a stand there at all it will no doubt be a desperate one. It is reported here that the rebel forces within 40 miles of Harpers Ferry amount to 20,000 men. We can move against them with a force much superior, attacking from various points. At Camp _____ very near Chambersburg they have had several deaths from what is known here as the spotted fever. It extremely dangerous and fatal. . . . As it is our first experience in camp life we have some little trouble pitching tents etc which experience and patience will dissipate entirely. . . . I will write you when we move again.

Affectionately,
Your Brother
James A. Beaver

Harrisburg Pa. 7 Sept 1862

My Dear Mother,

It's a little hard to be within four hours ride of home and not able to get there, but such is the case and as I never made any calculations for getting home until the war was over, I am less disappointed than I should otherwise be. Were I in the field I should of course think nothing of it. As it is I must confess to a little longing to see you if but for a minute. My resignation as Lieut. Col of the 45th P.V. has been accepted and I am here to take command of the 148th. I am very glad that I accepted the position ... Some companies of the regt. are from Carter County and sturdy fellows. Some of course tremendously raw, but with patience and hard work will work wonders. I saw Gib just before I left Washington, his health was excellent but rather shabby in appearance. They had marched every day and night for 14 days and were fighting more or less most of the time. Yet their regt. had not one man killed, and not a great many wounded. He thinks Genl Burnside will give their Regiment some position in which they can rest and recuperate.

... My regiment will probably get away on Wednesday. The Governor being anxious to keep it here until the truth in regard to the reports of the rebels having crossed into Maryland are confirmed or denied. I shall be kept busy night and day until I get away. I shall write you when I leave and my probable destination.

My love to the children
Affectionately
Your son
James A Beaver

Cockeysville Md 13 Oct 1862

My dear Mother,

Although not actually moved we came very near going to Chambersburg or Gettysburg to save Pennsylvania from being plundered. Gov. Curtin telegraphed me to prepare to move to Harrisburg on Saturday morning. Being under the command of Genl Wool and in the service of the United States I could not of course espouse the doctrine of 'States Rights' and obey the order of a Governor of a state, however much I may have wished to do so. Genl Wool came along early Saturday morning and ordered us to cook rations and distribute ammunition and await further orders. When the order came they directed us to remain quiet. I knew from the nature of the raid that the rebels would be gone before we could get there and consequently directed that no tents should be struck and nothing unusual done except the cooking. We were therefore very little inconvenienced by the 'raid.' We have again settled down to our accustomed quiet. Instead of Battalion Drill today I marched the Regt about six miles this afternoon. Not intending anything more than our usual drill I started on foot and per consequence feel somewhat tired.

Tomorrow I expect to have a grand Battalion Drill of all the companies of the Regt. except one at the camp at Gunpowder Bridge.... Genl Wool passed down the road to Baltimore again today, the fuss being all over and the rebels safe in Virginia with their plunder....

I wrote Rick Hairus a few days since sending him five dollars to pay the man who dug the grave in which Gib's body was laid.... Oh Mother! in all this terrible affliction how good God has been. Our loss having been decreed how many evidences of his goodness are manifest. How unequivocal the evidences of Gib's devoted piety. How literally was his prayer answered in being taken to God instantly, 'he suffered no pain.' ...All the circumstances attending his noble, heroic death are mitigating circumstances. Whilst we are called to mourn that he is not, we are called to rejoice that he has just begun to live....

With my love to you and the children.

Your devoted son,
James A Beaver

3rd May 1863 [Chancellorsville, Va]

My dear Mother,

Fearing that you may be anxious about me ... I will try and give you some idea of my situation. On the second day, Sunday, of the great battle on the Rappahannock which is still raging I advanced with my regiment through a thick woods to dislodge the enemy from a position which he held and from which in connection with others he was endeavoring to flank us. Genl Hooker led us to our position in person. We advanced on a line of dead rebel skirmishers, over a line of our own skirmishers, and were met all of a sudden with a most deadly discharge of musketry. Our boys returned the fire with deadly effect. I was struck very early in the engagement with a ball in the breast which fortunately hit the button on my coat and inflicted only a bruise which is somewhat sore to the touch but does not give me pain or uneasiness except when washed. After some time seeing that we were partially enfiladed by the fire of the enemy and seeing some confusion on my right I went in that direction but was prostated by a ball which struck me in the left side, passed around one of my ribs and came out about four inches from where it entered. I was carried off the field and brought here on a stretcher a distance of some three or four miles. I expect to leave here this morning and will perhaps be sent to the seminary hospital at Georgetown. My wound is not painful except when I move, and is not at all dangerous. I hope to be able to rejoin the regiment very soon. The boys behaved nobly. I Will Write you as soon as I reach Washington.

With much love,
Affectionately your son
James A Beaver

Jacob Gilbert Beaver about 1860. He became Lieutenant
of Co H 51st Pa., Infantry and was killed at the
battle of Antietam, MD, Sept. 17, 1862.
PHOTO COURTESY TOM MORGAN, GAULEY BRIDGE, WV

The Letters of Jacob Gilbert Beaver

York, May 10th 1861

My dear Mother,

    I am visiting Camp Scott for a short time, Wm. Duncan and I came here on Wednesday will leave tomorrow. Jim wrote to me and said if I would come down we might see them as they expected to start for some other point, but after coming here and seeing Jim I found out that they would not leave for some time yet. There are nearly 6500 soldiers snugly quartered here. Nearly all uniformed and armed for service.... There are but 13 in hospitals and none dangerously ill, one has pneumonia who is pretty sick it is a great wonder that more have not the same disease you see so many lying down on the damp ground having the sun pouring down on them, looking as though no danger might result in their carelessness. The late uniforms gotten up for the volunteers is not a very handsome one. Nor is it very expensive. Their pants is a sheep gray cold satinett cost about 75¢ a yd. Red flanel shirts and blue twilled flanel half sack coat. The parties have some very fine drills they were out this morning about 2 hours. Since dinner it has rained steadily and looks as though it would clear up in hurry. Comfortable lodging quarters are at Mrs. Spanglers and I am very glad that there is such a woman in existence as she gives to all friends who come by a hearty welcome. Mrs. Mitchell is staying here. Capt Mitchell and Jim put up here when they get tired or not on duty. Jim is here and will write the balance of this epistle. I expect a letter from you when I get home which I will answer when I receive it.

Affectionately your son,
J.G. Beaver

Camp Curtin Nov 12 1861

My dear Mother,

... Since my return I have confined myself to camp and am I think as well as well could be. I have an enormous appetite we have our mess fitted up and we eat plain victuals but a great variety. I have a very comfortable bed to sleep on it is an iron frame, canvas about 14 inches from the ground with a hair matrice which makes me feel as comfortable as if I was in the best of beds. I was one of the Officers of the Guard yesterday on duty 24 hours which kept me awake all night going the grand rounds visiting all the guards in camp. I came in contact with a soldier who had been placed on picket duty but had left his post and ... stolen his blanket full of cabbage, I had him arrested ... our company is attached to Col. Hartranft's 51st Reg. he is said to be one of the finest looking officers in camp ... the chaplain of the reg. is a young Presbyterian minister from Norristown ... our regiment is expected to leave this week destination unknown. ... our company is not quite full we expect to fill up by tomorrow ...

Your affectionate son,
JG Beaver

[John F. Hartranft was a prewar lawyer and colonel of a militia regiment which mustered into U.S. service April 20, 1861, as the 4th Pennsylvania Infantry, a three month regiment. Ninety days later, on the eve of the battle of First Manassas, the entire regiment marched to the rear claiming expiration of service. Hartranft volunteered for service with Gen. W.B. Franklin during the battle. As a result of that decision Congress gave Hartranft the Medal of Honor in 1886. Commissioned colonel of the 51st Pennsylvania Infantry on November 16, 1861, Hartranft served with distinction throughout the war. He was appointed a brigadier general May 12, 1864, and brevetted major general March 28, 1865. Hartranft became active in politics after the war, serving two terms as Governor of Pennsylvania. He died at Norristown, Pa., October 17, 1889.]

Camp Union Dec. 4th [1861]
2 miles from Annapolis

My dear Sister,

I received your letter a short time since. I also received one from Jim yesterday who is in camp at or near Fortress Monroe their destination is Port Royal. We were assigned today to the 2nd Brigade coast division we were disappointed as to our General. We thought we were to have Genl Foster but he has been assigned to the 1st Brigade coast division. . . . we expect to remain here for two weeks or more the vessals are to be prepared at New York with most of necessaries. I have understood that the vessals are to have quarters fitted up in them and we are to take no teams or tents. I suppose we are to go prowling along the coast and take up privateers, stragglers and do some bombarding as we are to be fitted out with Parrot guns which will carry four & five miles . . . I must put in a word about our Capt. J. Merill Linn . . . I have been with him since leaving Lewisburg I never have been with a more pleasant nor better privileged man than he is except one thing . . . that is he makes use of profane language once and awhile . . . we call the company after him, Linn Rifles. . . . we are very nicely fixed where we are now our wall tent is 9 feet square the ground covered with spruce brush we have a small stove which keeps us comfortable, four of us mess together, Capt 1st Lieut. Cap's clerk and myself. I have been making a fence around our tent . . . we spent our Thanksgiving on last Thursday, had preaching in the morning by our chaplain we had a Thanksgiving dinner of roast turkey, sweet potatoes, Irish potatoes, cranberry sauce, celary, coffee good bread and butter desert the peaches you gave me with some cream and pound cake. We almost live on oysters here they are right at our hand 50¢ a gallon . . . We buried a man today out of our company who died of Hemerage of the lungs, he leaves a wife who was very sick when he last heard of her . . . I have been able to attend P— [Presbyterian] church every Sunday evening since I have been here the congregation is very small their pastor Re. Patterson is a good preacher . . .

Affectionately Brother
Gib

Febry 9th 1862

My dear Mother,

I am at Camp Jordan Roanoke Island. We landed on the island on Friday night made an attack on the rebels in the woods and marsh. There was but one clear place for us to fight in which was the place that they had cleared before their masked battery. Our regt was on the right flank and part of the left there was but two men in our regt wounded. The fight lasted 4½ hours killed & wounded on our side 30 killed & 150 wounded as near as can be told. We scouted the rebels position then came upon their camps and took over 2500 prisoners, over 200 officers. Took 1 fort of 10 32 lb guns 1 fort of 5 32 lb guns and over 3000 stand of arms, camp equipage ammunition and a great many other articles of use. The killed of the rebels about 25 but they carried away as many as they could and chucked some of them in canal ditches to secret them from us. Their wounded is not known exactly. I waded through swamp and marshes up to my middle and was wet all day and did not suffer any from the effect of it. I will write Jim as soon as I get some paper.

Affectionately your son,
Gilbert

[The battle of Roanoke Island, N.C. occurred February 8, 1862, when a Union flotilla of nearly 100 ships commanded by Gen. Ambrose E. Burnside made an amphibious landing of 15,000 troops on the small island. Fewer than 3,000 Confederates and 7 gunboats defended the island. A series of small engagements ensued with the Confederates eventually forced to retreat. Outnumbered, with no escape avenues, Col. Henry M. Shaw surrendered his command of 2,500 men. Gen. Henry A. Wise, who earlier had overseen preparations for the island's defense, was not present at the time of the battle, thus escaping capture.]

Camp Burnsides
Roanoak Island N.C.
February 15th 1862

My dear sister,

    I wrote mother a short time after landing here but could only say to her where I was and how I was, and as I have but a little time to write I will make this letter do both of you send it to her after you have had the benefit of it. I was while we were at Annapolis a Signal Officer but when I found out that the Signal Corps were to go in one vessal I got permission to go with our company in the steamer Cossack. The Signal Corp were some time in getting to Hatures upon account of the storm, however when they came I was ordered to come aboard with them. I went to the schooner which they were in with my baggage I was shown to the officers cabin 25 bunked in it. I shook hands with the boys all around and took a seat quietly on a trunk and took a view of the cabin and its contense. A row of bunks were fitted up on each side of the vessal, trunks under the bunks behind the trunks empty demi johns and bottles, in the centre of the cabin btls and boxes. Here and there among the btls an empty ale keg. Thinks I they must have had quite a merry time. I felt out of place however I put in the day walking about the vessal. Night came and I retired early, and after hearing the most profane and vulgar language which came from these intelligent young officers, I thought almost loud enough to be heard if I am made a Colonel by being instructed in the signals of the army, with such men I will not be associated. I will make application in the morning for a discharge from the corp. I was so worried that I did not sleep any that night. However the long looked for day break came and I went out on deck and walked up and down until the commander of the corp made his appearance. I asked him for a discharge he said he would have to see Gen Burnsides first. In the afternoon he gave me a discharge and as it was very stormy I could not go to my former boat and was compelled to stay on board there an other night. That evening they went to the sutlers boat and brought on board 4 kegs ale and they had what they called a gay time. I put in another restless night and in the morning I was put aboard our old steamer Cossack, but I was glad. Enough of this however, I will tell you of our going to Roanoak Island. We had no trouble in going up the sound and the sight was beautiful, to see the fleet move slowly along each in turn. The gun boats took the lead we were about 2 miles to the rear of them. On last Friday at 11 am they arrived 4 miles from the fort at Roanoak and a little before noon the ball began. I presume you have read a full description of it in the papers but I will give it to you partly by way of variety. The rebels had 6 gun boats laying off about six miles from the fort and when the ball opened they came down a short distance. Our gun boats 20 in number began to play rapidly on the fort and also on their boats. We looked at the bombarding with great interest and anxiety. The most beautiful sight in the play was to see the shells explode in the air, splash and skip in the water and stir up the sand along the shore. After 2 hours firing a fire broke out in the barracks a little to the rear of the fort. That made the performance more exciting but the fire soon burnt out then nothing but the boom of the cannon kept up the excitement. As it grew near sunset the signal went up to send the troops to shore. The order was that the different vessels should fill their sury boats and hitch onto each other and towed by a tug. The Pilot Boy soon passed us with 25 or 30 sury boats all in a string floating from her steam, this was a beautiful sight, we sent from our vessal two boat loads holding 1 company. The firing was kept up briskly. On the shore near where our troops expected to land was quite a force of rebels but a shell or two from our gun boat scattered them. At dusk all the guns ceased firing. While we were at tea the gun boat Delaware came along side to take our troops to shore we hurried down ... I stood near the Col who said to me as I was appointed one of his aides, when we get to shore stick to me. Through thick and thin said I as long as I can. We loaded on to the boat without taking any blankets or any baggage, had 3 days rations in our haversacks. We soon reached shore landed safely and marched through a swamp over knee deep in some places so that most of us had wet feet to begin with. After we had gone about ¼ mile we came to an open space, a field of about 8 acres with a house in the centre which before we landed had about 800 rebels ... In 1 hours time 5000 troops were landed and formed by reg in close column arms stacked. After we had been there a while we got up a fire and dried a little. I then made a bed out of four 3 cornered rails and laid down did not sleep much but rested myself. About 12 o'clock it began to rain I roused up and went to the fire. We had then huddled on the 8 acres 10000 men, and although we expected a battle in the morning I wished for day break. Sure enough as usual day break came at the proper time. Just as we could see day a shot was heard in the woods and in 5 minutes the 10000 men were in their proper place under arms and ready to advance. Soon another shot was heard and another when it was clear day a volly went forth then another volly followed by a big gun. In the advance we had six field pieces. Our reg was on the left flank of 2nd Brigade but as there was but one narrow road through the woods and the men had to march in four ranks it was some time before we entered the woods. As we approached the woods a man was carried past us on a stretcher shot in the leg. The firing was going on at a pretty rapid rate. Before we entered the woods four wounded had been carried past us. We slowly advanced keeping close to the regt in front interrupted frequently by the wounded being carried by us. On each side of the road was deep, swampy, thick brushy woods so that we could not see what was before us. We passed on the road side . . . a tent used for a hospital there we saw quite a number wounded suffering and groaning, one man with both his legs shot off. We presently met Gen Reno's aid who told us to go 200 yards further and go to the left to cut off the rebels retreat in case they retreated. We arrived at the turning point, we went into the woods and the bush was so thick and the swamp so deep that we could scarcely get through. It was then I experienced for the first time bullets rushing past me. Col said he wished some one would climb that tree, I did not say that I was a good climber because the bullets were coming through and above us pretty sharp. 2 companies got into the left and they were ordered to advance on the left under Lieut Col. We were ordered to go to the right and out flank the rebels behind a battery. While crossing the road we passed in front of their battery, they fired their guns from the battery shot and shell, one shell exploded above Co D and part of a shell nocking off a bayonet. The others passed over us then they fired a volly of musketry but they went above us. We got to the right of their battery passing dead and dying all I could do was utter a silent prayer to God to cleanse us from all sin and iniquity in the blood of our saviour so that whether living or dying we might better live or die in the Lord. The swamp was so deep that men had to be pulled out occasionally. The companies got some what scattered, and as I was aid to the Col. I mounted a stump found where the officers of the scattering men were, dodging a bullet occasionally or at least going through the motion, and after getting them on the right track I pushed forward to the head of the column with the Col. Some places wading in water allmost to my middle and could scarcely see ten feet in front on account of the thick bushes. I presume however you will have a description of the battery and trap they had set for us by reporters who followed up. While we were getting through several companies from other regts made a charge on the battery and the rebels began to leave. Our regt was under fire about an hour and our report shows but two killed. When the regts were ordered to advance we advanced with five companies the others not quite ready to advance they were left in charge of our Major to bring along as soon as they were collected. We passed on the road clothes, cartridge boxes, ammunition, provisions, knapsacks, and arms. We advanced as rapidly as we could seeing nothing pretty [?] except the long spiked pines [?]. After we had marched about five miles one of Genl Burnsides aids stopped us and said all the other regts were to halt and we should advance. Thinks I, another fight expected. Col told me to stop there and hurry up the bal of the regt. I waited a long time and becoming impatient I started back for them. I had gone three miles passing here and there a worn out soldier when I met some of our regt who told me that the other part of the regt had been ordered to remain at the battery which we had taken. I twice found the advance of our regt. After I had passed some distance from where I had been left I saw the most beautiful hill I think ever witnessed it is about 80 or 100 feet above the level of the water pure and perfect buff sand spotted here and there with a green tree on it. I noticed a great many mens tracks and beyond it I saw a boat going toward Naggs Head. I suppose they were rebels making their escape. I passed along a little further, Genl. Foster came riding by and said we have taken 3000 prisoners. I took off my cap and gave three big cheers for our success. I soon arrived at the spot where the prisoners and our troops were. The rebels had prepared on the island, barracks of the most comfortable kind to accommodate 10000 men. The camp we came into they called Camp Georgia. We call it Camp Burnside it was formerly a heavy pine forest of 20 acres but now the ground is all cleared of stumps, on it the finest kind of barracks with all the conveniences to give comfort to a soldiers sore bones. Namely, rocking chairs, easy chairs, cots, good heavy matrices, with other improvements such as tables, desks, and many other articles which are very nice to have in camp. When I came to the camp I wanted to report to Col., went into a log cabin met some men there I asked who they were, they said staff officers of the 31st North Carolina Regt. The one who spoke to me said he was the man who carried out the flag of truce to your army. ——luck to it said he. I talked with them for some time and hunted up the Col. who said I should quarter with him as our baggage and cooking apparatus was not on shore. We made use of the cooking utencils and commissary of the rebels until our stores were landed. Col. met a class mate of his in the 31st Regt a captain, they got together and talked for some time in the evening as we sat by the chimney fire trying to dry our clothes which had been wet all day. This captain said that Genl. Wise had been on the island to try to get his son who was killed and he was so closely pursued that he left his overcoat behind. The next morning, Sunday, I went down to the fort now called Fort Reno it is a splendid fortification. Below it I visited Fort Park and below that Fort Foster, the one which our gun boats bombarded. The fleet expected to sail to some other point early in the week but the prisoners were so much trouble that we did not get away. The officers, over 200 in number, were put on board the steamer Spalding [?] and will likely sail soon for New York. The privates are all here yet in the 31st Regt there is scarcely 2 men dressed alike, the finest looking soldiers away. The whole party is a company in the Wise Legion called Richmond Blues. The men are all stout active looking men. We have some Ben McCulloughs Rangers, they are petted down considerably, On Monday I witnessed some places of interest the one most peculiar was a small frame house where I found I could have some washing done. Also accommodated with a nice tub of water, soap and towl. After taking a good scrub I left a six weeks wash and came out into the fresh air feeling like an other person. . . . I must give you a description of the knives the rebels carried, they are of a home manufacture 2½ inches wide 18 inches long, tapering 3 inches from the point. They did not get a chance to use them in this battle. I must say something about our commander Genl Burnside he is a brilliant man well able to command a body of men with skill and satisfaction to all who are under his control. Genl Reno our brigadier is a small man an excellent officer . . .

Your Affectionate Brother
J G Beaver Co H 51st P.V.
Burnsides Expedition via Fortress Monroe

Newbern May 27th 1862
My dear Mother,

. . . There is but little news in this department. Gov. Stanley arrived in last steamer. He in former years resided in this place and is well known in this neighborhood. . . . I saw some of our soldiers yesterday who had been taken prisoners in the three months service. Some were taken at Bull Run and others at Williamsport, they were taken to New Orleans to winter. They told me they had been in the prison at New Orleans and had not seen ground for four and a half months were kept on half rations and had to sleep on boards without covering they were sent to Sallisbury in this state in the opening of the spring at which place they have been until they were released or exchanged . . . Recruiting is still going on in some of the surrounding counties it is supposed that the 1st North Carolina Union Volunteers will soon be filled. . . . Capt Biggs has gone north for 500 horses to be used in wagons. Our sick are improving a great many of them have been taken to Beaufort N.C. to get the benefit of the sea breeze. I have entirely recovered from my sickness and have almost gained my former weight. . . . We drill about 3 hours during the day. . . . Citizens are coming back to their homes in town very slowly. I presume ere this the battle at Richmond has been fought, which battle I suppose will determine the period of the war. The drum has tapped for morning drill and I will have to close. . . .

Your affectionate son,
J G Beaver

Camp Reno June 23rd 1862

My dear Mother,

    Your letter of June 9th came to hand 21st inst and was very glad to hear from you.... You asked me how I was situated in the regiment. To this I take pleasure in reply, that having received promotion I am now 1st Lieut. of Co H vice Lieut. Sharkly appointed Adjutant, our orderly sergeant Wm T Campbell a worthy young man from our neighborhood has beet promoted 2nd Lieut. We all mess together get along very well... . Heretofore when I acted as aid to the Col it was only on marches and during battle on which occasions I have received and noticed in the papers in official reports a very complimentary notice.... The gun boats belonging to the expedition are scattered along the coast ... some were chartered vessels which we had in our coming here, most have been released while the other government transports and chartered ones make voyages to and from the north bringing mails absentees and stores ... our regimental camp is on a peninsula formed by Brices Creek which empties into Trent river about 3 miles from New Bern. The creek is wide and deep beautifully shaded on each bank by trees and shrubry of various kinds. The ground is about 15 feet above the level of the water .. . we have dug wells where we found good water and every thing about is convenient and comfortable ... The only things we have to contend with are deers in the morning and wood ticks mosquitos and gnats at night. We have been feasting on deer and mull berries black berries are not quite ripe.... We hear through contraband that the rebels are evacuating Kingston, a fortified town between this and Goldsboro. I think we will have but little more trouble in this state unless the rebels happen to escape McClellan and retreat through or to it. I think the large force of reinforcements sent him will enable him to trap them... .There was a grand review ... last Friday, the sight was grand. Genl Burnside received a sword on the occasion worth $1000 ...

Affectionately your son
J G Beaver

Newport News July 10 1862

My dear Mother,

    We left Newbern last Sunday arrived at Fortress Monroe Tuesday morning ... The greater portion of our expedition is here and it is supposed that G. Burnside is to have reinforcements and have a large command in cooperation with McClellan. Our troops are in pretty good condition ... McClellan has had a desperate time but has gained an excellent position before they were forced into swamp grounds and a great many of the troops were getting sick he is on high ground on the banks of the James river ... President L left here last evening. Our loss is not near as large as has been reported. I saw Col. Irvin of Lewiston yesterday he is on his way home he is completely worn out he said our troops behaved most gallantly he said there was no language that could describe the manner in which they fought he said some times as many as 50 cannon were fired on them at one time . . . he was on the field during all the battles he said the privates now have more confidence in McClellan than they ever had. . . . The sick and wounded are being sent north as fast as they arrive here. The accommodations for them in the Sanitary boats are good.

affectionately your son
JG Beaver

Camp Ferrero August 7th 1862

My dear Mother,

    I wrote you from Newport News 3 weeks ago. James also wrote you from that place. We left there on the 2nd inst our regiment was first to leave we did not know where we were going until we were in the Potomac River when we were told by our Col that we would disembark at Aquia Creek. At which place we arrived on the morning of the 4th inst we were immediately put aboard the cars and soon were underway for Fredericksburg. Being transported by railway was something new to us coast expedition boys and we enjoyed our short ride through the Virginia hills very much. We are encamped 1½ miles from Fredericksburg on a hill which from the brow can be seen the town and many miles of the surrounding hilly country. Genl Burnside has command of the 9th Army Corps the extent of his country I didn't know nor do I know the number of troops under his command. All those at Newport News left and are arriving daily I was told today that the 45th was guarding the railroad between here and Aquia Creek. The troops we met here which are a great many expressed some fear of "Stonewall Jackson" but on our arrival they asked who we were they were answered by many "Burnsides Boys." Then said they we are not afraid of "Old Jackson." An artillery company came in this morning which had been on a reconoitering expedition did not find out whether they saw anything of the enemy or not. We are in a healthy location water not very plenty we have commenced digging wells . . . Capt. Linn was ordered home on recruiting service I have command of the company . . . Quite a number of citizens left town yesterday most of them were conducted south. . . .

Affectionately your son,
JG Beaver

Popes Army 2½ miles from Culpepper Court House

My dear Mother,

    After marching 1 entire night and part of 2 days we arrived at this place Thursday evening. The weather was very favorable for our march and we had but little difficulty in getting along. I got along exceedingly well can walk all day and sleep soundly on the ground in the open air without the least interference with my constitution. I met Dr. Hayes who is a surgeon in the regular army he is from Lewisburg and now in Culpepper attending the wounded which are being brought in from the battle field of Cedar mountain he said he had a great many cases of amputation. A great many of the wounded were disabled and compelled to lay out in the field until their wounds had been filled with maggots and insects of various kinds. 9 cases out of 10 that were shot were shot in the legs. The battle was a desperate one although not many of our forces were engaged. After "Jackson" got permission to bury his dead he immediately began a retreat without burying any of his dead. A large portion of our cavalry and artillery are beyond the Rapidan in pursuit of Jackson. Pope has a very large force under his command and I think great good may result soon. There is but 2 Divisions of Genl Burnsides Corp here the 45th are guarding the rail road between Aquia Creek and Brooks Station ... Our regt is in fine health Capt. Linn has not returned yet, he has been ordered to recruit for 6 months ...When Dr. Hayes met me he said "you look rather hard, you look like a veteran." I had a picture taken the day we left so you can see whether he told the truth or not. Division after Division has been moving further south and our turn will come by and by....

                                    I am as ever your affectionate son
                                                        JG Beaver
                                                     9th Army Corps
                                               Genl Renno Division

[n.d. approximately 8/10/62]

Head Quarters 45th Regt. P.V. Sept. 28th 1862
One mile from Potomac River, Md.
Peter Beaver Esqr. Lewisburg, Pa.

Dr Sir,

    Having a few minutes to write this sabbath afternoon, I rode over to the camp of the 51st P.V. in order to learn more if possible, of the death of your nephew & my esteemed friend Lieut. Beaver. I had a long talk with Lieut. Campbell of the same company. He says they were making a charge upon the enemy when Gilbert was shot down, in front of him, as they were running down hill, from the bridge across Antietam Creek. He also informed me that Gilbert never spoke after being shot. When shot he exclaimed Oh! and that was all. He soon afterwards (Lieut. Campbell) sent a man back to his assistance, and remained with him until he died, when he took his money, watch, pistol, sword & etc, and took them to their company quarters, which was afterwards sent home by his brother of our regiment. Gilbert was shot through the neck, & I presume the carotid artery was severed, & he bled to death. This is my supposition of the case. When I first heard he was wounded, I was very busy with my own wounded about ½ mile from the battle field. I dispatched two men for him, to have him brought to me, so I would be able to render him assistance if no other surgeon was near him, but they returned saying he was dead & being cared for. I afterwards tried to see his remains, but being very busy & night coming on, I had little time to look for him. Besides I knew not where to go, to see him. I gave his brother my ambulance to carry his remains back from the field, & he took him clear into Frederick, from there to Baltimore and then sent him home. This is about the substance of my conversation with Lieut. Campbell. I afterwards talked with Col. Hartranft, he laments his loss very much & says he was always at his post, and was never found wanting when orders were given. He says he was brave and as good an officer as was in his regiment. All praise him, and all mourn his loss, he was beloved by all, as he always was at home. Col. H. told me he intended writing to his mother .

While there Lieut. Campbell gave me the enclosed letters for Gilbert. I told him I would send them home for him by Geo. W. Walls, who expects to go to morrow morning. He also informed me of several articles of clothing & etc. & said he would send them first opportunity to you. Here we have no facilities whatever for doing so.

I most earnestly sympathize with you all in this affliction, true, Gilbert is no more, he has fought his last fight & etc. he died the death of a true & pious soldier, he sacrificed his all, for that Country he loved so well, 'Peace to his ashes.' We are still lying in camp, doing nothing of much importance but picket duty & etc. We have probably 150,000 men here, we are within 5 miles of Harpers Ferry, & one of the Potomac.... My own noble regiment suffered severely in the two last battles. We lost in killed & wounded 25 killed & 147 wounded. Of the latter many has since died, they were both times much exposed. Remember me to all your family, & all enquiring friends. I am in excellent health & spirits.

Your friend & etc
Theo. S. Christ, Surgeon, 45th P.V.

The Letters of
Abraham Addams MacDonald

Camp Hale Oct 31st 1861

Dear Sister,

We have been so busy since we left Camp Curtin that I scarcely have had time to write to anybody. I wrote to Mother from Washington the night we arrived there. We were about 25 hours on the road from Harrisburg to Washington. We marched through part of Baltimore, on the road some little girls barefooted and bareheaded cheered us. I could not help comparing our reception with the reception they gave to the Pennsylvania and Massachusetts troops on the 19th of April last. They hand around bread and cheese at the depot. We had bread, meat, and coffee at Washington night and morning. The morning after we arrived in Washington we marched to an old camp about a mile and one half from the capitol. After we had got the camp in good order and after being in it only three days, we struck tents and got in readiness to march on last Saturday evening, hut for some reason or other we put up our tents again and struck tents on Sunday morning. We marched to another old camp on the site of the battle of Bladensburg, about one mile from Bladensburg. The place where the British landed is only about half a mile from the camp. There is a large rifle pit there now, built by Union troops. There is a large fort on a hill about one mile from camp. It is the highest hill around. All the country for seven miles around can be seen from it. It commands all the approaches to Washington from this direction. We were mustered into General Howards brigade today. The regiment was inspected today by General Howard and two of his staff together with the regimental officers. The regiment was reviewed in Washington on last Monday, by General McClellan and others, together with 10 other regiments. We are getting along finely down here. We get plenty to eat here. A loaf of bread weighing about 18 ounces everyday, besides pork and potatoes and coffee, sugar, hominy, and split peas. We have large tents. The sides are square but the ends are round. There are 13 in our tent. We sleep in two rows, with our heads all to the outside, rather towards the outside. We sleep in pairs throwing our overcoats under and blankets over us. Dr. Gibson, the chaplain of our regiment, is in our tent now, taking down all the names, and giving out a few tracts. We have just been called out to roll call and I must stop. . . .

                                        Your affectionate brother,
                                           A. Addams McDonald
                                           send this to mother

Camp 45th P.V.V.
10 miles N East of Richmond
June 5th 1864

Dear Sister,

    We have had another battle our regt suffered very much, losing 159 men killed & wounded.

    Our company lost one killed & 23 wounded, four of them so slightly that they have returned to duty. I was struck once with a spent ball but not hurt. All the privates of our company whose names commence with M were wounded. You will find a full list in the Lewistown Gazette. Our regt has lost 400 killed & wounded since the commencement of the campaign. Our company has had 2 killed & 41 wounded of whom 2 have since died. I merely wrote this to let you know I was unhurt. Carrell McManigal wishes me to say to you that he will be very much obliged to you, if you would tell his mother that he & James Gibbony are well & unhurt. I will send this by some of the wounded. I have not heard from you by letter since I came from home.

    Please write & send the photographs. I have not heard from James for more than a week. We are gradually pressing the enemy back. We are in good spirits & confident of success.

    Trusting in our own brave & determined comrades, our Generals, and in a kind & just God, we feel that we must conquer.

    Give my respects to my Milroy friends. With much love, your affectionate brother.

                                             A.A. McDonald

[McDonald is describing the battles of Cold Harbor, Va., June 1–3, 1864. Gen. U.S. Grant's army had numbered about 108,000 in early June; Gen. Lee's about 59,000. The battles ended June 3, when Grant ordered a frontal assault which failed miserably, costing him some 7,000 men, compared to a Confederate loss of about 1,500. The defeat caused Grant to alter his tactics, deciding he would make no more direct attacks on the Army of Northern Virginia. Instead, he broke away from Lee's front, crossed the James River, and marched to Petersburg, twenty-three miles south of Richmond.]

McKinney and his son, Jason, in 1995.

About the Author

TIM MCKINNEY has had a lifelong interest in the American Civil War. He was a history major in college and is a vice president of the West Virginia Historical Society. This is Mr. McKinney's sixth book, and his fifth book on the Civil War in West Virginia.

A career police officer with seventeen years' experience, Mr. McKinney is employed by the Department of Safety at the WVU Institute of Technology, Montgomery, W.Va. Mr. McKinney was first a military policeman with the Army's 101st Airborne Division. He can be written to at P.O. Box 157, Fayetteville, WV 25840. The West Virginia Historical Society may be written to at P.O. Box 5220, Charleston, WV 25361.